CRIMINAL JUSTICE ETHICS

CRIMINAL JUSTICE ETHICS

A Framework for Analysis

JOHN J. SLOAN, III
UNIVERSITY OF ALABAMA AT BIRMINGHAM

NEW YORK   OXFORD
OXFORD UNIVERSITY PRESS

Oxford University Press is a department of the University of Oxford.
It furthers the University's objective of excellence in research, scholarship,
and education by publishing worldwide. Oxford is a registered trade mark of
Oxford University Press in the UK and certain other countries.

Published in the United States of America by Oxford University Press
198 Madison Avenue, New York, NY 10016, United States of America.

For titles covered by Section 112 of the US Higher Education
Opportunity Act, please visit www.oup.com/us/he for the latest
information about pricing and alternate formats.

Library of Congress Cataloging-in-Publication Data

Names: Sloan, John J., author.
Title: Criminal justice ethics : a framework for analysis / John J. Sloan, III.
Description: New York : Oxford University Press, [2019] |
Includes bibliographical references.
Identifiers: LCCN 2018038171 (print) | LCCN 2018045656 (ebook) |
ISBN 9780190639181 (online ebook) | ISBN 9780190639136 |
ISBN 9780190639136 (paperback)
Subjects: LCSH: Criminal justice, Administration of—Moral and ethical aspects.
Classification: LCC HV7419 (ebook) | LCC HV7419 .S625 2019 (print) |
DDC 174/.9364—dc23
LC record available at https://lccn.loc.gov/2018038171

9 8 7 6 5 4 3 2 1
Printed by LSC Communications, Inc., United States of America

BRIEF TABLE OF CONTENTS

CONTENTS

ACKNOWLEDGMENTS

As is the case with any book-length undertaking, acknowledging the contributions of many people to its successful conclusion is called for. First, I want to offer my foremost thanks to my editor at Oxford, Steve Helba, who's now overseen two book projects with which I've been involved (talk about a glutton for punishment!). I can't imagine working with a better editor. I also thank Oxford's production team for their dedication to producing the highest-quality end product. Thanks, as well, to my colleagues and friends J. Heith Copes, Jason G. Linville, and Bonnie S. Fisher for their contributions. I also extend my sincerest thanks to those who reviewed drafts of the book, and whose critiques improved not only *what* I said , but *how* I said it. Reviewers included Marcel F. Beausoleil, Clairissa D. Breen, Greg Bridgeman, Gary Copus, Joel M. Cox, Sherri DioGuardi, William E. Harver, Galan Janeksela, Linda Keena, Stephen Mallory, Kerry L. Muehlenbeck, Gregory P. Orvis, Dylan Pelletier, David Polizzi, Gwenola Ricordeau, Michelle Rippy, Edward Sieh, Juyoung Song, William White, John T. Whitehead, Vanessa Woodward Griffin, and Glenn Zuern. Very special thanks to my spouse, Tavis, for her support during another book project (much of which was completed *after* I had allegedly "retired") and for the feedback she provided on the chapters. Finally, I thank the many undergraduate and graduate students at the University of Alabama at Birmingham who took my ethics classes over the years. They helped me not only hone my own thinking about ethics and criminal justice but also improve my teaching of it.

John Sloan
Orange Beach, AL
June 25, 2018

PREFACE

Let me begin with a disclaimer: I am neither a criminal justice practitioner, nor do I play one on television. I am also not a philosopher, nor am I an ethicist. In fact, I am a sociologist by training and a criminologist by specialization. "So," you may be saying to yourself, "what makes *him* qualified to write a textbook on criminal justice ethics?" One reason I'm qualified is that for over 30 years, I've conducted research on various aspects of the criminal justice system, the agencies that comprise it, and the people that staff them. As part of my research, I've studied how criminal justice practitioners exercise discretion; the organization and operation of police agencies, prosecutors' offices, and juvenile courts; and how appeals court judges reach decisions in the cases before them. I've also surveyed, conducted focus groups with, and interviewed hundreds of practitioners and learned what their professional lives involved, including the ethical issues they confronted. Additionally, for over 20 years at the University of Alabama at Birmingham (UAB) I taught a required course on criminal justice ethics to thousands of undergraduate students who majored in criminal justice, and for more than 10 years taught a graduate-level course on ethics to students pursuing a master's degree in computer forensics and security management. In preparation for teaching those courses, I've read about, studied, and discussed ethics with academic philosophers, psychologists, and others interested in ethics. I even received a grant from the National Science Foundation (NSF) in 2014 to convene a workshop on ethics and digital forensics that was attended by scholars and practitioners alike, all of whom were interested in ethics in the criminal justice context.

I say all of this not to pat myself on the back or to impress you (which I'm fairly sure I haven't managed to do—at least not yet—but give me a chance!). Rather, I share this introductory tale to advise you that the perspective guiding this book is *academic*, although its *tone* is supposed to be informal (but only you can judge how well *that* turned out!). What I mean is that the information presented in this book is based on scholarly research and commentary, rather than "war stories" or experience as might come from an author who'd spent time as a police officer, crime scene investigator, probation officer, judge, or prosecutor. On hearing this, some readers may at once dismiss the book as a fruitless exercise by a "pointy-headed academic," but let me add something. Over the 30 years I've conducted research on the criminal justice system, I have engaged in countless conversations with police officers (ranging from patrol officers and shift sergeants to multiple chiefs of police), prosecuting attorneys (including several district attorneys, US attorneys, and my late father, who was an assistant district attorney in Detroit), judges, probation officers—including those working with juveniles, prison wardens, and directors of state and federal prison systems. One common element in conversations with these practitioners involved/revolved around *ethics* and the sorts of ethical issues these people faced along the way and were willing to share with me. To a degree, then, the stories I've heard from and conversations I've had with those good people over the years both informed and shaped not only how I teach ethics to criminal justice and computer forensics students, but also how I *think* about ethics and criminal justice. This book is my attempt to share with you, in a conversational tone, what I have learned about criminal justice ethics over three decades and why I think ethics in the practice of criminal justice is a pretty important topic.

Because you are reading a book on criminal justice ethics, it's likely you are majoring in criminal justice, criminology, or some related field, like homeland security or law and society. Chances are also good that you are interested in pursuing a career in criminal justice, whether in law enforcement, forensic science, the courts, corrections, or perhaps even research. Your interest in criminal justice may have developed because you *love* so-called police procedurals (e.g., *CSI, NCIS, Law and Order SVU*) that are a staple of prime-time television, or so-called reality shows like *Cops Reloaded* or *North Woods Law*. You may have envisioned yourself, like one of the main characters in these shows, solving a case, arresting the "bad guys," and ensuring that "justice is done" for victims.

Perhaps your interest in criminal justice developed because someone in your family is working (or has worked) in the system as a police officer, probation officer, prosecutor, or other official, or you encountered someone who worked in the system who had a positive influence on your life. Because of these people, you decided the careers they had chosen were *important* on some level; that what they do is righteous, noble, virtuous, or honorable. These people give back to the community. They put their lives on the line to protect and serve others they don't even know. They work to ensure victims are not forgotten or that offenders who engage in crime are first punished, but also given a second chance. In short, you *respect* these people and what they do, and want to become one of them.

Alternatively, it could be that your interest in criminal justice arose because you or someone you knew experienced an *injustice* at the hands of a criminal justice practitioner. Perhaps you were unfairly pulled over by a police officer for "driving while black" (Bhatnagar, 2009) or saw corrupt criminal justice officials reaping benefits from the injustices they perpetrated. These experiences motivated you to learn more about the criminal justice system and ultimately helped you decide to try and change the system from the inside.

Regardless of your motivation for wanting to become a criminal justice practitioner, you probably view the system and its personnel as either just or good or as having the *potential* to become as much. You may see the people working in the system as good. Rather than seeking to destroy, they seek to build. Rather than caring only about self, they care about others. They are upright and virtuous. Additionally, you may perceive that what they do is also good. Fighting crime, helping victims, and ensuring that criminals are fairly punished for their behavior is good, at least in part because the result is preservation of the social order. Helping offenders "learn from their mistakes" and get a "second chance" is good as well, as it results in positive change for these individuals, who can then be welcomed back into the community.

Because you may perceive that both the people working in the criminal justice system and the duties and responsibilities they bear are good (or can *become* good), it is also likely you believe that police officers and prosecutors, defense attorneys and judges, and correctional officers and probation officers should be *ethical* in their dealings with the people they serve. They should, for example, strive for justice and treat the people they meet with respect. They should understand that their behavior has consequences not only for themselves and the people with whom they are directly interacting, but for *all* of us. The problem is that too often—and for a variety of reasons well beyond the scope of this text—we tend to hear only about the *unethical* behavior in which representatives of the criminal justice system have engaged. That behavior may involve police officers accepting bribes not to arrest drug dealers or using excessive force against suspects; prosecutors pursuing charges against factually innocent people; or judges sentencing offenders not because of *what they did* but because of *who they are*—the list, sadly, is nearly endless. Not only may the behavior involved be unethical *and* illegal, but it also, more importantly, erodes the trust that is necessary for the criminal justice system to function. Citizens are supposed to *trust* that law enforcement officials are not corrupt, that our prosecutors are not out simply to convict someone, anyone, so they can be reelected, or that our judges aren't out to simply "throw away the key" with offenders. Instead, we trust that they will both *be* good and *act* ethically.

This book is about criminal justice ethics. Its goal is to provide you, someone who is likely contemplating a career in the field of criminal justice, with an overview of what ethics *is* and what it means to *be* ethical as a criminal justice practitioner. To achieve that goal, the book provides you with basic information about ethics, including what ethics is; the relationship between morality and ethics; and various theories of ethics (what I call "systems of ethics") and their guiding principles that developed over hundreds of years and which have influenced each of us (even if we don't realize it) in developing our own personal ethics. The book both explores the notion of "moral dilemmas" and examines those often faced by criminal justice practitioners—where they are *forced* to choose between two courses of action—and how these dilemmas may be resolved. Further, the book explores moral reasoning, including why moral reasoning is important, and how to avoid errors in it. I also provide you with a template I developed over the 25-plus years I taught courses on criminal justice ethics that I designed to help students analyze various moral dilemmas confronting criminal justice practitioners. Finally, the book devotes chapters to discussing ethical issues involving key personnel in the criminal justice system, including police officers, defense attorneys, prosecutors and judges, correctional professionals, forensic scientists, and researchers.

Throughout the book, I provide examples and/or illustrations of ethical issues you will likely face as a criminal justice practitioner: Should you accept gratuities? How far should you go when prosecuting someone for a crime? How should you run your campaign to be elected as a judge? How do you justify working at a private prison that operates on a for-profit basis? What do you do when you realize the probation agreement signed by one of your clients is almost guaranteed to set her up for failure? How do you ensure the DNA analysis you're conducting is free from bias? Is it unethical for you to ignore what current research in the field of criminal justice is finding about the operation of the criminal justice system? The reason for doing this is to get you thinking about ethical issues you may face as a criminal justice practitioner *before* you actually face them. In doing so, you'll have the opportunity to explore how you *could* (note the operative) respond to them. Having the chance to think about how you *might* behave under certain circumstances allows you think through *why* you would act one way—as opposed to some other way—before you actually have to make that choice. In effect, you are practicing for a role you hope to occupy before you occupy it, what sociologists call *anticipatory socialization* (Merton, 1968; Wheeler, 1966). The benefit of anticipatory socialization is that it allows one, in effect, to practice a role (e.g., probation officer) before actually filling it. When practicing filling the role, one learns not only the specific behaviors associated with the role but also the norms, values, and beliefs of those who already occupy the role. While this book can't help you with the specific tactics you might adopt to efficiently track down an armed robber, it can help you begin to think about the ethics of using force *against* such an offender.

Once a criminal justice agency hires you, you'll undergo further anticipatory as well as actual socialization into your new role (Alpert, Atkins, & Ziller, 1979). You will receive specialized training that likely will include at least *some* attention to ethics. However, one problem with much of the training that occurs for both new criminal justice practitioners and those who've been on the job for a while is that the subject of ethics is either skipped or otherwise given short-shrift. For example, in my home state of Alabama, an Alabama Peace Officer Standards and Training (APOST)-certified police academy curriculum includes 520 hours of total training but includes only four hours of training in ethics (or less than 1% of the total hours in the curriculum) (Alabama Peace Officer Standards and Training, n.d.). In Michigan, where I was born and raised, the training academy for correctional officers includes 320 hours of instruction, but just two hours devoted to ethics; again, less than 1% of the total instructional time (Michigan Department of Corrections, n.d.). In California, one of the largest states in the nation, probation officers complete 196 total hours of training, of which just three hours is devoted to ethics (Board of State and Community Corrections, 2012).

Let me be clear about one thing: I am not saying these training academies or the agencies that hire their graduates don't care about ethics. They do. The problem they face is that new practitioners have much to learn about the "nuts-and-bolts" of the job in a brief period (usually 13 or 14 weeks). This results in ethics receiving less of an emphasis than it might were there more time.

Thus, the early socialization experiences of criminal justice practitioners really do not center on—or stress—ethics all that much. Instead, those coming to the job are expected to be "ethical" based partly on the results of extensive background checks routinely conducted on applicants (Equal Employment Opportunity Commission, 2012), combined with the results of relatively rigorous psychological testing they undergo (Ben-Porath, Fico, Hibler, Inwald, Krumi, & Roberts, 2011). There is also an assumption by high-ranking officials that agency "policy and procedure manuals" effectively guide decision-making by practitioners such that agency rules, more or less, help ensure ethical behavior by employees (Acevedo, 2013).

In reality, what often happens is rather than talking about ethics and how/why it is both important for and relevant to criminal justice practitioners, newcomers and veterans alike are left to "fend for themselves." Lawrence Sherman, one of the late-20th-century "giants" in police research, wrote an important article in the early 1980s about how police officers learn ethics that suggested they learn ethics one of two ways: (1) on the job, in the heat of battle, under the watchful eye of supervisors and peers, which limits frank and open discussion about the types of ethical issues police officers face and how to resolve them, or (2) off the job, and away from its pressures and supervisors (Sherman, 1982). Sherman argued that the latter situation is preferable, and I agree, but sometimes you take what you can get in order to achieve a greater goal, and the training has to take place at the police department or police academy. Regardless, in my experience, I found that officers attending police ethics training are *very* open to discussing, wrestling with, and making suggestions about handling the ethical issues they commonly face in their professional lives. I have experienced the same enthusiasm from state probation officers when I conducted training for them. They, too, were interested in ethics, but had little opportunity to talk about, consider, or work through—either by themselves or with their peers—the kinds of dilemmas they commonly encounter.

This book represents the culmination of my interest in both learning about and teaching ethics in the context of criminal justice. If it helps you develop and/or hone your critical thinking skills, provides you with an introduction to the kinds of ethical issues you will likely confront "on the street" as you go about performing your duties, and gets you thinking about how you'll address them, then it will have succeeded.

STRUCTURE OF THE BOOK

In assembling this book (yes, books are assembled—just like automobiles!), I tried to mirror its organization with how I have structured my ethics classes. As occurs in my class, material in the chapters builds on what has come before and moves from general information and topics in the early chapters to more specific and detailed information in the later ones. To give you an idea of what this means specifically, Chs. 1–5 provide you with an overview of ethics, including chapters that are devoted to (1) a general discussion of morality, ethics, and values; (2) systems of ethics; (3); moral dilemmas; (4) moral reasoning; and (5) a "template for analysis" that provides you with a way to identify and organize relevant information so that you can reach a reasoned conclusion about the ethics of your—or others'– behavior. The template consists of blanks you fill with information found in a scenario (what I dub a "case study"), including relevant ideals (notions of goodness or rightness to which we, as a culture, aspire to achieve), obligations of the main party in the scenario to him- or herself and to others, and possible consequences of the behavior described. Using this information, combined with applying guiding principles from various systems of ethics, allows you to reason through and develop an argument to support your conclusion that the main party acted ethically or not, as the case may be.

The remaining chapters examine common ethical issues confronting criminal justice practitioners, beginning with the police—the front end of the criminal justice system—and moving through the courts (prosecutors, defense attorneys, and judges) and ending with corrections (probation/parole officers and correctional officers). I also include chapters devoted to ethical issues relating to forensic science and criminal justice research. I conclude the book with my take on the future of criminal justice ethics.

Each chapter first provides you with an *outline* of the material to be covered and the specific *learning objectives* for the chapter to give you an idea of what should be your "take away." Chapters also include *boxes* that highlight or provide additional information on, or insight into, a concept or issue being discussed. Additionally, chapters include one or more *case studies* that describe an actual event that generated significant media coverage (e.g., misconduct by forensic technicians in one or more major crime laboratories) or present you with a "real-life" scenario and ask you to reach a conclusion about the ethics of the behavior described (e.g., a police officer accepts a free meal at a local eatery, or a judge running for reelection accepts campaign contributions from lawyers likely to appear before her). While the individuals and details found in some of the case studies are fictional, their substance is based on actual events that affected practitioners— who, in turn shared them with me, including me in my capacity as a criminal justice researcher. Chapters also contain one or more *thought exercises* meant to inspire further reflection on your part or discussion with classmates or your instructor about an issue or concept covered in the chapter. Further, at the ends of the chapters are *discussion questions* you can use to review the material covered in the chapter or that can generate discussion with classmates. Finally, each chapter includes a *summary* of the main points made; a list of *key terms* found in the chapter; and *additional resources,* such as books, scholarly articles, websites, videos, blogs, etc., that will help you learn more about the topics covered.

At the opening of one of my all-time favorite childhood TV sci-fi shows, *The Outer Limits,* the viewer is informed he or she is ". . . about to embark on a great adventure." Let's begin our adventure not into science fiction, but into moral philosophy, ethics, and the criminal justice system!

References

Acevedo, A. (2013). *Austin Police Department policy manual.* Austin, TX: City of Austin Police Department. Retrieved from http://austintexas.gov/sites/default/files/files/Police/ APD_Policy_2013-2_Effective_6-1-2013.pdf/

Alabama Peace Officer Standards and Training Commission (n.d.). 520-hour basic training curriculum. Retrieved from http://www.apostc.state.al.us/LinkClick.aspx?fileticket = u41o7IiGHbI%3d&tabid =58

Alpert, L., Atkins, B., & Ziller, R. (1979). Becoming a judge: The transition from advocate to arbiter. *Judicature, 62,* 325–335.

Ben-Porath, Y., Fico, J., Hibler, N., Inwald, R., Krumi, J., & Roberts, M. (2011). Assessing the psychological suitability of candidates for law enforcement positions. *The Police Chief, 78,* 64–70.

Bhatnagar, C. (2009). *The persistence of racial and ethnic profiling in the United States: A follow-up report to the U.N. Committee on the elimination of racial discrimination.* New York, NY: American Civil Liberties Union. Retrieved from https://www.aclu.org/ files/pdfs/humanrights/cerd_finalreport.pdf

Board of State and Community Corrections (2012). Probation officer core course. Sacramento, CA: Board of State and Community Corrections. Retrieved from http://www.bscc.ca.gov/downloads/2011_PO_Core_Manual_inc.policy_updates_effective_7.1.2013(rev_07-2013).pdf

Equal Employment Opportunity Commission (2012). EEOC enforcement guidance. Retrieved from http://www.eeoc.gov/laws/guidance/upload/arrest_conviction. pdf

Merton, R. (1968). *Social theory and social structure* (Rev. ed.). New York, NY: The Free Press.

Michigan Department of Corrections (n.d.). New corrections officer training curriculum. Retrieved from http://www.michigan.gov/corrections/0,4551,7-119-68918_28885-5509-00.html

Sherman, L. (1982). Learning police ethics. *Criminal Justice Ethics, 1,* 10–19.

Wheeler, S. (1966). The structure of formally organized socialization settings. In O. Brim & S. Wheeler (Eds.), *Socialization after childhood: Two essays* (pp. 5–20). New York, NY: Wiley.

LIST OF TABLES

LIST OF FIGURES

CRIMINAL JUSTICE ETHICS

CHAPTER 1

An Overview of Ethics

Chapter Outline

CHAPTER LEARNING OBJECTIVES:

1. Distinguish morality from ethics.
2. Contrast metaethics, normative ethics, applied ethics, and professional ethics.
3. Distinguish teleological systems of ethics from deontological systems of ethics.
4. Contrast terminal values with instrumental values.
5. Distinguish one's occupational career from one's moral career.
6. Describe the relationships among morality, ethics, and values.
7. Contrast the values-imported perspective from the values-learned perspective.
8. Identify and compare the values associated with the crime control and the due process models of criminal justice.

INTRODUCTION

Imagine you are a new police officer with a major urban department in this country working your very first shift. You and your field training officer (FTO), a 20-year veteran of the department, decide to stop for dinner at a local restaurant on your beat. As you finish your meal, you ask the server for the check. The server laughs and tells you that "meals for police officers are on the house, in appreciation for all the hard work you do." You are unsure how to react to this information since department policy expressly prohibits officers from accepting gratuities such as free meals. What do you do?

There are several ways you could respond. For example, you could just leave the full amount of the tab on the table and exit the restaurant. Or, you could give the server an oversized "tip" that covers both the meal and a gratuity. Finally, you could accept the gesture and return to your patrol duties. Which option would you choose?

The more important question from the perspective of ethics, however, is this: How *should* you respond? For example, an observer might say you should have paid the tab because the possible consequences of not doing so could be significant for both you and your partner. Accepting the gratuity would probably violate department policy and could subject the two of you to disciplinary action, including days off without pay—or worse. Thus, based on the severity of the potential negative consequences of accepting the gratuity, one might argue you should pay for the meal—it would be the "ethical" thing to do.

Every day, police officers, prosecutors, defense attorneys, judges, probation officers, and corrections officers face situations where they must decide what is the ethical thing to do as they go about their jobs: Should I use force against this suspect? Should I charge this defendant with every possible violation I can, in order to pressure her into accepting a plea bargain? Should I defend a client I know is guilty? As a judge running for reelection, should I accept campaign contributions from a political action committee (PAC) representing trial attorneys, some of whom may appear in my court? Should I overlook offenders' minor violations of a probation order? Should I reward this inmate with special privileges in exchange for information about a planned escape? What's the "right" choice, in moral or ethical terms, to make?

Regardless of how you feel about the above situations, the point here is that our lives involve having to make choices about how we *should* behave. Sometimes those choices are trivial: Should we wear a white shirt or a blue shirt to work today, or should that new car we're buying be red or black? At other times our choices can have potentially profound consequences for ourselves and others. For example, is it ever acceptable to lie to our spouse about an indiscretion in which we engaged, or treat another as the means to an end? It is those latter choices this book is most interested in, particularly as they relate to the behavior of criminal justice practitioners.

In this chapter, I begin exploring morality and ethics as they relate to the criminal justice system and those working in it. The goal of the chapter is to give you a starting point for considering ethics *and* criminal justice and why ethics *in* criminal justice is important. Over my years of teaching courses on criminal justice ethics, I've found that many students do not know what ethics *is*; the difference between, or the relationship of, ethics and morality; what role personal values play in morality and ethics; or why ethical behavior by criminal justice practitioners is important.

It's not that students don't care about these matters: they do, some very deeply. Most want to do the "moral" thing and act "ethically." They're just not sure what "doing the moral thing" or "acting ethically" entails. They need some guidance on how to tackle such matters so that they can "become more aware and open to moral and ethical issues" (Braswell, 2015, p. 7). So, to get started, let's see what morality *is*, and what it entails. I'll then examine ethics and the links between it and morality. I'll conclude the chapter by examining how personal values relate to both morality and ethics, paying attention to the interaction among them in the context of the field of criminal justice.

WHAT IS MORALITY?

In everyday parlance, people tend to think of morality as having something to do with "good" and "bad" or "right" and "wrong." You might say, for example, that "everyone knows it's 'bad' to lie, cheat, or steal." Indeed, much of early childhood socialization centers on learning about the difference between "good" and "bad" behavior: sharing toys with preschool classmates is "good" while grabbing a toy away from another child is "bad." What children are learning is that society has rules, what sociologists call norms (Jackson, 1965). These rules, according to sociologists, make social order possible—we all can't go around grabbing toys away from each other now, can we? Sociologists and anthropologists alike argue that some of these rules are formal, such as laws that are codified and involve formal social control mechanisms (the police) brought to bear against violators. Other norms are unwritten and are thus more informal and attend to matters ranging from rules about dress, etiquette, or marriage and procreation (Sumner, 1940). These culturally bound rules help members of the group learn what is "good" and "bad" behavior.

Importantly, the rules we learn are attached to various statuses we occupy during our lives. Sociologists have argued that a status is a position one occupies in a hierarchy of such positions, each of which has attached to it differing levels of power and prestige (Turner, 1988). For example, "college student" is a status in society that ranks relatively low on the hierarchy in terms of the amount of power and prestige associated with the position. However, compare the status of college student with that of "homeless person." A significant difference, yes?

Sociologists also argue that a status can be either ascribed—you are born into the position and have little to no control over it—or achieved—you earn the position based on merit and/or your achievements (Crossman, 2016). In the United Kingdom, for example, Prince Charles occupies the ascribed status of "heir to the throne" due to the fact he was born into the royal family and is the eldest son of Queen Elizabeth II (to lose this status, he would have to abdicate the throne). By contrast, the prime minister of England (currently Theresa May) occupies an achieved status—she was elected to the position.

Status also has a set of behavioral expectations associated with it that make interaction possible. For example, when you attend the first meeting of a class at the beginning of a semester, you don't expect the professor to come into the room, move into the corner, and stand on her head. Rather you expect the professor to introduce herself, review the course syllabus, answer questions, cover course policies, etc. Behavioral expectations that are associated with a status are known as "roles" (Giddens, 1993).

What's interesting is that while there are rules relating to a particular status that one occupies, such as a professor being discouraged (or even prohibited) from becoming romantically involved with a student, there are also rules that extend to all members of the group, regardless of an individual's status. Returning to our example of "it is 'bad' to lie, cheat, or steal," that rule covers everyone, regardless of status: mother, college student, professor, homeless person, or prime minister. Over the course of our lives, we learn not only the specifics of a larger "moral code" —the "don't lie, cheat, or steal" business—but we also learn that particular rules of conduct are tied to the status we occupy at a given moment, for example the rules for a professor when meeting a class the first day of a new semester.

DESCRIPTIVE AND NORMATIVE MORALITY

Norms thus provide us with a set of rules that govern our behavior. Morality, in turn, is tied to these rules. However, explicitly defining morality isn't that easy because philosophers have not adopted a consensus definition of the term. Rather, they tend to use the concept in either a descriptive or a normative manner (Gert & Gert, 2016). When using morality as a descriptive term, the philosopher is referring to codes of conduct developed and put forth by a group (e.g., Judaism) or codes accepted by an individual as binding on her behavior (e.g., a Hasidic Jew). When used normatively, philosophers are referring to morality as codes of conduct relevant only under specific conditions (e.g., a time of war) and would likely be agreed upon by most rational people (e.g., during war, the carpet bombing of civilian populations is morally wrong). Let me elaborate a bit on these notions.

Descriptive Definitions of Morality

In the descriptive sense, morality involves group members identifying which rules of conduct that have been put forward count as moral codes. But you may be asking yourself, "What other rules are there? Aren't all of the rules actually moral rules?" Sociologists and anthropologists alike agree that members of groups—even in small, homogeneous societies—distinguish rules along the following lines: morality, etiquette, law, and religion.

Etiquette, Law, and Religion

In many groups, etiquette may be considered part of the group's moral code, although members generally view the rules of etiquette as less important than rules more central to the group's overall moral code (Gert & Gert, 2016). In speaking of etiquette, the great English philosopher Thomas Hobbes (1588–1679) described it as "small morals" that involve "decency of behavior, as how one should salute another, or how a man [*sic*] should wash his mouth or pick his teeth before company," which he distinguished from "the qualities of mankind [*sic*] that concern their living together in peace and unity" (Hobbes, 1994 [1668], p. 56). However, note that etiquette is relative—its rules vary greatly across time, place, and group. Additionally, note that "there are no plausible conditions under which we could pick out the 'correct' rules of etiquette . . . that would be accepted by all rational beings" (Gert & Gert, 2016, p. 1). Thus, the rules of etiquette are not rules of morality.

Unlike etiquette, law involves explicit written rules, relatively significant penalties associated with violating them, and officials responsible for interpreting the rules and administering the penalties (Vago, 2012). Law is also tied—either explicitly or implicitly—to morality, which is then used to evaluate the law and, potentially, change it. Thus, just because some behavior is lawful does not make it moral. Finally, while the morality of a group may be based on a specific religion (e.g., Islam), the two are not the same. If morality is a guide to conduct, then religion is about much more: stories and parables; supernatural beings and events; and exemplary humans (sometimes called saints). Believers then use these components to explain or justify behavior required (or prohibited) by their religion. While there may be an overlap in the conduct prohibited or required by both religion and morality, in many cases religion requires or prohibits more than morality while also allowing some behavior that may be prohibited by morality (Gert & Gert, 2016). Even when morality is not regarded as the code of conduct that is put forward by a formal religion, it is often thought to require at least *some* religious explanation and justification. However, just as with law, some religious practices and precepts are criticized on *moral* grounds (e.g., a group's practice or precept that involves discrimination based on race, gender, or sexual orientation). Thus, when "morality" is used in the sense that it is referring to a general code of conduct put forward by a group or society that is distinguished from etiquette, law, and religion, morality is being used in a descriptive sense. It is also being used in the descriptive sense when it refers to widely held attitudes of individuals. Just as one can refer to the morality of "the Americans," so, too, can one refer to the morality of an American.

Normative Definitions of Morality

When used in the normative sense, "morality" refers to a code of conduct that would be accepted by anyone who meets certain intellectual and volitional conditions, especially the condition of being rational (Gert, 2005). That a person meets these conditions is typically expressed by saying that the person is a moral agent (Gert & Gert, 2016). Thus, for many philosophers, "morality" refers to a code of conduct that applies to all who can understand it and adapt their behavior to it, even if it is designed to protect the larger group rather than individual members. These same philosophers also argue that in a normative sense, morality would never be overridden.

A key point to make here is that philosophers differ on what is "rationality" and on the conditions whereby "rational" actors ultimately endorse the code of conduct that counts as "morality." Normative definitions may also diverge on what it means to "endorse" a code. Finally, philosophers differ considerably regarding to whom morality applies—that is, exactly whose behavior is subject to moral judgment— and evaluations of the "rightness" or "wrongness" of others' (and our own) behavior (see Willer & Simpson, 2017; I go into much greater detail on this point in Ch. 4). Thus, for some philosophers, "morality" applies only to those beings who have certain features of humans (e.g., fallibility and vulnerability) that make it rational for them to endorse morality. Others present morality as a guide to all rational beings, including God, even if they do not have human characteristics (Gert & Gert, 2016). For *our* purposes, then, let's say that morality, in the normative sense, relates to a code of conduct that applies to all who understand it and conform their behavior to it.

Morality, then, refers to an all-encompassing code of conduct that applies to all rational actors—what philosophers refer to as "moral agents"—who understand it and are willing to conform their behavior to it. The rules are taken as absolute and should not be overridden. The rules may be tied either implicitly or explicitly to etiquette, law, and religion although none of these, by itself, constitutes morality. To illustrate, Box 1.1 presents examples of moral values—deep-seated and enduring beliefs that specific kinds of conduct or end-states of existence are personally and/or socially preferable—common to people living in the United States (Rokeach, 1973).

If morality refers to an overarching code of conduct, then that code must specify how one should (or should not) behave. If, for example, a certain code of morality says that "lying, cheating, and stealing are wrong," there must be justification(s) for *why* those behaviors are wrong. Those justifications are found in the field known as ethics, to which I now turn my discussion.

BOX 1.1 Examples of Moral Values in the U.S.

Do not gossip	Tell the truth	Do not vandalize property
Have courage	Do not have sex before marriage	Keep your promises
Do not cheat	Treat others as you want to be treated	Be trustworthy
Do not judge	Be dependable	Respect others
Be forgiving	Keep your self-control	Have integrity

Source: Yourdictionary.com (2017)

WHAT *IS* "ETHICS?"

Ethics, also known as moral philosophy, is one of several major branches of philosophy devoted to the systematic study of what is right and wrong, and is divided into three major areas: metaethics, normative ethics, and applied ethics (Fieser, n.d.). To that, I am adding an additional subarea within applied ethics, what is called "professional ethics" (Center for the Study of Ethics in the Professions, n.d.). Figure 1.1 provides a schematic representation of the field. **Metaethics** involves the study of the origin, meaning, and logic behind the principles that shape ethics. Metaethicists examine abstract notions, such as whether there are universal truths; what is the will of God; what role is played by reason in making ethical judgments; and what is the meaning for self and others (Fieser, n.d.). Normative ethics tries to develop standards for morally acceptable conduct (e.g., "The Golden Rule") and uses logic and reason to justify the standards (Kagan, 1997). Applied ethics examines specific controversial issues such as abortion, euthanasia, eating meat, or capital punishment (Fieser, n.d.). What's crucial here is that applied ethics addresses questions about the right and wrong of specific behaviors, such as the state executing criminal offenders or the National Security Agency (NSA) "eavesdropping" on American citizens' international phone calls. Using the guiding principles and tools of both metaethics and normative ethics, applied ethics seeks to resolve such controversial issues as abortion, capital punishment, and euthanasia, among others. I add professional ethics as a subfield of applied ethics, as it is involved with developing rules or standards concerning the behavior of people who are professionals, such as doctors and lawyers (Center for the Study of Ethics in the Professions, n.d.). Let's explore these areas in greater depth.

METAETHICS

"Meta" means above or beyond, so metaethics concerns itself with issues that are "beyond ethics." What this translates to in practice is that **metaethics** concerns itself with the study of the meanings of the concepts or principles that are found in ethics.

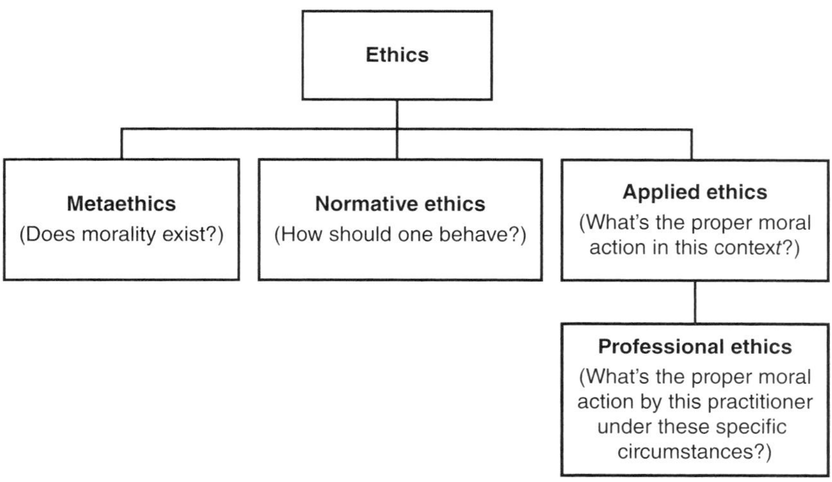

FIGURE 1.1 The Field of Ethics

Rather than attempting to show that a specific ethical orientation is "correct," metaethics seeks to understand from where important concepts originated and what they mean (Fieser, n.d.). Put another way, metaethics "steps back" from substantive debates over questions such as "Can police use of deadly force against suspects ever be justified?" to ask about the views, assumptions, and commitments shared by those engaging in the debate (Sayre-McCord, 2014). Metaethics thus involves "reflecting on the presuppositions and commitments of those engaging in moral thought, talk, and practice and so abstracting away from . . . moral judgments" (Sayre-McCord, 2014, p. 1).

Some philosophers suggest that at its most basic level, metaethics focuses on two principal issues: (1) determining if morality exists independent of human beings, (known as metaphysical issues), and (2) identifying the underlying psychological basis of moral judgments and the behavior in which we engage (identified as psychological issues) (Fieser, n.d.).

Metaphysical Issues

While there is no consensus among philosophers about what metaphysics means, for our purposes, let's say that metaphysics seeks to understand *why* things exist at all—in this case, morality, the principles that guide it, and what it means for morality to exist in the first place (Cline, 2016; van Inwagen & Sullivan, 2014). In metaethics, the issue is discovering "whether moral values are eternal truths that exist in a spirit-like realm, or [are] simply human conventions" (Fieser, n.d., p. 1). Some metaethicists argue that moral values are objective; that is, they exist beyond human conventions. They are absolute, eternal, and apply to all humans regardless of considerations like culture or time. For example, take the following equation: $2 + 2 = 4$. The objectivist would argue that this mathematical relationship is timeless (as are others like it), it never changes, and applies everywhere. The objectivist would say the same of moral values. Like mathematical relationships, moral values are unchanging, universal, and eternal. Plato, for example, argued that mathematics and moral values were absolute truths that existed as abstract entities and originated in a spirit-like realm. Other objectivists argue that morality is a divine command that originates in God's will, an orientation sometimes referred to as Divine Command theory (Fieser, n.d.). This theory argues that there is an all-powerful deity ("God") in control of everything. It is the deity's will that determines human morality, revealed to humans as commands (e.g., "Thou shall not commit adultery") or as found in sacred texts like the Christian Bible or the Jewish Torah (I explore Divine Command theory in greater detail in Ch. 2).

A different view held by some metaethicists denies the objective status of moral values (Mackie, 1977). While not rejecting moral values outright, these skeptics argue that all moral values are human creations. Known as **moral relativism**, this argument holds that people either create their own moral values and standards ("individual relativism") or that morality is grounded in the norms and values of the larger group or society of which individuals are a part ("cultural relativism"). Proponents of this orientation cite variability in moral values across cultures relating to such behavior as marriage, women's rights, or cannibalism as evidence of these values being culture-bound (Harrison & Huntington, 2000).

Psychological Issues

A second area of metaethics involves the psychology of moral judgments and behavior, particularly the question of why people are (or should be) moral. Psychologists suggest that people are moral for several reasons, including fear of punishment, desire for praise, to achieve happiness, to appear dignified, or simply to "fit in" with the group (Weir, 2012).

Egoism and Altruism

Researchers in moral psychology differ on what motivates people to be moral. Some scholars have argued that we are moral because doing so serves our own selfish interests and desires (Asher, 2012). This orientation is best illustrated by the 17th-century philosopher Thomas Hobbes in his classic work *Leviathan* (Hobbes, 1994 [1668]). In the book, Hobbes argued that selfishness motivates most human action. Even so-called charitable acts, like helping a homeless person or organizing a food bank, involve a reward, namely, exerting power over others. This view is known as psychological egoism. Scholars working in this tradition have argued that all humans have an instinctual self-interest that motivates behavior (May, 2011). Others, while agreeing that selfishness drives much human conduct, have also argued that we have an inherent capacity to show benevolence toward others. This view is called psychological altruism; its proponents argue that instinctual benevolence motivates at least some of our actions (Farside, 2007).

Emotion and Reason

Suppose I was to make the following statement: "Police use of deception during interrogation of suspects is morally wrong." Is that statement rational or is it an expression of an emotional feeling? The role played by emotion and reason when making moral judgments is the basis of a second area of interest in moral psychology. On one side are scholars who agree with the great 18th-century thinker David Hume that moral judgments are based solely on emotion. In the above example, I can tick off any number of reasons why police use of deception is morally wrong, but such a list—by itself—is not a true moral assessment. Rather, my emotional reaction to police using deception is the actual basis of my pronouncement, not my list of reasons. On the surface, my statement about police deception appears to be a factual description of a common tactic used by the police. In reality it is not. When considered carefully, my statement contains two elements: (1) my personal disapproval about police deception (an emotive element) and (2) my trying to get the police to stop engaging in the behavior (a prescriptive element) (Fieser, n.d.).

Other scholars, however, have rejected the notion that moral pronouncements and choices are based on emotion and have argued instead that moral assessments are (or at least can be) based on reason and are free from emotions and desires. Inspired by the great 18th-century Prussian philosopher Immanuel Kant, these scholars have argued that morality is based on reason. If I make a statement that it is "wrong to steal someone else's car," I should be able to justify my claim with an argument. For example, I might say that stealing causes pain to the owner of the property; that it violates the owner's property rights; or the thief risks being caught and punished (Fieser, n.d.). For these philosophers, moral decision-making involves offering the best reasons for one's position rather than providing one's emotional reaction to the behavior in question (I discuss the debate about emotion versus reason in moral thinking in greater depth in Ch. 4).

Male Versus Female Morality

A third area of interest in moral psychology extending beyond debates about egoism vs. altruism or emotions vs. reason in moral decision-making is whether morality is grounded in a distinctly male-centered (patriarchal) view of the world (Held, 1993, 2006). Scholars interested in this area suggest that men and women have different moral compasses, shaped by their lived experiences. For men, morality is grounded in and shaped by their involvement with traditionally male-dominated activities, such as acquiring wealth, entering business-related contracts, and governing societies (Fieser, n.d.). Systems of rules needed for trade and governance then became the model for creating relatively rigid, rules-based systems of morality that stress rights and duties (Held, 1993). Women, on the other hand, develop their moral compass from experiences that involve them in childcare and nurturing of others, both of which are far less rule-oriented actions. Because these activities involve greater spontaneity and creativity, systems of morality arising from these experiences stress caring and nurturance over rules, rights, and duties. As a result, in the "male model," the moral person performs the duties required of him and follows universalistic rules unaffected by circumstances. By contrast, in the "female model," the moral person responds to circumstances in a caring and nurturing manner. Rather than being distant, the moral person allows circumstances to touch them and uses creativity to respond in an appropriately nurturing fashion. Feminists (e.g., Held, 1993) have argued that a **care-based system of ethics**—concerned more with context and less with abstract rules—can either supplement "male-models" of morality or replace them entirely (I examine potential gender-based differences in morality in greater depth in Ch. 4).

NORMATIVE ETHICS

Normative ethics is the branch of ethics that seeks to develop standards for morally acceptable conduct (e.g., "The Golden Rule") and justify those standards using logic and reason (Kagan, 1997). A key assumption guiding normative ethics is either: (1) there is a single criterion that determines moral conduct or (2) there are sets of criteria that determine the morality of conduct (Kagan, 1997). Take the Golden Rule as an example. It consists of a single guiding principle against which the morality of behavior is compared: "Do unto others as you would have others do unto you." By using this single standard, I am able— at least in theory— to decide whether *any* possible action is right or wrong, ranging from lying, to cheating, to stealing, to physically harming others. In other instances, *sets* of guiding principles, such as those involving good character traits or possible consequences, become the standard for assessing morality. These lines of thinking are illustrated by three major systems of normative ethics, known as teleological ethics, deontological ethics, and virtue ethics.

Teleological Ethics

Have you ever been tempted to cheat on an examination in one of your classes? What helped you decide (either way)? If you focused on the possible costs (e.g., getting caught) and benefits (e.g., achieving a high grade) of cheating, you focused on the potential consequences of cheating (or not). In doing so, you relied upon a teleological system of ethics to decide what to do. **Teleological ethics** focuses on the potential outcomes of behavior, be they good or bad, to determine the ethics of the behavior (in Greek, the word *telos* means "end" or outcome of behavior). These theories first became popular in the 18th and 19th centuries, when philosophers sought a quick and (relatively) straightforward way of creating standards for judging the ethics of any behavior. Consequentialist theories are attractive since one can readily "envision" potential outcomes of behavior. In the case of cheating on the test, you can easily envision earning either an "A" or an "F" on the test—each is possible. There are competing teleological theories of ethics; my focus here is on two of them, known as ethical egoism and Utilitarianism.

One example of teleological ethics is known as **ethical egoism**. When determining whether behavior is ethical, this system focuses on the potential consequences of the behavior—good and bad—*for the actor alone*. If the potential negative consequences exceed the potential positive consequences, then the behavior is judged as unethical; if the opposite is true, the behavior is ethical. A second popular consequentialist theory is **Utilitarianism,** which holds that an action is moral if the possible positive consequences for everyone outweigh the possible negative consequences. As you will learn, the difference between the two theories is one of emphasis. Ethical egoism stresses the consequences for the person engaging in the behavior as important to the acceptability of the behavior. Utilitarianism, on the other hand, stresses the potential consequences for all involved as the key to whether the behavior is judged acceptable (I examine teleological ethics in greater detail in Ch. 2).

Deontological Ethics

Humans are social animals. That is, we seek the company of other humans and organize entire social systems around the relationships that develop. Depending on the specific nature of the relationship you have with other humans—friend, sibling, son or daughter, colleague, stranger—you incur certain obligations or responsibilities to those people (in other words, when you occupy a status, certain obligations to others arise). In **deontological ethics** (from the Greek *deon,* or duty), ethical behavior is not determined by the possible consequences of one's behavior. Rather, ethical behavior is determined by fulfilling the obligations people incur to others because of their relationship with them (Fieser, n.d.). Deontological ethics is sometimes referred to as nonconsequentialist because duties are obligatory, regardless of the consequences that might follow from an action. For example, from a deontological standpoint, it would be unethical for me to not care for my elderly, infirm parents, even if doing so resulted in great financial savings for my spouse and me.

Two examples of deontological theories of ethics include those based on the writings of the 18th-century Prussian philosopher Immanuel Kant and those relating to religious principles, referred to as Divine Command theory. Kant argued that that we have moral duties to self and others, but that there is one fundamental duty that is above all others, which he called the **categorical imperative**. This imperative—a command—says (1) treat others as ends, not as the means to an end, and (2) act in a way that you would want everyone to always act. Kant also distinguishes the categorical imperative from what he called **hypothetical imperatives** that relate to our desires, which he articulated as "if-then" statements, such as "If you want to earn an 'A' in this course, then you must work very hard," or "If you want a solid marriage, then remain faithful to your spouse." **Religious ethics** proponents argue that morality is (1) dependent upon the character of one or more supreme deities ("God") and (2) a function of obedience to God's commands revealed to us through parables or stories, along with sacred texts like the Christian Bible, the Jewish Torah, or the Islamic Koran. **Divine Command theory** views the morally right action as one that God commands of us—and that we are thus compelled (have a duty) to follow. The specific content of these divine commands varies based on the specific religion and views of the divine command theorist, but all versions of the theory hold in common the claim that morality and moral obligations are based on God (I discuss deontological ethics in greater detail in Ch. 2).

Virtue Ethics

The above systems of ethics focus on behavior and using rules to determine whether something is ethically permitted or not. While espousing different rules, each system's rules are based on reason. Therefore, people can learn them because people can reason. A third major system of ethics, called **virtue ethics**, suggests that that developing good habits or character is the key to living a proper life (Timpe & Boyd, 2014). Among the proponents of virtue ethics are some of the greatest philosophers of all time, including Plato, Aristotle, St. Augustine, and St. Thomas Aquinas, all of whom argued that ethics is fundamentally related to character. Plato, for example, identified four core (or cardinal) virtues: wisdom, courage, temperance, and justice. Other important virtues include fortitude, generosity, self-respect, good temper, and sincerity. In addition to advocating good habits of character, virtue theorists hold that we should avoid acquiring bad character traits, or vices (e.g., cowardice, insensibility, injustice, and vanity). Virtue theory also stresses that virtuous character traits develop through moral education, especially during childhood. Virtue ethics is among the oldest systems of ethics in the entirety of Western civilization, tracing its origins to ancient Greece (I discuss virtue ethics in greater detail in Ch. 2). Figure 1.2 summarizes the systems of normative ethics I've mentioned to this point.

APPLIED ETHICS

Under what circumstances is abortion morally permissible? What about physician-assisted suicide? Is human cloning morally acceptable? Is one *morally* obligated to help the homeless person begging for money on the street corner? Is eating meat morally permissible? These are just a few of the many thousands of questions that applied ethicists consider.

Applied ethics is the third major branch of ethics and is devoted to analyzing moral problems and the moral permissibility of specific actions or practices in specific areas of life, including economics and business, medicine, and law and policy (Collste, 2012). The field is distinct from other branches of ethics but is related to them in that it seeks answers to similar kinds of questions. The field is also varied— there are many kinds of research projects in applied ethics, including in the following substantive areas (Mastin, 2008):

- Medical ethics: moral values and ethical judgments as they apply to medicine;
- Bioethics: ethical controversies brought about by advances in biology and medicine;
- Legal ethics: ethical controversies relating to the practice of law;

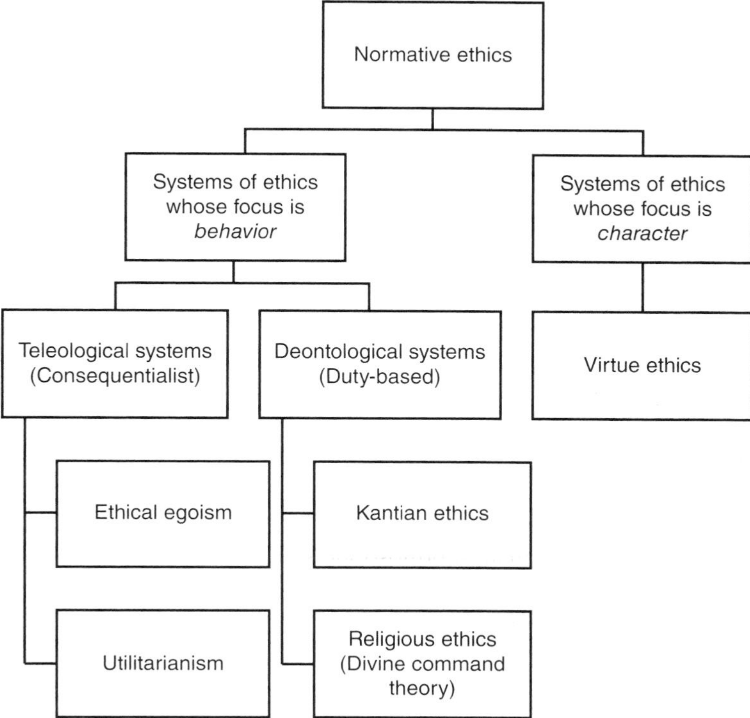

FIGURE 1.2 Systems of Normative Ethics

- Business ethics: ethical principles and problems arising in business;
- Environmental ethics: ethical issues relating to the relationship between humans and the natural environment;
- Information ethics: ethical issues arising from computers and information technologies;
- Media ethics: ethical principles and standards for journalism, advertisement, and entertainment.

One issue in applied ethics is which method or formula should be used to figure out the morality of a given practice, action, or policy (e.g., police use of deception to apprehend drug dealers). One approach is "top/down," where one starts with a normative theory, say, Utilitarianism, and moral actions are decided by the guiding principle(s) of that theory. One then assesses the action or practice using the principle(s) (Dittmer, n.d.). Another way is to use a pluralist approach, in which various moral principles are drawn from to decide the morality of the action or practice. A final choice is to use moral particularism, which defines the moral status of an action not on the basis of moral principles, but rather on the basis of morally relevant factors as they occur in a specific context, for example, in medicine or in law (Dancy, 1993). In criminal justice, applied ethics might deal with the ethics of such practices as plea bargaining; with police tactics like profiling and use of deception; or with judges running for election who accept campaign contributions from attorneys likely to appear in their courts.

Professional Ethics

How often have you used the word "professional" to describe how someone acted while occupying a specific status, such as plumber, nurse, police officer or architect? Meant to describe how well the individual performed his or her duties, in common parlance anyone can be a "professional." The reality, however, is much different.

As explained by Michael Losavio, Kathryn Siegfried-Spellar, and John Sloan (2016), sociologists distinguish among "jobs," "occupations," and "professions." A job is simply a way of earning money to cover one's basic needs, such as housing and food. In a job, the one doing the work may have little to no substantive interest in what he or she is doing, possesses minimal competency, and may be uncommitted to the position. An occupation, by contrast, involves much greater commitment to the work and the possession of minimum competencies and skills. "Police officer," for example, is an occupation that (at minimum) requires one to possess a high school diploma (or GED) and successfully complete a series of psychological and physical tests, graduate from a certified training academy, and endure a probationary period of on-the-job training. Finally, a profession involves entrance into an elite realm of work where the individual acquires specialized knowledge, training, and skills. Professionals engage in relatively autonomous, client-centered work, and follow a code of ethics that governs their work-related behavior. Table 1.1 presents the distinguishing characteristics of the professions.

TABLE 1.1 Distinguishing Characteristics of the Professions

Characteristic	Description
Knowledge	Specialized knowledge grounded in well-established theories and conceptual schemes that give intellectual coherence to specific facts and procedures; deeper and more sophisticated than that of an ordinary worker
Training	Specialized university-based training prepares individuals to be competent practitioners; university or professional school admissions policies and processes serve gatekeeping function
Value of the Work	Professional work is deemed of great economic and social value
Relations with Clients	*Credat emptor* ("let the buyer trust"), where the professional controls at least *some* aspects of the client's behavior (e.g., "doctor's orders")
Guidance of Professional Behavior	Presence of a code of ethics that defines the key values of the profession and provides general guidance for its practitioners; provides a process for investigating alleged unprofessional behavior, and provides sanctions, including expulsion from the profession for violating the code
Relations with Other Members of the Profession	Cooperative—professionals are participating in a common endeavor; competition for clients is frowned upon; public criticism of a fellow professional is avoided unless it serves some higher good; competitive relations (e.g., lawyers involved in litigation) are governed by accepted standards of professional practice
Level of Autonomy	Very high
Regulation	Self-regulation based on established standards and practices and licensing by the state

Source: Adapted from Volti (2012, pp. 153–156).

Professional ethics can be described as codified (written) sets of principles, standards, or rules that apply to professionals. The principles that guide the behavior of specific professionals, say, lawyers (including defense attorneys and prosecutors), can be developed in two separate ways (Dittmer, n.d.). One way is to find the key features of the profession and then, given these features, identify the major ethical issues associated with them. A second way would be to develop the principles by starting with important historical (as opposed to hypothetical) cases and then drawing out moral lessons and principles from them. Once members of the profession have adopted the principles, standards, or rules they are typically incorporated into a written code of ethics.

Codes of Professional Ethics

Andrew Abbott (1983) has noted that professionals such as lawyers, doctors, or engineers have two obligations: those to society and those to clients. In the former case, the professions have various service obligations to the larger society. Medicine, for example, has an obligation to help prevent and treat disease. Lawyers have an obligation to ensure justice is done. In case of clients, the professions have created rules— called "codes of ethics"— that outline members' societal obligations and articulate proper behavior when interacting with clients and others. In effect, these codes create rules for those in the profession to follow as they go about their everyday work.

In a classic study of professional codes of ethics, Abbott (1983) observed that they had several commonalities: (1) they are formally written and national in scope; (2) they are related to intraprofessional status (how members view other members and those outside the profession); (3) they stipulate an enforcement mechanism that includes disciplinary proceedings and sanctions for violations; (4) they are applicable to individual professionals and to individual occasions of professional behavior, rather than regulating aggregate professional performance or conduct (e.g., costs of service, quality of results, etc.); and (5) they identify obligations toward fellow professionals, clients, and others, with obligations toward fellow professionals predominating.

THE IMPORTANCE OF PROFESSIONAL ETHICS. Why are professional ethics important? One reason they matter is because most professionals have an informational advantage over their clients (Fisher, 2014). Because power imbalances between client and professional can be exploited to the professional's advantage, a corresponding obligation—articulated in the code of ethics—is needed to ensure that the professional does not exploit the client's trust. Such an obligation demands that the professional act in the client's best, long-term interests and take all necessary steps to ensure transparency in the relationship by revealing actual or potential conflicts of interest that could harm the client. Thus, professional ethics function to identify moral hazards for professionals, and either provide them appropriate strategies for avoiding them, or if they can't be avoided, provide ways to work around them (Fisher, 2014).

Second, professional ethics matter because most professionals are, at some point, new and inexperienced. Professional ethics for these individuals "represent a kind of collective, time-tested wisdom that is passed on to new professionals" (Fisher, 2014, p.1). Professional ethics warn those new to the profession what to watch out for and tell them what to do. In addition, as change occurs in law, technology, and professional norms, evolving standards "will help keep professionals informed of new ethical challenges, emerging responsibilities, and best practices" (Fisher, 2014, p. 1).

A third reason professional ethics are important is because they help serve as a "countervailing [balance] to organizational influence or the power of authority (say, from a supervisor or boss)" (Fisher, 2014, p.1). To illustrate, imagine an accountant for a successful company is calculating its quarterly earnings. Although accounting has a standard for calculating and reporting corporate earnings, there are also bosses who tell their accountants to "make the numbers work" to meet the earnings expectations of Wall Street. Professional ethics remind the individual accountant of his or obligations beyond those of helping ensure the financial success of the company (Fisher, 2014).

Finally, professional ethics play a role in disciplining those who engage in unethical conduct. Professional associations, like the American Bar Association (ABA), that create codes of professional ethics typically include a formalized process for pursuing sanctions against practitioners who do not follow the rules and enforce a sliding scale of penalties, ranging from censure to expulsion, for those found in violation of the rules.

THE RELATIONSHIP BETWEEN MORALITY AND ETHICS

Given what I've said to this point about morality and ethics, you may wonder how the two are related. Recall that, for our purposes, morality is an overarching code of conduct—a set of rules—that applies to all who understand the code and are willing to conform to it. Ethics, on the other hand, is the systematic study of what is right and wrong. An easier way to think about the two is this: morality refers to the customs, the special "dos and don'ts," that most people in a group or society share and accept as the standard for behavior, whereas ethics refers to reflections on these rules, including justifications for them (Gammel, n.d.). For example, a specific group or society may have rules against lying, and stress that "honesty is the best policy." Lying would thus be immoral. However, ethics might have a different take on lying, depending on which system of ethics and the guiding principle(s) consulted. For example, while a Kantian would agree that "lying is always wrong," the Utilitarian would assess the possible positive and negative consequences of lying before reaching a conclusion about whether the behavior was wrong. Additionally, morality has been shown to change over time and place—it is culturally relative (Prinz, 2011). To illustrate, prior to the 20th century in the United States, women were considered the property of their fathers and husbands; had limited legal rights; were limited in, or outright prohibited from, enrolling in certain professional schools, etc. Anyone who rejected these rules was considered "immoral." Today, however, discriminating against women would not only be considered immoral by most Americans, but such discrimination would also be patently illegal (Amnesty International, 2017). From the perspective of ethics, discrimination against women would be wrong—regardless of time or place. What this means is that there is not always *concordance* between morality and ethics. While morality tends to be fluid and variable over time and across place, ethics tends to be stable.

Table 1.2 distinguishes some of the key features of morality and ethics.

TABLE 1.2 Distinguishing Morality From Ethics

Key Feature	Morality	Ethics
Meaning	Beliefs shared and rules followed by members of a society or group as to what is right or wrong	Guiding principles that help individuals or groups decide what is good or bad behavior
Root Word	From the Greek word *mos*, which means "custom"	From the Greek word *ethikos*, which means "character"
Governed By	Social and cultural norms	Various systems/guiding principles
Deals With	Principles of right and wrong	What constitutes right and wrong conduct
Consistency	Morality may differ from society to society or group to group	Ethics are generally uniform.
Expression	Morality is expressed in the form of general rules and statements.	Ethics are expressed as abstract principles

Source: Adapted from Burhi (2015, p. 1).

MORALITY, ETHICS, AND THE CRIMINAL JUSTICE PRACTITIONER

Many of you want to pursue a career in the field of criminal justice, be it in law enforcement, as a defense attorney or prosecutor; in the field of institutional or community-based corrections; in forensics, whether natural (e.g., drug chemistry) or digital (the identification, recovery, preservation, and analysis of evidence stored on electronic equipment); or in research. Because many entry-level positions in the field of criminal justice require a bachelor's degree—at minimum—you're pursuing an undergraduate degree in criminal justice or a related discipline like sociology or psychology to qualify for those positions. Assuming you're successful in finding a position, you'll end up working in an agency setting, such as a municipal police department, county sheriff's department; or district attorney's office; in a regional crime laboratory; or with a federal agency like the Federal Bureau of Prisons (FBP). At that point, you'll join millions of others working in the tens-of-thousands of agencies that make up the criminal justice system in this country.

When you join the ranks of a criminal justice agency, you will bring with you a set of moral values—beliefs about right and wrong. Your values developed over time and have been shaped and influenced by your parents and friends; the community in which you were raised; your religious beliefs; and the law (Braswell, 2015). Additionally, one's values may take two forms: terminal and instrumental (Rokeach, 1973). Terminal values refer to socially acceptable end-states or goals, such as trust or safety, and are close to the center of one's core beliefs, whereas instrumental values are the preferred means, such as honesty or courage, to achieve socially acceptable ends (Conroy, 1979; Rokeach, 1973). Thus, the presumption here is that humans engage in specific modes of conduct to achieve desired end-states of being. For example, to be able to trust one another (an end-state) we do not lie, cheat, or steal from one another (preferred means). Milton Rokeach has argued that values are arranged into a value system that he described as "an enduring organization of beliefs concerning preferable modes of conduct or end-states along a

CASE STUDY 1.1 Discovering Personal Values

After graduating from high school, I began working full time as an automobile mechanic in a "mom-and-pop" service station (I had been working there part-time for about 18 months). I "clocked-in" six days a week at 2:00 p.m. and "clocked-out" at 10:00 p.m. After a year or so on the job, I realized that, long term, I could never really be happy doing this work. The reason for my dissatisfaction was probably that the all-boys Catholic high school from which I'd graduated had as one of its goals to "create men for others" who would "strive to be competent, religious, loving, open to growth, and committed to justice." Servicing cars to make my boss money while being paid just over the then-minimum wage hardly seemed to fit the bill. So, after three years, I quit my job and enrolled full-time at a regional university where I then spent the next five years earning a bachelor's and a master's degree in criminal justice. I then pursued a doctorate (Ph.D.) in sociology at a large research university in another state, which took another four years. Why did I do this? Because as I made my way through college and began to "find myself," I realized that serving others and being independent were core values of mine. It thus made sense for me to become a professor, as doing so would allow me to serve others by helping educate young people and train their minds, while also enjoying the enormous independence that came with the job. No more "punching clocks" for me!

continuum of importance" (Rokeach, 1973, p. 15). Finally, some scholars have contended that the number of values of primary interest to people is small, but nonetheless enhances decision-making by providing socially approved standards against which one compares one's actions (Ellwanger, 2015). Two of my values include service to others (an instrumental value) and independence (a terminal value). But realizing this took some time and effort on my part, as explained in Case Study 1.1.

Personal values are important, as they establish priorities in your life relating to career, marriage, children, politics, etc. They also will be the measure used to "take stock" of your life at various points and decide if it's turning out the way you wanted. When what you do for a living and how you behave while doing it are in harmony with your values, you'll feel satisfied. When there is disjuncture between them, you'll feel that something is wrong, become increasingly unhappy, and may decide that a change is necessary (Ellwanger, 2015).

THE NATURE AND SOURCE OF PRACTITIONER VALUES

There's an extensive line of research that explores the values of criminal justice practitioners and their impact on job performance. For example, Ellwanger (2015) has suggested that newly hired criminal justice practitioners (e.g., police officers) bring with them specific values that those choosing careers outside the criminal justice field do not necessarily possess. This occurs, in part, because criminal justice agencies actively screen for certain values (e.g., loyalty, conformity) held by prospective employees, and occupational socialization reinforces these values, modifies others, and replaces still others. What remains is a value system that finds expression in the practitioner's attitudes and behavior. In effect, this system is *imported* into the agency.

If this **value-predisposition perspective** is correct, which values are of importance for criminal justice practitioners? Research has identified several of them and described their sources (see Ellwanger, 2015). For example, conservativism and conformity are two key terminal values held by criminal justice practitioners, especially the police. Empirical research shows that police work typically attracts individuals from a local area who are family oriented and have working-class ("blue collar") economic roots. These individuals tend to see the world in "black or white" terms, have military experience (or come from military families), or come from families with members who are police officers. These individuals see their work as being important (i.e., "having a point") and having social significance. Other values include a commitment to make the world a safer place ("the noble cause"), utilitarianism (where the good of the many outweighs the good of the one), and crime fighting (which emphasizes questioning suspicious persons, making arrests, collecting evidence, and conducting interviews) (Ellwanger, 2015). Some scholars have even argued that police selection processes—with the polygraphs, drug tests, background investigations, and oral interviews—are specifically designed to screen out prospects who lack the above-mentioned values (Gaines & Kappler, 2011).

You should understand that these values have historical, cultural, economic, and social origins. For example, believing that "catching the bad guys" is important has its origins in individuals' prior life experiences, their families, and in "long-standing American values that have favored the underdog," the roots of which "are grounded in the idea that anyone can achieve the American Dream if they work hard enough" (Ellwanger, 2015, p. 52). These values are also the products of the perceived legitimacy of the law as it exists in a democracy and the perceived neutrality of its application. Finally, if the value-predisposition perspective is correct, social influences—especially those from popular media—affect practitioner values. Again, using the police as an example, media depictions of policing that stress crime fighting by individuals with almost superhuman abilities using sophisticated high-tech forensic devices that allow them to identify criminals and pinpoint their motivations reinforce "crime fighting" as the key role of police officers, which in turn attracts individuals with such an orientation (Ellwanger, 2015). Further, media depictions of police officers—along with other criminal justice practitioners—using "dirty means" to achieve "just ends" also influences the type of person drawn to the field of criminal justice. The result of all these influences may be that criminal justice agencies "feel pressured" to recruit and screen prospective employees in a way that retains those having values that approve of crime fighting and efficiency, rather than those possessing values that favor due process protections and shielding the innocent from the power of the state.

An alternative view of criminal justice practitioner values is the **values-learned perspective**, which argues that terminal and instrumental values possessed by criminal justice practitioners are not imported into the agency, but are instead learned through a process of socialization and enculturation (Ellwanger, 2015).This perspective suggests that through socialization, an agency "fuses" the practitioner to the organization by providing him or her "the rules, perspectives, prescriptions, techniques, and tools necessary to participate in the organization" (Ellwanger, 2015, p. 54). This results in the practitioner experiencing an occupational career during which one both learns what is expected of one and "becomes" a practitioner in the sense of that identity becoming crucial to one's sense of self.

The Occupational Career of the Practitioner

The **occupational career** of a criminal justice practitioner consists of several distinct stages (Ellwanger, 2015). The stages include choice, introduction, encounter, and metamorphosis. "Choice" relates to what the profession has to offer individuals, including the perceived importance and meaningfulness of the work, that is, the social benefit it produces, combined with job security and a relatively high salary with respect to the education requirements of the position. "Introduction" refers to the changes occurring in the recruit as he or she begins training and learning the skills necessary to do the job. Importantly, the novice learns what the job is "really like" and may begin experiencing a subtle shift in values during this phase of his or her occupational career. The high ideals and positive values brought to the job may begin to fade, replaced by distrust of the bureaucracy the novice encounters and the group loyalty and solidarity necessary to protect him or her from the hostilities of citizens and the administration of the agency for which he or she is working. The recruit's views on proper behavior may shift as a result of "war stories" told by academy instructors and field training officers that may explain how the novice can obtain "freebies," meet women (or men) while on duty, sleep on duty, and shirk responsibilities (Ford, 2003). "Encounter" describes the novice learning the difference between theory and practice, typically explained by a more senior officer responsible for training the novice and evaluating the novice's ability to do the job. Of note here is that the training officer helps redefine the reality of the work for the novice, much of which involves the mundane, and that only a few situations will involve "real" work, wherein danger is present and the rookie's willingness to use force to tamp down the threat is tested. In short, the novice is learning that most of what he or she thought was going to be commonplace, such as fighting crime, is rare. Finally, "metamorphosis" describes the psychological and sociological changes occurring in the new officer as he or she reorganizes his or her identity around the new role, which means leaving behind former ties to civilians and becoming increasingly immersed in a new world where practitioners are the primary system of support and former friends, and even family to some degree, are less important. Table 1.3 presents these components along with explanations.

The Moral Career of the Practitioner

In addition to his or her occupational career, the criminal justice practitioner experiences what Lawrence Sherman (1982) calls a **moral career**: how the practitioner reacts to the values he or she has learned. The practitioner's moral career involves the

TABLE 1.3 The Occupational Career of the Criminal Justice Practitioner

Stage	Description	Values
Choice	Desire and ability to become a member of the criminal justice field	Social significance of the position; desire to fight crime and become a member of an "elite organization"
Introduction	Learning necessary skills and behavior required to do the job	Loyalty; conformity; solidarity; cynicism for bureaucracy; distrust of superiors
Encounter	Bridging the gap between theory and practice (doing the job for the first time)	Distrust of citizens, media, agency administrators; increased cynicism; disenchantment with profession
Metamorphosis	Individual achieves "full status" as practitioner and reorganizes sense of self around the new role	Source of future transmission of learned values

Source: Adapted from Ellwanger (2015, p. 56)

individual slowly rejecting the positive values that moved her to join the field, while simultaneously beginning to accept and engage in behaviors contrary to agency, legal, and societal standards. Sherman's notion of a practitioner's moral career, in short, helps to explain how criminal justice practitioners may become corrupt ("bent") over time. Sherman argues that one's moral career consists of contingencies, moral experiences, apologia, and stages.

"Contingencies" describe the work environment of practitioners that encourages or discourages adopting unethical (and potentially illegal) behaviors. A variety of factors help to shape contingencies, including level and type of supervision of the practitioner by superiors. Type of work is also important. For example, a police officer working undercover with limited supervision, all things being equal, would be expected to be more likely than officers in other situations to adopt unethical practices that go undetected because of the opportunities and temptations that come with working undercover. "Moral experiences" describe specific challenges to one's morality, such as that occurring when one sees a colleague engaging in unethical or illegal conduct. Under such circumstances, the individual must choose between allowing and/or taking part in the behavior or reporting the colleague and facing ostracism from other members of the field. "Apologia" describe rationalizations that develop to explain away unethical or illegal behaviors to reduce the psychological or emotional discomfort they cause. Apologia are situation-specific and may vary depending on the nature of the behavior being rationalized. Finally, "stages" describe the overall transformational process of becoming corrupt, of moving from being virtuous and ethical to becoming corrupt. Table 1.4 presents the stages of the practitioner's moral career.

Each of us possesses a core set of values, such as respect, dependability, or forgiveness, arranged in a hierarchy. Those values, in turn, relate directly to our personal sense of morality, a personal code of ethics. That hierarchy includes the means we use to achieve a desirable end. For example, if we value respect, then when we meet others, we give them due consideration and treat them as worthy of our attention. When you become a criminal justice practitioner, you will not only bring a set of values to the new role you occupy (e.g., probation officer), but also learn from others—probation officials, police officers, or judges—the values that are considered important to *being* a probation officer (or a police officer, prosecutor, forensic scientist, etc.). You may find that others in the field have values like yours, largely because existing recruiting processes actively seek people possessing them. As you begin your occupational career, you'll be tugged in various directions and expected to engage in behavior that you may find problematic, such

TABLE 1.4 The Moral Career of the Criminal Justice Practitioner

Stage	Experiences
Contingencies	Factors associated with the type of work being done and level of supervision associated with the work that provide impetus for unethical behavior
Moral Experiences	Specific situations in which the practitioner's morality is challenged
Apologia	Rationalizations for unethical/illegal behaviors
Stages	The overall progression from being ethical to becoming corrupted

Source: Adapted from Ellwanger (2015, p. 63)

as using force or lying, to achieve some greater good. It's important that you understand there are connections between the values one has, and the means chosen to achieve them. Such connections can be illustrated by examining two views on how the criminal justice system should work and the kinds of behaviors that system enables.

VALUES IN ACTION: TWO MODELS OF THE CRIMINAL JUSTICE PROCESS

The values that one brings into one's role as a criminal justice practitioner has implications for how he or she does his or her job. For example, if a core value held by police officers is "conformity," they may frown on behavior the larger community being policed may accept, such as drinking alcohol in public. One way to try and ensure conformity is through negative sanctions imposed on those engaging in the proscribed behavior. Thus, the officer may choose to exercise his or her discretion and arrest people drinking alcohol in public. Indeed, one of the features of so-called broken windows policing is that minor, low-level offenses (such as public consumption of alcohol or social gatherings of small groups on street corners) will not be tolerated and will result in arrests being made (Center for Evidence-Based Crime Policy, 2013). The idea behind broken-windows policing is that punishing minor violations of the law deters prospective offenders from engaging in more serious types of crimes (Kelling & Wilson, 1982). Much like a vacant house where a single broken window left unrepaired leads to further acts of vandalism that continue until the house is destroyed, so too is there a relationship between allowing minor offenses to continue unabated and an increase in more serious crimes. By sanctioning minor offenders, the community sends the message to prospective offenders that a single broken window will not go unrepaired (Taylor, 2001).

Crime Control Model

One illustration of the importance of values in the operation of the criminal justice system is found in *The Limits of the Criminal Sanction* by Stanford University law professor Herbert L. Packer. In the book, Packer identifies two "models" of the criminal justice system that he labels the "crime control" and "due process" models. The models are "an attempt to abstract two *separate value systems* that compete for priority in the operation of the criminal process" (emphasis added; Packer, 1968, p. 14). According to Packer, key instrumental and terminal values of the **crime control model** include the following:

- *Crime repression*. The repression of crime and enhancement of public order are the essential functions of the criminal justice system. Order is a basic necessity for a free society.
- *Victims' rights*. The criminal justice system must protect the rights of victims throughout the process. Protecting defendants' rights is of much less importance.
- *Police powers*. The police must have the power to investigate crimes, search and seize evidence, arrest citizens, and convict the guilty.
- *Defendants' rights minimized*. Legal "technicalities" that constrain police powers, such as the exclusionary rule, *Miranda* warnings, etc., should be eliminated.

- *Efficiency.* To maximize its efficiency, the criminal justice process should operate like an assembly line, where cases are moved along swiftly to a conclusion.
- *Presumption of guilt.* In the event a citizen is arrested and had charges filed against him or her, the defendant should be presumed guilty because the outcomes of police and prosecutorial actions are highly reliable.
- *Establish guilt.* The primary aim of the criminal just process is to establish the factual guilt of the accused.

Due Process Model

Packer's **due process model** consists of instrumental and terminal values that, in general, run counter to those found in the crime control model:

- *Fundamental fairness.* The primary goal of the criminal justice process is to ensure fundamental fairness in its interactions with defendants. Due process of law is paramount.
- *Protect defendants' rights.* Police, courts, and correctional entities should concentrate on protecting defendants' and offenders' rights, as the Constitution expressly provides for such protections over those accorded to victims.
- *Constrain the police.* The power accorded the police should be constrained, as it too often leads to oppression of individual citizens.
- *Accountability.* Criminal justice authorities should be held accountable for protecting the rights of defendants and offenders, which ensures that due process of law is achieved.
- *Criminal justice as an obstacle course.* The criminal justice process should resemble an obstacle course, where procedural safeguards work as much to protect the innocent as to convict the factually guilty.
- *Legal guilt established.* Factual guilt is not enough to procure a conviction. Rather, defendants should only be found guilty if the government has properly followed legal procedures governing all stages of the criminal justice process from arrest to conviction.

Packer (1968) explained that accepting one model or the other is a value judgment on our part that is not necessarily guided by logic or scientific evidence. One can argue that the crime control model emphasizes "conservative" values that stress maintaining order and safeguarding the public good, while the due process model reflects values that are associated with "liberals" and stresses placing checks on governmental power and also ensuring fundamental fairness for defendants. Packer also noted that the larger political climate influences which model is preeminent. For example, during the politically liberal 1960s and into the 1970s, through a series of landmark decisions, the U.S. Supreme Court created significant checks on the power of the government to investigate, try, and convict its citizens of crimes. Thus, due process principles and policies were emphasized—and enforced—in the operation of the criminal justice system. Beginning in 1980, with the election of Ronald Reagan as president and continuing through today, the country moved to the political right and, as a result, the values espoused by the crime control model have held sway. Which model is closer to the values that *you* espouse?

SUMMARY

In this chapter, I introduced you to some foundational notions that will guide the rest of your journey into criminal justice ethics. As you've no doubt noticed, philosophy—along with sociology and psychology—have been very influential in identifying and describing these foundational issues. As your journey continues, I will again call upon these disciplines to help guide that journey, keeping in mind that your journey will not only be one of self-discovery but also one of understanding the implications of what you discover as a prospective criminal justice practitioner.

The chapter began by introducing you to the notion of "morality" and explaining that morality involves a set of rules ("norms") designed to guide our behavior—to tell us what is "right" and what is "wrong," acceptable and unacceptable. Sociologists and anthropologists alike observe that some of these rules are formal, such as laws that are codified and involve formal social control mechanisms (the police) brought to bear against violators. Other norms are unwritten and are thus more informal and attend to matters ranging from rules about dress, etiquette, or marriage and procreation. These culturally bound rules help members of the group label what is "good" and "bad" behavior. These rules are also attached to various statuses—the position one occupies in a hierarchy of positions that enjoy diverse levels of power and prestige—that we occupy over our lives. Finally, these rules help to make interaction possible by telling us what to expect of both self and other when meeting people in roles similar to, or different from, ours. I also argued that morality is variable, bound by time and culture.

Further, I explained that ethics and morality, often used interchangeably in everyday life, are *not* the same. Ethics is a subarea within the larger discipline of philosophy and concerns itself with a number of different questions, including whether morality even exists (metaethics), how we should behave (normative ethics), how character influences proper behavior (virtue ethics), how to reasonably address controversial issues such as abortion, climate change, and capital punishment that generate so much conflict (applied ethics), and what constitutes appropriate behavior for those working in the professions (professional ethics). I also introduced you to several systems of ethics, including consequentialist, Kantian, religious, and Virtue, along with their guiding principles. These systems have served as the foundations on which Western systems of normative ethics have been built over several millennia, stretching all the way back to ancient Greece. I emphasized that although offering different justifications for how one should behave, these systems are based on reason (as opposed to emotion) and have at their core some semblance of logic.

I then explored the role of values in morality and ethics, beginning with Rokeach's seminal work on values, including what they are, how they are ordered, and the distinct types that exist. I discussed the sources of values seen in criminal justice practitioners and offered two different perspectives on where these values come from—that they are imported into the field by those working in it or are learned through occupational socialization. Further, I illustrated how one's values as a criminal justice practitioner may change over time as one's occupational career and moral career play out. I also argued that values are important because they affect the way criminal justice practitioners go about their routines. I illustrated this point by reviewing the groundbreaking work of Herbert Packer, who characterized the criminal justice process as guided by two competing sets of values—crime control and due process.

Before moving forward with our journey into criminal justice ethics by learning more about the systems of normative ethics I introduced to you above, Thought Exercise 1.1 asks you to consider the ethical implications of the discretion that is exercised each day by police officers, prosecutors, judges, and correctional officials.

THOUGHT EXERCISE 1.1

ETHICAL ISSUES AND THE EXERCISE OF DISCRETION IN CRIMINAL JUSTICE

As you have likely learned in other criminal justice classes, discretion and its exercise are at the heart of how the criminal justice process—the various stages that begin with an arrest and continue post-conviction in American jails and prisons—operates. As a case winds its way through the process, at each stage an official must answer a basic question: What to do with this case? Police officers answer that question when deciding whether to issue a traffic citation to a motorist or arrest someone based either on a complaint filed by another citizen or on a warrant handed down by a court. Prosecutors do so when deciding what charges to bring against a defendant and how many charges to bring. Judges do so when deciding what sentence to give to a defendant who's either been found guilty at trial or has pled guilty. Probation officers do so when deciding whether to seek revocation of a probation agreement when one of their charges misbehaves. But what, exactly, *is* discretion?

Criminologists Shawn Bushway and Brian Forst have defined discretion in the context of criminal justice as "[the] latitude granted officials to act under a formal set of rules and in a public capacity" (Bushway & Forst, 2011, p. 1). The "rules" to which they refer are procedural laws relating to how crimes can be investigated, evidence seized, suspects arrested and interrogated, charges filed against them, etc. However, they make the point that even the most detailed rules "allow criminal justice personnel to countermand or contradict them" (Bushway & Forst, 2011, p. 1). Thus, there is not necessarily a one-to-one correspondence between what the rules say and how they are implemented. Bushway and Forst (2011) also point out that discretion may lead to *disparity*—instances in which similar cases are treated differently or different cases are treated similarly. For example, disparity in sentencing involves judges imposing *different* sentences on defendants in cases that appear the same on their merits or imposing the *same* sentence on defendants in cases that appear different on their merits.

From the standpoint of ethics, the question is whether such disparity can be rationally justified, not on *legal* grounds but on *moral* grounds. For example, is it ethically permissible to punish offenders who have been convicted of distributing "crack" cocaine more harshly than those convicted of distributing powder cocaine? Can the disparity in sentences created by certain types of "three-strikes laws" be justified? What about policies that mandate that individuals suspected of misdemeanor assault in cases of domestic violence be arrested by the police?

These questions are a matter of ethics and, as you progress through this book, should be answerable using available information, your capacity to reason, and logic.

KEY TERMS

Morality 6
Ethics 7
Metaethics 7
Moral relativism 8
Care-based system of ethics 10
Normative ethics 10
Teleological ethics 11
Ethical egoism 11
Utilitarianism 11
Deontological ethics 11
Categorical imperative 11
Hypothetical imperative 11
Religious ethics 12
Divine Command theory 12
Virtue ethics 12
Applied ethics 12

Professional ethics 15
Value-predisposition perspective 18
Values-learned perspective 19
Occupational career 19
Moral career 20
Crime control model 22
Due process model 23

DISCUSSION QUESTIONS

1. Work with one or more partners and identify an example where morality and ethics might reach a different conclusion about how one should act in a given situation, such as allowing an abortion in a case of rape or incest. Present your results to the class.
2. Pair off with another member of the class and pick one area in applied ethics. Next, identify a key issue associated with the area and debate the issue with one of you taking a "pro" side and the other taking a "con" side (even better, take the side with which you *disagree* and argue its case). Identify which of the approaches mentioned in the chapter (top/down, pluralist, moral particularism) the two of you used to inform your argument(s). Present your results to the class. Which approach was used most/least often?
3. Find your school's "code of ethics" for students and identify what the code stresses as important—from the perspective of ethics—to the role of "student" at your college or university.
4. Can you identify other instances in U.S. history when there was discordance between morality and ethics, besides the discordance involving women's rights? Explain.
5. Work with a partner to determine if there is an overlap between the *occupational* career of a criminal justice practitioner and her *moral* career. Present your findings to the class.

RESOURCES

***Psychology Today*'s** website (https://www.psychologytoday.com/basics/ethics-and-morality) has a great list of resources on morality and ethics including books, articles, blogs, etc.

The **American Psychological Association** (APA) has a website that is devoted to professional ethics for psychologists. The site includes the *APA Code of Professional Ethics.* http://www.apa.org/ethics/resources/

REFERENCES

Abbott, A. (1983). Professional ethics. *American Journal of Sociology, 88*, 855–885.

Amnesty International (2017). Gender-based discrimination. Retrieved from http://www.amnestyusa.org/our-work/issues/women-s-rights/gender-based-discrimination

Asher, L. (2012). Philosophy weekend: Rebooting the argument against egoism. Retrieved from http://www.litkicks.com/RebootingTheArgument

Braswell, M. (2015). Ethics, crime, and justice: An introductory note to students. In M. Braswell, B. McCarthy, & B. McCarthy (Eds.), *Justice, crime and ethics* (8th ed.) (pp. 3–9). Waltham, MA: Anderson Publishing.

Burhi, S. (2015). Difference between morals and ethics. Retrieved from https://keydifferences.com/difference-between-morals-and-ethics.html

Bushway, S., & Forst, B. (2011). Discretion in criminal justice. In B. Huebner (Ed.), *Oxford Bibliographies: Criminology*. Retrieved from http://www.oxfordbibliographies.com/view/document/obo-9780195396607/obo-9780195396607-0083.xml

Center for Evidence-Based Crime Policy (2013). Broken windows policing. Retrieved from http://cebcp.org/evidence-based-policing/what-works-in-policing/research-evidence-review/broken-windows-policing/

Center for the Study of Ethics in the Professions (n.d.). About the Center. Retrieved from http://ethics.iit.edu/about

Cline, A. (2016). What is metaphysics? Retrieved from http://atheism.about.com/od/philosophybranches/p/Metaphysics.htm

Collste, G. (2012). Applied and professional ethics. *Asian Journal of the Humanities, 19*, 17–33.

Conroy, W. (1979). Human values, smoking behavior, and public health programs. In M. Rokeach (Ed.), *Understanding human values: Individual and societal* (pp. 199–256). New York, NY: The Free Press.

Crossman, A. (2016). Sociology concept spotlight: Achieved status versus ascribed status. Retrieved from http://sociology.about.com/b/2011/03/25/sociology-concept-spotlight-achieved-status-versus-ascribed-status.htm

Dancy, J. (1993). *Reasons*. Oxford Blackwell.

Dittmer, J. (n.d.). Applied ethics. In J. Fieser & B. Dowden (Eds.), *Internet encyclopedia of philosophy*. Retrieved from http://www.iep.utm.edu/ap-ethic/

Ellwanger, S. (2015). Learning police ethics. In M. Braswell, B. McCarthy, & B. McCarthy (Eds.), *Justice, crime and ethics* (8th ed.) (pp. 47–71). Waltham, MA: Anderson.

Farside, T. (2007). The psychology of altruism. *The Psychologist, 20*, 474–477.

Fieser, J. (n.d.). Ethics. In J. Fieser & B. Dowden (Eds.), *Internet encyclopedia of philosophy*. Retrieved from http://www.iep.utm.edu/ethics/

Fisher, J. (2014). Why are professional ethics important? Retrieved from https://www.quora.com/Why-are-professional-ethics-important

Ford, R. (2003). Saying one thing, meaning another: The role of parables in police training. *Police Quarterly, 6*, 84–110.

Gaines, L., & Kappler, V. (2011). *Policing in America* (7th ed.). Boston, MA: Elsevier.

Gammel, S. (n.d.). Ethics and morality. Retrieved from http://www.philosophie.tu-darmstadt.de/media/philosophie_nanobuero/pdf_2/ethicsportfolio/ethics_morality bwnewfont.pdf

Gert, B. (2005). *Morality: Its nature and justification*. New York, NY: Oxford University Press.

Gert, B., & Gert, J. (2016). The definition of morality. In E. Zalta (Ed.), *The Stanford encyclopedia of philosophy* (Spring Edition). Retrieved from http://plato.stanford.edu/cgi-bin/encyclopedia/archinfo.cgi?entry=morality-definition

Giddens, A. (1993). *Sociology*. Chicago: University of Chicago Press.

Harrison, L., & Huntington, S. (Eds.) (2000). *Culture matters: How values shape human progress*. New York, NY: Basic Books.

Held, V. (2006). *The ethics of care: Personal, political and global*. New York, NY: Oxford University Press.

Held, V. (1993). *Feminist morality: Transforming culture, society and politics*. Chicago, IL: University of Chicago Press.

Hobbes, T. (1994 [1668]) *Leviathan* (E. Curley, Ed.). Indianapolis, IN: Hackett Publishers.

Jackson, J. (1965). Structural characteristics of norms. In I. Steiner & M. Fishbein (Eds.), *Current studies in social psychology* (pp. 301–309). New York, NY: Holt, Rinehart and Winston.

Kagan, S. (1997). *Normative ethics*. Boulder, CO: Westview Press.

Kelling, G., & Wilson, J. (1982, March 8). Broken windows: The police and neighborhood safety. *The Atlantic*. Retrieved from http://www.lantm.lth.se/fileadmin/fastighetsvetenskap/utbildning/Fastighetsvaerderingssystem/BrokenWindowTheory.pdf

Losavio, M., Siegfried-Spellar, K., & Sloan, J. (2016). Why digital forensics isn't a profession and how it can become one. *Criminal Justice Studies, 29*, 2–20.

Mackie, J. (1977). *Ethics: Inventing right or wrong*. New York, NY: Penguin Books.

Mastin, L. (2008). Applied ethics. Retrieved from http://www.philosophybasics.com/branch_ethics.html

May, J. (2011). Egoism, empathy, and self-other merging. *Southern Journal of Philosophy, 49*, 25–39.

Packer, H. (1968). *The limits of the criminal sanction*. Stanford, CA: Stanford University Press.

Prinz, J. (2011). Morality is a culturally conditioned response. *Philosophy Now, 82*, 5–9.

Rokeach, M. (1973). *The nature of human values*. New York, NY: The Free Press.

Sayre-McCord, G. (2014). Metaethics. In E. Zalta (Ed.), *The Stanford encyclopedia of philosophy* (Summer Edition). Retrieved from http://plato.stanford.edu/archives/sum2014/entries/metaethics/

Sherman, L. (1982). Learning police ethics. *Criminal Justice Ethics, 1*, 10–19.

Sumner, W. (1940). *Folkways*. Boston, MA: Ginn & Co.

Taylor, R. (2001). *Breaking away from broken windows: Baltimore neighborhoods and the nationwide fight against crime, grime, fear, and decline*. Boulder, CO: Westview Press.

Timpe, K., & Boyd, C. (Eds.) (2014). *Virtues and their vices*, New York, NY: Oxford University Press.

Turner, B. (1988). *Status*. Minneapolis, MN: University of Minnesota Press.

Vago, S. (2012). *Law and society* (10th ed.). Oxford: Taylor & Francis.

van Inwagen, P., & Sullivan, M. (2014). Metaphysics. In E. Zalta (Ed.), *The Stanford encyclopedia of philosophy* (Winter Edition). Retrieved from http://plato.stanford.edu/entries/metaphysics/

Volti, R. (2012). *Introduction to the sociology of work and occupations*. Thousand Oaks, CA: Sage Publications.

Weir, K. (2012). Our moral motivations. *Monitor on Psychology, 43*, 24–25.

Willer, R., & Simpson, B. (2017, April 10). Are moral judgments good or bad things? *Scientific American*. Retrieved from https://blogs.scientificamerican.com/guest-blog/are-moral-judgments-good-or-bad-things/#

Yourdictionary.com (2017). Morals. Retrieved from http://examples.yourdictionary.com/examples-of-morals.html

CHAPTER 2

Systems of Ethics

Chapter Outline

CHAPTER LEARNING OBJECTIVES:

1. Distinguish among teleological-, deontological-, and virtue-based systems of ethics.
2. Describe the guiding principles of Act and Rule Utilitarian ethics.
3. Identify the major criticisms of Utilitarian ethics.
4. Distinguish the categorical and the hypothetical imperative.
5. Describe the major criticisms of Kantian ethics.
6. Distinguish Divine Command Theory from Modified Divine Command Theory.
7. Identify the Euthyphro Dilemma.
8. Identify the major criticisms of Divine Command Theory.
9. Describe the guiding principles of virtue ethics.
10. Identify the major criticisms of virtue ethics.

INTRODUCTION

Suppose, for the sake of argument, you believe that capital punishment is morally wrong and that both the federal government and the states should abolish the practice. You might justify your position based on the actual (or potential) consequences of capital punishment, including the economic costs of executing someone; that a truly innocent person could be executed; that executing murderers does not deter others; and that executing a murderer does not bring closure to the family of the victim. Recall from Ch.1 that ethical justifications of behavior based on the possible consequences are *teleological*. Or, say that your opposition to capital punishment rests on a belief that executing people violates their inherent worth. This justification is in line with the a core guiding principle in deontological ethics that all humans have inherent value. Finally, your opposition to the death penalty may be based on your being compassionate toward others and forgiving of their wrongs. These are indications of your virtuous character, and thus your opposition would be based on virtue ethics. Using different systems of normative ethics, you could provide at least three different justifications for why the death penalty is unethical.

In this chapter, I elaborate on the introductory material on ethics and moral philosophy I provided you in Ch. 1. My elaboration involves going into much greater detail about systems of normative ethics and the core principles of these systems. In this chapter, I'll describe the historical roots of each system and identify the key individuals credited with developing them. I'll also share with you the criticisms philosophers have raised concerning these systems. I'll end the chapter by discussing the ethical issues associated with an increasingly popular idea: privatizing the police.

SYSTEMS OF ETHICS

In Ch. 1, I gave you a broad overview of the field of ethics, including a particular focus on normative ethics, one of the subareas within the larger discipline. You also saw that normative ethics consists of different "systems"—some of which were teleological, others deontological, and still others based on virtue, and that each of these systems contains guiding principles or rules to help one decide whether the behavior under scrutiny is ethical. Let's begin by making a distinction between systems that focus on *behavior* and those whose focus is *character*.

General Distinctions

Because normative ethics focuses on justifications for how people should behave, systems of ethics have developed different moral principles to help people make those decisions. For example, an ethicist might make the broad statement that lying is acceptable if and only if the lie does not significantly affect the emotional or physical well-being of the person being lied to. Such a statement is an example of a **moral principle**, a general statement about the conditions under which a behavior is either morally right or wrong (Timmons, 2013). Over the course of millennia, Western philosophers organized these principles into coherent **theories of ethics**, which have been be described as:

> . . . mechanisms for assessing whether a particular action or rule is ethically justified. [Theories of ethics] help us determine whether an action or a rule is ethically *right* (meaning it is required and must be performed and followed), *wrong* (meaning it must not be performed or followed), or *permissible* (meaning it may be, but need not be, performed or followed)
>
> —(emphasis added; Rowan & Zinaich, 2002, p. 8)

Theories of ethics provide guidance, in the sense that they tell us what we should do, as well as provide justifications for the action taken.

Theories of ethics tend to focus either on behavior or on character (see Bazerman & Gino, 2012). The former category includes systems of ethics whose focus is developing justifications for behavior based on a set of rules and reasons for them. The latter category addresses somewhat different questions involving how the moral worth of individuals is determined. Here, one is evaluating people and holding them accountable less for what they do than for the kind of person they are. When we say, "Sally is a 'good person,'" we engage in this kind of evaluation. The morally good person is one possessing positive character traits, called virtues, and therefore will act in accord with them. While theories of right conduct address *what to do*, theories of moral worth are interested in questions of *who to be*. Figure 2.1 depicts these two orientations.

Recall that systems of ethics seeking to identify morally acceptable behavior are typically classified as teleological (consequentialist) and deontological (duty-based). Teleological ethics identifies the consequences of behavior as key to determining the ethics of that behavior. In contrast, deontological systems focus on whether one's behavior corresponds with a duty one has to follow a moral law prescribed either by the group or by a deity. Examples of teleological systems of ethics discussed below include ethical egoism and Utilitarian ethics. Examples of deontological theories include

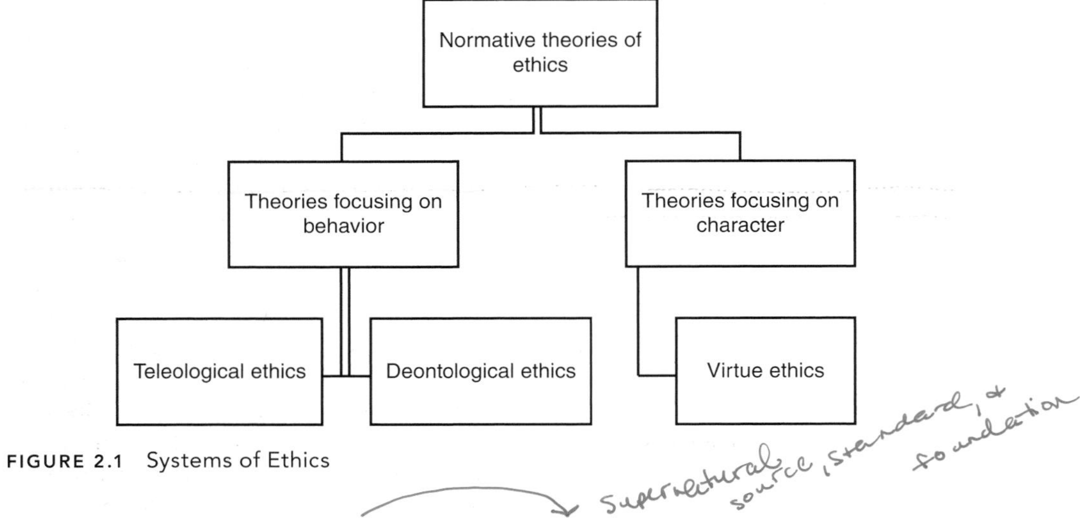

FIGURE 2.1 Systems of Ethics

Kantian ethics and religious ethics in the form of Divine Command theory. Systems of ethics that focus on one's character as the key to morality include virtue ethics. In the following sections, I explore these two categories of ethical theory in greater detail.

FOCUSING ON BEHAVIOR: TELEOLOGICAL ETHICS

Teleological theories of ethics were profoundly influenced by the writings of philosophers Jeremy Bentham (1748–1832) and John Stuart Mill (1806–1873). The guiding principles of teleological ethics they helped create tell us how we *should* behave and, in doing so, bring about good and avoid evil. The tasks teleological ethics tackles are to (1) define the principle(s) behind consequentialist moral judgments and (2) address how these principles can be applied. Recall from Ch. 1 that two well-known examples of teleological ethics include Ethical Egoism and Utilitarian ethics.

Ethical Egoism

A core principle of ethical egoism is simple: one should behave in a manner that is in one's best interests (see Field, n.d., p. 1). This is different from saying that people are motivated to act out of their own self-interests, which is a theory about why people act as they do, not a theory of how they should act. Thus, psychological egoism is different from ethical egoism (Feinberg, 1978; Gert, 1967). The former is an empirical or descriptive theory, while the latter is a normative theory (see Moseley, n.d.).

From the outset, let's be clear on what this theory is *not* saying. Ethical Egoism is *not* saying that one should never consider others. The logic is this: because doing what is good for others is typically also good for ourselves, the egoist would—under most circumstances—behave in a way that helped others as a way of promoting one's self-interests. The principle is also *not* saying that one should "do as one pleases" for the very reason that in so doing, one damages one's personal interests (Field, n.d.). What this principle *is* saying, however, is that moral behavior arises from *enlightened self-interest*. We should, based on the evidence available, act in a way that promotes our own best, long-term interests, both physically and psychologically. If doing so corresponds with the interests of others, then all the better.

Critique of Ethical Egoism

There are several problems with Ethical Egoism (Moseley, n.d.). For example, some critics have argued that pursuing one's personal "greatest good" often conflicts with another's pursuit of their greatest good. Assume for the moment you have a rich uncle. You may see *your* greatest good as coming from murdering your uncle. Your uncle, on the other hand, sees *his* greatest good as continuing to enjoy his money. Critics thus argue that such conflicts are an inherent problem, as the theory does not present a way to resolve such conflicts. Along similar lines, critics have charged that Ethical Egoism cannot resolve inherent contradictory obligations: when you act contrary to my interests, I have an obligation to prevent you from doing so (since I have an obligation to protect my interests). However, I also have an obligation *not* to prevent you from doing so, because you're doing what you're supposed to do. Thus, the contradiction and no answer for its resolution (Rachels, 2015). Finally, some critics have found a third problem with ethical egoism: it violates the principle that treating people differently can only be justified *if* it can also be shown that differences between them are relevant to justifying the treatment (Rachels, 2015). In effect, ethical egoism can result in treating people differently without justification, such as to achieve some greater good or because a religious precept commands me to do so.

Because some people are "turned off" by ethical egoism, they reject teleological ethics altogether. There are, however, other forms of teleological ethics that you might consider if you remain attracted to consequences as important for determining the ethics of behavior. These theories are known as Act and Rule Utilitarianism.

Act Utilitarianism

One of my favorite TV shows growing up in the 1960s was *Star Trek*, a weekly science fiction drama that featured the adventures of the starship *Enterprise* and its crew as they sought new life forms across the galaxy. The original *Star Trek* (1966–1969) eventually spawned five spin-off series, including, most recently, *Star Trek: Discovery* (2017–) along with a franchise of 13 successful films beginning in the 1980s and continuing through today.

In the second film that was based on the original series, *Star Trek: The Wrath of Khan* (Bennett, Phillips, Sallin & Meyer, 1982), the starship *Enterprise* is in imminent danger of destruction. Mr. Spock (played by the late Leonard Nimoy), the ship's science officer and second-in-command, enters a chamber that had been flooded with radioactive particles to try and fix the ship's engines so the crew can escape the danger. As Spock is dying from radiation poisoning, with his final breaths he says to his commanding officer Admiral Kirk (played by William Shatner), "Don't grieve, Admiral. It is logical. The needs of the many outweigh . . ." Kirk finishes for him, "The needs of the few." To which Spock replies, "Or the one" (cited in Armstrong, 2013, p. 1). Spock's words illustrate the core principle of Act Utilitarianism: the morally correct action is the one resulting in the greatest utility (happiness) for the greatest number of people, on a case-by-case basis. The Act Utilitarian thus considers the consequences of one or more choices and chooses the one that results in maximizing utility (Nathanson, 2011). Figure 2.2 depicts how an Act Utilitarian would engage in such decision-making.

Proponents of Act Utilitarianism point to three justifications for their theory (Nathanson, 2011). First, the theory calls for one to maximize the overall (net) utility of behavior. If one always chooses to behave in a way that maximizes utility, the cumulative effect of those choices over a lifetime produces the greatest utility that any one person could produce. If everyone else also chooses to maximize the utility of their behavior,

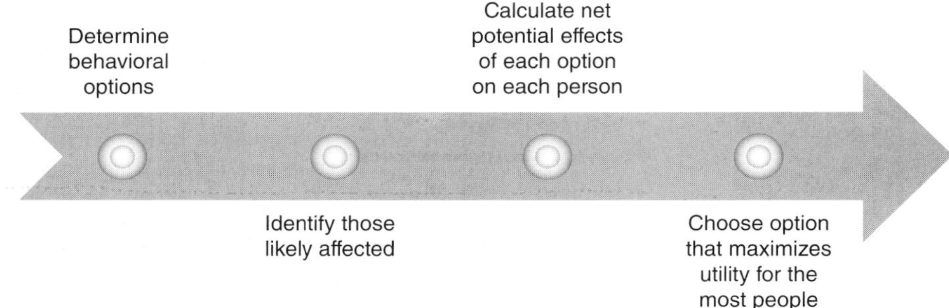

FIGURE 2.2 The Decision Process in Act Utilitarianism
Source: Adapted from Arsham (2015, p. 1)

the net effect would be to achieve the maximum possible overall utility for the entire group over its lifetime.

Second, the theory rejects rigid "rule-based moralities" that identify whole classes of actions as right or wrong but also provide exceptions (e.g., "Thou shall not kill" *except* during war). Act Utilitarians argue that identifying entire categories of behavior as either right or wrong ignores the fact that the effects of these actions vary under different circumstances. To illustrate: if a police officer used excessive force to arrest a suspect, the outcome of that behavior would likely be much different if no outsiders observed the officer, as compared to if it had occurred in front of a crowd. In the former instance, the officer "knows" she will be unlikely to face negative consequences for the behavior since it'll be her word against the defendant's and her superiors will be likely to believe her. In the latter instance, she "knows" she will likely be sanctioned by superiors due to so many people witnessing her behavior and corroborating the defendant's claim. For Act Utilitarians, morality must focus on the potential effects of individual actions because, in a given set of circumstances, it is the "likely effects" that determine whether the behavior is right or wrong. Act Utilitarians agree that general rules describing right and wrong behavior may be useful but argue that if the greater good can be achieved by violating a rule than by following it, the proper action would be to violate the rule.

Finally, supporters offer a third justification for the theory by arguing that the theory "shows how moral questions can have objectively true answers" (Nathanson, 2011, p. 1). In contrast to believing that morality is a function of belief or feelings, Act Utilitarianism provides evidence—specifically, foreseeable consequences of behavior—in support of which moral beliefs are true and which are not. If one can predict the level of happiness likely to arise from different behaviors, one can then know which action would be morally acceptable and which would not.

Before you dismiss this notion out of hand, consider that people predict the utility of behavioral outcomes all the time. Consider this illustration: say that two hospital patients are experiencing great pain, but there is enough medicine only for one of them. Because we can usually tell which of the two is in greater need of the drug(s), we can then assume we'll be doing the greatest good by giving the drugs to the patient suffering the higher level of pain. While this illustration is simplistic, it nonetheless shows how we can objectively find "true" answers to questions about the morality of behavior (Nathanson, 2011).

Critique of Act Utilitarianism

Act Utilitarianism is not without its critics (see Nathanson, 2011). Here, I consider three criticisms of the theory: (1) it offers wrong answers to questions involving the morality of behavior; (2) it undermines trust between people; and (3) it requires impartiality and equal consideration of all people's needs and interests.

Concerning the argument that Act Utilitarianism gives wrong answers to questions about morality, consider the following example. If a judge can prevent riots that will cause many deaths only by convicting an innocent person of a crime and imposing a severe punishment on that person, Act Utilitarianism would require the judge to convict and punish the innocent person (Nathanson, 2011). This example (and others like it) is used to illustrate how Act Utilitarianism accepts that certain acts would not only be morally permissible, but necessary, based on the circumstances and despite the fact the behavior violates other widely accepted rules (e.g., innocents should never be convicted of a crime they did not commit). The criterion that an act is morally wrong if and only if it fails to result in the greatest good can cause some acts that seem wrong not to be judged as such, while some acts that do *not* seem wrong can end up being judged as wrong (Nathanson, 2011). To illustrate, consider an act of murder that results in only slightly more good than any other action would likely have produced. According to Act Utilitarian ethics, this murder is *not* wrong because it produced the greatest amount of happiness for the largest number of people. Critics contend that a moral theory that condones actions resulting in the violation of other rules with which most people agree provides the wrong answer to questions about the morality of behavior.

Second, opponents of the theory contend that by criticizing rules that form the basis of various systems of ethics as "too rigid," Act Utilitarianism ignores the fact that "this alleged rigidity is the basis for trust between people" (Nathanson, 2011, p. 1). Consider: even though there is no magic in majorities, if most people believed that morality allowed for lying, cheating, breaking promises, or violating the law when doing so leads to good results, the result would be an inability to trust others to obey the very rules that frown upon lying, cheating, breaking promises, or violating the law. The implication here is that members of the group could not count on fellow members to follow the rules and/or act in accordance with them, which leads to everyone being unable to predict how others are going to act most of the time.

Finally, some have criticized Act Utilitarianism because it is impartial when considering the interests of those likely affected by the behavior (Nathanson, 2011). What this means is that from an Act Utilitarian perspective, the consequences of our behavior for complete strangers should be accorded the same weight as the consequences of the behavior for a close friend, a spouse, a sibling, or a parent. For proponents of Act Utilitarianism, the morality of behavior is a function of its consequences; we should thus always strive to maximize the utility (positive consequences) of our behavior for the greatest number of people. In practical terms this means that if you are sending your daughter to a private, college preparatory high school at a cost of $25,000 per year and it could be shown that the money spent on tuition could feed 5,000 people in sub-Saharan Africa for six months, the Act Utilitarian would say you should spend the money on African relief and send your daughter to public high school. As Nathanson (2011, p. 1) describes the situation, "[i]f more good can be done by helping strangers than by purchasing things for oneself or people one personally cares about, then Act Utilitarianism requires us to use the money to help strangers in need." Can you see a problem with this thinking? Most people would argue that we should first weigh the possible consequences of our behavior for those closest to us. In other words, when assessing the morality of their actions, most people would rank order the possible consequences based on the nature of the relationship the actor had with those affected by the behavior. The closer the relationship, the greater the weight accorded the consequences, whether positive or negative. As Nathanson (2011, p. 1) points out, ". . . most people would reject the notion that morality requires us to treat people we love and care about no differently from people who are perfect strangers."

As mentioned above, Act Utilitarianism is not the only consequentialist system of ethics. There is a second type of Utilitarian ethics, known as Rule Utilitarianism. Let's explore that system of ethics now.

Rule Utilitarianism

The guiding principles of Rule Utilitarianism include the following: (1) an act is morally wrong if and only if it is forbidden by rules that are justified by their consequences; (2) individuals should use rules for their moral decision-making that are justified by their consequences; and (3) moral sanctions should be rules-based and justified by their consequences (Hooker, 2015). Rule Utilitarians are saying that following certain rules helps ensure the maximum good (utility).

Consider the difference between a stop sign and a yield sign (Nathanson, 2011). Stop signs *prohibit* drivers from continuing through an intersection without coming to a complete halt, regardless of circumstances. A yield sign *permits* drivers to proceed through an intersection without stopping *if* approaching cars don't make doing so dangerous. The difference is thus the amount of discretion each sign, representing a particular rule, gives drivers. The stop sign illustrates Rule Utilitarianism: it tells drivers to STOP and doesn't allow them to figure out whether it would be better to not do so. Act Utilitarianism is like the yield sign. It permits drivers to decide whether there is a need to stop. Act Utilitarians see the stop sign as too rigid because it requires drivers to stop even when there is no need to do so, and thus utility is lost each time a driver stops when no other cars are approaching. Figure 2.3 illustrates these differences. Rule Utilitarians would not reject the stop sign analogy if (1) people could be counted on to drive carefully and (2) traffic accidents caused only limited harm (Hooker, 2015; Nathanson, 2011). The problem is neither of these is true—people often drive too fast and are inattentive while driving because they are talking, texting, listening to music, or tired. Thus, people can't be counted on to make good Utilitarian judgments regarding safe driving, resulting in many thousands of traffic fatalities and injuries each year. Rule Utilitarians would thus support using stop signs under most circumstances. Fixed rules—like stop signs—generate greater utility because they prevent more disutility than they create.

Critique of Rule Utilitarianism

Rule Utilitarianism isn't without its critics (Hooker, 2015; Nathanson, 2011). Common criticisms of this system are similar to those leveled at Act Utilitarian ethics. One criticism leveled against Rule Utilitarianism is that its proponents "worship rules." What is meant here is that critics contend Rule Utilitarians "blindly support the rules," even in instances where violating them would result in greater good than harm. For example, during the segregation era, police officers who "blindly" followed the rules requiring segregated public spaces were, in reality, promoting much harm for African Americans.

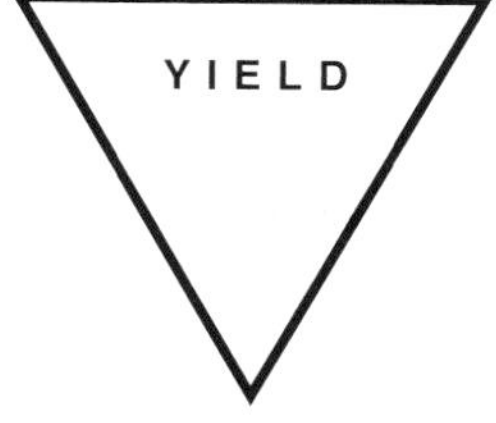

Rule utilitarianism

- You *must* stop at the intersection regardless of circumstances – there is no discretion afforded the driver
- You *must* maximize utility – there is no discretion when it comes to doing so, regardless of circumstances

Act utilitarianism

- You *should* stop at the intersection if circumstances warrant – use your discretion
- You *should* maximize utility, based on the circumstances

FIGURE 2.3 The Difference Between Rule and Act Utilitarianism

Had enough of them not enforced immoral segregationist laws, doing so would have resulted in the dismantling of those policies at a much faster pace, resulting in much greater good than harm.

A second criticism of Rule Utilitarianism is that it has "collapsed into the practical equivalence of Act Utilitarianism" (Hooker, 2015, p. 1). To illustrate, think about a rule that a Rule Utilitarian would condone, such as "do not steal." Now consider a situation where stealing would produce more utility (good) than would not stealing, such as the case of a CIA operative having the opportunity to steal North Korean plans for an intercontinental ballistic missile capable of striking the United States. What critics suggest here is that if Rule Utilitarians select rules on the basis of their expected utility (the good that results from following the rule), proponents would also be forced to admit that complying with a narrower rule—"Don't steal *except* when ________, or in the case of ________, or if ________ is occurring"—is actually better than complying with the simpler "do not steal" (Hooker, 2015). Critics are thus claiming that for every situation where compliance with a rule would not produce the greatest expected good, Rule Utilitarianism seems driven to favor instead compliance with an amended rule that also produces the greatest expected good. The result is that Rule Utilitarianism often mandates the *same actions* as those mandated by Act Utilitarianism (Hooker, 2015). The problem is that this creates a dilemma: what's the point of having a Rule Utilitarianism with infinitely amended rules if we can achieve the same result in a more efficient manner by simply following Act Utilitarianism?

The final criticism raised about Rule Utilitarianism is that it cannot avoid its weaknesses because it does not accept as legitimate common moral precepts such as justice, rights, and desert (Nathanson, 2011). Thus, Rule Utilitarians do not give adequate guidance for resolving moral dilemmas and justifying the choice(s) made when doing so. Ideals like justice and rights are often used to justify morality, but both Act and Rule Utilitarianism reject their importance. Instead, both systems focus only on the amount of utility generated by either specific behavior in specific instances, or by general rules governing behavior regardless of circumstances.

In summary, consequentialist systems of ethics, as the name implies, suggest that the key to determining the ethics of behavior is the end result—were the consequences favorable or not? If the potential consequences are mostly unfavorable, then the behavior is immoral. If the potential consequences are mostly favorable, the behavior is moral. However, as I illustrate in the following section, there is another way to assess the ethics of behavior that rejects the notion that all that matters revolve around consequences. Instead, based on another line of thinking, what matters in ethics is *duty*.

FOCUSING ON BEHAVIOR: DEONTOLOGICAL ETHICS

Recall that deontology translates to the "study of duty." For deontologists, the morally right action is one that conforms to the duty that one must follow a rule or principle. One example of a common deontological theory of ethics is found in the system developed by Immanuel Kant.

Kantian Ethics

The Prussian philosopher Immanuel Kant (1724–1804) made major contributions to multiple areas in philosophy and is considered one of the greatest philosophers of all time. Three of his most important contributions were in moral philosophy: *Groundwork of the Metaphysics of Morals* (1785), *Critique of Practical Reason* (1788), and *The Metaphysics of Morals* (1797). These works presented the foundation upon which Kant first constructed a system of ethics that philosophers later refined.

Kant's moral philosophy consisted of several important assumptions and principles. First, Kant argued that humans are autonomous beings capable of understanding the world around them through the laws of nature, and through reason, the capacity to

Immanuel Kant
Wikimedia Commons

consciously make sense of things, apply logic, and identify and verify facts (Rohlf, 2016). Reason allows us to think about what is true or false, cause and effect, or what is good or bad. Reason relates to our ability to change our beliefs, practices, traditions, and institutions and therefore relates to our capacity for freedom and self-determination (Glovitch, 1991). Morality cannot be solely a product of feelings because if it were, morality would vary from individual to individual, and even within individuals depending on their state of health and experience (Rickman, 2011). Kant also argued that the fundamental principle of morality is the moral law, what he called the categorical imperative, and upon which all moral duty is based (Cavalier, 2002; Folse, 2003; Kant, 1785/2008; Kant, 1788/1950; O'Neill, 1994). The categorical imperative is a product of both reason and our needs and wants. Kant argues that through reason, we "give the moral law to ourselves, just as we also give the general laws of nature to ourselves" (Rohlf, 2016, p. 1).

The duties that flow from this moral law command how we should act regardless of circumstances. For Kant, reflecting upon and following through on our duties lead us to the "highest good." In Kant's thinking, humans use the moral law to create the idea of a moral world guided by a general code of conduct. The categorical imperative is a formal principle (what Kant deemed a "maxim") that serves as the foundation of his system of ethics. It is a command without condition to behave in a certain way regardless of circumstances, goals one wants to meet, or desires. For Kant, the categorical imperative applies to all without exception or condition (Rickman, 2011). To illustrate, the rule "do not lie" remains in effect even if I could meet some desire or achieve a particular goal by lying.

The Categorical Imperative

In *Groundwork of the Metaphysics of Morals*, Kant (1785/2008) developed four formulations of the categorical imperative (CI), as follows:

1. CI-1: *The Formula of Universal Law*: "Act only in accordance with that maxim through which you can at the same time will that it become a universal law" (Kant, 2008, p. xvii);
2. CI-2: *The Formula of Humanity as an End in Itself*: "Act so that you use humanity, as much in your own person as in the person of every other, always at the same time as end and never merely as means" (Kant, 2008, p. xvii);
3. CI-3: *Formula of Autonomy*: "the idea of the will of every rational being as a will giving universal law" (Kant, 2008, p. xvii); and
4. CI-4: *The Formula of the Realm of Ends*: "Act in accordance with maxims of a universally legislative member for a merely possible realm of ends" (Kant, 2008, p. xviii).

Rickman (2011) explained these formulations as follows. For example, CI-1 tells us to act in a way that we would want everyone to act, if we could will them to do so, or if we could will the behavior in question (e.g., lying) to be a universal law. For example, when deciding whether to lie to your parents about whether or why you violated your curfew, Kant would ask whether you would you want *everyone* to lie to their parents (the implication being what kind of a world would be created if lying to parents was universally accepted behavior). CI-2 tells us never to use others as the means to an end, but to treat all people as ends in and of themselves. In other words, all humans have inherent worth and should never be used to achieve some end, even if the end is noble. CI-3 extends the earlier two conceptualizations by saying, in effect, picture yourself as a legislator writing the law for a new kingdom in which everyone must be treated as ends in themselves. You can't be hypocritical and say, "I'm going to write this new law that prohibits cheating on one's spouse *after* I've done so myself." You also can't legislate in a way that would allow people to be treated as means to an end, such as *allowing* a law to be passed that encouraged infidelity. Doing so makes it acceptable for all others to act in the same way, violating the principle that people should never be treated as a means to an end, and thereby creating a world in which spouses couldn't be trusted not to cheat on one another. CI-4 reiterates that the moral law that you're creating in your kingdom is rational and is therefore based on reason—the ability to consciously make sense of things and apply logic to them. It would not, for example, be either reasonable or rational to create a moral law that says that lying is acceptable behavior; you realize that lying damages trust and that trust between people is crucial to establishing and maintaining relationships. For Kant, reason dictates that the action we are morally bound to choose is the one motivated by adhering to a principle that could consistently apply to all rational actors (Folse, 2003).

Finally, Kant argues that morality and freedom are reciprocal. For Kant, acting morally is exercising one's freedom; the only way to be fully free is to act morally. Having the will to act in a certain manner at all arises from a maxim—what I'm doing and why I'm doing it. Although we may not be aware of our maxims, may be inconsistent in following them, or they may conflict with one another, they still guide our behavior as they help us to achieve some end or goal that may be as basic as fulfilling a desire ("I want to be rich") or something more complex, such as becoming a forensic scientist (Rohlf, 2016). When humans act to gratify a desire, they have simply chosen to act on a maxim to achieve that desire. For example, if I am hungry, I act on the maxim "visit a restaurant and purchase a meal" to gratify the desire.

The Hypothetical Imperative

Kant distinguished the categorical imperative, which he termed a formal principle that guides behavior, from the hypothetical imperative, which he termed a material principle that guides behavior (see Box 2.1). Hypothetical imperatives are rules that guide behavior

BOX 2.1 The Difference Between the Categorical and Hypothetical Imperative

Categorical Imperative	Hypothetical Imperative
Based in reason/rationality;	A material principle that is based on meeting some end or fulfilling a desire;
A formal principle—you must/must not act this way;	Framed as an "if . . . then" statement;
Circumstances do not matter— would you want everyone to act this way?	Considers circumstances;
Humans have inherent value—do not use them for your own ends;	Narrow in scope
Be consistent!	

to achieve a specific goal: if you want food, then you should go to a restaurant; if you want coffee, then you should visit a café. These imperatives are narrow and only apply when one chooses to gratify a specific desire. However, acting only on hypothetical imperatives does not mean that I am acting freely. It only means that I am acting out of the desire to satisfy a need that I have that is not ultimately within my control (for example, you can't really control when you're thirsty or hungry) (Folse, 2003; Rickman, 2011; Rohlf, 2016). In effect, Kant advises that we are free to either govern our desires or allow or desires to govern us. If we choose to act based on material principles, we have not "given the law to ourselves" and are allowing nature (our desires) to determine our behavior. As one scholar described it:

> The only way to act freely in the full sense of exercising autonomy is, therefore, to act on the categorical imperative, which is also to act morally. Kant does not mean . . . that we take no account of our desires, because that would be impossible. Rather, he holds that we typically formulate maxims with a view to satisfying our desires, but that 'as soon as we draw up maxims of the will for ourselves' we become immediately conscious of the moral law.
>
> —(Rohlf, 2016, p. 1)

Suppose you want to earn a good grade in your ethics class (a maxim). You could decide "if I want to earn a good grade in this class, then I should devote extra study time to it." Or, you could decide "if I want to earn a good grade in this class, then I should cheat whenever possible on the exams." What do you do? For Kant, what becomes important in your decision is this: which maxim (extra effort or cheating) would hold as a universal practical law? If you choose cheating, then your universal law would be for everyone to cheat in their ethics class to earn a good grade. However, because you are rational, you are at once aware that such a rule is infeasible as the grades everyone earned would be highly questionable. For Kant, a maxim is morally permissible only if it could be willed as a universal law. If your maxim fails this test, as this one does, then it is morally impermissible for you to act on it.

Critique of Kantian Ethics

Philosophers have identified both the strengths and the weaknesses of Kantian ethics. On the positive side, Kantian ethics stresses that all human beings have inherent value. Such a rule can become the basis for a system of human rights like that articulated by the United Nations in its *Universal Declaration of Human Rights* (United Nations, 2016). Kant also argued that some acts are always wrong, no matter the potential consequences. Thus, Kantian ethics also offers a sense of certainty that is lacking from Utilitarian-based ethics because consequences are not certainties, only possibilities. For Kant, if an action is a right action, then it should be done; if the action is not a right action, then it should not be done. Another positive aspect of Kantian ethics is that it considers intention and motive, something that most people consider important but something teleological theories ignore. Thus, if one did not intend the morally wrong action, one should not be open to criticism for engaging in the behavior. Additionally, taking account of intent allows moral rules to be narrowly tailored.

However, Kantian ethics is not without critics (Rickman, 2011). Perhaps the biggest criticism leveled at Kantian ethics concerns its absolutist orientation: if some behavior (e.g., lying) is wrong, it is always wrong—no exceptions. To illustrate this problem, imagine that you are home late one evening along with your spouse and children. You hear noises downstairs and investigate, only to be confronted by an armed burglar, who asks if you are there alone. Kant would say that lying to the burglar is morally wrong, since lying is always wrong. Critics point out that what would have to occur to remedy this problem would be to build a huge list of "exceptions" to each rule—in this case that lying is always wrong, except when it involves preventing harm to loved ones—which would be almost impossible. A second problem with Kantian ethics is that it has no problem with behavior that potentially makes the world less safe, good, etc. since it does not consider the consequences of our behavior as relevant to questions of morality. As the British philosopher A. C. Ewing once said about Kantian ethics, ". . . [I]t is hard to believe that it could ever be a duty deliberately to produce less good when we could produce more" (Ewing, 1947, p. 186). A final problem with Kantian ethics is that it cannot help us reconcile conflicting duties we may have—it accords the same moral "weight" to *all* duty.

In summary, Kantian ethics is a deontological system that justifies moral rules as being based on reason and offers guidelines/criteria for evaluating the moral worth of our behavior. Kant argued that behaving morally was a matter of fulfilling our duty (obligations), for which there could be no exception or loophole. For the Kantian, ends never justify the means; an action is itself either intrinsically good or bad, based on the categorical imperative. Kant also includes in his system what he dubbed hypothetical imperatives or dictates based on conditions or desires, as in "you should not lie if you want people to trust you." Hypothetical imperatives are framed as "if . . . then" statements that connect the command to an outcome. Critics have argued against the system's absolutist orientation—that it takes no account of actions making the world worse—and its failure to distinguish among duties owed to others, as a result of which it cannot help to resolve conflicts among them.

Let's now turn to a second deontological system of ethics—religious ethics. One well-known example of religious ethics is Divine Command theory (DCT), which says that we have a duty to follow rules created by a supreme deity (e.g., God, Allah) as revealed through sacred texts, stories, and traditions. In the next section, I provide details about this system and its principles.

Religious Ethics: Divine Command Theory (DCT)

Religious belief as the basis for ethics has a very long tradition that dates back over two thousand years with the world's three great Abrahamic religions: Judaism, Christianity, and Islam. These religions are considered Abrahamic because they are monotheistic (there is only one God) and revere Abraham, the biblical patriarch, as the ancestor of many peoples, including the Jews, Ethiopians, and Arabs (Hughes, 2013). Among Abraham's descendants are the major prophets depicted in the Christian Old Testament, the Torah, and the Qur'an. The land where Abraham and his descendants are believed to have settled is now called the Holy Land, a region on the eastern coast of the Mediterranean Sea that stretches between ancient Mesopotamia and Egypt and includes the modern states of Israel, Palestine, Jordan, Saudi Arabia, Yemen, and parts of Egypt, Iraq, and Syria (Douglass, n.d.).

Religious ethics answers what it sees as the basic question in morality: Is the source of, and ultimate justification for, morality religion or reason (see Hinman, 2013). Some religiously oriented ethicists take what is called the "religious supremacy position," which argues that if or when conflicts arise between religion and reason, religion provides the correct guide for morality and therefore takes precedence (Hinman, 2013, p. 74). The best example of this position is Divine Command theory (DCT), which says that morality, and therefore "good" behavior, is derived from God's commands. They tell us how we ought to behave (see Figure 2.4).

DCT presents three guiding principles, as follows: (1) morality originates with God; (2) morality is that which is "willed by God" and immorality is that which is "against the will of God"; and (3) because morality is based on divine will, not on reasons that exist independent of it, no further justifications for action are necessary (Pojman, 2013). For DCT, moral statements such as "always tell the truth" are defined in theological terms: God commands it (Wierenga, 1989). In one slight modification of the notion that moral principles are commands of God, some proponents of DCT suggest that God's commands, rather than telling us what is moral (as in a list), inform us about the content of morality more broadly (Austin, n.d.). The three Abrahamic religions—Christianity, Islam, and Judaism—epitomize DCT ethics, because they claim that God's will is both necessary and sufficient for determining the content of morality (Driver, 2007). In other words, whatever God commands must be good, even if it appears to contradict other rules or principles.

Illustrative of the guiding principles found in DCT are three stories from the Old Testament. The first involves Abraham and his son, Isaac, as described in the Book of Genesis. In the story, God orders Abraham to sacrifice his son, Isaac. Although Abraham loved Isaac, he was still willing to obey God and commit murder. At the last moment, as Abraham was about to plunge a knife into Isaac, God intervened and told Abraham he must not make the sacrifice. Abraham's faith was tested successfully, and Isaac's life was

God's will is the source of morality

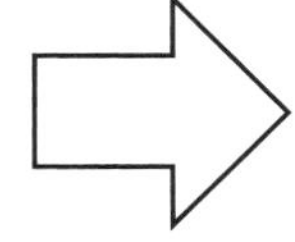

Moral actors (humans)

FIGURE 2.4 Divine Command Theory
ivan-96/iStockphoto
Created by Freepik

spared. The second illustration is God's command to the Israelites to plunder and loot the Egyptians, as described in the Book of Exodus. The third is God's command to Hosea to engage in sexual intercourse with a female adulterer. Each story involves God commanding individuals or groups to act in ways that appear to contradict one or more of the Ten Commandments, specifically, those prohibiting murder, stealing, and adultery. Rather than posing a problem for DCT, proponents point out that in each case God's will was revealed to the individuals or groups involved and therefore what they were doing—murdering, stealing, or committing adultery—could not be wrong because the behavior in which they were either going to engage or had engaged was what God commanded (Driver 2007). Thus, morality depends on God's will, even if it appears to violate some other standard, even one established by God. Thus, if God wills the behavior, it is good, no matter what. If God wills the behavior as bad, it is bad, no matter what.

The Euthyphro Dilemma

"Wait a minute," you may be saying. "Are proponents of DCT arguing that acts willed by God are morally good because they are morally good irrespective of God, or are they morally good because they are willed as such by God?" Philosophers have named this conundrum the **Euthyphro Dilemma** and traced it back to Plato's dialogue *Euthyphro*, in which Socrates asks Euthyphro, "Is the pious loved by the gods because it is pious, or is it pious because it is loved by the gods?" (Joyce, 2002). If the DCT proponent gives the first answer—that morally good acts are willed by God because they are morally good—she faces what's called the **independence problem**: if morally good acts are willed by God because they are morally good, then they must be morally good independent of God's willing them (Holt, 2008a). The independence problem, however, creates its own issues, namely, arbitrariness, emptiness, and the problem of abhorrent commands (Holt 2008b, 2008c, 2008d). "Arbitrariness" describes the problem that DCT seems to base morality on the "whims" of God. That is, how can arbitrary commands be the foundation of morality? "Emptiness" is the argument that in DCT, statements like "God is good" and "God's commands are good" are rendered as empty tautologies: "God acts in accordance with his commands" and "God's commands are in accordance with his commands." Finally, the problem of "abhorrent commands" is this: it appears DCT argues that if God were to command abhorrent acts (deception, cruelty, etc.), those acts become morally good. How can a system of morality be based on principles like deception and cruelty? So, in the end, the proponent of DCT is forced to choose the second response: the acts are morally good because they are willed as such by God.

Modified Divine Command Theory

In response to the problem of the Euthyphro Dilemma, proponents of DCT modified some of the core principles of the system and created what's now known as **Modified Divine Command theory** (MDCT) (Austin, n.d.). Robert Adams, for example, has claimed that MDCT assumes God loves us all equally and that an act is wrong "if and only if" the act is contrary to the will or commands of a loving God (Adams, 1987). Further, for MDCT proponents, not only the actions of people, but also their intentions are objective properties that possess moral wrongness. For example, lying to someone for the fun of it is objectively wrong, regardless of whether one believes lying is wrong since lying violates the will and commands of a loving God.

MDCT avoids the pitfalls of the first horn of the Euthyphro Dilemma because it argues that morality is based on the will of an unchanging, always-loving God, and therefore avoids the problem of morality being arbitrary. God's commands stem from benevolence that is never changing and therefore would never be arbitrary. MDCT avoids the second horn of the Euthyphro Dilemma because morality is a basic feature of God's character or internal to God. Since morality is internal to God, God is not subject to some other moral law? Rather, God *is* the moral law. For the proponent of MDCT, morality is thus grounded in the perfect nature of God (see Figure 2.5).

* interesting how he only criticized christianity, not Islam.

Critique of Divine Command Theory

There are many criticisms of DCT, but in this section, I present five of the more common (Austin, n.d.). First, critics have argued that morality cannot depend on the will of God because religion and morality are independent of one another—the "independence objection" (Austin, n.d.). While it may be "prudent" to obey God's commands, since God is, after all, omnipotent, it does *not* necessarily follow that obeying God is morally obligatory (Neilson, 1973). To illustrate: God must be good if His commands are relevant to

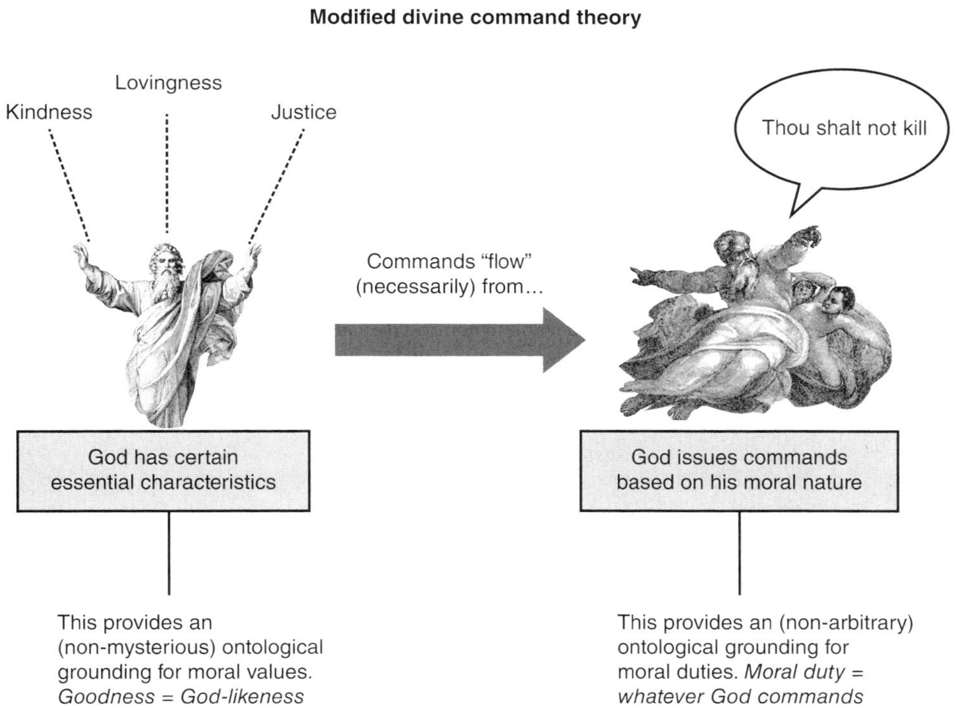

Modified divine command theory
Kindness
Lovingness
Justice
Thou shalt not kill
Commands "flow" (necessarily) from...
God has certain essential characteristics
God issues commands based on his moral nature
This provides an (non-mysterious) ontological grounding for moral values. Goodness = God-likeness
This provides an (non-arbitrary) ontological grounding for moral duties. Moral duty = whatever God commands

FIGURE 2.5 Modified Divine Command Theory
Source: http://philosophicaldisquisitions.blogspot.com/2012/10/divine-command-theory-and-metre-stick.html
ivan-96/iStockphoto
Nastasic/iStockphoto

moral obligations. While believers maintain that God is, in fact, good, what is the basis of this belief? The believer might say that the Bible teaches us this is the case or that there is evidence in the world around us of God's goodness. Such responses, however, show that the believer possesses logically prior criteria of goodness based on something apart from the mere fact that God exists or that God created the universe (Austin, n.d.). Further, how does the believer know that his or her other beliefs in the Bible or about the world support the belief that God is good?

A second problem with DCT is that it argues that not only would God not command cruelty for its own sake, but also that God could not do so. In response, critics take the position that this aspect of DCT ignores another core belief of the theory that God is omnipotent—the "omnipotence objection" (Austin, n.d.). How is it possible that an omnipotent being cannot do something, for example, overrule one of His own commands? DCT proponents suggest that this criticism is misguided. For them, to say that "God can do all things" is to say that God can do all things that are possible and not do those things that are impossible. For example, God cannot make the equation $2 + 2 = 5$ true, since this is impossible. Because the solution to this equation is a contradiction in terms—in much the same way as would be God making a round corner—it is better to say that making $2 + 2 = 5$ cannot be done, rather than saying God cannot make $2 + 2 = 5$ or make a round corner. Austin (n.d.) argues, however, that this response is insufficient for the issue at hand, namely, that per DCT, God neither would nor could command a "bad" action (e.g., murder, lying, or adultery) for its own sake. There is no logical contradiction here, as there is in the case of $2 + 2 = 5$ or a round corner. Cruelty, by its very nature, is contrary to omnipotence. Thus, saying that God cannot command an immoral action is not a limit on God's power, but is entailed by God's omnipotence. Thus, the view is that God cannot command cruelty because God is omnipotent.

A third criticism of DCT is that the theory argues an action is moral if God commands it. This means that God doing what God is bound to do is equivalent to His doing what He commands Himself to do. Critics, however, suggest this is incoherent and labels this criticism the "omnibenevolence objection" (Austin, n.d.). This criticism points out that while on the one hand God may well form an intention to engage in some act or judge that it would be good to do so, the notion that He commands Himself to do that action is incoherent. Moreover, God could not be seen as possessing moral virtues, because a moral virtue would be a disposition to do an action that God commands, which is also incoherent (Austin, n.d.). Some critics have pointed out that DCT proponents argue they can still make sense of God's goodness by noting that God has traits that are good, as distinguished from traits that are morally obligatory. God may well have the virtues of love, compassion, or fairness—all good, though not grounded in a disposition to obey God. If these dispositions are taken to be essential to God's nature, that is, if God possesses them in every possible world in which God exists, then, while it is still the case that whatever God does is good, "the range of 'whatever God were to do' includes no actions for which God would not be praiseworthy" (Wierenga, 1989, p. 222). Further, those who say that the moral obligation of telling the truth or not torturing kittens could not have been God's reason for commanding us not to lie or torture are in effect arguing that God doesn't have moral reasons for doing so, which does not follow, since the moral goodness of truth telling or not engaging in torture is a sufficient reason for God to command it (Wainright, 2005). Once commanded, telling the truth and not torturing kittens are not only morally good, they are moral obligations.

A fourth criticism of DCT involves autonomy. DCT argues that God's will governs our morality, thus denying us autonomy from God. This is labeled the "autonomy objection" of DCT and argues that moral law is imposed on us by God, which makes autonomy impossible since we are not imposing moral law on ourselves (Austin, n.d.). Supporters of DCT respond to this criticism by arguing that DCT *is* compatible with autonomy. DCT holds that we are responsible for either obeying or not obeying God's commands with understanding and applying those commands, and with "adopting a self-critical stance with respect to what God has commanded us to do" (Austin, n.d., p. 1). Relying on our independent judgment about which moral laws are compatible with God's goodness and commands makes us autonomous. We also subject ourselves to the law once we understand and accept it, even if the law is based in God's commands.

Finally, a common criticism of DCT involves how DCT proponents know which divine commands to follow, given the many religions that exist in the world. This criticism is known as the "religious pluralism objection" to DCT (Austin, n.d.). This criticism suggests that the many religions that exist—even those sharing a set of core beliefs, like Christianity or Islam—often disagree on, or offer conflicting accounts of, God's commands. For example, Orthodox Jews and members of Islam do not eat pork, citing God's command not to do so found in various parts of the Old Testament (e.g., Leviticus 11:7–8; Deuteronomy 14:8; Isaiah 65:2–5) and the Qur'an (Al-Qur'an 5:3). Yet members of other Jewish sects (e.g., Reform Judaism) and members of mainstream Christianity do not agree that eating pork is against God's command. Proponents of DCT respond by saying that one must decide for him- or herself how to interpret divine commands within a specific tradition, just as the secular moralist must decide which moral principles to adopt given the plurality of traditions (Austin, n.d.).

In summary, Divine Command theory (DCT) is a second example of a deontological system of ethics, as it is oriented around the duty to obey God's commands, whatever they may be. Exemplars of DCT are the three Abrahamic religions—Judaism, Islam, and Christianity—all of which teach that following God's will as revealed by His commands is both a necessary and a sufficient condition for determining the content of morality even if those commands contradict other rules or principles (Driver, 2007). God's commands are revealed through sacred scripture (e.g., the Bible in Christianity, the Torah in Judaism, the Qur'an in Islam), stories, and traditions. One problem that consistently is raised with DCT is the Euthyphro Dilemma: Is something good (or bad) because it is morally good (or bad) irrespective of God, or is it good (or bad) because God says it is? If the DCT proponent accepts the first proposition as true—that morally good acts are willed by God because they are intrinsically morally good, irrespective of God—then she faces the independence problem: if morally good acts are willed by God *because* they are morally good, then they must be morally good *independent of* God's will. If the supporter accepts the second question as true—that morally good acts are good because they are willed by God—the answer raises three new issues: arbitrariness, emptiness, and the problem of abhorrent commands. In response, philosophers, developed a Modified Divine Command theory (MDCT) that answers both "horns" of the Euthyphro Dilemma. Beyond the Euthyphro Dilemma, criticisms of DCT include (1) the independence objection; (2) the omnipotence objection; (3) the omnibenevolence objection; (4) the autonomy objection; and (5) the religious pluralism objection.

Returning to an overview of systems of ethics found in Figure 2.1, let's now turn attention to a third system of ethics, which focuses on character. Known as virtue ethics and traceable to the time of Aristotle and ancient Greece, this system focuses on developing character traits—the virtues—as the key to ethics and living a moral life.

FOCUSING ON CHARACTER: VIRTUE THEORIES

One way to discuss virtue ethics is to begin by examining the legal system in the United States. Political scientists have observed that ours is a nation of laws that tell us what we may and may not do (substantive law) and establishes specific procedures for dealing with law violators (procedural law) (Hinman, 2013). These laws are rules or commands that tell the police officer when she may search your car and whether what she finds there constitutes a violation. Thus, laws involve both rules and people. Importantly, we expect that the people enforcing the rules—police officers, prosecutors, judges, correctional officers—will be well-versed in them and enforce them fairly using good judgment. There cannot be one without the other. Ethics is like law: it, too, needs both rules and people to properly function (Hinman, 2013). Kantian and Utilitarian ethics provide us with rules on how to behave morally and are thus important. However, applying those rules depends on people who have solid character and good judgment. It is this latter point that is of greatest interest in virtue ethics.

Virtue Ethics

Virtue ethics focuses not on what constitutes moral *behavior*, but rather on what constitutes the moral *person*. For virtue ethics, the question is not "how should I behave?" but "how should I live?" Each of us answers that question by developing certain virtues or traits that become ingrained and, as a result, control our behavior. Aristotle observed that while each of us is born with ideal character traits, to become virtuous those traits have to be nurtured so they become a stable part of our psychological makeup. For example, the virtuous person is one who is kind (or compassionate or sincere—you get the picture) across situations and throughout life. Kindness is in this person's character; she is not kind because she seeks to maximize her own utility or that of the collective. Nor is she kind because she is following some command (as is the case with teleological or deontological systems of ethics). She is kind because that's who she *is*.

Most philosophers agree that virtue ethics can be traced to the works of Plato and Aristotle, as well as to ancient China (Wong, 2013). From ancient times through the Enlightenment, virtue ethics was the preeminent system of ethics in Western philosophy. Support for it then declined over the following centuries, but reemerged in the 20th century, particularly in America (Hursthouse, 2012). Its reemergence was apparently driven by ethicists' dissatisfaction with prevailing forms of deontology and consequentialism, as neither system paid much attention to the substance of the virtues (e.g., beneficence, honesty, trustworthiness), moral character and education, moral wisdom or discernment, and important questions about what sort of person one should be. "How should I behave?" deals with specific dilemmas; "How should I live?" is a question about an entire life.

Whereas deontology and consequentialism are based on rules, virtue ethics makes central the concept of *character* (Athanassoulis, n.d.). Modern virtue ethics remains inspired by Aristotle's emphasis on the role of virtue and character, that is, one's state of being. To illustrate, the virtue of honesty relates to not only how one *feels* about others, but also how one *acts* toward them. For Aristotle, one who possesses virtuous inner dispositions is likely moved *to act* in accordance with them. If one accepts honesty as an appropriate character trait, one will likely *behave* in an honest manner with others most of the time.

Arête, *Phronesis*, and *Eudaimonia*

At the core of virtue ethics are three important concepts: *arête* (virtue), *phronesis* (practical wisdom), and *eudaimonia* (flourishing) (Athanassoulis, n.d.). ***Arête*** refers to the fact that virtue is the sum of its parts, which can be learned. Those who lack it are not necessarily bad but are, instead, ignorant of what virtue is. ***Phronesis*** refers to prudence or practical wisdom, which Aristotle saw as involving knowledge of what is good and evil in practical terms. *Phronesis* also involves the capacity to act on one's knowledge about good and evil. For Aristotle, one possessing *phronesis* has (1) a general understanding of what is good or evil; (2) the ability to perceive, in light of that general understanding, what is required in terms of feelings, choices, and actions in a particular situation; (3) the ability to deliberate well; and (4) the ability to act on that deliberation (Lacewing, n.d.). Finally, ***eudaimonia***, or "happiness," is the "ultimate" good. Aristotle argued that differences of opinion exist about what is "good" for people. The task for ethics is to resolve those differences. For Aristotle, the purpose of ethics is not simply to ask what is good for humans, but instead identify how we are able to facilitate good if we understand what it takes for humans to flourish (Kraut, 2014). By asking "What is the good?" Aristotle is not seeking to develop a list; he assumes that such could be easily developed. The real question is whether some of the elements of such a list ("it is good to have friends, health, physical attractiveness, courage, wealth, etc.") are more desirable than others. What Aristotle seeks is to identify is the "highest good," which he believes (1) is desirable for itself, (2) is not desirable for the sake of some other good, and (3) all other goods are desirable for its sake. Aristotle argues that *eudaimonia* ("happiness") and *eu zên* ("living well") constitute the "highest good" (Kraut, 2014).

The Concept of Virtue

For proponents of virtue ethics, the meaning of virtue is traced to Aristotle's conceptualization presented in his *Nicomachean Ethics*. **Virtue** is a habit, involves feelings and actions, and seeks "the mean" in all things, where reason defines the mean (see Table 2.1; Hinman, 2013). Virtue promotes human flourishing while its opposite, vice, denotes weakness of character and impedes human flourishing (Kraut, 2014). Let's look more closely at these core ideas.

- *Virtue as habit*. Virtue is not innate, something with which we are born. Rather, we develop virtue through practice and experience. Moral education thus becomes important, as it helps us develop our fundamental character, what Aristotle believed was the soul (Hinman, 2013).
- *Feelings and actions*. Virtue arises from the blending of both feelings and actions. The honest person not only does not lie; he or she understands the feelings that

lying creates in those who have been lied to. The moral life thus includes an emotive component (Hinman, 2013).

- *Seeking the mean*. Aristotle conceptualized virtue as finding the mean (the average) between the two extremes of excess and deficiency. For example, compassion occupies a middle ground (the mean, in Aristotle's conceptualization) between cruelty (too little) and co-dependency (too much). Aristotle thus creates a three-legged framework: extremes of excess, extremes of deficiency, and the mean—what falls in between. We should always seek the middle state.
- *Defining the mean through reason and the prudent person*. Virtue ethicists suggest Aristotle provided us two different ways for determining the mean: (1) through reason and (2) through observation (Hinman, 2013). Reason allows us not only to "check" whether we are leaning toward one extreme or another but take necessary steps to change our orientation. On the other hand, observation allows us to learn from others who are prudent, and again, check ourselves. Through this process, we properly orient ourselves when it comes to virtue.

The temperate and the continent person

Aristotle draws a distinction between two types of people: the **temperate person** and the **continent person** (Hinman, 2013). Temperate people are individuals who do what is right because they *want* to. The continent person also does what is right but does so *reluctantly*. Thought Exercise 2.1 illustrates these concepts in the area of police use of force.

Critique of Virtue Ethics

Virtue ethics—like all normative theories in ethics—has its shortcomings. Critics have leveled various objections at the system: that the theory is self-centered, is not action-guiding, and leaves us hostages to luck (Athanassoulis, n.d.; Mastin, 2008). In this section, I present these criticisms and examine their meaning.

TABLE 2.1 Aristotle's Vices of Excess and Deficiency and the Virtuous Mean

Vice of Deficiency	Virtuous Mean	Vice of Excess
Cowardice	Courage	Rashness
Insensibility	Temperance	Intemperance
Illiberality	Liberality	Prodigality
Pettiness	Munificence	Vulgarity
Humble-mindedness	High-mindedness	Vaingloriousness
Want of Ambition	Right Ambition	Over-ambition
Spiritlessness	Good Temper	Irascibility
Surliness	Friendly Civility	Obsequiousness
Ironical Depreciation	Sincerity	Boastfulness
Boorishness	Wittiness	Buffoonery
Shamelessness	Modesty	Bashfulness
Callousness	Just Resentment	Spitefulness

Source: http://www.iep.utm.edu/aristotl/#H7

THOUGHT EXERCISE 2.1

USING FORCE: THE TEMPERATE AND THE CONTINENT POLICE OFFICER

Officer Matt Trez could be considered a temperate person when it comes to using force. He has thoroughly familiarized himself with department policy about using force, including raising questions about certain aspects of it and having supervisors provide him with scenarios illustrating different aspects of the policy. He keeps abreast of state and federal appeals court cases relating to use of force. He uses force only when other efforts have failed, and never uses levels of force beyond those necessary, given the circumstances. Officer Noah Fence, on the other hand, would be considered a continent person when it comes to using force. While he is familiar with department policy, he has not studied it in depth, nor has he asked questions about it. He keeps abreast of appellate court cases in the area, but grumbles about the effort needed to do so. He, too, uses force only when other efforts have failed but does so grudgingly—he'd really rather "punish the bad guy for 'pissing off a police officer.'" In other words, he really wants to "kick butt and take names" when it comes to using force.

For Aristotle, Officer Trez leads the better life, in moral terms, even though Officer Fence is, in fact, also restraining himself when using force. The difference is that Trez's behavior comes from both reason and feeling; he has reconciled the two because he has educated his emotions, which Fence has not done.

Some philosophers have argued that virtue ethics is self-centered because its primary concern is with one's own character and not with how one's actions affect others either in terms of consequences or failed duty (Athanassoulis, n.d.). For these critics, virtue ethics seems only interested in each of us acquiring different virtues so that we may each flourish. My acting virtuously simply because it will help me to flourish seems misdirected at best and smacks of Ethical Egoism at worst. While "seeking to flourish" *sounds* good and becomes a kind of "master virtue" to be achieved, in reality it is actually more like self-interest, which is at the core of Ethical Egoism. I will note that proponents of virtue ethics respond to this objection by pointing out that these critics miss the fact that real virtues are always other-directed. Compassion or kindness, as examples, are about how one responds to the needs of *others*. The virtuous individual is one who is concerned with engendering in him- or herself the proper character and allows a proper response to the needs of others. Compassion and kindness allow one to identify situations that require one to *act* kindly and do so in a reliable and stable manner. The virtue ethicist argues that self-good and the good of others are, in reality, inseparable (Athanassoulis, n.d.).

A second criticism leveled at virtue ethics is that since it isn't a rules-based system like Utilitarianism or DCT, it doesn't provide us with actual guidance about how we *should* behave and therefore fails as a theory of normative ethics. Defenders of virtue ethics respond by arguing that these critics have missed an important point: the virtuous person is a role model for others to emulate (Athanassoulis, n.d.). Because the virtuous person has developed a virtuous character, he or she will be highly likely to act per that character—they will *be* courageous, truthful, compassionate, etc. By observing people with fully-formed virtuous characters acting in accordance with their character, others learn to be virtuous. Unlike other systems, virtue ethics does not provide "easy answers" to questions of morality in the form of rules to be followed. This is because there are no easy answers, but also because finding answers to questions of morality is a long-term process of moral education and development. As Athanassoulis (n.d., p. 1) described it, "If virtue consists of the right reason and the right desire, virtue ethics will be action-guiding when we can perceive the right reason and have successfully habituated our desires to affirm its commands."

Finally, some critics have argued that virtue ethics leaves us hostages to moral "luck" (Friedman, 2009). Proponents of virtue ethics admit that moral development is a long and arduous process that includes developing and combining reason with emotion. Thus, the road to virtue is long, and the journey can be interrupted and affected by forces outside one's control. For the same reason that proper education, habits, influences, examples, and the like promote the development of virtue, opposite influences promote vice. What this means is that some people receive the help and encouragement needed to become virtuous, but others do not. Critics charge that it thus seems unfair to praise the virtuous and condemn the vicious given the role of outside forces in shaping character. Virtue ethicists respond to this criticism by pointing out that virtue theory recognizes how fragile is the good life; that it is, in fact, open to the negative influences of others, which can lead to the loss of virtue. However, its very fragility makes the virtuous life precious and achieving it even more valuable.

To summarize, unlike rules-based ethical theories, virtue ethics focuses on character and its development. Traceable to the ancient writings of Plato and Aristotle, these theories were predominant in Western philosophical thinking at least through the Enlightenment. After declining in popularity for several centuries, they saw a major resurgence beginning in the mid-20th century that continues today. Rather than focusing on rules or commands relating to how one should behave, virtue ethics focuses on who one should *become*. For the virtue ethicist, virtue is a habit that involves feelings and actions that comprise the middle ground between excess and deficiency. Moral development and education are crucial, and careful observation of the virtuous, who serve as exemplars to be followed, is important. Virtue ethics has, however, been criticized as being self-centered, non-action-oriented, and leaving all of us hostage to "moral luck."

SUMMARY

In this chapter, I shared with you an in-depth discussion of several systems of normative ethics. In doing so, I contrasted two competing strains: theories focusing on answering the question "how should I *behave*?" and those focusing on the question "how should I *live*?" As you saw, these are both very different questions, and the systems provide different answers to each.

I began by examining systems of ethics that answer the question "how should we behave?" I discussed teleological and deontological theories relating to how one should behave. While both rely on rules to guide behavior, their rules differ. Teleological systems emphasize potential consequences as the key rule to guide behavior; deontological theories focus on the fact we have a duty to follow a set of rules or commands. I then discussed specific examples of each category. Ethical Egoism and Utilitarianism are examples of teleological systems of ethics. The former emphasizes that ethical behavior is that which furthers one's personal interests, while the latter stresses that ethical behavior is that generating the most potentially positive consequences for the most number of people.

I then distinguished two types of Utilitarian ethics (Act Utilitarianism and Rule Utilitarianism) and contrasted them using the analogy of stop signs and yield signs.

I then turned my attention to deontological ethics and illustrated it by discussing Kantian ethics and religious ethics, specifically, DCT. In Kantian ethics, the key rule is the categorical imperative: to behave in a manner that you would want everyone, everywhere, to behave. In DCT, the core rule is to follow God's will as revealed in sacred texts, stories, and traditions, since God decides what is good and evil. I also presented what is perceived as the biggest issue with DCT, the Euthyphro Dilemma, and how MDCT was developed to address that issue. Finally, I examined systems of ethics whose focus is not on behavior, but on character. Here, I presented an overview of virtue ethics that emphasizes that the key to living a moral life is through the development of a virtuous character, which controls our behavior.

To conclude the chapter, let's consider an important issue that's been in the news for several years: privatizing the police. Thought Exercise 2.2 examines privatization and the ethical issues some have claimed that it raises.

THOUGHT EXERCISE 2.2

ETHICAL ISSUES AND PRIVATIZING THE POLICE

The following is an excerpt from a story filed by reporter Sam Scott of the Wilmington (NC) *Star News* on February 11, 2007:

> One chilly evening in November of 2004, Lopaka Bounds's troubles began when he tried to use a credit card to pay for an $11 meal at a cash-only restaurant. There was an ATM across the street, but the police officer guarding the Waffle House at 5041 Market St. demanded that Bounds first leave an ID before heading to the ATM. Bounds, then a member of Marines special forces, refused, offering his Visa credit card instead. The rising tensions peaked after another officer arrived. Bounds, who had cursed at the men, was pulled off his stool, pushed against a window, and handcuffed. Outside he was pepper-sprayed and forced to the ground when one of the officers snagged his wrist between Bounds and the chain of the cuffs. Whether Bounds was drunk and resisting or the sober victim of excessive force lies at the crux of his ongoing federal lawsuit. But the most noteworthy aspect of the arrest may be who the officers were. They didn't work for the city, the county, or any other public agency. They worked for Pinnacle Special Police, a private company that was practically the sheriff of the Waffle House that night. Under a unique North Carolina law, licensed firms have full police powers on properties they are hired to protect, including the power to write citations, to investigate, and to arrest. North Carolina is believed to be the only state that allows for-hire police, although some cities (e.g., Boston) have similar programs (see Scott, 2007).

Company Police Agencies and Officers

Pinnacle Special Police is not the only private police agency operating in North Carolina. For example, Capitol Special Police began its operations in August 2002 with the vision of providing the finest specialized law enforcement and security services in North Carolina and surrounding states, as a result of "local police and sheriff's departments [being] overwhelmed with calls for service" that diminished their ability to respond to citizen needs (Capitol Special Police, 2017, p. 1). According to Roy Cooper, then-Attorney General of North Carolina (he was elected governor in 2016), 51 company police agencies were operating in North Carolina during 2013, ranging in size from 1 to 60 officers (Cooper, 2013). Officers working for these companies "patrol and enforce the criminal laws of our state on private and public-school property, county and state hospitals, shopping centers, apartment complexes, office buildings, golf courses, recreational

continued

lakes and train stations" (Cooper, 2013, p. 2). These agencies and officers "are a *vital part of the criminal justice system's efforts* in this state, as they supplement state, municipal and county police agencies, thereby relieving them of some of the calls-for-service [burdens confronting] all law enforcement agencies" (emphasis added; Cooper, 2013, p. 2).

Company police officers in North Carolina must meet the same minimum standards required for employment and certification as a law enforcement officer, including completion of Basic Law Enforcement Training. Additionally, they must complete an examination on the law and administrative rules governing company police with a minimum score of 80%. If approved, an applicant will receive law enforcement certification from the North Carolina Criminal Justice Education and Training Standards Commission. Once the applicant has been officially sworn in by attesting to an oath of office, they will receive a commission from the Attorney General. *This commission will give the company police officer the same subject matter jurisdiction as other sworn law enforcement officers to make arrests for both felonies and misdemeanors, as well as to charge for infractions.*

The authority of company police officers is subject to strict jurisdictional limitations (Cooper, 2013). All company police officers, while in the performance of their duties of employment, have the same powers as municipal and county police officers to make arrests for both felonies and misdemeanors and to charge for infractions occurring on:

1. Property owned by or in the possession and control of their employer;
2. Property owned by or in the possession and control of a person who has contracted with the employer to provide onsite company police security personnel services for the property; or
3. Any other real property while in continuous and immediate pursuit of a person for an offense committed upon property described in (1) or (2), above.

Company police officers are all officers not designated as a campus police officer or a railroad police officer.

One observer of private policing agencies and officers has suggested that these entities pose a direct threat to democracy. Law professor David Sklansky has argued that the threat from private police is twofold (Sklansky, 2006, pp. 90–91). First, private police dampen political support for public law enforcement that is committed, at least nominally, to protecting everyone, resulting in a system of policing even less egalitarian than the one we have today. The second threat from private police is their aborting largely unrealized efforts to democratize public police departments. The result is a forfeiting of ways of making policing more effective, humane, and respectful of democratic processes (Sklansky, 2006, p. 91).

Can you justify on ethical grounds, the development and continuing expansion of private police—like those described in North Carolina? Are these entities a "threat to democracy," as Professor Sklansky cautions?

KEY TERMS

Moral principle 31
Theories of ethics 31
Euthyphro Dilemma 44
Independence problem 44
Modified Divine Command theory 44
Arête 49
Phronesis 49
Eudaimonia 49
Virtue 49
Temperate person 50
Continent person 50
Company police officers 54

DISCUSSION QUESTIONS

1. Conduct a survey of the class to identify the system of ethics to which your peers are most drawn. Have respondents identify why they are drawn to the particular system they chose and report the results.
2. Work with a partner to debate the following: "Resolved: Pursuing one's interests should *not* be used to gauge the ethics of behavior." One of you should pick the "pro" side and the other argue the "con" side.

3. One of the biggest criticisms of Kantian ethics is its universalism: if a particular behavior is wrong (lying, cheating, stealing), it is *always* wrong, regardless of circumstances. On the other hand, some critics have argued that teleological systems—like Utilitarianism—take circumstances into account almost *too* much and thus fail to provide a sound set of rules to guide us. Canvas the class about whether circumstances matter in assessing the ethics of behavior and why (or why not) such is the case.
4. Pick an issue that confronts college students, such as cheating on exams, "hooking up," using recreational drugs like marijuana, or taking Adderall (or other stimulants) to help them study. Then select a particular ethical theory and justify why that behavior is wrong—or not. Present your thoughts to the class.
5. Work with a partner to debate the following: "Resolved: Determining God's will on the basis of sacred texts, parables, and tradition is problematic."

RESOURCES

Basics of Philosophy (http://www.philosophybasics.com/). This website divides philosophy into manageable pieces and presents a concise yet competent overview of the various systems of ethics discussed in this chapter—and others not discussed.

Ethics Updates is a website hosted by the University of San Diego (http://ethics.sandiego.edu/) that provides accessible information on a variety of topics in ethics, including overviews of the systems discussed in this chapter.

The website for the **Center for the Study of Ethics in the Professions** at the Illinois Institute of Technology (http://ethics.iit.edu/teaching/utilitarianism) has an excellent discussion of Utilitarian ethics

The **British Broadcasting Company** (BBC) sponsors a website that deals with ethics (http://www.bbc.co.uk/ethics/guide/). Its discussion of Deontology (generally) and Kantian ethics (specifically) is well organized and well presented.

REFERENCES

Adams, R. (1987). *The virtue of faith and other essays in philosophical theology*. New York, NY: Oxford University Press.

Armstrong, A. (2013, September 12). Spock's illogic: The needs of the many outweigh the needs of the few. *The Objective Standard*. Retrieved from https://www.the objective standard.com/2013/09/spocks-illogic-the-needs-of-the-many-outweigh-the-needs-of-the-few/

Arsham, N. (2015). Ethics and decision making. Retrieved from http://home.ubalt.edu/nts barsh/opre640/partXIII.htm#rEthics

Athanassoulis, N. (n.d.). Virtue ethics. In J. Fieser & B. Dowden (Eds.), *Internet encyclopediaof philosophy*. Retrieved from http://www.iep.utm.edu/virtue/

Austin, M. (n.d.). Divine command theory. In J. Fieser & B. Dowden (Eds.), *Internet encyclopedia of philosophy*. Retrieved from http://www.iep.utm.edu/divine-c/

Bazerman, M., & Gino, F. (2012). Behavioral ethics: Towards a deeper understanding of moral judgment and dishonesty. *Annual Review of Law and Social Science, 8*, 85–104.

Bennett, H. (Executive Producer), Phillips, W. (Assistant Producer), Sallin, R. (Producer) & Meyer, N. (Director). (1982). *Star Trek: The Wrath of Khan* [Motion picture]. Country of origin: United States. Paramount Pictures.

Cavalier, R. (2002). Online guide to ethics and moral philosophy: Kant's ethics. Retrieved from http://caae.phil.cmu.edu/Cavalier/80130/part1/sect4/Kant.html

Cooper, R. (2013). *Company police study guide.* Raleigh, NC: North Carolina Department of Justice. Retrieved from http://www.ncdoj.gov/getdoc/255b13c2-17fb-45f9-b829-9565ecc24d9c/2010-Company-Police-Study-

Douglass, S. (n.d.). Historical background: The Abrahamic faiths. Retrieved from http://www. cmcuworkshops.net/wordpress/wp-content/uploads/8_historical-background-the-abrahamic-faiths.pdf

Driver, J. (2007). *Ethics: The fundamentals* (2nd ed.). Malden, MA: Blackwell Publishing.

Ewing, A. (1947). *The definition of good.* London, England: Routledge.

Feinberg, J. (1978). Psychological egoism. In R. Shafer-Landau & J. Feinberg (Eds.), *Reason and responsibility* (pp. 183–220). New York, NY: Wadsworth.

Field, R. (n.d.). Teleological ethical theory. Retrieved from http://catpages.nwmissouri.edu/m/rfield/274guide/274overview4.htm

Folse, H. (2003). Comments on Kant's ethical theory. Retrieved from http://www.loyno.edu/~folse/Kant.html

Friedman, M. (2009). Feminist virtue ethics, happiness, and luck. *Hypatia, 24*, 29–40.

Gert, B. (1967). Hobbes and psychological egoism. *Journal of the History of Ideas, 28*, 503–520.

Glovitch, T. (1991). *How we know what isn't so.* New York, NY: The Free Press.

Hinman, L (2013). *Ethics: A pluralistic approach to moral theory* (5th ed.). Boston, MA: Wadsworth.

Holt, T. (2008a). Philosophy of religion: The independence problem. Retrieved from http://www.philosophyofreligion.info/christian-ethics/divine-command-theory/the-independence-problem/

Holt T. (2008b). Philosophy of religion: The arbitrariness problem. Retrieved from http://www.philosophyofreligion.info/christian-ethics/divine-command-theory/the-arbitrariness-problem/

Holt, T. (2008c). Philosophy of religion: The emptiness problem. Retrieved from http://www.philosophyofreligion.info/christian-ethics/divine-command-theory/the-arbitrariness-problem/

Holt, T. (2008d). Philosophy of religion: The problem of abhorrent commands. Retrieved from http://www.philosophyofreligion.info/christian-ethics/divine-command-theory/the-problem-of-abhorrent-commands/

Hooker, B. (2015). Rule consequentialism. In E. Zalta (Ed.), *The Stanford encyclopedia of philosophy* (Winter Edition). Retrieved from http://plato.stanford.edu/archives/win2015/entries/consequentialism-rule/

Hughes, A. (2013, January 12). The Abrahamic religions: On the uses and abuses of history. *Oxford Scholarship Online.* Retrieved from http://www.oxfordscholarship.com/view/10.1093/acprof.oso/9780199934645.001.0001/acprof-9780199934645

Hursthouse, R. (2012). Virtue ethics. In E. Zalta (Ed.), *The Stanford encyclopedia of philosophy* (Summer edition). Retrieved from http://plato.stanford.edu/entries/ethics-virtue/

Joyce, R. (2002). Theistic ethics and the Euthyphro Dilemma. *Journal of Religious Studies, 30*, 39–75.

Kant, I. (2008). *Critique of pure reason* (M. Weigelt & M. Muller, Trans.). London, England: Penguin Classics. (Original work published 1787)

Kant, I. (1950). *Groundwork of the metaphysic of morals* (A. Wood, Trans.). New Haven, CT: Yale University Press. (Original work published 1785)

Kraut, R. (2014). Aristotle's ethics. In E. Zalta (Ed.), *The Stanford encyclopedia of philosophy* (Summer Edition). Retrieved from http://plato.stanford.edu/entries/aristotle-ethics/

Lacewing, M. (n.d.). Practical wisdom. Retrieved from http://cw.routledge.com/textbooks/alevelphilosophy/data/A2/Moral/PracticalWisdom.pdf

Mastin, L. (2008). Virtue ethics. Retrieved from http://www.philosophybasics.com/ branch_virtue_ethics.html

Moseley, A. (n.d.). Egoism. In J. Fieser & B. Dowden (Eds.), *Internet encyclopedia of philosophy.* Retrieved from http://www.iep.utm.edu/egoism

Nathanson, S. (2011). Act and rule utilitarianism. In J. Fieser & B. Dowden (Eds.), *Internet encyclopedia of philosophy.* Retrieved from http://www.iep.utm.edu/util-a-r/

Neilson, K. (1973). *Ethics without God.* Buffalo, NY: Prometheus Books.

O'Neill, O. (1994). A simplified account of Kant's ethics. In J. White (Ed.), *Contemporary moral problems*. Eagen, MN: West Publishing Company. Retrieved from http://people.morrisville.edu/~galuskwj/oneill.html

Pojman, L. (2013). *How should we live?* Belmont, CA: Wadsworth.

Rachels, S. (2015). *The elements of moral philosophy* (8th ed.) (pp.76–81). New York, NY: McGraw Hill.

Rickman, P. (2011). Having trouble with Kant? *Philosophy Now, 86*, 1–4. Retrieved from https://philosophynow.org/issues/86/Having_Trouble_With_Kant

Rohlf, M. (2016). Immanuel Kant. In E. Zalta (Ed.), *The Stanford encyclopedia of philosophy* (Spring Edition). Retrieved from http://plate.stanford.edu/archives/spr2016/entries/kant/

Rowan, J., & Zinaich, S. (2002). *Ethics for the professions*. Belmont, CA: Thompson Learning.

Sklansky, D. (2006). Private police and democracy. *American Criminal Law Review, 43*, 89–105.

Timmons, M. (2013). *Moral theory: An introduction*. Lanham, MD: Rowman & Littlefield.

United Nations (2016). Universal declaration of human rights. Retrieved from http://www.un.org/en/universal-declaration-human-rights/

Wainright, W. (2005). *Religion and morality*. Burlington, VT: Ashgate.

Wierenga, E. (1989). *The nature of God: An inquiry into divine attributes*. Ithaca, NY: Cornell University Press.

Wong, D. (2013). Chinese ethics. In E. Zalta (Ed.), *The Stanford encyclopedia of philosophy* (Spring Edition). Retrieved from http://plato.stanford.edu/cgi-bin/encyclopedia/archinfo.cgi?entry=ethics-chinese

CHAPTER 3

Moral Dilemmas in Criminal Justice

Chapter Outline

CHAPTER LEARNING OBJECTIVES:

1. Identify the components of the moral arena.
2. Describe the role of emotion in moral dilemmas.
3. Distinguish the three categories of moral dilemmas.
4. Differentiate among the different types of obligations we have to others.
5. Describe the characteristics of common-sense morality.
6. Identify examples of moral dilemmas involving the police, the courts, and corrections.
7. Explain whistleblowing and the moral dilemmas that give rise to it.

INTRODUCTION

More than a decade ago, I learned of a situation involving a patrol officer working for a local police department. It seems that Officer Sam Jones (not his real name) was being suspended without pay for leaving his beat (patrol area) one evening. What had happened was this.

Officer Jones, whose regular beat included a public housing community, had developed an extensive network of informants from whom he regularly received actionable intelligence about criminal activity occurring in the community. One evening, Jones learned from an informant that a major shipment of cocaine and marijuana was supposed to be arriving within the next few hours at a "no-tell-motel" several miles from his beat. The informant revealed that at least three suspected drug dealers operating in Officer Jones's beat would be meeting the people bringing in the shipment and the three would then "divvy" it up in the motel room. Jones had checked with other sources who, while not confirming all of the details he'd received, generally agreed that a large shipment was supposed to be arriving soon and that the motel was its destination.

Because the information was extraordinarily time sensitive, Jones decided he had to intervene. He contacted two friends on the force who worked the beat where the suspected shipment would arrive and informed them that he had a "hot lead" and would meet them at a restaurant near the motel. At the restaurant, Jones shared the information he'd received from his informants, which he described as "solid." The three officers then decided to put the motel under surveillance; soon after doing so, the intelligence Jones received panned out. Five individuals, including the three suspected dealers and two drug couriers, were arrested at the scene and about $100,000 worth of cocaine and marijuana, along with several illegal weapons, were also confiscated.

The precinct commander who oversaw both Jones's beat and the beat where the drug deal occurred arrived at the scene and learned that Jones had left his post to set up the surveillance. He also learned that Jones's proactive steps had paid off with the arrests and recovery of the drugs and weapons. He immediately informed Jones that he was suspended without pay, pending a full review of his actions.

Jones clearly had a very hard choice to make: pursue the lead and potentially disrupt the illicit drug network operating in his beat, or follow procedure, notify his superiors of the intelligence he'd received and let them handle it as they saw fit. Jones chose the former and suffered the consequences (my understanding is that he resigned from the force rather than accept the suspension). Jones faced a moral dilemma: act now and disrupt the drug sale or follow procedure and wait for others to respond to the intelligence and possibly not intercept the drugs. How *should* Jones have behaved? What would *you* have done, given the circumstances?

So far, I have discussed what ethics is and presented various systems of ethics that seek to answer either the question "how should I behave?" or the question "how should I be?" Once you venture into the world of criminal justice as a practitioner, you must sometimes make hard choices, like the one Officer Jones had to make.

Obviously, criminal justice practitioners make lots of decisions about how they are going to behave under various circumstances that are sometimes not only dramatic, but also life-changing, such as a police officer using deadly force against a suspect. Sometimes, practitioners find themselves in a situation where no matter what, it seems they'll end up doing at least some wrong. Such situations are what philosophers and psychologists have termed *moral dilemmas*, where, no matter what one does, it seems some wrong is likely to occur. In this chapter, I explore the concept of moral dilemmas in broad terms and then discus how conflicting obligations on the part of criminal justice practitioners sometimes lead to moral dilemmas. In doing so, I begin a discussion that I will repeatedly touch on throughout the rest of the book: how it is that you, me—all of us—resolve the moral dilemmas we face. Let's first begin by creating boundaries for assessing the morality of behavior.

THE MORAL ARENA

Before getting into a detailed discussion about moral dilemmas, I have found it useful in my teaching to create some boundaries for students—not every choice we make or behavior in which we engage becomes a matter of ethics. For example, think about all the choices you make during a typical day: what to eat and drink, how you are divvying up your time, with whom you're "hanging out"—you get the idea. In a typical day, however, how often do you confront a situation where, because of a choice you make, the relationship you have either with yourself or another is *significantly* affected, that is, the relationship could dramatically change. Deciding whether to call or text a friend is different from deciding, after a full evening of drinking, whether to drive yourself and your friend home from the bar. It is only in the latter situation that, because of your choice, something dramatic could happen to the relationship. The key is identifying situations where "a question of ethics" arises. Ordinarily, deciding to binge-watch the first three seasons of *Game of Thrones* is not a question of ethics. However, if you've been placed in charge of a sick child who's been running a fever, binge-watching the show's episodes may become a matter of ethics.

In my teaching, I tell students it's important to create a context for making moral judgments about our own and others' behavior. I call that context the **moral arena**. I use the term "arena" as a way of getting students to visualize a level area surrounded by seats where events like games, concerts, etc. occur. The open part of the arena where the performance or sporting event occurs is the "ethics" part. The seats that surround it stand for the "nonethics" area. As we sit in the seats, we observe and make judgments about what's going on in the "ethics" area. The question then becomes how to separate the "ethics area" from the "spectators' area." As I describe it to my students, distinguishing the two areas occurs in the following ways.

First, the moral arena always involves *behavior*. I make the point to my students that normative ethics doesn't concern itself with assessing ideas but with assessing behavior. While it may be morally wrong to harbor ill toward others for any number of reasons, until ill will translates into action, it is outside the moral arena.

Second, the moral arena involves *human behavior*. We do not make moral judgments about the behavior of nature—"Gee, that tornado sure acted unethically when it touched down in Billy-Bob's Mobile Home Park!"—or about the behavior of animals: "Well, it was certainly unethical for that German Shephard to bite that poor child!" Rather, normative ethics concerns itself with assessing the morality of human behavior because philosophers assume that only humans are rational actors and are therefore the only animals that have the ability to act out of reason (Rescher, 1988).

Third, the moral arena consists of human behavior that is the *product of free will* and rational choice (Narain, 2014). This means the behavior of young children and people with serious mental health issues—regardless of how dastardly their deeds may be—is outside the moral arena. If because of age or infirmity one does not have the capacity for rational thought, one cannot be held morally accountable for one's actions (although one can certainly be held *legally* accountable for the actions) (Wasserman, Asch, Bluestein, & Putnam, 2013).

Finally, the moral arena involves the potential for *significant harm* occurring to others, including nature, as a result of the human behavior. While I admit the term "harm" can be squishy, I'm referring to dictionary definitions of the word along the lines of "something that causes someone or something to be hurt, broken, made less valuable or successful, etc." (Merriam-Webster, n.d., p. 1). By adding the modifier "significant" I ask students to envision something other than a momentary slight that potentially causes minor emotional or physical discomfort. "Significant" means the possibility that much more harm, injury, or breaking has occurred: feelings have been seriously hurt, a relationship has been broken, or actual physical injury occurred. I include nature to remind students of the notion of interconnectedness—that we are all tied not only to each other but to this wonderful "big blue marble" we call Earth. To illustrate, Buddhism teaches about "dependent origination" (or *engi* in Japanese), which holds that nothing exists in isolation, independent of other life (Hoddings, 2005). Rather, all who occupy this planet are interconnected in a great fabric of being. Thus, the moral arena includes human behavior that, either directly or indirectly, affects not only other humans but other life forms. Figure 3.1 presents a graphical representation of the moral arena.

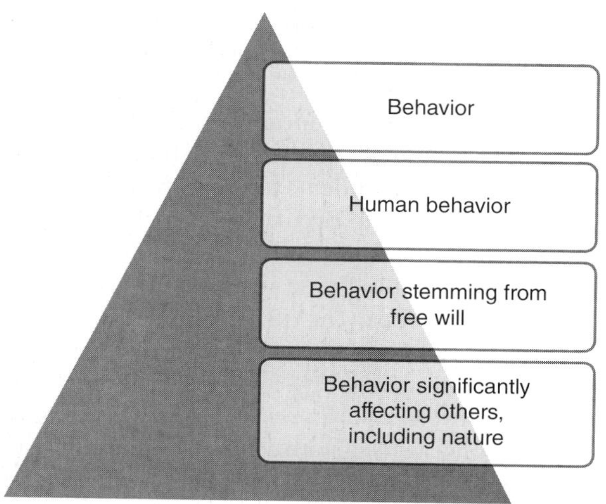

FIGURE 3.1 The Moral Arena

MORAL DILEMMAS

Suppose you were confronted with the following slight variation of a situation first described by Foot (1967, p. 1), which is now known simply as "the trolley-car problem":

> You are out for an afternoon walk and are crossing a bridge that overlooks a train track. The track splits in two a little way down from the bridge. You notice that on one of the tracks are five men playing a game of cards and eating lunch. On the other track is a solitary man who appears to be sleeping. As you look down on this peaceful scene your heart starts to race as you see a runaway freight car suddenly rounding a far corner of the tracks and heading your way. You quickly realize the freight car is going to hit the five men playing cards, a fact of which they are unfortunately oblivious. They are too far away for you to call out and warn them. In your panic, you look around for some way to alert the men and see that the track switch is a couple of feet away. It occurs to you that if you were to throw the switch, you would successfully divert the freight car's path onto the other track, where the sleeping man is located. He likely won't even know what hit him and you will have saved the lives of five men. Do you throw the switch?

While this scenario is often used in research efforts to distinguish people who are more Utilitarian in their moral orientation than they are deontological (Davis, 2015), for the moment, whether you lean toward a specific system of ethics to guide your behavior is not important (just to ask, *would* you throw the switch?). What is important is that the scenario describes a moral dilemma for the observer: if she does not throw the switch, five innocent people are killed. If she throws the switch, one innocent person is killed. And not acting isn't an option—the five men will likely be struck by the car. Regardless of what you do, death occurs.

When discussing a **moral dilemma**, ethicists are describing a situation where someone is required to do two or more actions, is able to do each of them, but cannot do both (or all) of them without potential harm occurring (McConnell, 2014; Sinnott-Armstrong, 1988). The person appears condemned to moral failure—no matter what, a wrong occurs. Returning to the Officer Jones example, no matter what, he faced moral failure—leaving his post (desertion) or allowing the drug shipment to arrive unimpeded when he could have stopped it (a crime committed).

Some philosophers have suggested that, regardless of their scope or intensity, moral dilemmas have certain shared characteristics, as follows (see Jones, 1991). First, there has to be a moral agent—the person facing the dilemma and having to choose one course of action over another. Second, the moral agent is making a decision that has implications for both the decision maker and for some larger community, no matter its size. Finally, there is a real possibility of harm occurring because of the chosen behavior. This third feature is what makes moral dilemmas so troubling: some harm is likely to occur no matter what choice is made. Further, the harm that occurs may not only touch the decision maker, but it may touch others as well.

The Role of Emotion in Moral Dilemmas

Philosophers have argued that emotion is an important dimension of moral dilemmas. That is, moral dilemmas generate negative feelings like guilt or remorse (called moral residue) in the moral agent and in those assessing the agent's behavior (Greenspan,1995; Marcus, 1980; McConnell, 2014; Williams, 1965).

A classic illustration of this notion is from the novel *Sophie's Choice* (Styron, 1979). In the story, Sophie and her two children find themselves in a Nazi concentration camp. One of the camp guards antagonizes Sophie by informing her that one child will be allowed to live while the other will be killed, and Sophie has to decide which child will be killed. Even worse, the guard tells Sophie that if she refuses to choose, both children will be killed. Sophie thus can prevent the death of one child by allowing the other one to die. The added consideration—both children will die—gives Sophie a compelling reason to choose one child, but also provides an equally compelling reason to not choose the child. Obviously, no matter what, Sophie will feel guilt and remorse, potentially for the rest of her life (if Sophie did not experience such guilt, we could rightly assume there was something wrong with her).

Those who argue that emotion is an important dimension of moral dilemmas make four claims. When resolving the dilemma (1) the person experiences guilt or remorse; (2) the guilt or remorse is appropriate; (3) had the person acted on the other of the conflicting requirement(s), the agent would again experience similar guilt or remorse; and (4) those emotions would be appropriate (McConnell, 1986). Effectively, no matter what, the person experiences similar levels of guilt or remorse. Further, these negative emotions consist of two components: the experiential (the actual negative feelings of guilt) and the cognitive (the person's belief that she has done something wrong and takes responsibility for it) (McConnell, 2014). What's interesting is this: the person feels these emotions even though she may not have done anything wrong from the perspective of others. To illustrate this point, consider the following hypothetical situation:

> The setting is a Midwestern village in 1958 on a snowy December day. Johnny and several of his friends are riding sleds down a narrow, seldom-used street, one that intersects with a busier, although still not heavily traveled, road. Johnny, in his enthusiasm for sledding, is not being very careful. During his final ride he slides under an automobile passing through the intersection and is killed. Bill was driving the car. He was driving safely, had the right of way, and was not exceeding the speed limit. Moreover, given the physical arrangement, it would have been impossible for Bill to have seen Johnny coming. Bill was not at fault, legally or morally, for Johnny's death. Yet Bill experienced what can be best described as remorse or guilt about his role in this horrible event.
>
> —(McConnell, 2014, p. 39).

On one level, Bill's feelings are not warranted: he did nothing wrong and therefore did not deserve to feel guilty. Yet, Bill also realized that he caused Johnny's death and that most would say such a realization was warranted. What if Bill's response had been different? Suppose he had said afterward that while it was terrible Johnny had died, it was not his (Bill's) fault, that he had nothing to feel guilty about, didn't owe anyone any apologies, and none would be made. What then? This leads us to an important question: is such intellectual objectivity about personal behavior even possible? McConnell (2014, p. 1) thinks not: "When human beings have caused great harm, it is natural for them to wonder if they are at fault, even if to outsiders it is obvious they bear no moral responsibility for the damage." The point is that your emotions and mine are not so "finely tuned" that when we cause harm we can shut down feelings of guilt or remorse, depending on the degree of moral responsibility we feel. An interesting point here is that feeling guilt and remorse, even when we're not morally culpable for our actions, is not necessarily a bad thing: those feelings help make us more aware of, and cautious about, our behavior; they make us more sensitive to our responsibilities and more empathetic to the plight of others (McConnell, 2014).

Categories of Moral Dilemmas

Let's consider two moral dilemmas. In the first case, Jimmy has borrowed a handgun from his good friend and neighbor Cliff to address an infestation of racoons. Early the next morning, Cliff rushes to Jimmy's house, pounds on the door, and starts screaming for Jimmy to give him back his gun. Cliff is also yelling, "I'm gonna KILL that whore!" seemingly referring to his spouse. Should Jimmy return the gun? Or what about this dilemma, developed by the great French philosopher Jean-Paul Sartre: during WWII, there was a French student whose brother had been killed by the Germans in an offensive in 1940. The student wanted to avenge his brother and fight the invading forces he regarded as evil. The problem was that he was living with his mother, who both depended on him and perceived him as her one consolation in life. Should the student join the Resistance and fight the Germans?

The first example is an illustration of a moral dilemma first described in Book I of Plato's *Republic*. There, Cephalous argues that "justice" involves both one's speaking the truth and repaying one's debts. Socrates rejects this argument, however, by suggesting that it would be morally improper to repay certain debts, for example, returning a borrowed weapon to a friend who is not in his right mind. The point Socrates makes isn't that repaying debts isn't important—it is. Rather, he is showing that it may not always be morally proper to repay a debt at exactly the moment when the one to whom the debt is owed wants repayment. What Socrates is showing us is a conflict between two obligations (repaying one's debt[s] and protecting others from harm) and how to resolve that conflict. Socrates would thus answer "no" to the question of whether Jimmy should return Cliff's weapon to him at that moment, because protecting others from harm—presumably, Cliff's spouse—is the more important obligation. Once Cliff has cooled off and satisfied Jimmy that he no longer poses a threat to his spouse, Jimmy should return the weapon. In the second example, there are again conflicting obligations. On the one hand, the student had a familial obligation to his mother that was of limited scope but certain efficacy; on the other hand, he had a citizenship obligation to help repel invaders of his country, an obligation much wider in scope but also one of uncertain efficacy (McConnell, 2014). While the examples from Plato and Sartre are among the most commonly used to illustrate that not all moral dilemmas are the same; there are obviously others.

If you reviewed the literature on moral dilemmas, you would find consensus among philosophers and psychologists alike that several different types of moral dilemmas exist, including those known as epistemic, ontological, self-imposed, other-imposed, obligation-based, and prohibition-based. Let's explore their characteristics.

Epistemic and Ontological Dilemmas

When philosophers speak of epistemic and ontological dilemmas, the primary contrast between them involves whether the individual "overrides" one or more of obligations in making the behavioral choice (McConnell, 2014). **Epistemic dilemmas** occur when one has conflicts between two (or more) obligations and the person cannot decide which obligation is the more important under the current circumstances. Most people would agree that in some situations, one obligation should take precedence over others, while in other circumstances, the same would not be the case. Thus, the conflict comes from having to weigh which obligation takes precedence. The assumption made here is that a hierarchy of obligations exists that allows one to rank them and choose the most important (e.g., a doctor's obligation not to harm patients). In an **ontological dilemma**, while there is the same conflict between two (or more) obligations, neither is overridden. This is not because the person doesn't know which is the more important, but because neither obligation is the stronger. Thus, there is no "clear" choice. *Sophie's Choice* illustrates an ontological dilemma.

Self-Imposed and Other-Imposed Dilemmas

Another distinction ethicists make is between moral dilemmas that are self-imposed and those that are other-imposed. A **self-imposed dilemma** occurs because of the person's own wrongdoing (Donagan, 1977, 1984; McConnell, 1978). For example, if a person made two promises that conflicted, such as offering to take her mother to the doctor and drive her son to the championship pee-wee football game at the same time, the person's own actions created a situation where she couldn't do both. In contrast, **other-imposed dilemmas** do not originate from the person's wrongdoing but from the wrongdoing of others. *Sophie's Choice* is a clear example of an "other-imposed" dilemma (McConnell, 2014).

Obligation-Based and Prohibition-Based Dilemmas

A final distinction is made between a dilemma in which more than one possible action is obligatory (**obligation-based**) and one where all feasible actions are forbidden (**prohibition-based**) (McConnell, 2014). An illustration of an obligation-based dilemma is the one involving the French student discussed above. *Sophie's Choice*, on the other hand, illustrates a prohibition-based dilemma.

Moral Dilemmas and Conflicting Obligations

As mentioned above, moral dilemmas involve conflicting obligations. The question then becomes, what are obligations? **Obligations** can be conceptualized as "moral requirements that people have, simply because they are moral agents" (McConnell, 2014, p. 1). Some ethicists have suggested that obligations consist of two types: general and role-related (Zimmerman, 1996). **General obligations** arise from the fact that because humans have free will (agency) and are rational actors, they have requirements to not engage in certain behaviors such as murder, theft, or sexual assault. **Role-related obligations** are moral requirements that accumulate because of the position one occupies or the occupation the individual has chosen ("assistant prosecutor"), or from a specific relationship the individual has with another person ("spouse," "brother," "parent") (Zimmerman, 1996). The classic example of a role-related obligation would be the lifeguard at the public pool. Because of her position, she is bound to render assistance to any swimmer in distress regardless of any other consideration, such as the swimmer wasn't authorized to be in the pool. The lifeguard still has the obligation to the swimmer.

Some ethicists speak to the fact there are instances when general obligations and role-related obligations may conflict. An example of this would be a student who knows that the final examination for his Introduction to Biology class has been stolen by two of his fraternity brothers. While he has a general obligation to report the theft to his professor, his roles of "fraternity brother" and "friend" say he is obligated to be loyal and not allow harm to befall his fraternity brothers. The obvious difficulty here is deciding which obligation takes precedence: not allowing an unfair advantage for the thieves or protecting them from the fallout the theft will generate. The choice is going to be based partly on the present circumstances and partly on the guiding principle(s) of the system of ethics looked to for guidance (McConnell, 2014).

Resolving Dilemmas: Common-Sense Morality?

Moral dilemmas involve conflicting obligations and a difficulty in choosing which takes precedence, given current circumstances. Recall from Ch. 2 that there are multiple systems of normative ethics that have been developed to help resolve dilemmas created by conflicting obligations. Some philosophers, however, have argued that people rarely choose one of these formal systems to guide them. That is, people are not strictly Utilitarian or virtue oriented, for example. Rather, they seem to use pieces from several of these systems to create what ethicists have labeled "common-sense morality" (Parfit, 1979; Slote, 1985).

Common-sense morality consists of rules or principles taken from several systems of ethics, including Utilitarianism, deontology, and virtue ethics, and combined into an overarching view of morality (Adler, 1970; Hooker, 2000; Sidgwick, 1907). "Common sense" refers to "the knowledge, judgment, and taste that is . . . universal and held . . . without reflection" (van Holthoon & Olson, 1987, p. 18). We rely upon common sense quite a lot in our daily lives. For example, common sense tells us to be a bit wary of the dog we're meeting for the first time (it may bite) and to look both ways before crossing the street (else risk being hit by a vehicle). Philosophers argue that common sense also plays a role in morality; "everyone" knows that lying, cheating, and stealing are morally wrong—although the specifics may vary because local customs and norms influence common sense (van Holthoon & Olson, 1987). Proponents of common-sense morality have suggested it has several key features (see Kahane, 2015), including:

- Not seeking to maximize the utility of the aggregate;
- Recognizing that multiple rules, principles, and considerations guide morality;
- Not treating rules as absolutely binding. In some instances, one of the rules outweighs or takes precedence over the others;
- Tending toward the deontological but not based on a set of absolute prohibitions;
- Emphasizing the prevention of harm and promotion of people's welfare;
- Giving moral weight to numbers: saving more lives is morally better than saving less; helping many is morally better than helping a few;
- Allowing for overruling a guiding principle if following it would lead to potentially significant harm. For example, while it may "wrong to lie" in general, if lying would prevent a murder, "common sense" dictates that the lie would be morally acceptable.

What all this is saying is that most people, most of the time, rely on some combination of rules to guide the hard choices involved in resolving moral dilemmas. This is not to say that morality is completely subjective (for example, **moral relativism** holds that "moral judgments are true or false only relative to some particular standpoint and that no standpoint is uniquely privileged over all others" (Westacott, n.d., p. 1)). Rather, common-sense morality involves both what the collective knows and the larger moral principles it holds dear. Both influence the individual choices that group members make when resolving moral dilemmas.

With this overview in mind, I'd now like to turn attention to examining moral dilemmas within the context of the criminal justice system. In the following section, I'll focus my discussion of moral dilemmas in criminal justice not by presenting you with a list of the kinds of moral dilemmas practitioners confront—such a list would be both arbitrary and likely omit at least some situations. Rather, I want to show you, and have you think about, how the moral dilemmas faced by criminal justice personnel are often grounded in the sometimes-competing functions of the agencies making up the criminal justice system, along with the sometimes-conflicting obligations that practitioners working in them may experience and be forced to resolve.

MORAL DILEMMAS AND CRIMINAL JUSTICE PRACTITIONERS

As you have now seen, moral dilemmas arise from conflicting obligations and the difficulty in deciding which obligation can be served. Over the years, I have found it useful to provide students a few examples—there are obviously many more that could be chosen—of moral dilemmas faced by criminal justice practitioners to illustrate the above discussion. Practically speaking, doing so tends to get them thinking about what moral dilemmas in criminal justice involve and how they might be resolved.

As I show below, in the criminal justice system, practitioners' moral dilemmas often arise from conflicts between general and role-related obligations. Indeed, an argument can be made that most dilemmas practitioners face are of the former variety. But criminal justice practitioners also confront moral dilemmas that arise from conflicts among role-related obligations. Further, practitioners also confront self-imposed and other-imposed dilemmas. Finally, some of the dilemmas are obligation-based while others are prohibition-based. The following discussion addresses all of these areas.

Moral Dilemmas and the Police

Scholars have argued that the police serve various functions in society (Bittner, 1979). For example, they enforce the law; they maintain order ("keep the peace") by ensuring that the activities of some do not disrupt or interfere with the larger public's ability to engage in normal, day-to-day routines (Sykes, 1986; Kelling & Wilson, 1982); and provide service to the community by being involved with noncriminal matters (e.g., providing directions to people who are lost, identifying for them where government offices are located, and helping people feel safe) (see Wilson, 1968). The above points can be boiled down to one of two key propositions about the functions of police: they are either "crime fighters" or "service providers." These conflicting views would then create conflicting obligations for police officers. On the one hand, if citizens want the police to "fight crime," it means that their time, energy, effort, and resources should be devoted to finding and arresting law-breakers and engaging in proactive, prevention-based activities to keep crime from happening (or reduce its seriousness when it does occur) (Rivero & Pepper, 2010). On the other hand, if citizens want the police to be service providers, their time, energy, effort, and resources should be devoted to activities other than controlling crime (Roberts, 1976).

These competing expectations also rear their heads when one considers the informal rules and values that guide the behavior of police officers (Van Maanen & Barley, 1984; Worden, 1995). Some police scholars have suggested that the police culture exists in response to the two work environments in which police officers find themselves: the occupational environment, which involves encounters with citizens on the street, and the organizational environment, which involves interactions with supervisors and other officers in the department (Paoline, 2003). The occupational (street) environment is dangerous, and the mandate there is to display one's coercive authority over citizens. The organizational (department) environment, by contract, is rife with supervisor scrutiny of patrol officers' decisions and role ambiguity—officers are expected to perform all police functions equally, but only enforcement is recognized and rewarded. Over time, patrol officers develop coping mechanisms, and those mechanisms represent the core of the police culture (Paoline, 2003).

What these dynamics translate to is officers quickly learning what is expected of them from other officers and their superiors—their obligations, in other words—while occupying the role of police officer (Paoline, 2003, 2001; Van Maanen, 1974). They have an obligation to fight crime while also being mindful of providing service to the community. They also learn they have major obligations to other officers, particularly loyalty to them and distrust of civilians.

Thought Exercise 3.1 presents a hypothetical situation in which an officer or officers used excessive force against one or more suspects and now faces a moral dilemma about what to do next. The exercise illustrates how conflicts between and among obligations help generate the moral dilemma.

THOUGHT EXERCISE 3.1

OBLIGATIONS AND MORAL DILEMMAS INVOLVING POLICE OFFICERS

General obligations:	Honesty, fairness, respect toward others
Role-related obligations (formal):	Enforce law, maintain order, provide service to community
Role-related obligations (informal):	Loyalty to other officers; distrust of superiors and outsiders (e.g., citizens, the press)
Behavior creating moral dilemma:	Use of excessive force against suspect(s)
Self-imposed moral dilemma:	*I* used excessive force against suspect(s)
Other-imposed moral dilemma:	*Other officers* use excessive force in my presence
Obligation-based moral dilemma:	Remain silent or inform superiors
Prohibition-based moral dilemma:	Remain silent—violates enforcing the law Inform superiors—violates loyalty to other officers

Moral Dilemmas and Prosecutors

Scholars have characterized prosecutors as the most powerful—yet hidden—figures in the criminal justice process (see Jacoby, 1980; Sloan, 1987). They are responsible for evaluating cases brought to them by the police and filing initial charges against defendants; in jurisdictions that use grand juries, they appear before the group and seek an indictment against the defendant; they are responsible for plea negotiations with defense counsel; they prepare cases for trial and represent the people at them; they make sentencing recommendations (should a defendant be convicted); they represent the people when defendants appeal their convictions; and last of all, they represent the people at parole hearings where convicted offenders seek release from prison prior to the expiration of their term of sentence. Effectively, they are involved in every aspect of a case (Green, 1991; Jacoby, 1980).

Prosecutors have multiple roles as administrators of justice, advocates, and officers of the court. According to the American Bar Association (ABA), prosecutors have a duty to seek justice, not merely to convict; to seek reform and improve the administration of criminal justice; and know and be guided by standards of professional conduct arising from professional traditions, ethical codes, and the law (American Bar Association, 1993). In effect, these are the obligations that come with the role, at least according to the ABA. However, after serving for 12 years as an attorney in the public defender's office in Washington, DC, and having thousands of interactions with prosecutors, Angela J. Davis (2009, pp. 10–11) observed that prosecutors held almost all of the cards and dealt them as they saw fit. Most wanted to win every case, and winning meant getting a conviction, without consideration of whether a conviction would result in the fairest or most satisfactory result for the victim. Not exactly in line with the ABA's standards for prosecutors!

Prosecutors also operate in a political environment. For example, the district attorney for a jurisdiction (usually a county) is typically an official elected to the office via partisan election and may result in office holders being shaped by local politics. As George Cole observed nearly 50 years ago: "Because the general public is a potential threat to the prosecutor . . . decision making occurs with the public in mind—will the course of action arouse antipathy towards the prosecutor rather than the accused?" (Cole, 1970, p. 341). Interestingly, one study of over 2,000 local elections of prosecuting attorneys found that incumbents rarely lost them, mainly because challenges were rare (Wright, 2009). Wright (2009, p. 1) suggested that such uncontested elections "short-circuit opportunities for voters to learn about the incumbent's performance and make an informed judgment about the quality of criminal enforcement in their district." Thus, while prosecutors may be mindful of the public, the public may not be nearly as mindful of prosecutors to the point that members would choose to run against incumbents.

Prosecutors also wield great power, based on the discretion they have in their decision-making (Howell, 2014; Jacoby, 1980; Kaplan, 1965). As mentioned earlier, prosecutors are involved in every post-arrest stage of the criminal justice process. At each stage, prosecutors make decisions about what to do with their cases: What initial charge(s) should be filed? How much information about the case should be shared with the press? Should a charge or a sentence bargain be offered? What witnesses should testify for the state at trial? What sentence shall we seek? Thought Exercise 3.2 illustrates a hypothetical moral dilemma for one or more prosecutors that might arise when deciding

THOUGHT EXERCISE 3.2

MORAL OBLIGATIONS AND MORAL DILEMMAS INVOLVING PROSECUTORS

General obligations:	Honesty, fairness, respect for the law; "do good"
Role-related obligations (formal):	Serve as counsel for "the people"; seek justice; serve as officer of the court; seek reforms in system where needed; convict the guilty
Role-related obligations (informal):	Achieve highest possible conviction rate ("batting average"); leverage charges into plea bargains; avoid jury trials due to uncertainty of winning; do not anger constituents
Behavior giving rise to moral dilemma:	Withholding evidence favorable to defendant believed guilty in a weak case
Self-imposed moral dilemma:	*I* withheld evidence
Other-imposed moral dilemma:	*Other prosecutors* withheld evidence
Obligation-based moral dilemma:	Remain silent or inform defense counsel/the court
Prohibition-based moral dilemma:	Remaining silent—violates seeking justice and duties as officer of the court Inform defense counsel/court—violates obtaining conviction of the guilty

to withhold evidence in a case that is legally weak, but where the prosecutors strongly believe the defendant is guilty. What to do?

Moral Dilemmas and Defense Attorneys

Despite the constitutional right of citizens to have counsel assist them when charged with a crime, many citizens are harshly critical of the work performed by criminal defense attorneys. Critics contend that defense attorneys are little more than manipulators who use legal "loopholes" (e.g., the Exclusionary Rule) to "get their clients off."

Years ago, a wise law professor at the University of Michigan told me that the real job of the defense attorney was to make sure "the state did it right." What this means in practical terms is that defense counsel is responsible for ensuring that the state, in its efforts to obtain a conviction, does not trample on a client's constitutional rights. As Richard Wasserstrom (1975, p. 8) described it, "The job of [defense counsel] is not to approve or disapprove of the character of his or her client. The task is, instead, to provide the competence the client lacks and the lawyer, as a professional, possesses." Jack Marshall (2005, p.1) goes even further when he says, "In a sense, the real client of a defense attorney isn't the defendant at all but the integrity of democracy and the justice system." Thus, one could argue that a defense attorney is professionally obligated to ensure that his or her client is not "railroaded" to jail or prison by police officers and prosecutors eager to obtain a conviction.

ABA standards indicate that defense attorneys constitute an essential component of the criminal justice process and are part of a "tripartite entity" involved in criminal cases that also includes the prosecutor and judge (American Bar Association, 1991). They are considered an officer of the court, just like prosecutors, and their primary duty is to serve as the accused's counselor. In addition, defense counsel are expected to be involved in efforts to improve and reform the legal system; they should not intentionally misrepresent matters of law or fact to the court; and they should be guided by standards of professional conduct defined by legal codes and canons of ethics (American Bar Association, 1991). Besides establishing standards for the defense function, the ABA has also established model rules of professional responsibility for practicing attorneys that constitute a set of ethical guidelines governing the professional behavior of these lawyers (American Bar Association, 2016). These documents outline in some detail the obligations of defense attorneys.

One of the biggest criticisms leveled against criminal defense attorneys is that they defend clients they "know" are guilty. The problem is that neither defense counsel—nor anyone else for that matter—can tell if a defendant is guilty just by looking at him or her. Further, for multiple reasons, people falsely confess their guilt not only to their lawyers, but also to others, such as police officers (Gudjonsson, 1992). Further, the 6th Amendment doesn't say that only the innocent or the popular are entitled to legal counsel. It says that *any citizen* facing possible incarceration is entitled to counsel. What every defense counsel "knows" about his or her client is that she is in trouble and needs help.

Not only do defense attorneys represent people whom they "know" are guilty, even worse, according to critics, they are expected to "zealously" defend these (guilty) clients. The problem is that except for knowingly violating the law, a defense counsel can seemingly

THOUGHT EXERCISE 3.3

MORAL OBLIGATIONS AND MORAL DILEMMAS INVOLVING CRIMINAL DEFENSE ATTORNEYS

General obligations:	Honesty, fairness, respect for the law, "do good"
Role-related obligations (formal):	Seek justice; Serve as officer of the court; Seek reforms in system where needed; Zealously defend client; Provide competent advice
Role-related obligations (informal):	Get client the best possible deal; Push the line for zealously defending client;
Behavior giving rise to moral dilemma:	Advise witness, whose testimony could implicate both the witness and the client in criminal behavior, to invoke 5th Amendment protections against self-incrimination when questioned by authorities which, although zealous, is legally questionable
Self-imposed moral dilemma:	I zealously defend my client by advising witness to invoke 5th Amendment protections
Other-imposed moral dilemma:	(Not applicable)
Obligation-based moral dilemma:	Advise witness to invoke 5th Amendment as strategy in zealously defending client. Do not advise witness to invoke 5th Amendment
Prohibition-based moral dilemma:	Remain silent and allow witness to answer questions—violates zealous defense strategy
	Advise witness to invoke 5th Amendment—may lead to sanctions for unethical/illegal actions

use any tactic she wishes to defend a client. This creates a problem relating to just how far they should go to defend a client. One observer describes the problem as follows:

> The duty of zealous advocacy exerts pressure on lawyers to take risks on behalf of clients that they ordinarily might not take on behalf of themselves. This pressure is particularly palpable in areas of practice such as criminal defense work. A criminal defense attorney will often find that his client's interests would be well served by conduct that, though not specifically proscribed by the ethical codes, approaches the gray line drawn by ambiguous criminal laws (Green, 1991, p. 778).

Thought Exercise 3.3 illustrates a hypothetical moral dilemma for defense counsel relating to zealously defending a client, and again describes conflicts involving general and role-specific obligations of defense counsel, both formal and informal, and the implications of those conflicts.

Moral Dilemmas and Judges

Our legal system is based on the principle that an independent, fair, and competent judiciary will interpret and apply the laws that govern us. Among the roles that practitioners play in the criminal justice process, judges wield both the most power and are the most visible. As the ABA describes their role, judges are highly visible symbols of government under the rule of law and must respect and honor the law, strive to enhance and maintain confidence in the legal system, and serve as arbiters of facts and law to resolve disputes (American Bar Association, 2007, p. 8).

As it did for prosecutors and defense attorneys, the ABA promulgated model rules for judicial conduct in the form of several canons (American Bar Association, 2003, p. 6):

CANON 1: A judge shall uphold the integrity and independence of the judiciary.
CANON 2: A judge shall avoid impropriety and the appearance of impropriety in all the judge's activities.
CANON 3: A judge shall perform the duties of judicial office impartially and diligently.
CANON 4: A judge shall so conduct the judge's extra-judicial activities as to decrease the risk of conflict with judicial obligations.
CANON 5: A judge or judicial candidate shall refrain from inappropriate political activity.

These rules outline the formal obligations of members of the judiciary, and while they do not have the authority of law, many states have incorporated them *into* law. The rules outline several areas of concern regarding judicial conduct, including acts that threatens the integrity and independence of the judiciary; conduct that is either improper or has the appearance of impropriety; conduct that shows or appears to show partiality; conduct that may create a conflict of interest; or political conduct that is inappropriate.

Judges, like prosecutors, also operate in a political environment. For example, 38 states now use popular election to select judges at the three levels of courts: the highest court in the state (usually called the Supreme Court), the intermediate appeals court, and trial courts of general jurisdiction (often called "circuit courts") (Corriher, 2012). Table 3.1 shows that among the 38 states, between six and eight—depending on the level of court—select judges via *partisan* election That is, candidates for judicial office publicly self-identify as being members of a political party, most often Democratic or Republican. Six of the states who elect Supreme Court justices do so using partisan elections: Alabama, Illinois, Louisiana, Pennsylvania, Texas, and West Virginia. Between 2000 and 2010, these states ranked among the "Top 10" in total judicial campaign contributions (Corriher, 2012). Two other states, Ohio and Michigan, use nonpartisan *elections* but partisan *nomination* processes to select candidates. Those two states were among the top six in campaign spending during the 2000–2010 period (Corriher, 2012).

With the large campaign contributions accompanying partisan elections also come scandals, calling into question the impartiality of candidates running for judicial offices (Corriher, 2012). For example, in 2004, a West Virginia coal company executive spent

TABLE 3.1 States Using Partisan Election to Select Judges

	Type of Court		
Selection Method	Highest Appeals Court (N=7)	Intermediate Appeals Court[a] (N=6)	Trial Court of General Jurisdiction (N=8)
Partisan Election	AL, IL, LA, NC, PA, TX, WV	AL, IL, LA, NC, PA, TX	AL, IL, LA, NY, PA, TN, TX, WV

[a] West Virginia does not have an intermediate appeals court.
Source: Adapted from Corriher (2012)

millions of dollars to help successfully elect a candidate to the state's Supreme Court. Subsequently, the same judge voted to overturn a $50 million verdict against the executive's company. Other states, including Illinois, Louisiana, and Texas, have experienced similar scandals arising from the influence of campaign contributions on judicial decision-making. Beyond the influence of campaign contributions on judicial decision-making, that these courts were majority Republican raised the taint of partisanship in decision-making (just as would be the case if the courts consisted of Democratic majorities). Because campaign contributions may "taint" judicial elections, members of some state supreme courts have publicly spoken against such contributions and argued that nonpartisan elections should be implemented (North Carolina did so in 2002 by creating public financing for judicial elections). Other members of the judiciary have expressed concerns over "hyperpartisanship," which they claim characterizes decisions coming from many state supreme courts. At least some judges, then, confront the moral dilemma of accepting campaign contributions—or not—when running for office involving partisan elections. They are also confronted with the effects of partisanship on post-election decision-making. Thought Exercise 3.4 replicates the previous exercises, this time for judges. The dilemma here is accepting campaign contributions.

Moral Dilemmas in Corrections

The final component of the criminal justice system (and process) involves corrections, either community-based or institutional. Every day, in thousands of jurisdictions around the nation, tens of thousands of probation and parole officers (PPOs) and correctional officers (COs) interact with millions of convicted offenders and monitor their behavior.

THOUGHT EXERCISE 3.4

MORAL OBLIGATIONS AND MORAL DILEMMAS INVOLVING JUDICIAL ELECTIONS

General obligations:	Honesty, fairness, respect for the law, "do good"
Role-related obligations (formal):	Impartiality; independence; diligence; seek justice
Role-related obligations (informal):	Partisanship
Behavior giving rise to moral dilemma:	Accept campaign contributions
Self-imposed moral dilemma:	If I accept campaign contributions I run the risk of appearing to be partisan in my decisions; if I fail toto do so, I may not get elected
Other-imposed moral dilemma:	Rules call for partisan elections, which forces me to have to choose whether to accept campaign contributions
Obligation-based moral dilemma:	Partisanship calls for candidate to accept contributions
Prohibition-based moral dilemma:	(Not applicable)

PPOs are key actors in community-based corrections (CBC) (McCarthy & McCarthy, 1991), an increasingly popular policy where offenders are sentenced to a term of monitored freedom in the community, where they receive various rehabilitative services. PPOs are involved with not only monitoring the behavior of offenders living in the community, but also with ensuring they receive services such as drug treatment, job training, or educational enrichment.

Probation is a frequent disposition in both adult and juvenile proceedings in this country. To illustrate, by yearend 2016 over 4.53 million adults in this country, a rate of about 1,810 per 100,000 adults, were under community-based supervision, including probation, parole, or some other community-based program (Kaeble & Cowhig, 2018). The most recently available figures for juveniles show that over 540,000 juveniles were on probation by year end 2009 (Livsey, 2012). Both probation and parole involve conditional freedom for offenders: they remain in the community provided they abide by a set of conditions. Some of these conditions are general and apply to all offenders, such as being employed, not associating with known offenders, refraining from using alcohol or illicit drugs, and not owning a firearm. Offenders may also receive special conditions tailored to their needs, such as attending substance abuse treatment, obtaining a GED or high school diploma, and having a curfew. The special conditions of probation/parole also stipulate the level of supervision for the offender, which can range from infrequent contact with the PPO to intensive supervision. Violation of either the general or specific conditions of probation may result, on recommendation from the PPO, in a judge revoking the agreement. Revocation can then result in the probationer or parolee being sent to prison to complete the remaining term of the sentence (Clear, Cole, Reisig, & Petrosino, 2015). CBC is supposed to save money by providing offenders with community-based services and resources and protect the community through offender supervision (Carlie, 2002).

PPOs face a delicate balance when supervising their charges (Clear, et al., 2015). On the one hand, probation/parole is a legal agreement between the court and the offender that must be enforced via surveillance of the offender and controls on his or her behavior. However, PPOs are also supposed to help in offender rehabilitation by identifying for, and providing to, their charges a range of services to meet their individual needs. This strain between the so-called law enforcement role of probation, which emphasizes surveillance and control of offenders' behavior, and the "social worker role," which emphasizes support and service provision, has to be resolved by individual PPOs. Thus, PPOs have to make choices concerning how they will interact with their charge and the kind of discretion they will exercise—just like police officers.

Thought Exercise 3.5 replicates the previous analyses of conflicting obligations and moral dilemmas, but its focus is on PPOs. Here, the dilemma is whether to revoke a client's probation. I again describe some of the general and role-specific obligations of probation/parole officers and examine the dilemma that arises from revoking a charge's probation.

COs are individuals employed by public and private correctional institutions (prisons) to supervise and control inmates confined to those institutions. As of yearend 2015, the American criminal justice system held more than 2.3 million people in 1,719 state prisons, 102 federal prisons, 2,259 juvenile correctional facilities, 3,283 local jails, and 79 Indian Country jails, as well as in military prisons, immigration detention facilities, civil commitment centers, and prisons in the U.S. territories (Wagner & Rabuy, 2015). These facilities employ thousands of COs.

THOUGHT EXERCISE 3.5

MORAL OBLIGATIONS AND MORAL DILEMMAS INVOLVING PROBATION/PAROLE OFFICERS

General obligations:	Honesty, fairness, respect for the law, "do good"
Role-related obligations (formal):	Enforce conditions of probation (protect the community); facilitate offender rehabilitation; use discretion wisely
Role-related obligations (informal):	Deter charges from violating probation; help to rehabilitate offenders; protect community
Behavior giving rise to moral dilemma:	Pursue probation revocation for a client as a result of his violating a specific condition of his probation
Self-imposed moral dilemma:	If I pursue revocation, likelihood of rehabilitation of this offender is reduced but deterrence for other charges is likely enhanced. If I don't pursue revocation, I may be seen as weak by both offender and other probationers in my caseload
Other-imposed moral dilemma:	Agency rules require revocation for failed drug tests
Obligation-based moral dilemma:	Enforcement obligation requires revocation Social work obligation does not require revocation
Prohibition-based moral dilemma:	(Not applicable)

The work of COs has certain features that are similar to the work of police officers. Mary Ann Farkas and Peter Manning (1997) explained that both police officers and COs: (1) are involved in "people work" that involves managing conflict, assessing risk, and addressing uncertainty; (2) need good judgment regarding when to conceal and when to reveal information and should be able to keep secrets; and (3) are embedded in occupations that are hierarchical in structure, paramilitary in character, rule-oriented, and punishment centered. Unlike policing, however, institutional corrections involve informal negotiations occurring between officers and inmates forced to share the same physical space.

COs, like their police colleagues, are members of an occupation that has a culture (Hemmens & Storr, 2000). The presence of this culture has led some scholars to suggest that—as was the case for police officers—this culture creates conflicting obligations for COs. The primary conflict involves officers' role as "hacks," that is, they are obligated to supervise inmates and maintain order within the prison, and their role as "human service providers," which obligates them to extend to, and assist inmates with, various rehabilitation-related services such as job training (Burke & Davies, 2011).

However unpleasant, the reality is that COs must rely, at least to some degree, on inmates to help them do their jobs. Consider the following:

- Officers work in an environment where they are outnumbered by inmates and forced to occupy the same physical space with them. Order is kept largely because the inmates wish it, not because officers impose it.

- Officers must get inmates to "do things"—obey the rules, arrive and leave areas where they work, eat, or engage in recreation—in a timely fashion (Farkas & Manning, 1997).
- Officers must constantly account for the whereabouts of the inmates, since escape is the single greatest threat to the security of the institution.

In prison, order may be likened to a commodity, the cost of which is negotiated between inmates and officers, and among officers themselves through informal arrangements, obligations, and relationships (Thomas, 1984). To achieve order, officers overlook minor violations of the rules, share information or material goods and services with inmates, or distribute special privileges. In return, inmates comply with the rules and assist officers in performing their duties. What can develop out of these relationships is COs relying too much on the inmates to help them do their jobs. This reciprocity in supervision develops out of the give-and-take relationships that exist between officers and inmates and may lead to corruption through friendship (McCarthy, 2015).

Thought Exercise 3.6 presents an examination of the obligations and moral dilemmas of corrections officers. Here, the dilemmas arise from reciprocity in supervision, which develops from the give-and-take relations that exist between inmates and officers.

THOUGHT EXERCISE 3.6

MORAL OBLIGATIONS AND MORAL DILEMMAS INVOLVING CORRECTIONS OFFICERS

General obligations:	Honesty, fairness, "do good"
Role-related obligations (formal):	Protect the security of the prison; provide inmates access to, and participation in, rehabilitation services; protect the community; maintain order; use discretion wisely
Role-related obligations (informal):	Maintain position of dominance over inmates; deter charges from violating institutional rules; do not inform on colleagues for misconduct; mistrust my superiors; prevent inmate e scapes at all costs
Behavior giving rise to moral dilemma:	How far do I go in developing give-and-take relationships with inmates?
Self-imposed moral dilemma:	How far do I go in allowing inmates to help me do my job? Too far, they are effectively in charge; not far enough, they will rebel against me and my authority
Other-imposed moral dilemma:	Institutional rules concerning personal relationships with inmates versus my own sense of what's appropriate appropriate
Obligation-based moral dilemma:	Security obligation requires my remaining dominant over inmates; social service provider requires development of trust with inmates
Prohibition-based moral dilemma:	Reciprocity undermines security—affords inmates too much influence Reciprocity undermines security—enhances possible conflict with inmates

SUMMARY

Normative ethics involves making assessments about morality (whether of behavior or of character). In this chapter, I began sketching for you the boundaries for deciding when such assessments are appropriate and presented the bricks that comprise the foundation for making these assessments.

I began the chapter by discussing the moral arena as the context for making assessments of morality. I explained that it establishes "when and under what circumstances" assessments of the morality of behavior are appropriate. I then turned my attention to exploring moral dilemmas, their place as a foundational aspect of understanding, and how to make assessments about the morality of behavior. I defined a moral dilemma as a situation where one is required to do two or more actions, is able to do each of them, but cannot do both (or all) of them. In other words, a moral dilemma is a situation involving conflict, where one has to commit to a course of action but is torn over which course to take and appears condemned to moral failure—no matter what, the person will either do some wrong or fail to do right. Resolving moral dilemmas always involves making a choice, the effects of which may significantly impact both the actor and some larger community. The choice made also involves the real possibility of harm occurring to either the actor or to others.

I then explored the emotional results of resolving moral dilemmas, the "moral residue" felt by both the decision maker (moral agent) and the community assessing the behavior. That residue includes feelings of guilt or remorse, which are both proper and occur regardless of the choice made. Those feelings are both experiential and cognitive—the belief by the moral agent that he or she has done something wrong. I concluded this discussion by pointing out that feelings of remorse or guilt arising from resolving a moral dilemma help make us more aware of, and cautious about, our behavior.

Next, I presented different categories of moral dilemmas and distinguished them. One key point here is whether the moral agent has the capacity to choose one particular obligation over others and whether the dilemma arises from the agent's own doing or from some outside cause(s). In some instances, more than one action is obligatory, but in other instances, all feasible actions are prohibited, which serves to enhance the feelings of remorse or guilt once the choice is made. I also folded into the mix a discussion of the role of conflicting obligations in moral dilemmas. We possess both general obligations—tell the truth; don't steal or cheat—and role-related obligations that arise from the relationships we have with others. I concluded the discussion about moral dilemmas by exploring common-sense morality as a path to resolve moral dilemmas and described common-sense morality as rules or principles taken from several systems of ethics and applied to the situation to help people decide what to do.

In closing the discussion, I offered illustrations of different moral dilemmas that sometimes confront criminal justice practitioners, including police officers, prosecutors, defense attorneys, judges, probation/parole officers, and corrections officers. In many cases, the dilemmas involve particularly strong conflicts between general and role-related obligations or among role-related obligations. I made the point that discretion and its exercise play a particularly relevant role in generating many of the moral dilemmas confronting criminal justice practitioners.

To conclude the chapter, let's examine a headline-grabbing issue: criminal justice professionals, such as police officers, "going public" (whistleblowing) with information about illegal or unethical activities occurring in their agencies. In nearly every case of whistleblowing by criminal justice practitioners, they faced a terrible choice: should I "go public" after efforts to get superiors to address illegal or unethical practices in my agency have failed? Case Study 3.1 examines the ethics of whistleblowing and offers a timeline of (in)famous whistleblower cases involving different criminal justice agencies. What would *you* do?

CASE STUDY 3.1 Whistleblowing in the Criminal Justice System

Whistleblowing involves an employee calling attention to illegal (or unethical) behavior occurring inside an organization, whether a government agency or large corporation. The Government Accountability Project (2015a) argues that there are four ways an individual might "blow the whistle" on unresolved illegalities or unethical behavior occurring in an agency or company: (1) report the wrongdoing to the proper authorities, such as a superior or an inspector general in the case of a federal government agency; (2) refuse to participate in the wrongdoing; (3) testify in legal proceedings about wrongdoing occurring in the organization; or (4) leak evidence of wrongdoing to the media, such as a major newspaper like the *Washington Post*.

Researchers studying whistleblowing suggest that "going public" is one's response to his or her understanding that behaviors occurring within the organization are *harmful*—they interfere with others' rights, detract from the common good, or are simply unfair (Nadler & Schulman, 2006). It's also worth noting that whistleblowing involves virtue: the courage to stand up and call attention to a wrong that is occurring and "take-the-heat" for doing so, including being ostracized, marginalized, or worse (Nadler & Schulman, 2006). Following is a list of prominent whistleblowers employed by different criminal justice agencies, including the illegal or unethical behavior they uncovered and about which they "went public" (Government Accountability Project, 2015b):

Frank Serpico (1970): Former detective with the New York Police Department (NYPD) reported widespread corruption in his precinct to superiors for several years but no action was taken; after approaching the *New York Times* with the story, New York City mayor John Lindsay was forced to establish a commission to investigate corruption in the police department.

Cathy Harris (1999): Former senior inspector for the U.S. Customs Service (USCS) at Hartsfield-Jackson International Airport in Atlanta. Harris disclosed to the media the USCS practice of discriminatory racial profiling. Her revelations resulted in a landmark General Accounting Office (GAO) study of USCS profiling practices, and federal legislation to reform them.

Jesselyn Radack (2002): Former ethics advisor to the United States Department of Justice (USDOJ) warned FBI agents of problems when they sought to interrogate "American Taliban" member John Walker Lindh without legal counsel present and advised them not to do so.

Coleen Rowley (2002): Former Special Agent with the Federal Bureau of Investigation (FBI) who went public with the agency's slow response time to reports of suspicious activity before the 9/11 attacks. She jointly held *Time* magazine's "Person of the Year" award in 2002.

Robert MacLean (2003): Former Federal Air Marshal (FAM) who revealed a cost-cutting plan to cancel FAM coverage from long-distance flights on the eve of a confirmed al-Qaeda suicide hijacking planned for the United States.

Thomas Tamm (2003): Former USDOJ attorney who became aware of a program that bypassed the 11-member Foreign Intelligence Surveillance Act (FISA) Court and allowed the then U.S. Attorney General to sign wiretap requests without the court's review. After Tamm's inquiries repeatedly ran into walls of silence, he contacted the *New York Times*, which ran a Pulitzer Prize–winning story about the case.

Frank Terreri (2006): Former FAM who joined the agency after the 9/11 attacks and disclosed numerous security problems on behalf of 1,500 air marshals. He questioned policies that helped identify undercover air marshals and challenged Justice Department endorsements of news segments that revealed methods air marshals use to prevent/respond to commercial airliner hijackings.

Christian Sanchez (2011): Former Immigration and Customs Enforcement (ICE) agent who alerted the major media outlets about overtime being paid to ICE agents when no extra work was being performed at the Port Angeles, Washington, office and briefed Congress about waste of taxpayer dollars on overtime paid by ICE.

Larry Alt and **Pete Forcelli** (2012): Both were formerly agents at the Bureau of Alcohol, Tobacco, Firearms & Explosives (BATF) and helped expose issues surrounding the *Operation Fast and Furious* scandal, the program that resulted in federally monitored guns ending up in the hands of Mexican drug cartels.

KEY TERMS

Moral arena 61
Moral dilemma 63
Epistemic dilemmas 65
Ontological dilemma 65
Self-imposed dilemma 65
Other-imposed dilemmas 65
Obligation-based dilemmas 66
Prohibition-based dilemmas 66
Obligations 66
General obligations 66
Role-related obligations 66
Common-sense morality 66
Moral relativism 67
Whistleblowing 79

DISCUSSION QUESTIONS

1. Using the moral dilemma depicted by *Sophie's Choice* and the "trolley-car problem," make the choice called for by each and use any of the systems of ethics discussed so far to guide your decision-making.
2. Can you think of a moral dilemma you experienced similar to any discussed in the chapter? Identify the nature of the conflict and how you resolved the dilemma.
3. Assess the validity of "common-sense morality." Does it make sense to you? Do you think students use common-sense morality to resolve their moral dilemmas? Explain why or why not.
4. Which group encounters moral dilemmas more frequently: probation/parole officers or correctional officers? Why do you think this is the case? Explain your thinking.

RESOURCES

The **Government Accountability Project** is a nonprofit, nongovernment agency that has worked since 1977 with, and on behalf of, whistleblowers from government and industry. Visit their website at https://www.whistleblower.org/our-history-and-mission

Institute for Criminal Justice Ethics is a university-based, nonprofit center set up to generate greater concern for ethical issues among criminal justice scholars and practitioners. Publishes the journal *Criminal Justice Ethics*. http://johnjayresearch.org/cje/about/purpose/

Markkula Center for Applied Ethics is a renowned academic unit at Santa Clara University whose work focuses on ethics, ethical decision making, and related topics. Visit their website at https://www.scu.edu/ethics/about-the-center/overview/

REFERENCES

Adler, M. (1970). *The times of our lives: The ethics of common sense*. New York, NY: Fordham University Press.

American Bar Association (2016). *Model rules of professional responsibility*. Retrieved from http://www.americanbar.org/groups/professional_responsibility/publications/model_rules_of_professional_conduct/model_rules_of_professional_conduct_table_of_contents.html

American Bar Association (2007). *Model code of judicial conduct*. Retrieved from http://www.americanbar.org/content/dam/aba/migrated/judicialethics/ABA_MCJC/approved.authcheckdam.pdf

American Bar Association (1993). *Prosecution function*. Retrieved from http://www.americanbar.org/publications/criminal_justice_section_archive/crimjust_standards_pfunc_toc.html

American Bar Association (1991). *Defense function.* Retrieved from http://www.americanbar.org/publications/criminal_justice_section_archive/crimjust_standards_dfunc_blk.html#1.2

Bittner, E. (1979). *The functions of the police in modern society.* Cambridge, MA: Oelgeschlager, Gunn & Hain Publishers.

Burke, L., & Davies, K. (2011). Introducing the special edition on occupational culture and skills in probation practice. *European Journal of Probation, 3,* 1–14.

Carlie, M. (2002). The goals of probation and parole. Retrieved from http://people.missouristate.edu/MichaelCarlie/what_I_learned_about/PP/goals.htm

Clear, T., Cole, G., Reisig, M., & Petrosino, C. (2015). *American corrections in brief.* Stamford, CT: Cengage Learning.

Cole, G. (1970). The decision to prosecute. *Law & Society Review, 4,* 331–344.

Corriher, B. (2012). *Partisan judicial elections and the distorting influence of campaign cash.* Washington, DC: Center for American Progress. Retrieved from https//cdn.americanprogress.org/wp-content/uploads/2012/10/NonpartisanElections-3.pdf

Davis, A. (2009). *Arbitrary justice: The power of the American prosecutor.* New York, NY: Oxford University Press.

Davis, L. (2015, October 9). Would you pull the trolley switch? Does it matter? *The Atlantic.* Retrieved from http://www.theatlantic.com/technology/archive/2015/10/trolley-problem-history-psychology-morality-driverless-cars/409732/

Donagan, A. (1984). Consistency in rationalist moral systems. *The Journal of Philosophy, 81,* 291–309.

Donagan, A. (1977). *The theory of morality.* Chicago, IL: University of Chicago Press.

Farkas, M., & Manning, P. (1997). The occupational culture of police and corrections officers. *Journal of Crime and Justice, 20,* 51–98.

Foot, P. (1967). The problem of abortion and the doctrine of the double effect. *Oxford Review, 5,* 1–7. Retrieved from http://www2.econ.iastate.edu/classes/econ362/hallam/Readings/FootDoubleEffect.pdf

Government Accountability Project (2015a). About Us. Retrieved from http://www.whistleblower.org/aboutus

Government Accountability Project (2015b). Timeline of prominent whistle blowers. Retrieved from https://www.whistleblower.org/timeline-us-whistleblowers

Green, B. (1991). Zealous representation bound: The intersection of the ethical codes and the criminal law. *North Carolina Law Review, 69,* 687–717.

Greenspan, P. (1995). *Practical guilt: Moral dilemmas, emotions, and social norms.* New York, NY: Oxford University Press.

Gudjonsson, G. (1992). *The psychology of interrogations, confessions, and testimony.* Oxford, England: John-Wiley & Sons.

Hemmens, C., & Storr, M. (2000). The two faces of the correctional role: An exploration of the value of the Correctional Role Instrument. *International Journal of Offender Therapy & Comparative Criminology, 44,* 326–349.

Hoddings, N. (2005). Educating citizens for global awareness: The Teachers College Model. *The Academy of Management Review, 16,* 366–395.

Hooker, B. (2000). Sidgwick and commonsense morality. *Utilitas, 12,* 347–360.

Howell, K. (2014). Prosecutorial discretion and the duty to seek justice in an overburdened criminal justice system. *The Georgetown Journal of Legal Ethics, 27,* 285–334.

Jacoby, J. (1980). *The American prosecutor: A search for identity.* Lexington, MA: Lexington Books.

Jones, T. (1991). Ethical decision making by individuals in organizations: An issue-contingent model. *The Academy of Management Review, 16,* 366–395.

Kaeble, D. & Cowhig, M. (2018). *Correctional populations in the United States, 2016.* Washington, DC: Bureau of Justice Statistics. Retrieved from https://www.bjs.gov/content/pub/pdf/cpus16.pdf

Kahane, G. (2015). Sidetracked by trolleys: Why sacrificial moral dilemmas tell us little (or nothing) about Utilitarian judgment. *Social Neuroscience, 10,* 551–560.

Kaplan, J. (1965). The prosecutorial discretion: A comment. *Northwestern University Law Review, 60,* 174–192.

Kelling, G., & Wilson, J. (1982, March 29). Broken windows. *The Atlantic.* Retrieved from http://www.theatlantic.com/magazine/archive/1982/03/broken-windows/304465/

Livsey, S. (2012). *Juvenile delinquency probation caseload, 2009*. Washington, DC: Office of Juvenile Justice and Delinquency Prevention. Retrieved from http://www.ojjdp.gov/pubs/239082.pdf

Marcus, R. (1980). Moral dilemmas and consistency. *The Journal of Philosophy, 77*, 121–136.

Marshall, J. (2005). The ethics of justice: Why criminal defense lawyers defend the guilty. Retrieved from http://www.ethicsscoreboard.com/list/defense.html

McCarthy, B. (2015). Keeping an eye on the keeper: Prison corruption and its control. In M. Braswell, B. McCarthy, & B. McCarthy (Eds.), *Justice, crime and ethics* (8th ed.) (pp. 277–298). Waltham, MA: Elsevier.

McCarthy, B., & McCarthy, B. (1991). *Community-based corrections*. Pacific Grove, CA: Brooks-Cole.

McConnell, T. (2014). Moral dilemmas. In E. Zalta (Ed.), *The Stanford encyclopedia of philosophy* (Fall edition). Retrieved from http://plato.stanford.edu/entries/moral-dilemmas/

McConnell, T. (1986). More on moral dilemmas. *The Journal of Philosophy, 82*, 345–351.

McConnell, T. (1978). Moral dilemmas and consistency in ethics. *Canadian Journal of-Philosophy, 8*, 269–287.

Merriam-Webster (n.d.). Harm. Retrieved from http://www.merriam-webster.com/dictionary/harm

Nadler, J., & Schulman, M. (2006). *Whistle blowing in the public sector*. Santa Clara, CA: Markkula Center for Applied Ethics. Retrieved from http://www.scu.edu/ethics/focus-areas/government-ethics/resources/what-is-government-ethicswhistle-blowing-in-the-public-sector/

Narain, V. (2014, October 21). Determinism, free will, and moral responsibility. *The Humanist*, November/December. Retrieved from http://thehumanist.com/magazine/november-december-2014/philosophically-speaking/determinism-free-will-and-moral-responsibility

Paoline, E. (2003). Taking stock: Toward a richer understanding of police culture. *Journal of Criminal Justice, 31*, 199–214.

Paoline, E. (2001). *Rethinking police culture: Officers' occupational attitudes*. New York, NY: LFB Publishing.

Parfit, D. (1979). Is common-sense morality self-defeating? *Journal of Philosophy, 76*, 533–545.

Rescher, N. (1988). *Rationality: A philosophical inquiry into the nature and the rationale of reason*. New York, NY: Oxford University Press.

Rivero, D., & Pepper, J. (2010). Proactive patrolling through the use of patrol scripts. *The Police Chief, 77*, 66–68. Retrieved from http://www.nxtbook.com/nxtbooks/Naylor/CPIM0910 index.php#/60

Roberts, R. (1976). Police as social workers: A history. *Social Work, 21*, 294–298.

Sartre, J.-P. (1957). Existentialism is a humanism. In W. Kaufman (Ed.), *Existentialism from Dostoevsky to Sartre* (pp. 287–311). New York, NY: Meridian.

Sidgwick, H. (1907). *The methods of ethics*. New York, NY: Macmillan.

Sinnott-Armstrong, W. (1988). *Moral dilemmas*. Oxford, England: Basil-Blackwell.

Sloan, J. (1987). *Retributive criminal justice: An empirical study of prosecutorial charge reduction and judicial sentencing decisions*. (Unpublished doctoral dissertation). Purdue University, West Lafayette, IN.

Slote, M. (1985). *Common-sense morality and consequentialism*. New York, NY: Routledge.

Styron, W. (1979). *Sophie's choice*. New York, NY: Random House.

Sykes, G. (1986). Street justice: A moral defense of order maintenance policing. *Justice Quarterly, 3*, 497–524.

Thomas, J. (1984). Some aspects of negotiated order, loose coupling, and mesostructure in maximum security prisons. *Symbolic Interaction, 7*, 213–231.

van Holthoon, F., & Olson, D. (1987). Common sense: An introduction. In F. van Holthoon & D. Olson (Eds.), *Common sense: The foundations for social science* (pp. 1–14). New York, NY: Lanham.

Van Maanen, J. (1974). Working the street: A developmental view of police behavior. In H. Jacob (Ed.), *The potential for reform of criminal justice* (pp. 83–103). Beverly Hills, CA: Sage.

Van Maanen, J., & Barley, S. (1984). Occupational communities: Culture and control in organizations. In B. Staw & C. Cummings (Eds.), *Research in organizational behavior* (pp. 287–365). Greenwich, CT: JAI Press.

Wagner, P., & Rabuy, B. (2015). *Mass incarceration: The whole pie, 2015*. Northampton, MA: Prison Policy Initiative. Retrieved from http://www.prisonpolicy.org/reports/pie2015.html

Wasserman, D., Asch, A., Blustein, J., & Putnam, D. (2013). Cognitive disability and moralstatus. In E. Zalta (Ed.), *The Stanford encyclopedia of philosophy* (Spring Edition). Retrieved from http://plato.stanford.edu/archives/spr2013/entries/cognitive-disability/

Wasserstrom, R. (1975). Lawyers as professionals: Some moral issues. *Human Rights, 5*, 1–24.

Westacott, E. (n.d.). Moral relativism. In J. Feiser & B. Dowden (Eds.), *The Internetencyclopedia of philosophy*. Retrieved from http://www.iep.utm.edu/moral-re/

Williams, B. (1965). Ethical consistency. *Proceedings of the Aristotelian Society, 39*, 103–124.

Wilson, J. (1968). *Varieties of police behavior*. Cambridge, MA: Harvard University Press.

Worden, R. (1995). Police officers' belief systems: A framework for analysis. *American Journal of Police, 14*, 49–81.

Wright, R. (February 9, 2009). How prosecutor elections fail us. Wake Forest University Legal Studies Paper No. 1339939. Retrieved from http://ssrn.com/abstract=1339939

Zimmerman, M. (1996). *The concept of moral obligation*. Cambridge: Cambridge University Press.

CHAPTER 4

Moral Reasoning and Criminal Justice Ethics

Chapter Outline

CHAPTER LEARNING OBJECTIVES:

1. Describe the steps involved in moral reasoning.
2. Explain how moral considerations can be identified and sorted, and conflicts among them resolved.
3. Explain how moral reasoning includes learning from experience and changing one's mind.
4. Describe moral dumbfoundedness and why it occurs.
5. Identify Kohlberg's levels and stages of moral reasoning.
6. Identify guiding principles for moral reasoning.
7. Describe common errors in moral reasoning.

INTRODUCTION

Is there a difference between these two situations: (1) a police officer's weapon discharged and (2) a police officer discharged her weapon? The short answer is "yes." The officer's weapon discharging could have resulted from any number of causes, some of which she had no control over. The officer discharging her weapon, on the other hand, implies consciousness of intent—she controlled the weapon and then fired it.

My little scenario illustrates what philosophers distinguish as an *occurrence* involving the weapon and an *action* involving it (Velleman, 2000, p. 1). "What" you may be asking yourself "does the difference between occurrence and action have to do with ethics and criminal justice?" Your question is legitimate. However, if you think about the difference between the two for a moment, I believe you'll see where I'm going: sometimes our behavior is *not* the product of conscious, reasoned thought, while at other times it is. In the realm of ethics, some philosophers have suggested that when we confront a moral dilemma, we are sorely tempted to "go with our gut" to resolve it, rather than thinking it through or discussing it with others (Harman, 2011). For example, when deciding whether I should report my new partner to the shift sergeant for using excessive force against an inmate during that evening's patrol, I may "go with my gut" and *not* report what happened; in such an instance, one could say that an "occurrence" has taken place. Or, I may carefully consider a variety of relevant factors and use guiding principles from Kantian ethics to reach a decision; thus, an action occurred. When confronting a moral dilemma like what to do about my partner's behavior, I make a decision that accounts for the end(s) I seek: Do I want to pursue justice for the arrestee or protect my partner? I have to decide which end is the more important and then act accordingly.

In this chapter, I share with you some thinking by philosophers and others about moral reasoning, including what it entails and why it matters in making decisions about how we ought to behave. I then examine the development of human capacity to engage in moral reasoning by reviewing with you one of the most important theories ever developed in moral psychology: Lawrence Kohlberg's theory of moral development. I then turn my attention to providing you with a guide to moral reasoning and share with you some common errors in it. I conclude the chapter by engaging in a little moral reasoning myself about Hebert Packer's "crime control model" of criminal justice that I discussed in Ch. 1. I will note for you that much of the substance found in this chapter serves as the foundation for material that will be covered in Ch. 5, where I provide you with a template I've developed for analyzing moral dilemmas. As you progress through the rest of the book, you'll have multiple opportunities to use that template to help you reason to a conclusion about ethical dilemmas associated with policing, the courts, and corrections.

MORAL REASONING

When faced with a moral dilemma we need to resolve, we consider our options and may look to guidelines from systems of ethics such as ethical egoism to help us reason through to a conclusion about how we should resolve the dilemma. We then make our choice and have to live with the potential consequences. This process is called *moral reasoning*. In this section of the chapter, I provide you with an overview of what moral reasoning involves, explain why it is important, and discuss an important contribution to the study of moral reasoning: Kohlberg's theory of moral development.

What Is Moral Reasoning?

The first consideration when discussing **moral reasoning** is defining it. What exactly *is* moral reasoning? While philosophers have formulated multiple formal definitions of "moral reasoning," they all seem to include the following considerations. Moral reasoning seems to involve some "moral agent" (you or I) deciding what to do to resolve a moral dilemma confronting them. Some set of standards or rules, such as those found in Utilitarianism or Kantian ethics, then guide the agent's decision-making.

With these two considerations in mind, let's say that for our purposes moral reasoning occurs when a moral agent formulates a judgment about what one ought to do in moral terms (Richardson, 2013). Some philosophers have described moral reasoning as a kind of "responsibly conducted thinking" wherein a moral agent, guided by an assessment of reasons for acting in one way (as opposed to another) makes a choice about how

BOX 4.1 An Example of Moral Reasoning

Smith should not have covered up his partner's use of excessive force against an inmate during the search of his cell. Covering up the truth constitutes a lie and lying is wrong	Moral judgment
Because lying causes great unhappiness	Rationale: reasons that appeal to or apply a guiding principle
And behavior that causes great unhappiness is wrong	Generalizable conclusion

to behave and then acts on that choice. When you or I engage in moral reasoning, we take what we believe is morally true (e.g., the morality of behavior is a function of its utility for the greatest number of affected individuals) and decide which course of action (i.e., behavior) should be taken. Box 4.1 illustrates this process.

When faced with moral dilemmas we often respond "from our gut" and act impulsively to resolve the dilemma. This is *not* moral reasoning. When, however, we pause to consider not only *what* we ought to do but *why* we ought do it, we are entering the realm of moral reasoning. In moral reasoning, the goal is to conform our behavior to a set of beliefs about why that behavior is "good" in moral terms. When we do so, we are acting rationally. We develop a well-supported answer ("I should not lie") to a well-defined question ("How do I resolve conflicting obligations to two friends to whom I've made promises I can't keep?). Moral reasoning involves a process of moving from finding relevant moral facts to applying specific principles and then deciding how well the principles "fit" the facts. One then reaches a conclusion about the fit and behaves accordingly. You might think of this process as moving along a road with signs, where each sign asks you an important question: What are the moral facts? What are the guiding principles you seek to apply? How well does the theory fit the facts? What is your conclusion?

The Process of Moral Reasoning

As I mentioned above, moral reasoning is a *process*, in much the same way a journey is a process: you begin at a certain point and along the way encounter various obstacles you must address; if you do this successfully, you arrive at your destination, as shown in Figure 4.1. Let's consider the obstacles as important questions you have to both ask and answer to ensure that your moral reasoning is sound.

Recognizing Moral Issues

Being aware of **moral issues**—the morally salient facts in any situation—is a crucial first step in the moral reasoning process because doing so requires that you possess both the ability to speak about morality and emotional awareness (Haidt, 2001; Mikhail, 2011). For some ethicists, the crucial first task for the moral reasoner is to identify the morally salient features of a situation. Say, for example, you face conflicting obligations between one or more duties owed to a parent and those owed your spouse. When you realize this,

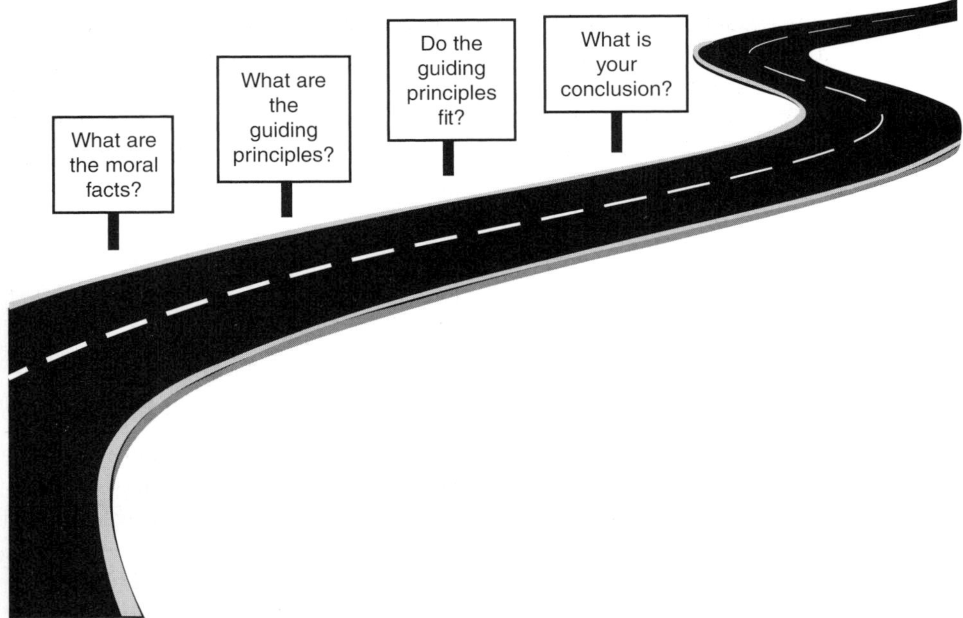

FIGURE 4.1 The Road to Moral Reasoning

you are assigning to that realization a level of moral importance that you would not assign to, say, the conflict that may arise when deciding whether to have eggs or cereal for breakfast. While what counts as a moral issue varies based on a particular system of ethics (e.g., not all systems would agree that loyalty to friends and country is a moral issue), no *legitimate* normative theory of ethics would claim that such a recognition isn't important (Richardson, 2013).

ATTENDING TO MORAL FACTS. In the world of our senses, it is a fact that Birmingham, AL, where I lived for nearly 30 years, occupies physical space at latitude 33.65° N and longitude –86.80° E and has an elevation of 644′ above sea level. As of this writing, its mayor is Randall Woodfin. All of these can be determined empirically using your senses or through mechanical extension of them. You may choose to *disagree* with them, but that doesn't change anything—these are facts. In ethics, however, there are not the same kind of facts that we can recognize using our senses or mechanical extensions of them. To illustrate, recall that normative ethics is concerned with *ought* and not *is*. Just because something exists doesn't mean that it ought to exist (this is similar to the notion that just because you have the ability to do something, doesn't mean that you should do it). As described by one scholar, "[P]hilosophers recognize that 'isness' doesn't imply 'oughtness.' This is why a scientist, who knows a great deal about the material world, isn't necessarily a good source of ethical guidance" (Dobrin, 2012, p. 1). What I'm speaking to here is the difference between possessing *knowledge* about the world and cultivating *wisdom* about it and its workings.

Moral facts are reality-based, but their reality is relational and not material. For example, if you have a brother, the material reality is this: you have a sibling. However, your relationship with your brother and the obligations arising from it occur within the context of human relations. In moral reasoning, what we need to do first is identify the nature of the relationship we have with another (i.e., our obligations) potentially being affected by our behavior. It is simply not enough to know that such relationships exist; we must identify what those relationships *mean* and factor them into our reasoning process (Richardson, 2013).

Sorting the Moral Considerations

Because moral dilemmas typically involve conflicting obligations, the moral agent needs to sort them and determine their relevancy. Obviously, while some obligations are not necessarily relevant when resolving the moral dilemma, others are extremely relevant. The trick is deciding into which category they fit.

REASONING BY ANALOGY. When engaging in moral reasoning, one tool you may use to sort relevant information and obligations from those that are not relevant is called **reasoning by analogy**. Analogical reasoning takes note of the fact that two or more things are similar in some respects and concludes, therefore, they are also similar in additional ways (Kemerling, 2011). To illustrate, let's return to the example of what I should do about my partner using excessive force on an arrestee . Here, using analogical reasoning, I would decide whether my lying about my partner's behavior is more like lying to protect the innocent (which, in general, is acceptable behavior) or whether I am lying to protect my own interests (the acceptance of which is not so clear). If you find yourself engaging in such thinking a lot, you are systematically using analogical reasoning to help you decide what moral choices to make. However, systematic analogical reasoning requires both stability in, and reflectiveness about, accepted moral norms (Richardson, 2013). Effectively, what's occurring is that you are satisfied that comparable cases are "settled"—that lying to protect the innocent is, in general, *always* preferable to protecting one's interests. You have now developed a "scheme" for identifying relevant information that you then use to resolve dilemmas, and that lends order to making appeals to analogous cases and the moral norms those cases represent.

Resolving Conflicts among Considerations in Moral Reasoning

When trying to resolve moral dilemmas through moral reasoning, you may find conflicts occurring between or among moral considerations or between or among moral principles. How can you best order your thinking to deal with these conflicts? One way to is found in the notion of ***prima facie* duty**, a moral theory developed by William Ross (Ross, 1988).

Sir William D. Ross (1877–1971) was a British philosopher whose best-known work combined elements and insights from several earlier moral theories and philosophical traditions, including virtue ethics and Kantian ethics, especially Kant's notions surrounding duty and obligations (Simpson, n.d.). When discussing *prima facie* duties, Ross was apparently focusing on the moral significance (or not) of relationships between people: benefactor-beneficiary, promiser-promisee, creditor-debtor, wife-husband, child-parent, friend-friend, etc. (Simpson, n.d.). These relations form the foundation for a *prima facie* duty, or an act that, by virtue of it involving morally significant relations between people, would otherwise be a simple duty (Dobrin, 2012). Table 4.1 illustrates some of Ross's *prima facie* duties.

Sir William D. Ross

TABLE 4.1 A Partial Inventory of *Prima Facie* Duties

Nature of the Duties	*Prima Facie* Duty
Duties stemming from *one's* previous actions	*Fidelity*: fulfill both explicit and implicit promises made or agreements entered into *Reparation*: make up for harms previously caused to others
Duties stemming from *others'* previous actions	*Gratitude*: repay others for their past favors
Duties stemming from possible mismatches between one's happiness and one's merit	*Justice*: prevent or correct such mismatches
Duties stemming from the possibility of improving the conditions of others with respect to virtue, intelligence, or pleasure	*Beneficence*: improve the conditions of others in these respects
Duties stemming from the possibility of improving one's condition with respect to virtue or intelligence	*Self-improvement*: improve one's virtues or intelligence
Special duty distinguished from the duty of beneficence (doing good for its own sake)	*Nonmaleficence*: do not injure others

Source: Adapted from Simpson (n.d., p. 1)

A *prima facie* duty is fundamentally different from a simple duty or obligation. When a moral decision must be made in a situation where more than one *prima facie* duty is applicable, Ross argues that the matter must be studied until it can be deduced under the present circumstances, that one *prima facie* duty is more incumbent than any other(s). The *prima facie* duty judged to be "more incumbent than any other" becomes the *actual* obligation that is owed (Ross, 1988, cited in Simpson, n.d.). While doing no harm is more important than doing good, Ross offers no ranking of *prima facie* duties, because, based on circumstances, each situation is judged separately.

Learning from Experience and Changing One's Mind

Does moral reasoning include learning from experience and changing one's mind? Some philosophers argue that this is indeed the case—that our "moral knowledge," including general principles and concrete conclusions, is imperfect. Some philosophers even suggest that enhancing our moral knowledge depends on the moral reasoning we use. Although some moral knowledge can be gleaned from the work of both ethicists (in particular) and philosophers (more generally), most of what we learn regarding morality occurs in the practical context of deliberating about new and difficult situations we confront (Richardson, 2013). Such deliberations may be purely instrumental—deciding on the most ethical means to get us through a particularly difficult dilemma—or they may target the ends themselves. While there is nothing special about learning which means lead us to morally acceptable ends, figuring out which ends are *acceptable* is an entirely different problem. The question now becomes, Does moral learning result from moral reasoning?

MORAL LEARNING FROM MORAL REASONING. Some philosophers and moral psychologists believe that moral learning from moral reasoning is possible (Millgram, 1997). Some of the learning arises from the emotions that factor into our reasoning. This is because our emotions help us become aware of moral considerations—such as sympathy or empathy—that are useful in moral reasoning. It could well be that one's capacity for anger or pleasure serves as a signpost, if you will, of both actions worth doing and morally wrong actions—even if one had not encountered a particular situation before (e.g., my lying about my partner's excessive use of force). In effect, emotions play a crucial role in moral reasoning, allowing us to generate moral insights we previously were not able to do. As we develop and exercise this skill, our capacity for moral judgment, guided by our emotions, can address increasingly complex moral situations, as we have *learned* from previous experience (Richardson, 2013).

Moral learning from moral reasoning can also occur as the product of after-the-fact reactions to a situation, or what some label "experiments in living," when we try something to see whether it "works" (Anderson, 1991). Note, however, that for after-the-fact moral learning to occur we must be open to what is meant by "works." For example, what are the important parts of happiness? What are the important parts of faithfulness? If we remain open to determining what works, we are then able to learn by experience what are the important parts of end-states such as faithfulness, truthfulness, etc

Overturning Moral Theories

If we accept that knowing about the extent and nature of an obligation is important in moral reasoning, not simply having the knowledge that the obligation exists, moral reasoning is not completed simply by knowing that some principle or principles are available to guide us. Again, knowledge is not enough. Rather, we must understand that moral theories are neither completely developed, nor do they exist in a vacuum. Instead, they develop and are perpetuated via moral convictions that are both systematic and consider a wide range of moral facts (Richardson, 2013). Unlike in biology or mathematics, where there are well-established theories and laws, what moral theory is trying to explain depends much more on provisionally accepted theories or revisions of them. At the same time, a specific moral theory (e.g., Act Utilitarianism) may be rejected after reasonable consideration because we conclude that its implications are unacceptable. What this means, in effect, is that circumstances matter. "Hard-and-fast" rules for how to act in all cases can leave us wanting, so we have to keep our reasoning flexible. Flexible reasoning is important because it leaves room for many possibilities, including conflicts among basic elements (Richardson, 2013). Priority rules are unlikely to fit all circumstances; an approach to moral reasoning is needed that extends beyond simply applying rules to the situation and being satisfied with the answer that develops.

Moral Dumbfoundedness

To make a final point about the process of moral reasoning, consider the following. I am confronting a moral dilemma that needs resolution. I could act instinctually and resolve the dilemma, but in doing so, I "takes my chances" because instincts are often incorrect (Kersting, 2005). Further, when acting instinctively, I may be unable to offer justification (or even explanation) for why I resolved the dilemma as I did. Ethicists refer to this condition as **moral dumbfoundedness** and describe it as someone confidently pronouncing a moral judgment, then finding that he or she has little to nothing to say in its defense (Sneddon, 2007). In other words, the moral agent is supremely confident in his or her judgment but is unable to articulate reasons to support it. Thus, moral reasoning is important because it helps avoid moral dumbfoundedness.

Some scholars suggest that moral dumbfoundedness occurs because we possess both a quick, emotionally based way of processing moral dilemmas and a slower, more cognitively oriented way of processing them, and we overrely on the former (Haidt, 2001). In effect, to resolve our dilemmas we often trust *intuition* rather than use *cognition*. Note, too, that moral dumbfoundedness may also arise from social norms interfering with our moral reasoning (Sneddon, 2007). This argument suggests that we—you, me, others—are perfectly capable of functioning, in a moral sense, when we possess superficial knowledge of what's right or wrong, what's permissible and what's not, along with knowing how to obtain more information when needed. However, when pressed on what we know, we are unable to explain what we know in any detail. Here's an analogy: say you claim to "know" how something works—for example, a toilet—but when *pressed* about the details of its workings, it turns out you really know very little about the device. The reason you think you know how the toilet works is perhaps because (1) you've been told about toilets by others—some of whom may have been plumbers; (2) you consulted a "how to" or "do it yourself" guide to toilets; (3) you inquired of the Internet; or (4) you read a book and "learned" about the workings of toilets. What's most important is that when the toilet malfunctions, you either know whom to consult for help or where to look for answers. Philosophers suggest that the same is true with making moral judgments: we carry around with us enough "moral knowledge to get by" but also know where to look for more answers and for better ones (Sneddon, 2007).

A third potential source for our moral dumbfoundedness arises from resolving similar moral dilemmas in different ways—in other words, we are inconsistent in our logic (Campbell & Kumar, 2012). For example, when deciding how to resolve a personal dilemma—say, what to do about my partner's using excessive force against an arrestee —I rely on guiding principles from ethical egoism. However, when making a judgment about the morality of the behavior of other police officers who use excessive force against citizens, I use principles from Kantian ethics to guide my assessment. The problem here is that I've used inconsistent logic in my assessment of the same behavior. When I do this—resolve similar cases in different ways—I violate what's known as the **law of noncontradiction** in formal logic, which says that for your arguments to be logical, they cannot conflict with one another (Harper, 2005). On the other hand, when I use the same reasoning to resolve similar cases the same way, I am engaging in what philosophers call **consistency reasoning**, which is important. It can, for example, influence not only my moral judgments but also my feelings about morality itself, which leads to moral growth (Campbell & Kumar, 2012).

THE DEVELOPMENT OF MORAL REASONING

Now that you have a grasp of what moral reasoning involves—identifying facts, considering guiding principles and how well they fit the circumstances of the moral dilemma, and reaching a conclusion that is not morally dumbfounded—I want to turn to how moral reasoning develops and grows in humans. Perhaps no other 20th-century thinker contributed more to our understanding of moral development and reasoning than did the psychologist Lawrence Kohlberg, who developed a theory of moral development. I present an overview of Kohlberg's arguments in the section that follows.

Kohlberg's Levels and Stages of Moral Reasoning

Lawrence Kohlberg (1927–1987) was a developmental psychologist whose groundbreaking work on the development of moral judgments in children drew from the disciplines of philosophy, anthropology, education, and psychology. Kohlberg was inspired by the work of the psychologist Jean Piaget, who had interviewed children and adolescents about morality and developed an influential theory of moral development (Piaget, 1932). Like Piaget, Kohlberg also interviewed a group of children—in this case, a sample of 72 Chicago boys

Lawrence Kohlberg
Photo by Lee Lockwood/The LIFE Images Collection/Getty Images

between the ages of 10 and 16—that he followed over the next 20 years, interviewing 58 of them every three years (Kohlberg, 1984). To study the subjects' moral development, his interviews involved presenting members of the group with scenarios that described various moral dilemmas, along with choices for resolving them, which he varied. For example, in some of the scenarios the choice was between the rights of an authority (e.g., the police) and the needs of an individual being treated unfairly (Kohlberg, 1958). One of the best-known dilemmas Kohlberg used involved a man named "Heinz," who lived somewhere in Europe:

> Heinz's wife was dying from a particular type of cancer. The doctors told Heinz that his wife might be saved by a new drug that a local chemist had discovered. Heinz tried desperately to buy the drug, but because the chemist was charging ten times the money it cost to make it, Heinz couldn't afford the amount needed to help his wife, even after family and friends gave him money. He explained to the chemist his situation and begged the man to let him have the drug. Heinz would give the chemist the money he'd raised and promised he'd give the man the rest of the money later. The chemist refused, telling Heinz that he had discovered the drug and intended to make money from the discovery. Heinz, to save his wife, broke into the chemist's store later that night and stole the drug.

Kohlberg then asked respondents a series of questions: Should Heinz have stolen the drug? Would it change anything if Heinz did not love his wife? What if the person dying was a stranger, would it make any difference? Should the police arrest the chemist for murder if the woman died? Each boy was given a two-hour interview that included asking them about 10 different types of dilemmas they had read, like the one involving Heinz (Kohlberg, 1984). Of primary interest to Kohlberg was not whether the boys judged the action of the main character in the scenario as right or wrong, but the *reasons* the boys gave to support their decision. Kohlberg found that the reasons given changed as the boys grew older.

From this research, Kohlberg identified three distinct levels of moral reasoning, each having two substages (see Table 4.2). He then argued that people pass through these stages in a specific order, with each new stage of reasoning replacing the type of reasoning associated with the earlier stage. He also argued that not everyone progressed through all the stages.

Criticisms of Kohlberg's Theory

While Kohlberg's theory has been very influential in the study of moral reasoning, the theory is not without criticism. Two broad categories of criticisms that have been made about Kohlberg's work are that (1) his methodology was flawed and (2) the theory itself fails to stand up to empirical scrutiny (see McLeod, 2013).

Methodological Issues

Some critics have argued that the scenarios Kohlberg used, and the resulting dilemmas they created, were both artificial and unfamiliar to his subjects (Rosen, 1980). Kohlberg's respondents were initially preteens and teenagers who had never been married nor had they experienced a situation even remotely like the Heinz scenario. Critics wondered if

TABLE 4.2 Kohlberg's Levels and Stages of Moral Reasoning

Level	Age Range	Stage	Nature of Moral Reasoning
Level I: Pre-Conventional Morality	Primarily seen in preschool children and most elementary school students	Stage 1: Punishment-avoidance/ obedience	Decisions made on the basis of what's best for themselves without regard for others' needs/feelings. Rules obeyed only if established by more powerful individuals. Rules disobeyed if perceived can get away with doing so. "Wrong" behaviors are those that will be punished.
		Stage 2: Exchange of favors	Recognition that others have needs. People will meet others' needs if their own are also met ("you scratch my back—I'll scratch yours"). Right/wrong continue to be defined in terms of consequences for themselves.
Level II: Conventional Morality	Seen in a few older elementary school students, some junior high school students, and many high school students	Stage 3: Good boy/girl	Decisions made based on what actions please others, especially authority figures and high-status people (e.g., teachers, popular peers). Concern with maintaining relationships through sharing, trust, and loyalty; able to empathize and take other people's intentions into account when making decisions.
	Typically, does not appear until high school years	Stage 4: Law and order	Society is looked to for guidelines about right/wrong. Understand that rules are necessary to keep things running smoothly. Belief that obeying rules is a duty. Rules perceived as inflexible. No understanding that as society's needs change, rules change.
Level III Post-Conventional Morality	Rarely seen before college	Stage 5: Social contract	Recognize that rules represent agreements among many individuals about appropriate behavior. Rules are seen as potentially useful for maintaining social order and protecting individual rights, rather than as absolute dictates that must be obeyed simply because they exist. People also recognize the flexibility of rules; those that no longer serve society's best interests can and should be changed.
	Extremely rare, even in adults	Stage 6: Universal ethical principle	Hypothetical, "ideal" stage that few people ever reach. People in this stage adhere to a few abstract, universal principles (e.g., equality of all people, respect for human dignity, commitment to justice) that transcend specific norms and rules. They answer to a strong inner conscience and willingly disobey laws that violate their own ethical principles.

Source: Adapted from McDevitt & Ormond (2010, p. 1)

it was reasonable to therefore assume the subjects would know what the main parties in the scenarios (e.g., Heinz) should do (McLeod, 2013).

A second methodological criticism is that Kohlberg's sample was *biased* because it included only males (McLeod, 2013). Because of this, it is entirely possible that the stages that Kohlberg identified are purely androcentric (male defined). Subsequent work by moral psychologists, including Carol Gilligan, among others, has shown that while men emphasize rules and justice as their guiding orientation when making moral judgments, women stress compassion and care in their judgments (Gilligan, 1977). These results suggest that there is not "a" morality, but a "men's" and a "women's" morality. The latter has been described as an ethic of care (or "care ethics") and suggests that the source of morality is found in the fundamental relationships and dependencies in which humans are involved. Care ethics speaks of networks of social relations that *should* promote the well-being of care-givers and care-receivers alike. Often described as being either practical or virtue-oriented, care ethics aims to promote and maintain a world where the needs of self and others—especially those who are most dependent and vulnerable—are met. One of the first works on care ethics is believed to be Milton Mayeroff's book *On Caring*, but the field's emergence as an alternative normative theory of ethics is generally attributed to the works of the psychologist Carol Gilligan and the philosopher Nel Noddings in the mid-1980s (Sander-Staudt, n.d.).

A third criticism raised about Kohlberg's methodology is that the scenarios themselves were contrived, which affected the judgments the subjects rendered (McLeod, 2013). This criticism makes the point that because the dilemmas were hypothetical, and his subjects knew this, the consequences of their choices were also hypothetical. By contrast, in real-life dilemmas, we know that choosing a particular course of action can result in consequences that are both real and significant. Critics have argued that if this had also been the case for Kohlberg's subjects—their choices had real consequences—the subjects might have chosen differently (McLeod, 2013).

Problems with Kohlberg's Theory

A second category of criticisms raised with Kohlberg's theory concerns the theory itself (McLeod, 2013). For example, some critics have raised the issue of whether there are, in fact, distinct and separate "stages" of moral development and, therefore, different types of moral reasoning associated with them (Gibbs, 1979). These critics are quick to point to empirical evidence found by scholars subsequently replicating Kohlberg's work that does not always agree with his conclusions about the presence of distinct stages of moral development. To illustrate this point, say we had a subject who justified his decision about the morality of the behavior depicted in a scenario using principled reasoning (post-conventional morality, stage 5 or 6). This same subject might then regress to conventional reasoning (stage 3 or 4) to justify his decision in a different scenario. In practice, it seems that moral reasoning about right and wrong depends more on the *situation* than on general *rules* (Kay, 1982). Additionally, people may not always progress through the different stages exactly as Kohlberg suggested. One study, for example, found that 1 in 14 subjects actually regressed as they confronted different scenarios, despite being older (Rest, 1979). Critics have also argued that the theory is biased toward values not necessarily shared by members of other cultures (Woolfolk, 1993). These criticisms have led some scholars to conclude that, overall, there is weak evidence (at best) to support Kohlberg's contention that there are levels and stages of moral reasoning and that people progress through them in a linear fashion (McLeod, 2013).

A second line of criticism with Kohlberg's theory questions whether moral judgment actually matches moral behavior (Woolfolk, 1993). Consider that although Kohlberg never explicitly argued there was a one-to-one relationship between moral thinking and moral behavior, the theory implicitly makes such a link. According to some critics, links between moral thinking and moral behavior are affected by long-term habits; whether people see situations as demanding their participation; the costs and benefits of behaving in a particular way; and competing motives such as peer pressure, self-interest and so on (Bee, 1994). Thus, moral behavior is quite possibly the result of not only moral reasoning but other factors, most of them external and social in nature.

A final criticism of Kohlberg's theory with which you should be familiar questions Kohlberg's conclusion that "justice" is the most fundamental moral principle (McLeod, 2013). Critics have argued that other principles, such as caring for others, are equally important (Gilligan, 1977). In various studies using Kohlberg's methodology, researchers have found that girls are typically at stage 3 in Kohlberg's system (good boy-nice girl orientation) whereas boys are at stage 4 (law and order orientation). Critics have contended that the traits marking girls and women "deficient" in terms of moral development also happen to be the traits that have traditionally defined their moral goodness (Gilligan, 1977). Critics thus claim that Kohlberg is suggesting that approaching moral problems from an "ethic of care" rather than from an "ethic of justice" is problematic. These critics, typically those arguing from a care ethics perspective discussed above, argue there is a sex bias in Kohlberg's theory that neglects the feminine voices of compassion, love, and nonviolence, all of which are associated with how girls are socialized in Western culture and are important to expectations for the behavior of girls and women.

Despite the criticisms leveled at Kohlberg's theory, it continues to be a highly influential approach to understanding moral development and moral reasoning. Consider, however, that even if we assume there are "stages" of development in moral reasoning, do they provide us with any guidance for moral reasoning? I tackle that issue in the following section of the chapter.

GUIDING PRINCIPLES FOR MORAL REASONING

When you or I engage in moral reasoning, we are engaging in a process where we establish (or attempt to establish) a position or claim that something is true ("stealing is wrong"); and base our claimed "truth" on one or more supportive premises (Field, n.d.). What's most important here is that the claim or conclusion supported by the reasoning is a moral judgment that the behavior in question is "right" or "wrong."

Philosophers and psychologists alike suggest that the most common form of moral reasoning is **moral deliberation**, where one attempts to establish the truth of a particular moral claim on the basis of one or more general moral principles (Field, n.d.). An example of this form of moral reasoning would be the statement "lying is always [morally] wrong." What one would then do is try to establish the truth of the claim that lying is never morally justified. For example, one could cite cases where, regardless of the situation, the negative consequences of lying *always* outweighed the positive. Here, the moral principle being relied upon is found in Utilitarian ethics: whether behavior is ethical is a function of its potential positive and negative consequences.

Moral deliberation has a structure that scholars have identified as involving general moral principles, factual claims, and derivative moral judgments. Let's now consider each of these in greater detail.

The Structure of Moral Arguments

In general, moral arguments typically consist of three components: a **general moral principle** (GMP), one or more **factual claims** (FC), and a conclusion that contains a **derivative moral judgment** (DMJ) (Callahan, 1988). The GMP provides a premise that constitutes the criteria used in the argument (e.g., "lying is wrong"). One or more FCs are then stated in support of the GMP (e.g., "lying consists of false statements"). The conclusion "states a DMJ that is more specific in application that is the principle stated in the [GMP]" (e.g., "deliberately speaking or writing a false statement is wrong") (Field, n.d., pp. 4–5). Note that this structure is *deductive* in nature: *if* the GMP is true *and* the FC correctly applies the moral criterion of the GMP, *then* the conclusion must be accepted (Field, n.d.). Thus, the general form of a moral argument can be represented as follows:

- GMP: Any action with properties A, B, C . . . is [right/wrong].
- FC: This action has properties A, B, C . . .
- DMJ: Therefore, this action is [right/wrong]

The properties of the action cited in the argument constitute the moral criterion or criteria defined by the principle. For example, temperance states that it is wrong to allow one's desire for physical pleasure to go unchecked (Jeffries, 1998). The "properties of the action" in this case are that (1) the action includes physical pleasure (e.g., eating, drinking, procreation, etc.) and (2) the action is unchecked. Another example would be honesty, which argues that it is wrong to utter or write false statements with the intent of deceiving another (Hursthouse, 2012). The "properties of the action" in this instance include (1) a statement that is false and (2) the speaker's or writer's intention to deceive another.

Because analyzing and understanding moral arguments can be challenging, there are some helpful tools you can use when interpreting moral arguments (Field, n.d.). Several of the more common include the following:

- *Identify* the derivative moral judgment (DMJ) or conclusion the writer or speaker is trying to support with his or her argument.
- *Decide* what general moral principle (GMP)—a general moral claim other than the conclusion—the writer or speaker offers as the basis for the argument.
- *Determine* whether the factual claim(s) (FC) the speaker or writer offers are relevant to the conclusion of the argument.

What should you do if the general moral principle or relevant factual statements are implicit or appear missing? You should try to state them explicitly or fill them in. For example, sometimes a speaker or writer will not actually provide the moral principle or relevant facts, because he or she thinks the principle or the facts are either so widely accepted they need no argument or that one or both are easily understood by most people and therefore don't need articulating. By filling in the blanks, you identify to your own satisfaction what exactly is being stated and can then respond accordingly.

Formal Principles of Moral Reasoning

When discussing **principles of moral reasoning**, I'm referring to a set of rules that philosophers and others have developed to help *guide* our thinking, not the content of *what* we are thinking about (Field, n.d.). In other words, regardless of the system of normative ethics you may choose to help resolve a moral dilemma, the guiding principles I'll share with you are intended to help you through the process of reaching a reasoned conclusion. To facilitate your understanding, I'm going to divide the rules into two categories—"general" rules and "specific" rules—based on their orientation (Field, n.d.). The general rules help *guide your thinking* regardless of the situation or the dilemma you may face while specific rules *identify errors* that often occur in our moral reasoning.

General Rules to Guide Moral Reasoning

The general rules I believe important include (1) accurately identifying valid normative claims in moral arguments and (2) being consistent in the perspective taken when resolving moral dilemmas (remember consistency reasoning, discussed above?). For example, if you agree that consequences are the most important consideration for determining the ethics of behavior, you should *always* consider consequences as the determining factor, circumstances notwithstanding.

Normative Claims

Valid moral arguments include a stated claim in the form of a general moral principle (GMP) and a set of factual claims (FCs)—that in combination are called **normative claims** (West, 1999). What this means is that no derivative moral judgment (DMJ) will follow simply from a description of the facts. For example, to conclude that lying is morally wrong simply by reciting a set of facts about the behavior—it involves a false statement; it is knowingly shared; it is intended to deceive another—is not a valid moral judgment. There must be more.

The notion that "there must be more than mere facts" was first articulated by the 18th-century English philosopher David Hume (1711–1776), who contended that saying how things *should be* based on *how things are* is not logical (Hume, 2007 [1738]). What Hume was arguing was that "no . . . evaluative conclusion whatsoever may be validly inferred from any set of purely factual premises" (Cohon, 2010, p. 1). For example, one cannot claim that we ought not to lie because lying involves stating a falsehood. The moral conclusion—"we should not lie"—does not follow from the) facts—"lying involves stating a falsehood." We must add a moral standard to the argument, such as "truth is something that all humans should seek."

Our argument would thus become:

- GMP: Humans should be honest, as honesty is a virtue.
- FC: Lying involves stating a known falsehood intended to deceive another.
- DMJ: Lying is morally wrong.

Philosophers dubbed this "Hume's Law" to describe an "is/ought" gap in moral reasoning (Cohon, 2010; Ridge, 2014).

Consistency in Thinking

A second guiding principle in moral reasoning is consistency reasoning. While some have argued that consistency in moral reasoning involves universalism ("if something is wrong, it's *always* wrong"), I depart a bit from this and argue that consistency in thinking

David Hume
National Galleries Scotland

relates to maintaining a consistent perspective when resolving dilemmas. For example, if one agrees with the notion that potential consequences should be the guide for determining the ethics of behavior, one should always use a Utilitarian perspective to resolve one's moral dilemmas regardless of their specifics. One should not, depending on the circumstances, choose a Kantian orientation while in other instances take a virtue ethics stance. Inconsistency occurs when, depending on the circumstances, an individual "picks-and-chooses" the system of ethics that allows her to reach the conclusion she wishes, or allows her to behave in a way she was leaning toward to begin with. Inconsistency can also occur when one does not fully understand what an ethical system is saying about how one should behave. By misinterpreting the meaning of a system's guiding principles, one could end up violating them by incorrectly applying them to the dilemma.

Specific Rules in Moral Reasoning: Avoiding Errors

Ethicists and psychologists alike have pointed out specific errors that people often make in their moral reasoning, referred to as **fallacies**. Fallacies are errors that prevent the reasons offered for why a conclusion should be accepted from actually supporting that conclusion (Tittle, 2011). While in-depth coverage of these errors is well beyond the scope of this book (one source I consulted listed *216* different fallacies in moral reasoning; see Dowden, n.d.), I do want to share with you some common fallacies in moral reasoning in the hope you will begin monitoring your thinking. Doing so is crucial to ensure that your thinking is not only logical, but also critical in orientation (Ruggiero, 2015). The common errors I'll discuss include: "mine-is-better" thinking, double standards, unwarranted assumptions, oversimplifications, hasty conclusions, *tu quoque* ("you also"), moral conventionalism, moral legalism, moral prudentialism, slippery slopes, arguments to the people, and red herrings (Field, n.d.; Tittle, 2011).

"Mine-is-Better" Thinking

The error of **"mine-is-better" thinking** is rooted in the reasoning many of us used as children that "my ____________ is ____________ than your ____________" (Ruggiero, 2015). For example, "my mother is *prettier* than your mother," "my teacher is *smarter* than your teacher," or "my bicycle is *faster* than your bicycle" are all examples of mine-is-better thinking. As we matured, however, most of us stopped making mine-is-better kinds of comparisons. However, the remnants of this thinking stay with us and may influence the way we consider the worth of both our own opinions and those of others. Mine-is-better thinking can pose an obstacle to keeping an open mind about opinions and perspectives that differ from ours. We then mistakenly assume our perspective is correct and anyone else's that is different is just plain wrong. The solution for this way of thinking is to check yourself by asking about the basis of your objection to the other's point of view or conclusion. If you are unable to articulate a substantive and reasonable objection, you're potentially engaging in mine-is-better reasoning.

Double Standards

The **error of double standards** occurs when we use one set of criteria for judging our behavior and another for judging the behavior of others (Ruggiero, 2015). What this error involves is either selectively considering or twisting evidence to serve our interests. Using a double standard is especially common when we have a strong commitment to a certain action, either because we have chosen it ourselves in similar instances and wish to avoid self-condemnation, or someone with whom we have a close relationship (e.g., a spouse or close friend) engaged in the behavior. What happens is that we set aside guiding principles and create rationalizations or irrational arguments to justify what we've done (Ruggiero, 2015). Similar cases should be judged similarly, regardless of who's involved: ourselves, our friends, or complete strangers. The best way to avoid this error is to ask yourself whether you have applied or used the same guiding principles regardless of who is involved in the situation at issue.

Unwarranted Assumptions

The **error of unwarranted assumptions** consists of our unconsciously taking too much for granted when assessing a moral argument or resolving our own moral dilemmas (Ruggiero, 2015). At the heart of this error is being sloppy: we carelessly "read into" a case certain facts that are omitted or misread/misinterpret facts in play. This results in our failing to distinguish what's *really* going on from what we *think* is going on. Does this mean one should never speculate about what is not known or stated? Not at all. However, you should do so responsibly. Take, for example, the following scenario. Here, I want you to make a judgment about whether the actions of the neighborhood committee were ethical:

> Residents of a poor neighborhood are plagued with a drug problem. Five pushers operate openly on their streets and brazenly try to entice neighborhood children to take free samples. A committee of residents has approached the police and begged them to arrest the pushers, but they have done nothing (there is good reason to believe some of the

> police are sharing in the proceeds of the drug trade). The residents decide that their only hope for a safe and decent neighborhood for their children is to take the law into their own hands. Accordingly, one calm summer night they unceremoniously execute the five pushers.
>
> —(Ruggiero, 2015, p. 97)

What facts are presented here? What assumptions might reasonably be made? What are some unwarranted assumptions? Illegal drugs being sold in a neighborhood is problematic for a variety of reasons, none the least of which is children being exposed to them. Also, as described, the identities of the drug dealers are known and been reported to police, who had not acted on the information. Finally, some unknown number of community members murdered the drug dealers. These are all facts. Here's what's problematic in the scenario: the statement that "there is good reason to believe some of the police are sharing in the proceeds of the drug trade." Why is this problematic? Because it might cause you to *assume* police involvement with the drug dealers was the reason they had done nothing about the problem. However, that assumption is not warranted, given the facts as stated in the case. Instead of assuming that the lack of police intervention was a function of their involvement with the drug dealers, you should ask yourself, "What is the reason to believe the police were involved with the dealers?" You should also ask yourself whether members of the community pursued other options for addressing the drug markets, such as contacting the county sheriff or state police and asking for their intervention. Further, you should ask yourself, "How do we know that 'they' (members of the community in which the dealers were operating) were the ones who murdered the dealers?" Is it not entirely possible that some other party or parties committed the murder, including the police?

Take heart, though! You can still make a reasoned assessment of the behavior in the scenario by including your questions in it. As suggested by Ruggiero (2015, p. 92), you might use an "if/then" format to develop the following argument: *If* the police *were* involved with the drug dealers and *if* the killers *were* members of the community, then their behavior (murdering the drug dealers) was not only unethical, it was highly illegal. Vigilantism, under most circumstances, is never acceptable behavior as it challenges the legitimacy of the law, which can lead to chaos. Further, community members could have sought help from other law enforcement agencies, such as the county sheriff or state police, before resorting to such an extreme solution if, indeed, one or more of the killers were members of the community.

Oversimplification

Sometimes when we're assessing the ethics of behavior in a case, we condense or "boil down" the case to some core set of facts to make the case manageable, which is fine. However, the **error of oversimplification** is problematic and occurs when we go beyond making the facts in the case manageable and end up distorting them. For example, we might omit some important criterion, such as obligations or consequences, in our assessment. Take, for example, police use of force. People often mistakenly believe that using force is a "cut-and-dried" matter for officers, when nothing could be farther from the truth. Choosing to use force—especially the level of force—is constantly evolving based on the intersection of the situation, the offender, and the officer. Rarely does an officer confront a suspect whose gun is drawn and he or she is firing at officers. Rather, as the officer interacts with the suspect, the officer encounters a somewhat fluid situation of the suspect responding to the officer's directions and the officer responding to the suspect's words and behavior. The perceptions of the officer can be affected by the "heat-of-the-moment," as can the perceptions of the suspect. That's why training for officers where they learn to defuse difficult encounters with citizens is so crucial to reducing police use of force (Prenzler, Porter, & Alpert, 2013).

The solution for oversimplification is being careful. When "boiling down" the case, don't "water it down." Make sure you include all the relevant facts and obligations, not just those that are obvious. Prepare yourself for what may be a complex matter and address it carefully when you find it (Ruggiero, 2015).

Hasty Conclusions

One of my "pet peeves" is people displaying knee-jerk reactions to situations, like concluding a police officer was "wrong" to use force against a suspect. When someone makes a snap judgment about such an event, I'm both saddened and angered. In ethics, snap judgments are known as hasty conclusions and involve one rendering a judgment about the ethics of behavior without fully or carefully examining all aspects of the case (Ruggiero, 2015). The **error of hasty conclusions** occurs for several reasons: people (1) either don't have (or won't take) the time necessary to conduct a thorough analysis of the case, (2) uncritically accept their first impressions, or (3) had already formed an opinion well before considering the specifics of the case (Ruggiero, 2015).

Having preconceived notions about certain people or situations is natural. When we encounter people and/or situations, we immediately try to "make sense" of the interaction. To do so, we draw upon "what we know," based on our experiences, what we've been told, or what we've read about such matters. We may then rush to a conclusion about what's occurred by fitting the present situation into the box we've created. The problem is that often, the case at hand may not fit neatly into the box we've created and labeled "similar situations."

How can you avoid making hasty conclusions? The best way is waiting to reach a final conclusion until *after* you have carefully studied the case. While there is certainly nothing wrong with arriving at a tentative conclusion based on a "first pass," you should resist turning that first impression into your final judgment. Instead, remind yourself of the various errors in moral reasoning that are common; recall the strategies you can use to avoid those errors; and conceive of yourself as both an idea producer, who creates many ideas about a case, and an idea evaluator, whose job is to scrutinize those ideas and choose the one that considers all aspects of the case. This approach will help you "form the habit of going beyond mere thinking to thinking about thinking" (Ruggiero, 2015, p. 93).

Tu Quoque

Another common error in moral reasoning occurs when one seeks to avoid responsibility for perpetrating a wrong (Field, n.d.). This **error of *tu quoque*** (pronounced "too quo-kwee," which is Latin for "you also") occurs when you argue that what you've done, although wrong, is still acceptable because others are either doing the same thing or something similar. This error often occurs when the accused argues that his or her accusers are guilty of the same wrongdoing and therefore have no legitimate basis for their accusation. The error here is that it is completely irrelevant whether others are guilty of wrongdoing—the actual issue is the guilt of the accused. As the old saying goes, "two wrongs do not make a right."

Moral Conventionalism

I'll bet that you've heard (and may have even used) this excuse when someone gets into trouble: "Why should I get into trouble! *Everyone's* doing it!" This is known as the **error of moral conventionalism**, which says that morality is a product of numbers: if a large portion of one's group is engaging in a particular behavior, that alone makes the behavior acceptable (Kekes, 1985). Effectively, this is ethics "by the numbers": if "many people" engage in (or at least do not object to) a certain behavior, the actions "must be morally acceptable."

There are two problems with this reasoning. First, the supposed "many people," on closer inspection, may not only not be true, the reality may be just the opposite (Ruggiero, 2015). A second problem with moral conventionalism is deeper: the argument's premise is that a group's "common practices" cannot be ethically impermissible is false on its face (Field, n.d.). Think about this for a moment: if it were true that a group's common practices cannot be unethical, then the institution of slavery—in place across the entirety of the southern United States prior to the Emancipation Proclamation—would have been ethically permissible simply because it was common practice.

Moral Legalism

Closely related is the flaw in moral reasoning known as the **error of moral legalism,** in which an appeal is made not to common practice(s) but to formal codes of conduct—including the laws of the state (Field, n.d.). One engages in this error when he or she argues that because a certain behavior is illegal, then it is immoral. The problem with moral legalism is twofold (Ruggiero, 2015). First, different types of law (e.g., civil or criminal) do not necessarily forbid all forms of behavior that can reasonably be regarded as ethically impermissible. There is good reason for this: efforts to legislate morality usually end up conflicting with the values of a free and open society. Think about what life in America would be like if in every case of moral wrongdoing (e.g., lying to your partner about a romantic affair in which you are involved) the government stepped in to sanction the violator. We would quickly find that our most personal beliefs and relationships would be subject to government oversight, resulting in diminished freedom and a demeaning of our dignity (Field, n.d.). "Legislating morality" is also quite impractical: the courts would quickly be overwhelmed with cases (Mooney & Lee, 1995).

Second, it does not logically follow that the mere fact that some legislative body decides certain behaviors are immoral *makes* those behaviors immoral (Field, n.d.). The converse is also true: a failure by the legislative or other group to make certain behaviors immoral does not make *those* behaviors *moral*. Let's consider a historical example to illustrate this point: the founding of the United States as a separate nation was an illegal act on the part of the Founding Fathers. However, in the Declaration of

Independence, its authors offer significant justifications for breaking away from England. Even in present times, one can find many examples of legally acceptable practices ranging from genocide to slavery that are, by any reasonable standard, immoral and unethical.

Moral Prudentialism

In general, "prudence" describes one's ability to act wisely when pursuing one's interests (Floyd, n.d.). For example, we exercise prudence when we tie our shoelaces, take prescribed medication, drive slowly when it's snowing, or read the directions before assembling a bicycle. The **error of moral prudentialism** occurs when one argues that certain behaviors or actions are morally permissible *because* those behaviors benefit (are prudent for) an individual or group (see Maclean, 2009). For example, one could make a morally prudent argument that members of a community who have suffered a catastrophic event such as a tornado do *not* have a moral duty to help others recover from the devastation if doing so detracts from their own recovery. Obviously, proponents of Ethical Egoism do not recognize moral prudentialism as an error in moral reasoning since its guiding principle is that the demands of prudence require moral agents to seek their own interests under all circumstances. Recall, however, that while some ethicists accept Ethical Egoism, a majority reject it as a legitimate system of normative ethics (Regis, 1980).

Slippery Slopes

How often have you heard the argument that "if we allow [action X] then [an even worse action] will occur"? For example, have you heard this argument? "If we allow intelligence-gathering agencies like the National Security Agency (NSA) to collect in bulk the incoming and outgoing emails of citizens to monitor these communications for discussions of terrorist activities, the next thing you know they'll be monitoring citizens' telephone calls!" (Liu, 2013). Similar kinds of arguments have been made for decades regarding the legalization of marijuana, where opponents have argued that legalizing marijuana would lead to the legalization of opiates like heroin and stimulants like cocaine (Messerli, 2011). In this line of reasoning, allowing one practice or behavior will automatically lead down a "slippery slope" to an even worse practice or behavior.

The problem with **slippery slope thinking**, and why it is considered an error in reasoning, is that the person making the argument usually does not establish that the undesirable consequences must occur (Field, n.d.). In recent years, for example, some observers have argued that sex education should be removed from high school curricula as once teens know about sex, they are more likely to engage in sexual explorations with each other. Thus, the argument is that sex education in high schools leads to (i.e., causes) promiscuity among teenagers (see Makow, 2015). Another argument one hears is that illegal immigrants perpetrate high levels of violence against native-born citizens. Here the argument is that lax immigration enforcement leads to (i.e., causes) violence against native-born Americans (von Spakovksy & Strobl, 2017). The reality, however, is that there is no legitimate empirical evidence to support either "slippery slope" contention (Ewing, Martinez, & Rumbaut, 2015; Rochman, 2012).

Argument to the People (also known in its Latin form, *Argumentum Ad Populum*)

During the 2015–2016 election cycle, then-presidential candidate Donald Trump made several promises concerning immigration policies he would adopt if elected president. These included building "a great wall along the Southern border of the United States" for which Mexico would be made to pay; and deporting massive numbers of illegal immigrants from the United States from the first day he took office. These promises specifically targeted a certain subgroup of the population, the so-called "base" of the Republican party, which enthusiastically endorsed them (Diamond & Murray, 2015; Newport, 2009). Candidate Trump was obviously appealing to the anti-immigrant prejudices of the Republican base.

An **argument to the people** involves appealing to certain popular prejudices and biases shared by members of a group (e.g., Islamophobia; homophobia) to inflame those prejudices and lead members to accept a certain moral conclusion (Field, n.d.). Consider the following example as illustrative: a conservative religious leader proclaims to his equally conservative congregation that "no one who is in the faith, and true to that faith, can accept the scourge of abortion perpetrated by godless heathens such as Planned Parenthood that are destroying our society." By identifying those who favor abortion as "godless heathens" working to "destroy our society," the preacher is encouraging his congregants to accept his unstated conclusion that abortion is morally wrong. The problem is, even if those who favor abortion are atheists and are engaging in activities designed to destroy the social fabric, those facts do not establish a valid reason why *abortion* is morally wrong (Field, n.d.).

Red Herrings

Say you are attending an event on campus where the keynote speaker is scheduled to talk about the issue of police-involved shootings of unarmed citizens. During her presentation, the speaker makes the following argument: "In many of these incidents, officers believed they were in imminent danger of death or great bodily harm. Blue lives matter!" What the speaker is doing is dangling what's known as a "red herring" in front of the audience. **Red herrings** (also known as the fallacy of the "irrelevant premise") are an error in moral reasoning where issues raised in an argument are not relevant to the conclusion drawn from them. The problem with this type of reasoning is that it diverts attention from the real issue(s)—that is, those needing to be addressed to evaluate the truth or falsity of the conclusion—to the phony issue(s). Importantly, red herrings are presented in such a way it is not clear to the audience that the issue or issues cited are false (Field, n.d.). If you were paying close attention to what the speaker was saying, you would see that she is dangling a classic "red herring." No reasonable person would say that the lives of police officers *don't* matter—of course they do! However, saying that "blue lives matter" is irrelevant to the morality of police using deadly force against unarmed citizens, which in some cases is actually illegal use of force against them. It does not follow that because "blue lives matter," no one else's lives matter!

To help you keep this material organized, Table 4.3 summarizes errors in logic reviewed here, along with how they can be addressed.

TABLE 4.3 Errors in Moral Reasoning

Name of Error	Nature of the Error	How to Fix It
"Mine-is-better"	Failing to keep an open mind about opinions/ perspectives different than ours	Keep your mind open to new ideas—they may just be correct
Double standards	Using a less stringent set of moral rules to judge our own behavior than we use to judge the behavior of others	Be consistent when applying moral rules
Unwarranted assumptions	Carelessly "reading into" a case certain facts that are omitted or misreading or misinterpreting facts, which results in a failure to distinguish between what's *really* going on and what we *think* is going on	Make a reasoned assessment of the case by including questions raised by unclear or omitted facts; use an "if/ then" format that includes unclear/ omitted facts to formulate your argument
Oversimplification	"Boiling down" the case to the point where important considerations are lost	Be careful to include subtleties or other considerations in your assessments
Hasty conclusions	"Knee-jerk" reactions to situations based on incomplete information	Avoid "knee-jerk" reactions; find facts that are missing; carefully assess the full case
Tu Quoque ("too quo-kwee")	The accused argues that his or her accusers are just as guilty of wrong doing and therefore have no legitimate basis for their accusations	Focus on the issue at hand and not side issues
Moral conventionalism	Behavior is morally acceptable because it is convention in society—most people accept it	Avoid "morality by the numbers" kind of thinking—there is no magic in majorities
Moral legalism	An argument is made that because something is *illegal* it is *immoral*	Avoid assuming that just because some behavior is illegal that it is immoral
Moral prudentialism	Arguing that certain behaviors are morally permissible *because* they benefit an individual or group	Focus your attention/argument on beneficence—the good of the many over the good of the one
Slippery slope	"If we allow X, then even worse things will happen—X^2"	Focus on outcomes that are either known or are reasonably likely to occur
Argument to the people	Appeals are made to certain popular prejudices and biases shared by large numbers of a group to inflame those prejudices and lead members to accept a certain moral conclusion	Be aware of your own personal biases and prejudices and do not draw on them to incite others to agree with your conclusion
Red herrings	Issues raised in a moral argument that are not relevant to the conclusion drawn from them; diverts attention from the *real* issues	Keep your focus on the actual—not side—issue(s)

Errors can plague moral reasoning. Some of these errors you may be familiar with, while others may be new. Common errors in moral reasoning revolve around faulty logic—trying to make connections that don't exist. The errors I've reviewed here pinpoint exactly where the fault lies and how you can avoid faulty thinking. By monitoring your thinking and paying attention to your logic, you should be able to identify when your thinking is problematic and what you can do to fix it. You can then be more confident in your judgments, whether they are being made about the morality of others' behavior or your own.

SUMMARY

In this chapter, I've presented to you a "foundation for judgment" that can be used to both logically resolve moral dilemmas you may be facing and properly assess the morality of others' behavior. The foundation is based on moral reasoning, where you reach a conclusion about a course of action by thinking about the dilemma, guided by principles. Unlike "reacting with your gut," moral reasoning can be described as "responsibly conducted thinking" during which you identify moral issues and considerations (e.g., one's obligations to others), sort the obligations into those that are most important given present circumstances (using, for example, analogical reasoning), resolve conflicts that may exist between or among them (by, for example, identifying *prima facie* duties), and reach a conclusion about what should be done or how one ought to behave. You then learn from this process and repeat it in the future, all the while building up your moral inventory but also critically evaluating your thought process and the guiding principles you've chosen to guide you. Importantly, by engaging in this process, you avoid moral dumbfoundedness, where you confidently pronounce your moral judgment but are unable to offer a defense for it.

You are capable of engaging in this process because, as Lawrence Kohlberg (among others) found, you are a rational creature able to make a claim ("All lying is morally wrong") and provide supporting evidence using premises. Most moral arguments consist of three components: you first articulate a general moral principle, make one or more factual claims, and reach a conclusion containing a derivative moral judgment explicitly (or implicitly) articulated in an "if/then" form. If the general moral principle is true and the factual claim correctly applies to the moral criterion of the general moral principle, then the derivative moral judgment is affirmed. When engaging in a moral argument with yourself or as part of an evaluation of others' arguments, identify the derivative moral judgment, decide which moral principle is offered as the basis for the argument, and determine whether the factual claim(s) is/are relevant to the argument. Finally, be aware of fallacies that reduce the effectiveness of your moral reasoning. Avoiding these errors involves monitoring your thinking: pay close attention to the claims you're making and whether the conclusions you draw are logically related to the premise(s) found in your argument. Be consistent in the rules you apply. Don't appeal to biases or prejudices. In doing so, your moral reasoning skills—with practice—will develop and become stronger.

To conclude this chapter, Thought Exercise 4.1 walks you through an example of moral reasoning in action. It questions whether the criminal justice system operating like an assembly line can be ethically justified (recall that Herbert Packer used this analogy in his discussion of the "crime control model" of criminal justice I shared with you in Ch. 1).

THOUGHT EXERCISE 4.1

THE ETHICS OF "ASSEMBLY-LINE JUSTICE"

Over 50 years ago, Hebert Packer developed what are now called "models" of the criminal justice process: "crime control" and "due process" (Packer, 1964, 1968). Intended more as a heuristic than an actual theory, these models suggest that there are two ways of viewing the operation of the criminal justice process. In the crime control model, the criminal justice process is likened to an assembly line, where speed and efficiency is stressed. As Packer uses it, "efficiency" refers to the ability of the criminal justice system to identify, apprehend, try, convict, and sentence a large portion of criminal offenders whose offenses are known to the police (Packer, 1968). The goal is to process cases quickly using plea bargains that result in large numbers of convictions. In the due process model, the criminal justice process is likened to an obstacle course, with the obstacles encompassing the legal protections afforded defendants based in the Bill of Rights.

Packer also argued that the two models emphasized different values. For example, the core value of the crime control model is social order: if the criminal justice system fails to repress crime, a breakdown in social order will occur and the right to be free from criminal victimization will vanish. There is also a presumption of guilt for those who make it through this "efficient" process. On the other hand, the core value of the due process model is the "primacy of the individual and the complementary concept of limitation on official power" (Packer, 1968, p. 8). Because the stigma and loss of liberty that occur upon conviction represent "the heaviest deprivation that government can inflict on the individual" (Packer, 1968, p. 8), there must be checks to ensure that *both* the factually innocent and the legally guilty are identified.

So, let's focus on the crime control model's analogy of the criminal justice process as an assembly line designed to maximize efficiency by identifying, arresting, trying, convicting, and sentencing large numbers of people. The question then becomes: Can such a system be *ethically justified*? As you have no doubt figured out, many of the dilemmas that criminal justice actors confront result from a conflict of obligations: those of the victims—such as bringing to justice those who have harmed them—and those of the accused—such as ensuring that their rights are protected. So, let's see if I can construct a moral argument about assembly line justice:

A. The criminal justice process should seek justice, since justice is a virtue.

B. A criminal justice process in which police officers, prosecutors, judges, etc.: (1) need only know how to do specific tasks and nothing more (e.g., arrest suspects; charge and get defendants to plead guilty; sentence them); (2) are not required to possess any vision or concept of the whole (e.g., treating equals equally and unequals unequally); and (3) are only required to master a specific set of skills, is unjust.

C. The criminal justice process is unjust.

Now, let's take apart my argument. First, I'm arguing from a virtue ethics perspective by stating a general moral principle (GMP) that "justice is a virtue." I then present a set of factual claims (FC) describing assembly line justice. I then state the derivative moral judgment (DMJ) or conclusion of my argument—the criminal justice process is unjust.

You may be surprised that a former criminal justice professor would make such an argument; you might have *assumed* I would make a different argument, which I *could do*. The point here is *not* whether you agree or disagree with the argument presented. The point is for you to understand how I arrived at the conclusion I did.

Is my reasoning sound? To counter my argument, you would need to "poke holes" in it. For example, you might counter my definition of justice with one that is less restrictive. You could also present data showing that police officers, prosecutors, and others need to have wide-ranging skills, and not just know how to arrest, charge and obtain guilty pleas from, or sentence defendants. Or, you could provide data showing that criminal justice actors *are* required to "treat equals equally and unequals unequally," by identifying appeals courts decisions that overturn convictions in which "justice" (as I defined it) was not achieved. By engaging in these actions, you counter my argument and therefore my conclusion.

As you progress through the rest of the book, you'll see more of these kinds of exercises and have the opportunity to begin honing your reasoning skills. I think you'll find that as you practice, your reasoning will improve.

KEY TERMS

Moral reasoning 86
Moral issues 87
Moral facts 88
Reasoning by analogy 89
Prima facie duty 89
Moral dumbfoundedness 92
Law of noncontradiction 93
Consistency reasoning 93
Moral deliberation 97
General moral principle 98
Factual claims 98
Derivative moral judgment 98
Principles of moral reasoning 98
Normative claims 99
Fallacies 100
"Mine-is-better" thinking 101
Error of double standards 101
Error of unwarranted assumptions 101
Error of oversimplification 102
Error of hasty conclusions 103
Error of *tu quoque* 103
Error of moral conventionalism 104
Error of moral legalism 104
Error of moral prudentialism 105
Slippery slope thinking 105
Argument to the people 106
Red herrings 106

DISCUSSION QUESTIONS

1. Evaluate your own "moral reasoning" processes by engaging in a mock debate with a classmate or friend over some moral issue, say same-sex marriage or mass deportation of illegal immigrants. As part of the debate, identify any errors in reasoning that you and your partner may make.
2. Have you ever been "morally dumbfounded?" Review the situation you identify as leaving you dumbfounded and use moral reasoning to reach a better conclusion.
3. Can you think of some examples of the *prima facie* duties of police officers, prosecutors, judges, etc.? Explain what they look like and why they might be important.
4. Sometimes, when two (or more) people engage in a moral argument, they end up "arguing past each other." What this means is that one side in the argument may present a teleological (consequences-based) argument, while the other presents a deontological (rules-based) or an ontological (virtue-based) argument. Pick a particular issue relating to criminal justice, such as the morality of legalizing prostitution, and develop an argument that includes a general moral principle (GMP), factual claims (FC), and a derivative moral judgment (DMJ) or conclusion based on deontology, teleology, and virtue.

RESOURCES

Three classic **"must-read" books** that have heavily influenced both philosophical and psychological thinking about moral development in children and adolescents include:

Piaget, J. (1997). *The moral judgment of the child*. New York, NY: The Free Press. Piaget's book chronicles how children's moral thinking evolves from preschool to adolescence by tracing how they conceive of lying, cheating, authority figures, and punishment and responsibility. First published in 1932.

Kohlberg, L. (1981). *The philosophy of moral development: Moral stages and the idea of justice* (Essays on Moral Development, Volume 1). New York, NY: Harper & Row.

Kohlberg, L. (1984). *The psychology of moral development: The nature and validity of moral stages* (Essays on Moral Development, Volume 2). New York, NY: Harper & Row.

Visit **Pixi's Blog** to practice your moral reasoning skills using **25 different moral dilemmas.** http://psychopixi.com/uncategorized/25-moral-dilemmas/

An amusing and clever lesson on logical fallacies can be found in Max Shulman's short story "**Love is a Fallacy**." You can read the story by visiting https://www.filozofia.bme.hu/sites/default/files/love_is_a_fallacy.pdf. Good commentary on the story is available at https://inkslingerblog.wordpress.com/2011/06/03/story-review-love-is-a-fallacy/

REFERENCES

Anderson, E. (1991). John Stuart Mill and experiments in living. *Ethics*, 102: 4–26.

Callahan, J. (Ed.) (1988). *Ethical issues in professional life*. New York, NY: Oxford University Press.

Campbell, R., & Kumar, V. (2012). Moral reasoning on the ground. *Ethics, 122*, 273–312.

Cohon, R. (2010). Hume's moral philosophy. In E. Zalta (Ed.), *The Stanford encyclopedia of philosophy* (Fall Edition). Retrieved from http://plato.stanford.edu/entries/hume-moral/

Diamond, J., & Murray, S. (2015, August 17). Trump outlines immigration specifics. CNN. Retrieved from http://cnn.com/2015/08/16/politics/donald-trump-immigration-plans/index.html

Dobrin, A. (2012, July 24). What are ethical facts? *Psychology Today*. Retrieved from https://www.psychologytoday.com/blog/am-i-right/201207/what-are-ethical-facts

Dowden, B. (n.d.). Fallacies. In J. Fieser & B. Dowden (Eds.), *The internet encyclopedia of philosophy*. Retrieved from http://www.iep.utm.edu/fallacy/

Ewing, W., Martinez, D., & Rumbaut, R. (2015). *The criminalization of immigration in the United States*. Washington, DC: American Immigration Council.

Field, R. (n.d.). Moral reasoning: Principles and problems. Retrieved from http://catpages.nwmissouri.edu/m/rfield/274guide/274overview2.htm

Floyd, S. (n.d.). Thomas Aquinas: Moral philosophy. In J. Feiser & B. Dowden (Eds.), *The internet encyclopedia of philosophy*. Retrieved from http://www.iep.utm.edu/aq-moral/

Gibbs, J. (1979). Kohlberg's moral stages theory. *Human Development, 22*, 89–112.

Gilligan, C. (1977). In a different voice: Women's conceptions of self and of morality. *Harvard Educational Review, 47*, 481–517.

Haidt, J. (2001). The emotional dog and its rational tail: A social intuitionist approach to moral judgment. *Psychological Review, 108*, 814–34.

Harman, G. (2011). Moral reasoning. Retrieved from https://www.princeton.edu/~harman/Papers/Moral_Reasoning_Current.pdf

Harper, S. (2005, September 14). The law of non-contradiction. *Philochristos*. Retrieved from http://philochristos.blogspot.com/2005/09/law-of-non-contradiction.html

Hume, D. (2007). *A treatise on human nature* (D. Norton & M. Norton, Eds.). New York, NY: Oxford University Press. (Original work published 1738).

Hursthouse, R. (2012). Virtue ethics. In E. Zalta (Ed.), *The Stanford encyclopedia of philosophy* (Fall 2013 Edition). Retrieved from http://plato.stanford.edu/archives/ fall2013/entries/ethics-virtue

Jeffries, V. (1998). Virtue and the altruistic personality. *Sociological Perspectives, 41*, 151–166.

Kay, S. (1982). Kohlberg's theory of moral development: Critical analysis of validation studies with the defining issues test. *International Journal of Psychology, 17*, 27–42.

Kekes, J. (1985). Moral conventionalism. *American Philosophical Quarterly, 22*, 37–46.

Kemerling, G. (2011). Analogy. Retrieved from http://www.philosophypages.com/lg/e13.htm

Kersting, K. (2005). Trust your first instincts: Fallacious folklore? Retrieved from http://www.apa.org/monitor/apr05/instincts.aspx

Kohlberg, L. (1984). *The psychology of moral development: The nature and validity of moral sages*. New York, NY: Harper & Row.

Kohlberg, L. (1958). *The development of modes of thinking and choices in years 10 to 16*. (Unpublished doctoral dissertation). University of Chicago, Chicago, IL.

Liu, E. (2013). *Reauthorization of the FISA Amendments Act*. Washington, DC: Congressional Research Service. Retrieved from http://fas.org/sgp/crs/intel/R42725.pdf

Maclean, A. (2009). *Autonomy, informed consent, and medical law: A relational challenge*. New York, NY: Cambridge University Press.

Makow, H. (2015, February 17). Promiscuity is hidden agenda of sex education. Retrieved from https://www.henrymakow.com/2015/02/Promiscuity%20is%20Hidden-Agenda-of-Sex-Education%20.html

McDevitt, T., & Ormond, J. (2010). Kohlberg's three levels and six stages of moral reasoning. Retrieved from http://www.education.com/reference/article/kohlbergs-moral-reasoning/

McLeod, S. (2013). Kohlberg. *Simply Psychology*. Retrieved from http://www.simply psychology.org/kohlberg.html

Messerli, J. (2011). Should marijuana be legalized? In a nutshell. Retrieved from http://balancedpolitics.org/marijuana_legalization.htm

Millgram, E. (1997). *Practical induction*. Cambridge, MA: Harvard University Press.

Mooney, C., & Lee, M. (1995). Legislative morality in the American states: The case of pre-*Roe* abortion regulation reform. *American Political Science Review, 39*, 599–627.

Newport, C. (2009, June 1). Republican base heavily white, conservative, religious. *Gallup Politics*. Retrieved from http://www.gallup.com/poll/118937/republican-base-heavily-white-conservative-religious.aspx

Packer, H. (1968). *The limits of the criminal sanction*. Palo Alto, CA: Stanford University Press.

Packer, H. (1964). Two models of the criminal process. *University of Pennsylvania Law Review, 113*, 1–48.

Piaget, J. (1932). *The moral judgment of the child*. London, UK: Kegan, Paul, Trench, Trubner & Co.

Prenzler, T., Porter, L., & Alpert, G. (2013). Reducing police use of force: Case studies and prospects. *Aggression & Violent Behavior, 18*, 343–356.

Regis, E. (1980). What is ethical egoism? *Ethics, 91*, 50–62.

Rest, J. (1979). *Development in judging moral issues*. Minneapolis, MN: University of Minnesota Press.

Richardson, R. (2013). Moral reasoning. In E. Zalta (Ed.), *The Stanford encyclopedia of philosophy* (Winter, 2014 Edition). Retrieved from http://plato.stanford.edu/archives/win2014/entries/reasoning-moral/

Ridge, M. (2014). Moral non-naturalism. In E. Zalta (Ed.), *The Stanford encyclopedia of philosophy* (Fall Edition). Retrieved from http://plato.stanford.edu/archives/fall2014/entries/moral-non-naturalism/

Rochman, B. (2012, March 9). Teen sex ed.: Instead of promoting promiscuity, it delays first sex. *Time*. Retrieved from http://healthland.time.com/2012/03/09/sex-ed-instead-of-promoting-promiscuity-it-encourages-teens-to-delay-first-sex/

Rosen, B. (1980). Moral dilemmas and their treatment. In B. Munsey (Ed.), *Moral development, moral education, and Kohlberg* (pp. 232–263). Birmingham, AL: Religious Education Press.

Ross, W. (1988). *The right and the good*. Indianapolis, IN: Hackett Publishers.

Ruggiero, V. (2015). *Thinking critically about ethical issues* (9th ed.). New York, NY: McGraw-Hill.

Sander-Staudt, M. (n.d.). Care ethics. In J. Fieser & B. Dowden (Eds.), *The Internet encyclopedia of philosophy*. Retrieved from http://www.iep.utm.edu/care-eth/

Simpson, D. (n.d.). William David Ross. In J. Fieser & B. Dowden (Eds.), *The internet encyclopedia of philosophy*. Retrieved from http://www.iep.utm.edu/ross-wd/#H6

Sneddon, A. (2007). A social model of moral dumbfounding: Implications for studying moral reasoning and moral judgment. *Philosophical Psychology, 20*, 731–748.

Tittle, P. (2011). *Critical thinking: An appeal to reason* (pp. 25–28). New York, NY: Routledge.

Velleman, J. (2000). *The possibility of practical reason*. New York, NY: Oxford University Press.

von Spakovksy, H., & Strobl, R. (2017, March 10). What the media won't tell you about illegal immigration and criminal activity. Retrieved from https://www.conservativereview.com/commentary/2017/03/what-the-media-wont-tell-you-about-illegal-immigration-and-criminal-activity#sthash.BT8pKBcF.dpuf

West, R. (1999). Taking moral argument seriously. *Chicago-Kent Law Review*, *74*, 499–516.

Woolfolk, A. (1993). *Educational Psychology*. Needham Heights, MA: Allyn & Bacon.

CHAPTER 5

A Framework for Analysis

Chapter Outline

CHAPTER LEARNING OBJECTIVES:

1. Describe the "totality of the circumstances" doctrine and why it is useful for assessing the ethics of behavior.
2. Identify examples of moral ideals and how they fit into assessing the ethics of behavior.
3. Differentiate substantive from procedural ideals.
4. Explain why the Principle of Respect for Persons is important when assessing the ethics of behavior.
5. Describe obligations and distinguish among the different types.
6. Summarize different types of consequences, including direct and indirect, short- and long-term.
7. Explain why impacts on the natural world should be included in assessments of the ethics of behavior.

INTRODUCTION

As you learned in Ch. 4, moral reasoning involves a process of justifying, defending, and arguing for a position you've taken for resolving a moral dilemma or assessing the ethics of others' behavior. The process, however, involves making sure that you account for several considerations: Did the behavior in question possibly violate a key virtue (e.g., justice)? Were obligations the party had to herself and others violated by the behavior (e.g., did the behavior potentially diminish a friendship between two people)? What about the potential benefits and harm to self and others that may occur? As I mentioned in Ch. 4, moral reasoning is analogous to undertaking a journey. The road signs you encounter pose questions relating to relevant considerations before you can reach your destination: a conclusion about the ethics of the behavior in question.

By taking these matters into account, you are considering what in the law is known as the **totality of the circumstances**, the notion that there is no single deciding factor when deciding whether the behavior at issue was illegal (or, in our case, unethical) (Mendelsohn, 1998). Rather, the judge must consider the facts, context, people, etc. and draw a conclusion from the whole picture. This is also what we need do when assessing the ethics of criminal justice practitioners' behavior—that of police officers, prosecutors, judges, and others. We must consider the entire picture. The problem is how to ensure that we don't overlook something that is relevant to helping us decide whether the behavior under scrutiny is ethical.

This chapter ties together what you've learned in the preceding four chapters and condenses that information into what I call a "framework for analysis" that identifies specific factors to consider when assessing the ethics of behavior: moral ideals, moral obligations, and the potential consequences of behavior. I also share a "template for analysis" that you can use to ensure you properly consider the totality of the circumstances surrounding the specific behavior by a criminal justice practitioner that has raised a question of ethics. This template is something I developed and have now used with success in dozens of undergraduate- and graduate-level criminal justice and computer forensics ethics classes over the past 20 years. I designed the template to help students "see the whole picture" when analyzing the behavior of a criminal justice practitioner that has raised a question of ethics. Using that picture, in conjunction with moral reasoning, allows you to reach a conclusion about the behavior in question: Was it ethical? As you'll see, the template includes pieces of information relevant to making a judgment about the ethics of behavior: the facts in the case; important details; the ethical issue in the case; and relevant ideals, obligations, and consequences. The template includes a section into which you insert your conclusion, which includes highlights of your analysis of the ideals, obligations, and consequences, along with some additional considerations. All this information is used to build an argument supporting a conclusion concerning whether the behavior you're assessing is ethical or not.

A FRAMEWORK FOR ANALYSIS

In Chs. 1–2, I presented to you an overview of normative ethics. In doing so, I created a context in which you will be working as you examine criminal justice ethics. In Chs. 3–4, I discussed moral dilemmas and the process of moral reasoning in relation to them. Taken together, the information presented in those chapters provided you with both a context and a guide to help you make decisions about not only the ethics of your own behavior but also that of others. In short, I created a framework for you to use when analyzing the ethics of behavior.

If you look up the word "framework" in a dictionary, it's likely defined along these lines: "a basic structure underlying a system, concept, or text" (Oxford Dictionary, n.d.). At present, the "structure underlying a system" is moral reasoning within the larger context of normative ethics as applied to the field of criminal justice and the behavior of practitioners like probation officers and judges. The structure consists of pieces that fit together and allow you to answer a simple question: Is this behavior ethical? So far, the pieces I have shared with you have included (1) systems of ethics; (2) moral dilemmas; and (3) moral reasoning.

Why is such a framework a good idea? One reason is because the framework consists of relevant considerations—the pieces—that should be included as you think about ethics and criminal justice. The framework also includes the processes associated with thinking about criminal justice ethics. The analogy here would be to that of building a house: one does not just show up one day and build oneself a house. Rather, there's a *process* involved: identifying the land on which the house would be placed and evaluating its fitness; hiring a reputable architect or builder to design the home for you; identifying a reputable builder to serve as the general contractor and be responsible for ensuring that proper permits are obtained, necessary inspections are completed, and warranties on the house are honored. Deciding on the ethics of the behavior of criminal justice practitioners involves a similar set of stages. The framework I've provided you serves as the "blueprint," if you will, for your thinking. But I've also developed a more practical way to keep the pieces of the framework from getting jumbled: a template that includes relevant information necessary for properly analyzing the ethics of behavior.

A TEMPLATE FOR ANALYSIS

In commonly understood terms, a template serves as a predefined format for some type of communication, such as a business letter or fax, or a document, such as an expense account. What's cool about a template—and its primary purpose—is that it can be used repeatedly. This means the letter, fax, or expense account can be easily replicated over many instances. Think about how many times you may have received a "form letter" from your college or university. That form letter followed a template and allowed your school to send out hundreds (if not more) of letters without the trouble of having to rewrite the letter for each recipient.

I'll grant you that form letters are very impersonal. However, there's also no doubt they enhance your school's ability to communicate with many people far more quickly than if the letter had to be physically rewritten hundreds or thousands of times! That's the idea behind the template for analysis I use in my ethics classes, which is based on material originally discussed by Vincent Ruggiero in his book *Thinking Critically About Ethical Issues* (Ruggiero, 2015). I've found that this template allows students to analyze many different scenarios involving questions of ethics without having to "rewrite the letter" many times over. All one need do is complete the various sections of the template and voilà! You now have the evidence you need to make your argument. You then use that evidence in conjunction with the guiding principle(s) of the system of ethics you've chosen to help guide you to a conclusion.

It's important that you understand something from the start: your using my template for analysis will not *cause* you to become ethical. Once you join the ranks of criminal justice practitioners, whether you behave ethically is not going to occur simply because you've studied and used this template. As I explained in Ch. 1, when you join the ranks of an agency like federal probation, you either bring with you (or learn) a set of values that, taken together constitute a system (Rokeach, 1973). Those values influence how you "see" the social world and the people in it. If your values are such that you believe people of color form an existential threat to "law and order," then when you are a prosecutor encountering a defendant who is a person of color, how you make sense of the interactions you have with him or her and, perhaps more importantly, how you behave toward him or her, aren't going to be influenced by my template. If your values lead you to distrust those who are different, you may deem them as "other" and treat them differently. Your encounters with those who are different as well as those who are similar are significantly influenced by the values and beliefs each party brings to the encounter—how each person socially constructs the event (Berger & Luckmann, 1966). Thus, the reality of your interaction is socially constructed, and your response to that reality—that is, your behavior—is a function of that construction. My template is simply intended to help you focus your thinking and follow a step-by-step process that moves you from initial impressions to reasoned conclusion.

By using the template, you're engaging in several activities that will help you develop your reasoning skills. First, you are synthesizing relevant information and entering it into the template. Second, you are applying guiding principle(s) from a system of normative ethics—for example, virtue ethics—to the case to guide you toward a conclusion. Third, you are constructing an argument that consists of premises and evidence supporting them. Finally, you are reaching a conclusion that answers the seminal question: Was this behavior ethical? So, without further ado, let's see what this template looks like—it's found in Box 5.1.

BOX 5.1 A Template for Analysis

I. Facts
II. Details
III. Issue
IV. Ideals
V. Obligations
VI. Consequences
VII. Conclusion

Facts

Assessing the ethics of behavior involves identifying the actual behavior that has raised the question of ethics, regardless of who engaged in it, where it occurred, etc. In effect, regardless of the scenario you're considering, whether it involves police officers, prosecutors, or probation officers, etc., you must be able to succinctly identify *what occurred*. Some scenarios are long and have a lot of information in them; others, not so much. Regardless of scenario complexity, if you can reduce it to its essence by stripping out unnecessary information like the names of the people involved, when and where the behavior occurred, people's motivations for the behavior, etc., then you'll have reduced the scenario to the basics of what happened and identified the **facts** of the case. Let's use Case Study 5.1 as the basis for our first analysis using the template and see if we can identify the facts in the case.

So, what happened here? *A police officer followed departmental policy.* How did I arrive at that answer? Let me identify key pieces of information from the case that will help you understand. First, the Port St. Lucia police department has a policy forbidding officers from accepting gratuities from citizens. Second, Gough is offered a gratuity by a local restaurateur—a free meal. Third, Gough rejects the gratuity by discreetly paying the tab. If we synthesize those pieces of information, Officer Gough, in paying for the meal, rejected the gratuity, and thereby followed departmental policy. If we remove nonessential information like people's names, the location where the behavior occurred, and the specifics surrounding the behavior, along with other nonessential information like the name of the department, the officer's partner, etc., the facts in this scenario were that *a police officer followed departmental policy*. What's valuable about this process is that once we've identified the facts in the case, we've also identified what will be the ethical issue: whether it was *ethical* for a police officer to follow departmental policy.

But wait! I'm guessing you may have already reached a conclusion that Officer Gough's behavior was/was not ethical. Not so fast! Remember from Ch. 4 the discussion about an error in reasoning called "hasty conclusions?" Regardless of what you decided, you've reached a hasty conclusion. Why is that? Because you've *not* considered other relevant information useful to helping you to reach a *reasoned* conclusion. Thus, we still have work to do, more "blanks" of the template to fill in. Let's move on and fill in the next part of the template: the details.

Details

According to the Merriam-Webster online dictionary, "detail" is defined as "a particular piece of information about something or someone" (Merriam-Webster, n.d.). In every scenario, there are particular pieces of information about the people, places, and

CASE STUDY 5.1 The Rookie and the Restaurant Tab

Jess Gough has just joined the Port St. Lucia (Louisiana) police department after earning a B.S. and M.S.W. from Louisiana State University. Gough is excited about the new job and has completed all the necessary prehiring training, including graduating first in his class at the police academy. For the past month, he has been assigned to the afternoon shift (3:00 p.m.–12:00 a.m.) and has teamed with a field training officer (FTO), Linda Hand, who's been with the department for 10 years and has the reputation of "going strictly by the book." He will work with her over the next 12 months while he's on probationary status. Her evaluation will go a long way to determining whether Gough is retained beyond the probationary period.

This evening, the two officers decide to get some dinner and agree that a local eatery, Al's Pizzeria, is as good a place as any—it's a bit pricey but has good food. They arrive and find the restaurant busy. The proprietor, Al Dente, is working and warmly greets the two officers. He finds them a table in the back corner of the restaurant "to give them some privacy" and takes their drink order. A bit later their server, Anna Fender, greets them and takes their food orders. They enjoy their dinner and continue getting to know one another. It turns out that Officer Hand's husband and brother had each graduated from LSU.

They finish their meal and prepare to resume their patrol duties. Anna approaches them to ask if they wanted dessert, but they decline. Jess tells her they "just need the check" and tells Linda that dinner is "on him." Anna gets a worried look on her face, which Jess notices. "What's wrong?" he asks Anna. "Gee, Officer Gough, there's no check—Al specifically told me that your dinner was 'on the house.'" "Just a minute," Jess says. "We pay our own way." Anna is now visibly shaken. "Officer Gough, you don't understand. Al was pretty firm with me on this—I'm liable to get fired for not complying with his wishes." Gough asks her to find Al and bring him to the table, which she does. Jeff tells him, "Look, Mr. Dente, it seems there's been a mistake. Anna tells me there's not a check to pay, but I wish to do so. Please give it to me so I can pay it and we can get back to work." Al laughs heartily. "Officer, in 15 years I haven't asked a police officer to pay a check in this establishment, and I'm not about to start now. Just be happy have a safe rest of your shift and tell your friends about Al's!" He then walks away, taking Anna with him. Throughout the exchange, Linda has remained silent. It seems that one of her favorite training exercises is bringing a rookie to Al's and having the new officer go through the routine with Al about the restaurant not charging officers for their meals. She wants to see how the rookie handles the situation in light of the department's policy of officers not accepting gratuities.

Gough asks Linda how much was her meal, and she tells him. He then figures the total tab for the meal, adds a 25% tip for Anna, and puts the money on the table under a plate. He then asks if she's ready to leave, which they do.

Did Gough act ethically?

behavior described that help you reach a reasoned conclusion about the ethics of the behavior you are assessing. Now that you've identified the facts in the scenario, let's examine the **details**, the "particular pieces of information" that help us identify who, what, where, when, and (possibly) why.

Let's return to Case Study 5.1 and see if we can identify the who, what, where, when, and why. The "who" are the key people in the scenario, in this case, and include Jess Gough (the rookie officer), Linda Hand (the FTO), Al Dente (the restaurant proprietor), and Anna Fender (the server). The "what" identifies the goings-on described in the scenario. Here, we have several pieces of information: (1) Gough is a rookie officer with the Port St. Lucia police department; (2) Gough is teamed with an FTO, Linda Hand; (3) Gough and Hand stop for dinner at a local restaurant, Al's Pizzeria; (4) the proprietor, Al Dente, has a policy of free meals for police officers (unbeknownst to Gough; Hand does know this); (5) Gough and Hand finish their meal and seek to pay for it; (6) there is no check; (7) Gough calculates the tab and gratuity and discreetly pays for it; (8) Hand has used this situation in the past as a training exercise for rookie officers. Next is the "where," which is easy to identify: it's the location where the behavior raising the ethical issue occurred. In the present case, all of the behavior occurred at Al's Pizzeria in Port St. Lucia (LA). The "when" is also available from information in the scenario: "this evening." Finally, there's the "why," which relates to the potential motivation of the person engaging in the behavior that's raised the ethical issue. So, let's consider some possible "whys" for Officer Gough's behavior: (1) he's aware of department policy about gratuities and simply wants to follow the letter of it, or (2) he *assumes* that paying the tab is what his FTO would want, and does so to please her. Which is the better deduction? That depends on the extent other details in the case support one explanation over the other, which should remind you about the pitfalls of falling prey to another error in reasoning: unwarranted assumptions (see Ch. 4). If you recall, unwarranted assumptions involve reading more into the case than is there. Returning to our "why" detail, you might have chosen the explanation "Gough assumes that paying the tab is what his FTO would want." However, where's the evidence to support this? All that's revealed in the scenario is that (1) Officer Hand "has a reputation of going strictly by the book" and (2) she has used this situation in the past as a training exercise for rookie officers. The essential point is that we simply don't *know* what Officer Hand thought—whether she believed Gough acted properly or not. All we *do* know is that Hand has a reputation among officers as "going strictly by the book." That's it. Sometimes people's reputations are correct; but sometimes they aren't. Remember you're trying to reach a *reasoned* conclusion to the question of whether Gough behaved ethically, which means you should avoid including "iffy" information. The better choice for why Gough acted as he did was because he was aware of the "no gratuity" policy and was simply following it.

Ethical Issue

Together, we've now filled two blanks in the template: the facts and some details. The third piece of information you'll need for the analysis is a statement of the **ethical issue** in the case, that is, the potential violation of ethics arising from the behavior identified in the scenario. When you identify the issue, you have articulated the target of your analysis, around which you will build evidence to support your conclusion.

For the purposes of our template (and from a purely practical standpoint), you can think of the issue as a *restatement of the facts in the form of a question*, adding the phrases "Is it ethical?" or "Was it ethical?" to the facts. To illustrate in the context of our present scenario, the issue would be: "Is it (Was it) ethical for a police officer to follow departmental policy?" And here's something else. You no doubt have noticed that if you correctly identify the facts in the case, you have also correctly identified the ethical issue! It's a "two-fer!" Who says professors can't be generous!

Identifying Moral Ideals

Let's review for a minute. I have now shared with you three valuable pieces of information to enter into the template—the facts, the relevant details, and the ethical issue. However, this information by itself will not allow you to reach a reasoned conclusion about whether it is ethical for a police officer to follow departmental policy. More information is needed. So, let's see if we can't fill in some more of the template. Let's continue doing so by identifying relevant **moral ideals** in the case.

Moral ideals shouldn't be thought of as rules or principles, for example, in the way the categorical imperative is a rule (see Ch. 2). Rather, ideals represent the fullest expression of basic values or culturally prescribed notions of ultimate "good"; they point to what society would be like under perfect conditions (DeMarco, n.d.). While moral ideals suggest unattainability, they nonetheless are culturally identified goals that members of the group strive to achieve (Ruggiero, 2015). For example, one commonly held moral ideal in American culture is *justice* (to some, the same as fairness). Rewards (e.g., material gain), punishments (e.g., incarceration), and entire institutions (e.g., our legal system) have been created to help us attain the ideal of justice. While the end-states described may be unattainable, they nonetheless serve the valuable function of serving as goals for each of us to strive toward.

Substantive and Procedural Ideals

Philosophers have suggested that moral ideals can be divided into two categories: substantive and procedural (DeMarco, n.d.). A **substantive moral ideal** is a depiction of how something or someone would be under ideal conditions; for example, an ideal judge, an ideal police officer, or an ideal probation officer. A **procedural moral ideal**, on the other hand, does not strive to describe some end. Rather, procedural moral ideals identify the optimal conditions under which choices are made concerning how we should behave or how a certain goal is achieved (DeMarco, n.d.). For example, you and I may both have in mind the "best"—in a moral sense—way to hire probation officers. Note we are *not* talking about the optimal moral or personal characteristics we believe probation officers should possess. Instead, we're talking about what would be the optimal moral conditions under which the person who'll occupy the position would be picked. What's relevant here is that when facing a moral dilemma—how to hire the "best" probation officer—and trying to make the right choice (in a moral sense), we may use ideal procedures to help us make the choice. One tactic we might use would be to first imagine what an "ideal" probation officer (or police officer, or judge, or prosecutor—you get the idea) would look like based on an "ideal" person with whom we're familiar—perhaps Martin Luther King, Jr., or Mother Theresa. We would then imagine the optimal conditions under which selecting such a person would occur. That is, what ideal procedures would be put into place to help ensure that someone like Martin Luther King, Jr., or Mother Theresa would be hired as a probation officer? The point is that we are looking outside ourselves to for guidance, and even if no such "ideal" probation officer exists, we can speculate on what their characteristics might be, how we could create procedures that would make their selection probable, and act accordingly.

Table 5.1 presents a list of moral ideals articulated by various philosophers from different eras in Western history (ancient, medieval, and modern—see Maslin, 2015). The list is hardly definitive, but I find it useful to share with students some of the ideals that Western philosophers have identified. You may note that several of the sources I included mention the same ideals, which shows that over the span of several centuries, there has been consistency in the moral ideals identified by Western philosophers and appearing in Western culture.

Principle of Respect for Persons

A final note for you to consider is this: not only in ethics, but also theologically speaking and in American culture, *respect*—especially for other people—is an important notion and likely rises to the level of a moral ideal. Philosophically speaking, one could argue that the **Principle of Right Desire**, which says that we ought to desire that which is really good for us, extends to include respect for other people (Adler, 1991). In other words, it

TABLE 5.1 A Sampling of Moral Ideals in Western Philosophy

Source	Important Moral Ideals
Plato	prudence, justice, fortitude, temperance
Aristotle	honesty, pride, friendliness, wittiness, rationality, friendships, scientific knowledge
St. Thomas Aquinas	chastity, temperance, charity, diligence, kindness, patience, humility
von Herder	sympathy, love, forgiveness, honesty, justice, and equality
C. S. Lewis	truthfulness, faithfulness, loving kindness, forgiveness
Ruggiero	fairness/justice, prudence, temperance, courage, honesty, compassion, loving kindness, forgiveness, repentance, reparation, gratitude, beneficence

is really good for us to respect others. Philosophers also argue that there is a theological basis for treating respect as a moral ideal (Ruggiero, 2015). Proponents of this orientation suggest that respecting others reinforces the notion that humans are created in the likeness of (God, YHWH, Allah, etc.) and are (his, her, its) children, despite their differences. One could also argue that despite its seeming decline in recent years, particularly in the political arena, respect is a core value in American culture (Baker, 2006). In popular culture, for example, the place of respect is potentially best articulated in a famous song by the American R&B artist Aretha Franklin, the refrain for which is "R-E-S-P-E-C-T, find out what it means to me." The U.S. Army (n.d., p. 1) includes respect as one of its formally articulated "core values" that soldiers are supposed to both learn and live by:

> Treat people as they should be treated. In the Soldier's Code, we pledge to "treat others with respect while expecting others do the same." Respect is what allows us to appreciate the best in other people. Respect is trusting that all people have done their jobs and fulfilled their duty. And self-respect is a vital ingredient with the Army value of respect, which results from knowing you have put forth your best effort. The Army is one team and each of us has something to contribute.

We have even taken to incorporating respect as a lesson in "values education" curricula that are found in K-12 public schools in both the United States and. elsewhere, like Australia (Halstead & Taylor, 1996).

In short, respect seems a "big deal" for Americans, the notion that someone (or something, say, a historically significant building) is important or serious and should be responded to as such. Because respect seems like such a core value in American culture, I would argue it is a moral ideal and should, therefore, be considered when we are assessing whether the behavior of criminal justice practitioners is ethical.

To facilitate this thinking, Errol Harris (1966) developed and articulated the **Principle of Respect for Persons** that can serve as a useful guide for helping us assess the ethics of behavior by considering its three tenets:

1. All people are worthy of sympathetic consideration (Don't "blow people off").
2. No person should ever be regarded as a possession, used as an instrument, or treated as an obstacle to another's satisfaction (Don't treat people as things to be used).
3. People should never be treated as mere expendables (Don't treat people as disposable).

As you'll see more fully below, where I discuss the concluding section of the template, incorporating the Principle of Respect for Persons into your analysis of the ethics of behavior formally denotes that you are considering respect an important moral ideal and believe that behavior that is disrespectful is problematic.

You have now progressed halfway through the template of analysis. So far, you have learned how to identify that facts and details; about the relationship between the facts and the ethical issue under scrutiny; and have a sense of what ideals are and why they should be included in your analysis. Let's continue exploring the template and see if I can't help you fill in another "blank," namely, the obligations the main party in the scenario has to self and others.

Identifying Obligations

Recall from Ch. 3 that because humans are social animals, we develop relationships with others, including nature. Some of these relationships are formal, such as between attorney and client; others are informal, such as between friends. Some relationships we have with others are fleeting, such as time spent sitting next to another passenger while traveling by commercial jet or interactions with a server at a restaurant. Regardless of the degree of "intimacy" that develops, with relationships come responsibilities. For example, with marriage come certain responsibilities like the spouses communicating with each other; decisions about whether to have children and if so, how to best raise them; fidelity on the part of each spouse to the other; etc. The responsibilities we have toward others are called **obligations** and extend to every person with whom we interact (see Ch. 3). In turn, the specific *nature* of the relationship with the other person defines the responsibilities that come with the territory. Obviously, you do not have the same obligations to the homeless person who stops you and asks for spare change that you do to your best friend. However, believe it or not, you have certain obligations to both your best friend and to the homeless person that are the same, including respect and courtesy. When assessing the ethics of behavior, you need to consider the obligations of the main party—the person who is engaging in the behavior that created the issue of ethics—to others with whom the party has a relationship.

Fidelity Obligations

Some types of obligations involve strict adherence to promises made, such as when one signs a contract (Ross, 2002 [1930]). These are known as **fidelity obligations** and may have not only moral implications if they are violated, but legal implications as well. For example, religious considerations aside, marriage between two people is a contract into which the parties enter and is recognized (and sanctioned) by the state. With that contract come certain obligations, such as to refrain from perpetrating abuse—whether physical or emotional—on the partner. Should abuse occur, the victim has legal recourse against the perpetrator, including divorce, which, if granted, results in the state approving the dissolution of the marriage contract. More broadly, fidelity obligations include those arising from formal promises found in situations such as employment, business relations, or certain personal relations; for example, a prenuptial agreement. In these instances, one party is promising to do (or not do) certain things; in exchange for a promise he or she will receive a benefit (e.g., fair wages for their work).

Nonfidelity Obligations

Other types of obligations are far less formal and can be considered **nonfidelity obligations**. These are still responsibilities to others, but they are less formally articulated by contract or a similar legal document. For example, you have an obligation to help a sibling in a time of need *because* of the relationship between the two of you. While you didn't choose to have the sibling, you do, nonetheless, have obligations to him or her simply because he or she exists and is part of the same family. Other types of nonfidelity obligations might include professional obligations arising from the specific occupation you have; citizenship obligations (although these may well be fidelity obligations under some circumstances); familial obligations (such as those to parents, siblings, and children); spousal obligations; friendship obligations; and obligations of beneficence (in effect, doing good for its own sake, such as picking up the empty soda can laying on the sidewalk and depositing it in the recycle bin or trash can).

One other type of nonfidelity obligation involves obligations to self, what I call personal obligations. Here, I'm not talking about instances where one is legally bound to live up to a responsibility one has or a promise one has made because of a contract or other legal agreement. Rather, I'm talking about responsibilities we have to ourselves, such as to continue to learn, to develop and nurture our conscience, to take care of our bodies, to keep an open mind to new ideas, to give our best effort, etc. These, too, should be considered when analyzing the obligations of the main party. Not fulfilling responsibilities to ourselves is just as problematic, from the perspective of ethics, as not fulfilling our responsibilities to others!

Obligations in the Template

Returning to the template for analysis, when analyzing obligations, the first thing you need do is identify all of the parties to whom the main party of interest has some kind of relationship. I have found that creating a simple list of those persons is an easy way to ensure that you capture all the relevant parties. Next, decide what *type* of obligation exists between the parties: personal? friendship? familial? employment? professional? Finally, identify the *nature* of the obligation(s) that exist between the parties. For example, returning to Case Study 5.1, if Gough (the main party in the scenario) has a friendship obligation to Hand (another party in the case), what *sort* of obligation(s) does it entail? To be honest with Hand? To trust Hand? To care for Hand? Thus, when working with obligations in the template, you're doing three things: (1) identifying other parties to whom the main actor has obligations, (2) determining the *type* of obligation(s) owed the other party, and (3) pinpointing the *nature* of the obligation(s) owed to the other.

By identifying and analyzing the obligations of the main party involved in the ethical question, you are compiling additional evidence—beyond that supplied by your analysis of the ideals—to support your final conclusion about whether the behavior in question was ethical. If, for example, you begin to see that the main party has apparently violated obligations to him- or herself and others, you are seeing a possible direction to go with your conclusion, keeping in mind that there are other pieces of information that also have to be considered.

WHEN OBLIGATIONS CONFLICT. There is one final point to be made about obligations. Sometimes the obligations to self and others may conflict (Ruggiero, 2015). For example, how many times have you encountered a situation where you have an obligation to a friend but also have an obligation to work or school? What do you do? For example, imagine that you are a police officer who has just stopped a driver for possibly driving under the influence of alcohol (DUI), only to discover that the driver is a childhood friend! On the one hand, you have an obligation to not knowingly harm your friend (which arresting him will surely do), but you also have a professional (if not an employment) obligation to enforce the law. Further, and to make matters even more interesting, there are also instances where *ideals* and *obligations* may be in conflict (Ruggiero, 2015). For example, in the courts, there are often conflicts between seeking justice for all and professional obligations to ensure that rules and procedures are followed, which *may* result in injustice (at least according to some observers).

How do we resolve such conflicts? In cases where obligations are in conflict, Ruggiero (2015) offers the following solution: we should consider the importance of each obligation and give preference to the more important one. "But wait a minute," you may be saying. "How do I determine the 'importance' of each obligation?" Ruggiero (2015) offers a solution here as well: consider the *relative* importance of each and give *preference* to the more important one. For example, if you owe a friend $200 that you borrowed six months ago, and today hear about a tornado that tore through a local neighborhood and for which the Red Cross has issued an urgent appeal for donations to help the victims, where should that $200 you just won playing the lottery go? To your friend or the Red Cross? Ruggiero suggests that to render a judgment on which obligation should take precedence, we must exercise a sense of proportion, in effect rank-ordering their importance. If we can partially serve them all, that's great, we should do so. However, if only one obligation can be served, we must choose the most important and serve it. I would argue that because the debt to the friend accrued well prior to the natural disaster, your obligation to repay your friend outweighs your beneficence obligation to help the disaster victims.

WHEN IDEALS AND OBLIGATIONS CONFLICT. What about instances where there is a conflict between ideals and obligations? How do we resolve them? A possible answer is found in the notion that we should choose the action that will achieve the greatest good (Ruggiero, 2015). Further, where the choice of actions is such that no good can be achieved, we should choose the action that will result in the least amount of evil. Consider this example (most professors have encountered it). It's the end of the semester and final grades have been posted. A student comes to see the professor, upset that she missed the higher grade "by only _____ (points/percent)." The student then asks, "Is there extra credit I can earn to make up the difference and earn the higher grade?" The professor (me, for the moment) is immediately faced with conflicting professional obligations to the class. On the one hand, I have an obligation to be fair to everyone enrolled, which means not knowingly affording one student an opportunity to improve his or her grade that is not also given to others in the class. On the other hand, I also have a professional obligation to help my students be successful, one measure of which is the final grade earned (since grades are the "coin of the realm" when it comes to keeping a scholarship, getting into graduate school, or finding a good job). What I have taken to doing to avoid this situation is two things. One, I do not grade work using percentages (e.g., 83%), so we avoid the whole "But Dr. Sloan, I *only* missed the higher grade by *1%*!" argument (which, depending on the total number of points available in the course and the difference between the higher and lower grade, can be substantial). Second, I make available to students "bonus points" that are based on class participation, extra work completed, attending a lecture outside of class, etc., and are available to *all* students in the class. Thus, when the student comes looking for "extra credit" at the end of the semester, what do you think my answer will be? Here, I have honored both my obligation to the class to be fair and to the individual student to help him or her be successful.

Obligations are responsibilities to others in our lives, regardless of how small or large a presence they may occupy. Some are formal, such as those spelled out in legal documents like contracts, and are known as fidelity obligations. Others are less formal and are associated with the mere fact that both parties involved in the relationship are human beings. By analyzing the obligations of the main party under scrutiny, we can begin developing a sense of the extent he or she may have acted (un)ethically. That becomes valuable ammunition to use when reaching a conclusion about the ethics of the behavior in question.

Identifying Consequences

Along with our responsibilities to others, we also should also pay attention to the potential outcomes of our behavior, both for ourselves and others. Some of those potential outcomes may be very pleasant, such as earning praise from one whose opinion we value or keeping a job we enjoy very much. Other consequences, however, may be significant harm not only to ourselves or to other people, but to the natural world as well. The potential outcomes of our behavior are the **consequences** they may generate and should be included in any assessment you undertake of the ethics of behavior . Note that I use the terms "may," and "potential" when speaking of consequences. I do that for a reason: consequences are probabilities rather than certainties. That is, any possible outcome of your behavior has a degree of certainty that ranges of from "0" (very little chance) to "1" (a near certainty). "But Dr. Sloan," you say. "What if I pointed a handgun at your head at point-blank range and pulled the trigger? Aren't you immediately dead from a gunshot wound to the brain?" My response is this: even here, we're *still* talking probabilities. For example, the probability of my dying from the aforementioned gunshot wound is zero if the weapon fails to properly function. All that happens when the trigger is pulled is **CLICK** rather than **BOOM**. And what if, at the last instant, your aim isn't all that steady? And what if I somehow duck? See what I mean? Each of these considerations reduces, in some cases a great deal, in others, not as much, the probability of my dying from a gunshot wound to the head after you aim your weapon at me and pull the trigger.

In ethics, consequences matter, so much so that entire systems of ethics (e.g., Utilitarian ethics; see Ch. 2) base judgments about what is ethical and unethical on the consequences of behavior (Bentham, 1996 [1789]; Haynes, 2015; Mill, 1998 [1861]). From a commonsense perspective (putting aside all the philosophical arguing and mumbo-jumbo for the moment), determining whether a particular behavior is ethical surely *must* consider the consequences of that behavior! So, let's do that.

Types of Consequences

When analyzing consequences, you should remember that behavior may have direct and/or indirect effects. The effects may also be short- and long-term in nature. Direct consequences are those specifically traceable to the behavior (e.g., my death from you shooting me in the head). Indirect consequences are ancillary effects of the behavior. Staying with the shooting example, an indirect effect could be my wife being forced to declare bankruptcy because, with the loss of my income, she can no longer afford our house payment each month. It's interesting that most times we are only interested in the possible direct effects of behavior and tend to ignore the indirect effects. When analyzing the ethics of behavior, I urge you, again in the interests of developing a reasoned conclusion, to consider both the possible direct and indirect consequences of the behavior in question.

Consequences may also be both short-term and long-term. Systems of ethics even take that distinction into account (recall from Ch. 2 "Act" and "Rule" Utilitarians). A typical Act Utilitarian analysis of the ethics of behavior emphasizes the importance of the possible short-term consequences while ignoring possible long-term effects. A Rule Utilitarian does just the opposite. However, a complete analysis considers both the possible short-term *and* long-term effects of behavior.

Finally, when analyzing the ethics of behavior, we must consider the potential consequences of the behavior not only for self and other people, but also for the natural world. Recall that one of the tenets of the moral arena (see Ch. 3) was that the behavior had to have "significant possible consequences for others, including nature." This speaks to the interconnectedness of humans and nature and to the fact our behavior, too often it seems, has implications for nature. To get into a "bigger picture" philosophical argument for a moment, consider the ethics of burning fossil fuels to produce electricity. Emissions from coal-fired power plants have been linked by scientists to the build-up of greenhouse gases in the planet's atmosphere; those gases, in turn, have been strongly linked to human-induced climate change (United States Environmental Protection Agency, 2015). Thus, we must consider the possible consequences for nature of the behavior under scrutiny.

The Principle of the Double Effect

One more thought on consequences. In some instances, the behavior chosen, while not evil in-and-of itself, may produce potentially serious harm (e.g., grievous injury to another) and some potential good (e.g., a much larger conflict is prevented). To illustrate using the criminal justice context, let's assume that three heavily armed robbers are currently holding 15–20 hostages inside a bank they were attempting to rob. The police were notified and quickly responded, trapping them inside the building. A police SWAT team has now arrived on the scene to potentially storm the bank and free as many hostages as possible. Talks between negotiators and the robbers break down and the SWAT team is ordered to rescue the hostages. During the raid, all the robbers, along with two hostages, are killed. Thus, the negative consequences included the loss of five lives (three robbers and two hostages) while the positive consequences included rescue of the remaining hostages, no deaths or injuries to police officers, and recovery of the stolen money.

The consequences arising in these types of scenarios are very difficult to analyze because of the level of their impact: for example, the deaths of multiple people but the rescuing of many hostages. What to do? According to the **Principle of the Double Effect**, sometimes it is permissible to cause potentially significant harm as a side effect (or "double effect") of bringing about a potentially good result, even though it would not be permissible to cause such potential harm as a means of bringing about the same possibly good end (McIntyre, 2014). In other words, in our bank robber scenario, as a very first step to potentially ending the robbery (a good end), the immediate storming of the bank and the killing of the robbers regardless of how many hostages and police officers were also killed would be hard to justify. Most ethicists would, however, be comfortable with the outcome as I have described it provided that (1) the good consequences are inseparable from the bad, (2) the good consequences outweigh the bad, and (3) the bad consequences are not directly intended (Boyle, 1980; Cavanaugh, 2006). Thus, when you're analyzing the consequences of the behavior under scrutiny, keep in mind that the Principle of the Double Effect can be a useful device for doing so.

Implicit Opposites when Identifying Consequences

One final thought on analyzing consequences. When identifying a specific potential consequence for one of the parties, whether in life or in a scenario, you do not need to include both the potential positive and the potential negative consequence. You need only consider one of them. The reason for this is because for every possible positive consequence there is also an *implicit opposite* possible negative consequence. So, for example, if a possible negative consequence of your friend lying to you is that you may be *less* likely to trust what your friend says, the implicit opposite consequence is that you may be *more* likely to trust what your friend tells you. You do not need to formally list (or consider) both.

The potential consequences of behavior, for self and others, are a very important consideration when assessing the ethics of behavior. And, regardless of whether the perspective you've taken is teleological or not (see Ch. 2), consequences are still part of the entire context and must be given full consideration before we can reach a reasoned conclusion about the ethics of behavior. Whether direct or indirect, short- or long-term, consequences, if for no other reason than common sense, simply must be considered.

The Conclusion

You've made it! You're now ready to fill in the final section of the template. Just to review where we've been, I have shared with you the key parts of what a reasonable assessment of the ethics of the behavior should include: a statement of the facts of the case; a consideration of the important details (the totality of circumstances); a statement of the ethical issue raised by the behavior in the case; and considerations of moral ideals, obligations of the main party to self and others, and the possible consequences of the behavior for the main party and others, including the natural world. Now it's time to pull all this together and construct an argument.

Typically, the question that arises in assessing behavior from the perspective of ethics is simple: Is (was) the behavior ethical? Answering that basic question is both a necessary and sufficient condition for your analysis to be reasonable. This means that the first thing to include in your conclusion is a straightforward answer to the question: "yes, the behavior was ethical" or "no, the behavior was not ethical." However, getting to "no" or "yes" is a product of producing evidence to support the stance you're taking. In other words, *why* have you concluded as you did that the behavior was (un)ethical and what reasons can you provide for doing so?

What I have found useful is to follow your opening statement ("yes, the behavior was ethical" or "no, the behavior was unethical") with an assessment of the extent to which the behavior in question violated one or more of the tenets of the Principle of Respect for Persons. Because respect is so important, ethically, theologically, and culturally, including your assessment of whether the behavior in question violated one or more of the principle's tenets shows that you are paying particular attention to an important moral ideal. Here, you should include a brief discussion of (1) whether the behavior violated one of more of the tenets, (2) which tenet or tenets the behavior violated, and (3) how the behavior violated the tenet(s). You might also include a discussion of whether, as well as how or why, the behavior might have also violated the Principle of Right Desire ("we ought to desire that which is good for us, and nothing else").

Next, provide a summary that highlights your analyses of the moral ideals, the main party's obligations to self and others, and the possible consequences for the main party and others in the scenario (those to whom the main party has obligations). However, not all of the ideals, obligations, or consequences are of equal importance. What you need to do is choose those that you see as particularly important (again, remember that you're assessing the extent to which the behavior in question may have violated the ideals and/or obligations and the overall nature of the behavioral consequences; were they generally positive or negative, all things considered?). Thus, in this section, you are identifying the most relevant ideals, obligations, and consequences.

Now that you've highlighted whether (and to what extent) one or more of the tenets of the Principle of Respect for Persons was/were violated by the behavior in question along with whether the behavior violated the Principle of Right Desire and you've provided highlights showing that the behavior violated one or more ideals and obligations (or not) and how it did so, along with possible (negative/positive) consequences of the behavior for all relevant parties, it's time to actually apply the guiding principle(s) from the system of normative ethics you've chosen to guide your analysis (e.g., Utilitarian ethics).

What seems to work best for this part of the conclusion is to briefly review the key principles of the system you've chosen. This shows that you are familiar with them and understand what they mean. You then apply them to the case and present the results of your analysis. To illustrate a full-blown analysis, I've provided a sample for you to consider in Case Study 5.2.

Congratulations! You have now seen how both the framework for analysis and the template for analysis can be used to engage in moral reasoning. In doing so, you fit together the pieces of the framework and then used the template to help you organize them and formulate an argument that included a conclusion that you supported with evidence. You're now well on your way to engaging in sound moral reasoning!

CASE STUDY 5.2 The Hostess and the Police Officer

April Schauer is the hostess at a local eatery, The Waffle Place, where she has worked for six years, first as a server and for the last eight months as hostess. On a recent Sunday morning on her shift, there is the usual long line of customers waiting to be seated when April notices a local police officer, Sherlock Holmes, and his family at the rear of the line and greets him loudly: "Hey Officer Holmes!" April has become acquainted with Holmes over the past several years because Holmes and his partner, John Watson, often eat breakfast at The Waffle Place before beginning their day shift. Both officers are always kind with their tips, which has endeared them to the restaurant's staff. They also inquire of April how she's doing, how are her three children, etc. When she notices Holmes, she quickly motions for him and his party to come to the front of the line, which they do. She then seats Holmes and his family before seating other parties who had been waiting for a table for a much longer time.

Did April act ethically?

I. Facts: Restaurant hostess gives preferential treatment to customer.

II. Details

- April Schauer is hostess at local eatery, The Waffle Place.
- April has worked at the restaurant for eight years as a server and hostess.
- Sherlock Holmes is a local police officer.
- Holmes works the morning shift with his usual partner, John Watson.
- Schauer, Holmes, and Watson are acquainted because Holmes and Watson are regular customers.
- Holmes and Watson are both liked by the restaurant staff.
- One recent Sunday Holmes and his family are in line for a table at the eatery.
- Schauer notices Holmes, waves him to the front of the line, and seats him and his party ahead of other customers who had been waiting for a longer period.

III. Issue: Is it ethical for a restaurant hostess to give preferential treatment to a customer?

IV. Ideals

- Fairness: Was it fair for April to give preferential treatment to a customer?
- Prudence: Was April being prudent in giving preferential treatment to a customer?
- Temperance: Was April showing temperance by giving preferential treatment to a customer?
- Courage: Was April being courageous by giving preferential treatment to a customer?
- Honesty: Was April being honest in giving preferential treatment to a customer?
- Compassion: Was April showing compassion by giving preferential treatment to a customer?
- Loving Kindness: Was April showing loving kindness by giving preferential treatment to a customer?
- Gratitude: Was April showing gratitude by giving preferential treatment to a customer?
- Beneficence: Was April being beneficent by giving preferential treatment to a customer?

V. Obligations

A. April Schauer to herself:
1. Personal obligation to be the best hostess she can.
2. Personal obligation to treat her customers fairly.

B. April Schauer to her customers (including Sherlock Holmes):
1. Professional obligation to seat them as quickly as possible and ensure their experience is positive.
2. Professional obligation to treat them fairly.

C. April Schauer to The Waffle Place:
1. Professional obligation to carry out her assigned duties as efficiently as possible.
2. Professional obligation to help create a pleasant work environment for her colleagues.
3. Professional obligation to help The Waffle Place be successful.
4. Employment/contractual obligation to carry out her assigned duties.

D. April Schauer to her children
1. Familial obligation to support her children—emotionally/financially—to the best of her ability.

E. April Schauer to her colleagues
1. Professional obligation to be a "team player."
2. Professional obligation to help them be successful at work.
3. Professional obligation to fulfill her assigned duties so she does not create added work for them.

VI. Consequences

April Schauer gives preferential treatment to a customer.

A. April Schauer

Positive: She may enhance her relationship with Sherlock Holmes into a friendship.

Positive: She could receive even bigger tips from Holmes and Watson in the future.
Negative: She may alienate the other customers.
Negative: She may be reprimanded for her actions.
Negative: She could jeopardize her job.

B. Customers
Positive: They could learn that familiarity breeds privilege.
Negative: They may be angry with April for her actions.
Negative: Their experience at The Waffle Palace may be sullied.

C. The Waffle Place
Positive: It could learn something important about how April treats her customers.
Negative: It could lose business in the short- and long-term.
Negative: It may have to reprimand or terminate a valuable employee.

D. April's children
Positive: They may learn a valuable lesson in how not to do behave at work.
Negative: Their mother could lose her job, which reduces her ability to support them.

E. April's colleagues
Positive: They may learn a valuable lesson in how not to behave at work.
Negative: They may bear the brunt of customer anger.
Negative: They may lose *their* regular customers.
Negative: They may earn smaller tips.

VII. Conclusion.

No. It was not ethical for April Schauer to give preferential treatment to a customer. In doing so, she violated several tenets of the Principle of Respect for Persons. First, she did not give due consideration to other customers who had been waiting in line longer than had Holmes and his party. Second, to a degree she "used" Holmes for personal gain, namely, to get him to come back and possibly leave even bigger tips. Finally, to a degree she treated her other customers as expendables, assuming they would not walk out or otherwise have a negative experience at the restaurant. She also likely violated the Principle of Right Desire because she failed to "desire" that which was right for her, namely, treating all customers the same.

April violated several ideals, including fairness, honesty, and compassion, by seating Holmes and his party ahead of the others. She also violated several obligations, including those to herself to be the best hostess she can and to not jeopardize her job, as well as obligations to colleagues and employer to be a "team player" and help them be successful. Finally, she violated her familial obligations to her children by potentially jeopardizing her job.

April's actions created far more potential negative consequences than positive for all involved. In particular, her actions potentially hurt business for the restaurant and hurt her colleagues' relationships with the customers. Her actions could also result in negative consequence for herself (reprimand/demotion/loss of job) and for her children.

From a Utilitarian perspective, the ethics of behavior is a considered a function of the potential consequences, positive and negative, for the greatest number. If the potential positive consequences outweigh the potential negative for the greatest number, the behavior is ethical. In this case, however, the possible negative consequences for all concerned—April, the customers more generally, her colleagues, her children, and the restaurant—far outweighed the potential positive consequences for the parties involved (e.g., April develops a better relationship with Holmes and by extension, Watson; positive lessons learned by customers, children, and colleagues). Further extending the analysis, from a Rule Utilitarian perspective, April's actions are setting a dangerous precedent that stresses that familiarity breeds privilege, something that could damage the restaurant even further in the long term).

For these reasons, April giving preferential treatment to a customer was *unethical*.

SUMMARY

Analyzing whether behavior by criminal justice practitioners is ethical involves a careful process of considering relevant information, determining what the information means, choosing a particular system of ethics to guide your decision-making, applying its principles to the case at hand, and reaching a conclusion. In this chapter, I provided you with both a framework for analysis and a template for analysis that tied together the material I shared with you in Chs. 1–4. Over the years that I have taught ethics classes, I have found that the framework helps students tie together various aspects of normative ethics and the process of moral reasoning to reach a conclusion about the ethics of behavior. I have also found the template a particularly useful tool for students that helps them organize necessary information when analyzing the ethics of behavior.

The framework for analysis stresses several considerations that ethicists typically believe are important for determining the ethics of behavior, including moral ideals, obligations, and consequences. Moral ideals can be considered as aspects of excellence, or goals that bring greater harmony within one's self and between self and others. Obligations are responsibilities that come with the relationships we have with others. Sometimes those responsibilities are formally articulated through a legal document (known as fidelity obligations), while in most cases the responsibilities are unstated, but understood nonetheless (what are called nonfidelity obligations). Obligations arise from responsibilities or promises made to others, including those formally articulated in legal documents like contracts, as well as those arising from other types of relationships like family, friendships, citizenship, etc. I noted that we also have obligations to ourselves, such as striving to be the best we can be, continuing to learn as we progress through life, and keeping an open mind to new ideas. Consequences are the potential outcomes of behavior—both positive and negative—and have clear implications for whether our behavior is ethical or not. Importantly, consequences are not certainties but instead are probabilities that may vary under different conditions. They include potential short- and long-term outcomes and possible direct or indirect effects of the behavior on self and others. Importantly, when considering consequences, the natural world should also be accounted for, as behavior may affect it as well.

I also shared a template for analysis with you that I designed and have used for years to assist students when engaging in moral reasoning. You should consider the template as a guide that helps you proceed through the process of moral reasoning with the goal of reaching a solid conclusion. The idea behind the template was to provide students like you a reusable form that contains key elements which a thorough (in my opinion) analysis should consider and which can be easily filled in. The template includes stating the basic facts of the case (what happened?), along with key details (who/what/where/when/why), identifying what is the ethical issue in the case, an assessment of the extent the behavior being analyzed *may* have violated one or more moral ideals and obligations, and identifying the possible consequences of the behavior for those involved, including the natural world.

Finally, the template includes a section into which your conclusion fits. In this final section, you "pull together" your analysis of ideals, obligations, and consequences by highlighting from each section those ideals, obligations, and consequences you thought were of special importance. This section will also include analysis of whether the behavior in question violated one or more tenets of the Principle of Respect for Persons, which allows you to assess the behavior in light of the moral ideal of respect, a core philosophical, theological, and cultural consideration when rendering a judgment about the ethics of behavior; it will also include discussion of whether the behavior violated the Principle of Right Desire. The remainder of the section involves you identifying the perspective you're taking—be it deontological or teleological—and identifying and applying the guiding principles of the normative system of ethics to the behavior at hand.

To finish this chapter, let's engage in some more moral reasoning, this time using Case Study 5.3, whose focus is on the ethics of judicial elections and campaign contributions to them.

CASE STUDY 5.3 The Ethics of Campaign Contributions for Judges

Judge Miriam Webster is currently a Superior Court judge in Mayberry County, N.C., a position she's held for 16 years (four terms). Webster earned a Bachelor of Arts degree in history from the University of North Carolina and her law degree from Duke University. After graduating from Duke, she clerked for three years with U.S. Supreme Court Associate Justice Anthony Kennedy and then worked for three years as an Assistant Attorney General for the State of North Carolina before running for judicial office in her home county.

Webster hates campaigning for office, but loves being a judge. She is well respected by the local defense bar, the police, and local prosecutors, who generally see her as being "tough but fair" in dealings with counsel and the police. She is a stickler for procedure and won't hesitate to throw out cases in which the police or prosecutors failed to follow procedure to a "T." She has also sanctioned defense counsel for antics she deemed inappropriate and pursued disbarment of two local attorneys for ethics violations.

One reason Webster, who considers herself a "moderate Republican," hates campaigning is that she has to raise money, which she believes is a corrupting influence in elections, particularly in judicial elections (she even wrote an op-ed piece for the *Charlotte Observer* decrying the Supreme Court's decision in the *Citizens United* case). She knows, however, that the reality is that she must spend money to get reelected, particularly this year, as she faces a stiff challenge from Andy Belham, who's running a "law and order" campaign that condemns "activist judges" and promises to "get tough on criminals" who come before him for sentencing. Belham has received endorsements from some local law enforcement professional associations and is running an ad that features him with prominent Republican leaders in the state.

Today, Webster is campaigning at an event sponsored by the local chapter of the Citizens for Better Government in North Carolina (CBGNC), an organization whose endorsement she is seeking (they have supported her previous reelection bids). However, the leadership of the organization has changed and there's a chance the endorsement she needs might not come if she doesn't impress the group with her take on crime and criminal justice. The leadership recently sponsored a similar event for her opponent that went very well but that sickened Webster with all the rhetoric about "courts paying too much attention to defendants' rights," "judges being 'soft' on crime," and how "liberal judges don't follow the Constitution." Webster knows that she's going to have to "talk tough" to impress an increasingly conservative group whose members may be leaning toward supporting her opponent.

While mingling with attendees before the event, she's approached by Doris Dickens, a well-heeled and well-known local entrepreneur whose political leanings are also well-known: she's a "dyed-in-the-wool liberal." Surprised at Ms. Dickens's presence at the event, Judge Webster asks why she's there. Doris tells her she's ready to write the campaign a $50,000 check on the spot if Judge Webster is willing to cancel her appearance at the event and not seek the group's endorsement as "they're a bunch of fascists." Dickens tells the judge that she has 10 minutes to make up her mind or the offer is withdrawn, and then walks away.

Webster is stunned: the money would fund most of her campaign and relieve her of having to continue appearing at events like these and asking for contributions. It would, however, significantly affect the judge's standing and reputation, as many would now see her as having been "bought" by a "liberal" who is "intent on destroying our way of life." Webster calls her wife, Nora (who's also her campaign manager), and tells her what's happened. Shocked, Nora reminds Miriam of Dickens's reputation and the negatives that would come with accepting the donation and advises Miriam not to take the money. Miriam reminds Nora how much she hates campaigning and says that if people think so little of her that they believe she can be "bought," then "to heck with 'em."

After further conversation, Miriam tells Nora of her decision and then searches for and finds Ms. Dickens. She tells her that she accepts her offer; Nora immediately writes a check for $50,000 to the campaign.

Did Judge Webster act ethically?

Let's tackle this one from a Kantian orientation and fill in the template:

I. Facts
   Candidate for public office accepts a campaign contribution.
II. Details:
   - Miriam Webster is the incumbent candidate for Superior Court judge in Mayberry County, N.C.
   - She holds a BA from UNC and a JD from Duke and is married.
   - Webster clerked for Associate U.S. Supreme Court Justice Anthony Kennedy and worked in the State Attorney General's office prior to first being elected to the bench.
   - Judge Webster has a good reputation among police officers, prosecutors, and defense attorneys – "tough but fair."

continued

- Webster is a stickler for following procedure in criminal cases and will dismiss cases where police/prosecutors fail to do so.
- The judge hates campaigning because it involves raising money, which she believes is corrosive in elections of all kinds and has written as much.
- Her opponent is Andy Belham, a much more conservative Republican than is Webster, who describes herself as a "moderate."
- Belham's platform is one of "law and order," which has resulted in endorsements from state-level Republicans and some local police groups.
- Webster is campaigning at an event sponsored by the local chapter of Citizens for Better Government in North Carolina (CBGNC), an increasingly conservative political action group whose endorsement Judge Webster seeks (CBGNC has previously endorsed her).
- Belham has already appeared at a CBGNC event that went well for him; Webster fears the group may be leaning his way.
- Webster is approached by Doris Dickens, a local, well-heeled, politically liberal entrepreneur who gives the judge 10 minutes to decide if she's willing to accept a $50K donation to her campaign and skip the CBGNC event, dooming any hope of an endorsement.
- The money would fund Webster's entire campaign.
- After discussing the situation with her wife (who's her campaign manager and thinks accepting the money isn't a good idea), Webster accepts the offer.

III. Issue

Is it ethical for a candidate for public office to accept a campaign contribution?

IV. Ideals

- Prudence: Was Webster being prudent in accepting the contribution?
- Justice: Was Webster pursuing justice by accepting the contribution?
- Temperance: Was Webster exhibiting temperance by accepting the contribution?
- Courage: Did Webster exhibit courage by accepting the contribution?
- Honesty: Was Webster being honest in accepting the contribution?
- Beneficence: Was Webster "doing good for its own sake" by accepting the contribution?

V. Obligations

A. Webster to herself

- Webster has a personal obligation of self-improvement.
- Webster has a personal obligation to do her best while on the bench.
- Webster has a personal obligation to not be corrupted (e.g., through favors granted to those contributing to the campaign).

B. Webster to her constituents (includes Dickens and CBGNC—see discussion below)

- Webster has a professional obligation to do her best while on the bench.
- Webster has a citizenship obligation to maintain the integrity of the courts.
- Webster has an employment obligation to properly execute the duties of her office.

C. Webster to her spouse (see discussion below)

- Webster has a fiduciary obligation to her spouse relating to their property, finances, etc.
- Webster has a spousal obligation to maintain communication with her.
- Webster has a spousal obligation to treat her with respect.

D. Webster to her campaign manager (see discussion below)

- Webster has a professional obligation to treat her fairly.
- Webster has a professional obligation to treat her with respect.
- Webster has a contractual obligation to her to abide by its parameters.

E. Webster to Belham

- Webster has a professional obligation to treat him with respect.
- Webster has a citizenship obligation to hold him accountable for his actions.

F. Webster to the judiciary

- Webster has a professional obligation to uphold the ideals of the judiciary.
- Webster has a professional obligation to follow rules applicable to the office.

G. Webster to Mayberry County

- Webster has an employment obligation to abide by the scope of work found in her contract.
- Webster has a contractual obligation to abide by the scope of work outlined in her contract.
- Webster has a professional obligation to not sully the office she occupies.

VI. Consequences

Webster accepts the campaign contribution.

A. For Webster
  - Negative: She may lose support from some constituents (see discussion above about *implicit opposites*).
  - Negative: She may lose possible endorsement from CBGNC and other conservative groups.
  - Positive: She may be able to pay for her entire campaign.
  - Positive: She may no longer have to fund-raise.
  - Positive: She may procure endorsements from more liberal groups.

B. For Webster's constituents
  - Negative: They may reduce/end their support for Webster.
  - Negative: Their belief that campaign contributions adversely affect elections may grow stronger.

C. For her spouse
  - Positive: Her happiness could be increased.
  - Negative: Her desire to be married to a judge may be affected.

D. For her campaign manager
  - Positive: Her trust could increase.
  - Positive: Her workload could be reduced since she would not have to schedule more fund-raisers.
  - Negative: She may have to reassure conservative supporters that Webster has not "sold out" to liberal interests, which may difficult.

E. For Belham
  - Positive: He may use the contribution as a "talking point" against Webster.
  - Positive: He could see increased support from conservative voters.
  - Negative: He may lose any chance at swaying less conservative voters to his side.

F. For the Judiciary
  - Negative: It may suffer reduced trust from citizens.
  - Positive: A "good" judge may still be reelected.

G. Mayberry County
  - Negative: It could suffer negative political fallout as the situation becomes public.
  - Negative: It may suffer reduced trust from citizens.
  - Positive: It may have a "good" judge returned to office.

VII. Conclusion

No. It was unethical for Judge Webster to accept a campaign contribution. In accepting the contribution, Judge Webster did *not* violate any of the tenets of the Principle of Respect for Persons: she seemed to give everyone due consideration, did not use anyone, and did not treat any party as mere expendables to be used up. For example, she listened to Dickens (when she did not have to); she did not use her (at least in the classic sense); she did not treat her as merely expendable. Further, she did not violate the Principle of Right Desire. In this case, given that Judge Webster is a "good" judge (i.e., she's fair, honest, and just in her decisions), getting reelected is really "good" not only for her but also for the people of the county.

Webster showed courage in accepting the contribution, given the larger political environment. There is no evidence of any dishonesty on Webster's part in accepting the contribution: no promises were made (or broken) by Webster. As for whether Webster was being prudent in accepting the contribution, given the larger political environment she faced it was likely *not* prudent to accept the contribution. Further, given the available evidence, Webster exhibited a certain amount of intemperance by accepting the contribution, given the election (circuit judge), its size ($50,000), and the nature of the campaign (local). Webster's acceptance of the contribution likely violated the ideal of beneficence, since no larger good was achieved by accepting the contribution and it may have exacerbated existing concerns about the corrosive influence of money in politics. Thus, Webster appears to have violated several ideals.

When reviewing Judge Webster's obligations, it appears she violated several of them. First, she had a personal obligation to "do her best" or "be the best judge" she could. Is accepting a $50K contribution fulfilling those responsibilities? Probably not, if for no other reason than doing so likely violated her responsibility to be trustworthy and accepting the contribution calls that into question. She likely violated her professional obligations to the county and to her constituents as well. Once her accepting the contribution becomes public (which it will), will she continue to be viewed as an "ideal judge?" Does an "ideal judge" accrue a debt to wealthy benefactors? Does an "ideal judge" contribute to a possible erosion of trust in the judiciary? While no promises were made or broken, and Webster gave her spouse/campaign manager and the donor due consideration and did not use them or treat them as expendables, she violated her duty to her constituents, her opponent, the county, and the judiciary more broadly to be fair, honest, and enhance trust in her court, the local government, her opponent, and the judiciary more broadly.

continued

As for the potential consequences of Webster's accepting the contribution, her primary need at the time was for contributions to fund her reelection bid and accepting the $50K resolved that need and was thus the greatest possible positive consequence. Accepting the contribution could also lessen her campaign manager's workload and enhance both communication with her spouse/campaign manager and trust between them, both of which are potential positives. The most important possible negative consequences for Webster included potential loss of the CBGNC endorsement and support from her constituents. Additionally, her actions could play into the larger narrative of campaign contributions sullying elections, the candidates running in them, and the profession the candidates represented, in this case, the judiciary.

From a Kantian perspective, the most important consideration is whether the behavior in question violates the categorical imperative that tells us to act in a manner we would want everyone to act and to not use others. In the present case, would we want all candidates for judicial office to accept campaign contributions? Also, did Webster *use* Dickens or any other party?

Webster desired to be reelected, which isn't a bad thing, since there's no evidence she wasn't a "good" judge (both morally and legally). However, she hated the drudge of the campaign, especially the part about raising money. Recall also that she was critical of the *Citizens United* decision and bemoaned the corrosive effects of money on political campaigns. Now, suddenly and unexpectedly, she is given an opportunity to fund her entire campaign and takes full advantage of it. In doing so, she meets an immediate need. One could thus argue she has fulfilled a *hypothetical* imperative: If you want to get reelected, accept campaign contributions from wealthy constituents. But recall also the hypothetical imperative is not the most important consideration in Kantian ethics—the categorical imperative is more important. While Judge Webster did not use Dickens, she nonetheless violated the categorical imperative: Would we want all judicial candidates at all times and places to accept campaign contributions? My answer is "no," because doing so may violate important ideals and obligations on the part of the candidate.

There is nontrivial evidence that the *Citizens United* decision, and the "dark money" that can't be traced to any single individual it allows, has led to a greater chance of, if not outright corruption in public office holders, then enhanced partisanship in their decision making. Corruption or partisanship are hardly ideals the collective desires for judicial office holders. Further, aren't judges obligated to fulfill responsibilities like enhancing trust in the judiciary? Obviously, judges should avoid becoming corrupt since becoming so is not only a personal vice, it erodes trust in an important institution—the judiciary. Because corruption and enhanced partisanship of judicial office holders is often tied to the campaign contributions they receive, Webster's accepting the contribution is both selfish (another vice) and contributes to erosion of her constituents' faith in the judiciary—a violation of one of her important obligations. Because we want our judges to be less corrupt and/or less partisan, we would not want all judges at all times and places to accept campaign contributions. In so doing, Judge Webster violated important ideals and obligations. Therefore, Webster acted unethically.

So, how did I do? Did I get the facts correct? Did I include all the relevant details (who, what, where, when, why)? What about relevant ideals? Were they all included? And how about the obligations of Webster? Did I include all the relevant parties? Did I identify the type of obligation Webster had to each party? The nature of the obligation to each party? And what about the potential consequences? Did I include those possible for the relevant parties? What about direct and indirect potential consequences? Were the short- and long-term possible consequences included? Finally, did my conclusion include a section about the Principle of Respect for Persons and the Principle of Right Desire? Did I provide supporting evidence in that discussion? Did I highlight important ideals, obligations, and consequences? What about my conclusion? Did it follow from Kantian guiding principles? How was my logic?

What if we were to change the orientation used to one involving Utilitarianism, say, Rule Utilitarianism? What would change? Not much in Sections I – VI. The facts, details, issue, ideals, obligations, and consequences would still be the same. In Section VII, you would again include discussion of the Principle of Respect for Persons and the Principle of Right Desire. The only substantive change would come where you discuss the guiding orientation. Now you would discuss the basics of Utilitarian ethics, including its emphasis on potential consequences as controlling. You'd discuss the difference between Act and Rule Utilitarianism. You would then identify and apply the guiding principles of Rule/Act Utilitarianism to the scenario and reach your final conclusion.

As I've noted previously, while this template may seem a bit much (as in too much doggone *work*!), it *is* comprehensive and as a result, will help you identify relevant information you can use to reason through to a logically solid conclusion.

KEY TERMS

Totality of the circumstances 115
Facts 118
Details 119
Ethical issue 120
Moral ideals 120
Substantive moral ideals 121
Procedural moral ideals 121
Principle of Right Desire 121
Principle of Respect for Persons 122
Obligations 123
Fidelity obligations 123
Nonfidelity obligations 124
Consequences 126
Principle of the Double Effect 128

DISCUSSION QUESTIONS

1. Compare how any two different systems of normative ethics include ideals and obligations (or not) as core concepts within their framework.
2. An enduring American ideal, according to some historians, politicians, and social commentators, is the notion of the "American Dream," which is described as "that that dream of a land in which life should be better and richer and fuller for everyone, with opportunity for each according to ability or achievement" (Adams, 1931, p. 404). What does the American Dream mean to *you* personally? Is there a *downside* to the American Dream?
3. What obligations do humans have concerning the production of food, given climate change and other challenges like overpopulation that face humanity (see Vermerr & Verbeke, 2006)?
4. If the consequences of one's actions are *unintended* does that relieve him or her from being considered morally blameworthy? Explain.

RESOURCES

Philosophy Talk is a high-quality website and podcast that "celebrates the value of the examined life." Each week, its hosts (who are philosophy professors at Stanford University) engage in reasoned conversation on a wide range of issues (e.g., science, morality, popular culture, religion). The talk and information are accessible, stimulating, and fun. Philosophy Talk is produced by KALW on behalf of Stanford University's Humanities Outreach Initiative. Visit the site at https://www.philosophytalk.org/

Vincent Ruggiero's *Thinking critically about ethical issues* (Boston, MA: McGraw-Hill) is an easily accessible and well-written short volume that provides a great overview of the role of critical thinking in assessing the ethics of behavior. The book contains short, concise discussions of ideals, obligations, and consequences and a concluding chapter that reviews normative ethics in Western philosophy from the ancient Greeks to modern times. Includes hundreds of short scenarios relating mostly to applied ethics, which are nonetheless useful for developing your critical thinking skills and moral reasoning.

If you are interested in learning more about the **American Dream**, check out an analysis by Matthew Warshauer that argues that the original values associated with the American Dream have been replaced with "get-rich quick" schemes. Visit http://www.americansc.org.uk/Online/American_ Dream.htm

REFERENCES

Adams, J. (1931). *The epic of America*. Piscataway, NJ: Transaction Publishers.

Adler, M. (1991). *Desires right and wrong: The ethics of enough*. New York, NY: Macmillan.

Baker, W. (2006). *America's crisis of values*. Princeton, NJ: Princeton University Press.

Bentham, J. (1996). *An introduction to the principles of morals and legislation* (J. Burns & H. Hart, Eds.). New York, NY: Oxford University Press. (Original work published 1789).

Berger, P., & Luckmann, T. (1966). *The social construction of reality: A treatise in the sociology of knowledge*. New York, NY: Random House.

Boyle, J., Jr. (1980). Toward understanding the Principle of Double Effect. *Ethics, 90*, 527–538.

Cavanaugh, T. (2006). *Double-effect reasoning: Doing good and avoiding evil*. Oxford, UK: Clarendon Press.

DeMarco, J. (n.d.). *Moral theory: A primer*. Retrieved from http://www.lawandbioethics.com/demo/Main/EthicsResources/Ideals__procedural.htm

Halstead, M., & Taylor, J. (Eds.) (1996). *Values in education and education in values*. Bristol, PA: Palmer Press.

Harris, E. (1966). Respect for persons. In H. Aiken (Ed.), *Ethics and society: Original essays on contemporary moral problems* (pp. 111–133). New York, NY: Anchor Press.

Haynes, W. (2015). Consequentialism. Retrieved from http://www.iep.utm.edu/conseque/

Maslin, L. (2015). *The basics of philosophy*. Retrieved from http://www.philosophybasics.com/historical.html

McIntyre, A. (2014). Doctrine of double effect. In E. Zalta (Ed.), *The Stanford encyclopedia of philosophy* (Winter Edition). Retrieved from http://plato.stanford.edu/archives/win2014/entries/double-effect/

Mendelsohn, A. (1998). Fourth Amendment and traffic stops: Bright-line rules in conjunction with the Totality of the Circumstances test. *Journal of Criminal Law and Criminology, 88*, 930–956.

Mill, J. (1998). *Utilitarianism* (R. Crisp, Ed.). New York, NY: Oxford University Press. (Original work published 1861).

Oxford Dictionary (n.d.). "Framework." Retrieved from https://en.oxforddictionaries.com/definition/framework

Rokeach, M. (1973). *The nature of human values*. New York, NY: The Free Press.

Ross, W. (2002). *The right and the good* (Stratton-Lake, P., Ed.). New York, NY: Oxford University Press. (Original work published 1930).

Ruggiero, V. (2015). *Thinking critically about ethical issues* (9th ed.). Boston, MA: McGraw-Hill.

United States Army (n.d.). The Army values. Retrieved from http://www.army.mil/values/

United States Environmental Protection Agency (2015). Learn about carbon pollution frompower plants. Retrieved from http://www2.epa.gov/cleanpowerplan/learn-about-carbon-pollution-power-plants

Vermerr, I., & Verbeke, W. (2006). Unsustainable food consumption: Exploring the consumer "attitude – behavioral intention"' gap. *Journal of Agricultural and Environmental Ethics, 19*, 169–194.

CHAPTER 6

Police Ethics—A Contextual Overview

Chapter Outline

CHAPTER LEARNING OBJECTIVES:

1. Contrast the theories of "rotten apples," "rotten barrels," and "rotten orchards" as explanations for unethical or illegal behavior by police officers.
2. Describe how police recruitment, hiring, and training processes work in concert to weed out "rotten apples."
3. Identify the core values of "the" police culture and how they influence the behavior of police officers.
4. Distinguish the various positions taken on police gratuities.
5. Identify the factors affecting the organizational climate of police agencies and how that climate relates to unethical behavior by police officers.

INTRODUCTION

Frank Serpico is best known for uncovering and fighting against corruption in the New York City Police Department (NYPD) in the late 1960s and early 1970s (see Maas, 1973). His promising career was cut short in 1971 when he was shot in the face during a drug raid that had gone bad. The bullet severed the auditory nerve to his right ear, causing him to lose hearing in it, and forced his retirement. Serpico claimed his wounding was payback from corrupt police officials he'd named in efforts to fight corruption in the NYPD.

Frank Serpico
Photo by Bill Tompkins/Getty Images

For years, Serpico had resisted inclusion in payoffs that officers in several precincts where he worked received from local drug dealers and racketeers. In 1967, he reported to senior-level commanders that credible evidence existed of widespread corruption in the agency, but no investigation was launched. In 1970, Serpico contributed to a front-page story in the *New York Times* about corruption in the NYPD that resulted in nationwide attention to the problem. Then-New York City mayor John Lindsay even created a five-person panel, the Knapp Commission (named for its chairperson, Whitman Knapp), to investigate Serpico's accusations of corruption and before which Serpico voluntarily testified about officers he believed were corrupt (Knapp, 1972). To this day, Serpico believes he was set up by colleagues involved in the raid as retaliation for his testimony before the Knapp Commission.

Serpico paid dearly for standing up to corruption in the NYPD. Beyond having his career cut short, he was ostracized by colleagues and forced to flee the country after he received an onslaught of death threats. Sadly, he *still* receives hate mail from misguided souls who claim he single-handedly "betrayed" the NYPD.

The Serpico case is useful for illustrating the ethical context of policing. On the one hand, there are *individuals* like Serpico, recruited into policing, and then hired and trained by departments who believe their recruits have the necessary skills and values to be police officers. Once trained, these individuals are then asked to perform various functions (e.g., fight crime, maintain order, and provide service to the community), that may involve using *tactics*, such as deception and racial profiling, that have raised ethical flags. There are also police *organizations*. These paramilitary-based bureaucracies feature a strong rank structure and a culture—values, attitudes, and norms—into which new officers are then assimilated. Finally, there are *communities*, like Brooklyn and the Bronx, with their own values, attitudes, and norms that are served by officers and their departments. For these reasons, I would argue police ethics is a multilayered phenomenon that should be approached as such: it involves individuals, organizations, and communities, each of which contributes a piece to the larger puzzle of police ethics.

This chapter begins a discussion of police ethics that continues in Ch. 7. Here, I present an overview of the context of police ethics that includes individuals, organizations, and communities. Included in this discussion is a theory of police ethics that uses an apple farm analogy to focus on "rotten apples," "rotten barrels," and "rotten orchards," along with analyses and discussion of ethical issues associated with (1) the recruitment, hiring, and training of police officers; (2) the culture of policing; and (3) the organizational environment of policing. I conclude the chapter by presenting a Thought Exercise that examines the ethics of the use of preemployment psychological assessment of prospective police officers. Ch. 7 continues the discussion of police ethics by examining ethical issues associated with police *tactics*—specifically, the use of deception during investigations, interrogations, and in court; and police use of surveillance, both active and passive forms. Before beginning a discussion of police ethics, let me first remind you about the functions of police in modern America.

THE FUNCTIONS OF POLICE IN MODERN AMERICA

To understand unethical and illegal behavior by police officers, you need to first understand the myriad functions police officers and agencies are expected to perform. Americans mistakenly perceive the police as "crime fighters" or "crook catchers" (Surette, 2015). These misperceptions arise because of media depictions of police officers showing them spending most of their time solving crimes and arresting "bad guys." These depictions no doubt influence some people to seek careers in law enforcement, mistakenly believing they'll be routinely involved in action-packed life-or-death situations. However, it's important to remember that shows like *CSI* and its offshoots are designed to entertain rather than give viewers an in-depth look into the reality of policing. Does this mean that police officers aren't involved in life-or-death situations? Of course not. But dealing with those situations is just one part of what police do.

If media depictions of the police are overblown (at best), then what exactly is it police officers do? Let's see if I can answer that question by asking you to imagine that you and I are partners on the afternoon shift of a police department employing several hundred sworn officers in a medium-sized American city. As we ready ourselves for the next eight to ten hours, we don our uniforms and slip into lightweight, durable, and supportive footwear. We put on our Kevlar vests (body armor) after checking them for wear and tear (such could make them useless). We spark-test our conducted electrical weapon (of which the Taser is the best known), and check our firearms, extra ammunition, heavy-duty flashlights, nylon ties, tactical pepper spray, handcuffs, batons, body cameras (if used), and radios to ensure that all are working properly. We check our "Sam Browne" duty-belt for wear and tear as it is what securely holds all our equipment (note that, with this gear, we've just added about 20 pounds to our current weight). We also check our vehicle—lights, siren, computer, radio, stored shotgun, etc.—and visibly inspect the car to ensure that no evidence has been left in it and determine if it had been damaged during the previous shift. After attending roll call with our shift supervisor, we're ready to hit the street.

What can we expect during our shift? As we engage in routine preventive patrol in our assigned geographic "beat" or sector, we'll be looking for evidence of crimes in progress, while also enforcing traffic laws. We'll also respond to dispatched calls for service. During these activities, we may arrest people suspected of engaging in one or more crimes or issue traffic citations to motorists. We'll also talk with people—including informants we've cultivated—who'll provide us information ("intelligence") about criminal activities occurring in our beat and likely perpetrators involved. We'll encourage a group of young men, congregating on a street corner while drinking alcohol and socializing, to disperse. We'll help Mrs. Jones, who has just moved into the area, find the post office; speak to Mr. Smith about how he can reduce the chance of his butcher shop being burglarized; and present a short program at the local middle school to educate students about the consequences of Internet-based bullying. In short, we can expect to enforce the law, maintain public order, and engage in service to the community (Wilson, 1968).

What the police do and how they do it tends to be determined by the department where they work. What a specific department emphasizes as important (e.g., enforcing the law) and the tactics its officers use in carrying out those functions (e.g., "zero-tolerance policing") matter, as both affect not only the trust of citizens, but the very legitimacy of the department. Trust and legitimacy connect the police with those being policed, and as recent years have shown, when those connections fray or are severed, the community distrusts the police and may outright reject the legitimacy of the department (President's Task Force on 21st Century Policing, 2015).

Prominent Features of American Policing

The most prominent feature of American policing is that it consists of a hodgepodge of thousands of agencies at the federal, state, and local levels of government. According to the most recent (although, admittedly, dated) statistics available, in 2008 at the federal level, 73 different agencies employed 120,000 individuals authorized to carry firearms and make arrests (Reaves, 2012a). These agencies (e.g., the Federal Bureau of Investigation [FBI], Immigration and Customs Enforcement [ICE], and the Bureau of Alcohol, Tobacco, and Firearms [BATF]) are organizational units of the federal government whose functions include preventing and detecting federal crimes and apprehending alleged offenders (Bureau of Justice Statistics, 2017). Further, all 50 states have a statewide law enforcement agency that in 2008 employed about 61,000 sworn officers. States may also have "special jurisdiction" agencies, such as Alcohol Beverage Control (ABC) officers, responsible for preventing illegal sales of alcohol to minors, or conservation officers responsible for enforcing hunting and fishing statutes (Reaves, 2011).

But it is at the local level of government—counties and cities—that one finds the bulk of police agencies and officers in this country. While exact numbers are unavailable, estimates are that there are over 3,000 county sheriff's departments that employ about 200,000 full- and part-time sworn (those with arrest powers) officers, and approximately 12,500 municipal police departments employing about 500,000 full- and part-time sworn officers (Reaves, 2011). There are also several thousand "special jurisdiction" police agencies at the local level, including college/university police departments, housing authority police, transit police, port authority police, or public-school system police, that also employ tens of thousands more sworn officers (Reaves, 2011). In total, there are over 15,000 local-level police agencies that employ about 800,000 sworn personnel. Because most police agencies and officers are found at the local level, my discussion about police ethics both in this chapter and in Chapter 7 concentrate on agencies and officers in local police and county sheriffs' departments.

Further, although most local police agencies are structured the same way (see Figure 6.1), there is, nonetheless, significant variability in their size, level of specialization, and

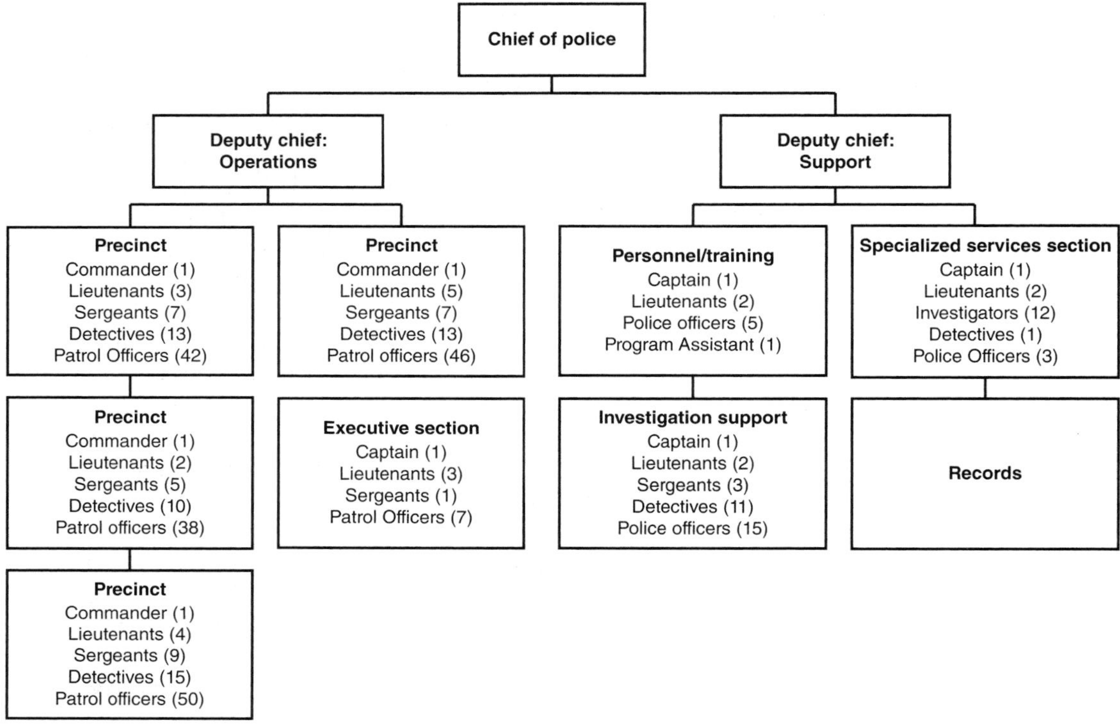

FIGURE 6.1 Organizational Chart of a Typical Municipal Police Department

communities served. For example, about 50% of all local agencies in 2008 employed fewer than 100 sworn officers (Reaves, 2011). In fact, while most police *agencies* are small—employing fewer than 100 sworn officers—most police *officers* work in large municipal departments like those found in major cities. The NYPD, for example, was projected to employ 35,000 sworn officers in 2016 and have an overall budget of $10 billion (Citizens Budget Commission, 2015). Variability in the size and complexity of these agencies, both across and within, has implications for police ethics and must be considered part of the larger context.

Importantly, the ethical questions that arise over the police and the moral dilemmas that officers confront do not necessarily relate to the functions of police *per se*. Rather, the issues and dilemmas confronting police officers tend to arise from these sources: (1) the recruitment, selection, and training of police officers; (2) the culture of policing; (3) the tactics of policing (examined in Ch. 7); and (4) the organizational climate of police departments. Further, the ethical issues confronting the police are rarely cut and dried. Rather, ethical issues involving the police exist in a world of shades of gray. Indeed, part of the problem—according to some—is that police officers often have values and a world view that do not account for shades of gray but are steadfast in seeing the world in terms of "right/wrong," "black/white," or "good guys/bad guys" (see O'Neill, Marks, & Singh, 2007; Rokeach, Miller, & Snyder, 1971). With these comments in mind, let's now turn our attention to the context of police ethics.

THE CONTEXT OF POLICE ETHICS

The context of police ethics involves multiple levels, ranging from individual officers and their personal characteristics, to the structure and culture of the organization employing them, to the community the organization serves (see Figure 6.2). The problem is that unethical (or even illegal) behavior by police officers is too often attributed to "rotten apples"—individuals circumventing built-in safeguards in the hiring process who became officers who violated the trust of the citizens being served. As you'll see, this is overly simplistic.

Are there rotten apples in policing? Of course, just as there are rotten apples in *any* occupation. But understanding why police officers engage in questionable behavior is far more complicated than simply saying a few "rotten apples have spoiled the barrel" and leave it at that. It's important that you understand that "rotten barrels" can just as easily spoil the apples! What I mean by this is that police departments, because they are complex organizations, have a structure and a culture that influence the behavior of the individuals working in them. If the organization's structure and/or culture is defective, opportunities for unethical and/or illegal behavior develop; if this behavior becomes normalized, the barrel itself then becomes rotten.

Finally, individual police officers and the departments for which they work serve communities. Those communities can be conceptualized as "orchards" replete with a culture that influences both the "barrel" and the "apples." In effect, if the orchard is rotten, shouldn't we expect both the barrel storing them and the apples themselves to be rotten? By depicting police ethics as involving rotten apples, barrels, and orchards, I present a perspective that is holistic and nuanced because it considers individual, organizational, and community-level factors' influences on police ethics. With that said, let's now explore the individual-level context of police ethics and the notion of "rotten apples."

The Individual Context of Police Ethics

The individual context of police ethics relates to the behavior of specific officers employed by an agency, say, the City of Miami Police Department. In turn, officers and their behavior are influenced by characteristics such as age, race, time-in-service, gender, etc.

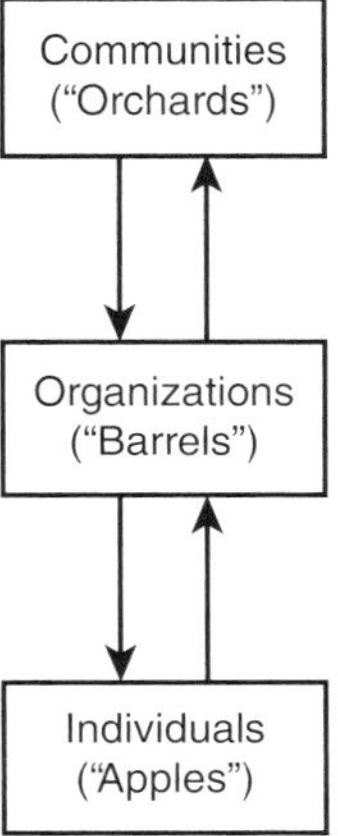

FIGURE 6.2 The Context of Police Ethics

Individual Characteristics and Police Ethics

Scholars studying police ethics have suggested that employment history, educational attainment, age, gender, and years-on-the-job affect police ethics, as measured by careers ended through dismissal, termination, or forced resignation. James Fyfe and Robert Kane, for example, compared the personal and career histories of all 1,543 officers involuntarily separated from the NYPD for cause between 1975 and 1996 with a randomly selected sample of academy classmates who remained on the job. Fyfe & Kane (2005) reported that officers with prior arrests, traffic violations, failure in other jobs, lacking at least an associate's degree or who had performed marginally at the police academy, or were white males were more likely to be involuntarily separated from the NYPD than officers who did not have those characteristics. Thus, focusing on the individual characteristics of officers engaging in unethical or illegal behavior involves efforts to find the "rotten apples" and get rid of them.

ROTTEN APPLES THEORY. A common refrain by citizens, and sometimes by ranking officials in police departments, is that officers caught engaging in unethical or illegal behavior are "rotten apples" and therefore, it's unfair to cast aspersions on officers in the department as biased, crooked, or otherwise inclined toward unethical behavior. This "**rotten apples theory**" of police misbehavior was the official line taken by the NYPD during Serpico's time on the force, as identified by the Knapp Commission:

> According to this [rotten apples] theory, which bordered on official department doctrine, any policeman [*sic*] found to be corrupt must promptly be denounced as a "rotten apple" in an otherwise clean barrel. It must never be admitted that his [*sic*] individual corruption may be symptoms of a larger underlying disease.
>
> —(Knapp, 1972, pp. 6–7)

Why is this theory so popular? One reason is that it's just plain easy: identify the rotten apple(s), denounce the officer(s), get rid of them, and move on. It's also easy because it doesn't involve challenging core practices relating to how police departments recruit, hire, and train new officers. As discussed more fully below, departments use various hurdles like background checks, polygraph examinations, drug tests, and psychological screenings to ensure that prospective officers possess high levels of integrity and, therefore, aren't rotten apples. Once you start questioning rotten apples theory as "the" explanation for unethical or illegal police behavior, you will find yourself either questioning the entire hiring process or looking at the organization itself as the root of the problem. It may indeed be that a "rotten barrel" has spoiled the bunch.

The Organizational Context of Police Ethics

As was depicted in Figure 6.2, police departments are complex and specialized paramilitary-oriented bureaucracies, replete with a solid rank structure (e.g., corporals, sergeants, captains, majors) and a top-down style of communication (i.e., orders flow from the top of the organizational hierarchy down to the street level). Knowing this, we can examine how organizational features of police departments affect the integrity and ethics of officers working in them. That is, a barrel that is rotten spoils the fruit.

Rotten Barrels Theory

Police scholars have shown that police organizations exert influence over the actions of individual officers (see Paoline, 2014). This influence occurs because police agencies have an organizational culture that affects the behavioral, emotional, and cognitive elements of group members' functioning. This culture is created by upper management (e.g., the police chief) and is imposed downward through organizational ranks (Schein, 1991).

In the early 2000s, Carl Klockars and his associates developed an organizational theory of police integrity known as **"rotten barrels theory"** using results from surveys administered to over 3,200 police officers in 30 American police departments (see Klockars, Ivković, & Haberfeld, 2004; Klockars, Ivković, Harver, & Haberfeld, 2000). Their work examined how the organizational features of police agencies—including department rules and responses to their violation, challenges posed by the "blue wall of silence" among officers, and the agencies' social and political environments—affected officer integrity and accountability as measured by officer willingness to report colleagues for infractions ranging from minor violations of rules to outright illegality. Klockars and colleagues' research is important because it showed that barrels can indeed become rotten if officers don't regard certain forms of misconduct as serious, regard discipline as too severe (or lenient), or silently tolerate misconduct by peers. An agency possessing a climate that tolerates deviance, fails to consistently enforce its own rules, and tolerates silence (at best) and coverups (at worst) about officers' unethical or illegal behavior has created a "rotten" environment. One would indeed be shocked if such an environment *didn't* spoil the apples!

The Community Context of Police Ethics

Local police operate don't operate in a vacuum. They are embedded as part of the institutional framework of a community, replete with social, economic, and political forces. How those forces affect police departments can be understood by examining police agencies' histories: some departments have a long, stable history of unethical and illegal behavior by its officers; others experience cyclical instances of scandal followed by reform; and still others have an equally long and stable tradition of minimal problems. What scholars suggest, as a result, is that community expectations about police departments' integrity and ethics exert pressures on police organizations which affects a department's ability to resist, confront, or combat questionable behavior by officers (Klockars et al., 2000, 2004).

Rotten Orchards Theory

To this point, I have suggested that the context of police ethics is one of individuals embedded in organizations. These individuals learn, through occupational socialization, what is expected of them both formally—from the standpoint of the organization—and informally—from the standpoint of other officers. In effect, they internalize the values, attitudes, and norms of the larger occupation and those of the organization. In turn, both affect officers' behavior and the ethical issues arising from that behavior. However, there is a third part of this context that is also important: the community in which the police agency and its officers are embedded. Indeed, some scholars posit a **rotten orchards theory** to help us understand police ethics. Let's first consider how a rotten orchard affects police behavior more broadly and then look at rotten orchards theory as it relates to police ethics.

In recent years, police scholars have explored how the socioeconomic and cultural characteristics of communities are related to police behavior such as excessive use of force, improper arrests, etc. For example, David Klinger (1997) developed an "ecology of patrol" perspective that explained the influence of neighborhood-based factors on officer behavior. This perspective suggests that the social and ecological aspects of patrol districts influence officers' perceptions of how "deserving" are those places to receive police services, which then influences the outcomes of police responses to calls for service. Places thus affect the norms that influence officer decisions and are inseparable from key aspects of legal or investigatory situations involving the police (see also Lum, 2010). Other researchers have found that neighborhood characteristics—including socioeconomic standing and racial composition—significantly affected officer arrest decisions, coercive use of force, and incident reporting (Morabito, 2007). In short, mounting evidence shows a relationship between socially disadvantaged neighborhoods and the behavior of the police officers serving them.

What are the implications of rotten orchards for police ethics? If the moral standards of the larger community tolerate certain behaviors, then officers will face pressure not to formally respond to those behaviors by arresting the people engaging in them. For example, if the community accepts large public gatherings featuring loud music and where alcohol is consumed in open containers, officers learn that dispersing such gatherings—despite their illegality—is *wrong* (in moral terms) and done at one's peril. The message to the officer is that under certain conditions, enforcing the law—assumed to be an indicator of the public's beliefs about the moral rightness and wrongness of behavior—*is problematic* and doing so may earn the officer a reprimand. As a more extreme example, let's say an officer is patrolling a part of the community that loathes drug dealers and supports the view that violence is acceptable for resolving conflict. In such places, residents may *not* object to officers using excessive force against drug dealers while arresting them as a way of "teaching them a lesson" in contradiction to department policy and ethical principles such as respecting the humanity of suspects. The rotten orchard thus erodes not only officer willingness to follow department policy, but their allegiance to guiding principles like fairness or respect for the rights of suspects. Table 6.1 summarizes the key features of the three contexts of police ethics and the theories associated with them.

ETHICAL ISSUES IN THE RECRUITMENT, SELECTION, AND TRAINING OF POLICE OFFICERS

Well before a person is sworn in as a police officer, she must first be recruited and then navigate a series of hurdles that results in her taking an oath of office and becoming a sworn officer. Critics of this process have identified numerous problems with it that raise ethical issues.

Police Recruitment and Selection

Between 1980 and 2001, the U.S. Army ran a hugely successful recruiting campaign via commercials with the tagline "Be All That You Can Be" penned by Earl Carter of the N.W. Ayer Advertising Agency (United States Army Recruiting Command, 2003). The 30-second

TABLE 6.1 Theories of Illegal/Unethical Police Behavior

Theory	Level of Analysis	Description	Limitation(s)
"Rotten Apples"	Individual	Individuals lacking *personal integrity* circumvent barriers like drug tests, background checks, or polygraphs as part of prehiring processes and become police officers	Does not question recruitment/selection/training processes; assumes processes can be "tweaked" to better predict "rotten apples;" ignores organizational factors or occupational/cultural factors that can foster unethical behavior
"Rotten Barrels"	Organizational	The *organizational culture* of police departments, including tolerance of deviant behavior, "code of silence" about officer deviance, or inconsistency in addressing officer misconduct, creates a work environment that fosters unethical/illegal behavior	Fails to accept that some "rotten apples" exist and will circumvent safeguards designed to exclude them; fails to recognize that community culture can influence organizational policies and individual officer behavior
"Rotten Orchards"	Community	*Community values* are such that using force, lying, etc. are acceptable behavior by members of the community and those values in turn influence officer behavior while on the job	Assumes the culture of the community is far more influential than it may actually be and/or that officer acculturation will negate personal morality

ads included images of soldiers and army equipment parachuting from cargo planes, catchy background music that included the lyrics "you're reaching deep inside," and a voiceover at the end of the commercial saying, "We do more before 9:00 a.m. than most people do all day." The images presented, combined with the jingle and the slogan ("be all that you can be"), were intended to attract people the Army believed could "fit in."

In general, recruiters—whether from the U.S. Army or "Big City Police Department"—use various tools, including images, video, and signage that depict an idealized picture of the organization, for purposes of attracting recruits who then apply for positions (Sycz, 2014). The tools used by recruiters to attract prospects are designed to find people of a certain ilk—those who appear able to master the skills necessary to become competent, but also those whose values match those the organization believes important. Just as in other contexts, person-organization fit is crucially important for any recruiter. In policing, as Caldero & Crank (2015) explained, recruiters are *not* seeking "just anyone." Instead, they are explicitly seeking prospects who are "squeaky clean," want to do something meaningful with their lives, have limited tolerance for wrongdoing, and carry a moral commitment to the **noble cause** of policing: to protect the innocent and identify and arrest criminals, even if doing so puts their lives in jeopardy. Some departments may work toward "selecting out" candidates by identifying flaws in them that would disqualify them from being hired, while other departments may work toward "selecting in" candidates by identifying positive qualities that would make a recruit attractive to the agency (Scrivner, 2006). Ultimately, what some scholars have suggested is that police recruitment and hiring is a value-neutral undertaking (e.g., Roberg, Crank, & Kuykendall, 2000), while others disagree and suggest that finding and hiring prospective police officers is very much a values-based activity (e.g., Ellwanger, 2015).

Scholars who support the **value-neutral perspective** on police recruitment and hiring argue that prospects are not screened for narrow or specific value predispositions they may possess, but rather are screened for character traits like honesty, psychological stability, and the lack of a criminal history. Proponents of this perspective argue that police officers should not carry or act out predispositions about social rights and wrongs, so screening is designed to weed these people out. Proponents then point to the fact many (most?) departments use the Minnesota Multiphasic Personality Inventory (MMPI), a paper-and-pencil test used to identify several dimensions of a recruit's psychological identity and assess her overall stability. The argument in favor of these complex procedures is straightforward: a thorough screening and testing process ensures that only the most highly qualified candidates will be hired as police officers (Caldero & Crank, 2015).

The argument that recruitment is a value-based activity is supported, at least in part, by the fact that those aspiring to careers in policing tend to share certain characteristics (Crank, Flaherty & Giacomazzi, 2007). For example, they often come from families that already have one or more members working in the field (or the military). They tend to come from "blue-collar" backgrounds and are (relatively) conservative in their political beliefs. They are inclined to see the world in terms of black and white, rather than shades of gray. People interested in police work also tend to see the career as one way of helping to maintain the values and traditions of American society.

According to the **values-predisposition perspective**, the recruitment and hiring of prospective police officers involves a process whose goal is to identify not only those who meet established minimum standards relating to character and background and possess skill sets that will help them be successful as police officers, but also those who possess "correct" values that can be fine-tuned via academy and on-the-job training (Caldero & Crank, 2015). Thus, recruitment and hiring is not necessarily about screening *out* prospective "bad apples." Rather, the process is about screening *in* those who have both the necessary skill sets *and* the "proper" values.

If the values-predisposition perspective is correct, you can think of the recruitment/hiring process this way. Aspiring police officers have chosen a career in policing from among competing options. Police agencies recruit them not only because they appear to meet established minimum standards relating to character, background, physical health, and skills sets, but also because they have the "proper" values. The agencies will then spend time fine-tuning the recruits' skills and values, including those emphasizing organizational loyalties and local practices. Especially during early occupational socialization experiences (e.g., in the academy and during post-academy field training), recruits hone their skills while interacting with and learning the police culture, as well as while encountering internal organizational pressures (e.g., making arrests). The end result is that the individual develops a fully formed "police" way of seeing the world.

Further, if it's true that the goal of police recruiters is to find those who meet minimum standards, possess a solid character, and possess "proper" values that can be shaped and refined during the first few years on the job, isn't it quite reasonable to argue that the entire process of recruitment and hiring is designed to maintain the status quo? That is, the point of recruitment and hiring is to attract and hire those whose skills, character, and values are *similar to those possessed by people already in the field*—even if doing so results in resistance to change (Guyot, 1979), fosters the continuation of the so-called "blue wall of silence" (Westmarland, 2005), or encourages racist or sexist attitudes toward others, both inside the field and out (Chang & Tchekmedyian, 2016).

That **recruiting to the status quo** occurred in American policing is well documented (see Potter, 2013). For most of the 20th century, for example, policing was the sole domain of white males largely because minimum physical standards for the job excluded women and males of Asian or Hispanic origin. Combined with the *overt* racism and sexism that openly ruled the day until the 1960s, you can see why there was so little diversity in the field and why discrimination in hiring was occurring. And yes, *major* change has occurred over the past 50 years that ended outright exclusion of women and certain minorities from the field, such that today the field is more diverse than it has ever been (United States Department of Justice, 2015). However, isn't excluding one who aspires to a career in policing based on whether or not he or she possesses the "proper" values—as defined either by the organization or the occupational culture—just as problematic? I would thus argue it is reasonable to raise the question of whether—as currently practiced—police recruitment and hiring processes are *ethical*.

Prehiring Procedures

Before one can be hired as a police officer, a recruit must navigate a series of hurdles designed to weed out the "rotten apples." The process begins with a prospect completing an application that lists background and personal information. That information is used as a preliminary screen to reject those not meeting established minimums for hiring (e.g., they do not meet minimum or maximum age requirements, have been convicted of a felony, have used drugs, or are in poor physical health). Some prospects will thus be rejected at this stage.

Assuming one meets the base criteria for hiring, most departments also require knowledge testing of applicants via a standardized examination that evaluates an applicant's reading comprehension, problem solving abilities and judgment, memory, and writing skills. Assuming a passing score is received on the test, applicants also must pass a physical examination that ensures they are in good enough health to complete required training that includes running, chin-ups, push-ups, and weight-lifting. Applicants must also pass background checks designed to assess the applicant's character, lifestyle, and past experiences, along with a polygraph examination to ensure the accuracy of the information they've provided.

The candidate is also subjected to psychological testing, known as **preemployment psychological evaluation** (PPE), a specialized examination to determine if a candidate "meets the minimum requirements for psychological suitability mandated by jurisdictional statutes and regulations [and] other criteria established by the agency" (International Association of Chiefs of Police, 2014, p. 1). PPE assesses a candidate's emotional stability and helps identify whether she possesses psychological traits believed relevant to future success (Sanders, 2008). Candidates also undergo an oral interview to assess their verbal communication and decision-making skills, demeanor, and level of self-confidence.

If the candidate makes it over these hurdles, she is hired, pending successful completion of training at an accredited police academy (where some number will "wash-out"). Those making it through the academy enter a probationary period where they are teamed with a Field Training Officer (FTO) and receive more training. Assuming the candidate receives favorable evaluations during FTO-based training, she becomes a full-fledged police officer.

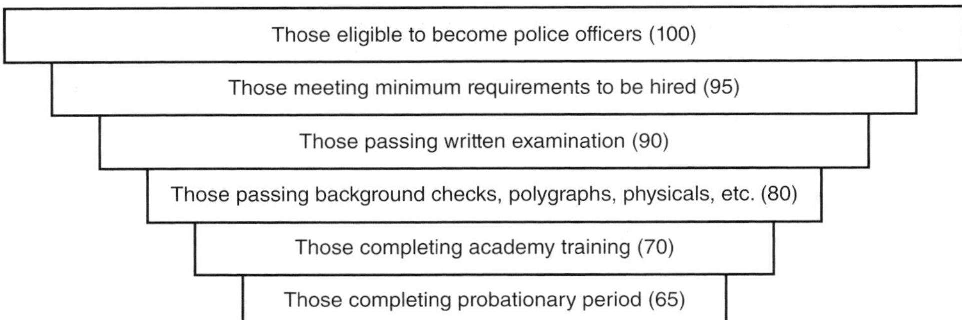

FIGURE 6.3 Hurdles to Becoming a Police Officer

This entire process can be likened to a funnel, where as one moves from the mouth of the funnel to its tip, fewer recruits remain. Figure 6.3 depicts this funneling process for a hypothetical pool of recruits. Numbers in parentheses represent estimates of the number of candidates remaining at each point in the process based on research conducted on the recruiting and hiring processes of police agencies by the RAND Corporation's Center on Quality Policing (see Wilson, Dalton, Scheer, & Grammich, 2010).

Police Academy Training

Police departments require that candidates complete training at an accredited police academy, which typically involves a 12- to 15-week-long (eight hours per day/five days a week) program of study. The program includes classes or skills-based learning in such areas as law, procedure, and evidence; forensics; vehicle operations; weapons training; physical fitness; report writing; traffic enforcement; etc. (see Table 6.2). While there is no consensus about what should be the outcome(s) of academy training (Marion, 1998), some have suggested trainees should emerge from the academy with certain competencies, including unbiased decision-making; an understanding of diversity; a team orientation; and good oral, written, and listening skills (see Muschler, 2016).

Academy training also involves values-based testing of candidates (Caldero & Crank, 2015). Does the candidate evidence loyalty? Can the candidate be trusted? Will the candidate back up other officers when called upon? Does the candidate's commitment to the "noble cause" of policing remain strong? Values-based testing typically involves instructors sharing their experiences with novices via war stories, or memorable personal experiences that typically include elements of danger, hardship, or adventure (Caldero & Crank, 2015). Robert Ford (2003) has analyzed academy war stories and found they contained both "manifest" (the overt message communicated by the story) and "latent" (the hidden or covert message the story communicates) content. Ford (2003, p. 91) illustrated manifest and latent content found in a war story an academy instructor used that described a white officer stopping an African American motorist for a traffic violation:

> The officer asks to see the driver's license and registration. The driver [claims] his license is in his wallet in the trunk. The officer opens the trunk to get the wallet; and as the officer reaches in, the driver, standing beside the officer, slams the trunk lid, barely missing officer's hands. And the fight is now on.

TABLE 6.2 Typical Police Academy Training Curriculum

Course Description	Minimum Hours	Approx. Percentage of Curriculum
Firearms/Chemical Agents	72	13
Arrest and Control	60	10
Investigative Report Writing	48	8
Vehicle Operations	40	7
Lifetime Fitness	40	7
First Aid, CPR, and AED	21	4
Crimes in Progress	20	3
Emergency Mgmt./Hazardous Materials Awareness	20	3
Policing in the Community	18	3
Traffic Enforcement	16	3
Cultural Diversity/Discrimination	16	3
People with Disabilities	15	3
Vehicle Pullovers	14	2
Controlled Substances	12	2
Laws of Arrest	12	2
Search and Seizure	12	2
Use of Force	12	2
Patrol Techniques	12	2
Traffic Collision Investigations	12	2
Crime Scenes, Evidence, and Forensics	12	2
Domestic Violence	10	2
Leadership, Professionalism & Ethics	8	1
Handling Disputes/Crowd Control	8	1
Victimology/Crisis Intervention	6	1
Property Crimes	6	1
Crimes Against Persons/Death Investigation	6	1
Presentation of Evidence	6	1
Unusual Occurrences	4	< 1
Missing Persons	4	< 1
Introduction to Criminal Law	4	< 1
Crimes Against the Justice System	4	< 1
Weapons Violations	4	< 1
Crimes Against Children	4	< 1
Sex Crimes	4	< 1
Juvenile Law and Procedure	3	< 1
Criminal Justice System	2	< 1
Alcoholic Beverage Control (ABC) Law	2	< 1
General Criminal Statutes	2	< 1
Custody	2	< 1
Information Systems	2	< 1
Gang Awareness	2	< 1
Minimum Instructional Hours	**577**	**100%**

Source: Adapted from California POST Commission (2017)

The manifest content here is obvious: during vehicle searches, keep vehicle occupants at a safe distance. But the latent content is even more interesting, as it *might* be construed as black motorists are more dangerous than are white motorists and more likely than whites to force officers into a fight.

These stories constitute parables that are used by veteran officers to share informal lessons with novices about working as a police officer. As Caldero & Crank (2015) have noted, manifest content helps candidates learn street skills, especially how to deal with danger. Through latent content, however, trainees are exposed to a department's local cultural values. Storytelling thus becomes a tool to socialize a new group of individuals into the local police culture. Instructors then gauge novices' reactions to the stories as part of the evaluation process. Note that one can do well academically at the academy but *not* graduate because of questions that instructors may have about a candidate's values.

Field Training

Once the candidate formally graduates from the academy, he or she takes the "oath of office" (see Box 6.1) and is a probationary officer for a fixed period, usually a minimum of six months. During that period, the new officer receives on-the-job training from a **field training officer** (FTO) with whom the novice is paired. FTO programs have existed since the 1970s and have been shown to produce both practical and legal benefits to departments using them, including standardizing personnel selection and training, enhancing work quality and morale, and reducing both civil liability lawsuits and Equal Employment Opportunity (EEO) complaints (Sun, 2002).

BOX 6.1 Police Officer's Oath of Office and Oath of Honor

Police Officer Sample Oath of Office[1]

I, [state your name], do solemnly swear (or affirm), that I will support the Constitution of the United States, and the Constitution and laws of the State of [name of state], that I will bear true faith and allegiance to the same, and defend them against enemies, foreign and domestic, and that I will faithfully and impartially discharge, the duties of a peace officer, to the best of my ability, so help me God.

Police Officer's Oath of Honor[2]

On my honor, I will never betray my badge, my integrity, my character, or the public trust. I will always have the courage to hold myself and others accountable for our actions. I will always uphold the Constitution, my community, and the agency I serve.

Understanding the Oath of Honor[2]

A public affirmation of adhering to an Oath of Honor is a powerful vehicle demonstrating ethical standards. Before officers take the Law Enforcement Oath of Honor, it is important that they understand what it means. An oath is a solemn pledge that individuals make when they sincerely intend to do what is said.

Honor means that one's word is given as a guarantee.
Betray is defined as breaking faith with the public trust.
Badge is the symbol of your office.
Integrity is being the same person in both private and public life.
Character means the qualities that distinguish an individual.
Public trust is a charge of duty imposed in faith toward those you serve.
Courage is having the strength to withstand unethical pressure, fear or danger.
Accountability means that you are answerable and responsible to your oath of office.
Community is the jurisdiction and citizens served.

[1] *Source:* Adapted from City of Phoenix (2017)
[2] *Source:* International Association of Chiefs of Police (n.d.)

According to Ivan Sun's ethnographic study of FTOs in Indianapolis during the late 1990s, FTOs were typically volunteers who were selected based on considerations like time-in-service, their attendance record, and the number complaints filed against them (generally on the low side). They had also completed a preliminary training program and passed written examinations relating to it and performed well in role-playing exercises, during oral interviews, and in presentations given to superiors concerning how they would supervise new officers. FTOs then received points toward promotion and a bump in pay when actively training new officers. Once certified as FTOs, to keep their certification, the officers had to complete annual in-service training programs (Sun, 2002).

Another example of research on FTOs is John Van Maanen's study of the dynamics of FTO and trainee interactions that is widely regarded as a classic ethnographic work in the field of policing. Van Maanen (1973, p. 411) described the relationship between rookie and FTO as follows:

> It is commonplace for the rookie to never make a move without first checking with [the] FTO. By watching, listening, and mimicking, the neophyte . . . learns how to deal with the objects of his occupation—the traffic violator, the drunk, the offender, the brass, and the criminal justice complex itself. A whole folklore of tales, myths, and legends surrounding the department is communicated to the recruit by fellow officers—conspicuously by [the] FTO. Through these anecdotes—dealing with mistakes or "flubs" made by policemen [*sic*]—the recruit learns to adopt the perspectives of more experienced officers . . . [and] learns that to be protected from mistakes, [the officer] must protect others [from theirs].

Van Maanen's work suggests that new officers are vulnerable to organizational pressure, represented by the FTO. Their vulnerability arises from the fact that during their probationary period, they have no job protection and can be fired if they don't meet FTO expectations. Simultaneously, the person who exerts the most influence on the new officer is the FTO—who stands for the organization. When the FTO speaks, it is effectively the department speaking to the trainee.

The role of the FTO can be characterized as twofold in nature. Formally, FTOs ensure trainees that are technically competent to do the job. Informally, the FTO ensures that the trainee not only learns, but also internalizes the norms and values of the occupation. Recall that the goal of the officer-selection process is identifying those recruits possessing "proper" values (as defined by the department), and that training helps highlight and fine-tune them. The fine-tuning begins in the academy with instructor war stories and extends through FTO-based field training. Through interactions with citizens (overseen by FTOs), during which trainees are given the opportunity to "do" policing (e.g., initiate a traffic stop; respond to a call for service; arrest a suspect), they receive formal and informal feedback on their performance. Additionally, through war stories shared by FTOs, trainees receive further socialization into the occupation. Further, because the trainee is hugely invested in making it through this probationary period, a trainee's need to be accepted by the group increases, and he or she is willing to do more to receive that acceptance. In short, it's unlikely a trainee would knowingly do something to jeopardize his or her becoming fully integrated into the organization, both formally and informally.

Here's the problem: what if the FTO's "messages" and feedback do not exactly mesh with organizational or community expectations of officers? What if the FTO's attitudes toward supervisors and the community are negative? From Day 1 the FTO engages in both formal and informal assessment of a trainee's competence, which includes evaluating not only the trainee's skills and knowledge, but also whether the trainee is loyal and whether she would back up other officers (Caldero & Crank, 2015). Of course, it's unlikely an FTO would allow a technically incompetent trainee to move forward and become a full-fledged police officer, if for no other reason than the FTO would be risking their own credibility. But isn't it just as reasonable to assume that no self-respecting FTO would allow a trainee to move forward if she didn't maintain "proper" values (e.g., loyalty to other officers and backing them up, no matter what)? The values expressed by trainees during the months of monitoring by the FTO matter at least as much, if not more, than the trainee's technical competence.

ETHICAL ISSUES IN FIELD TRAINING. I would suggest that this is the point where a poignant question should be asked about ethical issues relating to the training of new police officers: Why is so little attention paid to ethics training in police academy curricula and field training programs? Recall from Table 6.2 that if ethics is even offered in the academy, it is offered as a single course that lasts a few hours and constitutes less than 1% of total training. FTOs do not, to the best of my knowledge, evaluate trainees in terms of the ethics of their behavior. Why is this?

In response to this question, police administrators and supervisors will point out that:

> [From the beginning of the entire training process] novices are taught to avoid all forms of illegal behavior, even if others are engaging in them. They are taught to "resist and report" [illegal] actions. They're provided an elaborate, complicated set of written standards to guide their behavior. They learn that even the appearance of unprofessional conduct is to be avoided. They've been drilled in ethical conduct, including being scolded for even looking at a free meal. They may have even studied the Law Enforcement Code of Ethics from the International Association of Chiefs of Police.
>
> —(see Box 6.2; Caldero & Crank, 2015, p. 72)

Further, prehiring and hiring processes are supposed to weed out "bad apples." The assumption is that those who make it through the process possess the proper moral values, or else they would have "washed out." Thus, formal training in police ethics isn't necessary. But let's remember that the retaliation Serpico experienced when he "resisted and reported" the corruption flourishing around him is common (Blumberg, 2016). Let's also remember the influence FTOs have on their trainees. If an FTO was to say to a trainee, "Forget all that academy stuff, here's how we *really* do things around here," given the trainee's vulnerability it's unlikely she will express objections. If you think about it for a moment, Serpico's story could be used by an FTO either to illustrate what happens to officers—trainees or otherwise—"disloyal" to colleagues, or to show exemplary behavior of an officer adamant in his resolve to root out the forces crippling the NYPD. Isn't the moral of the story here a function of the FTO's perspective?

BOX 6.2 The Law Enforcement Code of Ethics

As a law enforcement officer, my fundamental duty is to serve the community; to safeguard lives and property; to protect the innocent against deception, the weak against oppression or intimidation and the peaceful against violence or disorder; and to respect the constitutional rights of all to liberty, equality and justice.

I will keep my private life unsullied as an example to all and will behave in a manner that does not bring discredit to me or to my agency. I will maintain courageous calm in the face of danger, scorn or ridicule; develop self-restraint; and be constantly mindful of the welfare of others. Honest in thought and deed both in my personal and official life, I will be exemplary in obeying the law and the regulations of my department. Whatever I see or hear of a confidential nature or that is confided to me in my official capacity will be kept ever secret unless revelation is necessary in the performance of my duty.

I will never act officiously or permit personal feelings, prejudices, political beliefs, aspirations, animosities or friendships to influence my decisions. With no compromise for crime and with relentless prosecution of criminals, I will enforce the law courteously and appropriately without fear or favor, malice or ill will, never employing unnecessary force or violence and never accepting gratuities.

I recognize the badge of my office as a symbol of public faith, and I accept it as a public trust to be held so long as I am true to the ethics of police service. I will never engage in acts of corruption or bribery, nor will I condone such acts by other police officers. I will cooperate with all legally authorized agencies and their representatives in the pursuit of justice.

I know that I alone am responsible for my own standard of professional performance and will take every reasonable opportunity to enhance and improve my level of knowledge and competence.

I will constantly strive to achieve these objectives and ideals, dedicating myself before God to my chosen profession . . . law enforcement.

Source: International Association of Chiefs of Police (n.d.)

The Police Officer's Occupational Career

As I've stressed to this point, the recruitment, training, and occupational socialization of police officers is a process. At its core is a change that occurs in the recruit's identity or sense of self as the candidate moves through the various stages of recruitment and academy and field training. The result is the candidate seeing him- or herself as a police officer. Recall from Ch. 1 the notion of one's **occupational career,** described by Steven Ellwanger as involving four stages: choice, introduction, encounter, and metamorphosis (Ellwanger, 2015).

CHOICE. Ellwanger (2015) explains that **choice** refers to the recruit's original decision to pursue a career in policing. That decision is partly a by-product of the recruit's values. But there's another factor in play: the type of work the field offers (Caldero & Crank, 2015). Police work is appealing to many because it is nonroutine, occurs outdoors, and is socially significant (the "noble cause"). One goes to work each day not knowing what events or circumstances will be encountered during a shift. Officers also exercise great amounts of discretion, which is appealing—it's not like the shift sergeant is following them around, and many circumstances confronting officers are too complex to be strictly regulated through standard operating procedures. These features are enhanced by relative job security and a reasonable salary with respect to education requirements.

INTRODUCTION. Once academy training begins, the recruit starts learning what policing is *really* like. As described by Ellwanger (2015), beyond the technical aspects of academy training, introduction involves the recruit learning—often through war stories from instructors—about the department's bureaucracy and how it works. The recruit may also learn that the department is very interested in controlling sworn personnel to ensure predictability, stability, and efficiency in operations. Lessons relating to the importance of group cohesion and solidarity are emphasized through uniforms worn, group exercises, war stories, and shared experiences. Recruits learn that because it's expected, good behavior goes mostly unnoticed, but problem behavior is punished, sometimes arbitrarily. The recruit thus learns how to operate "under the radar" and to employ various techniques of self-preservation from hostile and unsympathetic administrators and outside groups (Crank, 2004). While these forces are shaping the recruits, they also receive lessons in police work through instruction from veteran officers and outside experts to satisfy procedural requirements and reduce organizational exposure to civil liability (Buerger, 1998).

ENCOUNTER. As described above, the field training aspect of new recruits' socialization into policing is dominated by the FTO, who further shapes the recruit. Ellwanger (2015) characterizes encounter as the impact of various experiential aspects of field training on the recruit. For example, through the FTO, the recruit discovers differences between the "theory" of policing (as taught in the academy) and the "practice" of policing (what occurs on the street). The recruit may (mistakenly) believe that explaining the law to citizens is important until the trainee actually tries to do this, and the effort fails. The FTO then explains that trying to tell a motorist why there are laws against speeding and about its relationship to traffic accidents will only result in the motorist becoming angry and the officer frustrated (Van Maanen, 1974). The recruit also learns that the uniform and gun—key elements of policing—are symbols of power that provoke challenges, criticism, and taunts from citizens, especially juveniles and minorities (Kappeler & Gaines, 2009). Such responses do not mesh with a key reason the novice got into policing—to serve. Additionally, the recruit learns that some citizens will try to take advantage of the recruit's inexperience and that the department's administration, the broader legal system, and the media can be just as adversarial toward patrol officers as the public can be (Crank, 2004). As a result, and with the tacit approval of the FTO, the trainee begins to see supervisors, citizens, and the media as problems, as people who can't be trusted and who should be viewed with suspicion. Finally, continued testing by the FTO of the recruit's loyalty, willingness to use force (as necessary), and to back up other officers reinforces in the recruit the values of loyalty and trust.

METAMORPHOSIS. The final stage of the recruit's occupational career occurs when she completes her probationary period and "morphs"—socially and psychologically—into a full-fledged police officer (Ellwanger, 2015). It is here that the officer adopts the self-conception of "cop" that is in part the product of organizational and other forces that have influenced her over the many months of prehiring, training, and probationary hurdles she has navigated. Figure 6.4 depicts these stages and their core aspects.

Let me recap this discussion about ethical issues and police training by reminding you that: (1) recruits into policing are hired not only because they meet minimum criteria relating to intelligence and physical health, but because they possess "proper" values about society and the role of the police in it; (2) during training, recruits' values are honed, highlighted, and reinforced by academy instructors and later by FTOs, who exert enormous influence over their charges; (3) formal ethics training, if it occurs at all, generally ceases once the novice has completed academy training; and (4) enforcement of

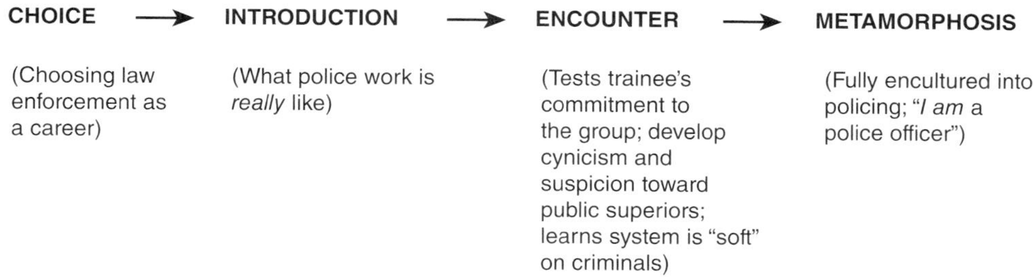

FIGURE 6.4 The Occupational Career of the Police Recruit

departmental ethical standards shifts to a system of oversight that includes standard operating procedures (SOPs) and other means (e.g., internal affairs) backed by sanctions. This is how police ethics is enforced, but not how police ethics is *learned* by officers (Caldero & Crank, 2015), which is discussed in Ch. 7.

ETHICAL ISSUES AND THE CULTURE OF POLICING

Beginning with the seminal work of William Westley in the 1950s, the fact that police officers share a culture—a set of values, attitudes, and behavioral norms into which they are socialized, is transmitted across generations of officers, and which affects their behavior—has been well established (Westley, 1970). Scholars suggest that this culture developed as officers "figured out" how to perform the various tasks and solved the problems they faced, resulting in their developing a set of shared attitudes, values, and behavioral norms related to problem solving and task performance (Van Maanen, 1974). As Eugene Paoline (2014) has observed, this **police culture** is an occupational phenomenon that developed as officers, individually and collectively, confronted the situations they did, including the ever-present potential of violence being perpetrated against them. This led to them creating a shared set of values, attitudes, and norms to guide them.

Adaptations to the Stresses of Policing

For over five decades, research on the culture of policing has described "the" police culture as being homogeneous in terms of its attitudes, values, and norms. It offers a coping mechanism for the stresses officers confront, including interactions with citizens that can be fraught with danger and suspiciousness and watchful and punitive supervisors who expect officers to perform all police functions but only recognize officers for their crime-fighting activities (see Paoline, 2003, 2014). For example, Steven Ellwanger identified the "core values" of the police culture as "using force," "time," "loyalty," "fringe benefits," "justice," and "discretion," as explained in Table 6.3. The consequences of "the" police culture are a socially isolated occupational group whose members are extremely loyal to each other and who strongly condemn those members daring to report to administrators or outsiders the unethical or illegal behavior of other members. This is known as the so-called *blue wall of silence* in policing (Marshall Project, 2017).

TABLE 6.3 The Core Values of the Police Culture

Core Value	Content of the Value
Use of force	Force should not be considered a last resort, but instead should be exercised as a way of deterring people from disobeying officers, conveying group solidarity, achieving a measure of justice, and showing the public the police are strong
Time	Officers can never respond too quickly to "real" calls for service that involve crime fighting, nor too slowly to "garbage" calls involving order maintenance or service to the community
Loyalty	Trust should only be placed in fellow patrol officers—the public, administrators, and media are "out to get you"
Fringe benefits	For what they do and the dangers to which they are exposed, police officers are underpaid. Therefore, rewards extended to them by the public for their service or in appreciation for what they have done constitute compensation that is both deserved and appropriated
Justice	Because the criminal justice system is both weak and untrustworthy, justice is sometimes best served on the street based on personal rather than legal considerations
Discretion	Except in the most serious instances, enforcing the law should be based not only on what it says but also on the characteristics of those involved

Source: Ellwanger (2015)

Recent scholarship, however, has challenged this depiction of "the" police culture by showing that increased diversity among members of the occupation and a move toward community-oriented policing have diminished the extent the values and attitudes of officers are monolithic (Manning, 1994, 1995). There is also evidence of variability in the extent of "buy-in" to "the" police culture across ranks (Farkas & Manning, 1997), and that the *organizational* culture of police departments may be a more important influence on how officers behave than is "the" police culture itself (Paoline, 2014). It is believed that as officers develop their own style of policing over time, they may depart from the values and behavioral norms found in "the" police culture (Bayley & Bittner, 1984). I will note that even if the police culture's influence on individual officers has waned, it is still important as its values and behavioral norms can lead officers to engage in wrongful behavior. Let's look at one example of an ethical issue relating to the influence of "the" police culture on officers: accepting gratuities from the public.

Police Gratuities

Imagine one evening you are in a local eatery and notice that two police officers (or sheriff's deputies—it doesn't matter) are seated in the booth next to yours. They appear to have just finished their meal and the server is talking with them. "Don't worry about the check, guys. We genuinely appreciate the work that you do. Consider the meal to be a token of appreciation from all of us to the two of you." How would you react? Be honest, here. Wouldn't you be at least a *little* irritated? Your irritation likely springs from a feeling that it's not *fair* for you to have to pay for your meal, while the officers get a "freebie." Or, your irritation might arise from feeling like the officers are *already being paid* a salary and the free meal is "double dipping" by them—in effect, being paid twice for doing their job. If you recall, one of the so-called core values of "the" police culture is "fringe benefits"—free stuff (or stuff at reduced cost) that police officers receive and that is perceived by officers as perfectly acceptable. The justification for such freebies is that because police officers are not compensated in a manner commensurate with the difficulties of the job they do, they deserve certain "fringe benefits," such as a free meal or reduced cost for goods and services.

Where does the public stand on this issue? While few studies have examined the topic, research that *has* been done shows that the public is concerned with police officer gratuities. Robert Sigler and Timothy Dees, for example, surveyed a random sample of adults in Reno, Nevada, about police gratuities and found that respondents saw gratuities as encouraging favoritism toward those providing them (Sigler & Dees, 1988). A more recent survey of residents living in Brisbane, Australia, found similar concerns by residents: accepting gratuities leads the giver to expect something in return from the police officer (Prenzler & Mackay, 1995). Thus, it's probably fair to assume that the public is skeptical not only of officers accepting gratuities, but of the people offering them to the officers.

One problem with studying police gratuities is with determining what exactly constitutes a "gratuity." Let's see if I can clarify. For our purposes, a **police gratuity** is something of economic value, be it goods or services, given by a member of the public to a police officer for any number of reasons. More formally, a gratuity is "any discount, gift or benefit one receives by virtue of their [being the member of a] profession" (Petrocelli, 2006, p. 1). In other words, the gratuity is given *because* the recipient is a police officer. The problem is that the economic value of gratuities is almost unlimited—a free soda and a new Ferrari can both constitute "gratuities" (I would suggest, however, that a new Ferrari would raise many more red flags than would a can of soda). To be reasonable, when I'm speaking of police gratuities, I'm referring to goods or services of minor economic value (less than $50) given to police officers. While you may say that $50 is arbitrary, you're right, it is to a degree. However, if the claim is that the gratuities of which I'm speaking are of "relatively small value," I'm confident most people would agree the $50 figure is a reasonable cut point.

Competing views on Gratuities

As you can imagine, the issue of police gratuities has generated a great deal of controversy. To my knowledge, just about every major police department, county sheriff's department, and state police agency in this country has a policy that forbids officers, deputies, and troopers from accepting gratuities *of any kind*. Both implicitly and explicitly, police agencies are skeptical of those giving and receiving gratuities, distrusting the motives of both parties. Justification for these policies can be found in the Law Enforcement Code of Ethics (Box 6.2, above), which explicitly prohibits officers from accepting them. Yet, almost every police officer, sheriff's deputy, and state trooper I've ever met—not to mention large-scale surveys of police officers—attest to the fact that law enforcement personnel routinely accept minor gratuities like free coffee or meals. Are *all* of these people corrupt?

If you reviewed the many writings on police gratuities, you would see there are two camps, one large and one small, but both vehement in the positions taken. On the one hand, there is a large group of academics and practitioners who argue that gratuities are antithetical to policing and therefore should *never* be accepted, period (see Withrow & Dailey, 2002). Objections from this group include (1) gratuities are inherently wrong; (2) they improperly obligate recipients to the givers; or (3) they inevitably lead recipients into corruption (see Kania, 1988).

This camp can be further subdivided into those adopting one of two positions. The larger group larger argues that gratuities form a "slippery slope" leading to the corruption of officers (Coleman, 2004a, 2004b; Ruiz & Bono, 2004a, 2004b). The logic here is that taking minor gratuities may not be a serious ethical breach by itself. However, doing so initiates a slow process wherein the recipient's integrity is gradually eroded, leading the officer to engage in more serious unethical (or even illegal) behavior, until finally the officer is corrupted (see Sherman, 1985). This line of reasoning is teleological in its orientation: acceptance of gratuities is not wrong in itself, but the possible consequences of bias, favoritism, and bribery are overwhelmingly negative. Therefore, accepting any and all gratuities should be prohibited.

The other group in the "antigratuities" camp takes a different line of reasoning that is more deontological. Here, the argument is that a gratuity is wrong because it constitutes unjustified enrichment for services that are already compensated by the public (Kania, 1988). Those taking this position argue that public employees are not entitled to anything beyond their salary for fulfilling the duties of their positions.

I will note that not all practitioners and academics (including me) oppose police officers accepting *minor* gratuities. Perhaps the best-known advocate for this view is Professor Richard Kania, whose 1988 article in *Criminal Justice Ethics* caused quite a stir. In the article, Kania (1988, p. 37) took what he called the "heretical position" that

> *the police . . . should be encouraged to accept freely offered minor gratuities and that such gratuities should be perceived as the building blocks of positive social relationships between police and the public, and not as incipient corruptors.*
>
> —(emphasis in the original)

In taking this position, Kania argued that teleological justifications for officers not accepting gratuities overemphasize the potential negative consequences (the "slippery slope" to corruption) and understate or even ignore the possible positive consequences, such as the social cohesion occurring when indebted citizens are given an opportunity to express their genuine appreciation to officers. Further, remember the degree to which hiring, academy, and field-training processes are designed to weed out the rotten apples? Given how many officers accept gratuities, opponents of gratuities seem to implicitly accept that those hurdles fail to weed out rotten apples, who then make it to the street. Kania makes the interesting observation that taking the position that any and every gratuity is corrupting creates a stigma of distrust that is then borne by a majority of police officers. Kania (1988, p. 47) continues by noting, "If a single free cup of coffee makes a public official corrupt, then nearly all police are corrupt," a claim for which there is simply no empirical evidence. Let's explore Kania's position in greater depth.

The Exchange Nature of Gratuities

For Kania (1988, 2004), gratuities can be conceptualized as an exchange between giver and recipient, and both have intentions or motivations for giving and receiving. He notes that some gratuities are given as a reward for services already rendered, as in a true gift that simply recognizes the officer's commitment to her duties and the community, or a "tip" for excellence in service rendered. Gratuities can also be given from ulterior motives (e.g., a bribe offered or an investment made). Kania argues that the perceptions of giver and recipient create a "dual scale of exchange-based relationships" of which some are certainly ethical, some are questionable, and some undeniably unethical. For too long, however, much has been made about the intent of the *giver* as being most important to figuring out the ethical quality of the exchange. Kania argues instead that it is the intent of the *recipient* that matters most and determines the ethical quality of the exchange. Further, the officer must "act in a manner that emphasizes his, not the giver's, perspective; otherwise, it is the giver's perception that will govern the exchange" (Kania, 1988, p. 44).

According to Kania (1988), when the giver and recipient have appropriately reciprocal intentions (the reason for giving and how the gratuity is received), the exchange is easily assessed. As Table 6.4 shows, when mismatches occur in perceptions, it is the perception of the recipient that is critical for categorizing the exchange as ethical. In his discussion, Kania (1988) points out that the officer must act in a manner that emphasizes the officer's, not the giver's, intentions. Otherwise, it is the giver's intention that matters. According to Kania (1988), the police officer who allows the giver to set the ethical terms of the exchange has abrogated her responsibilities. The problem is that in college courses and academy training, police officers are taught to do exactly that. Professors and academy trainers who emphasize givers' expectations determining the ethics of the exchange "deny the individual police officer control over the character of that relationship" (Kania, 1988, p. 47). Table 6.4 presents the possible combinations of intentions for giver and recipient and Kania's assessment of whether the exchange is ethical.

Before moving on, let me pose a question: If minor gratuities are acceptable, how does a police department develop a *policy* on them that does not stigmatize officers by banning all gifts, while remaining vigilant about their possible corrosive effects? Stephen Coleman (2004) tackled that very issue and, after presenting examples of acceptable gratuities, and solutions (e.g., banning officers from accepting gratuities from merchants), along with the problems created by both, reached the following conclusion:

> I would suggest that the only answer to these problems is to create a code that allows officers to exercise their own judgment about the acceptance of gratuities. Such a code would need to specify the sorts of gratuities that should be refused, and outline the sorts of situations in which they might be accepted. Since one of the major problems with the acceptance of gifts and gratuities is their hidden nature, such a code should also include a provision for the recording and audit of gifts of significant value . . . I would suggest that the best way to deal with the problem of gratuities is to provide police with guidelines in this area and then let them exercise their judgment.
>
> —(Coleman, 2004, p. 43)

Let's see how the gratuities issue stands up to scrutiny. Using the template I shared with you in Ch. 5, analyze the following scenario involving the giving and accepting of gratuities. Use a Rule Utilitarian perspective (Ch. 2) to guide your analysis.

The Moral Career of the Police Officer

If you'll recall from above, recruits experience an occupational career during which they metamorphose from "civilian" to "police officer." You will also recall that in Ch. 1, I discussed the notion of the criminal justice practitioner's moral career. Just as I did above in exploring the police recruit's occupational career, I now examine the police officer's **moral career** as described by Lawrence Sherman, who argues that it consists of

TABLE 6.4 The Exchange Nature of Police Gratuities

Category	Perception of Giver	Perception of Recipient	Ethical?
True Reward	Reward Given	Reward Received	Yes
True Gift	Gift Given	Gift Received	Yes
Ambiguous Gift	Gift Given	Gratuity Received	Yes
True Gratuity	Gratuity Given	Gratuity Received	Yes
Uncalled Debt	Gratuity Given	Understanding Reached	No
Bad Investment	Investment Made	Gratuity Received	Yes
An Understanding	Investment Made	Understanding Reached	No
A Bribe	Bribe Offered	Bribe Accepted	No + Illegal
An Arrangement	Arrangement Made	Installment Collected	No + Illegal
A Shakedown	Shakedown Paid	Bribe Extorted	No + Illegal

Source: Adapted from Kania (1988)

CASE STUDY 6.1 Police Gratuities

Officer Anne Chovee is a five-year veteran of the Eastaboga Police Department (EPD). She's recently transferred to a new precinct and has been working the afternoon shift for about 10 days. Once or twice during her shift, she stops at AA Liquor and Market, a convenience store on her beat, and picks up some fresh fruit or a smoothie. She's gotten to know the store manager, Al Pacca, who, it turns out, grew up in the same neighborhood as she did. They have even reminisced about mutual friends and childhood experiences in the neighborhood.

One day, when she stops at the market, Pacca is there and says to her, "Officer, you are welcome to anything in the store you want for free: food, drinks, even a lotto ticket!" She thanks him and grabs an apple and an energy drink before returning to her patrol duties. Several days later, Al is again at the market when she stops in. "Hey Officer Anne! How's it going today?" She responds that it's been a tough patrol—she had to respond to an accident earlier in the day that included serious injuries to multiple people. He then tells her, "I've been meaning to talk to you about a tough situation I've been experiencing. See, this group of kids keeps coming in here and is shoplifting from me. It's only small stuff, but hey, it adds up! I haven't caught any of them yet, but I know they're doing it and who they are by sight. If you would give me your cell number, I can then call you when I see them coming. You can then swing by and 'put the fear of God in them!'" She thinks about it for a moment and then tells him, "Sure. My number is 318-555-1212. Don't hesitate to call me when you see 'em coming."

Did the officer act ethically?

certain distinct experiences that can move officers from the "noble cause" of policing and the fundamental values underpinning their desire to protect person and property, to adopting behaviors contrary to departmental, legal, and greater societal standards. The moral career includes what Sherman has dubbed contingencies, moral experiences, apologia, and stages.

According to Sherman (1985), **contingencies** found in the officer's work environment produce opportunities and incentives that encourage unethical behavior. Contingencies operate at the individual, organizational, and community levels and may encourage (or discourage) unethical behavior. For example, at the individual level, an officer's lack of commitment to the values that pushed her into a career in law enforcement may "lead her into temptation." At the organizational level, both the type of work undertaken (e.g., undercover) and level of supervision associated with that work create opportunities for unethical behavior (Stephens, 2011). At the community level, the values and attitudes of people there create opportunities for unethical behavior. As the officer's values erode, the probabilities for unethical behavior increase.

Beyond contingencies, Sherman (1985) argues that police officers are faced with **moral experiences** that challenge their existing moral compasses and may result in a not-so-subtle shift in the bearing of the compass toward becoming corrupt, or what Sherman termed "becoming bent." Such moral experiences arise when, for example, an officer first witnesses other officers engaging in behavior violating department policy or legal standards (e.g., planting a weapon on a suspect) that run counter to the observer's personal ethics. In such instances, the observer must make a choice: keep silent, and in doing so condone the behavior; seek escape (e.g., request a transfer; quit their job); or confront the behavior either formally (by reporting it to superiors) or informally (by pulling the offending officer aside and letting him or her know that what they did will not be allowed to stand). A moral experience is a "moral crossroad" where one is forced to decide what the way forward will look like.

Moral experiences can also lead to unethical behavior when accompanied by what Sherman (1985) identified as **apologia**—rationalizations for the unethical or illegal behavior at hand. Apologia are situation-based and help reduce the psychological pain and sense of responsibility experienced by those engaging in behaviors incongruent with their ethical values and sense of responsibility. The classic example of apologia would be when an undercover officer steals money from the pile of cash she confiscated from a drug dealer and then uses the stolen money for some morally good end, such as paying for her son's college tuition or donating the proceeds to a local homeless shelter.

The final component is what Sherman referred to as **stages**. Here, Sherman is describing a progression from being an ethical police officer to "becoming bent." For Sherman, the process is akin to a slippery slope that begins with (relatively speaking) "benign" behavior like accepting gratuities or small bribes, progresses into rationalizing the unethical behavior, which then becomes increasingly more serious, until finally the officer no longer evidences any kind of moral compass and is willing to do just about anything: plant evidence, cover up other officers' misbehavior, lie under oath to obtain a conviction, or use excessive force against suspects. Table 6.5 presents the components of a police officer's moral career and brief descriptions of each.

TABLE 6.5 The Police Officer's Moral Career

Component	Description
Contingencies	Individual, organizational, and community-based forces that encourage or discourage ethical behavior by police officers
Moral Experience	Encounters with unethical behavior by colleagues that force the officer to accept the behavior, escape from it, or reject the behavior
Apologia	Situational-specific rationalizations for unethical (or illegal) behavior
Stages	The "slippery slope" involving an officer's descent into corruption

Source: Adapted from Sherman (1985)

THE ORGANIZATIONAL ENVIRONMENT OF POLICING

I have made the point that police agencies, in general, are examples of quasi-military-oriented bureaucracies, replete with a strong rank structure and clear lines of authority, varying degrees of specialization, secrecy, and a top-down communication process (orders flow from the chief to the line officers on the street). I have also suggested that this type of organizational environment has implications for the ethics of police officers; that is, the organizational environment of police departments affects the ethics of officers working there.

To illustrate, let's return to the immediate aftermath of Frank Serpico's uncovering of corruption in the NYPD. In its final report, the Knapp Commission recommended that certain changes occur in the recruitment and training of new officers, in supervision, and in internal control mechanisms for dealing with rule violations (Knapp, 1972). These solutions all related to changing the organizational environment or climate of the NYPD, rather than focusing on the individual officers who were corrupt. Similar recommendations have been suggested by other commissions investigating problems in departments in such cities as Los Angeles and Philadelphia (Christopher Commission, 1991; Pennsylvania Crime Commission, 1974). Let's consider how and why the organizational environments of police departments affect the ethics of their officers.

Factors Affecting the Organizational Environment of Police Departments

Research suggests that organizations perceived as unjust and unfair by employees are more likely to experience employee deviance (Wolfe & Piquero, 2011). Taking this cue, some police scholars have focused their attention on how organizational factors play a role in creating opportunities for police deviance of all forms. The assumption by these scholars is that ethical policing isn't solely a product of the moral fabric of individuals ("proper" values) but is rather a function of the moral fabric of the organization. In other words, if the climate of the organization is one that ignores violations of rules, inspires distrust of administrators, tolerates mistreatment of citizens by police, perpetuates the "blue wall of silence," etc., the department's moral fabric has been shredded and creates an ethical climate for officers that is also shredded. In this section, I recognize considerations that scholars have identified as influencing the organizational climate of police departments and, by extension, the ethical climate of the agency.

The Presence of Rules

As Ivković (2005) suggests, one consequence of police departments embracing a paramilitary orientation is that such organizations create many rules to control line (patrol) officers' behavior, particularly with respect to their use of force and, more specifically, use of deadly force. Just as an army creates "rules of engagement" for its soldiers (see French, 2015), so too do police agencies, through their policies and procedures (i.e., rules) that address (among other items) officer appearance, training, and behavior (Bittner, 1983).

The problem is this: because there are so many rules and despite their best efforts, many police officers unavoidably break some of them (e.g., accepting minor gratuities). The implication is that because officers—including supervisors—have themselves broken the rules, they may be reluctant to report (or sanction, in the case of supervisors) others' rule-breaking behavior. If allowed to flourish, this situation can result in uneven disciplining of rules violations and create an organizational climate accepting of officer deviance (Lim & Sloan, 2016).

The Police Chief

Beginning with the seminal work of James Q. Wilson (1968), research consistently shows it is the chief of police who creates (and ultimately enforces) the "rules of the road" for officers (Bureau of Justice Assistance, 2008). Through their leadership and management style, chiefs influence recruitment and training standards; the ethical climate of the department; accountability of, and standards for, supervisors; internal control mechanisms; discipline; and rewards (Ivković, 2005). The key is not only the chief's message and its sincerity, but also whether and how the chief "leads by example" (Murgado, 2011).

As Ivković (2005) described it, message sincerity depends on, among other things, the kind of behavior to which the chief reacts, to whom the chief's reaction extends, the intensity of the chief's response, and the severity of the reaction. Additionally, a chief who denies there's a problem in a department rife with them quickly undermines the trust of line personnel, who then question the honesty of the leadership, and distrust or even dismiss it as corrupt, incompetent, or unable to control officers' behavior. Further, the chief's actions are very important for addressing unethical or illegal behavior occurring in the agency (Pennsylvania Crime Commission, 1974). For instance, if the chief openly disparages gratuities, but is seen accepting a free meal at a high-end restaurant, the chief's credibility will almost immediately be destroyed (Rosoff, Pontell & Tillman, 1998).

If the chief fails to act against unethical behavior, he or she risks having minimum impact on the department's ethical climate and officer behavior. In such instances it is likely the chief failed to expand internal affairs personnel or assigned a high priority to the problem for investigators. The chief likely failed to create adequate mechanisms of supervision or enforced the accountability and responsibility of first-line supervisors. Vague or inconsistent agency rules were not rewritten, and streamlining or simplifying complaint processes failed to occur. The chief likely failed to develop performance measures designed to disrupt the "blue wall of silence." Finally, it was likely the chief failed to change personnel files so that they included both disciplinary records as well as honors and rewards (Ivković, 2005).

Supervisors

First-line supervisors—sergeants and corporals—are among the most important intermediaries in patrol officers' work environments (Sun, 2002). Yet, research has shown that relations between supervisors and their charges are poor. Surveys repeatedly show that first-line supervisors are perceived by patrol officers as disciplinarians doling out punishments erratically and unfairly and being "rules obsessed" while knowing full well that patrol officers' absolute adherence to the rules all the time is well-nigh impossible (Bittner, 1983; Kappeler, Sluder, & Alpert, 1999). The reality is that sergeants and corporals represent the closest supervisory authority in the agency and with whom patrol officers have the most frequent contact (Ivković, 2005).

Sergeants and corporals shape not only line officers' perceptions about, but also the agency's stance toward, unethical or illegal behavior, including the consequences line officers face for engaging in problematic behavior. Thus, first-line supervisors likely play a key role in both preventing and responding to problematic behavior of line officers

(Weisburd & Greenspan, 2000). Supervisors' actions alert line officers to what will and will not be tolerated and to discrepancies that may exist between "official" agency policy about specific behaviors (e.g., accepting gratuities) and the response to those behaviors (Mollen Commission, 1994). If first-line supervisors are more interested in whether their charges are being discreet with their unethical or illegal behavior than with whether line officers are honest and ethical, we can expect bad behavior to flourish (Ivković, 2005).

Department Resources

As public agencies, police departments receive funding from municipal governments. In theory, the funds are then budgeted to cover operating and other costs associated with the department. Although the municipality provides funds to the department, it is primarily the chief of police and his or her executive-level staff that determine how the funds are distributed within the agency. Importantly, decisions relating to resource allocation have implications for the organizational environment of police agencies and, by extension, the ethical climate of the agency.

As Ivković (2005) explains, cutting resources for recruitment, selection, and training may cause staff to cut corners by conducting less thorough background checks (which has implications for the quality of the pool of applicants), reducing incentives for FTO-related programs (which can affect their quality), or curtailing certain aspects of academy training. Resource allocation also has implications for first-line supervisors' ability to oversee patrol personnel. Pulling resources from this area may result in understaffing, lack of training for supervisors, and other problems. The result can be that even the most steadfastly honest sergeants and corporals face difficulties controlling the misconduct of their underlings.

Recruitment and Selection

There is strong evidence that police agencies with histories of problems like corruption, illegal/improper use of force, and racial animus toward the community being served continually fail in the recruitment and selection process of new officers (Sherman, 1980). The result: these agencies recruit and hire a greater share of prospects with problematic backgrounds, including adult or juvenile felony convictions, past membership in juvenile gangs, serious abuse of drugs, and erratic records of employment (Ivković, 2005). When personnel are overworked, understaffed, and pressured to lower hiring standards; to hire based on political connections; to hire to satisfy community pressure for additional police officers, or adjust hiring criteria, changes occur in the screening process such that those who make it through have questionable prospects for remaining honest. Finally, problematic departments also have a history of dragging their feet in completing background checks of applicants, which may allow prospects to enter and complete academy training or even become sworn officers without being properly vetted (Ivković, 2005; Mollen Commission, 1994).

Ethics and Integrity Training

Because police organizations can use training in ethics and integrity to identify dilemmas officers will confront, stress the importance of officer integrity, and clarify for both new and veteran officers the kind of behavior that won't be tolerated, agencies providing inadequate training in ethics and integrity can expect to have problems, all things being equal (Klockars, et al., 2000, 2004). By stressing "rotten apples theory," providing narrow and overly legalistic training content of questionable quality and short duration in the academy and failing to connect content with "real-life" experiences of officers, agencies can negatively impact officers' views of the administration, reveal a lack of commitment to ethics and integrity, enhance new officers' tendency to bow to peer pressure, and facilitate acceptance of the "blue wall of silence" (Ivković, 2005). By not providing officers legitimate training in ethics and integrity, not only in the academy but via in-service programs, the agency risks fostering an organizational culture that both facilitates and condones unethical and/or illegal behavior.

Internal Control Mechanisms

A consistent theme in the literature on police misconduct is this: unethical and illegal police conduct is helped when formal, **internal control mechanisms** break down (Ivković, 2005). In other words, the police fail to police themselves (Rentz, 2016).

Most police agencies have a formal internal control mechanism that consists of a way of submitting and receiving complaints (from both within and outside the organization), some kind of investigatory procedure (usually Internal Affairs), and a decision-making process (e.g., a board of inquiry). An agency characterized by widespread unethical or illegal behavior will usually also have experienced a breakdown of the formal internal control mechanism. Additionally, agencies that fail to create reward structures for those within the department willing to come forward and report rules' violations are also likely to experience problems. By not encouraging officers to come forward and not rewarding those who do, the agency is implicitly condoning unethical behavior.

Hopefully, you now understand that an organization has an ethical "climate" that can be significantly influenced by multiple factors. If a police department is experiencing unethical or illegal behavior by officers, looking beyond "rotten apples" and instead toward the structure and culture of the organization is a good strategy. By paying attention to such matters as the paramilitary orientation of police departments, the management style of the police chief, resource allocations, etc., one can identify not only the state of the organization's moral fabric but also understand how the ethical climate of a department is tied to the behavior of its officers.

SUMMARY

In this chapter, I presented you with a contextual analysis of police ethics that focused on individuals, organizations, and communities using the analogies of "rotten apples," "rotten barrels," and "rotten orchards." When discussing unethical or illegal behavior of police officers, we are easily seduced by the notion that such officers are a few "rotten apples" who violated the public's trust. The obvious solution is to then "purge" these apples from the proverbial barrel. However, as I tried to show, this notion is wrong-headed because it ignores other considerations that go beyond individuals, but that are crucial to understanding police ethics.

I then examined the processes of recruiting, selecting, and training new officers and emphasized that these processes assume that "rotten apples" can be identified and eliminated, but tend to maintain the status quo, at least in terms of the values and attitudes of officers, and thus discriminate against otherwise qualified prospects because they don't possess the "proper" values. I ended this discussion by noting that police recruits experience an occupational career, during which the individual moves from seeing him- or herself as a "civilian" to developing a new identity, that of police officer.

I then turned to the cultural context of police ethics by describing "the" police culture, including the content of its values, and questions that have been raised recently about whether "the" police culture exists as it once did. I also included an ethical issue associated with the culture of policing, namely, whether officers should be allowed to accept gratuities. Here, I presented arguments both for and against allowing officers to do so, and devoted particular attention to the arguments of Richard Kania in favor of allowing officers to do so. I ended the discussion by describing the moral career of police officers, suggesting that unethical and illegal behavior by police officers is part of a long-term process of becoming "bent."

The concluding section of the chapter examined the organizational context of police ethics. Here, I emphasized that police agencies have an organizational culture that sets the ethical "tone" for the department. If a specific agency is rife with unethical and illegal behavior, it has a deviant climate that facilitates inappropriate behavior. I also noted the several factors that help shape organizational environments, including rules, the police chief and supervisors, resources, recruitment, hiring and training standards, ethics and integrity training, and internal control mechanisms.

Before moving on to discuss ethical issues arising from the tactics used by the police, let's end this chapter by examining Thought Exercise 6.1, which concerns pre-employment psychological evaluations (PPEs) of recruits and ethical issues associated with their use.

THOUGHT EXERCISE 6.1

THE ETHICS OF PREEMPLOYMENT PSYCHOLOGICAL EVALUATIONS (PPEs)

As part of the hiring process, most police departments (more than 90%, by some estimates) require prospects to undergo psychological assessment, known as preemployment psychological evaluation (PPE). The ostensible purpose of this evaluation is to ascertain that a candidate is "free from any emotional or mental condition that might adversely affect the performance of safety-based duties and responsibilities and be capable of withstanding the psychological demands inherent in the prospective position" (International Association of Chiefs of Police, 2015, p .1). In combination with other prehiring requirements, PPE is intended to predict the risk posed by the candidate of, in the words of Lawrence Sherman, "becoming bent'" (Sherman, 1985). Makes sense, yes? At first glance, perhaps. But let's drill down a bit and see what the PPE involves and explore some ethical issues surrounding the PPE.

What PPE Involves and How It Works

As described by Timothy Roufa (2017), the PPE involves a battery of tests involving several components that can last over many hours. The PPE begins with a pretest self-interview that asks about the candidate's background and why he or she is interested in a career in law enforcement. A series of multiple-choice tests or surveys follow, designed to identify the presence of various personality traits, discovered using a tool like the Minnesota Multiphasic Personality Inventory (MMPI). Those traits include: impulse control, judgment, honesty, integrity, (lack of) personal bias, dependability, ability to deal with supervision, attitudes toward sexuality, and prior drug use. According to Roufa, (2017, p. 1), "These particular traits represent those that have been determined over time to be critical areas to explore when evaluating candidates of jobs in policing." Finally, there will usually be a sit-down interview with the clinical psychologist conducting the PPE.

Those conducting the PPE are required to follow the standards and "best practices" for such screenings as articulated by professional associations like the American Psychological Association (APA). These practitioners—licensed clinical psychologists (LCPs)—must also "be consistent in the methodologies and judgments they use in their assessment" (Steiner, 2017, p.1). What this means is that the LCP

> . . . has specific training and experience conducting pre-employment psychological evaluations as well as an understanding of general police psychology. The psychologist should be able to identify, describe and quantify police and public safety job responsibilities and potential stress of the public safety position.
>
> —(Steiner, 2017, p. 1)

According to some, the PPE serves as one more way to screen out candidates who may demonstrate unacceptable or undesirable personality traits. In conjunction with other information, the totality of the results of the PPE help the psychologist render a final opinion about the applicant's suitability in terms of their risk for engaging in unacceptable behavior (Roufa, 2017). That determination is expressed as a low, medium, or high risk.

Ethical Issues and the PPE

There are several ethical issues that arise from PPEs used by police departments in their hiring decisions. The issues I believe are particularly important relate to informed consent by the candidates and limitations on the evaluations, and normative standards for psychological testing.

INFORMED CONSENT AND LIMITATIONS ON THE EVALUATION. When one is being screened for employment purposes, it is imperative that the candidate understand, a priori, what's going to occur. Steiner (2017) argues that before the PPE begins, the candidate must understand the objectives of the evaluation, who will receive the results (not the applicant), limits on the confidentiality of the results (which 3rd parties might have access to the evaluation), and that the client is the *agency*, not the individual *applicant*. To ensure this occurs, the applicant should sign a form indicating that this information has been shared with him or her and that the candidate understands what's going to happen. Once the evaluation is completed, a written report should then be given to the hiring agency but not to the applicant. The LCP should avoid using clinical or psychiatric diagnosis or labeling unless relevant to the LCP's conclusions or where allowed by law. The LCP cannot include the use of genetic information such as family history when making employment decisions due to the *Genetic Information Nondiscrimination Act of 2008*. For example, a candidate cannot be excluded from consideration because of a family history of chronic diseases or mental illness.

NORMED STANDARDS FOR PSYCHOLOGICAL TESTING. To enhance the diversity of an agency, a police department might be willing to "make allowances" for members of protected groups based on such considerations as race, national origin, religion, sex, etc. However, doing so would likely be unethical and almost certainly illegal. As described by Steiner (2017), when conducting a PPE, neither the LCP nor the agency can use different norms or cut-off scores for protected persons. The *Civil Rights Act of 1991* reads in part:

> It shall be an unlawful employment practice for a respondent, in connection with the selection or referral of applicants or candidates for employment or promotion, to adjust the scores of, use different cutoff scores for, or otherwise alter the results of, employment related tests on the basis of race, color, religion, sex, or national origin.

The PPE report should focus on the applicant's ability to perform the essential job functions and position within police and public safety safely and effectively.

What all this means is that the PPE is a serious undertaking that should follow strict standards and ethical rules that govern clinical assessment for purposes of employment screening. Ensuring that candidates understand the mechanics of the process is crucial, as well as the fact the examiner works for the agency and will not be sharing the results of the assessment with the candidate.

KEY TERMS

Rotten apples theory 146
Rotten barrels theory 147
Rotten orchards theory 147
Noble cause 149
Value-neutral perspective 150
Values-predisposition perspective 150
Recruiting to the status quo 151
Preemployment psychological evaluation (PPE) 151
Field Training Officer (FTO) 154
Occupational career 157
Choice 157
Introduction 157
Encounter 158
Metamorphosis 158
Police culture 159
Police gratuity 161
Moral career 163
Contingencies 164
Moral experiences 165
Apologia 165
Stages 165
Internal control mechanisms 169

DISCUSSION QUESTIONS

1. It appears that prospective candidates seeking employment in police agencies must possess the "proper" values to get hired. Given the values associated with the police culture, are the "proper" values a potential roadblock to ensuring that police officers act ethically?
2. Why are we so hasty to identify "rotten apples" as the reason for police officer mis- or malfeasance and assume that getting rid of them solves the problem? Can you find examples outside of policing where "rotten apples" has been used to explain away unethical or illegal behavior?
3. Pick any one of the procedures commonly used in police hiring and subject it to an ethical analysis using the template I shared with you in Ch. 5. What did you conclude?
4. Critique FTO programs. What are their pros and cons? Perhaps, more importantly, can they be justified on *ethical* grounds?
5. Where do *you* stand when it comes to whether the police should be allowed to accept minor gratuities? Justify your position using any one of the various systems of ethics previously discussed.

RESOURCES

Michael Caldero and John Crank's ***Police Ethics: Corruption of Noble Cause*** provides great insight into why people get into policing, about the police culture and police agencies, and how laws and ethical standards get manipulated by many officers in the name of the "noble cause." I strongly recommend this book for anyone thinking about becoming a police officer.

James Q. Wilson's ***Varieties of Police Behavior***, while some 50 years old, contains important insights into how police chiefs and the communities being served affect the "style" of policing adopted by municipal law enforcement agencies. Truly a classic.

Edwin DeLattre's ***Character and Cops*** (first published in 1989 and now in its sixth edition) is another classic read in police ethics. The book illuminates literally hundreds of moral problems regularly faced by police officers and their supervisors and agency administrators and argues that without individuals of good character and institutions that apply high ideals to daily practice, liberty, public order, and justice cannot be achieved.

REFERENCES

Bayley, D., & Bittner, E. (1984). Learning the skills of policing. *Law and Contemporary Problems, 47,* 35–59.

Bittner, E. (1983). Legality and workmanship: Introduction to control in the police organization. In M. Punch (Ed.), *Control in the police organization* (pp. 1–11). Cambridge, MA: MIT Press.

Blumberg, N. (2016, June 20). Whistleblower cop on ending police 'code of silence.' *Chicago Tonight*. Retrieved from http://chicagotonight.wttw.com/2016/06/20/whistleblower-cop-ending-police-code-silence

Buerger, M. (1998). Police training as a Pentecost: Using tools singularly ill-suited to the purpose of reform. *Police Quarterly, 1,* 27–63.

Bureau of Justice Assistance (2008). Police chiefs desk reference: A guide for newly appointed police leaders (2nd ed.). Boston: McGraw-Hill.

Bureau of Justice Statistics (2017). Federal law enforcement. Retrieved from https://www.bjs.gov/index.cfm?ty=tp&tid=74

Caldero, M., & Crank, J. (2015). *Police ethics: The corruption of noble cause* (Rev. 3rd ed.). New York, NY: Routledge.

California POST Commission (2017). Regular basic course training specifications. Retrieved from https://www.post.ca.gov/regular-basic-course-training-specifications.aspx

Chang, C., & Tchekmedyian, A. (2016, May 3). Racial slurs by law enforcement are a legacy that's becoming more unacceptable. *Los Angeles Times*. Retrieved from http://www.latimes.com/local/california/la-me-sheriff-police-emails-20160503-story.html

Christopher Commission (1991). *Report of the independent commission on the Los Angeles Police Department*. Los Angeles, CA: Christopher Commission.

Citizens Budget Commission (2015). Facts about the NYPD. Retrieved from https://cbcny.org/research/facts-about-nypd

City of Phoenix (2017). Oath of office. Retrieved from https://www.phoenix.gov/police/neighborhood-resources/oath-of-office

Coleman, S. (2004a). When police should say "no!" to gratuities. *Criminal Justice Ethics, 23,* 33–44.

Coleman, S. (2004b). Police, gratuities, and professionalism: A response to Kania. *Criminal Justice Ethics, 23,* 63–65.

Crank, J. (2004). *Understanding police culture* (2nd ed.). Cincinnati, OH: Anderson.

Crank, J., Flaherty, D., & Giacomazzi, A. (2007). Noble cause: An empirical analysis. *Journal of Criminal Justice, 35,* 1–26.

Ellwanger, S. (2015). How police officers learn ethics. In M. Braswell, B. McCarthy, & B. McCarthy (Eds.), *Justice, crime, and ethics* (8th ed.) (pp. 47–71). Boston, MA: Elsevier.

Farkas, M., & Manning, P. (1997). The occupational culture of corrections and police officers. *Journal of Crime and Justice, 20,* 51–68.

Ford, R. (2003). Saying one thing, meaning another: The role of parables in police training. *Police Quarterly, 6,* 84–110.

French, D. (2015, December 21). How our overly restrictive rules of engagement keep us from winning wars. *National Review*. Retrieved from http://www.nationalreview.com/article/428756/rules-engagement-need-reform

Fyfe, J., & Kane, R. (2005). Bad cops: A study of career-ending misconduct among New York City police officers. Retrieved from ncjrs.gov/pdffiles1/nij/grants/215795.pdf

Guyot, D. (1979). Bending granite: Attempts to change the rank structure of American police departments. *Journal of Police Science and Administration, 7,* 253–284.

Ivković, S. (2005). *Fallen blue knights: Controlling police corruption*. New York, NY: Oxford.

International Association of Chiefs of Police (n.d.). Oath of honor. Retrieved from http://www.theiacp.org/oathofhonor

International Association of Chiefs of Police (2017). Code of ethics. Retrieved from http://www.theiacp.org/codeofethics

International Association of Chiefs of Police (2014). *Pre-employment psychological evaluation guidelines*. Retrieved from http://www.theiacp.org/portals/0/documents/pdfs/psych-preemploymentpsycheval.pdf

Kania, R. (2004). The ethical acceptability of gratuities: Still saying "yes" after all these years. *Criminal Justice Ethics, 23,* 54–63.

Kania, R. (1988). Should we tell the police to say "yes" to gratuities? *Criminal Justice Ethics, 7*, 37–49.

Kappeler V., & Gaines, L. (2009). *Community policing: A contemporary perspective* (5th ed.), New Providence, NJ: Matthew Bender.

Kappeler, V., Sluder, R., & Alpert, G. (1999). Breeding deviant conformity: Police ideology and culture. In V. Kappeler (Ed.), *The police and society* (2nd ed.) (pp. 238–264). Prospect Heights, IL: Waveland Press.

Klinger, D. (1997). Negotiating order in patrol work: An ecological theory of police response to deviance. *Criminology, 35*, 277–306.

Klockars, C., Ivković, S., & Haberfeld, M. (2004). The contours of police integrity. In C. Klockars, S. Ivković & M. Haberfeld (Eds.), *The contours of police integrity* (pp. 1–18). Thousand Oaks, CA: Sage.

Klockars, C., Ivković, S., Harver, W., & Haberfeld, M. (2000). *The measurement of police integrity.* NIJ Research in Brief (Document No. NCJ 181465). Washington, DC: U.S. Department of Justice.

Knapp, W. (1972). *The Knapp Commission report on police corruption*. New York, NY: G. Braziller.

Lim, H., & Sloan, J. (2016). Police officer integrity: A partial replication and extension. *Policing: An International Journal of Police Strategies & Management, 39*, 284–301.

Lum, C. (2010). Does the "race of places" influence police officer decision making? Retrieved from https://www.ncjrs.gov/pdffiles1/nij/grants/231931.pdf

Maas, P. (1973). *Serpico.* New York, NY: HarperCollins.

Manning, P. (1995). The police occupational culture in Anglo-American societies. In W. Bailey, (Ed.), *The encyclopedia of police science* (pp. 472–475). New York, NY: Garland Publishing.

Manning, P. (1994). Dynamics and tensions in police occupational culture. Unpublished manuscript, Michigan State University, East Lansing, MI.

Marion, N. (1998). Police academy training: Are we teaching recruits what they need to know? *Policing: An International Journal of Police Strategies & Management, 21*, 54–79.

Marshall Project (2017). Blue wall of silence. Retrieved from https://www.themarshallproject.org/records/605-blue-wall-of-silence#.YOA77jJc8

Morabito, M. (2007). Horizons of context: Understanding the police decision to arrest people with mental illness. *Psychiatric Services, 58*, 1582–1587.

Mollen Commission (1994). *Commission report.* New York, NY: Mollen Commission.

Murgado, A. (2011, November 18). Leading by example. *Police.* Retrieved from http://www.policemag.com/channel/patrol/articles/2011/11/leading-by-example.aspx

Muschler, V. (2016, November 11). Outcomes assessment: Southwestern Illinois College. Retrieved from http://www.swic.edu/sw-content.aspx?id=3663

O'Neill, M., Marks, M., & Singh, A. (Eds.) (2007). *Police occupational culture: New debates and directions.* Amsterdam, The Netherlands: Elsevier.

Paoline, E. (2003). Taking stock: Toward a richer understanding of police culture. *Journal of Criminal Justice, 31*, 199–214.

Paoline, E. (2014). Police culture. In G. Bruinsma & D. Weisburd. (Eds.), *Encyclopedia of criminology and criminal justice* (pp. 3577–3586). Berlin, Germany: Springer.

Pennsylvania Crime Commission (1974). *Report on police corruption and the quality of law enforcement in Philadelphia.* Saint David's, PA: Pennsylvania Crime Commission.

Petrocelli, J. (2006). Free cup of coffee? Retrieved from http://www.officer.com/article/10250436/free-cup-of-coffee

Potter, G. (2013). The history of policing in the United States—Part 5. Retrieved from http://plsonline.eku.edu/insidelook/history-policing-united-states-part-5

Prenzler, T., & Mackay, P. (1995). Police gratuities: What the public think. *Criminal Justice Ethics, 14*, 15–25.

President's Task Force on 21st Century Policing (2015). *Final report of the President's Task Force on 21st Century Policing.* Washington, DC: Office of Community Oriented Policing Services.

Reaves, B. (2012). Federal law enforcement officers, 2008. Retrieved from https://www.bjs.gov/content/pub/pdf/fleo08.pdf

Reaves, B. (2011). Census of state and local law enforcement agencies, 2008. Retrieved from https://www.bjs.gov/content/pub/pdf/csllea08.pdf

Rentz, R. (2016, August 10). Baltimore Police fail to police themselves, Justice Department finds. *The Baltimore Sun*. Retrieved from http://www.baltimoresun.com/news/maryland/baltimore-city/doj-report/bs-md-doj-accountability-20160810-story.html

Roberg, R., Crank, J., & Kuykendall, J. (2000). *Police in society* (2nd ed.). Prospect Heights, IL: Waveland Press.

Rokeach, M., Miller, M. & Snyder, J. (1971). The value gap between police and policed. *Journal of Social Issues, 27*, 155–171.

Rosoff, S., Pontell, H., & Tillman, R. (1998). *Profit without honor: White-collar crime and the looting of America*. Upper Saddle, NJ: Prentice Hall.

Roufa, T. (2017, June 4). Psychological tests and screening for police officers. *The Balance*. Retrieved from https://www.thebalance.com/psychological-exams-and-screening-for-police-officers-974785

Ruiz, J., & Bono, C. (2004a). At what price a "freebie"? The real cost of police gratuities. *Criminal Justice Ethics, 23*, 44–54.

Ruiz, J., & Bono, C. (2004b). Blinded by the lights and seduced by the sirens' song. *Criminal Justice Ethics, 23*, 65–67.

Sanders, B. (2008). Using personality traits to predict police officer performance. *Policing: An International Journal of Police Strategies & Management, 31*, 129–147.

Schein, E. (1991). What is culture? In P. Frost, L. Moore, M. Louis, C. Lundberg, & J. Martin, (Eds.), *Reframing organizational culture* (pp. 243–253). London, UK: Sage Publications.

Scrivner, E. (2006). *Innovations in police recruitment and hiring: Hiring in the spirit of service.* Washington, D.C.: U.S. Department of Justice, Office of Community Oriented Policing Services. Retrieved from https://ric-zai-inc.com/Publications/cops-p090-pub.pdf

Sherman, L. (1980). Three models of organizational corruption in agencies of social control. *Social Problems, 27*, 478–491.

Sherman, L. (1985). Becoming bent: The moral careers of corrupt policemen. In F. Elliston & M. Feldberg (Eds.), *Moral issues in police work* (pp. 253–273). Totowa, NJ: Rowman & Allanheld.

Sigler, R., & Dees, T. (1988). Public perception of petty corruption in law enforcement. *Journal of Police Science and Administration, 16*, 14–20.

Steiner, C. (2017, January 24). Ethics for psychologists: Pre-Employment Evaluations for police and public safety. *The National Psychologist*. Retrieved from http://nationalpsychologist.com/2017/01/ethics-for-psychologists-pre-employment-evaluations-for-police-and-public-safety/103601.html

Stephens, D. (2011). *Police discipline: A case for change*. Washington, DC: U.S. Department of Justice. Retrieved from https://www.ncjrs.gov/pdffiles1/nij/234052.pdf

Sun, I. (2002). Police officer attitudes toward peers, supervisors, and civilians: A comparison Between Field Training Officers and regular officers. *American Journal of Criminal Justice*, 27, 69–83.

Surette, R. (2015). *Media, crime and criminal justice: Images, realities and policies*. Stamford, CT: Cengage Learning.

Sycz, D. (2014). *Defining the ideal applicant: Examining patrol officer perspectives on police organizational recruitment standards* (Unpublished master's thesis). University of Waterloo, Waterloo, Canada.

United States Army Recruiting Command (2003). Former N.W. Ayer copywriter receives Army medal for "Be All That You Can Be." Retrieved from http://earlcarterawards.com/armypressrelease.pdf

United States Department of Justice (2015). *Diversity in law enforcement: A literature review.*Washington, DC: United States Department of Justice, Civil Rights Division. Retrieved from https://cops.usdoj.gov/pdf/taskforce/Diversity_in_Law_Enforcement_Literature_Review.pdf

Van Maanen, J. (1973). Observations on the making of policemen. *Human Organization, 32*, 407–418.

Van Maanen, J. (1974). Working the street: A developmental view of police behavior. In H. Jacob (Ed.), *The potential for reform of criminal justice* (pp. 83–130). Beverly Hills, CA: Sage Publications.

Weisburd, D., & Greenspan, R. (2000). *Police attitudes toward abuse of authority: Findings from a national survey.* Washington, DC: National Institute of Justice.

Westley, W. (1970). *Violence and the police: A sociological study of law, custom, and morality.* Cambridge, MA: MIT Press.

Westmarland, L. (2005). Police ethics and integrity: Breaking the Blue Code of Silence. *Policing and Society, 15,* 145–165.

Wilson, J. (1968). *Varieties of police behavior.* Cambridge, MA: Harvard University Press.

Wilson, J., Dalton, E., Scheer, C., & Grammich, C. (2010). *Police recruitment and retention for the new millennium: The state of knowledge.* Santa Monica, CA: RAND Corporation. Retrieved from https://www.rand.org/pubs/monographs/MG959.html

Withrow, B., & Dailey, J. (2004). When strings are attached: Understanding the role of gratuities in police corruptibility. In Q. Thurman & J. Zhao (Eds.), *Contemporary policing: Controversies, challenges, and solutions* (pp. 324–346). Los Angeles, CA: Roxbury.

Wolfe, S., & Piquero A. (2011). Organizational justice and police misconduct. *Criminal Justice and Behavior, 38,* 332–353.

CHAPTER 7

Ethics and the Tactics of Policing

Chapter Outline

CHAPTER LEARNING OBJECTIVES:

1. Identify the dimensions of police work and how various police tactics fit into them.
2. Describe how police use deception during investigations, in interrogations, and in courtroom proceedings, and provide examples.
3. Explain the legal limits imposed on police use of deception.
4. Contrast the subjective and objective tests for entrapment.
5. Discuss how the Reid technique creates psychological pressure on those being interrogated.
6. Discuss why people confess to crimes they have not committed.
7. Explain why police perjury occurs and the factors contributing to its perpetuation.
8. Explain how the ethics of police deception can be assessed.
9. Distinguish between explicit and implicit bias.
10. Distinguish profiling from racial profiling.
11. Describe how the ethics of police surveillance can be assessed.

INTRODUCTION

A crucial function of the police is to enforce the law, usually taken to mean "fight crime." To do this, the police use different tactics, some of which involve deception (e.g., undercover operations; "stings"), while others involve surveillance, either active or passive, of people and places. Consider the following examples:

Case #1: On July 15, 2015, motorists on a busy stretch of highway in the City of San Bernardino (CA) noticed people, apparently homeless, standing at different intersections holding up signs. Unlike the usual signs seeking work or a handout, these signs said:

In the space of just two hours that day, officers stopped 54 vehicles and issued 39 citations for distracted driving (CBS News, 2015)

Case #2: On December 1, 2008, on Worcester, MA, police had 16-year-old Nga Truong in an interrogation room. Her 13-month-old son, Khyle, had died the day before. "Now you said to me earlier you were going to tell the truth," a detective says from across one side of the table to the girl on the other side. "I'm waiting." "I did," she pleads. The detective is convinced Troung killed her son, but Truong continually denies it. After two hours of questioning, during which interrogators claimed they knew the truth about what happened; used the death of Truong's brother of sudden infant death syndrome (SIDS) years earlier as evidence she'd killed a baby before; and claimed the results of Khyle's autopsy showed the child had been smothered (in fact, there was no such evidence), detectives walked away with her confession, leading her to be charged with murder as an adult (Gavett, 2011).

Case #3: By analyzing data from all traffic stops in Raleigh, NC, between January 2009 and December 2014 obtained via a public records request filed with the state, Stanford University statisticians uncovered evidence of discrimination in police stops and searches of black and Hispanic drivers. These findings emerged after controlling for a variety of factors based on results obtained from three different advanced-level statistical analyses (Simoiu, Corbett-Davies &, Goel, 2017).

Case #4: Police in Baltimore and other cities have used a phone tracker, known as a "stingray," to locate the perpetrators of routine street crimes and frequently concealed that fact from suspects, their lawyers, and even judges. In the process they quietly transformed a type of surveillance billed as a tool to hunt terrorists and kidnappers into a staple of everyday policing (Heath, 2015).

The first two cases illustrate police using deception to uncover law violations and obtain a confession from someone charged with a crime. Cases #3 and #4 illustrate police use of passive and active surveillance to detect law breaking. Police tactics like deception and surveillance raise significant ethical issues and are the focus of this chapter.

This chapter concludes the discussion of police ethics that began in Ch. 6. It is divided into several sections, beginning with a review of the tactics of modern police work that includes a typology of that work originally developed by the American sociologist Gary Marx. In this typology, Marx argues that police work fits into two dimensions, defined by (1) the nature of the work—deceptive or nondeceptive; and (2) the nature of the operation—overt or covert. Marx's typology organizes the remainder of the discussion that follows around combinations of the dimensions from the typology: deception by police during investigation, interrogation, and in court; and police surveillance, both overt and covert. I then shift my focus and examine the teaching and learning of police ethics. I conclude the chapter by presenting to you a Thought Exercise examining the ethical issues associated with an emerging tactic in law enforcement known as "predictive policing."

MODERN POLICE WORK

Recall that the noble cause of policing involves a commitment by officers to "getting bad guys off the streets" (Caldero & Crank, 2015). To achieve that goal, the police use various tactics, including deception and surveillance. These have raised questions over not only their legality and effectiveness, but also whether such tactics are ethical. Before getting into specific examples of these tactics, let's first consider some dimensions of police work and where certain tactics they use will fit.

A Typology of Police Work

Police use various tactics as part of their law enforcement function. One way to examine these tactics is to identify commonalities found across them. This can be done by developing a **typology** of police work that groups together disparate things or activities based on shared characteristics. Gary Marx (1988) developed just such a typology of police work that classified officers' work along two dimensions: (1) whether the nature of the work is deceptive or nondeceptive; and (2) whether the nature of the operation at hand is overt or covert. This results in four combinations, as shown in Figure 7.1.

Turing to the figure, cell "a" involves police work that is nondeceptive and overt. An example of this would be traditional, uniformed, random, preventive patrol, where officers randomly appear at a specific location within a specific geographic area (a "beat" or

Nature of the work		Nature of the operation	
		Overt	Covert
	Non-deceptive	Uniformed random patrol (a)	Passive surveillance (c)
	Deceptive	Trickery by known officers (b)	Undercover operations (d)

FIGURE 7.1 A Typology of Police Work
Source: Adapted from Marx (1988)

"sector") during a 24-hour period and rapidly respond to 911 calls (Center for Evidence-Based Crime Policy, 2013). An example of work that is both deceptive and overt (cell "b") would be a police interrogator telling an arrestee who denies involvement in the crime at hand that "there is overwhelming evidence" against her (which is not true), that by cooperating with police "things will go better for her" (also not true), and that she "should just confess"—denying involvement in the crime is futile. An example of nondeceptive and covert work (cell "c") would be police installing at a busy intersection a high-speed camera capable of photographing the license tags of vehicles running red lights. Using computer software tied to the camera, tag numbers of offending vehicles are compared with Department of Motor Vehicle registrations lists and a citation is then mailed to the vehicle owner (Caputo, 2010). Finally, an example of police work that is *both* deceptive *and* covert (cell "d") would be police undercover operations targeting a drug dealer, during which officers pose as drug users and purchase the illegal substance from the dealer.

To begin my analysis of the ethics of police tactics, let's consider deception. As you'll see, the police use deception to (1) uncover crime and arrest those perpetrating it; (2) obtain confessions from arrestees that will enhance the chances of a conviction; and (3) help convict people being tried on criminal charges.

THE USE OF DECEPTION BY POLICE

A common tactic used every day by police is deception. But what does this mean exactly? As used in this chapter, **police deception** refers to "[the] intention to trick others by communicating messages meant to mislead and to make the recipients believe what the agent either knows or believes . . . is true" (Alpert & Noble, 2009, p. 238). Examples of police deception include undercover operations, known as "stings," designed to lure lawbreakers into the open and into the hands of law enforcement; the use of psychological coercion by police interrogators to convince defendants to confess to the charges on which they have been arrested; and lying during courtroom testimony to get juries to believe their version of the events that surrounded the arrests of defendants, so the jury will then convict defendants in these cases.

It's also true that police officers learn early in their careers that deception and lying are "part of the job," along with justifications for doing so, such as the noble cause of getting "bad guys" off the streets (see Barker, Friery, & Carter, 1994). Police officers also learn that deception *works*—it results in arrests, buoys prosecutors as they pursue a conviction, and convinces juries to convict defendants, sometimes wrongly. They also learn that deception, within certain limits, is *accepted by the courts*. Thus, they learn that the criminal justice system explicitly condones deception.

Deception During Investigation

Police use of deception during investigations has existed for as long as there have been police officers (Morton, 2011). Because many types of crimes (e.g., the sale and distribution of drugs) occur out of direct view, the police use **undercover operations** to identify persons involved with these crimes. These operations can vary dramatically in size (i.e., the number of officers involved), scope (i.e., the number of individuals targeted), length of time in operation (ranging from a few hours to years), and complexity (i.e., the techniques used, ranging from disguises to complex financial instruments) (Newman, 2007). One of the best-known examples of a police undercover operation is a "sting."

Police Stings

In a comprehensive analysis of **sting operations**, Graham Newman (2007) suggested that these operations target a variety of crimes and use different techniques. Newman (2007, p. 1) also identified four common features of stings. He argued they (1) either create an opportunity—or exploit an enticement—for someone to commit a crime; (2) target individuals and groups engaged in specific types of crime (e.g., burglary); (3) use an undercover or hidden police officer, a surrogate, or some other deception; and (4) include a key "gotcha" climax when police reveal themselves, arrests are made, and the operation then ends.

Police employ a variety of tools and techniques, including disguises, false storefronts, informants, and the Internet, during stings to generate deception and ensure positive outcomes (Newman, 2007). Stings are also resource-intensive: the greater their duration and complexity, the greater are the costs in personnel and other areas (e.g., rent, technology, etc.) (Newman, 2007). These costs can, however, be offset by recovering stolen property or seizing assets generated by the illegal behavior. Further, because stings require secrecy, little to no publicity occurs prior to or during their execution. A major publicity blitz *does* occur, however, following the successful execution of a sting. Finally, there are both positive and negative aspects of stings, as described in Table 7.1.

Legal Limits on Deception During Investigation

Perpetrators caught engaging in illegalities during sting operations may raise a claim that **entrapment** has occurred. Entrapment is a legal defense that argues that "but-for" the actions of the police through incentives offered or opportunities created, and because

TABLE 7.1 Possible Positive and Negative Aspects of Sting Operations

Positive	Negative
Facilitates investigations and increases arrests	Questionable long-term reduction in targeted crime(s)
Enhances image of police as "crime fighters"	May increase levels of targeted crime(s) by providing more opportunities for them to occur
Enhances police presence in known areas where targeted crime is occurring	Use of deception is simply another form of lying, and lying is morally wrong
Improves collaboration between police and prosecutors	Strong potential for government overreach—incentives used/opportunities created ensnare otherwise innocent persons
Conviction record is impressive	Privacy issues for third parties resulting from police surreptitiously collecting information about nonoffenders as well as offenders
Due to publicity, targeted crime (e.g., prostitution) may be reduced even without arrests	Entrapment issues
Improves ties to the community from working with businesses and others to set up and support sting operations	Expenses involved may not be justifiable
Improves community relations via recovery of stolen property for victims	Prevents consideration of other, more effective solutions that may be more difficult to implement
	High risk to the personal safety of officers

Source: Adapted from Newman (2007) and Kleinig (2008)

the offender is an otherwise innocent person, he or she would not have engaged in the illegal behavior of which she is accused (Colquitt, 2004). Therefore, the arrest violates the 14th Amendment's due process clause and should be thrown out by the court.

To decide if entrapment has occurred, courts use two "tests." The **subjective test for entrapment**, used in most state and all federal courts, focuses not on the behavior of the police but on the character and predispositions of the defendant (Marcus, 2009). Here, the court determines whether the defendant is, in fact, an "otherwise innocent person" not "predisposed" to engage in the crime for which he or she was arrested. To make that determination, the court considers such matters as the prior criminal record of the defendant. If the court does not find evidence of a defendant's predisposition to violate the law, it will rule that the police entrapped the defendant and negate the arrest (Storm, 2017).

A few states use the **objective test for entrapment**, wherein the court does not focus on the intent or predispositions of the defendant but instead on the actions and intent of the police (Colquitt, 2004). Here, the court decides if the police used tactics that would have induced an otherwise reasonable, law-abiding citizen, to engage in the illegal behavior. If police behavior created such an inducement, then entrapment has occurred, and the arrest will be negated (Storm, 2017).

In summary, police use of deception during investigations makes sense because deceiving people into engaging in illegal behavior is quite easy and doing so can pay large dividends, like removing offenders from the streets, enhancing department collaborations with prosecutors and media, and improving relations with the community. There are downsides to stings, however, including their posing high risks to the safety of officers involved and raising issues of entrapment. Note that the police do not use deception only during investigations—they also use it during the interrogation of arrestees. Let's consider that now.

Deception During Interrogation

Since the 1940s, police use of the so-called third degree to obtain confessions from arrestees—which included physical beatings of them; depriving them of food, water, and sleep; and keeping them isolated from family, friends, and legal counsel—has been replaced by the use of psychologically based coercion to obtain confessions (see Leo, 2004). Over time, these techniques have both expanded and been refined to a point where police interrogators (PIs) are trained not only in how to obtain confessions, but also how to detect deception by arrestees and "read" the offender's thinking (Leo, 2004).

Unlike the third degree, psychologically coercive interrogation techniques involve deceiving arrestees about what is occurring, manipulating them to undermine their own interests, and getting them to confess (Leo, 2017). To do this, the PI uses words and behavior to develop a minimal level of intimacy with the arrestee and deceive them into believing the PI is a "friend" "concerned" with the arrestee's best interests. If the PI gains the arrestee's trust, he or she can then exploit the arrestee's weaknesses and fears to undermine her self-interests and obtain a confession.

Police Interrogation Techniques

What specific techniques do PIs use to pressure suspects or defendants into confessing? How often are those techniques used? Those questions were answered by Saul Kassin and colleagues in the first study of its kind of PI techniques in 2007. In the study, Kassin and colleagues surveyed 631 investigators from 16 police departments in the United States and two Canadian provinces to examine police officials' beliefs about interrogations and the techniques they used during them (Kassin, Leo, Meissner, Richman, Colwell, Leach & La Fon, 2007). To identify interrogation techniques used by officers, respondents were instructed to indicate, on a scale of 1 to 5 (where "1" was "never used" and "5" was "always used"), how frequently they used a particular technique. Table 7.2 summarizes the techniques or tactics respondents reported they "always" used during interrogations. Note that officers may have "always" used more than one of them when interrogating defendants or suspects.

What Kassin and his colleagues showed was that physical isolation of detainees in a small room and identifying contradictions in detainees' stories were the most common techniques used by PIs. It turned out that many of the tactics PIs used are associated with a well-known interrogation strategy adopted by interrogators around the world. Let's explore that strategy in greater depth.

THE REID TECHNIQUE. Developed by the late John Reid and his friend and colleague Fred Inbau in the 1940s and subsequently refined over the next six decades, the **Reid technique** consists of a series of steps designed to isolate the arrestee, ingratiate the PI to him or her, and get the arrestee to confess. Since the early 1970s, the technique has been taught to over 500,000 investigators around the globe (Inbau, Reid, Buckley & Jayne, 2013).

While the Reid technique consists of three components—a *factual analysis* that includes a review of the facts and the evidence in the case; a *behavioral-analysis interview* with

TABLE 7.2 Frequency of Police Use of Various Interrogation Tactics

Interrogation Tactic	Percentage of Police Respondents "Always" Using This Tactic
Isolating suspect from family and friends	66
Conducting the interrogation in a small, private room	42
Identifying contradictions in the suspect's story	41
Establishing a rapport and gaining the suspect's trust	32
Confronting the suspect with evidence of his guilt	22
Offering sympathy, moral justifications, and excuses	13
Interrupting the suspect's denials and objections	13
Appealing to the suspect's self-interests	11
Minimizing the moral seriousness of the offense	8
Pretending to have independent evidence of guilt	7
Appealing to the suspect's religion or conscience	5
Showing the suspect photographs of crime scene	3
Having the suspect take a polygraph and telling him he failed it	3
Threatening consequences for not cooperating	2
Expressing impatience, frustration, or anger	1
Physically intimidating the suspect	1

Source: Adapted from Kassin, et al. (2007, Table 2, p. 388)

the arrestee to gauge the likelihood of guilt; and a full-blown *interrogation* of the arrestee—the most important of these is a structured interrogation consisting of nine steps that should only occur if the PI is "reasonably certain" of the arrestee's guilt (Inabu, et al., 2013). These nine steps are summarized below, based on analyses of the Reid technique by Hammill (2017) and Orlando (2014):

1. Direct confrontation. PI unequivocally tells the arrestee that the evidence demonstrates his or her guilt, while cutting off arrestee attempts at denial.
2. Theme development. PI presents a moral justification (or theme) for the offense, such as blaming outside circumstances, to minimize its moral seriousness and create an environment where arrestee feels comfortable telling the truth while also having the opportunity to couple admission with an excuse to save arrestee's self-respect.
3. Handling denials. Arrestee is likely to ask for permission to speak and denies the accusations. PI discourages all attempts to deny involvement.
4. Overcoming objections. When denials fail, an arrestee will then present objections in support of a claim of innocence (e.g., "I would never do that because I love my job"). PI should accept and use them to further develop the interrogation theme.
5. Procurement and retention of arrestee's attention. PI must maintain arrestee's attention and focus on the investigator's theme, rather than possible consequences for admitting guilt. One way to do so is to reduce physical distance between PI and arrestee.
6. Handling the arrestee's passive mood. PI intensifies the theme presentation and focuses on central reasons offered as psychological justification(s) for the crime while continuing to display sympathetic demeanor and urging arrestee to tell the truth.
7. Presenting an alternative question. PI presents two choices developed as an extension of the theme, with one alternative offering a better justification for the crime (e.g., "Did you plan this thing out or did it just happen?"). PI follows the question with a supporting statement encouraging arrestee to choose the more attractive alternative. Acceptance of either is a first admission of guilt.
8. Having the arrestee orally relate various details of the offense. After arrestee admits his or her guilt, PI responds with a statement of reinforcement that acknowledges the admission. PI then conducts brief review of events before asking more detailed questions.
9. Converting an oral confession to a written confession. PI converts arrestee's verbal confession to written or recorded form. Arrestee's own words are used.

CRITIQUE OF THE REID TECHNIQUE. While the Reid technique is probably the most popular tool used by PIs around the world to obtain confessions, it has also been widely criticized. For example, Timothy Moore and C. Lindsey Fitzsimmons (2011) have argued that Reid training improperly encourages investigators to trust their intuitions and rely on a hodgepodge of behavior, statements, and reactions from the arrestee that are *not* reliable cues to deceit. Additionally, they argued that the "guilt presumptive" nature of the process lends itself to having arrestees falsely confess to relieve psychological pressure they are experiencing. Moore and Fitzsimmons also raised concerns over whether those being interrogated fully understood their right to remain silent. Not understanding that right can lead them to which can lead them to unknowingly waiving it and submitting to interrogation. They concluded by noting:

> The Reid technique's vast edifice of pseudoscience, misinformation, self-delusion and outright deceit does not advance the objectives of the criminal justice system. In the 1950s, it was heralded as a vast improvement over the barbaric methods it replaced. Such justification stopped being applicable decades ago. There are viable alternatives to the Reid technique. It is time to start using and refining them.
>
> —(Moore & Fitzsimmons, 2011, p. 542)

Legal Limits on Deception During Interrogation

As was the case with investigative deception, there are also legal limits on using deception during interrogation. In general, the courts have concluded that lies, trickery, and deceit used by police interrogators are acceptable *if* the deception did not *coerce* a confession (Marcus, 2006). Safeguards to ensure that confessions are voluntary include the court determining that arrestees received their *Miranda* warnings before interrogation began and that confessions were not the product of coercion (physical or psychological), and as a result had "been given of free and unconstrained choice" (Hritz, 2017, p. 490). If there's a question about the voluntariness of a confession, the courts use the **totality of the circumstances test** to determine if that's the case. As the Supreme Court ruled in 1969 in the case of *Frazier v. Cupp* (394 U.S. 731), the test involves trial courts assessing whether police behavior (e.g., location and length of interrogation), personal characteristics of the individual being interrogated (e.g., age, maturity, intellectual functioning, and mental and physical condition), or some combination of the two resulted in the deception *coercing* the person to waive her rights and confess to the charges. Commentators have since argued that once the trial court is satisfied the defendant's waiver was not negatively impacted by police deception, they are reluctant to hold that the confession was given involuntarily (Hritz, 2017). Finally, in a 2010 ruling in the case of *Berghuis v. Thompkins* (560 U.S. 370), the U.S. Supreme Court held that:

- For a suspect to properly invoke his right to remain silent he must unambiguously assert this right. This could be accomplished by simply remaining silent or telling the police that he or she wishes to remain silent at the beginning of the interview or at any time during the interview;
- A waiver of *Miranda* rights may be implied through the defendant's silence, coupled with an understanding of his rights and a course of conduct indicating waiver;
- As a general proposition, the law can presume that an individual who, with a full understanding of his or her rights, acts in a manner inconsistent with their exercise has made a deliberate choice to relinquish the protection of those rights.
- The requirements of *Miranda* are met if a suspect receives adequate *Miranda* warnings, understands them and has an opportunity to invoke the rights before giving any answers or admissions. Any waiver, express or implied, may be contradicted by an invocation at any time. If the right to counsel or the right to remain silent is invoked at any point during questioning, further interrogation must cease (see Batterton, 2010, pp. 6–7).

I'll note here that several appeals courts have ruled that certain forms of deception (e.g., fabricating evidence) used to obtain confessions are *so* egregious as to constitute *prima facie* violations of the 5th Amendment *and* the due process clause of the 14th Amendment, and if used to obtain a confession render it invalid (Schwartz, 2003).

As you have no doubt concluded, the courts are relatively lenient in allowing the police to use deception to gain confessions. As the Supreme Court has said, its use is "strategic" rather than "coercive," but has also acknowledged that the psychological pressure that builds from police using deception *can* amount to coercion. While no one wants to see a guilty party escape prosecution and conviction for their crime(s), the problem—as noted above—is that police deception during interrogation can result in the innocent falsely confessing to something they did not do.

The Problem of False Confessions

In July of 1997 in Norfolk, VA, Michelle Moore-Bosko was brutally raped and murdered. Police soon after arrested a neighbor, Danial Williams, whom they interrogated for 11 hours and extracted a confession. The problem was that Danial Williams and three others (the "Norfolk Four"), also accused and later convicted of the crime on the strength of *their* confessions, were factually innocent (see Case Study 7.1).

CASE STUDY 7.1 Police Deception and False Confessions: The "Norfolk Four"

In July of 1997, Michelle Moore-Bosko was brutally raped and murdered in Norfolk, VA. Based on the hunch of a friend of Moore-Bosko's that her neighbor Danial Williams might have committed the crime, *investigators interrogated Williams overnight for more than 11 hours, eventually extracting multiple confessions from him to the horrific crime. During Williams' marathon interrogation, investigators repeatedly accused Williams of committing the crime; yelled at him; administered a polygraph examination and lied to him about the results; lied to him further by falsely telling him other evidence (DNA, hairs, witnesses) established that he had committed the crime when, in fact, no such evidence existed against him; poked him in the chest; threatened him with capital murder charges if he did not confess; promised him a lesser charge if he did confess; and educated him about the details of the rape and murder* (emphasis added).

Months later, forensic testing established that Williams' DNA did not match the sperm, blood or other genetic material recovered from the crime scene. Norfolk police would mistakenly suspect other innocent individuals of raping and murdering Michelle Moore-Bosko and would go on to extract false confessions from three more individuals: Joseph Dick, Eric Wilson and Derek Tice. Like Williams, Dick, Wilson, and Tice all confessed after lengthy, guilt-presumptive and accusatory interrogations in which they were repeatedly yelled at and called liars; physically touched (e.g., tapped or poked); lied to about non-existent evidence that supposedly irrefutably linked them to the crime, including bogus polygraph results; threatened with the death penalty if they did not confess; promised leniency and an end to grueling interrogations if they did confess; and shown crime scene photos and fed details of the crime. Importantly, as was the case with Williams, none of the others' DNA matched genetic material recovered from the crime scene.

Eventually DNA testing and other dispositive evidence established that Omar Ballard, a violent felon, had alone committed the murder and rape of Michelle Moore-Bosko, for which he confessed after a brief interrogation, pled guilty to committing, and received a life sentence. However, the fact of Ballard's demonstrable guilt and his conviction for the rape and murder of Michelle Moore-Bosko did not prevent Williams, Dick, Wilson, and Tice—who became known as the "Norfolk Four"—from being wrongfully convicted of the crime and spending many years in prison despite their provable innocence.

Source: Leo (2017, pp. 1–2)

According to The Innocence Project (2017), about one in four of the 325 wrongful convictions reversed because of DNA evidence the Project's team uncovered were based on false confessions, making them the third most common cause of wrongful convictions behind witness misidentification and invalidated forensic evidence. At this point, you may be asking yourself, Why in the world would someone confess to a crime they did not commit?

Before I answer the question, let's review where we are. Recall that confessions from defendants are extremely powerful evidence in criminal proceedings, so police are incentivized to obtain them and prosecutors to use them. Recall also that because police cannot use physical coercion to obtain confessions, they now use psychological pressure to lure defendants into confessing. These tactics, best exemplified by the Reid technique, assume that most defendants are guilty and will lie about their guilt, but that their deception can be identified and overcome using a combination of isolation, confrontation, and minimization to manipulate defendants into confessing. Finally, if the deception used did not "coerce" the defendant into waiving his or her right to remain silent or was not particularly egregious, the courts will usually accept the confession as voluntary.

THE PSYCHOLOGY OF FALSE CONFESSIONS. As more exonerations based on DNA evidence occur, combined with the fact many wrongful convictions result from false confessions, psychologists, legal scholars, and others have undertaken various research to (1) understand *why* people confess to crimes they did not commit and (2) determine *how* police interrogations contribute to false confessions.

A **false confession** is a "detailed admission to a criminal act the confessor did not commit" (Kassin & Gudjonsson, 2004, p. 48). Further, because neither an exact count of them nor an adequate method for calculating that number exists, ongoing debate over their frequency continues. As Kassin and Gudjonsson (2004) observed, part of the problem is that many false confessions are uncovered only before trial; they are not reported by police or prosecutors; and/or they are not publicized, all of which suggest that the problem may be much larger than is commonly assumed.

Lawrence Wrightsman and Saul Kassin (1985, 1993) developed a typology for false confessions using case studies of actual false confessions and drawing from social-psychological theories of attitude change. The pair identified three types of false confessions: voluntary, coerced-compliant, and coerced-internalized (see Wrightsman & Kassin, 1993). As it turns out, the scheme has proven useful, even to the point of it being incorporated into training materials for the Reid technique (Kassin & Gudjonsson, 2004).

In the Wrightsman and Kassin typology, **voluntary false confessions** are obtained not as a result of police pressures to confess, but because the individual may have an extreme need for notoriety; needs to release extreme feelings of guilt over previous wrongs; is unable to distinguish fact from fantasy; or desires to aid and protect the real criminal. **Coerced-compliant false confessions** occur when the arrestee acquiesces to the demand for a confession for purely instrumental reasons, such as escaping an aversive situation, avoiding explicit or implied threats, or gaining a reward. In other words, the confessor believes that the benefits of confessing outweigh the costs of continuing to deny their involvement in the crime. Incentives for compliance could include being allowed to sleep, eat, make a phone call, go home, or feed a drug habit. A desire to end the interview and avoid more confinement may be especially relevant for young people, and those who are desperate, socially dependent, or phobic of being confined. Finally, **coerced-internalized false confessions** occur when an innocent, but vulnerable, person not only admits to the alleged behavior but actually *believes* he or she committed the crime, based on false memories. These individuals evidence what Kassin (1997) labeled "memory distrust syndrome"—a profound distrust of one's own memories—which makes them vulnerable to influence by external cues and suggestions. During interrogation, an authority figure claims to have privileged insight into a defendant's past. Simultaneously, the individual is in a heightened state of malleability because interactions between the two occur in a private, socially isolated setting, absent from external reality cues. As a result, the PI convinces the individual to accept negative and painful self-insight by claiming the arrestee is simply repressing painful memories.

Despite the contribution the typology made to answering why people falsely confess, Kassin (2004) admits it has limitations. For example, the typology does not account for voluntary confessions resulting from pressures brought to bear in noncustodial settings by, among others, family members, friends, or clergy. The typology could thus be revised to distinguish between false confessions according to both the eliciting process and the source. Kassin (2004) also noted criticisms of "internalization" that have raised concerns over whether the confessor's beliefs really become entrenched rather than unstable as characterized by expressions that betray uncertainty (e.g., "I think I did" or "I probably committed the crime"). Thus, the question becomes whether an innocent confessor's false beliefs are ever fully internalized. Kassin (2004) noted that case studies of multiple false confessors evidenced internalization over lengthy periods (e.g., five months or longer after the confession) and internalization has been repeatedly found in laboratory-based studies of false confessions.

The crucial point for our purposes is not whether the above typology is "best" at classifying false confessions. Rather, the point is this: *there is no longer doubt that people falsely confess to crimes they have not committed*. Additionally, false confessions result in injustices, not only because innocents are convicted and punished, but because guilty parties remain free to offend again. It is also clear that the psychological pressure arrestees experience because of deception used on them during interrogations increases the risk for false confessions (Drizin & Leo, 2005; Leo, 2009).

As you have now seen, police deception during interrogation involves court-approved psychological pressures brought to bear against arrestees to gain a confession. These techniques revolve around isolating the arrestee, confronting him or her with false information, and minimizing the arrestee's denials. Further, proponents of the Reid technique swear by its ability to help interrogators identify deception and elicit confessions from arrestees. The problem is that the psychological pressures brought to bear against arrestees may result in false confessions, which lead to injustices that take decades to undo.

To conclude my discussion of police deception, let's consider one other instance where the police may use it: in testimony during pretrial and trial stages of the criminal justice process.

Deception in Court Proceedings

In its final report on a several years' long investigation into corruption involving the New York City Police Department (NYPD) during the early 1990s, the Commission to Investigate Allegations of Police Corruption and the Anti-Corruption Procedures of the Police

Department (known as the Mollen Commission, after its chairperson) made the following observations:

> Our investigation . . . focused on *testimonial perjury*, as when an officer testifies falsely under oath before a grand jury or at a court proceeding; *documentary perjury*, as when an officer swears falsely under oath in an affidavit or criminal complaint; and *falsification of police records*, as when an officer falsifies the facts and circumstances of an arrest in police reports. Several officers also told us that the practice of police falsification . . . is so common in certain precincts, that it has spawned its own word: *testilying*.
>
> —(emphasis added; Mollen Commission, 1994, p. 36)

The Commission noted that **testilying** by NYPD officers concealed "illegal steps taken for what officers perceived as 'legitimate' law enforcement ends," while falsification of police documents involved "officers presenting false information in official documents like arrest reports" (Mollen Commission, 1994, p. 37).

What the Commission was referring to was not "deception" by the police (as described above), but to the fact that police officers *lied* during their testimony and/or falsified documents to cover their lies. Lying is different from deception in that lying is an effort "to make a believed-false statement to another person with the intention that the other person believe that statement to be true" (Mahon, 2015, p. 1). If a police officer testifies in court (or writes on an arrest report) she recovered drugs from a defendant's vehicle because the drugs were in "plain view" during a routine traffic stop, but the drugs were actually planted by the officer, she is making a statement to the jury that she believes is false but is intended to have them believe otherwise.

Like people's reactions to defendants confessing to crimes they did not commit, many wonder why a police officer would flat-out lie during court proceedings or on official records. After all, hasn't the officer taken an "oath of office?" Isn't she familiar with the Code of Police Ethics? Isn't she supposed to have personal integrity? Doesn't she know full well that lying before a grand jury, on the witness stand during trial, or on official documents constitutes perjury, a violation of the very law she is sworn to uphold? Why *would* police officers lie about relevant facts in criminal cases?

Police Perjury

Officers giving testimony in court they *know* is false but is designed to influence members of a jury or a judge is common, and constitutes **police perjury** (Burns, 1998; Maclin, 1994; Uviller, 1988). Testimony by police—truthful or not—is accorded greater weight by juries in criminal cases than is testimony from other witnesses. As Gabriel Chin and Scott Wells (1998, p. 235) observed:

> Police are professional witnesses, perhaps the most experienced witnesses of any occupational group. Moreover, officers have special credibility. In a confrontation between a civilian and a "blue knight," a clear-eyed uniformed police officer, jurors may well bend over backwards to believe the person in blue.

Police perjury leads to two types of wrongful convictions: the conviction of those who are factually guilty but are convicted using illegal means (e.g., false testimony) and those who are factually innocent but are convicted using illegal means and endure punishments ranging from incarceration to possible execution (Chin & Wells, 1998).

CONTRIBUTING FACTORS TO POLICE PERJURY. Police perjury can be traced to several contributing factors: the power of the noble cause, the "blue wall of silence" associated with it, and the criminal justice system's failure to sanction police who lie during courtroom proceedings. Let's consider each of these in some detail.

Recall that the noble cause involves an officer's firm commitment to "getting the bad guys off the streets." As patrol officers go about their duties and arrest people for various crimes, they learn that "everybody" lies to them: the people whom they've pulled over for traffic violations; spouses who assault their partners; drug dealers who have "no idea" where the heroin came from that clogged the toilet while being flushed. Thus, many of the people with whom police interact are *factually guilty* of violating the law but lie about their involvement ("everyone lies"). These people also tend to be secretive, may have hurt others, may have a long record of offending, are implicated in the current offense, and want to get away with it (Caldero & Crank, 2015). The result, as Carl Klockars (1980) has argued, is that police officers may sometimes assume that (1) *everyone* lies and (2) as a result, *everyone's* guilty. What's problematic here is that officers may maintain these assumptions without supporting evidence (Caldero & Crank, 2015).

Officers also confront various constitutionally based procedural safeguards designed to protect the legal rights of individuals being investigated, searched, arrested, or interrogated. In some instances, these safeguards result in the court releasing people that officers steadfastly believe are guilty (but are lying about that guilt). Obviously, when this occurs, the police are not happy—someone they assume is guilty has now escaped his or her just desserts.

Given an assumption of guilt but faced with the possibility the courts will release the guilty on some "technicality," what is the officer to do to honor the noble cause of "getting the bad guys off the street?" The answer is to *lie*. On the report describing the circumstances surrounding the arrest. About the evidence recovered connecting the arrestee with the crime. About the deception used during the interrogation that led to the confession. From the officer's perspective, testilying and document falsification result not only in "justice" done but also honoring of the noble cause, as the "bad guy" is now off the streets (Mollen Commission, 1994).

The blue wall of silence. Another factor at work that explains testilying and document falsification by police officers is the **blue wall of silence**, a documented part of most local police cultures (Caldero & Crank, 2015; Kleinig, 2001; Skolnick, 1982). This code of silence can be characterized as an informal rule that says that "cops don't 'rat' on other cops" regardless of what the offending officer(s) have perpetrated. Coming forward and reporting violations of departmental policy or outright criminality constitutes a serious breach of loyalty to the occupation that is punished in many ways ranging from ostracism to outright violence. Thought Exercise 7.1 explores this area in greater detail.

Scholars, practitioners, and special commissions that have investigated police corruption have described not only the origins and characteristics of the blue wall of silence, but its harmful effects on the integrity of policing. By creating pressure on officers to *not* come forward with information about peers' testilying or falsification, such "sins of omission" can then lead to wrongful convictions of both the guilty and the innocent.

THOUGHT EXERCISE 7.1

POLICE OFFICER ATTITUDES TOWARD THE "BLUE WALL OF SILENCE"

In 2001, The Police Foundation released a report of the results of a national survey it conducted of a representative sample of 925 sworn police officers from 121 departments that employed 25 or more full-time, sworn officers (Weisburd, Greenspan, Hamilton, Bryant, & Williams, 2001). The sample consisted of a broad spectrum of officers that reflected the diversity of American police at the time. The purpose of the study was to query officers about their attitudes toward several topics/issues, including the blue wall of silence.

As reported by Weisburd, et al. (2001), more than 80% of respondents disagreed or strongly disagreed with the statement that the code of silence is "an essential part of the mutual trust necessary to achieve good policing." However, more than 66% of respondents strongly agreed or agreed that police officers would receive the "cold shoulder" from peers for reporting incidents of police misconduct. Further, more than one-half of officers reported it was not unusual for colleagues to "turn a blind eye" toward peers' improper conduct. Focus groups conducted as part of the study clarified that not only does the code of silence exist, it creates pressure on officers when deciding whether to report rules' violations—including serious misconduct—by peers.

Survey Items

The code of silence is an essential part of the mutual trust necessary to good policing

Response	Percentage
Strongly Agree	1.2
Agree	15.7
Disagree	65.6
Strongly Disagree	17.5

An officer who reports another's misconduct is likely given the "cold shoulder" by his or her fellow officers

Response	Percentage
Strongly Agree	11.0
Agree	56.4
Disagree	30.9
Strongly Disagree	1.8

Source: Adapted from Weisburd, et al. (2001, pp. 25–27)

Lack of sanctions. Police testilying and falsification are also perpetuated by a failure of the criminal justice system—especially prosecutors and the courts—to curtail them (Chin & Wells, 1998). Prosecutors, for example, have not dealt with police testilying or falsification very aggressively for several reasons: (1) they *know* the evidence is tainted by lies (which encourages them to not scrutinize prospective testimony or evidence to any great degree); (2) they want to avoid confronting "pro-police bias" on the part of judges and juries; (3) they understand that the blue wall of silence may make police witnesses unreliable; (4) they rely on police to do their investigations for them and want to maintain a good relationship; and (5) they approve of police testilying and falsification when it leads to a factually guilty person being convicted. Blame can also be laid at the feet of the courts, who seem reluctant to place police officers testifying before them into the same class of people as accomplices, drug addicts, or perjurers when it comes to weighing their credibility (Chin & Wells, 1998).

In summary, police officials who engage in testilying and falsification do so for many reasons, including staying true to the noble cause; as a result of pressure from local cultures of silence to not report colleagues who present false testimony in court proceedings; and because prosecutors and the courts are generally reluctant to pursue sanctions against officers who do so. In short, police officers use deception in court for the same reason they use it during investigations and interrogations: *it works*.

The Ethics of Police Deception

My discussion to this point has centered on police deception and lying (police perjury). Police deception involves officers tricking others by misleading them into believing what the officer knows is untrue. Police perjury (e.g., testilying and falsification of documents) is making a believed (or known) false statement to another while under oath, with the intention of making the other believe the statement is true. Jerome Skolnick (1982) has argued that police deception occurs during investigations, interrogations, and at trials and its legal acceptability varies from being most acceptable during investigations, to being moderately acceptable during investigations, to being least acceptable during trials. Skolnick thus not only describes when deception/lying is likely to occur but also argues that *legal* acceptance of deception varies based on when it is used. That does not, however, answer the question of whether police deception/lying is *ethical*.

You may find it useful here to examine *types* of lies, as they may matter when determining the ethics of police deception/perjury. Researchers have identified three common types of lies (Smith, 2017). **Black (antisocial) lies** are told to benefit oneself from possibly harming others (e.g., you deny going out with another person while you're in a committed relationship). **White (prosocial) lies** are told to benefit others (e.g., complimenting someone on their singing when in fact, the person can't carry a tune). **Blue (ingroup) lies** are told to benefit one's social group, while possibly harming members of other groups (e.g., President Trump describing mainstream media, such as the *Washington Post* and the *New York Times*, as "fake news" outlets). In the present context, police officers may tell black lies about the circumstances under which they arrested someone; white lies to a kidnapping victim's family that raise (false) hopes concerning the fate of the loved one; and blue lies about drug users to generate public support for draconian tactics to be used against them.

To assess the ethics of police deception/perjury, guidance can be found in what many scholars consider the most influential treatise on lying written in the past 30 years, Sissela Bok's *Lying: Moral Choice in Public and Private Life*. Among other topics, the book presents a set of criteria or a "test" to assess when and under what circumstances deception/lying (in this case, by police) might be morally acceptable. The test includes the following considerations: Are there alternative actions/tactics the police could use to address crime? What might be moral reasons supporting police use of deception/perjury and what reasons can be raised as counter-arguments? What might reasonable people say about police deception/lying? (Bok, 1999, pp. 105–106).

Alternatives to Police Deception/Perjury

For many people—including the police themselves—the use of deception is a "no brainer." Because those who violate the law do not generally turn themselves in, provide evidence of their crime(s), and confess to the illegality, the only way to detect them is to "lie to the liars," "deceive the deceivers," and "victimize the victimizers." However, isn't it plausible here that "only" is being confused with "easiest?"

Take, for example, offenses involving the sale, possession, and use of illicit drugs like cocaine, heroin, methamphetamine, etc. Undercover police operations routinely target individuals who buy, sell, and use these drugs, resulting in many arrests. Because drug deals usually occur out of direct view, police officers pose as users and purchase the drugs. Or, they pose as dealers or use other forms of deception, like becoming "friends" with leaders of drug cartels, to disrupt large-scale drug distribution networks (Marx, 1992). Is the "only"

way to address the problem of illicit drugs to have police develop undercover operations that target users, buyers, and sellers of drugs? John Kleinig (2008) suggested otherwise when he argued that treatment alternatives to incarceration are now available through drug courts. Additionally, as of this writing, 26 states and the District of Columbia have passed laws broadly legalizing marijuana in some form; three states will join them after recently passing measures permitting use of medical marijuana (Maciag, 2017). Kleinig (2008) reminded us that the present "war on drugs" (which has lasted 50 years) partly resulted from policies that criminalized illicit drugs rather than treating them as a public health problem, as has been done in many European countries (Hughes & Stevens, 2010). Are we thus not responsible for electing (and reelecting) lawmakers who created the "war on drugs" and its accompanying use of deception by police to target drug sellers, buyers, and users?

Moral Justifications for and Against Police Deception/Perjury

Systems of ethics address whether police deception/perjury is acceptable in different ways. Consequentialist systems like Utilitarianism focus on the possible positive and negative consequences of police deception/lying. For them, the question becomes, Which behavior—telling the truth or deceiving/lying—likely results in the greatest good (utility) for the greatest number? If deception/lying results in more potentially positive consequences than does telling the truth, police deception/lying is ethical. Duty-based systems such as Kantian ethics focus on whether deception/lying violates the officer's duty to citizens via the categorical imperative: would we want *all* police officers at *all* times and places to lie or deceive us? If yes, then police deception/perjury is ethical. Kant would also ask whether police deception/perjury uses others as the means to an end: if "yes," the behavior is wrong. Finally, virtue ethics would consider whether honesty is a virtue (it is) and what virtuous people do (not lie). If honesty is a virtue and the virtuous person does not lie, then police deception/perjury is not acceptable.

Case Study 7.2 offers a fuller assessment of the ethics of police deception. It is based on an actual "sting" operation conducted by federal agencies in the late 1980s that eventually made its way to the U.S. Supreme Court. Using the template found in Ch. 5, assess the ethics of the agencies' behavior in the case using one or more of the systems of ethics discussed and reach a conclusion about whether the behavior was ethical.

Public Attitudes about Police Deception/Perjury

Finally, Bok (1999) has suggested that public attitudes about the behavior in question are important considerations as well for assessing the ethics of lying. Here, the issue becomes to what extent does the public condone police deception/perjury? While a few studies have examined this question, and none of them included attitudes about testilying, the answer seems to be that the public generally supports police deception (see Ekins, 2016; Nicholson, 2013; Wasieleski, Whatley, & Murphy, 2009). Assuming that most people are reasonable, they seem to have little problem with police deception, at least outside the courtroom.

However, relying on public attitudes as one basis for supporting a particular tactic by police can lead us into the problem of **morality by majority** (Ruggiero, 2012). That is, if a majority identifies some behavior (e.g., police deception) as immoral, that's enough to claim the behavior is, in fact, immoral. The problem here is that there is no "magic" in majorities (Ruggiero, 2012). Recall that a "majority" simply refers to more

CASE STUDY 7.2 "Operation Heartland"

Sonny Crockett is an inspector with the U.S. Postal Service (USPS). Postal inspectors' primary duties are ensuring that no illegal material is sent through/received via the US mail, including pornographic books or magazines containing sexually explicit depictions of children in violation of the *Child Protection Act of 1984*. In February of 1985, he was briefed about a sting operation being undertaken by his office, "Operation Heartland," that targeted consumers of child pornography in the Great Plains states.

His boss, Manny Castillo, the inspector in charge of the operation, said it was an intelligence-gathering operation designed to watch producers and distributors of child pornography.

Castillo instructed Crockett to send a fictitious letter to all those the USPS knew had ordered such materials while still legal. The letter was to be from a fictitious organization called "The American Hedonist Society" that described itself in the letter as a "grass-roots" organization engaged in political lobbying "for the right to read what we want, discuss our interests with like-minded people, and to seek pleasure without restrictions placed on us by an outdated 'Puritan morality.'" Included with the letter was a survey designed to gauge the recipient's interest in various kinds of child pornography, including depictions of nude children; homosexual activities engaged in by children; and adults engaging in hetero- and homosexual intercourse and other activities with children.

Among the recipients of Crockett's letter was Keith Jacobson, a never married, 56-year-old U.S. Army retiree-turned-farmer who was living with his elderly parents in a small town in Nebraska. Prior to passage of the new law, Jacobson had ordered two magazines entitled *Bare Boys I* and *Bare Boys II* from Electric Moon, an adult bookstore in San Diego that had been raided by the FBI and shut down several months earlier after passage of the 1984 law. Jacobson indicated an "above average" interest in depictions of homosexual relations involving children, especially between males, but also stated he opposed depictions of adults having sex with children. Castillo and Crockett mutually decided he was not a promising target and left him alone.

Some eight months later, Calvin Comfort, a "prohibited mailing specialist" for the region, found Jacobson's name in another file, and the government decided to try again, this time as part of an operation aimed at purchasers of child pornography. In May 1986, they sent him mail from another fictitious organization, "Midlands Data Research," which was for those who "believe in the joys of sex and the complete awareness of those lusty and youthful lads and lasses of the neophyte age." Jacobson confessed to them that he was "interested in teenage sexuality," and asked for more information and that his name be kept confidential. This led to Jacobson getting mail from the "Heartland Institute for a New Tomorrow" (HINT), "an organization founded to protect and promote sexual freedom and freedom of choice. We believe that arbitrarily imposed legislative sanctions restricting your sexual freedom should be rescinded through the legislative process." Jacobson seemed to sympathize, writing in response that sexual freedom and freedom of the press were under attack by "right-wing fundamentalists." Along with a thank-you note from "Jean Daniels" of HINT also came a supposed list of others in the area with similar interests as possible pen pals. But Jacobson never wrote to any of them. So, Comfort, under the pseudonym "Carl Long," wrote back using a technique called "mirroring," claiming to have interests calculated to be similar to those believed held by Jacobson, and specifically, to be equally interested in depictions of sex acts between young boys. Jacobson said he, too, liked "good looking young guys (in their teens) doing their thing together." Neither Jacobson nor Comfort made any more explicit reference to pornographic materials and Jacobson stopped writing back after two letters. With no evidence that he had ever watched or possessed any child pornography, the USPS again dropped its efforts against him.

Those were renewed in March 1987 when the United States Customs Service sent similar exploratory material, supposedly from Canada, to Jacobson and others on the USPS's list, and he responded, placing an order that was never filled. A catalog from a "Far Eastern Trading Company" was sent instead, along with other written material bemoaning the infringement of sexual freedoms. This time Jacobson ordered *Boys Who Love Boys*, which the catalog said featured "11- and 14-year-old boys" who "get it on in every way imaginable. Oral, anal and heavy masturbation. If you love boys," it further read, "you will be delighted with this."

On June 16, 1987, Jacobson received a card in his mail telling him to go to the post office and pick up the envelope that supposedly contained *Boys Who Love Boys*. Comfort observed him doing so and obtained a search warrant for Jacobson's home on that basis. He was arrested shortly thereafter, *26 months after the postal inspectors had first contacted him.*

Were the agencies' efforts ethical?

Source: Adapted from *Jacobson v. United States*, 503 U.S. 540 (1992)

than 50% of members of some group. For convenience, their individual attitudes are grouped together and then translated into a number or percentage that creates the *impression* of authoritativeness and wisdom, both of which may be absent (Ruggiero, 2012). In fact, if you ask individual members of the majority about their attitudes toward police deception/lying under oath, you would find wide variation in (1) knowledge about these issues, (2) the degree and quality of consideration given them, and (3) the quality of judgment rendered about them (Ruggiero, 2012). To illustrate: just because public opinion polling during the 1940s consistently showed large majorities of white respondents favoring segregationist policies relating to education, employment, and even marriage, that did not make segregation morally right, nor did it ethically justify the enforcement of such policies by police and others. Sometimes the majority is just *wrong*.

Police deception, and to a lesser extent police perjury, raise significant questions about their acceptability from the standpoint of criminal justice ethics. Both involve potential harm not only to the person being deceived, but to the person doing the deceiving and to others as well (Bok, 1999). Developing an understanding about the "whys" and "wherefores" of both, along with a fuller appreciation of the dynamics of lying—including the possible harm to self and others—and subjecting the behaviors to a reasoned analysis (and encouraging both sides to engage in a public discussion about the morality of these behaviors) will not only shed greater light on the issues surrounding police deception and lying, but will hopefully lead to necessary reforms that address the negative consequences of these behaviors. Let's now turn attention to a different tactic by the police: surveillance, both passive and active.

SURVEILLANCE BY POLICE

In both America and around the world, surveillance is a huge industry that only grows larger each day. According to one recent estimate, each American taxpayer spends $574 annually to fund surveillance programs operated by the National Security Agency (NSA) (Hanke, 2013), while the FBI's Operational Technology Division (OTD) costs taxpayers between $600 and $800 million annually (the exact figure is classified) (Nakashima, 2015). Surveillance is also becoming increasingly sophisticated, as it involves audio and video monitoring of physical location, cell communications, the Internet, and biometrics (including speech and facial recognition) (Privacy International, 2016).

According to Anders Albrechtslund (2008), **surveillance** can be traced to the French word *surveiller*, which translates as "to watch over." Thus, the word infers a visual practice of one person looking carefully at another from above. However, in both ordinary language and academic circles, "watching over" has become a metaphor for all kinds of *monitoring activities* conducted by governments, business and industry, and even individuals. Surveillance is no longer limited to visual activity. It now involves all the senses, amplified by sophisticated technological innovations (Albrechtslund, 2008). As a result, social scientists speak of the current historical period as one dominated by the "surveillance society" (see Lyon, 2008) or the "maximum security society" (see Marx, 2005) wherein activity (surveillance) is occurring that involves "focused, systematic and routine attention to personal details for purposes of influence, management, protection or direction" (Lyon, 2007, p. 450).

Surveillance focuses on gathering details about people, including those relating to their behavior and beliefs, communications, friends and associates, travel, etc. It is also systematic and intentional, rather than random or arbitrary. Surveillance is also a routine part of the ordinary administrative apparatus that characterizes modern nation-states and has many purposes, including totalitarian domination, but far more typically involves subtler forms of influence over, or control of, people (Richards, 2013).

American police agencies and officers have become major spokes in the much larger wheels of the "surveillance society" that characterizes America, especially in the years following the September 11, 2001, attacks in New York and Washington, DC. My discussion now turns to police-related surveillance activities and the ethical issues surrounding them.

Police Agencies and Surveillance

On May 25, 2017, police in Atlantic City, NJ, held a formal opening of their new $12 million surveillance center that occupies the entire 4th floor of the Public Safety Building. The primary activities at the center are monitoring more than 200 closed-circuit television (CCTV) cameras located in the area—158 of which are found on the city's famous boardwalk. The system is monitored by officers 24 hours a day, seven days a week. The center is also part of PACT, or Protecting Atlantic City Together, which is a network that gives businesses and apartment complexes the ability to connect their privately owned cameras to the monitoring system. Officers in the center can switch views and locations that show up on the monitors, and zoom, rotate, tilt, and pan the cameras. The cameras can zoom to 90 times magnification and see as far as 20 blocks. During its first week of operation, center efforts resulted in 31 arrests and provided assistance to more than 100 investigations (Serpico, 2017).

In this new world of surveillance, local police officers and agencies engage in two forms of surveillance, active and passive, aided by ever-advancing technology. **Active surveillance** by police involves one or more officers surveilling a specific target suspected of involvement with criminal activities. The target is most often an individual, but the target can be a group, a specific residence or residential complex, a city park, etc. (Heibutzki, 2017). The key is officers reasonably believe the target has engaged in, is currently engaging in, or will engage in illegal behavior. The best-known example of active surveillance is when police suspect an individual of engaging in ongoing criminal behavior, such as distribution of illegal drugs. In such cases, the police obtain a warrant that allows them to "wire-tap" the suspect's phone line(s) and listen in on and record telephone conversations. Those recordings can then be used as evidence at any criminal cases that arise from the surveillance.

Passive surveillance is different, because it involves police engaging in a "fishing" expedition in the hope of catching unsuspecting people engaging in illegal behavior. For example, using traffic cameras strategically placed at busy intersections, municipal police can identify motorists who run red lights. The cameras, activated when a vehicle moves through the intersection after the light turns red, take photographs of the rear license tags of offending vehicles. That information is then transmitted to police, who use it to identify the registered owner of the vehicle and send the person a citation. Here, the police did not have any reason to believe a *specific motorist* would run the red light. They simply knew that such violations were common at the location and organized a surveillance operation to address the problem.

Passive surveillance that involves profiling of prospective offenders for police intervention has come under fire in recent years. Claims have been raised, supported by empirical evidence, that police pull people over, stop them on the street, etc. based on their race or ethnicity. So-called racial profiling occurs when criminal profiling, used by police to identify suspects in crimes, goes wrong.

Passive Surveillance and Biased Policing

For more than a decade, concerns have been raised by political commentators and scholars that certain kinds of passive surveillance by police result in **biased policing**. That is, the police stop motorists or pedestrians, conduct searches, and make arrests and other decisions based on factors outside those that are legally allowed to influence these decisions (Fallik & Novak, 2014).

There are two forms of bias that may be at work: explicit and implicit. **Explicit bias** is the traditionally accepted notion that people are consciously aware of their prejudices and attitudes toward members of certain groups (Community Relations Service, n.d.). Overt racism and racist comments are examples of explicit biases. Thus, if a police officer stops someone who is black because she hates blacks, that's explicit bias at work. **Implicit bias** is different and involves subconscious feelings, perceptions, attitudes, etc., we develop from prior influences (Kirwan Institute, 2015). It is an automatic positive or negative preference for a group, based on one's subconscious thoughts. Importantly, the individual may be unaware that biases are driving his or her decision-making. Implicit bias does not require animus; it only requires knowledge of a stereotype to produce discriminatory actions (Kirwan Institute, 2015). In policing, implicit bias might lead officers to automatically be suspicious of two young Hispanic males driving in a neighborhood where few Hispanics live. Implicit bias may even endanger officers; for example, if officers have an implicit bias based on gender, they might be "undervigilant" with women and miss clues suggesting that a particular woman may be dangerous (Fridell, 2013).

Profiling and Racial Profiling

Without question, police routinely use profiling as a tool in law enforcement. In its report on racial discrimination in the United States, the National Research Council (NRC) differentiated profiling from racial profiling used by officials in government and the private sector. **Profiling** is a screening process where some members of a larger group (e.g., motorists, pedestrians, airline passengers) are selected for investigation of possible illegal behavior(s) of interest, based on one or more observable characteristics (National Research Council, 2004, p. 187). The characteristics used in profiling depend on the situation and are based on prior instances of similar offenses being perpetrated by those with certain personality, behavioral, or demographic characteristics (Snook, Eastwood, Gendreau, Goggin, & Cullen, 2007). For example, at airports, people who buy one-way airline tickets using cash on the day of their flight may be "flagged" for further scrutiny by airport security personnel based on an assumption that such persons are more likely than others to pose a risk of perpetrating premeditated violence against airline passengers. When combined with other factors such as age, gender, national origin, volume of luggage checked, recent international travel destinations, etc., a "profile" of likely terrorists can be developed for use by airport security officials to further "screen" such individuals. **Racial** (or ethnic) **profiling**, on the other hand, is a screening process in which race (or ethnicity) is the primary observable characteristic used in the profile (National Research Council, 2004, p. 187). Racial profiling involves police using statistical generalizations about individuals based on characteristics of the group to which they belong. It also constitutes a type of statistically based discrimination against members of those groups.

Racial profiling illustrates implicit bias in action (Banks, Eberhardt, & Ross, 2006). In racial profiling, despite the fact an individual has not violated any law or is not otherwise implicated in a crime or other offense, such as a traffic violation, a police officer stops and questions the individual based on their race (or ethnicity) and not their behavior (Tyler & Wakslak, 2004). In other words, the person is "suspicious" *because* he is a young African American male driving through a mainly white neighborhood, rather than because the officer has information specifically implicating the person in a crime. During racial profiling, the police are using a tactic that takes racial or ethnic identity into account to (1) select "suspects" and (2) subject them to greater scrutiny. The operative assumption here is that the officer's behavior is preemptive—no crime or other illegal action has yet occurred—but the results of the officer's actions can turn deadly for citizens, officers, or both (Makarechi, 2016).

While a massive literature on racial profiling has developed in recent years, one particularly interesting study of the potential workings of racial profiling was done by Jennifer Eberhardt and her colleagues. For the study, researchers conducted several experiments that examined the psychological association between race and criminality (Eberhardt, Goff, Purdie, & Davies, 2004). In one part of the study, researchers exposed police officers to a group of African American faces and a group of white faces and asked, "Who looks criminal?" Results showed the officers not only identified more black faces than white faces as "criminals," but were most likely to identify black faces as "criminals" when they exhibited stereotypical features such as wide noses, thick lips, and dark skin. Eberhardt and colleagues also examined how stereotypical associations between African Americans and criminality operated in the context of racial profiling. Here, they investigated whether research participants would become more likely to be visually attuned to African Americans when subjects were first prompted to think about crime. Results of this experiment showed that both college student subjects and police officers, when first "primed" to think about violent crime, became more likely to look at a black face rather than a white face. Eberhardt and colleagues discovered that police officers who were primed to think about violent crime and who misremembered a black male image tended to recall that image as being more stereotypically black than it was.

While extrapolating these results to the behavior of people outside the laboratory must be done with caution, Eberhardt and colleagues' research highlighted the possibility that when looking for wrongdoers, police officers may be more inclined to look for blacks than whites. Further, blacks who have highly stereotypical facial features are likely to experience the greatest levels of police scrutiny, compared to other blacks and whites. Eberhardt and colleagues could not explain these results as a function of individual differences in subjects' levels of explicit racial bias, as subjects did not show signs of strong racial bias, based on results of several conventional measures of explicit bias.

The Problems with Profiling

Profiling refers to a general tool used by police to identify prospective offenders and subject them to greater scrutiny to determine if they are, in fact, "up to no good." Using certain known personality, behavioral, and demographic characteristics of offenders who have committed the crime(s) of interest in the past, police then "flag" people with those characteristics and pull them over, stop them on the street, etc., and subject them to questioning or additional interventions like searches. Racial (ethnic) profiling is a narrower form of profiling that relies upon race (ethnicity) as the primary characteristic used to identify prospective offenders, who are then subjected to enhanced police scrutiny.

A growing number of social scientists and legal scholars have questioned the reliability, validity, and utility of profiling, and by extension racial profiling (Godwin, 2002; Snook, et al., 2007). Maurice Godwin (2002) has noted that profiling is "vague and general and thus basically useless" and that "profiling is more an art than a science, and evidence for its validity is limited." Godwin (2002) argued that profiling relies on **confirmation bias**—selective thinking where one tends to notice evidence confirming one's beliefs and ignore contradictory evidence; suffers from the ***post hoc* fallacy** (the mistaken notion that simply because one thing follows another, the first thing was a cause of the second); and involves **illusory correlation** (the mistaken belief that unrelated variables are correlated). Snook and colleagues (2007), in a meta-analysis of the profiling literature, argued that profiling is just as likely to be hazardous to police as it is to be helpful, and that "profiling appears . . . to be an extraneous and redundant technique" (p. 448). Finally, in a recent study, Camelia Simoiu, Sam Corbett-Davies, and Shara Goel, using a new statistical procedure for identifying discrimination called a "threshold test," found that officers in the 100 largest police departments in North Carolina applied a lower threshold for stopping and searching African American and Hispanic motorists than officers used to stop and search white and Asian motorists (Simoiu, et al., 2017).

Profiling and its progeny, racial profiling, have been used as tools to either prevent crime or bring to justice those who have violated the law outside the observation of the police. The problem is that profiling involves discrimination in the name of public safety—members of racial or ethnic groups are singled out for extra scrutiny because they are members of these groups which have been deemed as more "crime prone" than other groups. Perhaps even more problematic is that there is no convincing evidence that profiling is either a valid or reliable tool for law enforcement. Instead, it can lead to distrust of the police by members of those groups and a fraying of larger institutional frameworks like the justice system.

The Ethics of Police Surveillance

Police surveillance involves focused watching of specific individuals or locations to identify law-violating behavior. The watching may be active or passive. In the former case, the police have reason to believe a specific person—a target—is engaging in (or has engaged in) criminal activity and they wish to build a case against the suspected offender. In the latter case, the police believe that a crime or some other legal violation is likely to occur at a location, such as a busy intersection, in a public parking deck or park, or some other venue. The location is then placed under surveillance to identify some unknown number of subjects who *may* engage in the behavior of interest. Often, the police use technology to enhance their ability to monitor individual targets, whether person, group, or place; whether through visual or auditory means, or through some combination of the two. Because technological developments have dramatically advanced the ability of law enforcement, and by extension the state, to monitor citizens, the ethics of surveillance has become topic of interest to philosophers, social scientists, and the police themselves.

Before considering determinants of the ethical nature of surveillance, it's important to first consider those areas most likely impacted by it. They include privacy, trust, and autonomy (Macnish, 2011, 2014). Above all else, surveillance affects privacy—what Supreme Court justice Louis Brandeis famously dubbed as the "right to be left alone" (Warren & Brandeis, 1890)—and is valued alike by individuals and the collective. As explained by Kevin Macnish (2011), privacy gives the individual both the space and the autonomy necessary to be who one is, while also protecting one's dignity. Privacy is also valued by the collective, as it facilitates interaction, protects political activities like voting, and keeps us from being overwhelmed by too much information. Closely linked to privacy, surveillance also affects trust—sometimes seen as the inverse of privacy (the more trust, the less privacy) (Macnish, 2011). If one of the elements is violated, however, the relationship suffers. Finally, surveillance affects autonomy. If the surveilled is suspicious, she might conform to the expected norm, but this will not necessarily reflect her true character.. Its presence pressures the surveilled to conform and so render her actions more predictable. Furthermore, if she does not conform there is the chance she will be subject to sanction. Surveilled people therefore can become more predictable if they fear reprisals for acting in ways that merit the disapproval of the surveillant (Macnish, 2011).

Ethical Surveillance

In a recent treatise, Kevin Macnish presented a way for us to judge the ethics of surveillance that borrows the guiding principles from **just war theory,** or moral justifications for the how and why of waging war between sovereign nations (see McMahan, 2012; Walzer, 1978), In his framework for ethical surveillance, Macnish (2014) argues that for surveillance to be ethical it must first be for a just cause (e.g., the security of the community). Further, the intent behind the surveillance must be "correct"—that is, not solely for personal gain or titillation but rather to serve a more noble goal such as the protection of vulnerable groups. Additionally, the entity engaging in the surveillance, in this case the police, must have the proper moral authority to do so (e.g., the police are a branch of a government that has been legitimately and democratically elected). Macnish also notes that the surveillance should be undertaken as a last resort after less harmful methods have been tried and failed (e.g., the use of informants). He also argues that surveillance is proper (e.g., police are attempting to deter automobile theft from public parking garages or armed robberies of convenience stores) if there is a formal declaration of the intent to carry out the surveillance so the citizenry is informed of the forthcoming actions. Finally, Macnish's justifications for surveillance also include the following criteria: (1) there should be a well-defined goal for the surveillance (e.g., reducing traffic fatalities caused by running red lights by 40% over a 12-month period); (2) the chances of achieving success should be high and well articulated; and (3) the foreseeable damage the inflict should be in proportion to the reason for which the surveillance was (is) undertaken, what Macnish termed "proportionality." Table 7.3 summarizes Macnish's framework.

TABLE 7.3 Considerations for Ethical Surveillance

Consideration	Description
Just cause	Surveillance should not be undertaken for salacious, trivial, or ignoble causes (such as protection of pride or of individuals in government, etc.)
Correct intent	Ulterior motives are not the motivating factor for undertaking the surveillance
Proper authority	Entity undertaking the surveillance has the moral authority to do so
Last resort	Decision to undertake surveillance must come after all other options have been tried and failed.
Formal declaration	Where appropriate (e.g., for deterrence purposes), a formal announcement that surveillance is being undertaken should be made (may be through signage)
Chance for success	The surveillance being contemplated must have a reasonable chance for "success" that has been well-articulated
Proportionality	Foreseeable damage inflicted by surveillance should be proportionate to the reason for it being undertaken

Source: Adapted from Macnish (2014)

Given that commonly used police tactics of deception and surveillance give rise to many ethical issues, how can we ensure that police officers are mindful of them? To conclude the chapter, let's consider how police agencies might help officers learn about ethics. In this discussion, I examine key questions: To whom should ethics be taught (e.g., new officers, those established in their careers, or both)? Where and how should ethics be taught to police? What should be the content and goals of this training?

TEACHING AND LEARNING POLICE ETHICS

As discussed in Ch. 6, if police are exposed to the ethical dimensions of their work, it is most often via an academy-based course taught by instructors who are veteran police officers. Rare is the police department that regularly offers in-service training on ethics to its officers, and if it does, the training is likely to occur at a police-related location. When I've been approached by police departments to conduct "ethics training" for officers, the department usually tries to establish restrictions on where, when, and how the training occurs, not to mention the content of the training, and to whom the training is directed, all of which I immediately try and negotiate, since they matter greatly.

In negotiating with police officials about ethics training, I first let it be known that I will approach the task guided by the following assumption: the officers involved in the training are already ethical people; they are committed to the noble cause, which includes a willingness to help others, even if doing so places their lives in jeopardy (Caldero & Crank, 2015). I can think of no higher ethical commitment than a willingness to lay down one's life for another, especially a stranger. Can you? To assume otherwise would be insulting both to the officers and to the department for which they work. Rather, I approach ethics training as an *opportunity* for officers to share with one another the conflicts and dilemmas they face and how they—and their colleagues—work through them. How the officers resolve their dilemmas can then be incorporated into a larger discussion about ethics (and, by extension, morality) that includes familiarizing them with deontological, teleological, and virtue ethics. I also let it be known that ethics training isn't just for line officers—it must include supervisors, through the executive level. However, I would break the training into two sessions, one for line officers and the other for supervisors/command personnel, since the content is slightly different for supervisors. Finally, the training would occur in a neutral setting, such as a conference center, and officers would not be in uniform.

Justifications for Teaching Police Ethics

The first issue to address is rather simple: Why is there a need for training in something called "police ethics?" John Kleinig (1990, p. 4) has offered what I think are the best answers I've yet seen to this question and are what I have used in my negotiations. First, the *need* for police ethics arises from the simple fact that police officers have been given the legal authority to use coercive force against citizens, including deadly force. Decisions made by police officers to use coercive force against citizens can quickly become matters of life and death. As a result, the police need to be taught to wisely exercise their enormous power, and ethics training can help them do so.

Second, the police routinely deal with breakdowns in normality: terrible accidents, brutal beatings, horrific mass shootings, etc. In such instances, the decisions the police make do not fit easily into "typical" moral responses to situations faced in everyday life. Instead, police officers must sometimes deal with people unconstrained by common moral sentiments or events too complex to handle with routine moral outlooks. The need for police ethics arises from an assumption that the moral nurturing officers received up to the point at which they became sworn law-enforcement agents isn't sufficient to help them address these outside-the-norm possibilities involving people and events.

Third, police officers are not only morally, but organizationally and legally, bound to intervene in a host of crisis situations that ordinary citizens can choose to ignore altogether without consequence. Because these situations *by definition* do not afford officers the leisure of thoughtful and extended contemplation, for them to respond wisely, it is important they encounter these crises well prepared and with appropriately sensitized dispositions.

Finally, the need for police ethics arises from the fact that officers confront far greater temptations than do most people, *most of the time*. While most people find it easy to be accepted as being "nice" by others, for police officers to be accepted as "nice" by citizens and/or by colleagues may potentially involve them in dereliction of duty or accepting ill-gotten gain. It is thus important that officers develop levels of moral courage that can effectively block these temptations. The *need* for training in police ethics thus stems from the fact that police officers must atypically respond to atypical situations for which the ordinary affairs of life give inadequate preparation (Kleinig, 1990).

To Whom Should Police Ethics be Taught?

The second issue to address is, Who should be the "target" of police ethics training? Those in the academy? Those under the supervision of FTOs? Line officers only? Commanders? The *snarky* answer obviously is "all officers." However, let me unpack a bit what "all officers" means.

Recruits enrolled in police academy training programs can benefit from police ethics training through the process of anticipatory socialization, which I've spoken about in previous chapters. Recall that the point of academy training is that recruits do not possess the necessary knowledge and skills to perform their jobs without first undergoing extensive training in areas such as law and procedure, firearms usage, forensics, and investigation. Why would we assume recruits are already prepared for the *moral* demands the job will place on them? By offering ethics as part of academy training, recruits can be exposed to and begin to understand and anticipate the moral demands they will confront well before they "hit the street" (Caldero & Crank, 2015; Kleinig, 1990).

Veteran officers can also benefit from police ethics training. If officers are required to attend annual in-service training designed to maintain or enhance their skills and knowledge in the tactical and legal aspects of policing, again, why shouldn't in-service training in ethics be included? As explained by Kleinig (1990, p. 5), veteran officers bring wisdom and the realism of exposure to the complexities of situations and the pragmatism of their world. More importantly, ethics training provides them with opportunities to critically reflect on the realities of their work, may provide clarity where situations have become confused, inspire new insights where an activity has left little room for appraisal, and provide them with the breathing space necessary to revitalize their commitment to the noble cause (Caldero & Crank, 2015).

There's another group who could benefit from police ethics training: citizens (Kleinig, 1990). Police officers routinely complain that citizens make impossible demands of them, don't fully understand or appreciate the work they do and the moral and ethical challenges it presents, and so forth (Caldero & Crank, 2015). Citizens in turn complain that the police are disengaged from the community and don't care about them. By making "police ethics" training available to citizens, they can develop both empathy with the police and sympathy for what it is the police do, the kinds of decisions they have to make, and the less-than-ideal circumstances under which those decisions often have to be made. Citizen engagement with police ethics and its many issues can enhance or even reinforce citizen willingness to grant legitimacy to the powers wielded by police. Engagement can also engender mutual understanding that can help to lower barriers that may exist between the police and the community.

Where Should Police Ethics be Taught?

The question "where should police ethics be taught?" seems easy to answer: the police academy. Just as law students learn law in specialized law schools, business students in business schools, and medical students in medical schools, so, too, should police officers learn police ethics in a specialized setting like a police academy. Or should they?

One argument in favor of the view that police academies are the best place for the teaching and learning of police ethics is that the academy setting is flexible enough to include simulation exercises, role-playing, and even field training (Kleinig, 1990). All these pedagogies involve experiences the trainees can share and form the basis for additional reflection and discussion. Sounds reasonable, doesn't it?

There are, however, complicating factors relating to academy-centered teaching and learning of police ethics (Kleinig, 1990). At best, academy-centered learning of police ethics is simulated, while actual ethical decision-making occurs in the "heat of the moment" under pressures created by time, peers (including supervisors and/or field training officers [FTOs]), and citizens with whom police officers must interact. Perhaps a more important, but subtle, problem with academy-centered teaching and learning of police ethics is that police academies are "partisan institutions"—while separate from police departments, they are nonetheless dedicated to a specific perspective and staffed by "insiders" (Kleinig, 1990). Recall from Ch. 6 that academies are designed to train new hires to become police officers not only in terms of developing in them the skills and knowledge necessary to do their jobs, but also in terms of transforming a recruit's identity from "civilian" to "police officer," ensuring their continued commitment to the noble cause, and maintaining (or enhancing) values like loyalty and a willingness to follow orders. As a result, recruits may lose a sense of the narrowness of their world view and of the moral ambiguity and complexity that often characterize police work (Kleinig, 1990).

Given the concerns with the academy as a setting for teaching/learning police ethics, it is thus at least arguable that police ethics teaching and learning should, therefore, occur "on the beat" (Kleinig, 1990). "On the beat" teaching and learning could involve a "buddy system" where newer officers are paired with more experienced partners who take the lead and are later "on hand" if a situation becomes too difficult. This apprenticeship style of training provides firsthand experience in real decision-making and, as a result, is preferable (Kleinig, 1990).

What Should be the Goals?

Another important question here is, What should be the goal(s) of police ethics training? To answer this question, a good starting point is to identify what teaching and learning police ethics should *not* seek as a goal, namely, providing a general moral education to officers (see Kleinig, 1990). As mentioned above, my starting assumption is that police recruits and officers are already ethical people with solid moral values. I am thus assuming that those involved in teaching and learning police ethics come to the topic with well-developed moral values and an existing framework of personal ethics. To do otherwise is to disrespect those choosing a career in policing and diminish the soundness of the noble cause as a reason for becoming a police officer.

Kleinig (1990) suggests several possible goals for police ethics training, including (1) to reinforce moral resolve in recruits/officers, (2) to sensitize the moral resolve of participants, and (3) to impart moral expertise. Reinforcing moral resolve refers to officers keeping their moral bearings or values and a continuing commitment to them despite the pressures and stresses of the work. The goal is thus to reinforce an officer's moral resolve to help others; to promote a correspondence between belief and action or intention and behavior. In doing so, the training counters a weakening of will or failure of moral nerve, and diminishes one's susceptibility to temptation (Kleinig, 1990). Sensitizing moral resolve refers to the goal of nurturing in recruits and officers a broader and deeper moral fabric. While new hires have already received "moral training" to a point, that training has been influenced by particular moral traditions and partisan biases that may not help them much when they encounter various crises. They will thus need to develop in themselves broader, "culturally universal" moral understandings better suited to police work such as those found in the Law Enforcement Code of Ethics and the oath of office. Ideals such as respect for all persons and obligations to protect the public from harm can help recruits and officers expand their moral horizons. Those sources may even become a core element of police ethics training. The ultimate goal of the training should be to broaden recruits'/officers' moral horizons by creating in them a greater sensitivity to the richness, diversity, and finer nuances of human interaction. Doing so can reduce cynicism and moral desensitization in them, while increasing their ability to reflect creatively on the complex circumstances of police decision-making (see Kleinig, 1990).

Finally, imparting moral expertise refers to shaping and deepening the respect for persons that is at the heart of moral sensitivity (Kleinig, 1990). Given that police officer decisions often have significant implications for the community (e.g., civil unrest generated by the perceived unlawful shooting of a citizen by police officers), and those decisions are sometimes both complex and problematic, officers must develop the ability to recognize the ramifications of their decisions while mediating competing claims that present themselves. Kleinig (1990) illustrates this point by using the example of an officer faced with accepting a minor gratuity (see Ch. 6). Both unthinking acceptance and brusque rejection can be problematic, particularly in the context of community policing. Brusque rejection may, for example, lead citizens to believe that the police are standoffish or unfriendly toward citizens. Outright acceptance may give the appearance of "mooching" by the officer. Both decisions can be further complicated by agency policy that forbids gratuities and by peers who routinely accept them. Officers who have critically reflected on the complexity of gratuities will be able to respond in a manner that results in enhancing the moral quality of the relationship between police and community. Until officers can do so, they may act in ways that either compromise or constitute outright violations of the norms that guide human interaction.

What Should be the Content?

Finally, what should be the substantive content of police ethics training? Again, I believe that Kleinig (1990) provides a reasonable answer. First, there should be a general introduction to moral philosophy that includes topics such as the difference between morality and ethics, the process of moral reasoning, and understanding the theoretical roots of moral decision-making. Second, the training should focus on the Law Enforcement Code of Ethics and variations of it that may exist. The point here would be to examine general statements of police ethical responsibilities and include specific directives for situations in which officers find themselves. As part of this examination, discussion of the background of the provisions and application of them to concrete situations could occur. The key is to go beyond mere recitation and memorization of code provisions by delving into what they mean, how they can be justified (or not), and how they work "on the street."

Third, the training should rely heavily on case studies of police behavior and the ethical implications of the behavior. A case-study approach enables recruits/officers to both envision and appreciate the complexity of the world in which they work by examining the many factors that influence the officer's choices, as described by the case study. Moreover, case studies provide the impetus for discussion, as well as for practicing their moral reasoning. Finally, training should focus on specific issues in police work (e.g., deception, resource allocation, whistleblowing, "noble cause corruption," etc.). Their general relevance to police work should be clear enough, and they should be sufficiently manageable to allow for several to be covered during a particular training session. They can also be tied not only to broader aspects of moral theory but also to easily understood concrete causes. This allows officers the opportunity to reflect upon and discuss the ethical implications of "real issues."

The teaching and learning of police ethics goes beyond simply reciting and memorizing provisions found in police codes of ethics, the oath of office, and agency policy. A training program organized along those lines fails to appreciate both the complexity of police ethics and its subtlety. Instead, teaching and learning police ethics should involve careful consideration of, and elaboration on why the training is important (i.e., justification for the training), who should be the targets (e.g., recruits, veterans, *and* citizens), where the training should occur (i.e., location, with on the beat preferable), and what should be the content (e.g., introduction to moral theory and moral reasoning; police codes of ethics; case studies; issues in police work).

SUMMARY

This chapter has examined ethical issues associated with common tactics used in policing, including deception and surveillance. I began the chapter by providing you with a typology of police work based on two dimensions: nature of the work and nature of the operation. Into the four cells can be placed different tactics in policing, including those involving traditional randomized, uniformed patrol; deception during investigations/interrogations; and surveillance activities by police, both active and passive. I then organized the remainder of the discussion on police tactics around two of the cells in that typology: deception and surveillance. Concerning deception, I explored its use by police during investigations, along with a specific tactic known as "sting operations." Here, I reviewed how sting operations work, positive and negative aspects of them, a key legal issue surrounding them (entrapment), and two tests used by the courts to establish whether police illegally coerced an otherwise innocent person into breaking the law.

I then examined police use of deception used during interrogations. I reviewed interrogation tactics used by police and highlighted the Reid technique. I also examined legal constraints imposed on police deception during interrogation. I then explored the connection between police deception used during interrogation and the problem of people confessing to crimes they did not commit, known as "false confessions." I provided you with an overview of the psychology of false confessions, including a well-regarded typology of them.

I next examined police deception in the courtroom in the form of "testilying" and falsification of official documents (e.g., arrest reports). In this section, I explained how and why the police lie during criminal proceedings. I also examined what factors contribute to police lying in court, including the "noble cause" and its progeny, the "blue wall of silence," along with a lack of sanctions imposed on police officers who lie. I ended the section by exploring the ethics of police deception, which included a brief discussion of types of lies, and presented a test developed by Sissela Bok for determining the ethics of deception/lying.

I shifted focus to another tactic of the police—surveillance—and differentiated active from passive forms of it. I shared with you one example of police surveillance in action, "racial profiling," and examined how it works and its potential impact on communities. I then discussed the ethics of police surveillance by sharing with you three areas most affected by it (privacy, trust, and autonomy). Following that discussion, I shared with you a "theory of ethical surveillance" recently developed by Kevin Macnish (2014) that borrowed its guiding principles from those found in "just war" theory. In combination, the principles constitute a test for determining the circumstances where surveillance by police can be ethically justified.

I concluded the chapter by exploring the teaching and learning of police ethics. In this section, I shared with you what I consider the most important considerations for this type of training, as first articulated by John Kleinig (1990). Important components of training in police ethics include justifying why such training is important, for whom the training is geared (i.e., the targets of the training), where the training should occur, and what should be the content of the training. The result is a training program that is comprehensive in scope, relevant in application, and one that promotes higher-order thinking about police ethics among participants.

To complete your journey into police ethics, I'd like for you to consider a newly popular tactic being adopted by police departments across America and Western Europe and its ethical implications.

THOUGHT EXERCISE 7.2

MINORITY REPORT AND THE ETHICS OF PREDICTIVE POLICING

Imagine a time when murder has been eliminated because it is now possible to see the future using images alluding to time and place and other details, and arrest and prosecute the offender just as the crime is being committed. This is the premise of 2002's *Minority Report,* which featured Tom Cruise as the main character Chief John Anderton, the head of the Department of Justice's "Pre-Crime Unit." Based on a story by famed writer Philip K. Dick, *Minority Report* is set in Washington, DC, in the year 2054 and chronicles how police utilize psychic-based technology to arrest and help convict murderers before they commit their crime. Sounds like science fiction, right? It should—Philip K. Dick was an award-winning science fiction writer. But consider this: in many major cities in both America and the European Union, police departments are combining "big data," geospatial technologies, and evidence-based interventions to reduce crime and enhance public safety using a tactic known as **predictive policing**.

Predictive Policing Explained

Predictive policing can be defined as "any tactic that develops and uses information and advanced analysis to inform forward-thinking crime prevention" (Uchida, 2009, p. 1). While it is not intended to replace traditional preventive patrol, predictive policing is supposed to enhance existing proactive approaches used by police (e.g., "hot-spot" policing). A presumed benefit of predictive policing comes from leveraging computer models—like those used in in business and industry to predict how market conditions or industry trends will evolve over time—to anticipate likely crime events and inform actions designed to prevent them. This is accomplished by focusing on key variables, including places, people, groups, or incidents. Enhancements also come from incorporating local demographic trends, parolee populations, and economic conditions—all of which affect crime rates—into predictive models (National Institute of Justice, 2014). Thus, predictive models supported by prior crime and environmental data inform interventions by police designed to reduce the number of crime incidents in a given location. Sounds promising, yes?

If predictive policing is one more application of "big data" to a problem—in this case, events like burglaries and murders—what sorts of issues arise with its use? William Isaac and Andi Dixon of the Human Rights Data Analysis Group have suggested that:

> At its core, any predictive model or algorithm is a combination of data and a statistical process that seeks to find patterns in the numbers. This can include looking at police data in hopes of learning about crime trends or recidivism. But a useful outcome depends not only on good mathematical analysis: *It also needs good data.* That's where predictive policing often falls short.
>
> —(emphasis added; Isaac & Dixon, 2017, p. 1)

The Problem of Biased Data

What Isaac & Dixon (2017) are concerned with is *bias* in the data used to make predictions about where and when crime occurs. They explain that algorithms used in machine-learning applications—like predictive policing—make their predictions by first analyzing patterns found in an initial "training" dataset. They then look for similar patterns in new data as that information becomes available. The problem is this: if the wrong patterns are gleaned from the training data, all later analyses will be flawed (Isaac & Dixon, 2017). Further, detecting bias in predictive models involving the police is hard because: (1) these data are not collected uniformly and (2) the events or individuals these data track may reflect decades' old institutional biases relating to social class, race, and gender (Isaac & Dixon, 2017). It's also true that large-scale victimization surveys show that many criminal victimizations remain unreported to police for various reasons (Fisher, Reyns, & Sloan, 2015). As a result, much crime data is not even available for use by the police, which means that predictions will be biased due to missing data (Belknap, 2015; Gelman, Fagan, & Kiss, 2007). Finally, "crime data" is often influenced by existing priorities, such as focusing resources to identify and arrest armed robbers or recidivist burglars operating in the community (Mosher, Miethe, & Hart, 2010). Again, the resulting predictions are biased because the data are overemphasizing certain crimes to the exclusion of others.

Fixing the Problem

Isaac & Dixon (2017) argued that this problem can't be fixed simply by using more sophisticated statistical computations—the math used in the predictions isn't the problem. The solution is data driven and involves rethinking how police data are collected and analyzed to address possible biases "baked into" the data. The solution is also personnel driven: police agencies have to do a better job of training their staff in the use of these data, including making them aware of the potential for bias when making predictions.

What do *you* think? Can predictive policing be justified on ethical grounds?

KEY TERMS

Typology 180
Police deception 181
Undercover operations 181
Sting operations 182
Entrapment 182
Subjective test for entrapment 183
Objective test for entrapment 183
Reid technique 184
Totality of the circumstances test 186
False confession 188
Voluntary false confessions 188
Coerced-compliant false confessions 188
Coerced-internalized false confessions 189
Testilying 190
Police perjury 190
Blue wall of silence 191
Black lies 193
White lies 193
Blue lies 193
Morality by majority 194
Surveillance 196
Active surveillance 197
Passive surveillance 197
Biased policing 198
Explicit bias 198
Implicit bias 198
Profiling 198
Racial profiling 198
Confirmation bias 200
Post hoc fallacy 200
Illusory correlation 200
Just War theory 201
Predictive policing 208

DISCUSSION QUESTIONS

1. Sting operations might be better viewed as tactics associated with police surveillance rather than as deception. Explain how stings might operate as examples of either active or passive surveillance by police. Does reclassifying stings as surveillance change the ethical issues associated with them?
2. One potentially major negative consequence of deception during interrogation

is generating a false confession. While these appear to be relatively rare events, are they so serious a consequence that police use of deception during interrogation should be *banned* entirely? Develop a moral argument for one position or the other.

3. Profiling, whether it's "criminal" or "racial," continues to be a controversial tool used by police that has many downsides and seemingly few benefits. Using moral reasoning, develop an argument that supports its abolition.
4. This chapter has reviewed the ethics of police deception and police surveillance, two "arrows in the quiver" to use in the fight against crime. Is there a tactic you can think of, either that I covered in this chapter or that you are familiar with based on other sources, that is always (or never) unethical? Discuss.

RESOURCES

Frontline, a long-running public broadcasting news and information series, did a comprehensive feature on the "Norfolk Four" (described above). The one-hour program is available to view at http://www.pbs.org/wgbh/pages/frontline/the-confessions/

The **Innocence Project** (founded in 1992 by Peter Neufeld and Barry Scheck at Cardozo School of Law) seeks to exonerate the wrongly convicted through DNA testing and reform the criminal justice system to prevent future injustice. Its website has an entire section devoted to false confessions that includes additional resources for those interested in learning more about the topic: https://www.innocenceproject.org/causes/false-confessions-admissions/

For over 30 years, Gary Marx, a sociology professor at the Massachusetts Institute of Technology (MIT), has been a leading scholar in the study of the "**new surveillance**" that governments have developed. For those interested in learning about him and his work, visit his website at: http://web.mit.edu/gtmarx/www/garyhome.html. There, you'll be able to access some of his writings on the "new surveillance."

REFERENCES

Albrechtslund, A. (2008, March 3). Online social networking as participatory surveillance. *First Monday*. Retrieved from http://firstmonday.org/ojs/index.php/fm/article/view/2142/1949http%3A

Alpert, G., & Noble, W. (2009). Lies, true lies and conscious deception. *Police Quarterly, 12*, 237–254. Retrieved from https://www.prisonlegalnews.org/media/publications/police__quarterly_lies_true_lies_and_conscious_deception_2008.pdf

Banks, R., Eberhardt, E., & Ross, L. (2006). Discrimination and implicit bias in a racially unequal society. *California Law Review, 94*, 1169–1190. Retrieved from http://scholarship.law.berkeley.edu/cgi/viewcontent.cgi?article=1255&context=Californalawreview

Barker, T., Friery, R., & Carter, D. (1994). After LA, would your local police lie? In T. Barker & D. Carter (Eds.), *Police deviance* (3rd ed.) (pp. 44–68). Cincinnati, OH: Anderson.

Batterton, J. (2010, June). Invocation of right to remain silent must be unambiguous: *Berghuis v. Thompkins*. Legal & Liability Risk Management Institute. Retrieved from http://www.llrmi.com/articles/legal_update/us10_berghuis_v_thompkins.shtml

Belknap, J. (2015). *The invisible woman: Gender, crime and justice* (4th ed.). Boston, MA: Cengage.

Bok, S. (1999). *Lying: Moral choice in public and private life*. New York, NY: Vintage Books.

Burns, R. (1998). Bright lines and hard edges: Anatomy of a criminal evidence decision. *Journal of Criminal Law and Criminology, 85,* 843–877.

Caldero, M., & Crank, J. (2015). *Police ethics: The corruption of noble cause* (Rev. 3rd ed.). New York, NY: Routledge.

Caputo, A. (2010). *Digital video surveillance and security.* Burlington, MA: Elsevier.

CBS News (2015, August 3). Calif. cops pose as homeless to nab distracted drivers. Retrieved from https://www.cbsnews.com/news/california-police-pose-homeless-sting-operation-catch-distracted-drivers/

Center for Evidence-Based Crime Policy (2013). Standard police tactics. Retrieved from http://cebcp.org/evidence-based-policing/what-works-in-policing/research-evidence-review/standard-model-policing-tactics/

Chin, G., & Wells, S. (1998). The 'Blue Wall of Silence' as evidence of bias and motive to lie: A new approach to police perjury. *University of Pittsburgh Law Review, 59,* 233–299.

Colquitt, J. (2004). Rethinking entrapment. *American Criminal Law Review, 41,* 1389–1437.

Community Relations Service (n.d.). *Understanding bias: A resource guide.* Washington, DC: U.S. Department of Justice. Retrieved from tttps://www.justice.gov/crs/file/836431/download

Drizin, M., & Leo, R. (2004). The problem of false confessions in the post DNA world. *University of North Carolina Law Review, 82,* 891–1007.

Eberhardt, J., Goff, P., Purdie, V., & Davies, P. (2004). Seeing black: Race, crime, and visual processing. *Journal of Personality and Social Psychology, 87,* 876–893.

Ekins, E. (2016). *Policing in America: Understanding public attitudes toward the police—results from a national survey.* Washington, DC: CATO Institute.

Fallik, S., & Novak, J. (2014). Biased policing. In G. Bruinsma & D. Weisburd (Eds.), *Encyclopedia of criminology and criminal justice* (pp. 154–162). New York, NY: Springer.

Fisher, B., Reyns, B., & Sloan, J. (2015). *Introduction to victimology.* New York, NY: Oxford University Press.

Fridell, L. (2013). This is not your grandparents' prejudice: The implications of the modern science of bias for police training. *Transnational Criminology.* Retrieved from http://cebcp.org/wp-content/TCmagazine/TC5-Fall2013

Gavett, G. (2011, December 9). A rare look at the police tactics that can lead to false confessions. Retrieved from https://www.pbs.org/wgbh/frontline/article/a-rare-look-at-the-police-tactics-that-can-lead-to-false-confessions/

Gelman, A., Fagan, J., & Kiss, A. (2007). An analysis of the New York City Police Department's "stop-and-frisk" policy in the context of claims of racial bias. *Journal of the American Statistical Association, 102,* 813–823.

Godwin, M. (2002). Reliability, validity, and utility of criminal profiling typologies. *Journal of Police and Criminal Psychology, 17,* 1–18.

Hammill, B. (2017). The nine steps of the Reid technique. Retrieved from http://slideplayer.com/slide/1526180/

Hanke, S. (2013, October 28). The NSA's rent is too damn high! Retrieved from https://www.cato.org/blog/nsas-rent-too-damn-high

Heath, B. (2015, August 24). Police secretly track cellphones to solve routine crimes. *USA Today.* Retrieved from https://www.usatoday.com/story/news/2015/08/23/baltimore-police-stingray-cell-surveillance/31994181/

Heibutzki, R. (2017). Types of surveillance in criminal investigations. Retrieved from http://work.chron.com/types-surveillance-criminal-investigations-9434.html

Hritz, A. (2017). Voluntariness with a vengeance: The coerciveness of police lies in interrogations. *Cornell University Law Review, 102,* 487–511.

Hughes, E., & Stevens, A. (2010). What can we learn from the Portuguese decriminalization of illicit drugs? *British Journal of Criminology, 50,* 999–1022.

Inbau, F., Reid, J., Buckley, J., & Jayne, B. (2013). *Criminal interrogations and confessions* (5th ed.). Burlington, MA: Jones & Bartlett.

Isaac, W., & Dixon, A. (2017, May 9). Why big data analysis of police activity is inherently biased. *The Conversation*. Retrieved from https://theconversation.com/why-big-data-analysis-of-police-activity-is-inherently-biased-72640

Kassin, S. (1997). The psychology of confession evidence. *American Psychologist, 52,* 221–233.

Kassin, S. (2004, April 26). Videotape police interrogations. *The Boston Globe*, p. A-13.

Kassin, S., & Gudjonsson, G. (2004). The psychology of confessions: A review of the literature and issues. *Psychological Science, 5,* 33–67

Kassin, S., Leo, R., Meissner, C., Richman, K., Colwell, L., Leach, A., & La Fon, D. (2007). Police interviewing and interrogation: A self-report survey of police practices and beliefs. *Law & Human Behavior, 31,* 381–400.

Kirwan Institute (2015). *Understanding implicit bias*. Retrieved from http://kirwaninstitute.osu.edu/research/understanding-implicit-bias/

Kleinig, J. (1990). Teaching and learning police ethics: Competing and complementary approaches. *Journal of Criminal Justice, 18,* 1–18.

Kleinig, J. (2001). The Blue Wall of Silence: An ethical analysis. *International Journal of Applied Philosophy, 15,* 1–23.

Kleinig, J. (2008). *Ethics and criminal justice: An introduction*. New York, NY: Cambridge University Press.

Klockars, C. (1980). The Dirty Harry problem. *The Annals of the American Academy of Political and Social Science*, 452, 33–47.

Leo, R. (2004). The third degree and the origins of psychological interrogation in the United States. In G. Lassiter (Ed.), *Interrogations, confessions, and entrapment* (pp. 51–98). New York, NY: Springer.

Leo, R. (2009). False confessions: Causes, consequences, and implications. *Journal of the American Academy of Psychiatry and the Law, 37,* 332–343.

Leo, R. (2017). Police interrogation and suspect confessions: Social science, law and public policy. In E. Luna (Ed.), *Academy for justice: A report on scholarship and criminal justice reform* (pp.1–34). San Francisco, CA: University of San Francisco School of Law.

Lyon, D. (2007). Surveillance, power, and everyday life. In R. Mansell, C. Avgerou, D. Quah, & R. Silverstone (Eds.), *The Oxford handbook of information and communication technologies* (pp. 449–472). New York, NY: Oxford University Press.

Lyon, D. (2008). Surveillance society. Retrieved from http://www.festivaldeldiritto.it/2008/pdf/interventi/david_lyon.pdf

Maciag, M. (2017). State marijuana laws in 2017. Retrieved from http://www.governing.com/gov-data/state-marijuana-laws-map-medical-recreational.html

Maclin, T. (1994). When the cure for the Fourth Amendment is worse than the disease. *University of Southern California Law Review, 68,* 1–70.

Macnish, K. (2011). Surveillance ethics. In J. Fieser & B. Dowden (Eds.), *The Internet encyclopedia of philosophy*. Retrieved from http://www.iep.utm.edu/surv-eth/#H9

Macnish, K. (2014). Just surveillance? Toward a normative theory of surveillance. *Surveillance and Society, 12,* 142–153.

Mahon, J. (2015). The definition of lying and deception. In E. Zalta (Ed.), *The Stanford encyclopedia of philosophy* (Winter Edition). Retrieved from https://plato. stanford.edu/cgi-bin/encyclopedia/archinfo.cgi?entry=lying-definition

Makarechi, K. (2016, July 14). What the data really says about police and racial bias. *Vanity Fair*. Retrieved from http://www.vanityfair.com/news/2016/07/data-police-racial-bias

Marcus, P. (2006). It's not just about *Miranda*: Determining the voluntariness of confessions in criminal prosecutions. *Valparaiso University Law Review, 40,* 601–644.

Marcus, P. (2009). *The entrapment defense* (4th ed.). New York, NY: LexisNexis.

Marx, G. (1988). *Undercover: Police surveillance in America*. Berkeley, CA: University of California Press.

Marx, G. (1992). Under-the-covers undercover investigations: Some reflections on the state's use of sex and deception in law enforcement. *Criminal Justice Ethics, 11,* 13–24.

Marx, G. (2005). Surveillance and society. In G. Ritzer (Ed.) *Encyclopedia of social theory,*

Vol II (pp. 734–739). Thousand Oaks, CA: Sage. Retrieved from http://web.mit.edu/gtmarx/www/surandsoc.html

McMahan, J. (2012, November 11). Rethinking the "just war." *New York Times*. Retrieved from https://opinionator.blogs.nytimes.com/2012/11/11/rethinking-the-just-war-part-1/

Mollen Commission (1994). *Commission report*. New York, NY: Mollen Commission.

Moore, T., & Fitzsimmons, C. (2011). Justice imperiled: False confessions and the Reid technique. *Criminal Law Quarterly, 57*, 509–542.

Morton, J. (2011). *The life and revolutionary times of Vidocq*. New York, NY: Overlook Press.

Mosher, C., Miethe, T., & Hart, T. (2010). *The mismeasure of crime* (2nd ed.). Beverly Hills, CA: Sage Publications.

Nakashima, E. (2015, December 8). Meet the woman in charge of the FBI's most controversial high-tech tools. *Washington Post*. Retrieved from https://www.washingtonpost.com/world/national-security/meet-the-woman-in-charge-of-the-fbis-most-contentious-high-tech-tools/2015/12/08/15adb35e-9860-11e5-8917-653b65c809eb_story.html

National Institute of Justice (2014). Predictive policing. Retrieved from https://www.nij.gov/topics/law-enforcement/strategies/predictive-policing/Pages/welcome.aspx#overview

National Research Council (2004). *Measuring racial discrimination*. Washington, DC: The National Academies Press. Retrieved from https://www.nap.edu/read/10887/chapter/1#ii

Newman, G. (2007). *Police stings*. Washington, DC: Office of Community Oriented Policing Services. Retrieved from http://www.popcenter.org/Responses/pdfs/sting_operations.pdf

Nicholson, J. (2013). Police deception: A survey of EKU Students. (Unpublished master's thesis). Richmond, KY, Eastern Kentucky University. Retrieved from http: encompass.eku.edu/cgi/viewcontent.cgi?article=1196&context=etd

Orlando, J. (2014). Interrogation techniques. Retrieved from https://www.cga.ct.gov/2014/rpt/2014-R-0071.htm

Privacy International (2016). *The global surveillance industry*. London, England: Privacy International. Retrieved from https://privacyinternational.org/sites/default/files/ global_ surveillance.pdf

Richards, N. (2013). The dangers of surveillance. *Harvard Law Review, 126*, 1934–1964.

Ruggiero, V. (2012). *Thinking critically about ethical issues* (8th ed.). New York, NY: McGraw Hill.

Schwartz, M. (2003). Compensating victims of police-fabricated confessions. *University of Chicago Law Review, 70*, 1119–1139.

Serpico, E. (2017, May 24). Atlantic City police, officials formally unveil surveillance center. *Atlantic City Press*. Retrieved from http://www.pressofatlanticcity.com/news/atlantic-city-police-officials-formally-unveil-surveillance-center/article_fe25b687-e917-57f1-9cf2-9907bc113411.html

Simoiu, C., Corbett-Davies, S., & Goel, S. (2017.). The problem of infra-marginality in outcome tests for discrimination. *The Annals of Applied Statistics, 11*, 1193–1216. Retrieved from https://5harad.com/papers/threshold-test.pdf

Skolnick, J. (1982). Deception by police. *Criminal Justice Ethics, 1*, 40–54.

Smith, J. (2017, February 8). What's good about lying? *Greater Good Magazine*. Retrieved from https://greatergood.berkeley.edu/article/item/whats_good_about_lying

Snook, B., Eastwood, J., Gendreau, P., Goggin, C., & Cullen, R. (2007). Taking stock of criminal profiling: A narrative review and meta-analysis. *Criminal Justice and Behavior, 34*, 437–453.

Storm, L. (2017). Entrapment. Retrieved from https://catalog.flatworldknowledge.com/bookhub/reader/4373?e=storm_1.0-ch06_s03

The Innocence Project (2017). Exonerate the innocent. Retrieved from https://www.innocenceproject.org/exonerate/

Tyler, T., & Wakslak, C. (2004). Profiling and police legitimacy: Procedural justice, attributions of motive, and acceptance of police authority. *Criminology, 42*, 253–282.

Uchida, C. (2009). *A national discussion on predictive policing: Defining our terms and mapping successful implementation strategies*. Washington, DC: National Institute of

Justice. Retrieved from https://www.ncjrs.gov/pdffiles1/nij/grants/230404.pdf

Uviller, R. (1988). *Tempered zeal: A Columbia law professor's year on the streets with the New York City Police*. Chicago, IL: Contemporary Books.

Walzer, M. (1978). *Just and unjust wars*. New York, NY: Basic Books.

Warren, S., & Brandeis, L. (1890). The right to privacy. *Harvard Law Review, 3*, 1–19.

Wasieleski, D., Whatley, M., & Murphy, S. (2009). The hindsight bias and attitudes toward police deception in eliciting confessions. *North American Journal of Psychology, 9*, 285–296.

Weisburd, D., Greenspan, R., Hamilton, E., Bryant, K., & Williams, H. (2001). *The abuse of police authority: A national study of police officer attitudes*. Washington, DC: Police Foundation.

Wrightsman, L., & Kassin, S. (1993). *Confessions in the courtroom*. Newbury Park, CA: Sage Publications.

Wrightsman, L., & Kassin, S. (Eds.) (1995). *The psychology of evidence and trial procedure*. Thousand Oaks, CA: Sage Publications.

CHAPTER 8

Ethics and the Courts

Chapter Outline

CHAPTER LEARNING OBJECTIVES:

1. Describe the courtroom workgroup, including its members, goals, and dynamics.
2. Describe the ABA's Standards for the Prosecution Function, including their purpose and organization.
3. Describe the ethical issues associated with prosecuting people.
4. Define prosecutorial misconduct and provide examples of the forms it can take.
5. Identify hurdles to curtailing prosecutorial misconduct.
6. Describe the ABA's Model Standards for the Defense Function, including their purpose and organization.
7. Identify the ethical issues associated with attorneys "zealously" defending their clients.
8. Describe two examples of model rules for the judiciary, including their purpose and organization.
9. Explain how caseloads, delegating decision-making, ambition, and "doing justice" are ethical issues for the judiciary.

INTRODUCTION

You're no doubt familiar with the litany of criticisms about the ethics of people affiliated with courts in this country: defense attorneys taking on clients they "know" are guilty; prosecutors who zealously seek to convict innocent people; judges running for election who spend large amounts of "dark money" doing so (and some of which has been contributed by trial attorneys appearing before them). Each constitutes an ethical issue relating to the behavior of defense attorneys, prosecutors, and judges—the people who make up the courts component of the criminal justice system, which is the focus of this chapter.

As I did in Chs. 6 and 7, I begin this chapter by presenting you with a context to help guide the discussion of ethics and the courts. Known as the courtroom workgroup (Eisenstein & Jacob, 1977), it consists of prosecutors, defense attorneys, and judges who work to process and dispose of criminal cases each day in courts across the nation. My discussion focuses on workgroup goals and describes their interactional dynamics. My purpose here is to set the stage for a fuller examination of ethical issues associated with each member of the workgroup, beginning with prosecutors, followed by defense counsel, and then judges. When discussing each member of the workgroup, I first describe their ideal functions as articulated by various codes of professional conduct or standards for behavior. Following this, I present examples of ethical issues associated with each member and efforts aimed at resolving them. I conclude the chapter by asking you to consider two different models for regulating the conduct of lawyers and decide which makes more "ethical" sense. Throughout my discussion on ethics and the courts, I emphasize the ideals that prosecutors, defense attorneys, and judges are supposed to be working toward and the obligations they have to the citizens they serve.

Let's start the discussion on ethics and the courts by exploring how the trio of prosecutor, defense counsel, and judge collaborate to process and dispose of the many cases they encounter each day in court.

THE COURTROOM WORKGROUP

Daily in this country's courts, preliminary hearings and arraignments are held; plea negotiations occur between prosecutors and defense attorneys; and trials happen. To give you an extreme example of local courts' caseloads, during 2015, in the seven courts that comprise the New York City Criminal Court system, 72 judges processed over 315,000 cases (Lindsey, 2016). That translates to 4,375 cases per judge, assuming an even distribution of the load. If there were 251 working days in calendar year 2015, each judge would need to dispose of 17 cases *per day*. Can you say pressure?

Americans tend to believe that their courts symbolize important ideals enshrined in the U.S. Constitution, such as "due process of law," "justice," and "fairness," and courtroom actors work to achieve them. Influenced by depictions found in media and novels, people often believe that prosecutors seek "justice" by getting defendants convicted and off the streets; that defense attorneys ensure "fairness" by checking the power of the state and providing the best defense for clients; and judges oversee what goes on in their courts as impartial and fair referees. Those are the ideals. The reality, as you know, is different. Because many courts face huge caseload pressures, it is simply impossible for all the cases to go to trial. As a result, depending on jurisdiction, about 95% of *all* felony cases in state and federal courts are disposed of through plea agreements negotiated by prosecutors and defense attorneys and approved by judges (Devers, 2011; Reaves, 2013). Rather than an **adversarial system** in which prosecutor and defense attorney litigate the merits of a case overseen by a judge and from which emerges "the truth," the reality is that most cases are disposed of via negotiated outcomes (plea bargains).

The existence of **negotiated justice** and its workings were chronicled extensively by James Eisenstein and Herbert Jacob (1977) in their now-classic book *Felony Justice: An Organizational Analysis of Criminal Courts*. In their study, Eisenstein and Jacob used quantitative and qualitative methods to examine factors affecting the processing of, and eventual results in, over 4,500 felony cases in Baltimore, Chicago, and Detroit, during 1972–73. Most importantly, they identified the role of the **courtroom workgroup** in processing and disposing of these cases. Consisting of individuals sharing a common workplace, interacting with one another in the performance of their jobs and disposing of cases efficiently and fairly, the courtroom workgroup and the negotiated justice it fosters constitute the reality in courtrooms everywhere (Eisenstein & Jacob, 1977; Nardulli, Eisenstein, & Flemming, 1988).

Goals of the Courtroom Workgroup

In working collaboratively to dispose of cases, the courtroom workgroup achieves several goals, including efficiency, reduced uncertainty at sentencing, and shared power (Gebo, Stracuzzi, & Hurst, 2006). Efficiency is achieved by working together to dispose of cases quickly and thus keep caseloads manageable. Reduced uncertainty at sentencing is accomplished by workgroups creating routines of informal negotiations that involve a going rate (i.e., a specific sentence) for certain crimes (Gebo, et al., 2006; Kramer & Ulmer, 2002). Defendants charged with these crimes are encouraged to plead guilty and receive the agreed-upon "routine" sentences "to reduce the guesswork in sentencing" (Gebo, et al., 2006, p. 426). Power-sharing is necessary to facilitate case processing and is accomplished by each member agreeing to give up some of the power they wield (Flemming, Nardulli, & Eisenstein, 1992). For example, prosecutors have the power to charge defendants as they see fit and offer negotiated settlements; defense attorneys have the power to take a case to trial and propose and accept negotiated settlements; judges have the power to rule on motions and objections, limit the admissibility of evidence, and approve negotiated settlements. If each member chose to exercise his or her maximum power, many more trials would occur, court resources would be stretched to the breaking point, and case backlogs would develop. By each member agreeing to give up some of his or her power and organize their interactions based on these constraints, many more cases can be processed and disposed of through "deals" that the members can live with.

Workgroup Dynamics

Three factors affect the dynamics of the workgroup: familiarity, similarity, and stability (Flemming, et al., 1992; Ulmer, 1995). Familiarity is important because it reduces uncertainty during negotiations and increases the chance of reaching a settlement in the case—a plea of guilty. Similarity refers to "shared pasts and the identities forged and sedimented through them" (Ulmer, 1995, p. 588) and includes background features of members (e.g., race and gender; college and law school attended; political party affiliation). Similar pasts and shared identities have been shown to generate cooperation in small groups—people tend to attach increased value to the contributions made by "similar" others (Hoskins-Haynes, Ruback, & Cusick, 2010). The greater the similarity of members, the greater is the cooperation among them. Finally, stability affects workgroup dynamics as well. Fewer changes in group membership leads to greater familiarity, which in turn leads to more interaction and reduced uncertainty, and more cases processed.

To summarize, in contrast to an idealized adversarial system of justice wherein the prosecutor zealously works to convict defendants, defense attorneys zealously defend people charged with crimes, and judges serve as impartial arbiters of the contest, the reality of the criminal justice process is one of negotiated justice. In this process, prosecutor, defense counsel, and judge form a courtroom workgroup whose purpose is to dispose of cases efficiently, effectively, and fairly. A stable roster of local prosecutors and defense attorneys regularly appearing before the same judge enhances the chances workgroup members agree to sacrifice some of the power they wield to reach negotiated settlements. They develop routines for these settlements, aided by the familiarity that comes with working together day-after-day; by members' similarity in background and experiences; and because of stability in the roster of people who are group members.

As you explore ethics and the courts, it's important that you keep in mind that, like the police, courtroom actors operate within a larger organizational context that creates opportunities, applies pressures, and imposes constraints on behavior. How prosecutors, defense attorneys, and judges navigate these organizationally based pushes and pulls creates moral dilemmas; how they are resolved creates questions of ethics.

Let's now turn our attention to prosecutors and explore some of the ethical issues associated with their roles as members of courtroom workgroups.

ETHICS AND PROSECUTORS

Prosecutors are among the most powerful actors in the criminal justice process. Their decisions profoundly affect the lives not only of defendants and victims, but also of their families. Remarkably, these sometimes-life-and-death decisions are largely discretionary and virtually unreviewable (Davis, 2007).

Local prosecutors' offices are typically headed by a district attorney (DA) elected to the office for a set term (Wright, 2009). The DA manages professional and paraprofessional staff working in one or more "divisions" or "sections" in the office. Staff include one or more chief deputies, appointed by the DA, overseeing one or more divisions; multiple assistant district attorneys (ADAs) handling charging decisions, appearing before grand juries, trying cases, or appearing at appeals; one or more investigators working with local police to compile evidence against defendants; one or more victim service officers (VSOs) keeping victims notified of important dates for their cases, offering emotional support to them, and assisting victims with necessary paperwork; information technology personnel assisting with trial-preparation activities and maintaining databases of cases and other records; and staff versed in public relations issuing press releases, handling media inquiries, etc. The DA will also have a chief of staff or executive assistant who keeps his or her calendar, organizes meetings, appears with the DA at public events, and the like. The professional and paraprofessional staff working in the DA's office are usually career people hired via civil service procedures. Collectively, the DA and his or her staff represent the interests of citizens living in the jurisdiction (typically, a county) in criminal matters (see Figure 8.1).

The Prosecution Function

Founded in 1878, the American Bar Association (ABA) is one of the world's largest voluntary professional organizations, with over 400,000 members. Besides accrediting U.S. law schools (which is probably why you've heard of it), the ABA's Center for Professional Responsibility (ABACPR) has developed model rules, along with commentary on them, for the practice of law that 49 states have adopted as regulations on the professional behavior of lawyers (American Bar Association, 2017a). The Center has also created professional standards and commentary on them for prosecutors, defense counsel, and the judiciary. For example, in 2015 the ABA updated an existing set of "black letter" standards relating to the prosecution function. Consisting of eight parts, the standards constitute "best practices" relating to the prosecution function, including general activities of prosecutors;

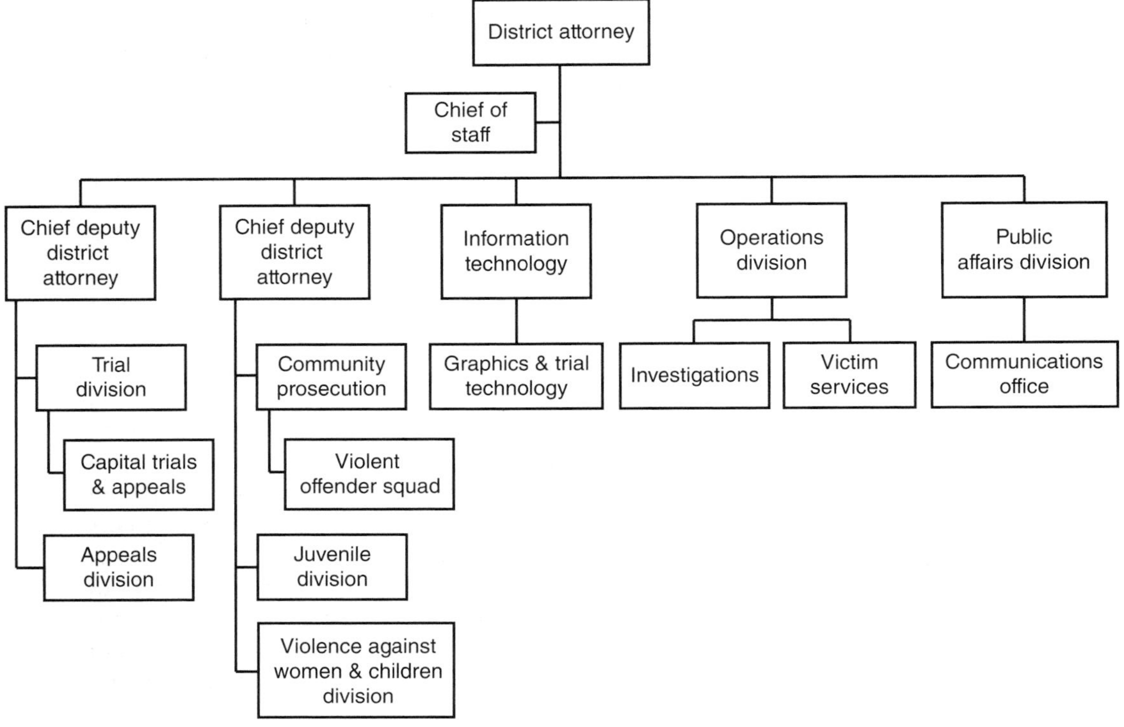

FIGURE 8.1 Organizational Chart of a Local District Attorney's Office

organization of district attorneys' offices; prosecutorial relationships; investigations, charging decisions, and grand jury appearances; pretrial activities and negotiated dispositions (plea bargains); court hearings and trials; posttrial motions and sentencing; and appeals (American Bar Association, 2015). Below, I highlight these standards to give you a sense of what the ABA believes the prosecutorial function *should* involve.

Standards for the Prosecution Function

The eight parts of the ABA's Standards for the Prosecution Function address separate aspects of how prosecutors should behave in relation to the citizens they serve, the courts, defendants, victims, and defense counsel (American Bar Association, 2015). Part I, for example, consists of 13 "best practices" relating to the general functions and duties of prosecutors. Part I makes it clear that prosecutors occupy three roles: administrators of justice, zealous advocates of the people, and officers of the court. As administrators of justice, they should exercise sound discretion and autonomous judgment in their charging decisions—only pursuing charges that are appropriate in number and severity—or when deciding not to file charges. As zealous advocates, they should represent the best interests of the people at all stages of the criminal process, from initial charging to post-conviction appeals. As officers of the court, they should seek justice, not just convictions; work to protect the innocent; and ensure that the rights of all defendants are protected.

Part II includes standards relating to the operation of district attorneys' offices. Best practices mentioned here include achieving excellence and diversity in the hiring, retention, and compensation of prosecutors; ensuring that necessary resources, such as those for investigative activities and experts, are available; and creating specific office policies and procedures relating to the exercise of discretion by prosecutors working there. The standards also say that prosecution authority should only be vested in a full-time public official who is an attorney in good standing.

Part III contains standards relating to prosecutorial relationships, including with other prosecutors' offices, the police, the courts, defense counsel, victims and witnesses, expert witnesses, and with physical evidence. These standards uniformly stress that prosecutors should develop strong relationships with these parties based on trust, sound judgement, reasonable exercise of discretion, and legal rules.

Part IV presents standards relating to investigations, charging decisions, and grand juries (I'll note here that in 2008, the ABA developed a stand-alone set of standards relating to prosecutorial involvement in investigations that are far more granular—see American Bar Association, 2014). For example, one set of standards addresses the decision to bring charges against defendants and suggests that charges only be sought if prosecutors "reasonably believe" they are (1) supported by probable cause; (2) supported by admissible evidence sufficient to convict beyond reasonable doubt; and (3) "in the interests of justice." Further, Standard 3-4.4 even lists *16* factors that prosecutors "may" consider when deciding to initiate, decline, or dismiss charges against defendants (e.g., strength of the case; defendant background and characteristics; victim views and motives; improper conduct by the police; and possible collateral consequences for third parties). Part IV standards also caution against overcharging defendants; that is, initiating or maintaining charges greater in number or seriousness than can be supported by the evidence, or than are necessary to fairly reflect the gravity of the offense or deter similar conduct (American Bar Association, 2015, p. 1).

Standards found in Part V relate to pretrial activities—especially the first appearance and preliminary hearing—and negotiated dispositions. Pretrial standards include prosecutors ensuring that defendants have been advised of their right to counsel and the procedure for obtaining same (if desired); ensuring that defendants are given a reasonable opportunity to obtain representation; and not allowing court proceedings to continue if a defendant desiring counsel does not have representation. Further, if the prosecutor has "reasonable concerns" with a defendant's mental competence, those concerns should be expressed to defense counsel and, if necessary, to the court. Additional standards found in Part V indicate that prosecutors *should* favor pretrial release of defendants "unless detention is necessary to protect individuals or the community" or a reasonable flight risk is present (American Bar Association, 2015, p. 1). Recommendations for release or detention should not be made categorically; rather, they should be based on the facts and circumstances of the accused and the crime at hand. The standards advise prosecutors to "work diligently" to identify and fully disclose to defense counsel any exculpatory evidence in the prosecutor's possession. Finally, standards in Part V advise that prosecutors should not agree to any plea bargains that, based on admissible evidence, would not support a conviction beyond reasonable doubt, nor involve a defendant waiving the right to appeal the terms of a sentence that exceeded an agreed-upon or reasonably anticipated outcome.

Part VI presents a group of standards relating to court hearings and the trial. Regarding trial, several standards indicate that prosecutors should be aware of, and receive training in, the legal rules governing juror selection, including rules prohibiting striking prospective jurors on the basis of certain personal characteristics (e.g., race). Additionally, questioning of prospective jurors during the jury selection process (the *voir dire*) should be done solely to obtain information relevant to formulating peremptory challenges or those for cause. Prosecutors should not use the *voir dire* to present the state's case to the jury or unduly ingratiate it to jurors. Once the jury has been struck, prosecutors should avoid even the appearance of engaging in improper communication with members. During trial, several standards advise that a prosecutor's opening statement should be confined to a fair summary of the state's case against the defendant. During the state's presentation of its case, prosecutors should not offer evidence or testimony they do not reasonably believe is true, and if discovered otherwise, they should take reasonable remedial steps. The prosecutor should also not bring to the attention of the jury or judge those matters the prosecutor knows to be inadmissible and should exercise strategic judgment when objecting to, or taking exception regarding, evidentiary rulings adverse to the state's case. Prosecutors should not use cross-examination to discredit or undermine a witness's testimony if the prosecutor knows the testimony to be true and accurate. At closing arguments, prosecutors should only present fair summaries of evidence and testimony comprising the state's case. Prosecutors should also respectfully accept acquittals.

Part VII's standards relate to the involvement of prosecutors in posttrial motions and sentencing. Of note here are several standards indicating that the severity of sentences imposed on convicted offenders should *not* be used as a measure of prosecutorial effectiveness. Further, the prosecutor should ensure that the sentence sought is consistent with office policy, and that the court renders a fair and informed sentencing judgment. Finally, prosecutors should be familiar with relevant laws and rules concerning victims' rights and facilitate victim participation in the sentencing process as permitted or required by law.

Finally, Part VIII includes standards concerning the prosecutor's involvement withappeals and challenges to convictions. While the standards indicate that prosecutors should defend convictions that were fairly obtained, they should *not* do so if the prosecutor reasonably believes the defendant is innocent, was wrongfully convicted, or that a miscarriage of justice has occurred. Prosecutors' offices should (1) designate one or more individuals to develop expertise regarding appellate law and procedure, along with developing contacts with individuals possessing such expertise working in other prosecutors' offices; and (2) develop consistent policies and positions regarding common bases for appeals. Standards advise that if a prosecutor becomes aware of new, credible, and material evidence creating a reasonable likelihood that a convicted offender was actually innocent of the charge(s) against him or her, the prosecutor *must* disclose that evidence to the appropriate court and to the offender—if he or she is unaware of it—and undertake (or cause to be undertaken) further investigation to determine whether the defendant was wrongfully convicted. In instances when a prosecutor *knows* of clear and convincing evidence that an offender was wrongfully convicted, the prosecutor *shall* seek to remedy the conviction. Finally, if at any stage of the process a prosecutor observes conduct or omissions by defense counsel that could reasonably constitute ineffective assistance, the prosecutor *should* (we're back to "should" rather than "shall") take reasonable steps to preserve a defendant's right to effective assistance and the public's interest in obtaining a valid conviction.

To summarize (see Table 8.1), the ABA's Model Standards for the Prosecution Function advise the prosecutor to seek justice, which may mean *not* charging someone with a crime or dismissing charges not supported by the evidence. Seeking justice also means that the prosecutor should ensure that a defendant's procedural and constitutional rights are protected, including instances where the prosecutor has discovered evidence that an offender was wrongfully convicted. In these cases, the prosecutor *must* (not "should") undertake efforts to undo the conviction.

Now that you have a sense of how prosecutors *should* behave, let's consider these standards in light of policies that prosecutors are asked to enforce. Those policies and the issues they raise have led some to questions the ethics of prosecuting people in the first

TABLE 8.1 ABA Standards for the Prosecution Function

Area	Summary of Standards
General function and duties	Exercise sound discretion and autonomous judgment in charging decisions; always represent the best interests of the people; seek justice, not merely convictions; work to protect the innocent and ensure the rights of all defendants are protected
Operation of DA's office	Achieve excellence and diversity in the hiring, retention, and compensation of prosecutors; ensure necessary resources are available; create office policies and procedures relating to the exercise of discretion; prosecution authority should only be vested in a full-time public official who is an attorney in good standing
Relationships with defense counsel, police, victims, etc.	Develop strong relationships with parties based on trust, sound judgement, reasonable exercise of discretion, and legal rules
Investigations, charging decisions, and grand juries	Initiate charges "reasonably believed" as supported by probable cause, admissible evidence, and are "in the interests of justice"; should not initiate or maintain charges greater in number or seriousness than can be supported by the evidence;
Pretrial activities	Ensure defendants have been advised of right to counsel and procedure for obtaining same; express to defense counsel and the court "reasonable concerns" about a defendant's mental competence; should favor pretrial release of defendants based on the facts/circumstances in the case; identify and disclose exculpatory evidence to defense counsel; should not agree to plea bargains that would not support a conviction beyond reasonable doubt
Court hearings and the trial	Receive training in the legal rules governing juror selection; avoid even the appearance of improper communication with jurors; should *not* offer evidence or testimony not reasonably believed true and if discovered otherwise take reasonable remedial steps; exercise strategic judgment when objecting to, or taking exception regarding, adverse evidentiary rulings; should *not* use cross-examination to discredit or undermine a witness's testimony if known to be accurate
Posttrial motions and sentencing	Severity of sentences imposed should *not* be used as measure of prosecutorial effectiveness; ensure sentence sought is consistent with office policy; ensure the court renders a fair and informed sentencing judgment
Involvement with appeals and challenges to convictions	Defend convictions *fairly* obtained; work to ensure wrongful convictions do not occur; remedy wrongful convictions; ensure that defendant's right to effective assistance is preserved

Source: Adapted from American Bar Association (2014)

place. Depending on how one answers the question whether prosecuting people guided by policies that may not be morally justified is ethical, the standards just reviewed may be little more than an intellectual exercise.

The Ethics of Prosecuting People

Recall that ABA standards say that prosecutors *should* be "zealous advocates" who "represent the interests of citizens in criminal matters." They *should* "stand up for victims." They *should* be "administrators of justice." They *should* act as "agents of the court." I think it could be reasonably argued that the standards represent *ideals* to which prosecutors should aspire: a *noble cause* of doing justice (heard that before?), standing up for victims, and representing the people as zealous advocates working to gain convictions of "bad guys" who have hurt others, stolen their property, or created disorder in their communities by selling drugs or engaging in other nefarious activities.

At bottom, however, what prosecutors really do is try and get people *punished* for violating the law. In doing so, prosecutors become the instruments by which anticrime policies created by state legislatures and the Congress (e.g., the "war on drugs") are implemented. In their everyday activities, prosecutors end up supporting the status quoand contributing to the myriad problems associated with it: overcrowded jails and prisons, substandard medical care for inmates, victimization of inmates by other inmates, and potentially draconian punishments for first-time and repeat offenders (Currie, 2013).

Importantly, prosecutors *know* the problems associated with these policies. Investigative journalists, various "think tanks," professional associations like the ABA, and academic researchers have all, for more than a decade, questioned the wisdom of such policies as the "war on drugs," "asset forfeiture," "three-strikes-and-you're-out," and mandatory sentences for offenders, along with bemoaning the enormously disparate impact these policies have had on people of color (Alexander, 2012).

The problem is whether prosecutors even *consider* the morality of the policies they enforce. I would argue most don't, not because they are "bad" or "unprincipled," but because they *believe they are doing good*. For example, they *believe* they are achieving "justice" by obtaining a conviction for crack cocaine possession that results in a 17-year-old African American male being sentenced to 25 years in prison. As Abbe Smith (2001, p. 378) observed:

> Perhaps this sense of righteousness is a good thing; it might reflect awareness on the part of an individual prosecutor that he or she is *obliged* to be righteous, no matter the competing impulses. But too often righteousness becomes self-righteousness. Too often prosecutors believe that because it is their *job* to do justice, they have extraordinary in-born wisdom and insight. Too oftenprosecutors believe that they *and only they* know what justice is (emphasis in original).

The ethics of criminal defense attorneys are routinely questioned (and addressed later in this chapter). Given the current backdrop of a criminal justice system that seems to disproportionately affect the lives of people of color (especially those who are young and living in disrupted communities), and that prosecutors' efforts to get "bad guys" off the streets help maintain this system, shouldn't the ethics of actually prosecuting people be questioned?

I agree with Abbe Smith who said that most prosecutors sincerely believe their professional actions to charge and convict people are motivated by conscience and guided by principle. However, like Smith (2001), I don't think it unfair to also accept the proposition that prosecutors sometimes come to believe they are the "sole agents of good" in the criminal justice system, that their actions, and theirs alone, determine whether "justice" has been served. In doing this, they lose sight of the fact that "justice" is very much in the eye of the beholder, varies from case to case, and that ethical standards can be negated when prosecutors claim—with supreme confidence—they have special insight into, or understanding of, what justice means.

Just as you saw with police officers, individual prosecutors engage in misconduct resulting in injustices (I'll examine that topic a bit later). But that's not what I'm talking about here. What I'm asking you to consider is whether, given the current state of criminal justice policy, prosecuting people can be *ethically justified*. In effect, can one be a morally good person and also a "good" prosecutor? That question is rarely asked; answering it requires examining the attitudes and values of prosecutors and how they exercise their power.

Narrowness and Cynicism

Like the police, prosecutors tend to have a world view that is rather narrow—something is either "black or white" or "right or wrong." As Smith (2001, p. 380) described it, "[P]rosecutors have a preference . . . for *what* happened over *why* it happened" as reflected in "the record" of a case (e.g., police reports; prior arrest history; forensic analyses; documentary evidence). Prosecutors heavily rely on "the record," believing that it "speaks for itself" and gives them the "who, what, where, when" and, possibly, the "why" of a case. As with the police, most prosecutors also believe that if someone breaks the law, he or she ought to be punished. If the law seems overly harsh, it's not their problem—that's the business of those who made the law to begin with. That "the record" may not reveal the full story or that a different story may exist altogether are considered details to be sorted at trial or during sentencing (Smith, 2001).

This narrow view may occur because prosecutors do not represent flesh-and-blood clients (Smith, 2001). Sure, they represent "the people," but "the people" are not standing next to them in court having emotional breakdowns when convicted. As Smith (2001) explains, although some prosecutors argue they "represent victims," the relationship between prosecutor and victim is complicated and *not* analogous to that of defense attorney and client. Victims in criminal cases are *witnesses, not clients*. Additionally, prosecutors are in the business of making judgments, upholding certain standards of behavior, and extracting a penance from people for their misdeeds. They are not in the business of empathizing with victims, like defense attorneys often do with their clients.

Smith (2001) argues that not having clients may also contribute to prosecutors acting like they have "heard it all before." This **prosecutorial cynicism** can lead them to reject, out-of-hand, alternative versions of "the record" such as exonerating or mitigating circumstances (Smith, 2001). Cynicism, in both style and substance, is a way for prosecutors to avoid being "played the fool." As a result, they become "suspicious, untrusting, disbelieving" as "the cultural and institutional presumption in most prosecutor offices is that *everybody is guilty*" (Smith, 2001, p. 384). Adopting a "letter-of-the-law" approach may create clarity and consistency for prosecutors, but taken to its extreme, may become "a kind of **moral fascism**" on their part as they assess cases (Smith, 2001, p. 385).

Discretion

Prosecutors exercise enormous amounts of discretion (Brownstein, 2003). Smith (2001) has even suggested that the discretionary power they wield draws at least some people into careers as prosecutors. However, the reality, at least according to Smith (2001), is that prosecutorial discretion may be more restricted and diffuse than is often believed. He argued (p. 386) that "there is [usually] someone higher up in the office hierarchy who must be consulted before a prosecutor can act," and there are some cases (e.g., assaults on police officers) where, no matter how experienced the prosecutor is, no discretion is available. Further, Smith (2001) suggested that sometimes prosecutors abdicate their discretionary authority, even in ordinary cases. Although they have the power to pursue prosecutions (or not), prosecutors do not engage in much soul-searching about these decisions. Instead, prosecutors may decide *not to decide* and thereby cede responsibility for doing so to the judge or jury (who can then be blamed, as appropriate) (Smith, 2001).

Winning

Practitioners and scholars alike have suggested that prosecutors have a strong interest in "winning," despite standards advising them to serve as "administrators of justice" and the ambiguity of what exactly constitutes "winning" (Davis, 2007). Is it "winning" when a prosecutor earns a conviction but refuses to back down when compelling evidence calls the conviction into question (Scheck, Neufeld, & Dwyer, 2000)? For some prosecutors—and their constituents—the answer is a resounding "yes!"

Because DAs are elected officials, they face political pressure to be successful which, for most constituents, translates into how many convictions the DA has obtained (known as a prosecutor's **batting average**; see Bradley, 2010). That pressure then filters into the trenches and impacts the ADAs working there, forcing them to not just win the "big" cases, such as capital murders, but *all* cases. Pressures to win thus arise from constituents expecting the prosecutor's office to take "bad guys" off the streets. But pressure to win also comes from office reward systems involving compensation and promotion (Smith, 2001).

The pressure on prosecutors to win can result in procedural unfairness for defendants (Smith, 2001). For example, during pretrial discovery, prosecutors are supposed to turn over to defense counsel *all* the evidence, not just evidence favorable to a conviction. Yet prosecutors continue to be reluctant to provide meaningful discovery to defense counsel (Smith, 2001). "Winning" can also taint plea negotiations, as illustrated by the habit of prosecutors making a generous plea offer in a weak case (Jonakait, 1987; Sloan, 1987). Finally, pressures to win may counter any reservations prosecutors may have about harsh sentences awaiting convicted offenders. From the narrow perspective of "winning," convictions obtained through procedural unfairness are not necessarily problematic (remember that "everyone is guilty"). What difference does it make how the "win" is achieved or its implications for offenders who may not be deserving of the level of sanction they receive?

The ethics of prosecuting people is thus more complex than it may first appear. If the culture of the criminal justice system and the offices where prosecutors go about their work are influenced by pressures to "win," and this pressure results in prosecutors abdicating their responsibilities as "administrators of justice" and "officers of the court," and fosters in them narrow views of defendants and cynicism about the forces that influenced their behavior, one may indeed question the ethics of the prosecution function, even with best practices in place.

Prosecutorial Misconduct

To this point, I have drawn parallels between "noble cause" corruption by police and ethical lapses by prosecutors. In both instances, serving the "noble cause" of getting "bad guys" off the streets and extracting a penance from them may lead to unethical or illegal behavior. In the case of prosecutors, misbehavior involves inappropriate actions taken during pretrial processes, at trial, or during sentencing, particularly in capital cases. Regardless of when it occurs, **prosecutorial misconduct** (PM) has consequences for defendants and their families and may result in the public absorbing additional costs of litigation associated with it (Ridolfi & Possley, 2010). Because PM threatens the perceived legitimacy of the criminal justice process, ethical and "best practice" standards created by the federal government and the ABA strongly discourage it.

Part of the challenge faced by those seeking to curb PM includes deciding when a prosecutor's actions constitute actual *misconduct*, determining how prevalent is PM, and identifying the hurdles to curbing it. I explore these issues below.

Prosecutorial Misconduct Defined

Prosecutorial misconduct is, to borrow from Supreme Court justice Potter Stewart's famous quote, a bit like obscenity—hard to define but "we know it when we see it." The problem is while we may "know it when we see it," to study and understand PM, we first need a definition of the topic at hand.

In trying to define PM, some have focused on prosecutor misbehavior occurring during trials, since those behaviors most directly contribute to wrongful convictions (Schoenfeld, 2005). Former prosecutor and law professor Bennett Gershman (1986) made such an effort when he defined PM as activity that sidetracked a jury from rendering a legitimate verdict through the process of weighing legally admitted evidence. But what about misbehavior occurring at other points in the process? There is wide agreement that PM can occur at *any* stage of the criminal process, so defining PM should take that into account (Green & Yaroshefsky, 2016). Sociologist Heather Schoenfeld (2005) did just that when she suggested that PM is a violation of the norms of trust that bind prosecutors to the courts and the public.

Perhaps the best way to define PM might be to do so in terms of the ABA standards that guide the prosecutorial function. Recall that prosecutors are supposed to serve as administrators of justice and officers of the court. They are also supposed to protect the constitutional and procedural rights of defendants. Whether intentional or arising from negligence, PM could thus be defined as any behavior by prosecutors during one or more of the stages of the criminal process that violates his or her duty to act as an agent of the court and protect the constitutional and procedural rights of defendants.

Types of Prosecutorial Misconduct

According to the Center for Prosecutor Integrity (2013), PM takes many forms and can occur at any stage in the criminal justice process. Examples the center identifies include: charging a suspect with more offenses than the evidence warrants; withholding exculpatory evidence from, or delaying its release to, the defense; deliberately mishandling, mistreating, or destroying evidence; allowing witnesses whom the prosecutor knows (or should know) are unlikely to be truthful to testify; pressuring defense witnesses *not* to testify; relying on fraudulent forensic experts; overstating the strength of the evidence during plea negotiations;

making statements to the media intended to arouse public indignation; and making improper or misleading statements to a jury. Some of these actions are intentional; most are simply mistakes. Regardless, they violate ABA standards and lead to injustice.

Prevalence of Prosecutorial Misconduct

No one knows the exact amount of PM that occurs each year, for several reasons, including the fact that much of what prosecutors do occurs behind closed doors and away from public or judicial scrutiny; because defense attorneys fail to report suspected PM; because some cases in which PM occurred are never appealed, so the record of the prosecutor's activities is never reviewed; or the case settles before trial, and since the defendant is pleased with the outcome, he or she is unlikely to complain about prosecutor misbehavior (Cunningham, 2016).

Prior to the 1990s, limited documentation existed on the prevalence of PM. That situation changed in 1999 when *Chicago Tribune* reporters Maurice Possley and Ken Armstrong published a five-part series that examined over 300 instances of PM in Illinois occurring between 1977 and 1998 (Possley & Armstrong, 1999). Their work inspired further investigation of PM by investigative reporters from other outlets, such as CNN (Griffin, Glover, & Black, 2016) and the *Arizona Republic* (Keifer, 2013; see Table 8.2). But the best estimates of the prevalence of PM may be found in two recent large-scale studies by the Center for Prosecutor Integrity (2013) and Henry Caldwell (2016). The Center for Prosecutor Integrity study estimated that between 1963 and 2013, there were 3,625 instances of PM that were confirmed by appeals courts in the United States. More recently, Caldwell (2016) analyzed 25 years of California State Supreme Court rulings in 926 criminal appeals that raised at least one claim of PM. In those cases, the court held that PM had occurred in 148 of them.

Hurdles to Controlling Prosecutorial Misconduct

Prosecutors engage in misconduct for two reasons: it works, and sanctions for engaging in it are minimal (Gershman, 1986). Focusing on the latter, two factors are noteworthy: the "harmless error" doctrine and the fact that prosecutors enjoy absolute immunity from civil lawsuits arising from cases in which PM occurs.

HARMLESS ERROR DOCTRINE. In an appeal claiming PM, the court first has to decide whether PM actually occurred and if it did, whether the misconduct affected the eventual outcome of the case (Bowman, 1997). To determine whether the behavior in question constituted misconduct by the prosecutor, appeals courts use a legal standard—a rule or guide. In California, for example, the standard used is whether the behavior involved "reprehensible" or "deceptive" efforts to persuade the court or a jury (Uribe, n.d.). A classic example of this would be a prosecutor inviting a jury to infer a defendant is guilty because she did not testify on her own behalf (Uribe, n.d.). I'll note that this type of legal standard limits PM to *intentional* behavior.

Regardless of the standard used, once the court finds that PM occurred, the next step is deciding whether the behavior negatively affected the case outcome. This is where the **harmless error doctrine** comes into play, which acknowledges that errors occur during case processing, but distinguishes those whose presence did not change the likely outcome in the case from those whose presence likely did. To decide into which category an error falls, appeals courts use one of two approaches (Boren & Fisher, 2004). The **guilt-based approach** requires reviewing records of the case to assess the

TABLE 8.2 Recent Analyses of Prosecutorial Misconduct

Source	Scope	Criteria	Years	Number of Cases	Number of Sanctions Imposed
Possley & Armstrong (1999)	United States	Homicide cases where appellate courts reversed a conviction due to prosecutorial misconduct	1963–1999	381	0
Gordon (2007)	United States	Cases in which prosecutorial misconduct affected the fairness of criminal proceedings or infringed constitutional rights of defendants	1970–2003	2,012	50
Heath & McCoy (2010)	United States	Cases in which judges determined that federal prosecutors violated laws or ethics rules	1997–2010	201	1
Veritas Initiative (2012a)	Arizona	Appellate court findings of prosecutorial misconduct	2004–2008	20	0
Kiefer (2013)	Arizona	Death-penalty cases reviewed by Arizona Supreme Court	2002–2013	16	2
Ridolfi & Possley (2010)	California	State and federal appellate rulings of prosecutorial misconduct	1997–2011	707	6
Veritas Initiative (2012b)	New York	Trial and appellate court findings of prosecutorial misconduct	2004–2008	151	3
Veritas Initiative (2012c)	Pennsylvania	Appellate court findings of prosecutorial misconduct	2004–2008	46	0
Veritas Initiative (2012d)	Texas	Trial and appellate court findings of prosecutorial misconduct	2004–2008	91	1
			Total	3,625	63

Source: Adapted from Center for Prosecutor Integrity (2013)

factual guilt or innocence of the defendant in light of the *untainted* evidence in the record. The **effect-on-the-verdict approach**, on the other hand, requires reviewing case records to determine whether the error swayed the jury and contaminated its verdict.

ABSOLUTE IMMUNITY FOR PROSECUTORS. In 1976, the Supreme Court decided the case of *Imbler v. Pachtman* (424 U.S. 409) and held that when prosecutors act within the scope of their legal duties they enjoy **absolute immunity** from civil damages arising from the conduct. The Court said in its ruling that "[p]rosecutors must be free to make discretionary decisions without constant dread of retaliation," but also acknowledged that their decision would "leave unredressed the wrongs done by dishonest [prosecutors]." More recently, in a 2011 ruling in the case of *Connick v. Thompson* (563 U.S. 51), the Supreme Court reiterated the *Imbler* standard by ruling (5-4) that absent a pattern of misconduct

CASE STUDY 8.1 Prosecutorial Ethics and Pursuit of the Death Penalty

In September of 1981, Thomas Thompson and his roommate, David Leitch, were arrested, charged with, and tried for the rape and murder of Ginger Fleischli. Leitch's attorney was able to sever his client's trial from that of Thompson, so the two were tried separately by the same prosecutor. Thompson was tried first.

At trial, the prosecutor's case was that Thompson alone had raped Fleischli in the apartment and killed her to prevent her from reporting the rape to police. Both crimes occurred before Leitch returned home. To support the theory, the prosecution presented testimony from two jailhouse informants, Edward Fink and John Del Frate. Fink testified that Thompson had confessed to him that he'd raped and murdered Fleischli; Leitch only learned of the murder when he returned home and had helped Thompson dispose of the body. Del Frate testified that only Thompson had stabbed Fleischli, causing her death. The testimony of the informants was the only direct evidence that Thompson had raped and killed Fleischli. Without the testimony, Thompson would have been ineligible for the death penalty.

The jury found Thompson guilty of rape and first-degree murder and sentenced him to death. In April of 1988, the California Supreme Court affirmed the conviction and sentence.

Months later, at Leitch's trial, the prosecution presented an *entirely different theory of the crime*. Here, the prosecutor argued that Leitch and Fleischli had been dating; that Leitch wanted Fleischli dead because she was interfering with his efforts to reconcile with his ex-wife; that Leitch was the only person with a motive to kill Fleischli; that Leitch had recruited Thompson to help kill her; and that both men were directly involved in both the killing and disposal of the body, although it was unclear who had actually stabbed Fleischli. The prosecutor did not call either Fink or Del Frate to testify. *Instead, he called three other jailhouse informants who had been defense witnesses at Thompson's trial whose testimony he had objected to*. However, as each left the stand in Thompson's trial, the prosecutor issued them a subpoena to testify at Leitch's trial. The prosecutor then relied heavily on the three to establish for the jury that (1) Leitch had previously threatened Fleischli; (2) Leitch had a long history of violence toward women; and (3) only Leitch had a motive to kill Fleischli. The jury found Leitch guilty of second-degree murder, and the judge sentenced him to fifteen years to life in prison.

Thompson was executed in August of 1997 after a series of failed appeals in the federal courts.

Was the prosecutor's behavior in the Leitch trial ethical?

Source: Adapted from Minsker (2009)

in a DA's office, a single instance of PM by a prosecutor in that office precluded the victim from suing the DA's office for damages.

In summary, PM can devastate defendants, lead to injustices such as wrongful convictions, and force taxpayers to pay for extended litigation from appeals in which PM is alleged. Prosecutors know that most times, however, their misbehavior does not rise to the level of misconduct, and even if it does, appeals courts are likely to rule the misbehavior as "harmless error." Further, if the courts find PM occurring, defendants cannot then sue for damages caused by the misbehavior because prosecutors enjoy absolute immunity.

Let's conclude discussion of prosecutorial ethics by having you assess whether the behavior of a prosecutor in a capital murder case, described in Case Study 8.1, was ethical.

ETHICS AND DEFENSE COUNSEL

Sometime during the early morning hours of May 23, 1987, Kenneth Parks drove 14 miles to his in-laws' house and attacked them, fatally stabbing his mother-in-law. He then drove to the nearest police station and surrendered, telling officers he thought he'd badly hurt some people but had no recollection of the event. His defense counsel proposed that Parks had committed the murder while sleepwalking and therefore could not be held responsible. As you can imagine, the authorities were skeptical of Parks' "sleepwalking defense" to the murder and aggravated assault charges he faced. However, the charges against Parks were dropped when it was determined he had, in fact, committed the offenses while sleepwalking (see Koenig, 2009).

A wise law professor who had also been a successful criminal defense attorney once told me the job of defense counsel is to ensure that the state "does it right." What he meant is that the defense counsel's job is to ensure the state follows procedural rules and standards of professional behavior and does not violate a defendant's rights. He also told me a defendant being guilty should be "irrelevant" to defense counsel. "It's not counsel's job to *judge* the defendant; it's counsel's job to *represent* him." In this section, I turn my attention to the second member of the courtroom workgroup—defense attorneys—and examine the defense function and ethical issues surrounding it.

The Defense Function: Model Standards

As it did for the prosecution function, the ABA has created model standards for the defense function (American Bar Association, 2015). Consisting of nine parts and 64 specific standards, the ABA's Criminal Justice Standards for the Defense Function cover everything from general functions/duties of defense counsel to defense attorneys' activities during post-conviction proceedings. I'll note here, as was the case for the standards relating to prosecutors, the standards for defense attorneys are *aspirational*, meaning, they are ideals that defense attorneys should strive to achieve; they are *not* fixed rules. As I did for the prosecution function, here I will highlight for you some of the important standards relating to the broad functions of defense counsel; their relationships with clients; their activities during litigation; and their activities post-conviction.

Broad Functions of Defense Counsel

Standard 4-1.2 outlines, in broad terms, the function of defense counsel in the criminal justice process. For example, the standard indicates that defense counsel is an "essential" component in the administration of justice and serves as both an officer of the court and a "loyal and zealous advocate for . . . clients." The standard also says that defense counsel should engage in efforts to reform and improve the administration of justice. Finally, in capital cases the standard indicates that defense counsel "should make extraordinary efforts on behalf of the accused" to ensure that the client's rights are protected.

Relationship with Clients

Standard 4-3.1 outlines the kind of relationship defense counsel should have with clients. For example, counsel should work to create a relationship with a client based on trust and confidence. It should include frank and open discussion of relevant facts (protected, except under certain specific circumstances, by attorney-client privilege), the goals of representation, and through which stage(s) counsel will represent the client. Counsel should also consider whether a client suffers from a mental impairment or other disability that could adversely affect the representation, and in such instances, decide whether a psychiatric examination would be in the client's interests. Finally, according to Standard 4-5.1, defense attorneys should keep clients regularly informed about the status of their case, and before significant decisions are made, should "advise the client with candor concerning all aspects of the case, including an assessment of possible strategies and likely as well as possible outcomes."

Ideals that counsel should pursue to protect a client's interests are found in Standard 4-3.7. For example, counsel should, at the earliest opportunity, explain to the client his or her rights (e.g., right to remain silent; right to counsel; right to a jury trial) and "promptly seek to obtain and review" all relevant information in the matter, including material or information possessed by the prosecutor and that counsel should ensure is preserved. The attorney should also "work diligently" with the client to develop strategies relating to investigating the case and a defense strategy. If counsel has evidence showing innocence or mitigation, this should be discussed with the client along with deciding whether approaching the prosecution with the evidence is in the client's interests. Counsel should also decide whether an opportunity to "benefit from cooperation with the prosecution" could be lost if not quickly accepted, and if so, discuss with the client and decide whether such cooperation is warranted. Counsel should not simply follow rote procedures learned from previous cases, but instead consider the procedural and investigative steps to take and motions to file relevant in each case.

Standards for Defense Counsel During Litigation

Parts IV through VII address defense counsel responsibilities and activities relating to pretrial actions, trial preparation, and the trial itself. During pretrial stages, defense counsel has a *duty* to promptly investigate all cases to determine the presence of sufficient facts to warrant criminal charges, as well as determine whether a client's interests would be served by engaging experts in consultation with the client. If the client cannot afford these resources, counsel should take up the matter with the court. Defense counsel should know and follow the law and rules of the jurisdiction regarding victims and witnesses, and seek to interview all witnesses, including the victim or victims, without using means (e.g., misrepresentation) that have no substantial purpose other than to embarrass, delay, burden, or violate their legal rights. Counsel should also give witnesses reasonable notice of when their testimony is expected and know relevant rules governing expert witnesses.

Standard 4-5.2 relates to defense counsel control of, and direction taken in, the case and advises that some decisions relating to the conduct of a case are for the accused to make, while counsel should make others. Additionally, while these decisions are "highly contextual," counsel should give great weight to strongly held views of a competent client regarding all decisions (e.g., proceeding without representation; waiving a jury trial; pleas to enter; plea offers received; testifying; speaking at sentencing). Standard 4-5.2 notes that all strategic and tactical decisions should be made in consultation with the client.

Standard 4-6.1 states that counsel has a "duty to explore disposition without trial." More specifically, the standard advises that defense attorneys be open, at every stage of a criminal matter and after consultation with the client, to discussions with the state concerning disposition by guilty plea. During plea negotiations, counsel should: (1) keep the client advised of developments; (2) promptly explain proposed plea bargains offered, while reminding the client such an offer does not mean the state is unwilling to go to trial; (3) ensure that the client understands any proposed disposition agreement, including its direct and possible collateral consequences (e.g., loss of voting rights, exclusion from certain occupations); (4) not recommend acceptance of a disposition without completing an appropriate investigation of the disposition and its consequences; and (5) not knowingly make false statements of fact or law during disposition discussions with the state.

The model standards also address defense counsel relationships with the court. Standard 4-7.2, for example, says that defense counsel should "support the authority and dignity of the court" by following codes of professionalism and through a courteous and professional attitude but also "maintain . . . an *independent relationship*" with the court (emphasis added). Counsel should "avoid unnecessary personalized disparagement" of opposing counsel and develop and maintain courteous working relationships with judges and prosecutors, including working with them to solve ethical, scheduling, or other issues.

At trial, counsel should not strike prospective jurors based on impermissible criteria (e.g., race, sex, religion, national origin, disability, sexual orientation, or gender identity) and once the jury is struck, avoid actual or the appearance of improper communication with jurors. Outside court, counsel should minimize his or her proximity to, or contact with, jurors. Counsel should give an opening statement that is "confined to a fair statement of the case from counsel's perspective," including discussing evidence counsel legitimately believes will be offered and admitted at trial. During presentation of the state's case, counsel should challenge perceived misconduct by objecting to the court or through other avenues, not by engaging in improper retaliatory conduct. In presenting its case, counsel should not "knowingly offer" false evidence as being true or fail to take remedial steps upon discovery of falsehoods in the evidence offered. Counsel should examine witnesses "fairly and with due regard for dignity and legitimate privacy concerns" and not intimidate or humiliate them. I note that Standard 4-7.7 says that even when defense counsel believes (or knows) a witness is telling the truth, counsel should still vigorously cross-examine the witness *even if doing so casts doubt on the veracity of the testimony* (emphasis added). Finally, before making a closing argument, counsel should first review all the evidence in the case and then at closing, make only "reasonable" inferences from the evidence and avoid arguments that appeal to prejudices that may be held by jurors. If the defense receives an adverse court ruling or jury verdict during trial, counsel should not criticize either entity and instead express "respectful disagreement" with the ruling or verdict, maintain the client's innocence, and indicate an intent to seek appellate relief. Conversely, counsel may "publicly praise" a favorable court verdict or ruling; compliment participants, supporters, and others who aided counsel; and note the verdict or ruling's social or legal significance.

Post trial, defense counsel should only file motions that have a "non-frivolous, legal basis," and at sentencing, counsel should familiarize him- or herself with the court's practices and potential issues that could affect sentencing (e.g., client's background, sentencing laws and rules, and options). Defense counsel should also consider whether consultation with sentencing experts would be useful.

Standards for Defense Counsel Post-Conviction

Finally, Part IX of the standards offers guidance for defense counsel relating to post-conviction appeals. For example, several standards indicate defense counsel should promptly explain to the client the meaning and consequences of conviction, along with his or her right(s) concerning an appeal. Counsel should offer the client his or her best judgment about pursuing an appeal, potential grounds for doing so, advantages and disadvantages of appealing the verdict, and probable outcome of doing so. If, at some later date, counsel becomes aware of "credible and material evidence" creating a reasonable likelihood a client (or former client) has been wrongfully convicted, sentenced, or was actually innocent, counsel has "some duty to act," even after counsel's representation has ended. In such instances, counsel should (1) evaluate the information, investigate if necessary, and decide what potential remedies are available; (2) advise and consult with the client; and (3) determine what action if any to take, including how best to notify the prosecution and the court of the evidence.

Taken collectively, the model standards for the defense function outline how defense attorneys *should* interact with clients, the court, prosecutors, and juries. They also offer guidance to ensure that counsel provides "zealous" representation of a client, while advising that counsel adopt a respectful attitude toward, but independent orientation from, the court. Table 8.3 summarizes the model standards for defense counsel.

Defense Tactics and the Ethical Issues They Raise

Battered woman syndrome, and its progeny, posttraumatic stress disorder (PTSD); XYY ("super male") syndrome and postpartum depression; the "Twinkie defense" and "gay panic"; all of these approaches have been used, to widely varying degrees of success, by attorneys as novel defenses in criminal cases (Forsythe & Miller, 2014; see Table 8.4). Novel defenses are usually justified under the auspices of "zealously" defending clients, but they also raise questions of ethics. In this section, I examine the ethics of a "zealous" defense in a criminal case, and the tactics used by defense attorneys that have raised ethical concerns.

In a famous quote about zealous advocacy by attorneys, the 19th-century English Lord Chancellor Henry Brougham observed:

> An advocate, in the discharge of his duty, knows but one person in all the world, and that person is his client. To save that client by all means and expedients, and at all hazards and costs to other persons, and, amongst them to himself, is his first and only duty; and in performing this duty he must not regard the alarm, the torments, the destruction which he may bring upon others. Separating the duty of a patriot from that of an advocate, he must go on reckless of consequences, though it should be his unhappy fate to involve his country in confusion.
>
> —(Allibone, 1880, p. 41)

In several places, ABA standards for the defense function say that "defense counsel ha[s] the challenging task of serving both as officer of the court and as loyal and *zealous* advocate for [a] client" or that "defense counsel should act *zealously* within the bounds of the law and standards on behalf of their clients" (emphasis added; American Bar Association, 2015, p. 1). In the ABA's Model Rules of Professional Conduct, commentary

TABLE 8.3 ABA Standards for the Defense Function

Area	Summary of Standards
Functions and Duties	Defense counsel serves as an officer of the court and zealous advocate for clients; should engage in efforts to reform and improve the administration of justice; in capital cases should make "extraordinary efforts" to ensure client's rights are protected
Relationship With Clients	Create a relationship based on trust and confidence; engage in frank and open discussion of relevant facts, goals of representation, and through which stage(s) counsel will represent client; should consider whether client suffers from a mental impairment or other disability and decide whether a psychiatric examination is warranted; should keep clients regularly informed about status of the case; should advise client with candor about possible defense strategies and likely outcomes
Protecting Client's Interests	Should explain to client her rights and promptly obtain and review relevant information in the matter; should work diligently with client to develop strategies relating to investigating the case and strategy; discuss with client evidence showing innocence or mitigation, along with whether to approach prosecution with the evidence; should also decide whether cooperation with prosecution is warranted and discuss same with client; should not simply follow rote procedures learned from previous cases
Pretrial and Trial	Determine presence of sufficient facts to warrant criminal charges and whether experts should be retained; follow rules regarding victims and witnesses; give witnesses reasonable notice of when their testimony is expected; know rules governing experts; give weight to strongly held views of competent clients regarding strategic and tactical decisions; explore disposition without trial; support the authority and dignity of the court and avoid disparaging opposing counsel; do not strike prospective jurors using impermissible criteria; avoid actual or the appearance of improper communication with jurors; opening statements should be confined to fair overview of the case; challenge perceived misconduct by opposing counsel by objecting to the court; should not knowingly offer false evidence; fairly examine witnesses; make only reasonable inferences from the evidence at closing and avoid appealing to juror prejudices; express respectful disagreement with court rulings or the verdict; maintain client's innocence and indicate intent to seek appellate relief; publicly praise favorable verdicts or rulings
Post Trial	Should only file motions that are non-frivolous and have a legal basis; should be familiar with the court's practices at sentencing, potential issues that could affect it; should also consider whether consultation with sentencing experts would be useful
Post-Conviction Appeals	Promptly explain meaning and consequences of conviction for the client, along with her right(s) concerning appeal; offer best judgment about pursuing an appeal, potential grounds for doing so, advantages and disadvantages of appealing the verdict, and probable outcome; if becomes aware of "credible and material evidence" of wrongful conviction, counsel has a duty to act even after representation has ended

Source: American Bar Association (2015)

on Rule 1.3 about "diligence" in the lawyer-client relationship states: "A lawyer must also act with commitment and dedication to the interests of the client and with *zeal* in advocacy upon the client's behalf" (emphasis added; American Bar Association, 2016). The problem is neither the ABA nor the courts, law professors, or practitioners have developed a definition of what constitutes "zealous" defense of a client.

TABLE 8.4 Novel Defenses to Criminal Charges

Defense	Description	Result
Amnesia	Defendant claims he or she experienced a partial or complete memory loss and does not remember the crime	Courts are *very* unsympathetic to this defense
Posttraumatic Stress Disorder	Developing severe symptoms including flashbacks, nightmares, extreme alertness, etc., after exposure to a traumatic event such as combat during war.	Often successful as a mitigation strategy
Battered Woman Syndrome	Group of symptoms a woman may develop over time resulting from repeated physical and/or psychological abuse by spouse or significant other.	Often successful as a mitigation strategy
Multiple Personality Disorder	A mental illness in which a person has more than one distinct personality, each of which take turns controlling the person's behavior. Defendant may claim that one of the "other personalities" committed the crime	Very rarely successful due to so few documented cases
Postpartum Depression	A condition involving severe depression that a woman may suffer after she has given birth that may lead her to injure the child, herself, others, or commit other crimes.	Successful primarily in supporting insanity defense
Gay Panic	Describes a reaction a person might have when discovering that her/his date or significant other is of the other sex, contrary to their appearance and behavior. As a result of learning this, defendant is suddenly overtaken by strong emotion and engages in the alleged crime.	Successful primarily in supporting diminished capacity claim

Source: Adapted from Forsythe & Miller (2014)

"Zealously" Defending Clients

To understand the "Z" words ("zeal," "zealously," "zealous," or "zealousness"), one way to begin is with how the words "zeal," "zealously" "zealous" and "zealousness" are used in everyday discourse. I would imagine that when most people are talking about "zeal," they are talking about intense emotion compelling one to pursue a goal, be it success, fame, wealth, etc. The problem with zeal is that it puts blinders on us—we become so engrossed in achieving the goal we've set that we sacrifice others, either intentionally or unwillingly: "In her zeal to become president of the company, she sacrificed relationships with those about whom she cared the most." It's the blinders that matter and that cause the potential harm.

Returning to defense counsel, recall that around 95% of all felony cases are settled via negotiated plea agreements. That means about 5% of felonies end up going to trial, and this is where the proverbial "gloves" come off. Once members of the courtroom workgroup are unable to reach a negotiated settlement, the dynamic changes and they assume different roles. In the case of the lawyers, they become *litigators*; in the case of the judge, he or she becomes a much more formal *arbiter*. In assuming these alternative roles, participants become keenly aware of the stakes and, as a result, assume a much different posture. When assuming these alternative roles, perhaps it is here that the reasons for becoming a prosecutor, or a defense attorney, or a judge drive each individual to "go the distance." Particularly for the attorneys, "winning" becomes a far more important end. The guns are loaded and the hammer cocked: it's "time to go to war."

"RAMBO" LITIGATION. Some attorneys have likened litigation to war (Whitmer, 2007). As Keith Lee (2014) explained it, studying military strategy and tactics such as those described in Sun Tzu's *Art of War* or Carl von Clausewitz's *Vom Kriege* (*On War*) can provide useful tips for litigators. For example, von Clausewitz argued there are three main objectives of war: (1) conquer/destroy the armed power of the enemy; (2) take possession of the enemy's material and other sources of strength, and (3) gain public opinion. For Lee (2014), these goals align closely with those of litigation. The attorneys involved engage in a contest where they seek to best the opposing party, while both sides seek to win the opinion of not only judge and jury, but also the media, by presenting a narrative most favorable to their side.

To be successful, there are four rules to be followed, based on von Clausewitz's ideas about fighting war (Lee, 2014). First, if warfare (litigation) is to be pursued, it should be done with all the resources that can be summoned. This means that defense counsel must be organized, prepared, and develop and execute a plan. Each argument, motion, and letter must be drafted with the intent to win. Full attention and effort are mandatory to putting up a good fight. Second, defense counsel must execute a strategy that finds and exploits weaknesses in the other side's arguments, evidence, experts, facts, etc. Third, counsel must never waste time. Unless important advantages can be achieved via delay, strike hard and fast. Finally, follow up on successes energetically. For example, successful objections by defense counsel and favorable rulings by the judge to motions on behalf of the client create patterns revealing the judge's thinking that can be used strategically when formulating new objections or filing new motions.

In recent decades, however, legal practitioners and scholars have become increasingly vocal in their concern about the negative impact "litigation as war" has had on the practice of law (Freedman & Smith, 2016). So-called Rambo tactics or Rambo litigation—named after the fictional character John Rambo (played by Sylvester Stallone), a one-man army who successfully takes on the North Vietnamese army and corrupt officials in the United States during the Vietnam conflict—have become entrenched, and have caused not only a loss in civility between opposing counsel, but have enhanced already-negative attitudes held by Americans about the honesty and ethics of lawyers (Gallup, 2016; see Table 8.5). **Rambo attorneys** "employ whatever tactics [are] necessary for victory" (Wilbert, 2008, p. 1129) and believe they aren't accountable for the tactics because they are being used to "zealously" represent clients. This attitude of nonaccountability includes (1) belief by counsel that it's in both their interests and those of their clients to make an opponent's life miserable; (2) disdain for common courtesy and civility because they ill-befit the "true warrior"; (3) manipulating facts and engaging in revisionist history; (4) willingly filing unnecessary motions and using discovery to intimidate; and (5) counsel putting him- or herself at center stage, rather than the client or the client's cause (Harris, 2002). What these lawyers are saying is that they are not legally, professionally, or *morally* accountable for either the means used or the ends achieved (Freedman & Smith, 2016). As is the case in war, incivility during litigation becomes the norm in the name of "zealously" defending clients.

TABLE 8.5 Public Ratings of Honesty/Ethics in Various Fields

	Rating				
Field	**Very High %**	**High %**	**Average %**	**Low %**	**Very Low %**
Nurses	29	55	13	2	1
Pharmacists	15	52	26	6	2
Medical doctors	15	50	29	5	2
Engineers	13	52	29	4	1
Dentists	10	49	34	5	2
Police officers	16	42	29	10	3
College teachers	10	37	32	12	6
Clergy	12	32	39	9	4
Psychiatrists	6	32	45	9	3
Chiropractors	5	33	45	10	3
Bankers	2	22	46	22	8
Journalists	4	19	34	23	18
Lawyers	**3**	**15**	**45**	**26**	**11**
State governors	2	16	45	27	8
Business executives	2	15	50	23	9

Source: Adapted from Gallup (2016)

RETURNING CIVILITY TO LITIGATION. Those who bemoan the seeming entrenched incivility that characterizes litigation have also proposed solutions to the problem. For example, attorney Jayne Reardon (2014) suggested that incivility can be reduced by (1) educating attorneys about the fact that client satisfaction is strongly tied to counsel acting civilly during interactions with opposing counsel and the court; (2) enhanced monitoring of incivility by attorneys and sanctioning of such behavior by state and local regulatory authorities, including state supreme courts; (3) revising the "lawyer's oath" (taken when one is first admitted by the state to the practice of law) to include civility clauses; and (4) state and local bar associations creating training and mentoring programs for attorneys (particularly those new to the practice of law) that show how zealousness and civility are not mutually exclusive. One additional solution I've seen discussed among practitioners and scholars includes "civility training" as part of the required course on professional responsibility offered in law schools around the nation (Brown, 2007).

You have now seen how the "Z" words, ostensibly promoting a standard to which defense counsel should aspire, can be used to justify nearly any tactic conceived by criminal defense attorneys. More importantly, they have also created a kind of "Frankenstein's monster" where litigation is viewed as war, civility is set aside, and innumerable sorts of "Rambo" tactics are used, reinforced by a belief that "Rambo" lawyers using them should not be held professionally accountable.

Let's end this section by revisiting in Case Study 8.2 a high-profile case from the late 1990s in which a local defense attorney agreed to defend a New York City police officer accused of brutally sodomizing an immigrant who had the misfortune of being in the wrong place at the wrong time. How is one to defend the indefensible?

CASE STUDY 8.2 Defending the Indefensible

On August 9, 1997, a Haitian immigrant, Abner Louima, who was living in New York City, was arrested by NYPD officers in the 70th Precinct in Brooklyn for participating in a disturbance outside a local nightclub. He was transported to the station, where Officer Justin Volpe sodomized him using a broken broomstick handle. As a result, Mr. Louima suffered a torn rectum, a ruptured colon and bladder, and was hospitalized for two months.

To obtain a strong defense in the resulting criminal case, Officer Volpe hired a local experienced and well-known attorney, Marvin Kornberg. Reports at the time said the officer insisted he was not guilty—the allegations against him were untrue or overblown—and that he wanted to go to trial to clear his name.

Let's assume for the moment that Mr. Kornberg probed his client's story to learn as much as he could about what happened; familiarized himself with the government's case; and developed possible defenses to the charges facing Officer Volpe. Let's also assume that Mr. Kornberg did not believe his client, while keeping in mind that Officer Volpe (1) was entitled to a lawyer, (2) was presumed innocent until proven otherwise beyond reasonable doubt, and (3) the burden to prove his guilt beyond reasonable doubtwas on the state. Recall also that Mr. Kornberg had a duty to "zealously defend" his client in what became a *very* high-profile case.

Based on what he learned from his client and from the evidence the state intended to present, Mr. Kornberg fashioned a defense that attacked the credibility of Mr. Louima; discredited the government's witnesses (many of whom were police officers); and offered alternative explanations for the government's physical, medical, and scientific evidence. He first took his case to the press and shared with them the defense theory that the victim could not seem to keep his story straight and was a "liar," a "trouble maker," and a "mercenary." Mr. Kornberg claimed that police officer

informants, crucial to the state's case, had not been present during the incident, had no direct knowledge of what had happened, and were motivated by their own self-interest. He also claimed that the physical injuries Mr. Louima suffered could have occurred in a manner other than what was alleged. *He also took this theory to court.* With rare exception, according to most observers, Mr. Kornberg's cross-examinations of witnesses were intense and aggressive.

It is the last aspect of the defense theory having to do with the source of Mr. Louima's injuries that became controversial. Mr. Kornberg claimed the victim's injuries resulted not from Officer Volpe's brutality, but from consensual anal sex with another man, and laid out this theory to the jury by emphatically saying in court, "[T]he injuries sustained by Mr. Louima are not, I repeat, not consistent with a nonconsensual insertion of an object into his rectum." In making this statement, he thus set the groundwork for arguing that consensual homosexual sex was what had caused the injuries. Mr. Kornberg noted in court "that a trace of Mr. Louima's feces found in the police station bathroom contains the DNA of another male," and told the jury, "'[y]ou are going to be shown how somebody else's DNA can get into another individual's feces." In effect, Mr. Kornberg used a "rough-sex defense" to rebut the state's case.

One legal commentator at the time noted that Mr. Kornberg's "rough-sex defense" played on an expectation that members of the jury would see homosexuality as vile and violence as normal in homosexual intercourse; it offered a "plausible" explanation for Mr. Louima's injuries.

Both during and after the trial, Marvin Kornberg was roundly criticized for using the "rough-sex" defense. Media pundits characterized him as a "racist," a "villain," a "liar," an "opportunist," and a "publicity seeker." Even defense attorneys were critical of the "rough-sex" defense, saying it was solely intended to play on jurors' potential anti-gay biases.

(Note: Halfway through the trial, Officer Volpe changed his plea to guilty and was sentenced to 30 years in prison).

To what lengths should a lawyer go to defend the indefensible?

Sources: Smith (2000) and Chan (2007)

ETHICS AND THE JUDICIARY

My late father had an interesting legal career that spanned 60 years, and included stints as a corporate attorney, a solo practitioner, an ADA , and magistrate judge. As magistrate judge for a decade, Dad faithfully served the people of the jurisdiction by holding initial appearances and preliminary hearings for those arrested on felony charges and presiding over bench and jury trials of people charged with misdemeanors. One thing Dad liked was that he was *appointed* as the magistrate judge, serving at the pleasure of the presiding judge of the district court. Dad believed that politics and money held major sway in judicial elections in his home state of Michigan and hated it. On more than a few occasions he told me, "Thank God I don't have to run for this office!"

Judges are the third members of the courtroom workgroup and it is to them I now turn my attention. As described below, judges enjoy great power as managers of their courts and in the ideal, serve as impartial arbiters of activities occurring in them. As I did when discussing prosecutors and defense attorneys, I've organized this section on judges around several topics, including the function(s) of the judiciary, standards/rules that guide the professional conduct of judges, and ethical issues affecting the judiciary. Let's begin this section by reminding you of the functions served by the judiciary in the modern American system of justice.

Function(s) of the Judiciary

As you'll recall from your introductory course on the criminal justice system, the judicial branch is one of the three branches of government, along with the executive and legislative. It serves as a check on the others; its power is grounded in Article III of the U.S. Constitution ("The judicial power . . . shall be vested in one Supreme Court, and in such inferior courts as the Congress may . . . establish") and Supreme Court precedent. As the states were created, based on their constitutional arrangements, they developed their own judiciaries.

Courts serve various functions (National Association for Court Management, 2017). One function they serve is to provide a public forum where disputes between or among individuals and entities (e.g., corporations; states) are resolved, individuals are protected from arbitrary use of government power, and a record of their legal status is created and maintained. Courts also function as impartial and independent institutions, designed to earn public trust and confidence as they balance the need for social order with that of individual freedoms. Courts also function as institutions that are interdependent with other branches of government—it is from them that courts receive necessary resources to run efficiently and effectively.

But what of the judges who preside over courts? As you saw with prosecutors and defense counsel, model standards—in this case, model rules—have been promulgated to guide judges in their professional activities.

Model Standards for the Judiciary

Just as it did for lawyers more broadly, the ABA created and published a set of Model Rules for the Judiciary (American Bar Association, 2011; see Box 8.1). Additionally, the Administrative Office of the United States Courts (AOC) developed what might be viewed as a parallel set of rules for the federal judiciary (Administrative Office of United States Courts, 2017). Let me provide you with some highlights of both sets of rules.

ABA Model Code of Judicial Conduct

As presented in Box 8.1, there are four canons articulated in the ABA Model Code of Judicial Conduct that guide and serve as criteria to evaluate the professional behavior of judges. Additionally, there are specific "black letter rules"—sometimes many, other times

BOX 8.1 Canons of the American Bar Association Model Code of Judicial Conduct

CANON 1
A judge shall uphold and promote the independence, integrity, and impartiality of the judiciary, and shall avoid impropriety and the appearance of impropriety.

CANON 2
A judge shall perform the duties of judicial office impartially, competently, and diligently.

CANON 3
A judge shall conduct the judge's personal and extrajudicial activities to minimize the risk of conflict with the obligations of judicial office.

CANON 4
A judge or candidate for judicial office shall not engage in political or campaign activity that is inconsistent with the independence, integrity, or impartiality of the judiciary.

Source: American Bar Association (2011)

few—that accompany each canon and articulate specific activities either encouraged or prohibited in pursuit of the relevant canon. For example, Canon 1 says that judicial behavior *shall* (i.e., must) promote core ideals of the judiciary (e.g., independence, integrity, and impartiality). while avoiding even the appearance of impropriety. Associated rules say that this canon can be achieved by a judge following the law and inspiring public confidence in the judiciary by not abusing the privilege or prestige of the office for personal gain and participating in activities promoting ethical conduct and professionalism within the judiciary and access to justice for all. Public confidence can also be inspired by initiating and participating in public outreach efforts that enhance the public's un-

derstanding of and confidence in the legal system.

Canon 2 stresses that judges must not show favor (impartiality); must have proper legal knowledge, skills, thoroughness, and preparation (competence); and must devote proper resources and time to the matters coming before him or her (integrity/diligence). This includes the judge undertaking reasonable efforts to ensure that attorneys, staff, and litigants cooperate with the judge to dispose of matters promptly and efficiently.

Canon 3 relates to activities involving judges that occur outside the courtroom. The canon says that judges, when undertaking such activities, should do so in a way that minimizes actual or potential conflicts with their judicial obligations (independence, integrity, and impartiality). Rules developed for this canon stipulate that activities like public lectures, writings, or scholarly research on the law or administration of justice are acceptable, as is participating in nonprofit educational, religious, charitable, fraternal, or civic activities. Participating in these activities helps integrate judges into the community and enhances public understanding of, and respect for, judges and the legal system. I'll note here that in recent years, investigative reporters have begun scrutinizing judges' extrajudicial activities, especially those of several U.S. Supreme Court justices, and minor scandals have erupted over some of those activities (Williams, 2017).

Canon 4 offers guidance for judges either running for office or involved in campaign activities of others seeking office and points out that such involvement may jeopardize a judge's impartiality, integrity, and independence. When judges actually fall prey to political pressure (or appear to do so), citizen confidence in the independence and impartiality of the judiciary erodes. The canon thus stipulates that judges and judicial candidates must be free from political pressures or the appearance of bending to such pressures. Associated rules prohibit judges and judicial candidates from making public speeches on behalf of any political organizations or those that endorse or oppose candidates for public office. Rules also say that when seeking elected office, judges and judicial candidates must be scrupulously fair and accurate in all statements made either by them or by campaign committees. Judges and judicial candidates are also prohibited from making statements that could negatively impact the fairness of pending judicial proceedings. Finally, while judges and judicial candidates may make campaign pledges relating to judicial organization or administration and court management, pledges or promises inconsistent with the impartial performance of adjudicative duties of the office are prohibited.

Code of Conduct for Federal Judges

Box 8.2 presents the Code of Conduct for judges serving in federal district and circuit courts of appeal—justices of the U.S. Supreme Court are not bound by this code (Slaughter, 2014). According to the AOC, the code was developed to provide guidance to federal judges and judicial nominees based on "reasonable" rules (Administrative Office of the United States Courts, 2014, p. 1). The AOC also says the rules "should be applied consistently with constitutional requirements, statutes, other court rules and decisional law, and in the context of all relevant circumstances" (Administrative Office of the United States Courts, 2014, p. 1). The code provides guidance for judicial behavior inside and outside the courtroom.

As you saw with Canon 1 of the ABA code, Canon 1 of the AOC code also speaks to judges keeping and enforcing high standards of conduct to maintain the integrity and independence of the judiciary, and public confidence in both. Canon 2 of the AOC code and its commentary mirror themes found in the ABA code—federal judges must respect and comply with the law at all times to promote public confidence in the integrity and impartiality of the federal judiciary. Further, to inspire public confidence in the federal judiciary, judges should not allow outside relationships with family, friends, or others to influence either their personal or professional conduct or decision-making. Finally,

BOX 8.2 **Code of Conduct for Federal Judges**

Canon 1: A Judge Should Uphold the Integrity and Independence of the Judiciary.

Canon 2: A Judge Should Avoid Impropriety and the Appearance of Impropriety in All Activities.

Canon 3: A Judge Should Perform the Duties of the Office Fairly, Impartially and Diligently.

Canon 4: A Judge May Engage in Extrajudicial Activities That are Consistent with the Obligations of Judicial Office.

Canon 5: A Judge Should Refrain from Political Activity.

Source: Administrative Office of the United States Courts (2014)

members of the federal judiciary should not hold membership(s) in organizations(s) that practice discrimination on the basis of race, sex, religion, or national origin, as doing so creates an impression of partiality.

Canon 3 and its commentary speak to judicial fairness, impartiality, and diligence in discharging official duties. As was true of the ABA judicial code, the AOC code stresses the need for federal judges to show competence in discharging their duties, which includes having the necessary skills, knowledge, and experience to do so. Federal judges should promptly dispose of the business before them and avoid making public comments about the merits of cases pending before them. Diligence and impartiality extend to the circumstances under which a federal judge should recuse him- or herself from a case, as in "[when] the judge's impartiality might . . . be questioned" (Administrative Office of the United States Courts, 2014, p. 1).

Canon 4 of the code and its commentary stipulate that members of the federal judiciary "may engage in extrajudicial activities" (e.g., law-related, civic, charitable, educational, religious, social, financial, fiduciary, and governmental) and speak, write, lecture, and teach about law-related and nonlegal subjects (Administrative Office of the United States Courts, 2014, p. 1). Judges should not, however, engage in extrajudicial activities that demean the dignity of the office, interfere with a judge's ability to complete her official duties, lead to frequent disqualification from matters pending before the judge or jeopardize her impartiality.

Finally, Canon 5 of the AOC judicial code addresses federal judges' involvement in political activities. According to the canon, federal judges should not lead or hold office in any political organization or make speeches for political organizations or candidates, including publicly endorsing or opposing a candidate for public office. Judges should also refrain from fund-raising activities associated with, paying assessments to, or making contributions to either a political organization or a candidate. They should also not attend or purchase tickets to events sponsored by political organizations or candidates. The canon also stipulates that judges should resign from their office if they become a candidate for any office in a primary or general election. For purposes of this canon, a "political organization" includes a party or group affiliated with a party, a candidate for public office, or any entity whose primary purpose is to advocate either for or against political candidates or parties that are connected to elections for public office.

You have now been exposed to two examples of "black-and-white" rules for the judiciary developed by the ABA and the federal AOC. While several themes run through both, of primary importance for judges is that their conduct inside and outside the court does not impinge on the impartiality, independence, and diligence of these offices. Both examples provide guiding ideals and articulate judicial obligations that support achieving the ideals.

SUMMARY

This chapter examined ethics and courts, the second component of the criminal justice system. Similar to what I presented when discussing ethics and the police, ethical issues and the courts are embedded in a larger organizational context, that of the courtroom workgroup. Consisting of prosecutors, defense attorneys, and judges, the courtroom workgroup processes and disposes of the many criminal cases flowing into courts around the nation. Unlike idealized notions of adversarial justice—where prosecutor and defense attorney "go at it" hammer and tong, overseen by an impartial arbiter—the vast majority of criminal cases in this country are disposed of via negotiated outcomes involving the three members of the workgroup. In doing so, each member agrees to give up some of the power they have to achieve a common goal—disposing of the case—while also ensuring that a kind of rough justice is achieved for defendants in them.

Each member of the workgroup is supposed to adapt their professional behavior to a set of standards created by professional associations like the American Bar Association (ABA). For example, the ABA has created a set of standards for the prosecution function stressing that prosecutors should not merely seek to convict, but should seek to achieve justice, even if doing so means not charging people with crimes, reducing charges pending against them, or helping undo an injustice that's occurred in the case. Prosecutors are also embedded in a larger organization, headed by an elected official—the district attorney—and staffed by professionals (e.g., assistant district attorneys) and paraprofessionals (e.g., investigators, victim service officers, and IT experts). Prosecutors are also more than just the "people's lawyers": they are officers of the court and as such have certain obligations, such as seeking justice, reforming the system, and ensuring that they do not allow politics or other pressures to cause them to veer in inappropriate directions and become guilty of prosecutorial misconduct. Prosecutorial misconduct is related to pressures to win, knowledge that harmless error will protect prosecutors from being disciplined, and the absolute immunity prosecutors enjoy from civil lawsuits and the damages that arise from their misconduct.

The ABA also developed a set of standards for the defense function that likewise stresses ideals such as competence, developing good relationships with clients, and zealously defending them to the best of one's ability. The three "Z" words—zeal, zealously, and zealousness—often give rise to claims that defense attorneys are behaving unethically in representing their clients. Contributing to this is a larger belief in the profession that litigation is the equivalent of war, although the use of "Rambo" tactics results in practitioners, professional associations like the ABA, and legal scholars decrying such tactics and pointing to law school curricula, continuing education, and other methods as ways to help reduce "Rambo"-style litigation and restore civility to litigation.

Finally, judges are the third member of the courtroom workgroup and they also have sets of rules (e.g., the ABA Model Code of Judicial Conduct and the Code of Conduct for United States Judges) designed to ensure that the judiciary remains independent, impartial, and diligent, clearly notable ideals. Ethical issues confronting judges arise from mundane, everyday activities in which they engage, and include devoting proper time to both big and small cases, not delegating too many of their responsibilities to support staff, checking their professional ambitions, and potentially bending the law to ensure that injustices are avoided. Codes of judicial ethics typically fail to offer guidance on these matters.

To conclude this chapter, consider Thought Exercise 8.1, which addresses how lawyers' professional activities are regulated. Here, I will ask you to consider two different regulatory "models" and then decide which would have more of a positive impact on the ethical issues arising from the practice of law.

THOUGHT EXERCISE 8.1

REGULATING THE PRACTICE OF LAW

I've spent a good portion of this chapter reviewing for you different standards and rules for lawyers—be they prosecutors, defense attorneys, or judges—designed to regulate their professional lives. While "best-practice" standards and concrete rules contain embedded ideals and obligations, they are also based on a set of assumptions about the practice of law in the broadest sense, including that lawyers are *amoral agents* and their clients seek to preserve or obtain their self-interests, with neither caring much about the common good (see Fisher, 2008). You also saw how these standards and rules, it could be argued, are ineffective at discouraging misconduct or providing guidance for lawyers facing moral dilemmas in their professional lives. But what if there was an alternative way to regulate the behavior of lawyers based on different assumptions? Would such a model be more effective as a regulatory tool? More importantly, would it encourage more *ethical* behavior by lawyers?

The Guiding Assumptions of "Black Letter Rules"

In a much-cited article published in the *Harvard Law Review*, former U.S. Supreme Court chief justice Oliver Wendell Holmes, Jr., defined law as simply "a prediction about how particular cases might be decided" (Holmes, 1897, p. 458) and illustrated how such an instrumental approach would work in practice, using the metaphor of a "bad man." This individual is interested only in avoiding legal penalties for his behavior and now seeks legal counsel to defend him. In this world, an attorney is an amoral facilitator or defender of the "bad man" client's wishes and should do everything in his or her power to do so. Holmes contrasts this "bad man" not just with someone who consciously tries to conform his or her behavior to the "right" side of the law, but with one guided by a developed and deeply considered moral judgment. Holmes's "good man" is a person of good conscience; his "bad man" is not.

Beginning in the 1980s, law schools and their students found that instrumentalism in the practice of law resonated with them, via what was the then-trendy and influential "law and economics" movement led by federal judge Richard Posner (Posner, 1987). It also turns out that instrumentalism was influential in developing rules for the professional conduct of lawyers, as reflected in the ABA's Model Rules of Professional Conduct, its predecessors, and its various progeny (American Bar Association, 2016). Under these **black letter rules**, lawyer and client are *assumed* to be rational, autonomous, actors: clients are pursuing their self-interests with little regard for those of the community; lawyers serve as extreme partisans for their clients' interests, also with little regard for the interests of the larger public (Fisher, 2008). As a result, *both* lawyer and client had become Holmesian bad men and women seeking to get away with what they could within the letter of the law and professional rules (Pearce & Wald, 2012). As Fisher (2008) and Pearce and Wald (2012) described it, the "black letter rules" of ABA codes (1) created a framework that legitimated and encouraged lawyers to become "neutral partisans" for their clients; (2) jettisoned the notion of lawyer as "counselor" and downplayed the importance of engaging in behavior to "benefit the common good"; and (3) prescribed many discretionary duties that allow lawyers to apply their own perspectives to the situation at hand.

Where did this get us? Russell Pearce and Eli Wald (2012), among others, argued that this instrumentalism impaired the occupational culture from becoming supportive of compliance, since lawyers who believe they are autonomously self-interested individuals view rules instrumentally and assume it acceptable to try and "get away with" what they can when representing clients. Second, lacking a culture that promotes adhering to the rules as ends-in-themselves, compliance became overly dependent on actual enforcement (or the fear of it), an expensive and inefficient undertaking that ended up mostly targeting rules' violations also subject to civil or criminal penalties (e.g., negligence, crimes, or fraud). Finally, in this model, disciplinary authorities overly relied on reactive strategies, namely, responding to complaints, rather than proactively developing ways to encourage conformity.

The Guiding Assumptions of a Relational Model

In response to the "black letter rule" model, over the past 40 years an alternative model for regulating the professional conduct of lawyers has developed and gained traction among practitioners and scholars (Fisher, 2008; Green & Pearce, 2009; Pearce, 2006; Pearce & Wald, 2012). At its heart, this model builds on the notion that regulating the professional

continued

conduct of lawyers should be based on the *relational nature of what lawyers do* (Simon, 1978). Such a **principles-based regulatory model** was developed and implemented in Australia and the United Kingdom to regulate lawyers; in America, efforts to do so reflect a growing commitment by members of the bar to embrace the relational context of lawyers' work and design regulatory approaches that reflect this fact (Pearce & Wald, 2012).

What's important here is this: 50 years ago, a large percentage of lawyers worked as *solo practitioners*; today, more and more lawyers work in *firms*. What this means is that they are interacting with colleagues a great deal and developing relationships with them far more than used to be the case (Schneyer, 2011). Under a principles-based regulatory model, those relationships become the basis for standards of professional conduct. Firms are then tagged with enforcing the standards they create, resulting in a reciprocal relationship developing between the regulated and the regulators.

In explaining a principles-based regulatory model, Pearce and Wald (2012) suggested that the model assumes (and promotes the notion) that lawyers are *relationally self-interested actors* bearing at least some responsibility for enhancing the public good. In effect, the model posits that lawyers "exist within a web of relationships" that include clients, colleagues in the firm, adversaries, friends, families, and agents working in the legal system (Pearce & Wald, 2012). Fostering relational self-interest thus becomes an important and achievable goal of regulation and can occur when leaders of the bar work to educate members on the relational nature of the practice of law and the value of relational (as opposed to autonomous) self-interest.

Pearce and Wald (2012) described the framework of this model as including multiple dimensions. Instead of focusing exclusively on relationships between regulator and regulated, it focuses on firms developing and enforcing *their own ethical identities*. In doing this, firms ensure that all attorneys (including new associates) and staff are involved with creating, implementing, and enforcing an ethical infrastructure that includes committing to a relational ethic within the firm, along with creating and implementing necessary training, mentoring, etc. to develop intrafirm relationships based on mutual respect. Firms' regulatory goals then include creating and enforcing "black letter rules" grounded in ethical aspirations that are based on relational self-interest. In doing this, a firm helps create solid ground for attorneys (and staff) to make a commitment to professional values, including civility, the public good, *pro bono* service, and civic engagement, service, and leadership.

Pearce and Wald (2012) note that in this model, regulators and bar associations would work to create a mechanism for small firms and solo practitioners to benefit from firm-type regulation. For example, a local bar association could organize a working group that would be charged with creating an alliance of small firms and solo practices who would then cooperate to develop their own ethical principles and regulatory plans, including mechanisms for assisting and monitoring each other without breaching duties of confidentiality and loyalty.

Where would such a model get us? For proponents like Pearce and Wald (2012), it would help change the notion that lawyers are autonomous, partisan agents, willing to do pretty much anything to represent their client(s). In its place would be a realization that the "context of lawyering" is a web of relationships. That attorneys already understand this is shown by their admitting, when pressed, that the successes they have accumulated have resulted from the relationships they developed with clients, colleagues, and even adversaries (Schneyer, 2011). Pearce and Wald (2012) further argued that the "vocabulary" of relational self-interest allows lawyers—whether seasoned litigators or new associates—to learn that achievements and ethical obligations are tied to relationships. The two also suggested that many lawyers who are "burned out" or otherwise dissatisfied with their careers are unhappy because of the disjuncture they have experienced between the relational way they live their lives and the autonomous way they engage in their work as lawyers. For these people, the language of *relational* self-interest would enable them to understand how their lives and their work can be harmonious. By promoting a sense of community among lawyers and a commitment to the public good, a principles-based model of regulation may well prove both more effective and efficient at regulating the professional conduct of lawyers.

Now that you've been exposed to both models, which do *you* prefer and why?

KEY TERMS

Adversarial system 217
Negotiated justice 217
Courtroom workgroup 217
Going rate 218
Prosecutorial cynicism 225
Moral fascism 225
Batting average 226
Prosecutorial misconduct 227
Harmless error doctrine 228
Guilt-based approach 228
Effect-on-the-verdict approach 229
Absolute immunity 229
Rambo attorneys 237
Work allocation
Work delegation
Doing justice
Black letter rules 245
Principles-based regulatory model 246

DISCUSSION QUESTIONS

1. Do you think that model standards or codes of conduct like those developed by the ABA are effective at "policing" the professional ethics of prosecutors, defense attorneys, and judges? Explain.
2. Review the professional conduct of the prosecutor(s) and defense counsel in any of the following "high-profile" criminal cases and assess the ethics of that behavior: the OJ Simpson double murder trial (1995); three members of the Duke University lacrosse team being prosecuted for sexual assault (2006); the Scott Peterson double murder trial (2005); the Casey Anthony murder trial (2011).
3. Should members of the U.S. Supreme Court be bound by the same code of conduct as the rest of the federal judiciary? Why or why not?
4. Is it ethical for a prosecutor or judge to advocate, whether publicly or in their writings, for policies that empirical evidence shows have little to no effect on crime (or may even cause backfire effects)? Explain your position.

RESOURCES

American Bar Association's Center for Professional Responsibility (ABACPR). According to the Center's website, the ABACPR was created in 1978 and "advances the public interest by promoting and encouraging high ethical conduct and professionalism by lawyers and judges." https://www.americanbar.org/groups/professional_responsibility.html

National District Attorneys Association (NDAA). This professional association was formed in 1950 by local prosecutors to give a focal point to advance their causes and issues at the national level. http://www.ndaajustice.org/#

National Trial Lawyers (NTL). A professional organization composed of the premier trial lawyers from across the country who exemplify superior qualifications as civil plaintiff or criminal defense trial lawyers. This national organization provides networking opportunities, advocacy training, and the highest-quality educational programs for trial lawyers. http://www.thenationaltriallawyers.org/

American Judges' Association (AJA). According to its website, the AJA is the largest judges' organization in North America and is dedicated to "Making Better Judges" through quality education programs and publications, such as the quarterly published *Court Review*. http://aja.ncsc.dni.us/

REFERENCES

Administrative Office of the United States Courts (2017). U.S. courts of appeal: Judicial caseload profile. Retrieved from http://www.uscourts.gov/sites/default/files/data_tables/fems_na_appprofile0331.2017.pdf

Administrative Office of the United States Courts (2014). *Code of conduct for United States judges*. Washington, DC: Administrative Office of United States Courts. Retrieved from http://www.uscourts.gov/judges-judgeships/code-conduct-united-states-judges

Allibone, S. (Ed.) (1880). *Prose quotations from Socrates to Macaulay*. Philadelphia: J. B. Lippincott Co.

American Bar Association (2017). State adoption of the ABA Model Rules of Professional Conduct. Retrieved from https://www.americanbar.org/groups/professional_responsibility/publications/model_rules_of_professional_conduct/alpha_list_state_adopting_model_rules.html

American Bar Association (2016). *Model rules of professional conduct*. Washington, DC: American Bar Association. Retrieved from https://www.americanbar.org/groups/professional_responsibility/publications/model_rules_of_professional_conduct/rule_1_3_diligence/comment_on_rule_1_3.html

American Bar Association (2015). *ABA standards for the prosecution and defense function* (4th ed.). Washington, DC: American Bar Association. Retrieved from https://www.americanbar.org/groups/criminal_justice/standards/DefenseFunctionFourthEdition-TableofContents.html

American Bar Association (2014). *ABA standards for criminal justice: Prosecutorial investigations* (3rd ed.). Washington, DC: American Bar Association. Retrieved from http://www.americanbar.org/content/dam/aba/publications/criminal_justice_standards/Pros_Investigations.authcheckdam.pdf

American Bar Association (2011). *Model code of judicial conduct*. Washington, DC: American Bar Association. Retrieved from https://www.americanbar.org/groups/professional_responsibility/publications/model_code_of_judicial_conduct.html

Bowman, D. (1997). A matter of life and death: Revising the Harmless Error standard for *habeas corpus* proceedings. *Washington University Law Review, 72*, 567–610.

Boren, J., & Fisher, M. (2004). Fear of a paper tiger: Enforcing Louisiana's procedural and statutory rules in the wake of harmless error analysis. *Louisiana Law Review, 64*, 5–20.

Bradley, B. (2010, July 31). Prosecutors' batting average. *ABC7 Notes from the Newsroom*. Retrieved from http://abc7chicago.typepad.com/going_for_the_games/2010/07/prosecutors-batting-average.html

Brown, L. (2007). "Lawyers" not "liars": A modified traditionalist approach to teaching legal ethics. *Saint Louis University Law Journal, 51*, 1119–1133.

Brownstein, R. (2003, January 1). Are there limits to prosecutorial discretion? *Intelligence Report*. Retrieved from https://www.splcenter.org/fighting-hate/intelligence-report/2003/are-there-limits-prosecutorial-discretion

Caldwell, H. (2016). Everybody talks about prosecutorial conduct but nobody does anything about it: A 25-year survey of prosecutorial misconduct and a viable solution. Retrieved from https://papers.ssrn.com/sol3/papers.cfm?abstract_id=2761252##

Center for Prosecutor Integrity (2013). *An epidemic of prosecutor misconduct*. Rockville, MD: Center for Prosecutorial Integrity.

Chan, S. (2007, August 9). The Abner Louima case—10 years later. *New York Times*. Retrieved from https://cityroom.blogs.nytimes.com/2007/08/09/the-abner-louima-case-10-years-later/

Davis, Angela (2007). *Arbitrary justice: The power of the American prosecutor*. New York, NY: Oxford University Press.

Devers, L. (2011). *Plea and charge bargaining*. Washington, DC: United States Department of Justice.

Eisenstein, J., & Jacob, H. (1977). *Felony justice: An organizational analysis of criminal courts*. Boston, MA: Little, Brown.

Fisher, K. (2008). Repudiating the Holmesian "bad man" through contextual ethical reasoning: The lawyer as steward. *Journal of the Professional Lawyer*, 13–43.

Flemming, R., Nardulli, P., & Eisenstein, J. (1992) *The craft of justice: Politics and work in criminal court communities*. Philadelphia, PA: University of Pennsylvania Press.

Forsythe, S., & Miller, M. (2014). Novel defenses in the courtroom. Retrieved from http://www.thejuryexpert.com/2014/08/novel-defenses-in-the-courtroom/

Freedman, M., & Smith, A. (2016). *Understanding lawyers' ethics* (5th ed.). Durham, NC: Carolina Academic Press.

Gallup (2016). Honesty/ethics in professions. Retrieved from http://www.gallup.com/poll/1654/honesty-ethics-professions.aspx

Gebo, E., Stracuzzi, N., & Hurst, V. (2006). Juvenile justice reform and the courtroom workgroup: Issues of perception and workload. *Journal of Criminal Justice*, *34*, 425–433.

Gershman, B. (1986). Why prosecutors misbehave. *Criminal Law Bulletin*, *22*, 131–145.

Gordon, N. (2007). Misconduct and punishment. The Center for Public Integrity. Retrieved from https://www.publicintegrity.org/2003/06/26/5532/misconduct-and-punishment

Green, B., & Yaroshefsky, E. (2016). Prosecutorial accountability 2.0. *Notre Dame Law Review*, *92*, 51–116.

Green, B., & Pearce, R. (2009). Public service must begin at home: The lawyer as civics teacher in everyday practice. *William & Mary Law Review*, *50*, 1207–1250.

Griffin, D., Glover, S., & Black, N. (2016, December 22). Jeff Sessions' office accused of prosecutorial misconduct in the '90s. CNN Politics. Retrieved from http://www.cnn.com/2016/12/21/politics/jeff-sessions-prosecutorial-misconduct/index.html

Harris, A. (2002). The Professionalism crisis, the "Z" words, and other Rambo tactics: The Conference of Chief Justices' solution. *University of South Carolina Law Review*, *53*, 549–600.

Heath, B., & McCoy, K. (2010, September 23). Prosecutors' conduct can tip justice scales. *USA Today*. Retrieved from http://usatoday30.usatoday.com/news/washington/judicial/2010-09-22-federal-prosecutors-reform_N.htm?csp=usat.me

Holmes, O. (1897). The path of the law. *Harvard Law Review*, *10*, 457–518.

Hoskins-Haynes, S., Ruback, B., & Cusick, G. (2010). Courtroom workgroups and sentencing: The effects of similarity, proximity, and stability. *Crime & Delinquency*, *56*, 126–161.

Jonakait, R. (1987). The ethical prosecutor's misconduct. *Criminal Law Bulletin*, *23*, 550–567.

Kiefer, M. (2013, October 28). Prosecutors under scrutiny are seldom disciplined. *Arizona Republic*. Retrieved from http://archive.azcentral.com/news/arizona/articles/20131027wintory-prosecutor-conduct-day-2.html

Koenig, J. (2009). The seven most baffling criminal defenses (that sort of worked). Retrieved from http://www.cracked.com/article_17470_the-7-most-baffling-criminal-defenses-that-sort-worked.html

Kramer, J., & Ulmer, J. (2002). Downward departures for serious violent offenders: Local court "corrections" to Pennsylvania's sentencing guidelines. *Criminology*, *40*, 897–932.

Lee, K. (2014). The 4 rules of warfare (and litigation). Retrieved from http://abovethelaw.com/2014/07/the-4-rules-of-warfare-and-litigation/

Lindsey, L. (2016). *Criminal court of the City of New York Annual Report*. New York, NY: Office of the Chief Clerk, City of New York Criminal Court.

Minsker, N. (2009). Prosecutorial misconduct in death penalty cases. *California Western Law Review*, *45*, 373–404.

Nardulli, P., Eisenstein, J., & Flemming, R. (1988). *The tenor of justice: Criminal courts and the guilty plea process*. Urbana, IL: University of Illinois Press.

National Association for Court Management (2017). *Purposes and responsibilities of courts*. Williamsburg, VA: National Center for State Courts.

Pearce, R. (2006). The legal profession as a blue state: Reflections on public philosophy, jurisprudence, and legal ethics. *Fordham Law Review*, *75*, 1339–1357.

Posner, R. (1987). The law and economics movement. *The American Economic Review, 77,* 1–13.

Possley, M., & Armstrong, K. (1999, January 11). The verdict: Dishonor. *Chicago Tribune*. Retrieved from http://www.chicagotribune.com/news/watchdog/chi-020103trial1-story.html

Reardon, J. (2014, September 15). Civility as the core of professionalism. *Business Law Today*. Retrieved from https://www.americanbar.org/content/dam/aba/publications/blt/2014/09/civility-professionalism-201409.authcheckdam.pdf

Reaves, B. (2013). *Felony defendants in large urban counties, 2009—Statistical tables.*Washington, DC: Bureau of Justice Assistance.

Ridolfi, K., & Possley, M. (2010). *Preventable error: A report on prosecutorial misconduct in California (1997–2009)*. Sacramento, CA: Northern California Innocence Project.

Scheck, B., Neufeld, P., & Dwyer, J. (2000). *Five days to execution and other dispatches from the wrongly convicted*. New York, NY: Doubleday Publishers.

Schneyer, T. (2011). On further reflection: How professional self-regulation should promote compliance with broad ethical duties of law firm management. *Arizona Law Review, 53,* 577–628.

Schoenfeld, H. (2005). Violated trust: Conceptualizing prosecutorial misconduct. *Journal of Contemporary Criminal Justice, 21,* 250–271.

Simon, W. (1978). The ideology of advocacy: Procedural justice and professional ethics. *Wisconsin Law Review, 1978,* 29–90.

Slaughter, L. (2014). Supreme unaccountability: The nine federal judges to whom no code of ethics applies. *Stanford Law & Policy Review, 28,* 9–15.

Smith, A. (2001).Can you be a good person and a good prosecutor? *Georgetown Journal of Legal Ethics, 1,* 355–400.

Smith, A. (2000). Defending defending: The case for unmitigated zeal on behalf of people who do terrible things. *Hofstra Law Review, 28,* 925–961.

Ulmer, J. (1995). The organization and consequences of social pasts in criminal courts. *The Sociological Quarterly, 36,* 587–605.

Uribe, S. (n.d.). *A primer on alleging prosecutorial misconduct on appeal*. Sacramento, CA: Central California Appellate Program.

Veritas Initiative (2012a). Prosecutorial oversight forum: Court findings of prosecutorial error and misconduct in Arizona. Retrieved from https://www.innocenceproject.org/panel-discussion-at-phoenix-school-of-law-addresses-prosecutorial-misconduct/

Veritas Initiative (2012b). Prosecutorial oversight forum: Court findings of prosecutorial error and misconduct in New York State. Retrieved from https://www.innocenceproject.org/innocence-project-research-illustrates-lack-of-accountability-for-prosecutors-who-commit-misconduct/

Veritas Initiative (2012c). Prosecutorial oversight forum: Court findings of prosecutorial error and misconduct in Pennsylvania. Retrieved from https://www.innocenceproject.org/pennsylvania-stop-on-national-tour-addressing-prosecutorial-error-tonight-in-pennsylvania.

Veritas Initiative (2012d). Prosecutorial oversight forum: Court findings of prosecutorial error and misconduct in Texas. Retrieved from https://www.innocenceproject.org/new-research-illustrates-lack-of-accountability-for-prosecutors-in-texas/

Whitmer, F. (2007). *Litigation is war: Strategies and tactics for the litigation battlefield*. Minneapolis, MN: West Publishers.

Wilbert, J. (2008). Muzzling "Rambo" attorneys: Preventing abusive witness coaching by banning attorney-initiated consultations with deponents. *Georgia Journal of Legal Ethics, 21,* 1129–1141.

Williams, J. (2017, June 9). The ethical honor system. *U.S. News & World Report*. Retrieved from https://www.usnews.com/news/the-report/articles/2017-06-09/supreme-court-justices-play-by-their-own-ethics-rules

Wright, R. (2009). How prosecutor elections fail us. *Ohio State Journal of Criminal Law, 6,* 581–610.

CHAPTER 9

The Ethics of Legal Punishment

Chapter Outline

CHAPTER LEARNING OBJECTIVES:

1. Describe recent trends in the correctional population of the United States.
2. Identify the features of legal punishment and define the concept.
3. Explain the ties among the state, legal punishment, and crime.
4. Contrast major justifications for legal punishment.
5. Describe the major criticisms that have been raised with justifications for legal punishment.
6. Identify how race and wrongful convictions raise ethical issues with the death penalty in America.
7. Contrast legal punishment in America with legal punishment in Scandinavia.

INTRODUCTION

Have you ever heard the phrase "don't do the crime if you can't do the time?" According to the Urban Dictionary, the phrase was a popular expression in the 1960s and 1970s, warning people not to do something risky if they weren't willing to fully accept the consequences (Poppyjoe, 2005). Judging from recent trends in American corrections, many people either ignored the adage or were willing to "do the time." (Figure 9.1).

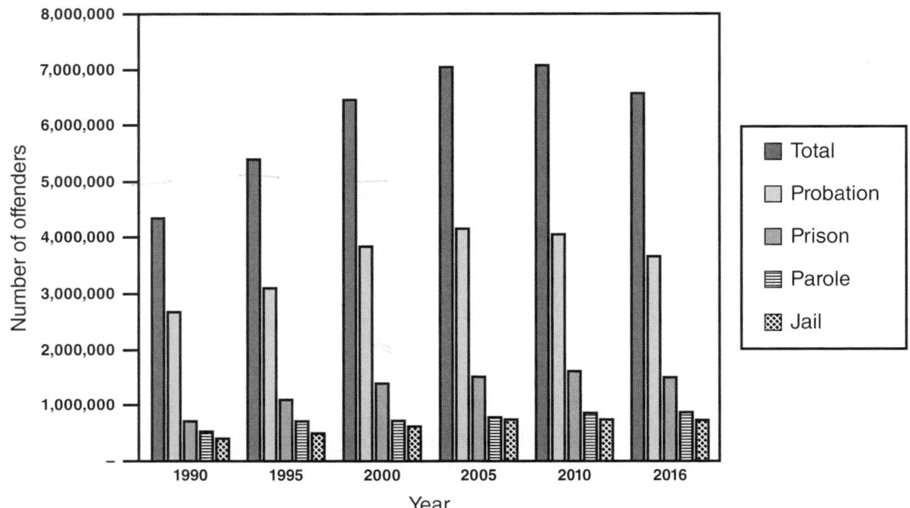

FIGURE 9.1 Trends in the U.S. Correctional Population: 1990–2016
Source: Adapted from Jankowski (1992), Hester & Hinds (1997), Kaeble & Glaze (2016), Kaeble & Cowhig (2018)

Figure 9.1 reveals several important trends in legal punishment over the past 25 years in this country. First, between 1990 and 2016, the total correctional population grew by about 51%—about 2 million people, or roughly the population of Houston, TX. Indeed, if you consider that the average annual size of the correctional population—those in prison or jail or on probation or parole—in this country was about 6.15 million people, that population *by itself* would constitute the second most populous city behind New York (the population of which, in 2018, was estimated to be about 8.55 million people; see Barron, 2018). Put another way, on average, over this period, about 1 in every 38 adults in this country was under some form of correctional supervision (Kaeble & Cowhig, 2018). Second, probation was the most common criminal sanction used over the period. On average, between 1990 and 2016 , about 58% of the total correctional population each year consisted of people on probation. Third, between 1990 and 2016 there was an explosion in the prison population. To illustrate, in 1990 there were about 773,000 inmates in the nation's prisons; by 2016 there were about 1.5 million inmates, a nearly 200% increase. In 2016 , by themselves, prison inmates would constitute the sixth-largest city in the United States, about the population of Phoenix, AZ. Finally, the *use* of imprisonment changed. In 1990, the prison population was approximately 17% of the total correctional population, but by 2016, it was about 23% of the total. Each year between 1990 and 2016, on average, the prison population was about 1.31 million people, or about the same number of people that live in San Antonio, TX.

Figure 9.2 focuses on the people who were imprisoned between 1990 and 2016, so let's focus on that. Recall that over the period, an average of about 1.31 million people were incarcerated in state and federal prisons in this country each year (there are about 1,800 of these facilities). Figure 9.2 translates the annual raw numbers of inmates into the number of prison inmates per 100,000 people or the rate of imprisonment. On average, over the 25-year period, about 500 people were imprisoned annually per 100,000

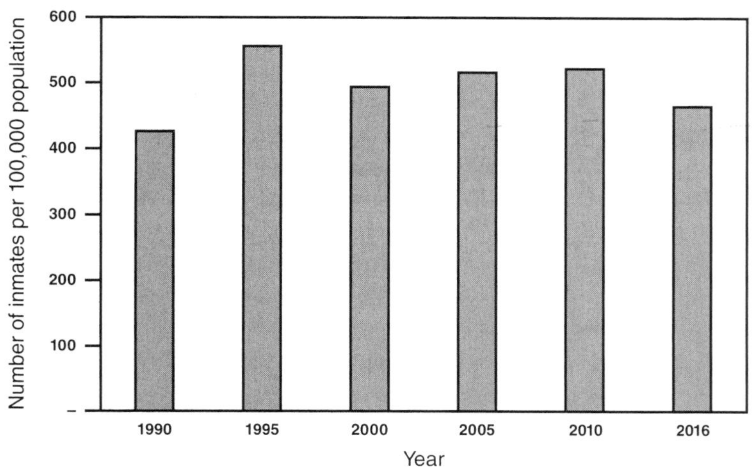

FIGURE 9.2 Imprisonment Rates in the United States: 1990–2016
Source: Adapted from Jankowski (1992), Hester & Hinds (1997), Kaeble & Glaze (2016), Kaeble & Cowhig (2018)

population. To put that figure into a global context, the U.S. imprisons people at a rate much higher than is the case for the Russian Federation, Cuba, and Iran, not to mention Canada, Australia, Germany, and France (Walmsley, 2015). Compared to many of those countries, the U.S. rate of imprisonment is four to five times higher.

But sanctioning criminals is not the only context where Americans seem to relish punishing wrongdoers. For example, consider how we administer punishment in the K-12 public school context. While corporal punishment (e.g., paddling) is banned by about every state, it nonetheless occurs in most of them. In fact, despite the states banning it, seven of them (Mississippi, Texas, Alabama, Arkansas, Georgia, Tennessee, and Oklahoma) accounted for some 80% of all public school corporal punishment events in the United States during 2015 (Startz, 2016). Further, a recent study by the Center for Civil Rights Remedies (Rumberger & Losen, 2016) showed that during the 2011–2012 school year, around 10% of all sophomores in public high schools in this country reported they had received either an in-school or out-of-school suspension during the first semester of the school year. Don't fool around in school!

Finally, looking to the family context and how parents punish their children, Murray Straus and Julie Stewart examined parental use of various forms of corporal punishment on children, including slaps of the hand or leg; spanking the buttocks; pinching or hitting the buttocks with a belt or paddle; and slapping of the face. Using data collected from a nationally representative sample of nearly 1,000 parents in 1995, Straus and Stewart (1999) found that 35% of the parents in their sample admitted they had used *any* of these types of corporal punishment during the previous year on infants; about one-half had used any of these forms of corporal punishment on children aged three to five; over one-half of parents had hit their children at age 12, one-third did so at age 14; and 13% indicated they had hit their children at age 17. The data also revealed that parents who hit their teenage children did so an average of about six times during the year. Severity of the corporal punishment, as measured by hitting the child with a belt or paddle, was greatest for children in the age 5–12 category, where over one-fourth (28%) of parents admitted they had used a paddle or belt on children in this age group (Straus & Stewart, 1999). Spare the rod and spoil the child, indeed!

The point here is not to dazzle (or baffle) you with statistics. The point is simple: America is an *incredibly* punitive country. We not only criminally sanction our population at levels unprecedented in the world, we also suspend our children from school and routinely use corporal punishment against them, both inside and outside of school settings. As you can imagine, not only does punishment raise important psychological and sociological issues, it also raises important *ethical* issues. It is to those issues, arising from the third and final component of the criminal justice system—corrections—that this and the following two chapters are devoted. I devote the present chapter to examining broad-based ethical issues arising from the punishment of criminal offenders. I then devote Ch. 10 to discussing ethical issues involving institutional corrections (prisons and jails), while Ch. 11 examines ethical issues surrounding community-based corrections (probation and parole in particular).

I begin the present chapter with an overview of the legal punishment of offenders. Included is discussion about what legal punishment involves and how it can be defined. I also explore ties among the state, legal punishment, and crime. Much of the rest of the chapter is then devoted to examining various justifications for legally punishing offenders, including justifications that are guided by teleological (consequentialist) and deontological (retributivist) systems of ethics, as well as justifications that focus on offenders losing the right to *not* be punished and, finally, those based on virtue ethics. I also offer critiques of each justification for legal punishment. Next, I consider a special case of legal punishment: the death penalty. Here, I share with you some facts about capital punishment (CP) in America, briefly examine key legal aspects of CP, and discuss two prominent issues surrounding CP: the role of race in the death penalty and the problem of executing innocents. I finish this section by discussing the "death" of CP in America. I then conclude the chapter by contrasting legal punishment in America with that found in Scandinavia, and ask you to consider which of the two is more ethically justifiable.

THE LEGAL PUNISHMENT OF CRIMINALS

In an excellent overview of legal punishment, Antony Duff and Zachary Hoskins (2017) described how the legal punishment of criminals raises various issues about the role of the state, its relationship with its citizens, and about the role of criminal law in society. They suggested that when one considers legal punishment, one should understand that it is both *burdensome* and *condemnatory*. Legal punishment is burdensome because it involves unwelcome or unpleasant impositions made upon, or extractions taken from, people. Punishment deprives people of something they value, such as their time, freedom, or money (in the case of criminal fines levied against them). It also requires something of them they wouldn't ordinarily do, such as reporting to a probation or parole officer or engaging in unpaid labor that benefits the community (e.g., removing graffiti from a building). Punishment is also condemnatory. That is, the offender is condemned in a public forum—the trial—for what she has done. Legal punishment is thus more than a mere "penalty" paid by an offender for her misbehavior (Feinberg, 1970). Take, for example, a parking ticket or a traffic citation. These are penalties imposed on people who violate the law, in part to recoup some of the costs associated with the proscribed behavior. However, a parking ticket or a traffic citation does not involve condemnation in a public forum like a court, which is what criminal offenders must endure. Rather, the fine can be paid by mail or online, and no one need know the violation has occurred. Because legal punishment is intentionally burdensome and condemnatory, the question becomes, How can legal punishment be ethically justified?

The great legal scholar H. L. A. Hart (1968) once argued that legal punishment raises three important questions relating to its justification. First, what justifies our creating and keeping a system that is both burdensome and condemnatory? Or, as Duff & Hoskins (2017) reformulated the question, what *good* can the system of punishment do? What duty can it fulfill? What moral demands are satisfied by the system? The second question Hart (1968) asked was twofold: who may be punished by this system and what principles guide allocation of the punishments that it dispenses? Finally, Hart (1968) asked how, in this system, should the appropriate amount of punishment be determined? This question actually addresses not only how much or how severe the punishment should be, but also the form the punishment should take (e.g., incarceration).

As Duff & Hoskins (2017) observed, a single ethical foundation (e.g., consequentialism) could well answer these questions. However, it could just as well be that legal punishment can only be justified by addressing different and conflicting values that surround it, using multiple systems of ethics. Finally, it could just as well be that no system of ethics can satisfactorily justify legal punishment, an important point not often considered when discussing the morality and ethics of legal punishment. Duff & Hoskins (2017) noted that too often discussions about the ethics of legal punishment assume that a system of legal punishment can, in fact, be justified and that one's primary task is to establish and explicate that justification. The reality, however, is that this system *may not be justifiable*.

Scholars within and outside criminology and philosophy have increasingly developed an "abolitionist" orientation that argues that the legal punishment of criminal offenders as it is now understood *cannot* be justified and, therefore, should be abolished. Note that the argument here is not merely that existing penal practices are unjustified. Rather, the argument is that considering many ethical theories, existing penal practices—particularly those involving incarceration or execution—are not merely imperfect "but so radically inconsistent with the values that should inform a practice of punishment that they cannot claim to be justified" (Duff & Hoskins, 2017, p. 1). For those who think that legal punishment can, in principle be justified, this means simply (and hardly surprisingly) that our penal practices need radical reform if they are to become justified. The abolitionist critique, however, goes much deeper to argue that legal punishment cannot *ever* be justified, even in principle.

You have now seen some of the "big questions" raised by the legal punishment of criminal offenders. Let's now examine some underlying dimensions of legal punishment that involve crime, the state, and the criminal law.

Crime, Legal Punishment, and the State

For legal punishment to exist, there must first be *law*—codified norms that articulate proscribed behaviors whose occurrence triggers the imposition of negative sanction(s). The existence of law presupposes the existence of the state—the entity possessing the political authority to create and enforce law and impose sanctions for its violation (Duff & Hoskins, 2017). One type of law (there are many) is *criminal* law, or a codified set of rules that define certain behaviors as being so wrong as to threaten the larger social order, and whose violations trigger formal mechanisms of social control (e.g., the police) to be activated and begin a process of imposing sanctions on violators. Violations of the criminal law are called *crimes*, which are, at minimum, socially proscribed wrongs—conduct that is condemned as wrong by an authoritative social norm (Duff & Hoskins, 2017). The wrongs are not behaviors affecting only those directly involved. Rather, the behaviors involve the whole community that, through its law(s), claims the right to declare the behavior is wrong. A criminal case is thus a conflict that has arisen between the whole political community—the state and/or its people—and the person engaging in the wrongful conduct, the defendant. As Duff & Hoskins (2017, p. 1) described it, "[t]he wrong is 'public' in the sense that it is one for which the wrongdoer must answer not just to the individual victim, but to the whole polity through its criminal courts." Duff & Hoskins (2017) noted that one can argue that crimes are "public" wrongs because they injure the whole community (e.g., they threaten social order, involve taking advantage of those who follow the law, or undermine the trust necessary in social life). Or, one might argue that crimes are "public" wrongs because they flout the community's core values. Here, the "victims" are not the specific people harmed by the conduct, but the entire community that sees itself as sharing in the wrong that has been done (Duff, 2007; Marshall & Duff, 1998).

In summary, legal punishment requires the existence of law, one form of which is criminal law. A crime is a violation of that particular type of law and subject to sanction by a politically authorized authority, namely, the state. Crimes are considered "public" wrongs, in the sense that the violative behavior has threatened the stability or morality of the entire community. The state's response to that violation—imposition of criminal sanctions—thereby (at least in theory) represents the will of the community.

Now that you understand that the roots of legal punishment lie with the state and criminal law, let's consider how scholars have defined the concept "legal punishment."

Defining Legal Punishment

Scholars cannot seem to agree on a definition of "legal punishment," which may strike you as odd since so many disciplines (e.g., law, philosophy, psychology, sociology, literature, theology) are interested in the topic. I can, however, share with you some *common features* of legal punishment, and based on those features, present to you a working definition of the concept.

Zachary Hoskins (n.d.) has suggested that there are five features of legal punishment. First, it involves inflicting a burden on someone (e.g., monetary sanctions; loss of, or restrictions on, freedom, privacy, and association with others). Second, the burden inflicted is intended; that is, it does not occur by accident or mistake but occurs at the end of a formal process (arrest and trial). Next, punishment is intentionally imposed on one presumed (or found) to be guilty of committing an offense. Thus, punishment is not imposed on the innocent. If that occurs, those individuals are now considered *victims*. A fourth feature of punishment is that it is expressive: an offender is condemned or censured, unlike in nonpunitive penalties such as parking tickets or fines for littering (Feinberg, 1970). Finally, punishment is imposed by a properly constituted legal authority, the state, which distinguishes legal punishment from the victimization people suffer at the hands of vigilantes. If these features are combined, **legal punishment** can be defined as the state's imposition of intended burdens that express social condemnation of people guilty of crimes, in response to those crimes.

You've now learned that legal punishment is the state's imposition of intended burdens that express social condemnation on those (believed to be) guilty of crimes. Crimes are public wrongs, punishable by the state, that are grounded in the law, which is created by a politically authorized authority. Let's next consider how legal punishment can be ethically justified.

JUSTIFICATIONS FOR LEGAL PUNISHMENT

Moral justifications of legal punishment, when closely examined, typically try to address one or more of the following areas: (1) the presumed function(s) of punishment; (2) whether punishment violates the moral rights of those being punished; (3) which principles and considerations guide the severity of the punishment received; (4) which principles and considerations guide the form that punishment takes (e.g., a monetary fine); and

(5) why the state is the proper agent to administer punishment (Hoskins, n.d.). Further, there is wide agreement among scholars that most justifications for punishment are either consequentialist or retributivist, although there are additional justifications that are based on legal theory and virtue ethics. Let's examine these justifications and how they address the five areas listed above.

Consequentialist Justifications for Legal Punishment

Recall from Ch. 2 that consequentialist (Utilitarian) theories of ethics argue that the rightness or wrongness of a behavior is based solely on its potential consequences: if the potential positive consequences outweigh the potential negative, the behavior is considered ethical. A consequentialist justification of legal punishment would thus argue that the potential consequences of having a system of legal punishment are better than are the consequences of *not* having such a system (Hoskins, n.d.). Further, for the consequentialist, punishment is instrumental. What this means is that by punishing people, some ultimate end or goal is sought: less crime, greater social cohesion, protection of property or person, etc. (Hoskins, n.d.). Note, however, that in traditional Utilitarian thought punishment is considered "evil" since it involves inflicting pain on another person (McHugh, 2008). Therefore, for punishment to be justified it must result in other, valuable consequences outweighing the "evil" done through punishment.

Deterrence

Consequentialists typically posit there are three socially desirable ends of legal punishment: deterrence, incapacitation, and/or rehabilitation (Murtagh, n.d.). Deterrence, for example, assumes that humans are rational creatures who weigh the costs (pain) and benefits (pleasure) of their behavioral choices. In the case of a specific crime, say theft, if the person perceives that the benefits of keeping or selling the stolen item(s) will outweigh the costs (the chance of being caught, convicted, and punished), the person will engage in the theft. **Deterrence** occurs when the perceived costs of crime outweigh the perceived benefits (National Research Council, 2012).

Deterrence also takes two forms: specific and general (Kennedy, 2010). **Specific deterrence** occurs when an individual offender, after being caught and punished, learns that the costs of criminality—arrest, conviction, and incarceration—outweigh its benefits and thus desists offending. **General deterrence** occurs when others contemplating breaking the law see what happened to those who have been arrested, convicted, and punished, and decide the costs of crime outweigh the benefits and choose not to engage in the contemplated behavior.

According to traditional consequentialist thought, for deterrence to work, punishment must be swift, certain, and severe (National Research Council, 2012). Swiftness (known as **celerity**) refers to how long in time after the behavior occurs is the punishment administered. **Certainty** refers to the perceived probability of being caught and punished. **Severity** refers to the intensity or form of the punishment received (e.g., incarceration). Thus, to be deterred, offenders must be punished quickly, the punishment must occur with a high degree of certainty, and the punishment (costs) must be severe enough to outweigh benefits gained from the crime.

Incapacitation

A second potential justification of legal punishment is **incapacitation** (see Blumstein, Cohen, & Nagin, 1978). Incapacitation occurs when an offender is removed from the community by incarcerating her, which makes the offender unable to continue victimizing it. For incapacitation to be successful, however, the offender must be locked up long enough so she is "past her prime," in terms of offending. We need to know for how long (on average) is an offender's "career" and in how much annual criminality (on average) does a particular offender engage to determine the effect of punishing a particular offender. In doing so, we can then figure out how much crime was prevented and thus identify the social benefits gained by locking up the offender (Gottfredson & Hirschi, 1986). These considerations determine the offender's sentence.

For example, if Smith is 20 years old and has been convicted of burglary, we would need to figure out for how much longer Smith would keep burglarizing people (e.g., another 20 years) as well as how many annual burglaries (on average) Smith perpetrates (e.g., 15). The former tells us for how long we need to lock Smith up (assuming the punishment used is incarceration); the latter, how many burglaries will be prevented by doing so. This information gives us an indicator of the utility gained from the punishment. In our example, if we lock up Smith for 20 years (until the age of 40), doing so would prevent as many as 300 burglaries.

Rehabilitation

A final justification of legal punishment is that it alters the forces causing the offender to engage in the behavior (Allen, 1981). By identifying those forces (e.g., drug addiction) and developing a treatment plan to address them, the offender desists (Cullen & Gilbert, 2015). In **rehabilitation**, the assumption is not that criminality is the product of rational choice but is instead a product of forces over which the individual has little control. Proponents also assume that experts (e.g., psychiatrists, counselors, and social workers) can identify those forces, and through a carefully designed treatment program eliminate them (or at least reduce their influence). By subjecting the offender to a process of diagnosis and treatment—that includes punishment in the form of incarceration or other restrictions on their liberty—the offender desists from future criminality and thus the community is protected.

One last point I need to make about consequentialist justifications of punishment: they are *forward looking* in their orientation (Hoskins, n.d.). In other words, the consequentialist is saying that for punishment to be justified, it must look to the future and toward achieving some presumed end. We are thus doing something to offenders *now* (e.g., incarcerating them) to achieve some end *later* (e.g., lower crime rates).

Critiques of Consequentialist Justifications for Legal Punishment

Let's assess consequentialist justifications for punishment in terms of their ability to answer the five questions posed above. Consequentialist justifications clearly answer the "what is the function of punishment" question—to deter, to incapacitate, or to rehabilitate (or some combination of these). They also answer the "which principles and considerations are being used to guide how severely the punishment should be" question, by suggesting that punishment be *proportionate* to the wrong perpetrated—lesser crimes are punished less severely than are more serious crimes (in part to encourage prospective offenders to choose the less serious crime).Finally, consequentialist justifications explain why the state is the proper agent of punishment by arguing that the only *true* punishment is that which is imposed by a *legitimate* legal system representing a *legitimate* state. Vengeance or "vigilante justice" is not punishment—it is victimization of the offender by other citizens.

I note here that some critics have argued that consequentialists *would* allow punishment of the innocent *if* doing so would result in positive social utility (Hoskins, n.d.) Here's the classic illustration of this concern: Suppose for a moment, in the wake of the rape and murder of an 8-year-old girl, a small-town sheriff has to determine whether to arrest and seek conviction of, and punishment for, a resident whom the *townspeople* believe is guilty of the crime, but the *sheriff* knows is innocent if doing so is the only way of preventing rioting (McCloskey, 1957). Critics charge that the consequentialist would be committed to punishing the innocent person if doing so quieted the residents and prevented potential riots and the carnage they would bring. Since most people would consider it an injustice to knowingly punish an innocent person, consequentialist justifications thus become problematic. In response, Hoskins (n.d.) noted that consequentialists argue (1) in such a case, *legal* punishment is *not* being imposed because of the illegitimacy of the process involved and (2) such an example is extremely far-fetched and, as a result, constitutes unfair criticism.

Where consequentialists appear to run into problems is with the two remaining questions: whether punishment violates the moral rights of those being punished and the considerations used to guide the form that punishment takes. Regarding the former, critics have argued that consequentialist justifications for punishment treat offenders as *means to an end* (rather than as ends-in-themselves). Offenders are labeled "dangerous outsiders" that law-abiding people simply *must* deter or incapacitate to protect public safety (Duff, 2007). In doing this, consequentialists are treating offenders as being less-than-human, which violates their basic dignity. It also encourages officials to enhance punishment: because offenders are "animals," they should be treated as such.

On the latter question, consequentialists argue that proportionality guides punishment—that is, lesser crimes receive lesser punishment and worse crimes receive harsher punishment, in terms of both severity and form Critics point out, however, that proportionality ignores the fact that there are the additional costs associated with punishment (particularly, incarceration) that potentially outweigh its presumed benefits. These costs include the burdens that punishment imposes on offenders' families and communities, and the economic costs to taxpayers, who are asked to pay billions of dollars to build and maintain prisons and jails (Hoskins, n.d.).

In summary, consequentialist justifications for legal punishment argue that sanctions like incarceration achieve some greater end (e.g., lower crime rates). In doing so, they address some of the important issues relating to punishment, by establishing that it serves a particular function, that it is guided by proportionality, and that only the state can legitimately punish offenders. Where consequentialists run into problems are with whether offenders are treated as means-to-an-end and the possibility of ignoring additional societal costs the come with the form that punishment takes. These could overshadow legal punishment's presumed benefits. There is, however, an alternative justification for punishing offenders that argues that legal punishment is *deserved* by offenders. Let's examine that perspective.

Retributivist Justifications for Legal Punishment

A second moral justification for punishing offenders is that the punishment is deserved by those who violate the law (von Hirsch, 1985). While various forms of this justification exist, such as those saying the offender deserves to be punished because she gained an unfair advantage over those who don't offend, or because the offender has violated the trust of the collective, there is agreement that deservedness is the primary justification for legal punishment. Note here that retributivist justifications view punishment as an end-in-itself and thus reject consequentialist notions that punishment is instrumental. While deterrence, incapacitation, or rehabilitation may well occur through punishment, even if they didn't, legal punishment would *still* be justified because it is deserved.

Retributivist justifications tend to take two forms: positive and negative (Walen, 2016). **Positive retributivism** suggests that the state must punish those found guilty of a crime (or believed to have committed one) because they have gained an unfair advantage over others or violated the collective trust. That gain must be rectified by punishing offenders. **Negative retributivism** takes a different tack by suggesting that only the guilty deserve to be punished. In other words, the state must be *constrained* to punishing only those who are guilty.

Guiding Principles of Retributivism

The core guiding principles in retributivism are **proportionality** and **fairness** (Walen, 2016). The retributivist argues that the state must punish the guilty because it is deserved, but punishment must also be proportionate to the harm done. Here, there is agreement with consequentialists that a sliding scale of punishment should exist based on the seriousness of the harm inflicted. But retributivists also argue that proportionality involves not only the harm done by the criminal act, but also the *moral blameworthiness* of the offender as evidenced by her prior criminal history (see Appleman, 2007). The retributivist is thus saying that prior offending is proof the offender is inclined to continue violating the social contract. She is, therefore, worthy of greater moral blame than an offender with no prior record. Proportionality is thus achieved by considering both the seriousness of the conviction offense (based on the harm it caused) *and* the prior record of offending (as evidence of increased moral blameworthiness).

The other guiding principle in retributive justifications for punishment is fairness (von Hirsch, 1985). Part of what is meant here is that similarly situated offenders must receive similar punishments in both form and term. For example, two offenders convicted of the same offense having similar criminal records must receive the same sentence, not only in terms of the length of the term received, but in terms of the form of punishment received (e.g., incarceration). It would be unfair in the case of two convicted thieves with similar records for one to receive probation and the other a term of incarceration, or for one to receive a fine and the other to receive a term of probation. Both must receive not only the same form of punishment, but a similar amount of time, in terms of sentence length.

SENTENCING GUIDELINES. To illustrate how a retributive punishment scheme would work in practice, Box 9.1 presents sentencing guidelines used in the State of Minnesota as of August 1, 2017 (Minnesota Sentencing Guidelines Commission, 2017a). The guidelines are presented in grid form, consisting of an X-axis, which represents the seriousness of the conviction offense on a scale of 1 to 11 (where "1" is the least and "11" the most

BOX 9.1 State of Minnesota Sentencing Guidelines (August 1, 2017)

Presumptive sentence lengths are in months. Italicized numbers within the grid denote the discretionary range within which a court may sentence without the sentence being deemed a departure. Offenders with stayed felony sentences may be subject to local confinement.

Severity level of conviction offense (Example offenses listed in italics)		Criminal history score: 0	1	2	3	4	5	6 or more
Murder, 2nd degree (intentional murder; drive-by-shootings)	11	306 *261–367*	326 *278–391*	346 *295–415*	366 *312–439*	386 *329–463*	406 *346–480*[2]	426 *363–480*[2]
Murder, 3rd degree Murder, 2nd degree (unintentional murder)	10	150 *128–180*	165 *141–198*	180 *153–216*	195 *166–234*	210 *179–252*	225 *192–270*	240 *204–288*
Assault, 1st degree controlled substance crime, 1st degree	9	86 *74–103*	98 *84–117*	110 *94–132*	122 *104–146*	134 *114–160*	146 *125–175*	158 *135–189*
Aggravated robbery, 1st degree controlled substance crime, 2nd degree	8	48 *41–57*	58 *50–69*	68 *58–81*	78 *67–93*	88 *75–105*	98 *84–117*	108 *92–129*
Felony DWI	7	36	42	48	54 *46–64*	60 *51–72*	66 *57–79*	72 *62–84*[2]
Controlled substance crime, 3rd degree	6	21	27	33	39 *34–46*	45 *39–54*	51 *44–61*	57 *49–68*
Residential burglary simple robbery	5	18	23	28	33 *29–39*	38 *33–45*	43 *37–51*	48 *41–57*
Nonresidential burglary	4	12[1]	15	18	21	24 *21–28*	27 *23–32*	30 *26–36*
Theft crimes (over $5,000)	3	12[1]	13	15	17	19 *17–22*	21 *18–25*	23 *20–27*
Theft crimes ($5,000 or less) check forgery ($251–$2,500)	2	12[1]	12[1]	13	15	17	19	21 *18–25*
Sale of simulated controlled substance	1	12[1]	12[1]	12[1]	13	15	17	19 *17–22*

[Unshaded box] Presumptive commitment to state imprisonment. First-degree murder has a mandatory life sentence and is excluded from the guidelines under minn. stat. § 609.185. See guidelines section 2.E. Mandatory sentences, for policies regarding those sentences controlled by law.

[Shaded box] Presumptive stayed sentence; at the discretion of the court, up to one year of confinement and other non-jail sanctions can be imposed as conditions of probation. However, certain offenses in the shaded area of the grid always carry a presumptive commitment to state prison. Guidelines sections 2.C. presumptive sentence and 2.E. mandatory sentences.

[1] 12[1] = One year and one day

[2] Minn.stat § 244.09 requires that the guidelines provide a range for sentences that are presumptive commitment to state imprisonment of 15% lower and 20% higher than the fixed duration displayed, provided that the minimum sentence is not less than one year and one day and the maximum sentence is not more that the statutory maximum. Guidelines section 2.C.1-2. Presumptive sentence.

Source: Minnesota Sentencing Guidelines Commission (2017a)

serious category of offenses), and a Y-axis, which represents the criminal history score of the offender (i.e., number of prior felony convictions). You'll also note that some of the grid is shaded, which indicates a presumptive sentence of something *other* than imprisonment ("out" of prison), while the nonshaded area indicates a presumptive sentence of imprisonment ("in" prison).

At sentencing, a judge first identifies the seriousness level of the conviction offense, then looks at the offender's criminal history and determines whether the box at the intersection of the two includes a presumptive "in" or "out" disposition. That box also contains three numbers: the *median* sentence (the single number, in months, found at the top of the box) and a *range* of months (the italicized numbers found in the guidelines). The judge is then presumed to give the offender the median number of months (either "in" or "out") shown in the box but *must* give the offender a sentence that falls within the range, and either "in" or "out" based on grid shading.

To provide a concrete example, say we have an offender who has been convicted of 1st-degree assault (a "level 9" crime on the seriousness scale) and the offender has one prior felony conviction. If you look at the intersection of the X and Y axes on the grid, you'll see first, the presumptive sentence involves imprisonment (the box is in an unshaded area of the grid). Second, you'll see the median sentence is 98 months (or just over eight years) and the range for the sentence is between 84 and 117 months. The presumptive sentence in this case would be 98 months in prison, but the required sentence would be between 84 and 117 months in prison (or between seven and about 10 years). If the judge was to depart from either the "in" or "out" presumption or the number of months given the offender, the judge has to file a "sentence departure form" with the Minnesota Sentencing Guidelines Commission within 15 days of the date the sentence was entered into the record, justifying the departure on reasonable grounds—for example, the personal circumstances of the offender (Minnesota Sentencing Guidelines Commission, 2017b).

Critiques of Retributivist Justifications for Legal Punishment

Just as I did with consequentialist justifications for punishment, I review here how well retributivist justifications fare in terms of our five questions relating to the function(s) of punishment, the moral rights of those being punished, guiding principles, including those relating to the form punishment takes, and the state as the proper agent of punishment.

Retributivists articulate both the function of punishment and the guiding principles for its imposition. Punishment is an end-in-itself—it is deserved for violating the social contract or disrupting the equilibrium of the collective. The offender is not being used as an instrument to achieve some larger goal, which protects the offender's moral right to be treated as an end-in-herself. Both the severity and form of punishment are guided by principles of proportionality and fairness. Finally, retributivists argue that rather than allowing victims to seek vengeance against offenders—which would only lead to perpetual strife—the state and its laws become the agents of punishment through the social contract the state has with its citizens (Rawls, 1971).

Despite their seeming ability to justify the imposition of punishment generally and theseverity and form it takes more specifically, retributivists have been subjected to several criticisms, the most important of which, I would argue, is their belief that fixed, deserved sentences for offenders are possible and can be achieved using sentencing guidelines (Hudson, 1987). This criticism directly challenges the extent to which punishment can be both proportionate and fair (Smith, 2013; Spohn, 2014). Empirical evidence supporting this criticism comes from multiple studies of sentencing, that examined sentences before ("pre" guidelines) and after ("post" guidelines). These studies reveal that significant departures have occurred from both presumptive and required sentences (Kramer & Ulmer, 2009). This criticism also voices concerns that fixed sentences may be disproportionately harsh. Consider, for example, that for years, federal guidelines for sentences in drug cases involving powder and crack cocaine involved weight-based penalties for crack that required 100 times as much powder cocaine to trigger. The result was substantial racial disparities in sentencing, as African Americans were more likely to be involved with crack cocaine–related offenses (Steiker, 2013).

In summary, retributivist justifications for punishment revolve around the notion of deservedness: an offender who has broken the law *deserves* to be punished and is morally blameworthy for her behavior. Retribution, however, is not vengeance, because the punishment administered is by the state under legal authority, rather than by victims or their families. Retribution is guided by both proportionality—let the punishment fit the crime—and fairness—only the behavior and its effects should be considered when administering punishment, not other factors such as the offender's personal circumstances.

Other Justifications for Legal Punishment

Because of criticisms leveled at both consequentialist and retributivist accounts for why punishing offenders is justified, philosophers, legal scholars, and social scientists have developed other justifications for punishment (Hoskins, n.d.; Murtagh, n.d.). Two of the more interesting efforts I've seen are what are called rights forfeiture theory and moral education theory. The former argues that because an offender has violated the law, he or she forfeits the right of all citizens to *not* be punished by the state, while the latter claims that punishment actually confers a benefit on offenders, that of moral education. Let's now consider both arguments.

Rights Forfeiture Theory

The best way to begin discussion of **rights forfeiture theory** is with a scenario presented by Christopher Wellman (2012) that highlights the theory's logic:

> [I]magine that Victim and Bystander are eating their lunches, when suddenly, without provocation, Criminal punches Victim in the face and then runs off with Victim's briefcase. All that the rights forfeiture thesis alleges is that Criminal's moral status has changed in such a way that Victim (or perhaps the authorities) may now treat Criminal in a way that would have been impermissible before Criminal struck Victim and stole her briefcase. That is, before Criminal violated Victim's rights, Victim (or the authorities) could not permissibly do anything to Criminal that she could not also do to Bystander, but this is no longer the case. Finally, the rights forfeiture theorist claims that the reason Victim (or the authorities) may now treat Criminal in ways that she (or they) cannot treat Bystander is because, in acting the way she did, Criminal forfeited her rights.
>
> —(Wellman, 2012, p. 377)

Wellman thus presented the basic argument of rights forfeiture theory: violating the legal rights of others alters the moral status of wrongdoers and therefore allows them to be punished. Wellman claimed that the foundations of this argument can be found in scholarly writings relating to citizen rights and duties, in social contract theory, and in basic notions of fairness. He also argued that the purpose of the theory is to answer the question, "Why is punishment justified?" rather than other questions, such as those involving guiding principles and why the state should serve as the agent of punishment. For rights forfeiture theory, the sole justification for punishment is that offenders have lost their right to *not* be punished, and that punishment functions as a way of identifying a change in the status of the offender from that of being a citizen who should not be punished, to being a citizen who should. Punishment is appropriate when one's moral status changes because one has victimized others and the larger community (Wellman, 2017).

Critique of Rights Forfeiture Theory

Wellman (2017) also reviewed criticisms that have been raised about rights forfeiture theory, which include the problems of (1) authorization, (2) relatedness, (3) suitability, and (4) durability and depth. I consider each of these below.

Critics contend that rights forfeiture theory doesn't articulate *who* is allowed to punish an offender. That is, under the theory, who is authorized to carry out the punishment? Because of this omission, critics contend the theory would allow vigilantes to punish offenders. Wellman (2017) responded by arguing that "who is allowed to punish" is separate from whether legal punishment, regardless of who is administering it, is *justified* and is, therefore, permissible. While some claim that the state cannot punish, others argue the opposite. These are, however, questions more relevant to political theories about the state than they are a criticism of the notion that offenders forfeit their right to *not* be punished, which is a question of morality and ethics.

As to the relatedness criticism, Wellman (2017) provides the following illustration of what relatedness entails. Let's say that I have stolen your identity, but no one has discovered the theft. Let's also say that the punishment for stealing your identity is the same as the punishment for stealing a car. Under rights forfeiture theory, can I then be punished for stealing a car that I didn't steal? In other words, does the theory permit the perceived injustice of being punished for something one did not do? The theory seems to answer in the affirmative: because I stole your identify, I've forfeited my right to *not* be punished by the state. Since the punishment for stealing your identity is the same as for stealing a car, when I'm arrested and incarcerated for a crime I did not commit (automobile theft), there's not a problem.

Wellman (2017) answered this concern as follows. It is possible we should adopt a "limited-reasons" account of rights forfeiture that would work along these lines. Say you have given a surgeon the right to operate on you as she deems necessary to treat your condition. You have thus waived your right to decide what the surgeon does during the operation—she is allowed to do as she sees fit to treat the condition. You waiving your right and giving the surgeon free rein does not, however, mean that the surgeon can choose the most financially lucrative option during surgery or choose the option that would make her famous, were it to work, and thus enhance her reputation as a surgeon. If we accept that people can waive their rights in such a way that others can only act toward them for certain narrow reasons (e.g., treating a medical condition), then when a criminal forfeits the right *not* to be punished, the offender forfeits only the right not to be punished *for the right reason*. Thus, if I steal your identity but not your car, as long as the punishment is the same for both, I forfeit my right *not* to be punished. I retain, however, my right not to be punished for actions whose punishment is not the same, say armed robbery or murder.

Suitability has to do with the form that punishment takes. The suitability criticism of rights forfeiture theory is that the theory appears to be saying the state can murder murderers, rape rapists, steal from thieves, etc., because these offenders have forfeited their right not to be murdered, tortured, or stolen from. Wellman (2017) suggested, first of all, that murdering murderers, etc. may not actually be wrong. People can well disagree about what constitutes proper punishment for offenders. However, that disagreement doesn't nullify the basic principle that offenders forfeit their right to not be punished once they break the law. Second, Wellman argues that the theory is not saying that we *should* institute these punishments. Determining the proper punishment for offenders can be based on several reasons ranging from the practical (e.g., avoiding torturing the wrong person), to the principled (e.g., the state shouldn't ever torture anyone; no person should ever murder or torture another, because doing so dehumanizes them). Finally, Wellman argues that the theory does not say that an offender forfeits the right to not be treated in the same way as the offender treated the victim.

Duration and breadth address for how long punishment lasts and available options for it (Wellman, 2017). What rights *do* you forfeit when you commit a crime? For *how long* do you forfeit them? For example, if I kidnap you for a week, does that mean I go to prison for only a week as punishment? Most people would say that's not nearly a long enough prison stay, given the seriousness of my actions. Or, say I steal $100 from you. Does that mean I can be fined the value of all the property I own, or just $100? The former seems excessive if I'm well off, while the latter seems too little. Wellman (2017) admitted there was no easy answer to these questions but does point out that the length and form of punishment is also a problem for retributivists. He cautions that what may be needed, rather than a simple "one size fits all" punishment (both form and length) for burglars, rapists, or arsonists, is to carefully consider the relevant circumstances in each case and impose punishment accordingly. Wellman also reminds critics that the goal of the theory is to provide justification for punishing offenders. Other questions concerning the type, form, or function of punishment are beyond the intended scope of the theory.

To summarize, rights forfeiture theory is an alternative to commonly given justifications for punishing criminal offenders. Rather than justifying punishment based on consequentialist or retributivist principles, rights forfeiture takes more of a legalistic stance by arguing that punishing offenders is justified because in violating the law, these individuals have given up their right to not be punished by the state, a right that all law-abiding people enjoy. While still existing on the fringes, the theory is gaining some traction, particularly as Christopher Wellman and others continue to hone the theory as they write about it in books and scholarly articles.

Moral Education Theory

A second alternative to typical justifications for punishing criminal offenders has its roots in an article by Jean Hampton that appeared in *Philosophy & Public Affairs* in 1984 and was titled "The Moral Education Theory of Punishment." In the article, Professor Hampton argued that "punishment should not be justified as a deserved evil, but rather as an attempt, by someone who cares, *to improve a wayward person*" (emphasis added; Hampton 1984, p. 237). Hampton's **moral education theory** of punishment thus suggests that punishment is justified as a way of teaching a *moral lesson* to not only those who commit crimes, but also the broader community. Central to the theory was Hampton's notion that those committing crimes are **moral agents** who have the capacity to reflect on, and respond to, moral reasons for not engaging in the illegal behavior. Because of this, the function of punishment is to communicate to the offender that his or her illegal action was forbidden *because* it was morally wrong and for that reason should not have been done. In learning this lesson, the offender realizes that he or she should change (reform) his or her behavior (Hampton, 1984). While the goal of reforming the offender is similar to what a consequentialist might argue, the justification for punishment is the moral education that results from learning the lesson that criminal behavior is morally wrong.

Critique of Moral Education Theory

Critics have raised various objections to moral education theory (see Hoskins, n.d.). Some are skeptical about whether punishment is the most effective means to achieve moral education, while others point out that most offenders do not appear to need moral education: at the time of the illegal act (or shortly thereafter), they *knew* what they were doing was wrong but did it anyway. Finally, some critics have argued that moral education theory is inappropriately paternalistic. It argues that the state is justified in coercively restricting offenders' liberties as a means to conferring a benefit (moral education) on them. Many theorists seem uncomfortable with the idea that the state may coerce one of its citizens for her own benefit.

In summary, moral education theory suggests that punishment can be justified because it serves the function of moral education by teaching offenders that criminal behavior is not just legally wrong, it is morally wrong. The state is justified in punishing offenders to educate them about the immorality of crime and the moral value of victims. Moral education theory thus combines elements of both consequentialist and retributivist justifications for punishment.

You've now been exposed to various justifications for punishing criminal offenders, including the principles guiding their reasoning and critiques of these theories. Let's focus now on a particularly controversial form of legal punishment and the ethical issues it raises: the death penalty.

CAPITAL PUNISHMENT: A SPECIAL CASE

Tackling the morality and ethics of capital punishment in a short amount of space means I can share with you only the most basic aspects of this controversial form of legal punishment, including a general overview of capital punishment (CP), its legal aspects, justifications for capital punishment and critiques of it, two key ethical issues associated with capital punishment, and an interesting analysis that suggests the coming "death" of capital punishment in America.

Capital Punishment: An Overview

Among the 196 United Nations' recognized countries on this planet, 58 (30%) of them have capital punishment in either law or practice (Smith, 2016); among Western, industrialized, liberal democracies, the United States is the only one (Amnesty

International, 2017). In America, as of late 2017, the federal government and 31 states allowed capital punishment; however, four states (Colorado, Oregon, Pennsylvania, and Washington) were under gubernatorial-imposed moratoria on executions (Death Penalty Information Center, 2017a). The primary method of execution is through lethal injection, although most CP states have alternative methods such as electrocution, hanging, or firing squad (Death Penalty Information Center, 2017b). In 2016, the most recent year for which data are available, a total of 20 individuals were executed in this country, the fewest since 1991 (Death Penalty Information Center, 2017c). Longer term, between 1976—when a Supreme Court–ordered moratorium on executions was lifted by that court—and May 17, 2018 (the most recent date for which data are available) there have been 1,476 executions, with 81% of them occurring in the South (Death Penalty Information Center, 2018c). Texas leads the nation with 538 executions between 1976 and year-end 2017, followed by Virginia, Oklahoma, Florida, and Missouri (Death Penalty Information Center, 2018c). Finally, just 15 counties in four states—Texas, Oklahoma, Missouri, and Arizona—were responsible for upwards of 30% of all executions occurring in the U.S. between 1976 and 2013 (Death Penalty Information Center, 2018c).

Legal Aspects of Capital Punishment

In 1972, the Supreme Court instituted a moratorium on executions by ruling in the case of *Furman v. Georgia* (408 U.S. 238) that, as it was administered at the time, the death penalty constituted cruel and unusual punishment in violation of the 8th and 14th Amendments to the U.S. Constitution because it was applied in an unequal, discretionary, and haphazard manner. Four years later, in the case of *Gregg v. Georgia* (428 U.S. 153), the court reaffirmed the constitutionality of the death penalty but required the states to implement changes to the capital case process. The changes included requiring separate guilt (trial) and sentencing phases. In the latter phase, the jury had to now apply (and weigh) statutorily defined aggravating and mitigating circumstances before imposing a death sentence. Subsequent Supreme Court decisions have held that individuals under the age of 18 at the time they committed the capital offense cannot receive the death penalty, nor can those who are developmentally disabled (Acker, 2014). Finally, since 1976, repeated challenges to the constitutionality of capital punishment on various grounds, including that of racial bias in application, have failed (Breyer, 2016).

Justifications for Capital Punishment

Those who support capital punishment invoke the same justifications as those invoked for justifying legal punishment more generally. Some proponents argue that the death penalty can be justified on consequentialist grounds, including that it serves as a deterrent to future crimes or has an incapacitation effect, whereas others justify the death penalty on purely retributivist grounds.

Capital punishment opponents argue that there is no evidence that it serves as a deterrent, mainly because it is not consistently and promptly applied and cannot ever be administered in a way that meets these conditions (American Civil Liberties Union, 2017). Additionally, these critics argue that life without parole (LWOP) is just as effective at incapacitating offenders at far less of a cost (Acker, 2014). Opponents also argue that capital punishment is unfair and violates the ideal of due process of law, based on a growing body of evidence showing tremendous disparity in capital sentencing that renders the death penalty both arbitrary and racially biased (Acker, 2014). Further, opponents point to a large body of evidence from the modern era (post 1972) showing that innocent people are often wrongfully convicted of crimes—including capital crimes—and that some of these offenders have been executed. To illustrate this point, as of April 19, 2018 the Death Penalty Information Center identified 162 individuals who, since 1973, had been wrongfully convicted of capital murder and sentenced to death but had ultimately been exonerated and released from prison (Death Penalty Information Center, 2018d). A 2014 study concluded that "if all death-sentenced defendants remained under sentence of death indefinitely, at least 4.1% of them would be exonerated" (Gross, O'Brien, Hu, & Kennedy, 2014, p. 7230). I discuss this issue in greater detail below.

Race and Capital Punishment

One of the most troubling aspects of the death penalty is the fact that people of color, particularly African Americans, are disproportionately charged with and convicted of capital crimes, and sentenced to death. To illustrate the troubling connection between race and capital punishment, Table 9.1 presents results of an analysis by the NAACP Legal Defense Fund of all executions that have taken place since 1976 and the racial or ethnic characteristics of the offenders and victims in these cases (Fins, 2017). The key here is to look at the combination of race/ethnicity of offender and victim. In general, more than three-quarters of the offenders (78%) who were executed post 1976, regardless of their race/ethnicity, had murdered *white victims*. Compare that figure to offenders executed for murdering nonwhite victims, and you'll see a huge disparity: only 13% of offenders executed since 1976 had murdered African American victims, and just 7% of the offenders had murdered a victim who was a Latino/a, 2% had murdered Asian victims, and 1% had murdered Native American offenders have been executed since 1976. Among them, 60% had murdered a white victim.

TABLE 9.1 Racial/Ethnic Characteristics of Executed Offenders and Victims: 1976–2017[a]

	Race/Ethnicity of Victim					
Race/Ethnicity of Offender	**White % (N)**	**African American % (N)**	**Latino/a % (N)**	**Asian % (N)**	**Native American % (N)**	**Total (N)**
White	68 (747)	1 (20)	1 (17)	1(6)	0 (0)	56 (790)
African American	26 (284)	12 (167)	1 (20)	1(15)	0 (0)	34 (486)
Latino/a	5 (51)	1 (3)	4 (48)	1(2)	0 (0)	7 (104)
Asian	1 (2)	0 (0)	0 (0)	1 (5)	0 (0)	1 (7)
Native American	1 (14)	0 (0)	0 (0)	0 (0)	1 (2)	1 (16)
Total[b]	78 (1098)	13 (190)	7 (95)	2 (28)	1 (2)	100 (1413)

[a] Figures do not include 35 defendants executed for the murders of multiple victims of different races/ethnicities.

[b] Total may not add to 100% due to rounding.

Source: Adapted from Fins (2017, p. 6)

What Table 9.1 indicates is that offenders murdering white victims are more likely to be executed than offenders who murdered victims belonging to all other racial or ethnic groups. The table also shows that African Americans, in particular, are far more likely to be executed for murdering whites. Several studies, using very sophisticated statistical analyses that controlled for a multiplicity of legal and extra-legal factors have found that African American offenders who murder white victims are, in general, three to five times more likely to be charged, prosecuted, and convicted of capital murder, and sentenced to death for the crime, than any other combination of victim/offender racial/ethnic characteristics (Baldus, Woodworth, Zuckerman, & Weiner, 1998). If such racism in the administration of the death penalty exists, it raises the question of whether CP is not only unethical, but also illegal.

Executing Innocents

Another pressing issue concerning the death penalty is whether a *truly* innocent offender has ever been executed (Radelet & Bedau, 1998). We know, for example, that for two centuries stretching well past the segregation era in this country, lynch mobs murdered thousands of African American men—not to mention boys, girls, and women—in this country (see Dray, 2002). That's not what is at issue here, as those incidents were little more than racist, mob-inspired, *murders*. What I'm talking about is whether, after duly-sanctioned legal proceedings that included appellate review of the case, the government, at either the state or federal level, has executed someone who later turned out to be innocent—either factually or legally—of the crime(s) for which he (or she) had been convicted (Norris, 2017). If innocents have been (or will likely be) executed for crimes they did not commit, whether capital punishment is ethical or legal must, again, be seriously questioned.

We know, for example, that between 1972 (when the Supreme Court ordered a moratorium on executions as a result of its decision in *Furman v. Georgia*) and April of 2018, a total of 162 offenders in 27 states who had been sentenced to death were exonerated and released from death row, the most recent (as of this writing) being **Vicente Benavides**, who was released on April 19, 2018 in California after 25 years on death row (Death Penalty Information Center, 2018e). We also know that wrongful convictions in capital cases are caused by multiple factors, including official misconduct by police and prosecutors, false accusation, improper admission of forensic evidence , inadequate legal defense, false confessions, and eyewitness misidentification. To give you an idea of precisely how frequently these factors are involved, as of 2018, official misconduct had occurred in over 80% of cases resulting in exonerations; false accusations, in over 70% of the cases; false confessions, in over 30% of the cases; inadequate legal defense, in about 25% of the cases; improper forensics, in about 20% of the cases; and eyewitness misidentification, in about 10% of the cases (Death Penalty Information Center, 2018f). Thus, we know that errors occur resulting in wrongful convictions of capital case defendants. It is also entirely possible that some individuals we have executed, were in fact, wrongfully convicted.

To give you an idea of how we might have executed people who were actually not guilty of the crime(s) for which they had been convicted, Table 9.2 presents a description of five cases of offenders who have been executed in two different states since 1989 for which there is reason to doubt they committed the crime(s) for which they had been convicted. The sample is taken from a larger group of 13 offenders the Death Penalty Information Center (2017) identified as likely being innocent but who were, nonetheless, executed by several

TABLE 9.2 Sample of Potentially Innocent Offenders Executed Since 1989

Offender	State	Year Convicted	Year Executed	Reason(s) Offender May Have Been Innocent
Carlos Deluna	TX	1983	1989	Four investigations conducted between 2004 and 2006 uncovered new evidence that cast reasonable doubt on DeLuna's guilt and pointed to another man as the offender
Ruben Cantu	TX	1985	1993	Two-part investigative series by the *Houston Chronicle* cast serious doubt on Cantu's guilt; Prosecutor and jury forewoman in the case have expressed doubts about his guilt; Eyewitness in the state's case and Cantu's co-defendant have both claimed he was innocent
Joseph O'Dell	VA	1986	1997	New DNA blood evidence creates reasonable doubt as to O'Dell's guilt; In one of his appeals, three U.S. Supreme Court justices said they did not believe he was guilty
Cameron Willingham	TX	1992	2004	Four arson experts concluded that the original investigation in Willingham's case was flawed; State relied on testimony from jailhouse "snitch," a known drug addict taking antipsychotic medication; the snitch claimed Willingham had confessed to him, but evidence discovered years later showed that the prosecution had given the snitch favorable treatment and had elicited perjured testimony from him that he had not been promised or given anything in exchange for testifying in the case
Richard Masterson	TX	2002	2016	Prosecutors concealed evidence that the pathologist performing the autopsy was unqualified; falsified his credentials; botched the autopsy; and gave false testimony; Two pathologists who examined autopsy data said the victim died of a heart attack; Masterson may have falsely confessed to the crime

Source: Death Penalty Information Center (2017)

different states. The Center's arguments about actual innocence comes from reevaluations of the offenders' cases by technical experts, police officials, judges, and legal scholars. Have we perhaps executed as many as 13 innocent people in the last 30 years alone?

To summarize, the United States is the only Western, liberal democratic, developed nation to use capital punishment (CP). You have also seen that while a majority of states and the federal government continue to use CP, trends are indicating that ever fewer death sentences and executions are occurring each year. You have also seen that while the death penalty is justified using the same arguments as those used to justify legal punishment more generally, there are legitimate critiques of these justifications. You have also seen how, since 1976, the Supreme Court (and the states) have continued to "tinker" with CP in the hope of somehow perfecting it. Finally, as you have also seen, there are more than a few issues—both legal and ethical—that surround the death penalty in America that include legitimate questions being raised about the death penalty being racist in its administration and that one or more innocents may have been executed. Given all of these considerations, are we witnessing the slow death of capital punishment?

The Death of Capital Punishment?

In a June 8, 2015, cover story, *Time* magazine's David Von Drehle argued that capital punishment would soon end in the United States for five reasons (Von Drehle, 2015). First, despite decades of effort, we're not getting any better at executing offenders. The technological innovations relating to execution—electric chair, gas chamber, lethal injection—have not reduced the chance of botched executions occurring (see especially, Sarat, 2014). Second, plunging crime rates have led to declines in public support for the death penalty and increased support for alternatives such as LWOP. One indicator of this is the fact that since 2007, seven states have abolished CP and four more are under gubernatorial moratoria on executions. Third, there are dwindling justifications for CP. For example, supermax prisons are just as effective deterrents as capital punishment and equally effective as a tool to incapacitate the "worst of the worst." Fourth, cash-strapped governments can no longer afford the "luxury" of the death penalty—it costs far more to execute an offender than to keep him or her incarcerated for LWOP. Finally, Von Drehle argues that the Supreme Court will be forced to rule that the death penalty violates "evolving standards of decency" and is unconstitutional by considering state actions to abolish it ; declining public support for it; arbitrariness in its application; length of time between sentence and actual execution (as of 2012, about 16 years—see Snell, 2014); and realizing that its 40-plus years of "tinkering with the machinery of death" has gotten us nowhere.

In conclusion, capital punishment is an extremely volatile subject, with staunch supporters and detractors raising claims and counterclaims. The problem for proponents is that evidence is mounting that the administration of the death penalty is seriously flawed and that no amount of "tinkering" can hope to alleviate the myriad problems that plague it. Perhaps more to the point: Is it ethical for citizens of this country to continue to allow a flawed system of punishment that takes lives to continue operating when other, just as effective forms of punishment that do not involve killing people are available? What do *you* think?

SUMMARY

This chapter, the first of three to address the "back-end" of the criminal justice system—sentencing and punishment—presented you with arguments about legal punishment. Over the course of the chapter, I provided you with an overview of the process that results in people being sanctioned for their illegal behavior. In this overview, I provided you with facts about legal punishment, and arguments about the ethics of a system of punishment that includes sanctions ranging from restrictions on offenders' freedom, to loss of that freedom, to the loss of offenders' lives via capital punishment. As you saw, America is a punitive country—we criminally sanction millions of our citizens annually, which creates the need to justify restricting or taking people's liberty, not to mention taking people's lives in certain cases. You learned that from the standpoint of ethics, the state being allowed to impose burdens upon, or elicit extractions from, citizens must be justified, and that several different justifications have been offered that claim to do so. Some of these justifications focus on the possible positive consequences of legal punishment, such as reductions in the volume or seriousness of crime. Others argued that retributive justice demands offenders be punished—they deserve legal punishment because they have violated the social contract and/or gained an unfair advantage over those who abide by the law. Still other justifications argue that legal punishment is justified because offenders forfeit their right to *not* be punished when they engage in criminality, while other justifications suggest that legal punishment is actually a benefit accrued by offenders—they learn a moral lesson. I provided you with critiques of these justifications that may ultimately lead you to conclude that, as we currently understand legal punishment, it cannot be either morally or ethically justified. I also included discussion of the ethical issues surrounding the ultimate criminal sanction—the penalty of death—and shared with you some facts on the death penalty and ethical issues surrounding it. I also suggested that current trends indicate that capital punishment is experiencing a slow death. It may even be that in the not-too-distant future, the U.S. Supreme Court may well rule, finally, that all things being considered, the death penalty is not only illegal, it is also immoral.

To conclude the chapter, let's explore how another part of the world, Scandinavia, uses legal punishment to sanction criminal offenders. You may be both surprised and befuddled to learn how, as described in Thought Exercise 9.1, compared to the United States, countries like Denmark, Finland, Iceland, Norway, and Sweden respond to violations of the criminal law. You may also conclude that legal punishment can take forms that are much different from those found in this country and, as a result, may be more ethically justifiable.

THOUGHT EXERCISE 9.1

LEGAL PUNISHMENT IN SCANDINAVIA: A DIFFERENT RESPONSE

Let me begin with a disclaimer: the Scandinavian countries (Denmark, Finland, Iceland, Norway, and Sweden) are *very* different places than the United States, so comparing legal punishment there with legal punishment in the United States is somewhat problematic. Beyond matters such as population (Scandinavia has about 10% the population of the United States) and geographic area (Scandinavia is about 10% the size of the United States), the five Scandinavian countries have a strongly shared cultural heritage that includes multiple related languages (Maples, 2017). Additionally, three of the countries—Denmark, Norway, and Sweden—are constitutional monarchies (Iceland and Finland are republics). The countries that comprise Scandinavia also typify so-called welfare states, as their governments play a major role in protecting and promoting the social and economic well-being of citizens (Garland, 2016; Rector, 2015). Scandinavian countries also have much lower levels of income inequality than does the United States; feature powerful labor unions; and evidence low unemployment rates (Mulvad & Stahl, 2015). None of the countries in Scandinavia has the death penalty. Perhaps most importantly, the countries that comprise Scandinavia have much lower rates of violent and property crime than does the United States (Farrington, Langan, & Tonry, 2004). With all that being said, let's consider how Scandinavia uses legal punishment to respond to its "crime problem."

Legal Punishment in Scandinavia

To examine legal punishment in Scandinavia, I present descriptions of the length of sentences handed down in the region, along with information about the forms legal punishment usually takes, and a rather in-depth exploration of prisons in the region.

LENGTH OF SENTENCES IN SCANDINAVIA. Compared to the United States, legal punishments in Scandinavia are more lenient (Lappi-Sappala, 2007). The most severe term of sentence in Denmark, Finland, and Sweden is life imprisonment (although in practice, this translates to about 16 years in Denmark, 12–17 years in Finland, and 17–20 years in Sweden) and is reserved for a very small cadre of offenders who are either serious recidivists or engaged in particularly

continued

egregious offenses such as mass murder. Norway abolished life sentences and replaced them with a 21-year maximum term. In Denmark, the maximum term of imprisonment for a single offense is 16 years, in Finland 12 years, and in Sweden 10 years (Lappi-Sappala, 2007).

FORMS OF PUNISHMENT IN SCANDINAVIA. In Scandinavian countries, imprisonment is used only for the most serious offenses; a majority of penalties are less severe alternatives, with monetary fines constituting the principal form of legal punishment (Lappi-Sappala, 2007, 2008). For example, Denmark, Finland, and Sweden rely heavily on day fines that seek to "ensure equal severity of the fine for offenders of different income and wealth" (Lappi-Sappala, 2007, p. 223). The number of day fines imposed is based on the seriousness of the offense, while the amount of the fines depends on the financial situation of the offender. As a result, similar offenses committed by offenders of different income levels result in roughly similar overall severity of the sanction. Lesser offenses (e.g., minor traffic violations) result in fines imposed via fixed penalties. If a fine is not paid, the sanction may be converted to imprisonment through separate proceedings (Lappi-Sappala, 2007).

PRISONS IN SCANDINAVIA. Unlike in the United States, in Scandinavia one finds a large number of small prisons typically housing less than 100 inmates (Pratt, 2008). For example, according to Pratt (2008), in 2006 there were 86 prisons in Sweden, 47 in Norway, and 38 in Finland. Pratt (2008) noted that in 2006, Sweden had the largest prison in the region, which held about 350 inmates (compare these figures with the U.S., which in 2006 had 1,821 prisons that housed an average of 785 inmates ([Stephan, 2008]). Prisons in the region are either open or closed institutions (see the next two sections). According to Lappi-Sappala (2007, 2008), open institutions typically house 20%–40% of the prison population in the region. There are also no private prisons in Scandinavia, nor has there been any momentum to develop them (Pratt, 2008). Finally, a system of early release (parole) of inmates is routine in Scandinavia (Lappi-Sappala, 2007). In Finland, for example, practically all prisoners are released on parole after serving one-half to two-thirds of their sentence; in Sweden, inmates are eligible for parole after serving two-thirds of their sentence. Parole revocations occur generally because of a new offense committed rather than from violating the conditions of parole, known as "technical violations" (Lawrence, 2008).

Open prisons in Scandinavia. The presence of **open prisons** in Scandinavia more broadly can be traced to penal policy developed in Finland during the 1930s, where inmates were permitted to work on nearby farms for wages comparable to those paid to regular laborers (Pratt, 2008). In his visits to these facilities during 2006, Pratt (2008) noted they have minimal physical barriers or none at all. There were no bars on windows; in some facilities, prisoners locked their own doors. After finishing work or classes, inmates were allowed to freely walk around prison grounds and were sometimes allowed to walk into local communities. From the wages they earned, inmates paid taxes and rent, bought food, and sent money to families and victims. In some open prisons, inmates were allowed to keep the jobs they had prior to their conviction. In one such facility in Sweden, there was a parking lot reserved for inmates' vehicles. Pratt (2008) noted that the social distance between open prisons and the outside world was very small.

Closed prisons in Scandinavia. Pratt (2008) also visited **closed prisons** across Scandinavia. In doing so, he noted that the external appearances of these facilities were unexceptional; their architecture spanned all stages of prison development from the mid-nineteenth century onward. He noted that these facilities had external security precautions and controlled exits and entrances; some used airport-like security checks for visitors, inmates, and staff as they moved around the institutions. At one maximum-security prison in Sweden, Pratt (2008) noticed that an electrified fence had been strung between two perimeter walls.

Once inside the facility, Pratt (2008) noted there were familiar looking wings and long corridors with unit-based divisions between them. Double-bunking of inmates was uncommon; most cells had internal sanitation. Pratt (2008) further observed that most facilities featured common rooms or lounges in each unit, with communal television and cooking facilities available for light meals. In the main, meals were eaten in a canteen, also used by prison staff, or at a communal table in the unit, where prisoners might be joined by officers for midday meals. Many of the facilities possessed a solarium to help reduce Vitamin D deficiencies that could develop in inmates during the long winter months. Pratt (2008) noted that "[the presence of a solarium] has become so unremarkable a feature of prison life that, unless a visitor specifically asks, there is unlikely to be any mention of [it]" (Pratt, 2008, p. 121). Pratt (2008) added that offering such facilities showed that prison authorities recognized and were trying to address chronic health problems (or prevent them), rather than limiting prison health care to emergency or acute care.

CONDITIONS OF CONFINEMENT IN SCANDINAVIA. As described by Pratt (2008), unlike in the United States, which generally locates its prisons well away from urban areas, Scandinavian prisons afforded most inmates the opportunity to be near home and family. Prisons were also administered to stress *normalization*. For prison authorities in Scandinavia, liberty is the only thing the offender loses; various services, such as health care, are provided via community resources rather than by the Scandinavian equivalent of a department of corrections. The social distance between inmates and staff is minimal; correctional officers are well-trained and earn a reasonable salary; inmates have direct input into prison governance, including (in Sweden) the right to meet with the warden to discuss issues of mutual interest and to present their views. In Norway, prisoners are included in a yearly "meeting in the mountains" where prison policy is worked through and determined by all interested parties (see Ugelvik & Dullum, 2012).

Pratt (2008) further observed that, in these facilities, the personal space and relative material comfort of most inmates was much greater than in prisons in the United States or the United Kingdom. He noticed no "institutional smell" in the facilities he visited. Prisoners had state-provided televisions in their cells. Movement within the institution was comparatively relaxed, prisoner loitering was unusual, and units were, generally, quiet. Most prisoners worked or received full-time education well beyond the remedial level—inmates were encouraged to pursue undergraduate degrees via distance education (and for which they paid using the wages earned from working). Pratt found that the food available to inmates seemed nutritious and the servings were generous. Inmates wore their own clothes during visits with family or friends, and conjugal relations were both encouraged and facilitated (most prisons provided accommodations where partners and children of inmates could stay free of charge and unsupervised for entire weekends, typically at monthly intervals). Pratt suggested these arrangements helped reduce institutional tensions as well as the rate of sexual assaults occurring in the facilities. Scandinavian prisons also did not (generally) hold inmates younger than age 18, which, Pratt claimed, reduced the potential for bullying and sexual assault.

So, let's compare legal punishment in the United States. and Scandinavia. In the United States, we imprison at a rate unsurpassed in the world; in Scandinavia, they rely primarily on day fines. In the United States, we typically have a few prisons in each state, including one or more federal institutions, located well away from cities, that hold an average of 785 inmates. Scandinavia, by contrast, uses lots of small prisons that typically house 50–100 inmates and are close to towns and cities. In the United States, we sentence people to long terms of incarceration, including life without parole. We also have the death penalty. About 60% of states use parole, but not the federal government. In Scandinavia, "life in prison" is a sentence of about 20 years; parole is widespread, with most inmates being paroled after serving one-third to one-half their sentences. Parole revocation in the United States is commonly for "technical violations" of the parole agreement; in Scandinavia, revocations usually occur because of new offenses committed. Scandinavia has no death penalty nor does it allow life without parole. In the United States, we want inmates to suffer the "pain of imprisonment," which includes multiple losses, including that of freedom, identity, ties to friends and family, personal possessions, etc. In Scandinavia, prisons stress normalization, which includes maintaining one's identity, being paid a living wage, retaining at least some freedom of movement, having access to conjugal visits that are both encouraged and provided for, etc. In Scandinavia, community resources take care of services, rather than the department of corrections as done in the United States. In Scandinavian prisons, unlike in the United States, social distance between staff and inmates is small; unlike in the United States, which wants prisons located well away from any significant population center, in Scandinavia social distance between prison and community is small.

Which system of legal punishment do *you* think is more easily justified on either moral or legal grounds?

KEY TERMS

Legal punishment 257
Deterrence 258
Specific deterrence 258
General deterrence 258
Celerity 258
Certainty 258
Severity 258
Incapacitation 259
Rehabilitation 259
Positive retributivism 261
Negative retributivism 261
Proportionality 261
Fairness 261
Rights forfeiture theory 264
Moral education theory 267
Moral agents 267
Open prisons 274
Closed prisons 274

DISCUSSION QUESTIONS

1. Based on the material provided in the chapter, explain how/why the United States may be the most retributivist country among those in the developed world.
2. Debate with another student the utility of different forms of legal punishment available in this country, including incarceration, probation, house arrest, etc. What are the presumed benefits (utility) of these sanctions? What are the possible negative consequences associated with each?
3. Explain why legal punishment *cannot* be ethically justified, using any of the systems of ethics you have examined to this point.
4. How would you explain to a supporter/critic of capital punishment why the practice is not/is ethically justified? In other words, play "devil's advocate" for each side of the argument.
5. Explain to a skeptic how the Scandinavian use of legal punishment, so different from ours, can be ethically justified. Pick any system of ethics discussed to this point to use in your argument.

RESOURCES

The **Bureau of Justice Statistics** (BJS) (https://www.bjs.gov/), a component of the Office of Justice Programs in the U.S. Department of Justice, collects, analyzes, publishes, and disseminates information on crime, criminal offenders, victims of crime, and the operation of justice systems at all levels of government. BJS routinely compiles excellent data on corrections in this country, including conducting trend analyses of imprisonment, probation, etc.

The **Stanford Encyclopedia of Philosophy** (https://plato.stanford.edu/) and the **Internet Encyclopedia of Philosophy** (http://www.iep.utm.edu/) are peer-reviewed sources that have multiple entries relating to the philosophy of legal punishment, incarceration, and the death penalty.

If you are looking for **resources on capital punishment**, the Death Penalty Information Center (https://deathpenaltyinfo.org/) may be the single best resource available for providing timely information on capital punishment. See also Pro Death Penalty.com (http://www.prodeathpenalty.com/) for a different take on capital punishment.

One of the best talks I've ever heard on the death penalty was by University of Houston law professor **David Dow** (who also defends people accused of capital murder) in 2012. His TEDx Talk on capital punishment will move you, regardless of the position you take on the matter. The 18-minute-long presentation is available by visiting: https://www.ted.com/talks/david_r_dow_lessons_from_death_row_inmates/transcript?language=en

REFERENCES

Acker, J. (2014). *Questioning capital punishment.* New York, NY: Routledge.

Allen, F. (1981). *The decline of the rehabilitative ideal.* New Haven, CT: Yale University Press.

American Civil Liberties Union (2017). The case against the death penalty. Retrieved from https://www.aclu.org/other/case-against-death-penalty

Amnesty International (2017) Death penalty. Retrieved from https://www.amnesty.org/en/what-we-do/death-penalty/

Appleman, L. (2007). Retributive justice and hidden sentencing. *Ohio State Law Journal, 68,* 1307–1385. Retrieved from https://kb.osu.edu/dspace/bitstream/handle/1811/71138/1/OSLJ_V68N5_1307.pdf

Baldus, D., Woodworth, G., Zuckerman, D., & Weiner, N. (1998). Racial discrimination and the death penalty in the post-Furman era: An empirical and legal overview with recent findings from Philadelphia. *Cornell Law Review, 83,* 1638–1772.

Barron, J. (2018, March 22). New York city's population hits a record 8.6 million. *New York Times.* Retrieved from https://www.nytimes.com/2018/03/22/nyregion/new-york-city-population.html

Blumstein, A., Cohen, J., & Nagin, D. (1978). *Deterrence and incapacitation: Estimating the effects of criminal sanctions on crime rates.* Washington, DC: National Academy Press.

Breyer, S. (2016). *Against the death penalty.* Washington, DC: Brookings Institution.

Cullen, F., & Gilbert, K. (2015). *Reaffirming rehabilitation* (2nd ed.). New York, NY: Routledge.

Death Penalty Information Center (2018a). States with and without the death penalty. Retrieved from https://deathpenaltyinfo.org/states-and-without-death-penalty

Death Penalty Information Center (2018b). Methods of execution. Retrieved from https://deathpenaltyinfo.org/methods-execution

Death Penalty Information Center (2018c). Number of executions by state and region since 1976. Retrieved from https://deathpenaltyinfo.org/number-executions-state-and-region-1976.

Death Penalty Information Center (2018d). The innocence list. Retrieved from https://deathpenaltyinfo.org/innocence-list-those-freed-death- row

Death Penalty Information Center (2018e). Innocence and the death penalty. Retrieved from https://deathpenaltyinfo.org/innocence-and-death-penalty#inn-yr-rc

Death Penalty Information Center (2018f). Causes of wrongful conviction. Retrieved from https://deathpenaltyinfo.org/causes-wrongful-convictions

Death Penalty Information Center (2017). Executed but possibly innocent. Retrieved fromhttps://deathpenaltyinfo.org/executed-possibly-innocent

Dray, P. (2002). *At the hands of persons unknown: The lynching of Black America.* New York, NY: Random House.

Duff, A. (2007). *Answering for crime.* Oxford, UK: Hart Publishing.

Duff, A., & Hoskins, Z. (2017). Legal punishment. In E. Zalta (Ed.), *The Stanford encyclopedia of philosophy* (Fall Edition). Retrieved from https://plato.stanford.edu/archives/fall2017/entries/legal-punishment/

Farrington, D., Langan, P., & Tonry, M. (2004). *Cross-national studies in crime and justice.* Washington, DC: Bureau of Justice Statistics.

Feinberg, J. (1970). The expressive function of punishment. *Monist, 49,* 397–423.

Fins, D. (2017, April 10). *Death row USA.* Washington, DC: NAACP Legal Defense Fund.

Garland, D. (2016). *The welfare state: A very short introduction.* New York, NY: Oxford University Press.

Gottfredson, M., & Hirschi, T. (1986). The true value of lambda would appear to be zero: An essay on career criminals, criminal careers, selective incapacitation, cohort studies, and related topics. *Criminology, 24,* 213–234.

Gross, S., O'Brien, B., Hu, C., & Kennedy, E. (2014). Rate of false conviction of criminal defendants who are sentenced to death. *Proceedings of the National Academy of Sciences, 111,* 7230–7235.

Hampton, J. (1984). The moral education theory of punishment. *Philosophy & Public Affairs, 13,* 208–238.

Hart, H. (1968). *Punishment and responsibility.* Oxford, UK: Oxford University Press.

Hester, T., & Hines, I. (1997). *Correctional populations in the United States—1995*. Washington, DC: Bureau of Justice Statistics.

Hoskins, Z. (n.d.). The moral permissibility of punishment. In J. Fieser & B. Dowden (Eds.), *The Internet Encyclopedia of Philosophy*. Retrieved from http://www.iep.utm.edu/m-p-puni/

Hudson, B. (1987). *Justice through punishment*. New York, NY: St. Martin's Press.

Jankowski, L. (1992). *Correctional populations in the United States—1990*. Washington, DC: Bureau of Justice Statistics.

Kaeble, D. & Cowhig, M. (2018). *Correctional populations in the United States—2016*. Washington, DC: Bureau of Justice Statistics.

Kaeble, D., & Glaze, L. (2016). *Correctional populations in the United States—2015*. Washington, DC: Bureau of Justice Statistics.

Kennedy, D. (2010). *Deterrence and crime prevention*. New York, NY: Routledge.

Kramer, J., & Ulmer, J. (2009). *Sentencing guidelines: Lessons from Pennsylvania*. Boulder, CO: Lynne Rienner.

Lappi-Sappala, T. (2008). *Crime prevention and community sanctions in Scandinavia*. Helsinki, Finland: National Research Institute of Legal Policy.

Lappi-Sappala, T. (2007). Penal policy in Scandinavia. *Crime and Justice, 36*, 217–295.

Lawrence, A. (2008). *Probation and parole violations: State responses*. Denver, CO: National Conference of State Legislatures.

Maples, T. (2017, June 6). Scandinavia fast facts. *TripSavvy*. Retrieved from https://www.tripsavvy.com/scandinavia-fast-facts-1626712

Marshall, S., & Duff, A. (1998). Criminalization and sharing wrongs. *Canadian Journal of Law & Jurisprudence, 11*, 7–22.

McHugh, J. (2008). Utilitarianism, punishment, and ideal proportionality in penal law. *Journal of Bentham Studies, 10*, 1–16.

McCloskey, H. (1957). An examination of restricted Utilitarianism. *The Philosophical Review, 66*, 466–485.

Minnesota Sentencing Guidelines Commission (2017a). 2017 sentencing guidelines and commentary. Retrieved from https://mn.gov/sentencing-guidelines/guidelines/

Minnesota Sentencing Guidelines Commission (2017b). Departure report form. Retrieved from https://mn.gov/sentencing-guidelines/forms/departure-report/

Mulvad, A., & Stahl, R. (2015, August 4). What makes Scandinavia different? *Jacobin*. Retrieved from https://www.jacobinmag.com/2015/08/national-review-williamson-bernie-sanders-sweden/

Murtagh, K. (n.d.). Punishment. In J. Fieser & B. Dowden (Eds.), *The Internet Encyclopedia of Philosophy*. Retrieved from http://www.iep.utm.edu/punishme/

National Research Council (2012). *Deterrence and the death penalty*. Washington, DC: National Academies Press.

Norris, R. (2017). *Exonerated: A history of the innocence movement*. New York, NY: New York University Press.

Poppyjoe, P. (2005, July 4). Don't do the crime if you can't do the time. *Urban Dictionary*. Retrieved from http://www.urbandictionary.com/define.php?term=Don%27t%20do%20the%20crime%2C%20if%20you%20can%27t%20do%20the%20time

Pratt, J. (2008). Scandinavian exceptionalism in an era of penal excess. *British Journal of Criminology, 48*, 119–147.

Radelet, M., & Bedau, H. (1998). The execution of the innocent. *Law and Contemporary Problems, 61*, 105–124

Rawls, J. (1971). *A theory of justice*. Cambridge, MA: Harvard University Press.

Rector, R. (2015, September 16). *Poverty and the social welfare state in the United States and other nations*. Washington, DC: The Heritage Foundation. Retrieved from http://www.heritage.org/welfare/report/poverty-and-the-social-welfare-state-the-united-states-and-other-nations

Rumberger, R., & Losen, D. (2016). *The high-cost of harsh discipline and its disparate impact*. Los Angeles, CA: The Civil Rights Project.

Sarat, A. (2014). *Gruesome spectacles: Botched executions and America's death penalty*. Stanford, CA: Stanford University Press.

Smith, K. (2013). Principles, pragmatism, and politics: The evolution of Washington State's sentencing guidelines. Retrieved from http://digitalcommons.law.yale.edu/cgi/viewcontent.cgi?article=5979&context=fss_papers

Smith, O. (2016, September 1). The 58 countries that still have the death penalty. *The Telegraph*. Retrieved from http://www.telegraph.co.uk/travel/maps-and-graphics/countries-that-still-have-the-death-penalty/

Snell, T. (2014). *Capital punishment 2012—Statistical tables*. Washington, DC: Bureau of Justice Statistics.

Spohn, C. (2014). Twentieth-century sentencing reform movement: Looking backward, moving forward. *Criminology & Public Policy, 13*, 535–546.

Startz, R. (2016). *Schools, black children, and corporal punishment*. Washington, DC: Brookings Institution.

Steiker, C. (2013). Lessons from two failures. *Law & Contemporary Problems, 76*, 27–52.

Stephan, J. (2008). *Census of state and federal correctional facilities—2005*. Washington, DC: Bureau of Justice Statistics. Retrieved from https://www.bjs.gov/content/pub/pdf/csfcf05.pdf

Straus, M., & Stewart, J. (1999). Corporal punishment by American parents: National data on prevalence, chronicity, severity, and duration, in relation to child and family characteristics. *Clinical Child and Family Psychology Review, 2*, 55–70.

Ugelvik, T., & Dullum, J. (Eds.) (2012). *Penal exceptionalism? Nordic prison policy and practice*. New York, NY: Routledge.

von Hirsch, A. (1985). *Past or future crimes*. New Brunswick, NJ: Rutgers University Press.

Walen, A. (2016). Retributive justice. In E. Zalta (Ed.), *The Stanford encyclopedia of philosophy* (Winter Edition). Retrieved from https://plato.stanford.edu/entries/justice-retributive/

Walmsley, R. (2015). *World prison population list* (11th ed.). London, UK: Institute for Criminal Policy Research. Retrieved from http://prisonstudies.org/sites/default/files/resources/downloads/world_prison_population_list_11th_edition_0.pdf

Wellman, C. (2017). *Rights forfeiture and punishment*. New York, NY: Oxford University Press.

Wellman, C. (2012). The rights forfeiture theory of punishment. *Ethics, 122*, 371–393.

Von Drehle, D. (2015, June 8). The death of the death penalty. *Time*. Retrieved from http://time. com/deathpenalty/

CHAPTER 10

Ethics and Institutional Corrections

Chapter Outline

CHAPTER LEARNING OBJECTIVES:

1. Explain crime control theology.
2. Describe who is incarcerated in America and the ethical implications of those findings.
3. Distinguish prisons *as* punishment from prisons *for* punishment and the ethical implications of both.
4. Explain how codes of ethics can guide the behavior of correctional officers and treatment staff.
5. Identify ethical issues associated with correctional officers and treatment staff.
6. Explain how the Lucifer Effect can lead to unethical or illegal behavior by correctional staff.
7. Describe how jails can be misused in this country and the ethical implications of that misuse.

INTRODUCTION

As you saw in Ch. 9, incarceration as punishment for violating the criminal law is but one of many sanctions available in the criminal justice system. Incarceration is also associated with two very different kinds of institutions: jails and prisons. Jails are locally operated facilities whose primary purpose is to securely hold, for short periods, people who have been arrested and are awaiting trial and those sentenced to a short term of incarceration. Prisons, on the other hand, are state-run facilities whose purpose is to hold people convicted of relatively serious crimes for a lengthy period. During their time in prison, the offender's behavior is corrected and she is prepared for a return to the community. Scholars describe jails and prisons as examples of "institutional corrections." Ethical issues associated with institutional corrections, especially prisons, are the focus of this chapter.

I begin the chapter by providing you with a context for the discussion that follows, namely, why imprisonment became so popular over the past 40–50 years and who it is that's been imprisoned. I then devote much of the chapter to examining two issues and their ethical ramifications: prisons *as* punishment and prisons *for* punishment. The former topic explores issues like the conditions of imprisonment, what the imprisoned deserve, whether the government should allow for-profit corporations to build and run prisons, and whether—given their abysmal history—prisons as they are currently known should continue being used. The latter topic focuses more on questions arising from the day-to-day operation of prisons and focuses on the behavior of two key groups of practitioners, correctional officers and treatment staff (e.g., correctional psychologists) and the ethical issues they confront as they go about fulfilling their daily responsibilities. Included here is discussion of ethical standards, promulgated by professional associations affiliated with correctional officers and treatment staff, that are intended to help guide these practitioners. I then briefly discuss jails in this country and explore whether jails are being misused and, if so, what are the ethical ramifications of doing so. I conclude the chapter by examining the ethics of the increasingly widespread practice of isolating jail and prison inmates in solitary confinement. Let's get started by first examining the context of ethics and institutional corrections, beginning with why prisons have become such a popular mechanism for punishing criminal offenders.

INSTITUTIONAL CORRECTIONS AND PUNISHING OFFENDERS

> First off, we need to remind ourselves that people are sent to prison *as* punishment and not *for* punishment.
>
> —(emphasis in original; Kleinig, 2008, p. 224)

For too long, American crime control policy has relied on what Samuel Walker dubbed **crime control theology**, which involves both political conservatives and liberals—and the representatives they elect—peddling "nonsense" about how to best address street crime. Crime control theology consists of articles of faith, based on assumptions about human nature and idealized world views, that include proponents' greatest hopes and their deepest fears (Walker, 2015). For example, conservative crime control theology aspires to a world of "discipline and self-control in which people exercise self-restraint and subordinate immediate gratification to their long-term interests. It is a world of limits and clear rules about human behavior" (Walker, 2015, p. 27). By contrast, liberal crime control theology "emphasizes the social context of crime [wherein] behavior is largely the result of social influences" (Walker, 2015, p. 27). Because of these assumptions, conservatives tend to favor incarceration to punish offenders, the goal of which is to deter and/or incapacitate them. Liberals, however, favor less restrictive alternatives to incarceration (e.g., probation) for most offenders, preferring that prison be reserved for only the worst (e.g., robbers). In both instances, efforts should be undertaken to change (i.e., rehabilitate) offenders.

For the past 40 years, political conservatives have controlled criminal justice policy in this country, resulting in a well-documented explosion in rates of incarceration (see Ren, Zhao, & Lovrich, 2008). The problem is not necessarily with prisons (or jails) *as* punishment. Moral justifications for using incarceration as punishment involve the same as those for criminal punishment more broadly. Instead, the problem is that collectively we have agreed that incarceration is some sort of a "magic bullet" for reducing crime, despite mixed—at best—empirical evidence on its effectiveness. When increased use of incarceration fails to achieve that primary goal, the solution has then been to make imprisonment available to an *even wider* group of offenders (e.g., those convicted of low-level drug possession) while also making it harsher on inmates. For example, during the late 1990s, a **no-frills prisons and jails** movement developed in this country that sought to restrict or end inmate access to personal items (e.g., TVs or radios), computers, and weightlifting equipment; eliminated federal financial aid for inmates in the form of Pell grants that allowed them to pay for college; reduced visitation of inmates by family or friends; and increased healthcare co-pay requirements for inmates (Finn, 1996). More recently, "frills" like air conditioning and access to sufficient amounts of water during the height of summer heat have either been eliminated or have had restrictions placed on them (as of this writing, these issues are being litigated in the federal courts—see Speri, 2016). As the conditions of confinement become ever harsher, prison then becomes not something that is given *as* punishment, but something given *for* punishment. What's lost in doing so (or worse, ignored entirely) are both the moral (e.g., freedom from torture or degrading treatment) and legal (e.g., the 8th Amendment's ban on "cruel and unusual" punishment) constraints that supposedly ensure prisons don't become inhumane.

Who's Incarcerated?

As you've no doubt noticed, I like to provide context for discussing ethical issues. As you begin exploring the ethics of institutional corrections, I believe it important you first have a clear understanding of who's incarcerated in the nation's prisons and jails and why they are there. Yes, these people (at least most of them) are indeed both factually and legally guilty of the crime(s) they committed and for which they were convicted and should receive *some* punishment. Whether incarceration is the ethically justified form that their punishment should take is open to debate. Keep in mind that prison inmates are *human beings* (even if they have behaved like animals), with families and friends, who, at least at one point in their lives, had hopes and dreams. The impact of incarceration on them, their families, their communities, and society at large has both ethical and legal ramifications often glossed over in the rush to "lock 'em all up."

The Characteristics of Incarcerated Persons in America

At year end 2016 (the most recent year for which data are available), there were about 2.131 million adults incarcerated in this country: 1.316 million housed in state prisons, 188,400 living in federal prisons, and about 740,700 residing in local jails (see Figure 10.1). This translates to a rate of incarceration of about 850 people per 100,000 population age 18 or older, or about 1 in every 117 adults (Kaeble & Cowhig, 2018).

Looking more closely at these inmates, Figure 10.2 shows that, based on their share of the population, adult males and people of color were disproportionately incarcerated in 2016 (Kaeble & Cowhig, 2018; Zheng, 2018). Turning to the offenses for which adult

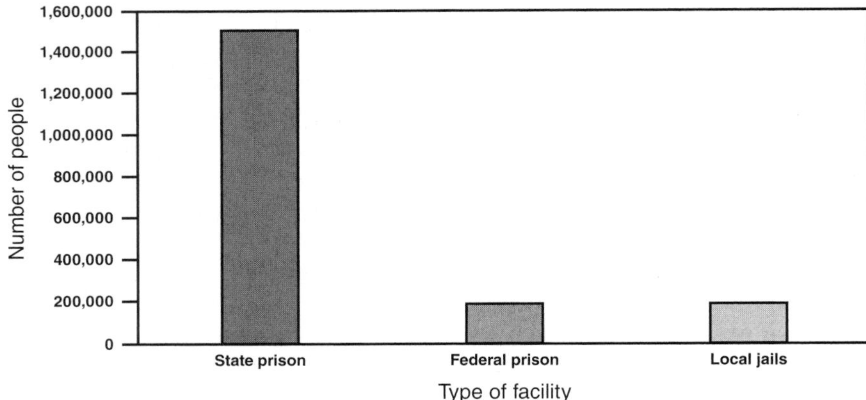

FIGURE 10.1 Number of People Incarcerated in the United States (2016)
Source: Adapted from Wagner & Rabuy (2017)

inmates had been incarcerated, Figure 10.3 shows that over one-half (55%) of state prison inmates in 2016 had been convicted of a violent offense (e.g., murder, manslaughter, rape/sexual assault, robbery, or assault); about 1 in 5 (18%) had been convicted of a property crime (e.g., arson, burglary, auto theft, or larceny/theft); 15% had been convicted of a drug offense (e.g., possession, distribution, or trafficking); and the remaining 13% had been convicted of some other type offense such as those involving DUI or public order (conviction offense is most serious charge on which an offender was convicted if multiple charges were involved).

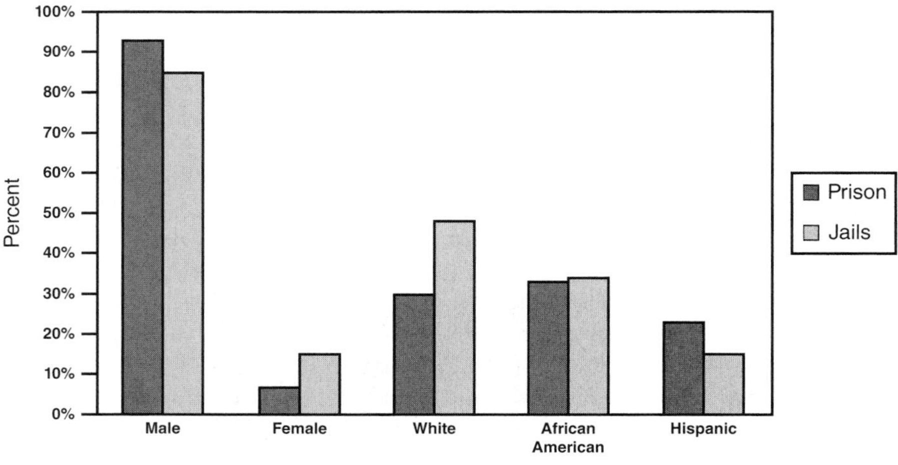

FIGURE 10.2 Personal Characteristics of Prison and Jail Inmates in the United States (2016)
Source: Adapted from Carson & Anderson (2016) and Minton & Zeng (2016)

Patterns for conviction offenses of inmates in federal prisons were quite different during 2016: only about 8% of inmates had been convicted of violence, around 6% had been convicted of property crimes, almost one-half (47%) had been convicted of drug offenses, and 39% had been convicted of other offenses (e.g., weapons, immigration violations). Data on jail inmates (also found in Figure 10.3) reveal that 21% had been convicted of a violent offense, 25% had been convicted of a property offense, 25% had been convicted of a drug-related offense, and the rest had been convicted of some other offense. Importantly, fully 71% of people in jail at year end 2015 had *not* been convicted of any crime—they were awaiting trial and either had not made bail or no bail was available in their case (Wagner & Rabuy, 2017).

Unpacking these data leads to several conclusions about "who's incarcerated" in this country. First, most inmates are incarcerated in state prisons (the ratio of inmates in state prison to federal prison is about 7 to 1). This means the states have "reaped what they have sown." Sure, the states bear the greatest burden to (1) house, clothe, feed, and monitor inmates; (2) build and maintain the physical plants of prisons, and (3) recruit and retain prison staff (COs, treatment staff, support personnel). But it was also state-level policies (e.g., mandatory minimum sentences, abolition of parole and "good time," "three strikes" laws, etc.) that significantly contributed to the mass incarceration phenomenon of the past four decades. Second, the overwhelming majority of those incarcerated are men (among prison inmates, they outnumber women by a factor of about 8 to 1). This indicates that crime—at least the kind that lands you in prison (or jail)—is, generally, the purview of men. One could thus argue that the causal forces at work in criminality appear to affect men in ways not experienced by women. Third, while more than one-half of *state* prison inmates are incarcerated for committing a violent crime, about one-half of inmates in *federal* prisons are incarcerated for

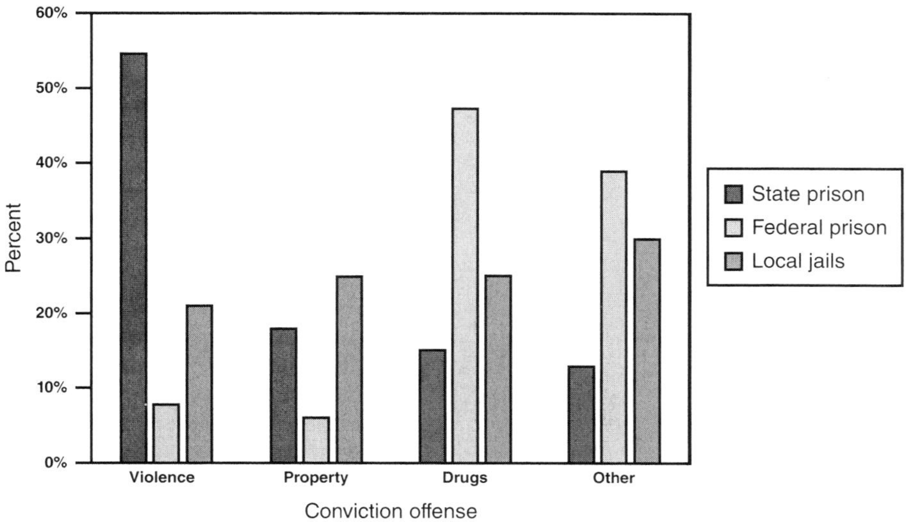

FIGURE 10.3 Inmate Conviction Offense (2016)
Source: Adapted from Wagner & Rabuy (2017)

drug offenses. Thus, policies geared toward reducing the sale and use of illegal drugs are directly tied to the explosion that occurred in the number of people incarcerated in federal prisons. Finally, these data show that incarceration has seemingly become a new system of "Jim Crow" (Alexander, 2010). Anticrime policies adopted by the states and Congress that fueled mass incarceration have disproportionately affected people of color, particularly males, and resulted in massive negative consequences for offenders, their families, and their communities.

Critics of incarceration often overlook the fact that many inmates really *are* "bad dudes"—career burglars or robbers—who pose legitimate threats to community safety. These critics must address how to deal with such offenders if reliance on incarceration were reduced. Proponents of incarceration, including its expanded use, must be able to justify the direct and the indirect costs to society of locking up so many offenders, such as damaged social networks (including those of family and friends), distorted social norms, and the destruction of social citizenship (Clear, Rose, Waring, & Scully, 2003). They must also justify policies relating to the "war on drugs" that contributed so much to exploding prison populations at the federal level. These are the sorts of issues that must be addressed in any discussion relating to the ethics of locking people up (Kleinig, 2008).

Ethical Issues and Prisons

For the past 40 years, imprisonment has constituted the tip of the spear of crime control efforts in this country. Politicians and political commentators that favor "locking 'em up" helped ensure the nation's prisons were full to the breaking point, created a prison-building binge that racked up billions of dollars in public debt, and turned over the state's punishment function to for-profit corporations (Garland, 2013). However, those advocating imprisonment tend to ignore (or are ignorant of) these facts (Kleinig, 2008):

- Imprisonment did not become socially acceptable punishment until a century *after* the founding of this country;
- Prisons were first developed as a "more humane alternative" to the then-widespread practice of corporal (e.g., beatings and whippings) and public (e.g., the pillory) punishments;
- As public attitudes about the body changed during the 18th and 19th centuries, confining people—in combination with subjecting them to potentially incapacitating forced labor—became favored by most citizens, along with a way of supplying cheap labor to various industries through such programs as "convict leasing" (Morris & Rothman, 1998);
- During the 19th century—mostly because of efforts by religiously based reformers—the *penitentiary* was introduced as a short-lived vehicle for remorse by, and rehabilitation of, inmates, who were forbidden to speak to one another, were housed in solitary confinement, and wore distinctive uniforms that "marked" them as miscreants;
- Although imprisonment as a form of legal punishment is a state function, especially since the 1980s, implementation of that function has occasionally been given to private, for-profit corporations to build and/or run prisons to meet increasing demand for prison space; in response to court orders relating to institutional overcrowding; or to address ever-tightening state budgets;

- Western-style prisons have *rarely* lived up to the rehabilitative goals envisioned for them, and instead, became sources of cheap labor or warehouses for societies unable (or unwilling) to address their crime problem and its causes in a constructive manner (see Weiss, 2001).

To say that the history of prisons in this country is abysmal is an understatement. That they are dehumanizing (Zimbardo, 2007), breed violence and victimization (Gilson, 2016), tend to be corrupt and corrupting (Center for the Advancement of Public Integrity, 2016), and are little more than giant warehouses for deviant members of the underclass (Irwin & Owen, 2004) has been well documented. Also, well documented is the fact that in many communities, imprisonment of their members has become so normal that those remaining "live in the first genuine prison society in human history" (Wacquant, 2001, p. 121). Further, the idea that prisons effectively deter or incapacitate (Roberto & Francesco, 2012) or that their programs rehabilitate offenders (Cullen & Gilbert, 2015) has been the subject of ongoing, often fierce, debates. These concerns, combined with a continuing preference by many Americans to "lock 'em up," raises important ethical and legal questions that must be addressed.

Questions about the morality and ethics of prisons seem to fit into two groups (Kleinig, 2008). The first group involves questions about **prisons *as* punishment** and includes issues like who should be imprisoned, what do the imprisoned deserve, whether corporate entities should be allowed to run and profit from prisons, and whether prisons should be abolished. The second group involves questions about **prisons *for* punishment** and focuses on issues involving the personnel working in them and their day-to-day activities (like supervision), corruption, and the delivery of services to inmates.

PRISONS *AS* PUNISHMENT

When speaking of prisons *as* punishment, what I am referring to is the way in which a specific punishment—the loss of one's liberty—occurs through incarceration in a long-term setting. Used here, "as" is a conjunction that means "in accordance with" or "the way in which" something occurs (Merriam-Webster, 2017). So, for example, fines, asset forfeiture, jail, imprisonment, and house arrest are all criminal sanctions used *as* punishment for those who break the law, in much the same way detention is used *as* punishment for students who misbehave in school. Prison is simply a specific type of criminal punishment that is used against certain offenders, given the magnitude of their illegal behavior.

Who Should Be Imprisoned?

When using prisons as punishment, the first issue involves who should be eligible for *this* sanction—as opposed to something else. When imposing complete loss of freedom on an offender, the person is subjected to various "pains" or deprivations that, beyond loss of liberty, also include loss of goods and services, identity and personal autonomy, and security (Sykes, 1958). One could thus argue that because of these "pains," imprisonment should not be imposed on everyone who breaks the law—it should be reserved only for certain offenders. The question then becomes, What standard should be used in making that determination?

Some scholars have argued that the standard used should be the "risk" an offender poses to the security of the community (Bonta & Andrews, 2007). More specifically, given an offender's past record of felony convictions and the nature of these offenses (e.g., violence, property crime, drugs), one could argue that such offenders pose the gravest risk to the community of continuing to engage in serious, illegal, behavior and that only imprisonment can effectively address the risk these offenders pose (Kleinig, 2008). We should use caution, however, when arguing in favor of using risk as the standard, since many times criminality is a stage rather than a permanent condition (Gottfredson & Gottfredson, 1994). Using evidence-based criteria to predict risk would seem preferable, since those criteria account for the fact that criminality may be a stage in, rather than a permanent feature of, an offender's life (MacKenzie, 2000).

What Do the Undeserving Deserve?

Once we decide who should be imprisoned—those posing the greatest risk to the community—the next question is figuring out what kind of life these people should have while in prison. For some, prison is more than simply a tool being used to punish offenders by stripping them of their liberty. They argue there should be more to imprisonment than "just" restricting inmates' freedom of movement and ability to associate with family and friends. For these folks, the conditions of confinement should remind the prisoner each day that she has offended the moral sensibilities of the larger society and must pay a price for doing so. Thus, prison should be as unpleasant as possible. The question then becomes how unpleasant is *too* unpleasant? For example, is air conditioning during summer (or heat during the winter) or access to enough water to avoid heat exhaustion a "frill?"

In 1948, in the wake of World War II, the United Nations General Assembly passed its Universal Declaration of Human Rights (see Box 10.1). The Declaration lists 30 basic rights that all people enjoy, including the right to *not* be tortured or subjected to degrading treatment (United Nations, 2017). For those wishing prison to be as unpleasant as possible by enhancing the pain already caused inmates being stripped of their freedom, isn't subjecting them to forced labor on chain gangs (such as what occurred in Alabama during the 1990s and in Arizona more recently) or restricting their access to water during the height of summer heat not violating at least some of these basic rights? Perhaps more importantly, isn't doing so treating inmates as less than human?

The question here is really one about what the undeserving among us—in this case criminals—deserve. Some have argued that inmates should not receive any benefit that is greater than those available to the law abiding (Keim, 2013). To illustrate: should the convicted robber serving time in the Northern Correctional Facility—a maximum-security prison located in Moundsville, WV—have access to food, clothing, and other necessities of life that an ex-coal miner living in Fayette County, WV (the "heart of coal country") who has never broken the law and is barely eking out a life without running water or indoor plumbing does not?

The difference here is that the ex-coal miner has his freedom (although it may be limited by his life circumstances), while the inmate does not. What this means is that the ex-coal miner can move freely about without asking permission and can read, speak, or worship (or not) as he pleases (although there are some limits on these, such as not being free to yell "fire" in a crowded theater), while the inmate has much greater restrictions imposed on him in these areas. It is these impositions on his freedom that constitute punishment for the inmate. But how far should those restrictions go? What should be the conditions of confinement?

BOX 10.1 Thirty Basic Human Rights—*Universal Declaration of Human Rights*

Right to Equality
Freedom from Discrimination
Right to Life, Liberty, Personal Security
Freedom from Slavery
Freedom from Torture and Degrading Treatment
Right to Recognition as a Person before the Law
Right to Equality before the Law
Right to Remedy by Competent Tribunal
Freedom from Arbitrary Arrest and Exile
Right to Fair Public Hearing
Right to be Considered Innocent until Proven Guilty
Freedom from Interference with Privacy, Family, Home and Correspondence
Right to Free Movement in and out of the Country
Right to Asylum in other Countries from Persecution
Right to a Nationality and the Freedom to Change It
Right to Marriage and Family
Right to Own Property
Freedom of Belief and Religion
Freedom of Opinion and Information
Right of Peaceful Assembly and Association
Right to Participate in Government and in Free Elections
Right to Social Security
Right to Desirable Work and to Join Trade Unions
Right to Rest and Leisure
Right to Adequate Living Standard
Right to Education
Right to Participate in the Cultural Life of Community
Right to a Social Order that Articulates this Document
Community Duties Essential to Free and Full Development
Freedom from State or Personal Interference in the above Rights

Source: Adapted from Human Rights Resource Center (2017)

The Conditions of Confinement

Most people agree that prison should not be "easy"—otherwise, where's the punishment? But many of these same people would accept that prison should not be overly harsh and note that there are supposed to be safeguards against it becoming so, such as the 8th Amendment's prohibition on cruel and unusual punishment or the U.N.'s Declaration of Human Rights. But do these safeguards really impose constraints on harshness?

In an interesting observation on prison conditions, John Kleinig (2008, p. 223) has suggested that among criminal justice officials and the courts there is an unspoken commitment to a doctrine of **penal austerity**, or the view that conditions inside prison should be no better than those an inmate would experience on the outside. At the core of this doctrine, according to Kleinig (2008), is the notion that punishment is an *imposition* on, not a *benefit* gained by, offenders. The problem becomes one of the imposition being confinement versus confinement *plus* additional hardships like forced labor on chain gangs, lack of access to healthcare, or continual harassment by correctional officials. Kleinig (2008) noted that because imprisonment results in the state and its representatives (i.e., correctional officials) gaining almost complete control over an inmate's life and the conditions surrounding it, the state *explicitly* takes on the obligation to make sure the conditions of confinement do not humiliate or degrade those subjected to them. If one had experienced a harsh existence outside prison—like our ex-coal miner—that is no reason to make the prison experience even harsher and then justify doing so based on the notion of penal austerity. Kleinig (2008, pp. 224–225) summarizes this view by arguing:

> We should not resent the fact that, despite the discipline of confinement, people can be better off in prison than outside it. What we ought to seek is a prison experience that, in

> addition to confining the person, also prepares that person to function more responsibly than before. Although advocates of penal austerity have given it potent political form when they complain of "country clubs" and "vacation spas," the doctrine of penal austerity [is] an inappropriate benchmark for determining prison conditions.

In short, the conditions of confinement should not be such that the basic dignity of the inmate is jeopardized through humiliation, intimidation, or exploitation.

Privatization

The United States has a long history dating back to the 1800s of delegating to private, nonprofit entities the building and/or the running of prisons (Selman & Leighton, 2010). Much more recently, during the 1980s, there occurred an explosion in the number of states, along with the federal government, delegating their penal function to private, *for-profit,* corporations (Simonds & Wright, 2016). Some of these corporations, such as Wackenhut, expanded into corrections from a core of operations that had been grounded in private security, while others (e.g., CoreCivic, formerly known as Corrections Corporation of America) were founded exclusively to venture into corrections (Kleinig, 2008). In the case of CoreCivic, its founding partners created a company that could "design, finance, build, operate and manage correctional facilities of many types . . . [and] tailor correctional solutions based on [government] needs, with budget, population, policies and procedures in mind" (CoreCivic, 2017).

Kleinig (2008) has suggested that proponents of for-profit privatization of prisons argue that these companies, beyond their being able to respond in a timely fashion to urgent government needs, represent efficient and economical responses to the need for more prisons, while properly managing scarce public resources. Proponents also claim that state contracts with for-profits to operate prisons can be fashioned to provide protections for inmates from the kinds of abuses that had occurred in prisons operated by nonprofits during the late 19th and early 20th centuries. Opponents argue it is unseemly for corporations to profit from the "business of punishing others" and that too often, profit motives encourage cost-cutting measures, leading to diminished quality in correctional services (Kleinig, 2008).

Kleinig (2008) suggested that, in the broadest sense, legal punishment of offenders *should* involve their humane treatment and an opportunity for them to maximize their potential while incarcerated. However, relying on profit-making organizations to do so is problematic on two levels. First, doing so could change citizen expectations, such that "profit" or "profitability" becomes associated with imprisonment. Were this to occur, corporations running private prisons might then be tempted to employ fewer personnel who are paid less money and are less well-trained than are personnel in nonprivate prisons, and "scrimp" on rehabilitative programs in the interests of security. Second, it is almost certain that these companies would oppose state and/or federal policies that were aimed at decarcerating imprisoned offenders or reducing the use of prisons as a tool for punishing them (see Scull, 1977). Even if it could be shown that prisons operated by private, for-profit corporations were "just as good as" state-operated prisons, Kleinig (2008) suggested that such a standard is hardly something about which to be proud. What this really means is that private prisons can be "just as bad as" state-run prisons.

Abolition

If you accept there are many chronic problems with prisons *as* punishment, along with the fact that policy makers are unlikely to devote needed resources to address them, then prison abolition may seem a logical next step (McLeod, 2015). In a recent article in the *UCLA Law Review*, Professor Allegra McLeod described prison abolition as:

> [The] end of the use of punitive imprisonment as the primary means of addressing what are essentially social, economic, and political problems, dramaticallyreducing reliance on incarceration, and building the social institutions and conceptual frameworks that would render incarceration unnecessary.
>
> —(McLeod, 2015, p. 1172)

McLeod goes on to say that abolition is more than simply calling for the immediate opening or tearing down of all prison walls. Instead, abolition involves developing a network of alternative regulatory frameworks that are nonpenal in nature and an ethic that recognizes the moral wrong inherent in any action that includes caging, chaining, or controlling people by penal force.

Calls for abolition are based in Quaker ideals and exist along a continuum, as follows (Simon, 2007). On one end are those who see absolutely no value in incarceration and characterize punitive responses to crime as spinning a false tale about offenders and criminality revolving around "personal responsibility" for behavior and an "objective moral order" (Kleinig, 2008). Other abolitionists accept limited use of incarceration to incapacitate but believe that most offenders currently imprisoned should be subjected to alternative sanctions (Kleinig, 2008). Finally, still others point to incarceration as exacerbating existing, structurally based inequalities across individuals and groups, leaving inmates either as they were or worse than before they were imprisoned, and offer this as the reason prisons should be abolished (Kleinig, 2008).

Regardless of location on the continuum, abolitionists face major hurdles to achieving their goal(s), even with supporting evidence like that found by the Vera Institute's Commission on Safety and Abuse in America's Prisons (Gibbons & Katzenbach, 2006) showing that violence occurring in America's jails and prisons is being brought back to the community by former inmates and correctional officials alike. Imprisonment is now "deeply etched into our way of doing things," in much the same way that capital punishment is ingrained into our attitudes about murder and its control (Kleinig, 2008, p. 232). Just as has been alleged about the death penalty, we continue to "tinker" with the machinery of mass incarceration rather than committing ourselves to ending imprisonment as it is now practiced.

To summarize, prisons *as* punishment addresses broad issues that surround stripping offenders of their freedom, and includes questions relating to who should be incarcerated, the conditions of confinement, the extent to which the state is justified in delegating its punishment function to private, for-profit corporations, and whether prisons—as currently known—should be abolished. Prisons *as* punishment raises questions about whether incarceration violates basic human rights, including the right to not be tortured or subjected to degrading treatment.

In the following section, I consider prisons *for* punishment, which raise issues surrounding the people responsible for ensuring that offenders are punished: the correctional staff, particularly correctional officers (COs) and the professionals and paraprofessionals that work with inmates daily.

PRISONS *FOR* PUNISHMENT

If prisons *as* punishment deals with broad ethical issues relating to incarceration, prisons *for* punishment deals more with issues surrounding the day-to-day operation of prisons, including supervision and delivery of services. The focus is on the people charged with *implementing* imprisonment; that is, the people charged with monitoring and providing a range of services to millions of inmates serving sentences in state and federal prisons. In this discussion, I focus on two groups of people: correctional officers (COs) charged with ensuring that inmates do not escape and limiting inmate contact with the outside world; and treatment staff, primarily psychologists and counselors, charged with delivering services to inmates.

Correctional Staff in this Country

According to the most recent data available, at year end 2005, there were just over 278,000 COs and a little over 54,000 treatment staff working in state and federal prisons (see Table 10.1). To obtain a more current estimate, if you extrapolate an average 3% annual growth in these numbers, by 2015 there were over 374,000 COs and nearly 73,000 treatment staff working in approximately 1,800 federal and state prisons in this country. The 2015 numbers translate to an inmate-to-officer ratio of 4:1, and an inmate-to-treatment-staff ratio of 20:1, keeping in mind the ratios are affected by institutional resources, which tend to be loaded more toward security than treatment (Henrichson & Delany, 2012).

In exploring ethical issues confronting correctional personnel, I will focus first on COs, who share many characteristics with police officers (Farkas & Manning, 1997). For example, both groups have similar minimum requirements for hiring (e.g., high school diploma or GED) and training (e.g., completion of an academy). Both groups attract people with a strong public service orientation who believe that rules are important and

TABLE 10.1 Correctional Personnel in State and Federal Prisons (2005)

Type of Facility	Total Facilities	All Employees	Correctional Administrators	COs	Educational	Professional/ Technical
Public	1,406	393,699	8,290	262,718	9,827	39,618
Private	415	25,938	1,864	15,680	1,041	3,770
Federal	102	29,755	900	14,165	922	4,855
State	1,719	389,882	9,254	264,233	9,946	38,533
Total	1,821	419,637	10,154	278,398	10,868	43,388

Source: Stephan (2008)

see behavior as clearly "right or wrong." Members of both groups perceive their job as involving a noble cause (only in the case of COs, it's not getting "bad guys" off the streets, it's keeping them locked up) and a willingness to take and follow orders. Additionally, both police and COs are part of an occupational culture that contains similar values and norms, particularly keeping silent about peers' misbehavior.

The ethical issues involving COs arise primarily from their supervisory activities, and include reciprocity and corruption. Ethical issues confronting treatment staff, particularly professional psychologists and counselors, mainly revolve around the care they administer to inmates and how that care raises ethical issues such as respect for the dignity of inmates, professional competence, and the integrity of inmate relationships. Let's examine these issues in more detail.

Ethics and Correctional Officers

Inside prison, COs are crucially important because it is they who interact daily with inmates, monitor inmate behavior for rules' violations, implement sanctions should infractions occur, and maintain order. Their primary job is to keep inmates from escaping and the outside world from getting in. That is, they are the "front line" when it comes to the security of the facility.

Correctional Officer Duties

COs have multiple duties, just as you saw was true of police officers. For example, the Florida Department of Corrections (n.d.) describes the primary duties of its correctional officers as including supervising inmates; maintaining and demonstrating proficiency in the use and care of firearms, nonlethal weapons, and physical restraint methods and equipment; conducting inspections of inmate living quarters and work areas; conducting regular and impromptu inmate counts; maintaining control over, and discipline of, inmates using physical restraint and/or devices (e.g., restraint chairs or desks—see Wheeler, 2017); and maintaining inventories of equipment and supplies in their section of the facility.

Correctional Officer Skills

Because COs work in highly stressful environments populated by people who (generally) dislike and distrust them, not to mention outnumber them, officers must rely on more than brute force when dealing with inmates. Good COs possess certain skills that help them overcome the fear and distrust on the part of inmates, and foster respect (Fox, 2015). For example, officers must possess effective communication skills, both verbal and written. Being a good communicator helps facilitate teamwork and fosters camaraderie with colleagues. Because they must quickly evaluate potentially explosive situations, and identify the correct response, officers must also be good problem solvers. They must also be decisive, which means being able to "handle uncertainty, process information quickly, weigh evidence with intuition, and take action in a timely manner" (Fox, 2015, p. 1). Officers must also be resilient; that is, able to learn from mistakes or setbacks (and not repeat them). Finally, officers should be selfless, open-minded, and dedicated to the position.

The responsibilities of COs often create opportunities to engage in unethical or illegal behavior. This is particularly true of officers' supervisory activities, which may allow them to form close relationships with inmates for assorted reasons, some illegitimate. Supervision is also associated with the greatest ethical challenge for COs, namely, reciprocity in supervision—the proverbial "you scratch my back and I'll scratch yours." But it is also true that COs, like their police colleagues, have a code of ethics to help guide them as they engage with inmates. The code also speaks to skills that officers should possess and enhance through continuing education and in-service training.

The Occupational Culture of Correctional Officers

As you saw with police officers, COs likewise belong to an occupational culture, and share certain values, beliefs, and behavioral norms associated with a specific occupation (Farkas & Manning, 1997). In turn, those values, beliefs, and norms affect how one handles the duties and interactions that come with the occupation. For example, officers daily encounter people that are hostile toward them; some, in fact, wish harm to befall officers. Yet, unlike the police, COs are unarmed, outnumbered, and can't leave the scene. They must thus learn to manage and supervise inmates, and much of that knowledge is contained in the officers' occupational culture. Translating various aspects of the culture into how the job is done can then be used to classify COs as fitting into different "kinds" of officers.

TYPES OF CORRECTIONAL OFFICERS. Mary Ann Farkas (2000), for example, has argued that there are certain "types" of COs, each of which can be identified based on their orientation toward rule enforcement and negotiation or exchange in working with inmates; the extent they support norms of mutual obligation with colleagues; and their desire or interest in human service delivery (Farkas, 2000).

Farkas (2000, p. 438) characterized **rule enforcers** as being "rule bound, inflexible in discipline, and as having an *esprit de corps* with others sharing their enforcement philosophy." For these officers, invoking rules was a prerequisite for maintaining order and teaching inmates discipline. They advised new officers to quickly learn the rules and know them inside and out—rule ignorance allowed inmates to manipulate them. Rule enforcers were unwilling to negotiate with inmates to gain compliance. They also perceived rule violation as a direct affront to officer authority and would not tolerate it. Finally, Farkas (2000) observed that norms of mutual obligation were especially strong for these officers: they would not contradict colleagues in front of inmates, supervisors, or administrators and strongly supported actions colleagues took with inmates, even if the actions were inappropriate.

The **hard liner** CO constituted an extreme of the rule enforcer (Farkas, 2000). The hard liner was aggressive, sought power, was highly inflexible with rule enforcement, and possessed few interpersonal skills. These officers strongly supported formal goals and values of the facility. Hard liners also strongly endorsed paramilitary aspects of the job, including "distinction and deference to rank, chain of command, and authority vested in the position" (Farkas, 2000, p. 439). They perceived that acting hard and tough was the way COs were *supposed* to act to maintain order and control. Hard liners had negative views of the inmates, strictly enforced the rules to both punish them and show off their authority and were unwilling to negotiate for inmate compliance with rules because doing so was a sign of weakness. They strongly identified with other officers, especially those sharing their negative orientation toward inmates, whom they viewed as having it "too easy" in prison.

Farkas (2000) described **people workers** as officers trying to be professional, sociable, and responsible while carrying out their duties. These officers adjusted both the formal goals of the unit or facility and played down the militaristic aspects of the job. Instead, they were flexible in rule enforcement and disciplinary measures and developed their own informal system of rewards and punishments, while seeking inmate compliance through interpersonal communication and personalized relations. People workers were more concerned with why a rule was broken than with the actual breaking; their response depended on the circumstances and the inmate's attitude. Norms of mutual obligation toward colleagues were less developed for these officers. They would intervene in altercations between inmates and coworkers for the sole purpose of resolving the conflict, even if doing so might bruise coworkers' egos or potentially undermine their authority over inmates.

Synthetic officers emphasized larger organizational directives and interpersonal skills as important to being a CO (Farkas, 2000). While following rules and procedures closely, they also accounted for circumstances while not straying too far from procedure to cover for themselves. In handling inmates, their strategy was to strictly sanction serious rules' violations, but in cases of lesser violations, they would talk to inmates and figure out what was going on. They also expressed less distrust of inmates and were less cautious working with them than were the other types of officers. For synthetic officers, a "good" CO was one who treated inmates fairly and respected them, but also didn't take any nonsense from them. Norms of mutual obligation were evident: they backed colleagues and did not want to see them in trouble with either inmates or supervisors.

Loners were identified by Farkas (2000) as those who closely followed rules and procedures out of fear of being criticized. They accepted and identified with formal goals and values articulated by the administration, but neither identified with, nor felt a sense of loyalty toward, coworkers. In conforming with rules and procedures, their motivation was providing validation of their authority to inmates and colleagues and avoiding errors. Loners felt their job performance was more closely watched because of their status—most were female and/or African American—and as a result they felt they had to continually "prove" themselves. They were unwilling to negotiate with inmates for rule compliance out of fear they'd be viewed as "soft" or "unable to handle themselves" (Farkas, 2000, p. 443), and/or because they felt doing so left them open to manipulation by inmates. Loners did not feel accepted by colleagues, and did not identify with them, thus rejecting norms of mutual obligations. They were also wary of inmates, mistrusting and even fearing that inmates were "always trying to set officers up or take advantage of them" (Farkas, 2000, p. 443).

This typology of officers illustrates some of the values and norms that are components of the CO occupational subculture: don't trust inmates; have strong bonds with coworkers; rules and their enforcement are paramount; don't appear weak. How those values translate into interactions with inmates can lead to positive results, where inmates view officers as firm but fair, or to negative outcomes, where officers are seen as tormentors. There is, however, another source COs can consult for guidance: the code of ethics for correctional professionals.

Correctional Officer Code of Ethics

The American Correctional Association (ACA), one of the oldest professional associations for corrections officials, created a Code of Ethics for members in 1994 (condensed in Box 10.2). As you have seen with other such codes, it presents a set of ideals to which members should aspire, such as honor, respect, selflessness, and dignity. It also provides an overview of the obligations to which they are bound, including protecting civil and privacy rights of inmates and the confidentiality of information they possess; being transparent in their dealings with inmates and third parties; avoiding conflicts of interest; reporting unethical or illegal behavior to the proper authorities; and engaging in nondiscriminatory behavior. One could certainly argue that in contrast to the CO occupational culture, the code offers better guidance for officers that (one would hope) would lead to generally positive outcomes with inmates.

As you have now seen, COs have two "standards," if you will. On the one hand are those arising from the norms and values of the occupational culture to which COs belong

BOX 10.2 American Correctional Association (ACA) Code of Ethics[a]

The American Correctional Association expects of its members unfailing honesty, respect for the dignity and individuality of human beings and a commitment to professional and compassionate service. To this end, we subscribe to the following principles.

Members shall respect and protect the civil and legal rights of all individuals.

Members shall treat every professional situation with concern for the welfare of the individuals involved and with no intent to personal gain.

Members shall maintain relationships with colleagues to promote mutual respect within the profession and improve the quality of service.

Members shall make public criticism of their colleagues or their agencies only when such is warranted, verifiable, and constructive.

Members shall respect the importance of all disciplines within the criminal justice system and work to improve cooperation with each segment.

Members shall honor the public's right to information and share information with the public to the extent allowed by law subject to individuals' right to privacy.

Members shall respect and protect the right of the public to be safeguarded from criminal activity.

Members shall refrain from using their positions to secure personal privileges or advantages.

Members shall refrain from allowing personal interest to impair objectivity in the performance of duty while acting in an official capacity.

Members shall refrain from entering into any formal or informal activity or agreement which presents a conflict of interest or is inconsistent with the conscientious performance of duties.

Members shall refrain from accepting any gifts, services, or favors that are or appear to be improper or imply an obligation inconsistent with the free and objective exercise of professional duties.

Members shall differentiate between personal views/statements and views/statements/positions made on behalf of the agency or Association.

Members shall report to proper authorities any corrupt or unethical behaviors in which there is enough evidence to justify review.

Members shall refrain from discriminating against any individual because of race, gender, creed, national origin, religious affiliation, age, disability, or any other type of prohibited discrimination.

Members shall preserve the integrity of confidential information; they shall refrain from seeking information on individuals beyond that which is necessary to implement responsibilities and perform their duties; members shall refrain from revealing nonpublic information unless expressly authorized to do so.

Members shall make all appointments, promotions, and dismissals in accordance with established civil service rules, applicable contract agreements, and individual merit, rather than furtherance of personal interests.

Members shall respect, promote, and contribute to a work place that is safe, healthy, and free of harassment in any form.

[a] Adopted by the Board of Governors and Delegate Assembly in August of 1994

Source: American Correctional Association (2017)

that emphasize rules and their enforcement, occupational norms that stress not allowing inmates to"get away with anything," even if the inmate's violation was a product of circumstances, and norms of mutual obligation among officers. Importantly, like police (and prosecutors, for that matter), circumstances don't usually matter—the causes of inmate behavior are best left to others, like the treatment staff, to figure out. On the other hand, the ACA Code of Ethics clearly articulates a set of ideals and obligations that suggest honesty, respecting the dignity of inmates, avoiding conflicts of interest, and reporting colleagues' unethical or illegal behavior are important behavioral norms for COs. Which do you think is the better guide?

Now that you have a sense of the occupational world of COs, let's consider the world inhabited by the other important group of people that work with inmates: the treatment staff.

Ethics and Treatment Staff

Treatment staff include the professionals (e.g., psychiatrists and psychologists) and paraprofessionals (e.g., counselors) who oversee institutional programs designed to prepare inmates for their return to society (about 95% of all prison inmates will be released through mandatory or discretionary parole or end-of-sentence) (Bureau of Justice Statistics, 2017). These individuals conduct needs assessments of inmates, oversee programs and the delivery of services associated with them, and work with COs and institutional administrators to ensure inmates are prepared to reenter the community. As with COs, there is also a code of ethics for treatment staff.

Treatment Staff Code of Ethics

The International Association for Correctional and Forensic Psychology (IACFP; formerly the American Association for Correctional Psychology) recently published its latest set of standards for psychology services in jails, prisons, correctional facilities, and agencies (International Association for Correctional and Forensic Psychology, 2010). The revised standards published in 2010—previous standards were published in 1980 and 2000—represent a guide for treatment staff that makes reference to professionally accepted and recognized mental health services practices in prisons, jails, and other facilities. Beyond including a statement of general principles and specific standards relating to such areas as the administration and operation of treatment services, staffing and professional development, services and programs, records, and research, the code includes a set of ethical principles relating to treatment services by mental health professionals and paraprofessionals.

The IACFP Code (see Box 10.3) contains nine standards, beginning with general guiding principles, as well as specific standards relating to mental health resources, professional competence, documentation, confidentiality and limits on it, informed consent, involuntary treatment, and employer/staff conflicts of interest. The standards make clear that treatment staff are bound by professional codes, state and federal law, and international agreements to (in general) ensure that inmates' dignity and autonomy are preserved, that emotional or physical harm is minimized, and inmates are respected. What this means in practice is that service providers must not use involuntary treatment as punishment, that inmates' mental health records are confidential and maintained in separate files with "right-to-know" access by nontreatment personnel, and that inmates understand the potential risks and benefits of treatment received. The standards also recognize that while the inmate is a client *of* the treatment professional, the treatment provider works *for* the institution (i.e., the state), which creates a "duty to warn"

BOX 10.3 Ethical Standards for Mental Health Practices in Correctional Contexts

1. *General Principles*: All mental health services will comply with the prevailing professional rules (e.g., codes of ethics), licensing agency requirements, state and federal law, and international treaties, and with basic principles recognizing offenders' rights to dignity, respect, autonomy; to avoiding or minimizing emotional and physical harm; and advocating for competent mental health services and research.
2. *Mental Health Resources*: Mental health resources are provided only for clearly defined mental health purposes in compliance with the ethical principles of these standards.
3. *Competence*: Psychologists and other mental health service providers limit their services to their supervised or demonstrated areas of professional competence.
4. *Documentation*: All mental health services, contacts generating clinically relevant information, and mental health information, will be maintained in a confidential file in compliance with current professional, legal, and administrative standards.
5. *Confidentiality of Files/Records*: (a) All mental health services files and records are confidential to the detainee/inmate in accordance with current professional guidelines and relevant laws and administrative codes; (b) A documented policy and process exists to ensure confidentiality of all mental health services files, records, and test protocols along with a documented access process/policy for non-psychological services staff. This process is supervised by an on-site mental health records custodian and all staff are trained in this policy; (c) Each organization/ agency has its own policy regarding the transport of mental health records from one institution to another for routine or emergency facility transfers that ensure record confidentiality during the process.
6. *Limits of Confidentiality*: All detainees/inmates are informed, verbally and in writing via appropriate form signed and dated by the offender and/or the mental health services' provider, of the limits of confidentiality and legally or administratively mandated "duties to warn" prior to receiving any psychological service that places their confidentiality at risk. This documentation will be placed in the offender's confidential file.
7. *Informed Consent*: All psychological screenings, assessments, treatments, and procedures (e.g., audio/video recording, observation of treatment for training and research procedures) are preceded by an "informed consent" process and documented on the appropriate consent form. The form includes explanation of the diagnosis, available options, risks (including nontreatment), anticipated outcomes, and time frames and is signed by both client (or designated guardian) and the mental health services professional and placed with the offender's mental health services confidential file.
8. *Involuntary Treatment*: Involuntary treatment (e.g., administration of psychotropic medication, placement in an observation status, and the use of restraints) is undertaken only by a qualified mental health professional under the auspices of relevant practice guidelines federal and state law, and administrative codes. Written policies and procedure clearly articulate the role and responsibilities of qualified mental health professional in these procedures that are advocated and/or maintained only after initial and ongoing assessments to determine necessity. Mental health services professionals refuse to participate in such processes if they are inconsistent with legal, professional, or ethical standards; are utilized for disciplinary or punitive purposes; or are contrary to prisoner/detainee constitutional rights or conflict with international agreements on prisoner/detainee treatment.
9. *Employer/Staff Conflicts of Interest*: There exists a documented and implemented policy regarding the resolution of ethical/professional conflicts between the employing correctional facility, organization, or agency and mental health services staff.

Source: International Association for Correctional and Forensic Psychology (2010, pp. 769–776)

institutional administrators of, for example, security threats posed by an inmate receiving treatment or being assessed.

You have now seen that both correctional officers and treatment staff have guiding codes of ethics to help in their day-to-day decision-making while interacting with inmates. They stress that inmates, although being punished for sometimes horrific behavior, are still human beings worthy of having their dignity respected and their autonomy preserved as much as possible in the closed environment of a prison (or jail). You have also seen that in the case of COs, the occupational culture and its values and norms—along with how those are translated into the actual behavior of these officers—may pose a threat to the larger ideals and obligations contained in the codes. In the following section, I present examples of specific kinds of ethical issues faced by COs, most of which are tied to the supervision of inmates. I then examine examples of ethical issues for treatment staff.

Ethical Issues and Correctional Officers

COs and how they carry out their responsibilities and duties represent the fine line between prisons *as* punishment and prisons *for* punishment. While they have little control over the design and overall physical condition of the prison in which they work—some of these institutions are more than 100 years old and have physical plants that leave much to be desired—because officers implement and enforce institutional rules and policies, they have much control over the general conditions of confinement experienced by inmates. On the one hand, if they aspire to achieve the ideals and accept the obligations of the position as outlined in the ACA code, they will protect the dignity and humanity of the inmates. If they lose sight of those ideals and obligations, a much different landscape awaits inmates. More practically, in losing sight of these ideals and obligations, the institution will be vulnerable to litigation over the conditions of confinement and potentially face intervention by the federal courts, the U.S. Department of Justice, or both, into institutional operations. Besides the economic costs associated with these interventions, the negative press that accompanies them does little to inspire citizen confidence in the state's punishment function.

Reciprocity in Prison

The warden of a maximum-security prison (which also housed death row inmates) once told me the only reason any given prison doesn't descend into complete chaos is because the inmates have chosen not to rebel *that particular day*. Prison rebellions are the absolute worst-case scenario for anyone working in a prison (Adams, 1994). During such uprisings, inmates and staff alike can be injured or killed and the facility can suffer major damage, even to the point of rendering it inoperable. Prison wardens and staff are thus keenly aware of the reality they face: they are outnumbered, they can't simply leave if a major problem arises, and they do not have easy access to firearms. As a result, they have to develop ways to maintain order other than using brute force.

Reciprocity in the context of prisons (and jails) refers to COs developing relationships with inmates that revolve around mutual benefit: you do something for me, I'll do something for you (Griffin & Hepburn, 2005). Inmates and officers interact in exchange relationships—a give-and-take that (generally) proves beneficial to both.

For example, if an officer does not report an inmate's rules' violation or imposes less than a maximum punishment for the violation, the inmate has benefited. The officer, in turn, looks to the inmate to provide him or her with a benefit such as alerting the officer to the presence of contraband in the unit or plans for an assault on a new African American inmate by a group of white inmates. When the exchange is in balance, there is little incentive for either officer or inmate to disrupt the relationship. However, in some cases, the relationship becomes unbalanced because, for example, the inmate and officer become too friendly, the officer abuses his or her power, or the officer becomes lazy or disconnected and relies too heavily on inmates to supervise themselves. Reciprocity can thus become problematic and threaten not only the security of the facility, but the larger conditions of confinement if power relations are so out of balance that inmates are being exploited as officers become little more than bullies. Beyond threatening security, ethically speaking, reciprocity can threaten the dignity and autonomy of inmates, while also negating the legitimate authority of the officers to manage, control, and supervise inmates.

Prison Corruption

Scholars of institutional corrections have often written about the corruption that occurs inside America's prisons (Souryal, 2009). In those writings, corruption is described as an erosion or circumvention of the goals of the correctional process for the benefit of prison administrators and/or staff. With that in mind, let's say for purposes of our discussion, **prison corruption** can be defined as "intentional violation of organizational rules and/or procedures by public employees for personal gain" (McCarthy, 2015, p. 281). Thus, corruption involves individuals (e.g., COs) functioning as public employees whose behavior violates formal institutional rules/policies/procedures, and is done for personal, material, benefit. As explained by McCarthy (2015), these features distinguish corruption from other forms of misconduct, such as officer use of excessive force.

Examples of corruption abound, but let's consider some of the more common. **Misuse of authority** occurs when corrections officials intentionally abuse their discretion for personal gain (McCarthy, 2015). For example, COs might accept "payoffs" from inmates to receive choice cells or work assignments, to protect operations designed to bring contraband into the facility and distribute it, or to avoid being punished by officers (i.e., extortion). Correctional administrators taking bribes from local contractors in the form of "sweetheart contracts" for goods or services needed by the facility is another form of misuse of authority (Hunter, 2007). Finally, sexual misconduct involving staff and inmates is another form of misuse of authority and involves staff exercising their power in exchange for sexual favors.

A second example of corruption involves the trafficking and smuggling of contraband. Here, COs conspire with inmates (or colleagues) to import contraband (e.g., alcohol or illegal drugs) into the facility and distribute it (McCarthy, 2015). The scope and complexity of these operations vary, ranging from a single officer and one or two inmates being involved to an entire prison. In recent years, trafficking in illegal cell phones has become "big business" in the nation's prisons (Wilson, 2011).

A third example of corruption involves theft or embezzlement. Here, prison officials illegally take inmate (or visitor) property or convert state property for personal use (McCarthy, 2015). Theft is usually opportunistic and involves single, discrete events; embezzlement, on the other hand, involves the systematic stealing of money or materials (e.g., building materials, tools) from state accounts, state property, or state warehouses.

Classifying Correctional Officer Misconduct

Reciprocity and corruption involve specific behaviors, but these behaviors fit into one of three broad categories of CO misconduct (McCarthy, 2015). **Misfeasance** involves improper performance of duties that one is legally expected or required to fulfill. Essentially, misfeasance involves an officer misusing his or her legal authority for personal gain. An example of misfeasance would be accepting monetary "kickbacks" from inmates for better cell assignments or work details. **Malfeasance** refers to outright illegality by COs, administrators, or other staff. An example here would be theft, embezzlement, or trafficking in contraband. Finally, **nonfeasance** involves an officer failing to fulfill his or her responsibilities or duties—in other words, acts of omission. Examples of this behavior could be officers selectively ignoring rules' violations or permitting colleagues to engage in misconduct (e.g., failing to stop or report a colleague's sexual involvement with an inmate).

Understanding Correctional Officer Misconduct

To understand unethical/illegal behavior by COs, Stanford psychology professor Philip Zimbardo's work on the dynamics of imprisonment offers great insight. His now (in) famous **Stanford Prison Experiment** (Zimbardo, 2007; Zimbardo, Haney, Banks, & Jaffee, 1972) was a simulation conducted in 1971 that vividly revealed the effects of imprisonment on guards and inmates alike.

Briefly, in mid-summer of 1971, a group of Stanford undergrads were recruited for a two-week study and randomly assigned into two groups as "prisoners" (10 volunteers) or "guards" (11 volunteers). They were then placed into a "prison" setting (the basement of the psychology building at Stanford University), where the inmates occupied "cells" (converted offices) and the "guards" watched over them in three "shifts" each day. After only six days, the experiment had gone awry: "guards" were abusing "inmates" and at least one "inmate" became suicidal, necessitating a premature end to the study. Subjects took their roles seriously, interactions became heated, and the interpersonal dynamics of "guards" and "inmates" became imbalanced as "guards" exerted their authority over "inmates" in increasingly harsh ways, fueled in part by the physical setting. The project highlighted what social psychologists have argued repeatedly about the power of situation to shape behavior, thoughts, and feelings. However, as Zimbardo pointed out, if this were a true prison, most observers would forget the dehumanizing and deindividuating nature of the environment and attribute everyone's behavior (guards and prisoners) to personal disposition and psychology (Whitbourne, 2013).

THE LUCIFER EFFECT. Decades later, Zimbardo wrote *The Lucifer Effect*, which contains his reflections on good and evil, and how ostensibly good people can engage in horrific evil, such as genocide, massacres, mass suicides, etc. He devotes the entire second half of the book to the abuses uncovered at the Abu Ghraib prison in Iraq in 2003 (and

Philip Zimbardo
CTK via AP Images

about which he testified at a military court martial involving one of the soldiers/COs). In the illustrations he used, Zimbardo made the point that typically good people had succumbed to the social and psychological dynamics of the situation, resulting in the worst possible outcome. He also pointed out how, in each instance, observers typically (but mistakenly) concluded that the pathologies evidenced were the work of a few bad apples, when in fact the bigger problem was the nature of the barrel into which they had been placed. Psychologists call this misinterpretation the **fundamental attribution error**, or the tendency to explain the bad behavior of others by overstating the importance of personality traits or disposition and underestimate the power of situational forces.

For Zimbardo, the power of the situation involves certain crucial dynamics, all of which were in evidence during the Stanford Prison Experiment and at Abu Ghraib (see Box 10.4). The first of these is **obedience to authority**. Stanley Milgram famously showed in his experiments how far people would go to inflict pain on others under the guidance or auspices of an authority figure such as a laboratory scientist (Milgram, 1974). In the case of COs, especially those who are relatively new to the job, the authority figure could be a supervisor or someone even higher in the chain of command who approves of strip searches, physical restraint desks, or other humiliating actions against inmates. A second important dynamic is the power of **group conformity**. As described above, the diverse types of COs were fairly consistent in their negative views of inmates as manipulators, seeking to taking advantage of COs. As a result, inmates *cannot* be allowed to "show up" officers, because in doing so, the officers come off as being weak. One way to avoid this is to exploit the power that officers have over inmates. Officers unwilling to do this are then ostracized by the group.

Deindividuation is a third dynamic in prison, and involves people losing their sense of individual identity (Cook, 2012). For example, most people refrain from aggression

BOX 10.4 The Dynamics of the Lucifer Effect

- Provide people with an ideology to justify beliefs for actions.
- Make people take a small first step toward a harmful act with a minor, trivial action and then gradually increase those small actions.
- Make those in charge seem like a "just authority."
- Transform a once-compassionate leader into a dictatorial figure.
- Provide people with vague and ever-changing rules.
- Relabel the situation's actors and their actions to legitimize the ideology.
- Provide people with social models of compliance.
- Allow dissent, but only if people continue to comply with orders.
- Make exiting the situation difficult.

Source: Ditmann (2004, p. 1)

because they fear being held to account for their actions. However, in situations like crowds, such restraints may be lessened and aggression may occur. Zimbardo (2007) argues that another way to lose one's sense of individual identity is through wearing a uniform—just as COs (and police officers) do. Wearing a uniform can disguise one's usual appearance, which in turn promotes anonymity and reduces personal accountability. This is especially so if the setting (i.e., prison) grants permission to enact one's impulses or to follow orders or implied guidelines that one would usually disdain. As Zimbardo (2007, p. 219) described this dynamic:

> When . . . members of a group . . . are in a deindividuated state, their mental functioning changes: they live in an expanded-present moment that makes past and future distant and irrelevant. Feelings dominate reason, and action dominates reflection. In such a state, the usual cognitive and motivational processes that steer their behavior in socially desirable paths no longer guide people. Instead, their rationality and sense of order yield to excess and even chaos. Then it becomes as easy to make war as to make love, considering the consequences.

Finally, **bystander apathy** ("the evil of inaction") is also a potent force in the situational dynamics of prisons. Bystander apathy describes occurrences where individuals are less likely to offer help to a victim when other people are present than they would had others not been there (Zimbardo, 2007). In effect, we don't do what we *know* we should do because we fear the consequences of doing so—ridicule, being mocked, etc. If COs allow a colleague or colleagues to abuse, exploit, or use inmates—when they know that doing so is victimizing the inmate—they are exhibiting bystander apathy.

In summary, prisons create dynamics affecting the behavior of both inmates and COs and may result in officers exploiting, using, and even abusing inmates. In turn, these dynamics can also lead to prison rebellions by inmates who initiate violence to express their displeasure with the actions of COs or other officials. Zimbardo's point is that situational dynamics commonly found in prisons—obedience to authority, group conformity, deindividuation, and bystander apathy—rather than the individual pathology of COs and other officials goes a lot further to helping us understand the unethical and sometimes illegal behavior of these officials.

Responding to Correctional Officer Misconduct

Efforts to prevent correctional officials' misconduct are being undertaken at prisons around the country. Increasingly, state departments of corrections are realizing that training of, and professional development for, correctional staff—particularly COs—not only reduces staff attrition but can also reduce costly litigation arising from their illegal or unethical behavior.

Bernard McCarthy (2015) has suggested several steps that can be taken to help prevent corruption, especially that involving COs. For example, the state department of corrections can both create and enforce a strict, zero-tolerance policy on corruption, and implement and communicate a strong and forceful anticorruption policy to all those working in state prisons. Anticorruption training for employees that includes information on the nature, causes, impact, and consequences of corrupt behavior should be integrated into preservice and in-service training. Employees that are charged with corruption should be thoroughly investigated and prosecuted (if warranted), not merely asked to resign.

A second step that can be taken is for the state to create a proactive mechanism designed to detect and investigate corruption occurring within prisons (McCarthy, 2015). Included here would be establishing an internal affairs unit in each prison, along with procedures that encourage employees, inmates, and civilians to report alleged staff misconduct. The state could also randomly order routine and special audits of prisons that would include interdiction investigations to search for contraband. Individual wardens could also order that inmates, staff, and civilians be subject to random screening and drug testing.

A third action that states could take would be improving the management of material practices in each prison in its system (McCarthy, 2015). This type of reform is designed to improve control of the organization, which reduces opportunities for corruption. One example here would be using guidelines to structure the exercise of CO discretion and reduce the opacity of low-level decision-making. To illustrate: specific criteria for, and supervisor review of, all cell changes, job assignments, and transfers or temporary releases would be established. The process of disciplining inmates should also be opened to review by supervisors to ensure accountability. Other steps include (1) upgrading employee-selection procedures to include more extensive psychological testing and formal preservice training to screen out questionable prospects, (2) expanding preemployment checks to include in-depth investigations, and (3) improving CO working conditions (e.g., enhance job responsibilities, broaden participation in decision-making) and salaries to raise the quality of those being hired.

McCarthy (2015) recommends a final strategy for controlling misconduct that relates to the political environment of prisons. He notes that while correctional administrators have little control over political and community attitudes toward prisons and prisoners, they can take steps to insulate employees from external pressures to act in a way that benefits a constituent or campaign donor seeking to intervene on behalf of an inmate (McCarthy, 2015, p. 292). Requiring merit-based selection and promotion of employees reduces the impact of political interference in the operation of the prison.

As McCarthy (2015) has observed, controlling prison corruption requires correctional administrators—wardens and those higher in the chain of command—to provide leadership by creating high standards of ethical conduct, communicating and enforcing those standards, and holding personnel accountable for their actions. Leadership also includes improving and upgrading the general correctional environment to protect employees from political pressures and replace a tendency toward complacency with a concern for accountability.

To conclude this section of the chapter, I turn my attention to ethical issues involving treatment staff. As you will see, those issues directly arise from the day-to-day work they do that involves delivering various services to inmates that are designed to prepare them to return to the community.

Ethical Issues and Treatment Staff

Recall that treatment staff typically consist of professional psychologists or psychiatrists, along with social workers and counselors, who work on a team that develops treatment programs for inmates intended to prepare them to return to the community. You saw in Box 10.3 a set of standards developed for the practice of correctional psychology and it is that aspect of treatment to which I devote this section of the chapter. But before sharing with you some of the ethical issues confronting correctional psychologists (and, by extension, other members of the treatment staff), I want you to again consider the context in which these people are working.

Prison psychologists/psychiatrists often experience a conflict in fundamental values, given where they work. While these professionals usually value (and stress) cooperation not only with colleagues, but also with patients, their work is often performed in the context of an adversarial system and unique social microcosm (Haag, 2006). As described by correctional psychologist Andrew Haag (2006), treatment staff confront a paramilitary-based staff hierarchy; an "us-versus-them" separation of staff from offenders; separation from mainstream society; a perceived hierarchy among offenders often linked to their crimes; the obvious presence of criminal gangs; and social pressures faced by offenders to conform their behavior to antisocial values. As a result, treatment staff generally and correctional psychologists more specifically must be keenly aware of, and explicit about, the value system in which they are working.

What this entails, according to Haag (2006), is possessing a standard that goes well beyond self-awareness about one's values, to possessing a sensitivity about the values not only of one's clients but also those of the correctional context itself, replete with its emphasis on security and maintaining order. Thus, treatment staff should recognize that the services provided in one value system could well be interpreted much differently by another value system.

With these introductory comments in mind, let's now examine some of the more important ethical issues confronting those working in the treatment arena.

Respect for the Dignity of Persons

Recall that IACFP standards for psychological practice in correctional contexts (Box 10.3) stress that mental health services should comply with basic principles that recognize offenders' rights to human dignity and respect, autonomy, and to avoiding (or minimizing) emotional and physical harm (International Association for Correctional and Forensic Psychology, 2010). This standard gives rise to three issues: who's the client, confidentiality of inmate treatment records, and inmate refusal of services.

Who's the Client?

Perhaps the biggest issue for correctional treatment staff is recognizing that, depending on the service being provided, "the client" varies. For example, when conducting risk assessments for purposes of classifying inmates or engaging in rehabilitative services that involve risk, the client is the *government* (Haag, 2006). In such a situation, the psychologist is obligated to clarify her relationship with the offender at the onset, including the fact that information compiled as part of the assessment will be shared with prison authorities. In instances where the treatment professional is providing traditional psychotherapeutic services to the offender, the client here is the *inmate*, although again, safety and security risks posed by the inmate will be shared with the prison authorities (Haag, 2006).

Confidentiality

One of the most important standards in psychological practice is to maintain the confidentiality of client records. Issues of patient confidentiality almost never come up in a community setting. However, in a correctional setting, confidentiality is often a prominent issue and one that creates dilemmas for treatment staff (Haag, 2006). The classic illustration of such dilemmas is when, during treatment services, the inmate reveals that a prison escape plan is ready to be executed. Should the therapist inform institutional authorities of the plan and therefore reveal the client's identity to others in the institution (which will almost certainly be learned by inmates)? Consider that if a prisoner escapes and serious harm occurs during the escape, the treatment professional with foreknowledge of the escape would almost certainly be charged with failing to alert prison authorities. On the other hand, if the psychologist warns institutional officials and the client is assaulted by other inmates because he or she is a "rat," this is also problematic. As recommended by Haag (2006), treatment staff, before beginning treatment, must be explicit with inmates about how situations like escape plans, planned assaults, taking of hostages, etc., will be addressed.

Refusal of Services

A third issue relating to maintaining the dignity of inmates is an inmate's refusal to consent to the process of psychological assessment (Haag, 2006). Should the therapist ignore such a refusal and proceed with an assessment anyway because of interests of the larger society (for example, a risk review of a dangerous offender)? According to Haag (2006), such questions raise a very important question concerning whether the psychologist should, in fact, engage in the activity. Haag (2006) points out that adding weight to this issue is the fact that actuarial measures from third-party sources—those not requiring responses from the client being assessed—are generally better indicators of risk than are clinical judgments. Haag (2006) makes the point that an argument can be made that conducting the clinical assessment could hinder the accuracy and objectivity of the risk assessment.

Responsible Care

Responsible care in the correctional environment mainly involves the competency of the treatment staff delivering the services. Recall from the IACFP standards that mental health service providers will limit their services to demonstrated areas of professional competence (International Association for Correctional Forensic Psychology, 2010).

COMPETENCE. Psychologists generally agree that they should only deliver treatment or services in the area(s) in which they are competent, which means they are clearly aware of the boundaries of such competence (Haag, 2006). A key question that is often raised in the correctional context is this: At what point is the person competent to serve as a correctional psychologist? Haag (2006) observes that many psychologists have neither been trained in forensic psychology nor have they acquired supervised psychological experience in a correctional setting. While there is obvious overlap between many of the activities undertaken by both "regular" and "correctional" psychologists, there are also numerous unique aspects to working in a correctional setting.

Haag (2006) recommends that competent correctional psychologists will have had at least one year of supervised practice experience in a correctional environment so that they develop a firm understanding of the issues involved in correctional practice. He also recommends that new correctional psychologists receive in-service training about these issues. In addition, correctional psychologists should regularly consult with colleagues or recognized experts about the daily issues they confront. Haag (2006) argues that the process of ensuring demonstrable competence involves active self-evaluation and keeping current in areas of correctional practice, both intellectually and emotionally. He argues that "one needs to be constantly cognizant of what one is doing, and why, in any given situation" (Haag, 2006, p. 103).

Integrity in Relationships

The final area of ethical concern relating to treatment staff involves integrity in the relationships they have with inmates, other correctional staff, and third parties, such as family members of inmates, based on a specific role or roles they may be playing at any given time: assessor, therapist, etc.

MULTIPLE RELATIONSHIPS. Haag (2006) has suggested that the issue of multiple relationships most often occurs when the psychologist mixes their therapist and assessor roles with the same client or service recipient. He points out that, practically speaking, these situations will often lead to problems with maintaining rapport with clients, but more importantly, such practices likely embrace two separate value systems with the same client. Haag (2006, p. 105) claims that occupying these "dual roles" can (1) lead to confusion as to the role of the psychologist, (2) create ambiguity in terms of who is benefiting from the psychological relationship, and (3) lead to a blurring of professional boundaries. He recommends that, to avoid these issues, whenever possible, separate psychologists be used to perform separate psychological roles, but if this is not possible, the psychologist needs to explicitly clarify that there is a conflict in the roles in a manner that is easily understood by the client.

You have now seen how not only correctional officers, but also treatment staff encounter ethical issues while performing their duties and responsibilities. In the case of treatment staff, the ethical issues they face are often created by the correctional context in which they are working. Issues such as determining who is the client, client confidentiality. and refusal of services, along with competence in service delivery and the relationships created by the varying roles played by correctional psychologists (e.g., assessor and therapist), are confronted daily and require that treatment staff be both prepared for them and have reasonable resolutions for them as they occur.

In the following section, I briefly touch on jails as another part of the institutional corrections landscape. Beyond providing you with some basic information about them,

I address what is a growing concern that jails are being misused such that they have become the new "asylums" and "debtors' prisons" in this country.

ETHICAL ISSUES AND JAILS

Jails are among the oldest secure facilities in human history, dating back to ancient times. As a place of detention prior to trial for those accused of crimes, jails can be traced to the earliest forms of civilization and government in ancient Greece and Rome. From the beginning, jails have served several functions, including custody, coercion, and punishment. In the United Kingdom and this country, they have also been distinctly local institutions (unlike prisons), typically administered by county sheriffs' departments. There are lots of jails in America—over 3,100 of them, which means there's at least one in each county—that vary greatly in the number of inmates housed, from as few as 50 to over 17,000 held in the Los Angeles County Jail during 2015 (Hare & Rose, 2016). Further, at year end 2015, nearly three-quarters of jail inmates had not been convicted of a crime—they were awaiting trial (Wagner & Rabuy, 2017).

Because the terms are commonly confused, let's be clear: jails and prisons are not the same. While both are secure facilities that physically confine residents and deprive them of certain freedoms, the difference between them is twofold. First, jails are *local* correctional facilities typically run by county governments and administered by the country sheriff. Prisons are *state* operated and administered (typically) by a state-level agency, such as a department of corrections, housed in the executive branch of government. Second, jails are designed as *short-term facilities* where people awaiting trial are held or where people convicted of a crime are ordered to serve a sentence of less than 12 months incarceration. On the other hand, prisons are designed as *long-term facilities* that house people who have been convicted of a crime and received a sentence of greater than 12 months. They are also designed to provide a variety of rehabilitative services to inmates.

In recent years, scholars have expressed increasing concern that U.S. jails are being misused, and because of this are becoming full of two groups of people: those suffering from mental illnesses and the poor. Let's examine these claims more closely.

The Misuse of Jails in America

According to recent data, some 11 million people are admitted annually to jails in this country while daily populations are around 800,000 inmates (see Figure 10.4). **Jail churn** describes the steady flow of admissions (and releases) occurring in the nation's jails and, in the opinion of a growing number of correctional scholars, should be the focus of attention when it comes to understanding jails (Irwin, 2013). By focusing on jail churn, one can develop a better understanding of (1) who is coming to jail and (2) why they end up there. As Nicholas Turner, President of the Vera Institute, was quoted in a 2015 Institute report on jails:

> [T]oo often we see ordinary people, some even our neighbors, held [in jail] for minor violations such as driving with a suspended license, public intoxication, or shoplifting, because they cannot afford bail as low as $500. Single parents may lose custody of their children, sole wage-earners in families, their jobs—while all of us . . . pay for them to stay in jail.
>
> —(Subramanian, Delany, Roberts, Fishman, & McGarry, 2015, p. 2)

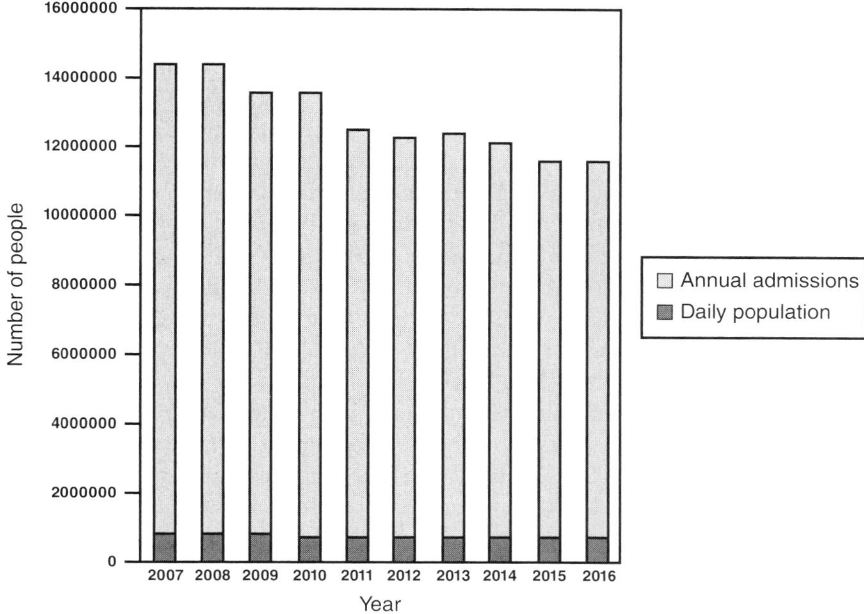

FIGURE 10.4 Daily Jail Admissions and Population in the United States (2007–2016)
Source: Adapted from Wagner & Rabuy (2017)

The concern of critics is that because they are being misused, jails are becoming the institutional personification of the criminalization of poverty (Foster, 2017). When jail churn is studied, one learns that jails in this country are little more than warehouses for those too poor to post even minimal ($500) bail or evidencing significant mental health issues that are too much for existing community resources to manage (Foster, 2017). In a recent report for the Vera Institute, Ram Subramanian, and colleagues Ruth Delaney, Stephen Roberts, Nancy Fishman, and Peggy McGarry (2015), explored the misuse of jails and how they have become the "gateway" into the American criminal justice system. They found that while jails do hold people accused of serious, violent crimes, nearly 75% of the population of both sentenced offenders and pretrial detainees are in jail for nonviolent traffic, property, drug, or public order offenses. The problem is that these relatively minor offenders end up in facilities that are overcrowded, noisy, chaotic, and, most of all, dangerous (Ruddell, Decker, & Egley, 2006).

Two issues raised about the misuse of jails is that they have become the new (1) "insane asylums" and (2) "poor houses" or "debtors' prisons" for America (Foster, 2017). According to the report from Subramanian, et al. (2015), the largest group of disadvantaged people spending time in jails are those suffering from mental illness. For many of these people, jails become their primary source of treatment, with the closing of state psychiatric hospitals. Subramanian, et al. (2015) noted that schizophrenia and major depression affect an estimated 1 in 6 men and 1 in 3 women jail inmates, rates four to six times higher than are rates in the general population. Further, they noted that over one-half (60%) of jail inmates self-report having experienced a mental health disorder in the previous year. Inmates experiencing serious mental health issues also tend to be poor, homeless, and substance abusers, and prone to committing the very public order offenses and minor crimes targeted by "zero-tolerance policing" in recent years.

Subramanian, et al. (2015) also argue that jail design, operations, and resources are not equipped to handle the mental health problems of so many inmates. Jails, especially large ones, can fairly be characterized as being brightly lit and noisy, having an ever-changing flow of admittees, and presenting an atmosphere of nearly constant threats and violence—hardly ideal conditions for those with mental health issues. When combined with very limited availability of mental health treatment programs, jail time is more likely to result in exacerbation of mental illness, not in gaining control of it. The lack of treatment options—combined with a chaotic environment—contributes to the use of solitary confinement for jail inmates with mental health issues, either as punishment for rules' violations or for protection from other inmates who might be inclined to victimize them. As discussed in Thought Exercise 10.1, these are exactly *not* the kinds of people who should be placed in solitary confinement.

Beyond jails supplanting psychiatric hospitals as the new asylums, Subramanian, et al. (2015) argue that jails are becoming "debtors' prisons" for the nation's underclass, despite such institutions being outlawed 200 years ago. Did you know that jails charge fees for the services they provide (e.g., clothing and laundry, room and board, medical care, and even the costs of formal booking)? Jails also contract with third parties for telephone and video-conferencing services used for visitation purposes. While the *individual* fees for all these services are generally small, they can quickly become thousands of dollars when combined with fines levied against inmates. Fees may continue accruing after release as well. The result is that necessary payments become impossible to make. People spending more than a few days in jail, who typically work in low-wage jobs, risk both losing those jobs and not finding new employment, particularly if they have a conviction or have supervision and programming obligations that interfere with work. This, in turn, increases their vulnerability to being incarcerated again. Although the use of incarceration for failure to pay a debt is unconstitutional absent evidence that a person willfully refuses to pay despite an ability to do so (and that alternative punitive measures are unavailable), guidelines are lacking for how judges should evaluate a defendant's ability to pay, resulting in both inconsistency in the application of this rule, and a risk that people are returned to custody simply for being poor.

Many jails may truly be, as Erving Goffman (1961) once wrote, the worst "total institutions"—places in which large numbers of people, cut off from the wider community for long periods, lead highly structured, formally administered routines—one can imagine existing in modern society. Overcrowded, noisy, and dangerous, they charge their inmates—some of whom have not been convicted of anything—for their housing, clothing, and numerous services, which can lead to insurmountable debt for inmates, a good portion of whom suffer from mental health problems along with being substance abusers. Clearly, the use of jails as America's new asylums and debtor's prisons raises ethical questions.

SUMMARY

This chapter has explored various ethical issues associated with institutional corrections—prisons and jails. I began the chapter by presenting to you the context of institutional corrections: who's incarcerated and the offenses that got them that way. I then devoted much of the rest of the chapter to addressing two areas of ethical concern: prisons *as* punishment and prisons *for* punishment. Prisons *as* punishment involve ethical issues such as who should be imprisoned and what standard might be used to make that determination, what do the undeserving deserve, privatization of prisons using for-profit companies, and abolition of prison as it currently exists. Prisons *for* punishment involve ethical issues surrounding the people who work in prison (and jails) and their duties. The two groups on which I focused included correctional officers (COs) and treatment staff (particularly correctional psychologists).

In examining ethical issues relating to COs, I first gave you a sense of how many of these practitioners work in the criminal justice system. I then provided you with information about the duties of COs and the skills they need. I also shared with you the fact that COs and police officers are typically recruited from similar groups of people and have similar minimum hiring requirements. COs also are influenced by an occupational culture, as was the case with police officers. The values and norms of that culture are then translated into different ways of carrying out the responsibilities and duties of COs, as shown in different types of officers. I also shared with you the fact that COs can look to the ACA Code of Ethics for guidance—that a different standard exists from that solely found in the CO occupational culture. I then discussed treatment staff and the fact they, too, have a code of ethics to help guide their professional behavior.

Following this, I shared some specific examples of ethical issues relating to the activities of COs and treatment staff. In the case of COs, their unethical or illegal behavior often arose from their supervisory responsibilities, with two of more commonly occurring forms of misconduct involving reciprocity and corruption. I also shared with you a classification scheme for officer misconduct and discussed the Lucifer Effect as one way to understand why good people do bad things. I ended that discussion by describing various efforts being undertaken in prison to respond to and prevent CO misconduct.

I then examined ethical issues associated with treatment staff, especially those involving correctional psychologists. Here, I discussed how issues relating to respecting the dignity of inmates, to responsible care, and to the integrity of relationships between staff and inmate manifest themselves in several ways, such as deciding who is the client, confidentiality of treatment information, refusal of services, competence in the care given, and keeping separate the different roles that treatment staff may play with the same inmate.

Finally, I shared information with you about jails in this country, and explored how their claimed misuse is turning them into asylums and debtors' prisons, the likes of which have not been seen in this country for over 200 years.

To conclude the chapter, I'd like for you to consider the ethics of an increasingly common—and controversial—practice in institutional corrections: solitary confinement of prison and jail inmates. After considering Thought Exercise 10.1, where do *you* stand?

THOUGHT EXERCISE 10.1

THE ETHICS OF SOLITARY CONFINEMENT

Consider the following scenario, which plays itself out daily in many of the nation's prisons:

> Imagine you live in a space that is 60 sq. ft. in size (about 10′ × 6′). The cell walls and floor are made of steel-reinforced concrete. You are not allowed to tack anything to the walls, not even a calendar. You are not allowed to purchase a radio or TV. The cell door is solid metal with a slot for a food tray, and two thin Plexiglas rectangles that allow officers to see in. Your entire life is confined within the four corners of this room. You eat sitting on the floor or on the bed. You sleep on a steel bunk along one wall, covered in a thin plastic mattress. You go to the bathroom in the toilet that's in the corner. Most days, your only contact with another human being is the hand that slides your food tray through the slit in the cell door. Weeks pass in which you never see another person's face or look another in the eye. You can only talk to people by shouting to them through the concrete walls. There is no window in your cell. Your field of vision is limited to peering through the Plexiglas slit in the cell door to the door of the cell opposite yours. You have not seen the stars in a decade. You struggle to fall asleep at night—you average about four hours, partly because the fluorescent light hanging from the ceiling remains on constantly. The cell block constantly echoes with screams because some of the men confined in neighboring cells have gone insane, cutting themselves or eating their own feces. The noise can be overwhelming. Prison regulations require that officers take you outside your cell for one hour a day, four days a week to exercise in a "recreation yard"—a space not much larger than your cell that is covered with bird droppings—where are, again, you are alone. Even though you want to better yourself, you are prohibited from attending counseling sessions, from classes, from any services other inmates can use
>
> —(adapted from American Civil Liberties Union of Texas, 2015, pp. 2–6).

Solitary confinement (SC) (also known as "isolation," "segregation," or "cellular confinement") occurs when inmates are held alone in a cell between 22.5 and 24 hours per day. They have no contact with the outside world or other prisoners, and limited contact with staff (Shalev, 2011).

In the late 1990s, with the advent of so-called "supermax" prisons—large, high-tech/high-security institutions designed for strict and prolonged isolation of prisoners deemed as high risk for escape and/or as difficult to control—growing debate has occurred about the legal and humanitarian concerns related to SC, including its use in managing prison inmates (Smith, 2016). Proponents claim that SC is a necessary tool in the continuum of placement options in institutional corrections, especially for inmates posing a threat to themselves or others (Igne-Bianchi, n.d.). Opponents of SC assert that it is one of the most restrictive, harsh, and stressful settings that an inmate can ever experience, and as a result its use violates basic human rights (Wiltz, 2016), and characterize the practice as "cruel and unusual punishment" because of objectionable conditions accompanying it (e.g., lack of windows, 24-hour lighting, minimal opportunities for exercise and recreation, restricted interpersonal contact, removal of privileges, denial of personal items, and limited therapeutic services) and its long-documented negative effects on inmate psychological and physical well-being (see Shalev, 2011).

During the 1800s, this country introduced the world to the use of SC during prolonged periods of incarceration. With the invention of the penitentiary in Philadelphia in the early 1800s, proponents believed they had uncovered the key to rehabilitating criminals: keep them in solitary confinement, where they were forced to think about and do "penance" for their wrongdoings. We were quite proud of our invention, as prison officials invited observers from Europe and elsewhere to visit and see first-hand the positive results of the penitentiary (Rothman, 1971). This system, originally labeled the "Pennsylvania System," involved almost exclusive reliance on SC during incarceration; it also became the predominant mode of incarceration, both for postconviction and pretrial detention, in several European prison systems that emulated the American model (Johnson, Finkel, & Cohen, 1994).

That the Pennsylvania System didn't survive all that long was because officials discovered that prolonged periods of SC literally drove inmates insane (Grassian, 2006). Typical psychological disturbances involved an inmate becoming agitated and confused, experiencing paranoia and auditory and visual hallucinations, and random, impulsive, often self-directed violence. These disturbances were frequently observed in inmates with no prior history of psychiatric disorders.

Over the past 25 years, as the use of SC increased in state and federal prisons as well as in local jails, a flood of litigation arose in both federal and state courts over whether SC constituted "cruel and unusual punishment" in violation of the 8th Amendment to the U.S. Constitution. According to a recent review of case law in the area, while the courts have recognized the damaging effects of prolonged SC, its use is considered both a legitimate and a constitutionally acceptable practice (Shalev, 2011). Further, when assessing the use of SC in particular cases, the courts have typically balanced the reasons for its use against its damaging effects and ruled that the reasons for its use outweigh the damage it causes (Shalev, 2011).

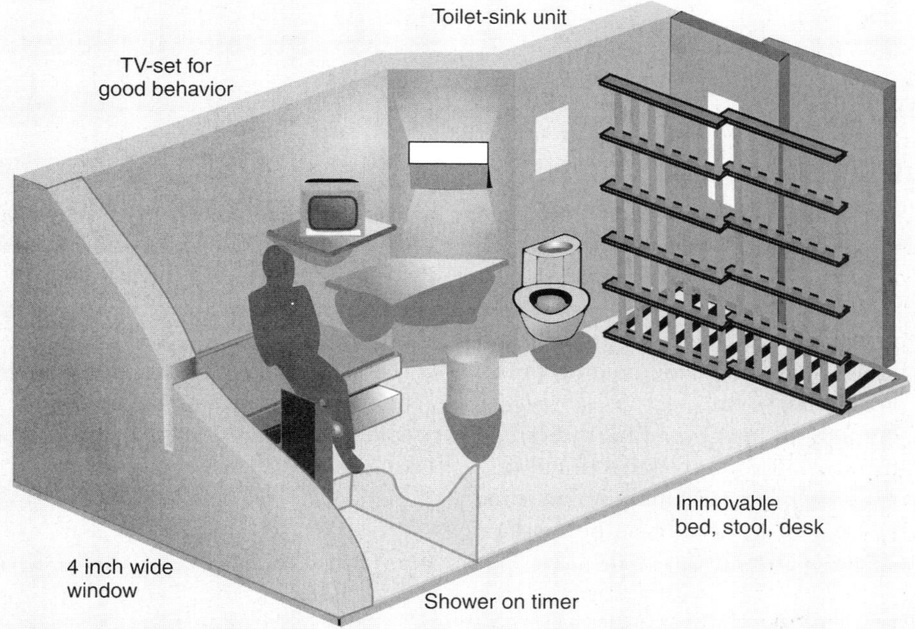

In an interesting analysis of the ethical foundations of existing federal appeals court opinions relating to SC, Heather Bersot and Bruce Arrigo (2010) found that principles tied to Utilitarian and Kantian ethics often informed the courts' decision-making. Specifically, the courts used an interest-balancing approach in which the needs of correctional administrators and the public were weighed against the rights of inmates. In other words, the legal opinions overwhelmingly weighed the greater good for the majority over the rights of the minority. Bersot and Arrigo (2010) also discovered that the courts' jurisprudence focused on their commitment to upholding a duty as outlined by Kantian ethics. In some cases, the court argued its duty was to defer to correctional administrators, while in others the bench argued its duty was to ensure preservation of the inmates' dignity as human beings, notwithstanding their being segregated both from society and/or from other prisoners.

Where do *you* stand on the use of SC? How would you justify its use based on any of the systems of ethics you've learned about to this point?

KEY TERMS

Crime control theology 282
No-frills prisons and jails 283
Prisons *as* punishment 287
Prisons *for* punishment 287
Penal austerity 289
Rule enforcers 294
Hard liners 294
People workers 294
Synthetic officers 295
Loners 295
Reciprocity 299
Prison corruption 300
Misuse of authority 300
Misfeasance 301
Malfeasance 301
Nonfeasance 301
Stanford Prison Experiment 301
Fundamental attribution error 302
Obedience to authority 302
Group conformity 302
Deindividuation 302
Bystander apathy 303
Jail churn 308

DISCUSSION QUESTIONS

1. Select several of your classmates and have a debate over the ethics of incarceration. Have each member of the group select a different system of ethics and present an argument either for or against incarceration using the guiding principles of that system.
2. Identify how much training is required in your state for new correctional officers (COs). Can the amount of training required of these officers be justified on *ethical* grounds? Explain.
3. If the entire criminal justice system can be justified on ethical grounds, is it possible for an ethical system to engage in unethical practices, such as incarceration? Discuss.
4. Using a specific system of ethics, develop an argument for or against the use of solitary confinement as a tool for controlling and/or managing inmates.

RESOURCES

For almost 150 years the **American Correctional Association** (ACA) has helped shape corrections in America. Its website is full of information about institutional and community-based corrections. The ACA also publishes the bi-monthly journal *Corrections Today*. http://www.aca.org/ACA_Prod_IMIS/ACA_Member/Home/ACA_Member/Home.aspx

Since 1981, the **American Jail Association** (AJA) has offered training for jail officials and local governments, and sponsored research on jail operations and issues. It publishes the bi-monthly trade journal *American Jails*, which, according to the AJA's website, "has the distinction of being the only [trade publication] geared solely to jail issues with articles covering both the American and foreign jail scenes." http://www.americanjail.org/

Philip Zimbardo is Professor Emeritus in the Department of Psychology at Stanford University and, for over 40 years, has been a leading scholar on the psychology of imprisonment. More recently, his attention turned to the psychology of evil and heroism in his bestseller *The Lucifer Effect* (2007). His TED talk in February of 2008 shared his insights into the Abu Ghraib scandal and is well worth watching. https://www.ted.com/talks/philip_zimbardo_on_the_psychology_of_evil

To learn more about the **Stanford Prison Experiment**, check out the 2015 docudrama of the same name. Emery, B. (Producer), & Alvarez, K. (Director). (2015). *The Stanford prison experiment* [Motion Picture]. United States: Abandon Pictures.

Another docudrama film I recommend that depicts the dehumanization that can occur in prison is ***Brubaker***, which stars Robert Redford as the warden of an Arkansas prison farm who faces major obstacles in his efforts to reform the facility. The 1980 film is closely based on the actual experiences of former prison warden Thomas Murton (1928–1990) who wrote about them in the 1969 book *Accomplices to the Crime: The Arkansas Prison Scandal* published by Grove Press. Murton also wrote the 1982 treatise *The Dilemma of Prison Reform*, published by Irvington Publications. An entry on his tenure as a warden in Arkansas is found in the online *Encyclopedia of Arkansas*. http://www.encyclopediaofarkansas.net/encyclopedia/entry-detail.aspx?entryID=7697

REFERENCES

Adams, R. (1994). *Prison riots in Britain and the USA* (2nd ed.). New York, NY: Macmillan.

Alexander, M. (2011). *The new Jim Crow*. New York, NY: The New Press.

American Civil Liberties Union of Texas (2015). *A solitary failure: The waste, cost and harm of solitary confinement in Texas*. Houston, TX: ACLU Texas.

American Correctional Association (2017). ACA Code of Ethics. Retrieved from http://www.aca.org/ACA_Prod_IMIS/ACA_Member/About_Us/Code_of_Ethics/ACA_Member/AboutUs/Code_of_Ethics.aspx?hkey=61577ed2-c0c3-4529-bc01-36a248f79eba

Bersot, H., & Arrigo, B. (2010). Inmate mental health, solitary confinement, and cruel and unusual punishment: An ethical and justice policy inquiry. *Journal of Theoretical and Philosophical Criminology, 1*, 1–82.

Bonta, J., & Andrews, D. (2007). *Risk-need-responsivity model for offender assessment and rehabilitation*. Ottawa, Canada: Public Safety Canada.

Bureau of Justice Statistics (2017). *Reentry trends in the U.S.* Retrieved from https://www.bjs.gov/content/reentry/releases.cfm

Carson, E., & Anderson, E. (2016). *Prisoners in 2015*. Washington, DC: Bureau of Justice Statistics. Retrieved from https://www.bjs.gov/content/pub/pdf/p15.pdf

Center for the Advancement of Public Integrity (2016). *Prison corruption*. New York, NY: Center for the Advancement of Public Integrity.

Clear, T., Rose, D., Waring, E., & Scully, K. (2003). Coercive mobility and crime: A preliminary examination of concentrated incarceration and social disorganization. *Justice Quarterly, 20*, 33–64.

Cook, S. (2012, May 15). Deindividuation. *Revise Psychology*. Retrieved from https://revisepsychology.wordpress.com/2012/05/15/2-deindividuation/

CoreCivic (2017). The CCA story. Retrieved from http://www.cca.com/our-history

Cullen, F., & Gilbert, K. (2015). *Reaffirming rehabilitation* (2nd ed.). New York, NY: Routledge.

Ditmann, M. (2004). What makes good people do bad things? *Monitor on Psychology*. Retrieved from http://www.apa.org/monitor/oct04/goodbad.aspx

Farkas, M. (2000). A typology of COs. *International Journal of Offender Therapy and Comparative Criminology, 44*, 431–449.

Farkas, M., & Manning, P. (1997). The occupational culture of corrections and police officers. *Journal of Crime and Justice, 20*, 51–68.

Finn, P. (1996). No-frills prisons and jails: A movement in flux. *Federal Probation, 60*, 35–44.

Florida Department of Corrections (n.d.). Correctional officer careers: Examples of duties and responsibilities. Retrieved from http://fldocjobs.com/paths/co/duties.html

Foster, L. (2017). Injustice under law: Perpetuating and criminalizing poverty through the courts. *Georgia State University Law Review, 33*, 695–724.

Fox, H. (2015, July 21). Eight skills of successful COs. *CorrectionsOne*. Retrieved from https://www.correctionsone.com/corrections/articles/8685690-8-skills-of-successful-correctional-officers/

Garland, D. (2013). Penality and the penal state. *Criminology, 51*, 475–517.

Gibbons, J., & Katzenbach, N. (2006). *Confronting confinement*. New York, NY: Vera Institute.

Gilson, D. (2016). What we know about violence in America's prisons. *Mother Jones*. Retrieved from http://www.motherjones.com/politics/2016/06/attacks-and-assaults behind-bars-cca-private-prisons/

Goffman, E. (1961). *Asylums*. New York, NY: Doubleday.

Gottfredson, S., & Gottfredson, D. (1994). Behavioral prediction and the problem of incapacitation. *Criminology, 32*, 441–474.

Grassian, S. (2006). Psychiatric effects of solitary confinement. *Washington University Journal of Law & Policy*, 22, 325–385.

Griffin, M., & Hepburn, J. (2005). Side bets and reciprocity as determinants of organizational commitment among COs. *Journal of Criminal Justice, 33*, 611–625.

Haag, A. (2006). Ethical dilemmas faced by correctional psychologists in Canada. *Criminal Justice & Behavior, 33*, 93–109.

Hare, B., & Rose, L. (2016, September 26). Pop. 17,049: Welcome to America's largest jail. CNN. Retrieved from http://www.cnn.com/2016/09/22/us/lisa-ling-this-is-life-la-county-jail-by-the-numbers/index.html

Henrichson, C., & Delaney, R. (2012). *The price of prisons*. New York, NY: Vera Institute.

Human Rights Resource Center (2017). Human rights here and now. Retrieved from http://hrlibrary.umn.edu/edumat/hreduseries/hereandnow/Part-5/8_udhr-abbr.htm

Hunter, G. (2007, February 15). Correct Rx a new major player in the prison drug industry. *Prison Legal News*. Retrieved from https://www.prisonlegalnews.org/news/2007/feb/15/correct-rx-a-new-major-player-in-the-prison-drug-industry/

Igne-Bianchi, J. (n.d.). In the hold: Is solitary confinement justifiable? Kenan Center for Ethics at Duke University. Retrieved from http://kenan.ethics.duke.edu/teamkenan/encompass/ current-issue/e14-in-the-hole-is-solitary-confinement-justifiable/

International Association for Correctional and Forensic Psychology (2010). Standards for psychology services in jails, prisons, correctional facilities, and agencies. *Criminal Justice & Behavior, 37*, 749–808.

Irwin, J. (2013). *The jail: Managing the underclass in American society*. Berkeley, CA: University of California Press.

Irwin, J., & Owen, B. (2004). *The warehouse prison*. New York, NY: Oxford University Press.

Johnson, N., Finkel, K., & Cohen, J. (1994). *Eastern state penitentiary: Crucible of good intentions*. Philadelphia, PA: Philadelphia Museum of Art.

Keim, B. (2013, July 10). The horrible psychology of solitary confinement. *Wired*. Retrieved from https://www.wired.com/2013/07/solitary-confinement-2/

Kleinig, J. (2008). *Ethics and criminal justice*. New York, NY: Oxford University Press.

MacKenzie, D. (2000). Evidence-based corrections: Identifying what works.*Crime & Delinquency, 46*, 457–471.

McCarthy, B. (2015). Keeping an eye on the keeper. In M. Braswell, B. McCarthy, & B. McCarthy (Eds.), *Justice, Crime & Ethics* (8th ed.) (pp. 277–296). Cincinnati, OH:Anderson.

McLeod, A. (2015). Prison abolition and grounded justice. *UCLA Law Review, 62*, 1156–1239.

Milgram, S. (1974). *Obedience to authority: An experimental view*. New York, NY: Harper Collins.

Minton, T., & Zeng, Z. (2016). *Jail inmates in 2015*. Washington, DC: Bureau of Justice Statistics. Retrieved from https://www.bjs.gov/content/pub/pdf/ji15.pdf

Merriam-Webster (2017). As. Retrieved from https://www.merriam-webster.com/dictionary/as

Morris, N., & Rothman, D. (Eds.) (1998). *The Oxford history of the prison*. New York, NY: Oxford University Press.

Packer, H. (1964). Two models of the criminal process. *University of Pennsylvania Law Review, 113*, 1–68.

Ren, L., Zhao, J., & Lovrich, N.(2008). Liberal vs. conservative policies on crime: What is the comparative track-record during the 1990s? *Journal of Criminal Justice, 36*, 316–325.

Roberto, G., & Francesco, D. (2012). Deterrent effects of imprisonment. Retrieved from https://halshs.archives-ouvertes.fr/hal-01073676/document

Rothman, D. (1971). *The discovery of the asylum; Social order and disorder in the new republic*. New York, NY: Little,Brown.

Ruddell, R., Decker, S., & Egley, A. (2006). Gang interventions in jails. *Criminal Justice Review, 31*, 33–46.

Scull, A. (1977). *Decarceration*. Englewood Cliffs, NJ: Prentice Hall.

Selman, D., & Leighton, P. (2010). *Punishment for sale*. New York, NY: Rowman & Littlefield.

Shalev, S. (2011). Solitary confinement and supermax prisons: A human rights and ethical analysis. *Journal of Forensic Psychology Practice, 11*, 151–183.

Simon, J. (2007). *Governing through crime*. New York, NY: Oxford University Press.

Simonds, L., & Wright, K. (2016). Private prisons. In K. Kerley (Ed.), *The encyclopedia of corrections* (pp. 345–353). New York, NY: John Wiley and Sons.

Smith, P. (2016). Toward an understanding of "what works" in segregation: Implementing correctional programming and re-entry-focused services in restrictive housing units. In N. Rodriquez (Ed.), *Restrictive housing in the U.S.: Issues, challenges, and future directions* (pp. 331–366). Washington, DC: National Institute of Justice.

Souryal, S. (2009). Deterring corruption by prison personnel. *The Prison Journal, 89*, 21–45.

Speri, A. (2016, August 14). Deadly heat in U.S. prisons is killing inmates and spawning lawsuits. *The Intercept*. Retrieved from https://theintercept.com/2016/08/24/deadly-heat-in-u-s-prisons-is-killing-inmates-and-spawning-lawsuits/

Stephan, J. (2008). *Census of state and federal correctional facilities, 2005*. Washington, DC: Bureau of Justice Statistics. Retrieved from https://www.bjs.gov/content/pub/pdf/csfcf05.pdf

Subramanian, R., Delany, R., Roberts, S.,Fishman, N., & McGarry, P. (2015). *Incarceration's front door: The misuse of jails in America*. New York, NY: Vera Institute.

Sykes, G. (1958). *The society of captives*. Princeton, NJ: Princeton University Press.

United Nations (2017). *Universal declaration of human rights*. Retrieved from http://www.un.org/en/universal-declaration-human-rights/index.html

Wacquant, L. (2001). Deadly symbiosis: When prison and ghetto meet and mesh. *Punishment and Society, 3*, 95–133.

Wagner, P. (2015, August 14). Jails matter. But who is listening? Retrieved from https://www.prisonpolicy.org/blog/2015/08/14/jailsmatter/

Wagner, P., & Rabuy, B. (2017). *Mass incarceration*. Northampton, MA: The Prison Policy Initiative. Retrieved from https://www.prisonpolicy.org/reports/pie2017.html

Walker, S. (2015). *Sense and nonsense about crime, drugs, and communities* (8th ed.). Belmont, CA: Wadsworth.

Weiss, R. (2001). Repatriating low- wage work: The political economy of prison labor reprivatization in the postindustrial United States. *Criminology, 39*, 253–292.

Wheeler, L. (2017, July 28). Federal prisons want to increase use of restraints. *The Hill*. Retrieved from http://thehill.com/regulation/343762-federal-prisons-want-to-increase-use-of-restraints

Whitbourne, S. (2013, July 20). The rarely told true story of Zimbardo's prison experiment. *Psychology Today*. Retrieved from https://www.psychologytoday.com/blog/fulfillment-any-age/201307/the-rarely-told-true-story-zimbardo-s-prison-experiment

Wilson, M. (2011, February 15). New epidemic: Contraband cell phones in prison cells. *Prison*

Legal News. Retrieved from https://www.prisonlegalnews.org/news/2011/feb/15/new-epidemic-contraband-cell-phones-in-prison-cells/

Wiltz, T. (2016, November 21). Is solitary confinement on the way out? *Stateline*. Retrieved from http://www.pewtrusts.org/en/research-and-analysis/blogs/stateline/2016/11/21/is-solitary-confinement-on-the-way-out

Woolley, K. (2015). After a guilty verdict. Retrieved from http://slideplayer.com/slide/4170444/

Zheng, Z. (2018). *Jail inmates in 2016*. Washington, DC: Bureau of Justice Statistics. Retrieved from https://www.bjs.gov/content/pub/pdf/ji16.pdf

Zimbardo, P. (2007). *The Lucifer effect*. New York, NY: Random House.

Zimbardo, P. G., Haney, C., Banks, W. C., & Jaffe, D. (1972). *Stanford prison experiment: A simulation study of the psychology of imprisonment*. Stanford, CA: Philip G. Zimbardo, Inc.

CHAPTER 11

Ethics and Community-Based Corrections

Chapter Outline

CHAPTER LEARNING OBJECTIVES:

1. Distinguish the three pillars of community-based corrections.
2. Compare the development and purpose(s) of probation, parole, and intermediate sanctions in this country.
3. Contrast the administration of probation and parole.
4. Explain the purpose(s) of intermediate sanctions.
5. Describe the characteristics of probation/parole officers and their training.
6. Explain the importance of ethical standards for probation/parole officers.
7. Describe the duality of the role of probation/parole officer and its ethical implications for supervising offenders.
8. Explain why acceptable penal content is an ethical issue in community-based corrections.
9. Distinguish caseloads from workloads of probation/parole officers and the ethical implications of each.
10. Describe why arming probation/parole officers is an ethical issue.
11. Identify the ethical issues associated with offender-funded corrections and for-profit privatization of community-based corrections.
12. Identify the ethical issues associated with electronic monitoring.

INTRODUCTION

Ripley County, IN (pop. 28,568 in 2010), a rural area in the southeast corner of the state, has boasted a recent success: its community corrections program (Raver, 2016). Initiated in August of 2015 as an alternative to imprisonment for select, nonviolent offenders who "need more than probation," the program includes house arrest with home detention; an intensive outpatient drug treatment program that meets twice weekly run by a certified drug treatment counselor; community service; and an alcohol treatment program called "Soberlink" that includes "breathalyzers on demand" for some offenders. The program employs two probation officers, one of whom is the program coordinator and the other is the "field officer" who monitors 27 offenders, the maximum the program can enroll. No local taxpayer money is earmarked for the program—it is funded primarily by a $170,000 grant from the State of Indiana that must be reapplied for every two years. Additional funding comes from fees charged to enrollees in the program. According to Ripley County Superior Court judge Jeff Sharp and District Attorney Ric Hertel, the program is a "collaborative undertaking that brought together county prosecutors and judges, along with probation personnel, the sheriff's department, and an advisory board, all of whom are vested in the program" (Raver, 2016, p. 1).

As you saw in Ch. 9, at sentencing, judges have a range of sanctions they can impose on offenders. Prior to the 1970s, however, judges were limited in their sentencing decisions to incarceration—prison or jail—and conditional freedom for offenders (probation) that allowed them to remain in the community provided they followed a set of rules. Beginning in the 1970s state legislatures (and later, Congress) adopted new sentencing provisions that allowed for the attachment of additional sanctions to probation and parole agreements. These additional punishments are known as *intermediate sanctions* and include, among others, house arrest, electronic monitoring, residential treatment programs (for drug-addicted offenders), and "boot camps" for juveniles. Proponents of intermediate sanctions argued that they offered judges punishments that provided varying levels of restriction on offenders' liberty (to protect community safety), while also affording opportunities for offenders to be rehabilitated (Morgan, 2016). The point was to change the traditional "probation vs. prison" dichotomy by giving sentencing judges options that would not involve incarceration, but nonetheless would restrict offenders' freedom. Not only would these options offer proportionate sanctions to offenders based on the seriousness of the conviction offense, they would also help to save money by keeping offenders in the community. Over time, intermediate sanctions, along with probation and parole, came to be lumped together into what scholars dubbed *community-based corrections* (CBC) (Abadinsky, 2018; Alarid, 2017; Morgan, 2016). This chapter concerns itself with ethical issues associated with CBC and its practice.

I begin the chapter by briefly reviewing CBC and its pillars of probation, parole, and intermediate sanctions to give you context for the chapter's discussion of ethical issues in community corrections. I then turn my attention to the practitioners of CBC— probation and parole officers (PPOs). Here, as I did for police officers and corrections officers, I examine the hiring and training of these officials, their occupational culture, and the role conflict PPOs confront as they enforce probation/parole agreements and serve as treatment facilitators. I also explore ethical standards for PPOs. I then turn my attention to ethical issues surrounding CBC, including whether CBC-related programs constitute ethically acceptable penal sanctions; PPO caseloads and workloads; arming PPOs; offender-funded corrections; and for-profit privatization of CBC. I conclude the chapter by considering the ethics of the electronic monitoring of offenders, a commonly used "tool" in community corrections.

AN OVERVIEW OF COMMUNITY-BASED CORRECTIONS

Community-based corrections is an umbrella term referring to options available to judges at sentencing designed to both punish and rehabilitate offenders while allowing them to remain in the community (Alarid, 2017). The theory behind CBC is that *most* offenders can be held accountable for their crimes without incarcerating them. Practically speaking, community-based sanctions confer benefits on both offenders and communities (Abadinsky, 2018; Alarid, 2017). By remaining in the community, offenders maintain legitimate employment; continue paying taxes; meet child support obligations; compensate victims and community through restitution and community service; and are shielded from the violence and victimization found in prisons and jails. While some CBC options occur pre-adjudication, most are imposed after a defendant has either pled guilty or been found guilty at trial (Morgan, 2016; my focus in this chapter is with post-adjudication CBC). Regardless of when imposed, CBC-related sanctions exist on a continuum of restricting offenders' freedom (see Figure 11.1), ranging from unsupervised probation to residential programs like juvenile boot camps.

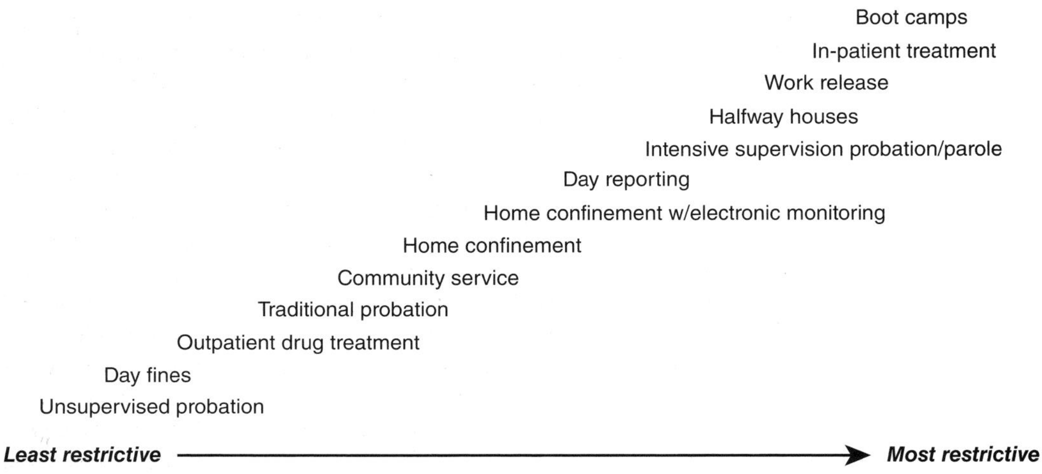

Boot camps
In-patient treatment
Work release
Halfway houses
Intensive supervision probation/parole
Day reporting
Home confinement w/electronic monitoring
Home confinement
Community service
Traditional probation
Outpatient drug treatment
Day fines
Unsupervised probation

Least restrictive → ***Most restrictive***

FIGURE 11.1 Continuum of Restrictiveness in CBC Programs
Source: Alarid (2017)

As mentioned above, the three pillars of community-based corrections include **probation**—a court-approved agreement allowing offenders to remain in the community provided they follow certain conditions; **parole**—state-sanctioned, early release of imprisoned inmates provided they follow certain conditions; and **intermediate sanctions**—a continuum of criminal punishments that extend beyond traditional probation but do not involve incarceration for certain offenders (see Table 11.1). In this section, I provide you with an overview of the pillars as they constitute the organizational backdrop for CBC and the ethical issues associated with it.

Probation: Its History and Administration

Even with the mass incarceration boom of the past 40 years, probation remains the most common court-imposed criminal sanction for felony offenders in this country. Probation has a long history dating back to 16th-century English courts' use of the **judicial reprieve**—a temporary suspension of an offender's sentence to appeal it to the Crown and seek a pardon. Envisioned as a temporary postponement of a sentence and the

TABLE 11.1 The Pillars of Community-Based Correctional Programs

Program	Characteristics
Probation	Court-enforced agreement between offender and jurisdiction that allows offender to remain in community in exchange for meeting certain general and specific conditions; available at the federal, state, county, and municipal levels of government
Parole	Early release from prison after offender serves a portion of her sentence; supervised and conditional; available in 34 states but not at the federal level
Intermediate Sanctions	A continuum of criminal sanctions that extend beyond traditional probation but do not involve imprisonment; exist at federal, state, and local level; available for both juveniles and adults

Sources: Adapted from Layton, McFarland, & Kincaid (2010); Mackenzie, Gover, Armstrong, & Mitchell (2001)

punishment associated with it, judicial reprieve became what we now know as a suspended sentence—the court never actually imposes the sentence and accompanying punishment on an offender. Judicial reprieve made its way to America during the late 1800s, and in 1916 the U.S. Supreme Court, in the case *ex parte United States* (242 U.S. 27), ruled that federal judges did not have the authority to suspend sentences, but through legislation, Congress could authorize judges to suspend sentences temporarily or indefinitely. This case set a precedent for creating probation statutes across the country.

As it is understood today, probation is an American invention that began with the work of John Augustus (1785–1859) in Boston during the 1850s. He coined the term "probation" to describe a practice of bailing defendants from jail, followed by a period of supervised living in the community that included helping defendants find work. When defendants returned to court, Augustus would report to the judge on offenders' progress toward rehabilitation and recommend dispositions in the cases that judges accepted most of the time. Over a 15-year period, Augustus is supposed to have bailed out and supervised over 1,900 defendants (Alarid, 2017). Enabling legislation for probation was first passed in Massachusetts in the late 1870s; the rest of the New England states followed suit. By 1920, probation was being used by the federal government and from there, it spread to the rest of the states (Abadinsky, 2018).

Probation is complex in its administration: it exists across levels of government (e.g., local, state, and federal) and is administered by both the executive (as a separate agency) and judicial (as part of the courts) branches. Its twin purposes of rehabilitation and protecting community safety remained stable over time; how those goals are achieved, however, has undergone sustained change as seen in different "models" of probation (see Alarid, 2017). The current model—"neighborhood-based supervision"—stresses zip-code-based supervision of offenders and establishing meaningful and professional relationships with them (Alarid, 2017).

Parole: Its History and Administration

As was the case with probation, parole—community-based supervision of previously imprisoned offenders released before completing their sentence—has a long history and has experienced flux in both its administration and its functions. The word "parole" is taken from the French term *parole d'honneur*, which means "word of honor" (although the French prefer the term "conditional liberation"—see Alarid, 2017). Parole's origins can be traced to late 18th-century France; it then spread to Spain, Germany, the United Kingdom, and finally to this country. In 1876, New York began the practice of early release with inmates incarcerated at the Elmira Reformatory (Abadinsky, 2018). Parole in the federal system was first implemented in 1910 and became formalized across the entire federal system in 1930, when it was brought under the control of the attorney general's office, before finally moving to the U.S. Department of Justice (Abadinsky, 2018; Alarid, 2017). Currently, a total of 34 states use parole; the federal government abolished parole in the 1980s.

Most of the 34 states that still use parole administer it from a centralized, state-level office that is part of the executive branch of government (Abadinsky, 2018). The **independent model** of parole administration involves a parole board responsible for making release and revocation determinations and for supervising persons released on parole. The other way parole is administered is under the **consolidated model**. Here, the parole board is an autonomous panel within a department that also administers correctional institutions (e.g., a state department of corrections) and is responsible for both parole release and parole revocation.

Parole occurs in one of two ways (Abadinsky, 2018). **Mandatory release** occurs when a legislature dictates that an inmate must be released from prison back into the community upon serving a predetermined amount of the sentence they received, minus time earned for good behavior (i.e., "good time" reduction in sentence length). Thus, mandatory parole is *automatic release* from prison based on legislative guidelines. The other way parole occurs is through **discretionary release** according to a recommendation given by a **parole board** (a panel of experts appointed by the governor to a specific term of years) who determines an offender has *earned the privilege* of early release into the community under the supervision of a parole (or probation) officer under certain stipulations or conditions.

Parole tends to be justified on four grounds (Alarid, 2017). First, parole encourages and rewards good behavior by inmates. What this means is that inmates know that by following the rules they can earn time shaved from their sentences. Second, parole allows for supervision of released inmates who would otherwise return to the community without resources and under no scrutiny. Third, the practice allows for the adoption of indeterminate sentencing, a crucial foundation of the rehabilitative ideal. Finally, proponents justify parole in practical terms: it reduces the rising costs of imprisonment by allowing early release of inmates.

The primary functions of parole include: (1) supervising parolees and enforcing the restrictions and controls placed on them by parole authorities; (2) providing to parolees the necessary services that help reintegrate them back into both the community and a noncriminal lifestyle; and (3) enhancing public confidence in, and the responsiveness of, parole services (Alarid, 2017). In recent years, a fourth function of parole has appeared: to control prison overcrowding (Alarid, 2017). What this means is that in the states still using it, parole serves as a "safety valve" to, or a "back door" for, relieving pressures placed on a correctional system's ability to deliver basic services to inmates because of prison overcrowding.

Intermediate Sanctions: History and Purpose

The final pillar of CBC includes intermediate sanctions, or criminal sanctions that "reduce the need for prison beds and provide a continuum of [punishment] that satisfies the . . . concern for proportionality in punishment" (Tonry & Lynch, 1996, p. 100). Beginning in the 1970s, corrections officials and policy makers realized that not every offender "deserved" imprisonment. They also realized that there were serious economic costs associated with imprisoning so many people, and these costs were negatively impacting state budgets. The problem was probation was the only alternative to imprisonment, and for many, such a sanction seemed inappropriate—it was "too lenient." The solution was finding a way to appropriately punish offenders without sending them to prison and presented itself when penal experts and policy makers developed new forms of criminal sanctions that included residential and nonresidential graduated sanctions, and economic- and restorative justice–based sanctions for offenders (see Table 11.2). Intermediate sanctions could be used with both probationers and parolees and, according to proponents, would reduce recidivism, lower correctional costs, and diminish pressures on correctional systems to produce more prison beds (Tonry & Lynch, 1996).

TABLE 11.2 Examples of Intermediate Sanctions

Sanction	Description
Intensive Supervision Probation/Parole (ISP)	More restrictive probation or parole for higher-risk offenders that includes intensive surveillance
Boot Camps	A type of residential program designed for high-risk young offenders that provides highly structured, military-like environment and activities that focus on discipline, physical labor, and education
Day Reporting Centers	Nonresidential placement that combines high levels of control with intensive delivery of services; Requires offenders to report to a specific location on a routine, prearranged basis
Home Confinement/House Arrest	Requires that offenders remain under curfew in their homes for a specified number of hours per day; May be allowed to leave for approved activities (e.g., work)
Electronic Monitoring	Mechanism for monitoring offender's location; Used with home confinement and other sanctions such as ISP
Fines	Financial penalties that require offender to make payments to the court
Restitution	Compensation for victim's financial, physical, or emotional losses
Community Service	Required, uncompensated labor by offender for a certain number of hours
Halfway Houses/Community Correctional Centers	Minimum-security residential facilities that provide offenders with housing, some treatment services, and access to community resources

Source: Adapted from Caputo (2004, pp. 11–12)

Research on intermediate sanctions indicates they were designed to serve two primary purposes: (1) reduce skyrocketing costs of corrections by diverting offenders from prison while simultaneously reducing prison overcrowding, and (2) create a continuum of criminal sanctions that meet the proportionality requirement at the core of the justice model of corrections (see Table 11.3; Abadinsky, 2018; Alarid, 2017; Caputo, 2004; Tonry, 1996; Tonry & Lynch, 1996). Intermediate sanctions save money and reduce prison overcrowding by diverting offenders into the community without sacrificing the deterrent or incapacitative effects of punishment. Sanctions like residential placement, intensive supervision probation (ISP), house arrest, and electronic monitoring provide almost as much supervision of offenders as that available in prison, at lower costs, some of which can be borne by offenders (Abadinksy, 2018).

Additionally, by diverting offenders from prison, overcrowding would be reduced. This would mitigate the need for judicial intervention and potential court orders mandating reductions in the number of incarcerated persons in any prison system (Tonry & Lynch, 1996). Finally, given the flexibility that intermediate sanctions provide to sentencing judges, their ability to tailor sentences commensurate with the seriousness of the harm caused by the offender (in conjunction with her prior record of offending) would meet the requirement of proportionality in criminal sanctions.

I've now provided you with a basic overview of CBC and its three pillars: probation, parole, and intermediate sanctions. My attention now turns to the practitioners involved with CBC. As I did with the police and correctional officers, I examine hiring and training of PPOs, ethical standards relating to the practice of probation and parole, and how those standards create ideals to which PPOs should aspire and obligations that accrue

TABLE 11.3 Purposes of Intermediate Sanctions

Purpose	Example
Restrict offender's behavior	Limit with whom offender may associate, ability to travel, ability to own firearms, driving privileges, use of alcohol; Direct surveillance; Electronic monitoring
Monetary/economic penalties	Restitution; Fines; Supervision fees; Court costs
Work-related measures	Community service; Gainful employment
Education-related measures	Enrollment in academic (e.g., GED) or vocational training programs
Treatment-related measures	Enrollment in substance abuse treatment program; Attend psychological/ psychiatric counseling; Attend outpatient treatment center
Physical confinement measures: Partial/Intermittent	Home confinement; Day reporting center; Halfway house; Intermittent incarceration (e.g., every third weekend spent in jail for specified period)
Physical confinement measures: Full/Continual	Boot camp; Home confinement; Residential treatment center; Halfway house

Source: Adapted from Caputo (2004, p. 5)

concerning the treatment of clients. Following that discussion, the remainder of the chapter is devoted to specific ethical issues that have arisen with CBC, especially those involving the twin pillars of probation and parole.

COMMUNITY CORRECTIONS OFFICERS

Probation and parole officers (PPOs) are the practitioners involved with community-based corrections (CBC) each day. It is they who supervise offenders, connect them with resources, and sanction those who violate the conditions of their community placement. PPOs—as you saw with police and correctional officers (COs)—are also committed to the "noble cause" of rehabilitating offenders while protecting the community from further victimization. And, like police and COs, they are subject to ethical standards and experience role conflict.

Characteristics of Probation/Parole Officers

Most people drawn to careers in CBC as PPOs desire to help people and protect the community (Deering, 2010). To a degree, PPOs possess values that revolve around a commitment to the "noble cause" of helping people and reducing the harmful effects of crime on the community—just as you saw with police and COs. Like their police and CO peers, PPOs are typically hired through civil service processes that stress merit in hiring decisions. In most instances, hiring requirements include candidates having at least a college degree, no criminal record, a satisfactory background (based on prehiring investigation), and American citizenship (Alarid, 2017). There may be additional requirements for getting hired, such as passing drug tests and/or polygraph examinations. Finally, those drawn to, and having successful careers in, CBC tend to possess certain characteristics (Alarid, 2017). For example, they tend to be confident people who possess high levels of integrity, are good managers of their time, and understand different cultures. They possess solid knowledge about human behavior and local programs and resources and know how to connect with them. They evidence good oral and written communication skills, build relationships with others, and establish rapport with them. Most important, they are able to treat people fairly, consistently, firmly, and with respect (Ireland & Berg, 2008).

Probation/Parole Officer Training

In general, PPOs undergo two types of training (Abadinsky, 2018). **Preservice training** occurs when PPOs are first hired and may take place in an academy-type setting, comparable to what occurs with police and COs. This training serves as the groundwork for helping PPOs understand the "nuts and bolts" of their job and its responsibilities. Typical preservice training for PPOs includes topics like legal issues encountered on the job; building relationships with clients; managing caseloads; protecting themselves; professional conduct and ethics; and various other topics (see Table 11.4). Preservice instruction may also include firearms training, as some 40 states and the federal government allow PPOs to be armed, especially those supervising adult clients (American Probation and Parole Association, 2006). On average, PPOs can expect to complete between 150 and 200 hours of preservice training before starting their position (Alarid, 2017). **In-service training** occurs annually, and is designed to keep PPOs abreast of developments in one or more areas relating to their jobs, such as changes in relevant laws, innovations in cultural competency or counseling, advances in brokering local resources for clients, etc. The American Correctional Association recommends 40 hours per year of in-service training for PPOs (Alarid, 2017).

Ethical Standards for Probation/Parole Officers

About 10% (12 hours) of preservice training for PPOs involves coursework and other activities relating to "professional conduct and ethics." "Professional conduct" refers to the *practice* of probation and parole—that is, strategies used by PPOs to supervise clients, connect them with resources, oversee their progress, and, if necessary, sanction them for violating the conditions of their probation or parole agreement. It also includes the *bureaucracy* of probation—the forms and files, case management systems, and other tools used daily. Finally, professional conduct relates to PPO responsibilities to the courts, including when PPOs are testifying.

The larger piece of professional conduct training relates to the *ethics* of the practice of CBC by PPOs. To give you an idea of the ethical context for CBC practitioners, let's look to the American Probation and Parole Association (APPA), an international professional association whose members are actively involved with CBC in both adult and juvenile justice, as well as the public and private sectors (American Probation and Parole Association, 2009a). APPA's mission is to "serve, challenge and empower members . . . by educating, communicating, and training; advocating and influencing; [and] acting as a resource and conduit for information, ideas and support . . ." (American Probation and Parole Association, 2009a).

Among other initiatives, APPA developed a code of ethics for members that provides a good overview of how CBC personnel *should* comport themselves (see Box 11.1). As you have seen with other such codes, the APPA code identifies a set of *ideals* to which PPOs should aspire, as well as outlining for them the obligations they accept as part of the practice of CBC. For example, the code identifies such ideals as "public service," "dignity," "inherent worth," "decorum," "cooperation and competence," and "dedication" as relevant to the practice of CBC. The code also identifies *obligations* PPOs have to

TABLE 11.4 Preservice Training for Probation/Parole Officers

Training Area	Hours
I. OVERVIEW	**4**
Overview of Community-Based Corrections	*4*
II. LEGAL ISSUES	**14**
Presentence Investigations and Reports	*4*
Technical Violations, Sanctions, Hearings	*4*
Search, Seizure, and Arrest Procedures	*6*
III. OFFICER–CLIENT RELATIONS	**38**
Understanding Offender Behavior	*4*
Cognitive-Behavioral Counseling	*6*
Crisis Intervention and Home Visits	*4*
Offenders with Drug Addictions, Mental Health Issues	*12*
Motivational Interviewing	*4*
Evidence-Based Practices	*4*
Community Resources	*2*
IV. CASE MANAGEMENT	**44**
Targeting Offender Risk and Needs	*8*
Treatment Plans and Offender Supervision	*20*
Parole/Probation Violations and Revocations	*6*
Report/Technical Writing	*10*
Targeting Offender Risk and Needs	*8*
V. DEFENSIVE PROTECTION	**18**
Controls, Restraints, Defensive Techniques	*8*
Verbal De-escalation	*10*
VI. PROFESSIONAL CONDUCT AND ETHICS	**20**
Scenario-Based Role Plays and Ethics	*12*
Courtroom Demeanor and Testifying	*8*
VII. OTHER	**12**
Drug/Alcohol Identification	2
Gang Identification	2
Employee Wellness/Stress Reduction	2
Written and Oral Exams	6
Total Hours of Training	**150**

Source: Alarid (2017)

themselves, the criminal justice system, their clients, the community at large, and the practice of CBC. Using the APPA code as a model, academy training in the ethics of CBC would provide PPOs with classroom-based as well as role-playing and other active learning strategies to impress upon PPOs the importance of ethical standards in the performance of their probation/parole duties. Ethics training could also be part of annual in-service training activities for PPOs.

BOX 11.1 Code of Ethics for Probation and Parole Officers

- I will render professional service to the justice system and the community at large in effecting the social adjustment of the offender.
- I will uphold the law with dignity, displaying an awareness of my responsibility to offenders while recognizing the right of the public to be safeguarded from criminal activity.
- I will strive to be objective in the performance of my duties, recognizing the inalienable rights of all persons, appreciating the inherent worth of the individual, and respecting those confidences which can be reposed in me.
- I will conduct my personal life with decorum, neither accepting nor granting favors in connection with my office.
- I will cooperate with my co-workers and related agencies and will continually strive to improve my professional competence through the seeking and sharing of knowledge and understanding.
- I will distinguish clearly, in public, between my statements and actions as an individual and as a representative of my profession.
- I will encourage policy, procedures and personnel practices, which will enable others to conduct themselves in accordance with the values, goals and objectives of the American Probation and Parole Association.
- I recognize my office as a symbol of public faith and I accept it as a public trust to be held.
- I will constantly strive to achieve these objectives and ideals, dedicating myself to my chosen profession.

Source: American Probation and Parole Association (2009b)

To this point, I have shown you the commonalities shared by PPOs and their colleagues in policing and institutional-based corrections in personal background and values, selection and hiring, and training. The final area of comparison involves the occupational culture of PPOs and that of police officers and COs. Once again, you will see commonalities in occupational values—and the impact of them on the behavior of PPOs.

The Occupational Culture of Probation/Parole Officers

Recall that all criminal justice practitioners—police, courts, corrections—are members of (at minimum) an *occupation*. Recall, too, that over time, occupations develop certain values and norms that provide continuity to members over time and "help them do their jobs." For example, in policing, much of the occupational culture revolved around the "noble cause" of policing—to protect the community by putting "bad guys" in jail, while among COs, much of the occupational culture focused on the "noble cause" of "keeping the 'bad guys' in and the world out." In both cases, certain dichotomies develop concerning the "proper" role of members. In policing, the dichotomy involved law enforcement versus service. In institutional corrections, the dichotomy involved security versus treatment. As you'll now see, there is also a certain dichotomy that has developed in the occupational culture of CBC: rule enforcement versus treatment on the part of PPOs.

Duality in the Role of Probation/Parole Officer

Since the 1950s, when systematic studies were first undertaken of PPOs, research has continually identified an ongoing duality in their role (Miller, 2015). On the one hand, PPOs have a duty to protect the community from further criminality. PPOs are thus entrusted with enforcing probation/parole agreements that allow clients to remain in the community, which means that in some instances PPOs will pursue revocation of a client's community placement. PPOs are thus **enforcers**. On the other hand, community placement also involves a treatment component (i.e., rehabilitation of the offender). Thus, the PPO is likewise bound to identify community resources (e.g., drug/alcohol treatment, education and job training, mental health counseling), link clients with these resources as necessary, and work with the client to change her behavior. They are thus **treatment enablers**. The problem becomes balancing the two.

In studies that have been conducted of how PPOs balance the duality of enforcement versus treatment, typologies of PPOs have been developed. These efforts have identified different "types" of PPOs, based on where on the continuum of enforcement and treatment the officer falls by way of practical emphasis. Implicit in this work is an assumption that such duality creates **role conflict** in PPOs as they switch from a pure enforcement mode in some instances to a treatment mode in others (Alarid, 2017).

Ethical Implications of PPO Duality

What do these findings mean for the *ethics* of the practice of probation and parole? First, one could argue that the ideals guiding probation and parole are changing as CBC moves toward more of a neighborhood-based model. No longer is the "noble cause" served by putting clients in jail (or returning them to prison) when they violate the conditions of their release into the community. Rather, the "noble cause" involves PPOs working to ensure that probationers and parolees are successful—they reintegrate back into the community, they do not reoffend, and they leave behind the people and contexts that created opportunities for them to do so (Miller, 2015). Second, as the guiding ideals of probation and parole change, so too do the obligations PPOs have toward their clients. Rather than having an obligation that overly stresses ensuring a client meets the conditions of probation or parole in the interests of community protection, the PPO is now obligated to help ensure that the client is *successful*—which, by extension, results in protecting the community (Miller, 2015). Finally, with these changes should come a reorientation of occupational values away from those stressing punishment, surveillance, and control, to those stressing human dignity, caring, and consistency in treatment (Miller, 2015).

In summary, PPOs share many of the same personal values as do police officers and COs, and their occupational culture stresses the "noble cause" of protecting the community and reducing the level of crime in it. You have also seen that members of all three groups face certain role conflicts that revolve around the duality of enforcement versus treatment. In the case of PPOs, the duality involves enforcing the conditions that govern release into the community while also helping rehabilitate offenders in their charge. For decades, research developed various typologies of PPOs based on how much they stressed enforcement over treatment. As probation/parole moves toward new models, ethics training for PPOs should adapt such that training stresses the ideals and obligations associated with these new models.

I have briefly touched on the ethical issues that accompany the duality of PPOs roles as enforcers and treatment enablers. But what are some of the ethical issues that involve CBC more broadly? I devote the remainder of the chapter to exploring those issues.

ETHICAL ISSUES IN COMMUNITY CORRECTIONS

When discussing CBC, you may be tempted to believe that because these sanctions do *not* involve imprisonment, there are no ethical issues surrounding them. The reality is because CBC-based programs involve deprivations suffered by offenders, they do raise ethical questions. This section examines several of the ethical issues with CBC sanctions, beginning with the content of CBC-related programs and whether that content can be ethically justified.

Acceptable Penal Content

Recall from the discussion in Ch. 9 about criminal punishment that it involves the state extracting from offenders valued commodities (e.g., liberty, economic resources, time, etc.). Recall also that criminal punishment can be ethically justified based on teleological, deontological, and virtue-based grounds. Further, as you saw in Ch. 10, prison—one type of criminal sanction—is supposed to be given *for* punishment, not *as* punishment. What many people don't realize is that CBC raises some of these same ethical issues. CBC-related programs involve both extracting valued commodities from offenders, as well as imposing deprivations on them. As penologist and legal scholar Andrew von Hirsch (1990, p. 163) observed, CBC "often involve substantial deprivations" that curtail freedom, exact forced labor, or inflict substantial economic loss on offenders.

Consider, for example, an offender sentenced to a term of home confinement (house arrest) with electronic monitoring (EM). This sanction effectively involves an offender being incarcerated in her own residence for some period, combined with enhanced surveillance of her movements through EM. In this case, potential benefits accrue to the state while the offender suffers certain deprivations. Beyond any crime-reducing effects of the sanction, the primary benefits accrued to the state are cost savings. First, the state avoids the costs of imprisoning the offender, which can run upward of $30,000 annually per inmate. Second, the state can also save money on the costs associated with EM if, as a condition of the sentence, the court requires the offender to pay for the equipment itself and/or the per-diem costs of using the equipment (e.g., an offender in Washington, DC, in 2014 paid a per diem of about $5.50 for the wristlet or anklet worn; see Development Services Group, 2014). Deprivation(s) suffered by the offender include loss of freedom and economic resources. The question then becomes whether these deprivations can be ethically justified.

In addressing that question, von Hirsch (1990) first worried that too often, policy makers and practitioners accept the "they *could* have gotten prison" argument to justify CBC programs that are highly intrusive, such as intensive supervision, EM, home confinement, boot camps, etc. The problem is that such an argument is off-point: what they could have received does not address the issue of whether what they actually received is ethically justified. Further, von Hirsch reminded us that offenders are still people, members of the "moral community," and should be treated as such. For von Hirsch (1990) the problem is this: on the one hand, an offender's status as a person rules out insulting or demeaning treatment. On the other hand, punishment itself not only includes deprivations but also conveys blame or censure to the offender for what she has done. The key, from the view of ethics, is striking a balance between ensuring the dignity of the offender is supported while still subjecting her to the deprivations that come with criminal punishment.

Von Hirsch (1990) has suggested that the answer involves determining what constitutes **acceptable penal content** of CBC programs, along with determining whether ancillary enforcement functions associated with the programs are acceptable. As described by von Hirsch (1990, p. 167), acceptable penal content is a sanction devised in such a way that its intended penal deprivations are administered in a manner consistent with an offender's dignity. Unless one is confident that this is the case, the sanction should not be allowed. Von Hirsch (1990) argued that certain kinds of CBC-based sanctions that include deprivations of property (if not impoverishing), compulsory labor (if served under humane conditions), community service (not including chain-gangs), and limitation of freedom of movement *are* acceptable because they do *not* impinge on offender dignity, while offering crime-reducing outcomes. Regiments intended to humble or make offenders feel ridiculous (e.g., DUI offenders required to plaster bumper stickers on their vehicles indicating their drinking habits) do *not* pass ethical muster.

Von Hirsch (1990, p. 168) also observed that ancillary enforcement functions relating to the conditions of probation or parole may include additional deprivations and, as a result, should also be scrutinized:

> Once we have specified the acceptable penal content of the sanction, we may also have to permit certain ancillary deprivations as necessary to carry the sanction out. Imprisonment, for example, involves maintaining congregate institutions and preventing escapes or attacks on other inmates and staff. Segregation of some violent or easily-victimized offenders for limited periods may be necessary for such purposes, even if not appropriate as part of the intended penal content in the first place. But these must be essential to maintaining the sanction.

To illustrate ancillary deprivations arising from enforcing a CBC program, von Hirsch used the example of random home visits undertaken by PPOs. He argued that such visits would not generally be acceptable penal content by observing that without any other need for them, the punishment for a given type of crime should not be that state agents periodically snoop around in an offender's residence. These visits *can* be ethically justified, however, as a mechanism by which PPOs enforce a primary sanction, such as community service, that meets the standard of acceptable penal content. Thus, if community service is acceptable, then using home visits to ensure attendance at work sites and/or to check on absences may be an acceptable part of the enforcement routine. But von Hirsch also cautioned that in this example, home visits can only be justified as an ancillary enforcement mechanism *if* they are limited in scope and no more intrusive than necessary to enforce the primary sanction (here, community service). For example, they should only occur when the offender fails to appear and be used to determine her location. For von Hirsch (1990, p. 169), "the less connected and the more intrusive [ancillary deprivations] become, the more they are suspect."

Finally, von Hirsch (1990) raised an interesting point about whether CBC-based sanctions interfere with the dignity of *third parties* and if this consideration should be raised when CBC-based sanctions are being imposed. Von Hirsch's concern was that "[n]oncustodial penalties reintroduce the . . . offender into settings in which others live their own existence. As a result, the offender's punishment spills over into the lives of others" (pp. 170–171). For example, home visits, EM, and intensive supervision affect not only the offender, but anyone else living with her—the residence is just as much theirs as it is the offender's. These people are being affected because they have a consensual relationship with the offender.

Von Hirsch (1990) offered guidance for how to reduce the impact of CBC-related sanctions on third parties by suggesting that (1) ancillary enforcement mechanisms used with them should not become a ruse for investigating whether third parties may be violating the law, and (2) when imposing CBC sanctions and several options are available for an offender, judges should choose the sanction that affects third parties the least. For example, if the choice in a case is between house arrest enforced by EM and a stiff schedule of community service enforced by home visits, if the judge concludes the home visits would be more disturbing for and intrusive into the lives of third parties, house arrest combined with EM would be the better option.

In summary, questions about the ethical acceptability of penal content are usually raised with prisons and the conditions of confinement found in them. However, such discussion is also relevant for CBC and its many programs. Some scholars have argued that acceptable content in CBC-related programs should only include sanctions whose deprivations (e.g., restraints on freedom, monetary costs for offenders) can be both devised and administered in a manner that does not demean an offender's dignity. Additionally, ancillary enforcement mechanisms associated with CBC programs must also be assessed in terms of how *they* impact on the dignity of offenders—the less connected and the more intrusive ancillary mechanisms become, the more they are suspect. Finally, because CBC-related sanctions can negatively affect the privacy and dignity of third parties, when multiple CBC-related options are available for an offender, judges should choose the sanction least likely to do so.

Let's now look at some specific ethical issues associated with CBC, including PPO caseloads and workloads, arming PPOs, CBC-related fees, and privatizing CBC.

Probation/Parole Officer Caseload and Workload

If the scope and content of CBC programs can be justified as ethically acceptable, what about actually *implementing* the programs? As you know, it is PPOs who work toward promoting community safety and offender rehabilitation through a balance of surveillance, treatment, control, and enforcement (DeMichelle & Payne, 2007). As you also probably know, not only do PPOs supervise many offenders (the PPO's **caseload**), they have multiple tasks to complete as part of the activities in which they engage (surveillance, treatment, and enforcement) and only so many working hours each day to do so (the PPO's **workload**) (DeMichelle & Payne, 2007). Thus, while a PPO's caseload may vary as changes occur in offender populations in the officer's jurisdiction, her workload remains relatively constant since it involves fixed time parameters (Jalbert, Rhodes, Kane, Clawson, Bogue, Flygare, Kling, & Guevara, 2011).

The ethical issue here relates to how caseloads and workloads impact a PPOs ability to fulfill her obligations of surveillance, treatment, and enforcement. In her recent study of PPOs, Faith Lutze (2014) concluded that (1) excessive caseloads and workloads resulted in PPOs being unable to properly monitor, engage, or record activities according to policy or offender needs; (2) large caseloads inhibited PPOs' ability to develop meaningful professional relationships with offenders and be proactive in addressing offenders' risks and needs; (3) excessive caseloads dramatically reduced the time PPOs had to engage with the community, something they were both expected to do, and enjoyed; and (4) PPO workload—especially administrative tasks—was directly tied to ever-changing agency (or state-level) policies. One of the PPOs that Lutze (2014, p. 122) interviewed nicely summarized how caseloads and workloads affected him:

> Reduce the caseload. If I could change that, then I could focus on doing a better job, focusing on people. Feel like they're not just a number passing through the system, because with so many people, you can hardly remember what their needs are. When they're in and out and, you know, you're dealing with 80 to 90 people; 10% you're dealing with full time because they are the problem, then when the other 90% comes up, it's like, "What was your name again?" So, I'd like to lower caseloads if that could ever be done.

What Lutze's research showed was that PPO caseloads and workloads are intertwined and permeated with challenges relating to administrative tasks, changing policies, and a desire by officers to have more meaningful contacts with offenders. In turn, overwhelming caseloads result in the neglect of crucial duties, inadequate supervision, and fear of liability when mistakes occur. Further, as their responsibilities shift, PPOs may be forced to devote greater time and attention to surveillance and enforcement and reduce efforts devoted to treatment. As a result, PPOs are unable to fulfill their obligation to help offenders change their behavior.

Years ago, a colleague of mine who had been a juvenile probation officer in Atlanta for several years told me flat-out that "we're setting them up to fail." What she meant was that for many reasons, most probationers and parolees should *reasonably be expected to fail*. This is not due to unwillingness to change (although for some, that's obviously true), but results from structural deficiencies in CBC organization and administration, especially deficiencies tied to PPO caseloads and workloads. This leads to an interesting question: Is it ethical to *knowingly* set offenders up to fail? Case Study 11.1 lets *you* be the judge. Use the template for analysis (see Ch. 5) and take a Kantian perspective (see Ch. 2) to guide your analysis.

Arming Probation/Parole Officers

According to results of a 2006 survey conducted by APPA, PPOs in 85 of 94 federal judicial districts were authorized to carry firearms (American Probation and Parole Association, 2006), while Alarid (2017) reported that at the state and county level, about one-half of all jurisdictions in this country *required* adult PPOs to carry firearms. Further, in jurisdictions where PPOs may be armed, probation/parole departments mandate that officers buy and maintain their firearms and related equipment (e.g., holster and ammunition) without reimbursement.

In most jurisdictions where PPOs are armed, they are authorized to carry a firearm *only* when they are on the job (but may carry when "off the clock" if they have a permit as a private citizen). In jurisdictions permitting PPOs to be armed, before being allowed to carry a firearm officers must first complete Peace Officer Standards Training (POST), which could mean as much as 500 additional hours of instruction at a police academy that includes proficiency in the use of their weapon (Alarid, 2017). Once trained, officers who carry firearms must then annually requalify in the proficiency of using their weapon (Alarid, 2017). Finally, policies concerning PPO use of firearms usually restrict officers to actually using their weapon in either self-defense or defense of a colleague (including police officers), or if the officer reasonably believes she or a colleague is in imminent

CASE STUDY 11.1 The PPO's Dilemma

Tiffany Lampe is a Senior Probation Officer (SPO) in Auckland County, MA, with a caseload of 55 offenders, ranging from those convicted on minor charges like public intoxication to eight parolees who have served time for offenses like burglary, auto theft, and robbery. Most (80%) of her clients have at least one prior felony conviction and about 40% have two or more prior felony convictions. A majority (75%) are men, and just over one-half of them (53%) are African American. A majority of her clients have substance abuse problems (either drugs, alcohol, or both), lack a high school diploma or GED, have spotty employment histories, and don't have much of a social support network.

She has recently been reviewing her "failures" during the past two years—that is, clients whose probation or parole had been revoked by the court for violating the conditions of their probation/parole—and was struck with a pattern. It seems the treatment services to which she had connected these clients were located on the other side of town from where they lived. On checking further, she found that most clients who'd failed did not have a valid driver's license, let alone own a car or have access to a ride. They were, instead, forced to use the public transportation system, long known for its dysfunctionality—routine break downs, not running on time, ever-rising fares, etc. She also found that only one or two of those whom she'd recommended for revocation had been arrested on a new charge. The rest had repeatedly violated the special conditions of their sentence, like working toward a GED, receiving outpatient drug/alcohol treatment, or getting job training and finding gainful employment, to the point where she had no choice but to recommend revocation. "Wait a minute," she muttered to herself. "let's see how these clients compare to my 'successes'" (that is, clients who'd completed all terms of their probation or parole and were released). Of course, she found exactly the opposite for those clients. The "successes" generally had fairly strong social support networks; had found stable housing; had routine access to transportation or lived relatively close to the agencies providing the services they needed. It then dawned on her that "the system" was setting up her clients to fail. She created a spreadsheet containing a representative sample of clients from the past 10 years and found the same general pattern concerning "successes" and "failures." "OK," she said to herself, "I'm taking this to the Chief" (meaning, the Chief Probation Officer [CPO] for the county).

A few days later, she meets with the CPO and shares with him the results of her analysis, including showing him a pin-map of where both groups of clients had lived and where most of the service providers were located. She had figured out, on average, clients lived about 10 miles from service providers and that a bus ride would take between 30 and 45 minutes to get there, depending on traffic and weather conditions. She also noted that bus fares over the period had risen 166% from \$.75 to \$2.00 (each way, in 2017 dollars). The CPO considered everything but was silent. "Don't you see, Chief? It's not them—it's US. We're setting them up to fail by not ensuring they have easier access to service providers and reliable transportation, and a strong support network. It's **OUR FAULT** they are failing." The CPO audibly sighed and said "You're right, Tiffany. I've known this for years. In fact, I've even done my own analysis of successes and failures and came to the same conclusion. It's our fault." Tiffany explodes, angrily shouting at him "YOU'VE KNOWN THIS FOR YEARS AND KEPT IT TO YOURSELF? HOW IS THAT POSSIBLE? WHAT WERE YOU THINKING?" The CPO sighs again and whispers "There's not really anything I *can* do about it." Angry and discouraged, Tiffany resigns.

Did Tiffany act ethically?

danger of death or serious bodily harm; PPOs may not discharge their weapon in the aid of third parties (Alarid, 2017).

What ethical issue(s) arise from arming PPOs? Some have argued that doing so fundamentally alters the role of PPOs to one that overemphasizes surveillance and enforcement, and diminishes the role of PPOs as agents of treatment, rehabilitation, and change (see Roscoe, Duffee, Rivera, & Smith, 2007). Thus, arming PPOs results in a shift in their obligations to clients and the public. Opponents also argue that with the arming of PPOs comes major liability issues for officers and agencies, not to mention having to develop policies relating to training, qualification, requalification, and use of weapons by officers (Alarid, 2017).

In response to these concerns, proponents of arming PPOs argue that protecting officer safety is becoming paramount as caseloads increase and include larger numbers of offenders convicted of serious crimes, combined with officers using home visits during evening hours or being involved with intensive supervision of offenders (Abadinsky, 2018). These shifts translate to officers having greater contact with more serious and potentially violent offenders and thus call for PPOs being armed while on duty. As one proponent of arming officers described it, "[B]etter to be judged by 12 than be carried by 6" (Brown, 1990, p. 23). What do *you* think? Is it ethical to arm PPOs?

Offender-Funded Corrections

If you recall, CBC—especially probation and intermediate sanctions—developed as an option to incarceration, especially imprisonment. In recent years, however, scholars have noted that as part of offenders' sentences, courts are now requiring them to also pay fees associated with CBC-related programs to help jurisdictions recoup at least some of the costs associated with running these programs (see Human Rights Watch, 2014). These fees—sometimes referred to as **court costs**—can be described as reimbursements imposed on offenders that are paid directly to the court to defray administrative costs associated with community correctional programs (American Probation and Parole Association, 2011). Fees, in turn, may be classified as *mandatory* or *discretionary* (see Table 11.5). **Mandatory fees** are imposed on *all* offenders receiving certain community-based sanctions (e.g., probation), while **discretionary fees** accrue only if specific services are used (e.g., DUI classes; drug testing; electronic monitoring).

Imposition of fees on offenders has become so common as to be described by observers as constituting **offender-funded corrections** (see Shapiro, 2014; Teague, 2016, 2011).

TABLE 11.5 Sample Fees Imposed on Offenders Sentenced to Community-Based Programs

Category	Examples	Cost
Mandatory	DNA sample	$100
	Attorney's fees (if client is not indigent)	$1,000–$5,000
Discretionary	Probation	$60–$75 month
	Radio frequency (RF) electronic monitoring	$20 month
	Global positioning system (GPS) electronic monitoring	$75 month
	Ignition interlock system	$60 month
	Antabuse (prescription medicine to prevent alcohol use)	$80 month
	DUI class	$35 per class
	CBC administration fee	$100 month
	Residential placement (e.g., halfway house)	$400 month
	Drug test	$10 per test
	Diagnostic testing (e.g., mental health, substance abuse)	$75 per test
	Outpatient treatment (e.g., substance abuse)	$40–$75 month

Source: Adapted from Alarid (2017, p. 242)

For example, Ruback and Bergstrom (2006) found that county-level probation departments, particularly those located in rural areas, rely more heavily on fees for operating revenue than do departments in urban counties (this is akin to law enforcement agencies relying on asset forfeitures to help fund their agencies; see Bernick, 2014). Additionally, in many areas probation departments (1) keep most of the fees they collect; (2) use collected fees as an incentive to collect more of them; and (3) include fee-collection rates as part of PPO annual evaluations (Peterson, 2012). Courts have even extended an offender's probation for nonpayment of fees (Alarid, 2017). These patterns have raised concerns on the part of scholars and practitioners alike that offender-funded corrections is turning PPOs into revenue-generating agents; offenders are becoming fearful of having their probation extended or revocation proceedings initiated for nonpayment of fees; and offenders who pay their fees in a timely fashion may either be released early from their probation sentence or, worse, have their probation extended, since they are providing revenue for the agency (Alarid, 2017).

Michael Teague (2016, 2011) has argued that charging offenders fees to support CBC raises two ethical questions: (1) Are they compatible with the overall philosophy of CBC? and (2) Do they impede successful conclusion of a term of supervision? Teague then argued that fees are both incompatible with CBC philosophy *and* they impede completion of supervision. For example, say an offender is faced with thousands of dollars in fees that accrued during an early period of supervision. Say also the offender has not found gainful employment, nor does she have a support system to which she can turn for help. Her PPO is after her to pay up; she soon realizes she is unable to do so. What's the solution? If the offender fears the PPO will pursue revocation for failure to pay the fees, the offender realistically doesn't have many options. They could, for example, avoid scheduled meetings with their PPO, which will likely result in the officer pursuing revocation. Or, they may decide to commit additional crimes to raise the funds. If they are caught, their PPO will immediately pursue revocation due to arrest for a new crime. So, what we have, in effect, is a price being placed on CBC that many offenders may not be able to pay (American Probation and Parole Association, 2011).

While Teague's arguments are insightful, other observers have argued that the central issue with offender-funded corrections is this: the longer it takes offenders to pay their debt, the longer they stay on supervision. The longer they remain on supervision, the more they end up paying in fees. In other words, the poorer the offender, the more they pay and the longer they must live with the threat of revocation hanging over their heads. This boils down to a basic question of *fairness*, as wealthier offenders can avoid these possibilities altogether (Human Rights Watch, 2014).

For-Profit Privatization of Community-Based Corrections

The final issue to share with you involving CBC is whether privatizing these programs through government contracts with for-profit corporations can be ethically justified (see Southern Poverty Law Center, 2016). Recall from Ch. 10 that private prisons, especially those run by for-profit corporations, have become both an ethical and a fiscal issue. Recall also that two ethical issues concerning privatization of prisons involving for-profit companies were that citizen expectations could change such that profitability became associated with imprisonment, and that the companies involved would oppose policies aimed at decarcerating offenders or reducing the use of prisons as a tool for punishing them.

Privatization of CBC-related programs involving for-profit companies is also occurring, especially in probation and parole service provision (Diller, 2010; Human Rights Watch, 2014; Southern Poverty Law Center, 2016). The attraction is this: moving to a private, for-profit service-delivery model costs governments next to nothing, since the companies involved assume responsibility for all service delivery—including offender supervision and fee collections. But can this movement be ethically justified?

Michael Nellis (2013) has explored the normative dimensions of CBC programs; that is, their "rightness" or "wrongness" in ethical terms. He has argued that even if CBC programs are ethical, the delivery of CBC-related services by for-profit companies constitutes an ethical issue worthy of its own discussion, reflection, and analysis. For example, Nellis (2013) argued it is both morally and politically desirable to continue developing (and implementing) alternatives to imprisonment for many types of offenders (e.g., low-risk petty or persistent offenders; those suffering mental health problems; and juveniles). One reason this is desirable is that these efforts align with those geared toward not only decarcerating offenders, but better matching rehabilitative programs and services with them. To that point, CBC privatization involving for-profits *could* help achieve those goals because private, for-profits would be incentivized to pursue the very innovations to which Nellis refers, and companies that developed such programs would be the "winners" and receive service-delivery contracts. By encouraging innovation and awarding contracts to companies able to provide relevant CBC-related programming, governments would thus fulfill their obligation to pursue alternatives to incarceration while enhancing efforts to rehabilitate offenders. Sounds good, yes?

In theory, this is true. However, both media accounts and scholarship on CBC-related programs indicate that the reality is much different. When a public function like corrections is privatized, the first thing that often occurs is that employees in the field are paid lower salaries and lose benefits (Nellis, 2013). In turn, private managers and executives receive a large share of the "savings" that accrue, not CBC workers. Take, for example, a recent analysis of privately operated prisons in Arizona that have been run by private, for-profit companies. It turns out that these facilities, in the long term, ended up costing *more* to operate than they did when they were run by the state (see Oppell, 2011). There are also issues of corruption that cloud privatization of government services. Consider the results of a 2017 U.S. Department of Justice Office of Inspector General audit of the first five years of a $697 million, 20-year contract by CoreCivic (formerly Corrections Corporation of America) to run a detention facility in Leavenworth, KS, for the U.S. Marshal's Service. The audit found that:

> [O]ne of CoreCivic's employee fringe benefits called the "sick account" contained excess funds that could be interpreted as "cash equivalents" that should have been paid to employees on a regular basis. Because CoreCivic's benefits administrator *withheld these funds for months or years* before disbursement to employees, *it is questionable whether the sick account is compliant with applicable labor standards for federal service contracts* . . . Core Civic also *improperly requested*—and the USMS improperly paid—*$103,271 in salaries and benefits for commissary positions not funded through the . . . contract*. These unallowable payments have a compounding effect over time because they are incorporated into each monthly invoice until the contract ended.
>
> — (emphasis added; U.S. Department of Justice Office of Inspector General, 2017)

Salaries that should have been paid; benefits that should have been disbursed; improper payments made to contractors; and lack of oversight are some of the potential pitfalls that come with governments contracting with private, for-profit, service providers for correctional services. While it is true that private providers can be fined by the state for not providing agreed-upon levels of service, or contracts may not be renewed if the company is underperforming, it does not seem reasonable to place additional oversight burdens on governments simply because of a (potentially mistaken) belief the private sector can "always do things better" than can government (Schnurer, 2015). Consider also that privatization of government services, let alone turning over such functions to for-profit companies, can leave governments open to the risk of damaging the entire public service enterprise that extends well beyond corrections and includes police and security services (Cohen & Eimicke, 2000). Along with encouraging innovation and lowering costs, privatizing CBC-related programming creates the possibility that ideals like concern for others, values such as "honor" and "justice," and the notion that those working in CBC are pursuing a secular calling could all be jeopardized in the name of profit (Cohen & Eimicke, 2000). Additionally, as Alarid (2017) has suggested, the need to provide *effective* correctional services often tends to be at odds with a profit-making agenda. Privatization—especially where for-profit companies are involved—both intrudes upon and competes with government's traditional, core responsibility to carry out punishment fairly (see Schnurer, 2015). Alarid (2017) also argued that the private sector is ill-equipped to offer the range of services necessary when caseloads involve relatively serious offenders and, as a result, may only be able to take on low-risk offenders requiring little, if any, monitoring.

An additional issue is the fact that private-sector service providers, including for-profit companies, may not have to demonstrate qualifications such as licensing and experience (depending on jurisdiction) and tend to lack uniform methods of monitoring probation conditions or ensuring that victim restitution is collected (see Schloss & Alarid, 2007). These companies may also circumvent statutory stipulations concerning minimum hiring requirements for employees, thus leading to the possibility their employees receive less training, have less opportunity for career advancement, and experience higher turnover than is true of public-sector staff involved with CBC. As a result, the specter is raised of private, for-profit service providers employing ill-trained and ill-committed PPOs who monitor offenders in a haphazard fashion. One can certainly argue that such a situation hardly fulfills the twin goals of CBC, which involve working to ensure offenders are rehabilitated while also protecting the community.

In conclusion, just as you saw with privatization of institutional corrections, privatization of CBC-related services, especially when for-profit companies are involved, creates ethical issues relating to oversight, damaging the entire public service enterprise that extends beyond CBC, circumventing minimum requirements for PPO hiring and training, and jeopardizing the twin goals of CBC to enhance rehabilitation efforts of offenders and protect the community from further criminality.

SUMMARY

This chapter has examined ethical issues involving the second prong of corrections in America, programs and services involving community-based corrections (CBC). I first presented you with an overview of the variety of programs and services that constitute

CBC. I then discussed the history, administration, and purpose of the three "pillars" of CBC—probation, parole, and intermediate sanctions. Following that discussion, I examined community-based correctional officers and the practice of CBC by discussing the characteristics and training of PPOs, along with ethical standards developed for them by the American Probation and Parole Association. What you learned was that PPOs evidence many of the same values as those possessed by police officers and correctional officers, values that involve the "noble cause" of helping people while also reducing crime. Ethical standards for PPOs, like those previously discussed for police officers and correctional officers, stress certain ideals and obligations intended to help PPOs not only do their jobs but do them ethically. I concluded that discussion by exploring the occupational culture of PPOs and the role conflict they face as both agents of change and rules enforcers. I showed how that role conflict, caused by conflicts between ideals to which PPOs are supposed to aspire and obligations they have to their clients, the community, and the courts, creates ethical issues for PPOs.

Following that discussion, I then shared with you five ethical issues relating to CBC more broadly, including whether the penal content of CBC-related programs is ethical; the ethical implications of PPO caseloads and workloads for larger ideals and the obligations they have; the ethics of arming PPOs; ethical issues arising from offender-funded corrections; and the ethical implications of privatizing CBC using for-profit companies.

To conclude the chapter, Thought Exercise 11.1 examines the ethics of one type of CBC program: electronic monitoring (EM). Where do *you* stand regarding the ethics of this sanction? Is it an ethical form of punishment?

THOUGHT EXERCISE 11.1

THE ETHICS OF ELECTRONIC MONITORING (EM)

Imagine for a moment that you are a probation or parole officer and that technology exists that allows you to monitor an offender's movements 24/7/365 in near real time because your client is wearing a device that broadcasts a signal to a base linked to a satellite that is orbiting thousands of miles above the Earth. The signal broadcasts the offender's latitude and longitude coordinates (which can then be translated into a specific address or location) that are tracked by the satellite. If the signal is interrupted for some reason or if the offender's location changes beyond whatever limits have been placed on her movements, you are notified by the monitoring agency and can take appropriate action.

You may be skeptical that such technology exists, but it does. More importantly, the technology is not only being used, its use is expanding. According to a report from the Pew Charitable Trusts published in 2016: (1) all 50 states, the District of Columbia, and the federal government use electronic devices to monitor the movements and activities of pretrial defendants or convicted offenders on probation or parole; (2) during 2015, about 131,000 defendants and offenders were being monitored using these devices; (3) about 2% of all offenders under some form of correctional supervision were being tracked via electronic monitoring (EM) in 2015; (4) between 2000 and 2015, the number of offender-tracking devices in use in the United States increased 140%; and (5) although some research suggests that EM reduces recidivism, expanded use of EM has occurred largely in the absence of demonstrable evidence that EM is an effective tool for different types of offenders at different stages of the criminal justice process (Fahy, Gelb, Gramlich, & Stevenson, 2016).

EM developed in the early 1980s in Florida and New Mexico, inspired by a Spiderman comic that appeared in the 1960s (Gable, 2007; Nellis, 2006). EM devices are typically ankle bracelets worn by offenders or smartphones equipped with EM technology that are carried on the person of offenders whose movements are restricted as a condition of probation or parole. For example, convicted sex offenders are typically barred from locations like schools or playgrounds, while those convicted of domestic violence crimes are prohibited from approaching their victims' homes or places of employment. When monitored offenders enter such exclusion zones, GPS devices alert supervising agencies, which can then act. Because EM allows tracking of the physical location of offenders, it is considered a restrictive intermediate sanction (Payne & Gainey, 2000).

The Ethics of Electronic Monitoring

In a recent paper published in the journal *Science and Engineering Ethics*, William Bulow (2014) identified six ethical issues associated with EM. The first is the potential harm EM could do to an offender, such as invite retaliation from co-defendants or their associates, or from vigilantes. Such harm would (at least in theory) be less likely to befall an offender who was imprisoned, which she might then choose if given the option. Such a choice defeats the whole purpose of intermediate sanctions and leads to questions about the legitimacy of EM as a CBC-related tool.

The second potential ethical problem with EM involves not *who* is designing and implementing EM—such as a private, for-profit company—but *how* EM is implemented. According to Bulow (2014) the issue is developing ethically sound conditions for using EM—an argument similarly made by von Hirsch (1990) while expressing his concerns over acceptable penal content in CBC.

The third ethical issue raised by Bulow is whether the overtly intrusive nature of EM can be ethically justified. Bulow (2014, p. 510) explains that the right to privacy, understood as the "right to limit and control access to information about oneself, one's personal thoughts, and one's body," is usually considered a *moral* right. From that perspective, any action or practice intruding into a person's privacy is morally permissible *if and only if* the benefits of the intrusion are sufficiently justifiable. The question then becomes, What is considered a "sufficient justification?" Answering this involves (1) identifying and justifying the purpose of the infringement and (2) determining whether acquiring information from the offender via EM is crucial to meeting the purpose of the sanction. Bulow suggested that if EM's purpose can be proven to be both rehabilitative and to protect community safety, EM can be justified as an infringement on privacy. He also suggested that insofar as EM only monitors information about an offender's whereabouts, it does not pose any great threat to one's privacy and neither does it pose a greater threat to privacy than would humane forms of imprisonment. As a result, he does not believe that EM is overly intrusive, nor that it is unethical.

A fourth ethical issue with EM that Bulow described is the risk of stigmatization of offenders. What Bulow is referring to here is the fact that wearing the EM device may reveal to others the fact the individual is an offender, which may result in both social disadvantages and social exclusion (Bulow, 2014). He also suggested this problem is solvable by making the device more discreet or embedding it in another device, such as a smartphone (which can be done).

The fifth concern with the ethics of EM Bulow raised is that EM is patently unfair. What Bulow is getting at here is that for punishment to be fair, there must be proportionality between the sanction and the crime committed. The problem is that not all offenders perceive EM in the same manner—some perceive it as "no big deal" while others are horribly shamed. These differing perceptions cause some individuals to be punished far more severely than is warranted, given their offense, while others feel they are not really being punished at all. If one compares the minimum severity of imprisonment, we can be reasonably assured it's the same for most imprisoned offenders. The same cannot be said of EM. Problematic here also is that EM allows punishment of those who previously were not punished at all; that is, EM has "widened the net." Bulow (2014) suggests these are difficult issues that involve culpability, desert, and decreased recidivism. He also observes that justice and fairness are important values and the use of EM should respect the constraints imposed by them.

The final ethical issue Bulow identified is whether EM is a morally permissible form of criminal sanction. The answer to this depends on what end is achieved by the punishment, which is, in turn, dependent on the normative theory of punishment advanced: consequentialist, retributivist, or virtue ethics. Regardless of which theory of punishment is chosen, it should be apparent that normative assumptions regarding the justification for and the targeted effect of punishment on offenders affects how EM programs ought to be developed (Bulow, 2014).

KEY TERMS

DISCUSSION QUESTIONS

1. Given the mixed history, administration, and purposes of probation and parole, can they be justified as ethical forms of punishment? Explain.
2. Imagine that you are a probation or parole officer. How would you resolve the role conflict seemingly inherent to the position and yet remain true to the ideals and obligations described by the APPA's ethical standards for probation and parole officers?
3. Can intermediate sanctions be ethically justified? Choose any system of ethics and subject that particular form of community-based corrections to scrutiny.
4. Increasingly, it appears that "cash-register justice," "offender-funded justice" and similar descriptions typify community-based corrections. If these descriptions are true, is the ethical legitimacy of community-based corrections in jeopardy? Explain why or why not.
5. Andrew von Hirsch's notion of *acceptable penal content* is very important to discussions about corrections in America. Why do you think that's the case? Explain.

RESOURCES

The **National Institute of Justice** (NIJ) maintains a website devoted to community-based corrections. Available from the site are reports, case studies, scholarly works, and other resources. Visit https://www.nij.gov/topics/corrections/community/Pages/welcome.aspx

The **National Institute of Corrections** (NIC) is an agency within the U.S. Department of Justice, Federal Bureau of Prisons. The Institute is headed by a director appointed by the U.S. attorney general and advised by a 16-member board, also appointed by the attorney general. According to the Institute's website, the NIC provides training, technical assistance, information services, and policy/program development to federal, state, and local corrections agencies. Visit the Institute's website at: https://nicic.gov/aboutus

The **American Probation and Parole Association** (APPA) is an international association composed of members from the United States, Canada, and other countries actively involved with pretrial, probation, parole, and community-based corrections, in both criminal and juvenile justice arenas. According to its website, APPA has become the voice for thousands of pretrial, probation, and parole practitioners and providers of services and provides training and technical assistance for its constituents and constituent partners. Visit them at: https://www.appanet.org/eweb/Start Page.aspx

REFERENCES

Abadinsky, H. (2018). *Probation and parole: Theory and practice* (13th ed.). New York, NY: Pearson.

Alarid, L. (2017). *Community-based corrections* (11th ed.). Boston, MA: Cengage Learning.

American Probation and Parole Association (2011). *Supervision fees.* Lexington, KY: American Probation and Parole Association.

American Probation and Parole Association (2009a). Introduction and mission. Retrieved from https://www.appa-net.org/eweb/DynamicPage.aspx?WebCode=IA_Introduction

American Probation and Parole Association (2009b). Code of ethics. Retrieved from https://www.appa-net.org/eweb/DynamicPage.aspx?WebCode=IA_CodeEthics

American Probation and Parole Association (2006). *American Probation and Parole Association adult and juvenile probation and parole national firearm survey* (2nd ed.). Retrieved from https://www.appa-net.org/eweb/Resources/Surveys/National_Firearms/docs/NFS_2006.pdf

Bernick, E. (2014). *Law enforcement's dependence on civil asset forfeiture in Georgia and Texas.* Washington, DC: Heritage Foundation.

Brown, P. (1990). Guns and probation officers. *Federal Probation, 54,* 21–27.

Bulow, W. (2014). Electronic monitoring of offenders: An ethical review. *Science & Engineering Ethics, 20,* 505–518.

Caputo, G. (2004). *Sanctions in corrections.* Denton, TX: University of North Texas Press.

Cohen, S., & Eimicke, W. (2000). Assuring public ethics in privatized public programs. Paper presented at the 61st Annual Meeting of the American Society of Public Administration, San Diego, California, April 1–4, 2000.

Deering, J. (2010). Attitudes and beliefs of trainee probation officers: A new breed? *Probation Journal, 57,* 9–26.

DeMichelle, M., & Payne, B. (2007). Probation and parole officers speak out: Caseload and workload allocation. *Federal Probation, 71,* 30–35

Development Services Group (2014). *Home confinement and electronic monitoring.* Washington, DC: Office of Juvenile Justice and Delinquency Prevention. Retrieved from https://www.ojjdp.gov/mpg/litreviews/Home_Confinement_EM.pdf

Diller, R. (2010). *The hidden costs of Florida's criminal justice fees.* New York, NY: Brennen Center for Justice.

Fahy, S., Gelb, A., Gramlich, J., & Stevenson, P. (2016, September). *Use of electronic offender-tracking devices expands sharply.* Washington, DC: The Pew Charitable Trusts.

Gable, R. (2007). Electronic monitoring of offenders: Can a wayward technology be redeemed? In Y. de Kort, W. Ijsselstein, C. Midden, B. Eggen, & B. Fogg (Eds.), *Persuasive technology* (pp. 100–104). Berlin, Germany: Springer.

Human Rights Watch (2014). *Profiting from probation: America's offender-funded probation industry.* Washington, DC: Human Rights Watch.

Ireland, C., & Berg, B. (2008). Women in parole: Respect and rapport. *International Journal of Offender Therapy and Comparative Criminology, 52,* 474–491.

Jalbert, S., Rhodes, W., Kane, M., Clawson, E., Bogue, B., Flygare, C., Kling, R., & Guevara, M. (2011). *A multi-site evaluation of reduced probation caseload size in an evidence-based practice setting.* Cambridge, MA: Abt Associates, Inc.

Layton, L., McFarland, D., & Kincaid, D. (2010). *An elected official's guide to community corrections options* (2nd ed.). Lexington, KY: Council on State Governments.

Lutze, F. (2014). *Professional lives of community corrections officers.* Thousand Oaks, CA: Sage Publications.

MacKenzie, D., Gover, A., Armstrong, G., & Mitchell, O. (2001). *A national study comparing the environments of boot camps with traditional facilities for juvenile offenders.* National Institute of Justice *Research in Brief,* NCJ 187680. Washington, DC: Office of Justice Programs, U.S. Department of Justice.

Miller, J. (2015). Contemporary modes of probation officer supervision: The triumph of the "synthetic" officer? *Justice Quarterly, 32,* 314–336.

Morgan, K. (2016). *Probation, parole, and community corrections work in theory and practice.* Durham, NC: Carolina Academic Press.

Nellis, M. (2013). Surveillance, stigma and spatial constraint: The ethical challenges of electronic monitoring. In M. Nellis, K. Bevens, & D. Kaminski (Eds.), *Electronically monitored punishment: International and critical Perspectives* (pp. 193–210). New York, NY: Routledge.

Nellis, M. (2006). The limitations of electronic monitoring. *Prison Service Journal, 164*, 3–12.

Oppell, R. (2011, May 16). Private prisons found to offer little in savings. *New York Times*. Retrieved from http://www.nytimes.com/2011/05/19/us/19prisons.html

Payne, B., & Gainey, R. (2000). Electronic monitoring: Philosophical, systemic, and political issues. *Journal of Offender Rehabilitation, 31*, 93–111.

Peterson, P. (2012). Supervision fees: State policies and practice. *Federal Probation, 76*, 40–45.

Raver, D. (2016, March 16). Community corrections program a success. *The Herald-Tribune*. Retrieved from http://www.batesvilleheraldtribune.com/news/local_news/community-corrections-program-a-success/article_0523d06c-f84c-5dea-ac80-4723c69f75f5.html

Roscoe, T., Duffee, D., Rivera, C., & Smith, T. (2007). Arming probation officers: Correlates of the decision to arm at the departmental level. *Criminal Justice Studies, 20*, 43–63.

Ruback, R., & Bergstrom, M. (2006). Economic sanctions in criminal justice: Purposes, effects, and implications. *Criminal Justice & Behavior, 33*, 242–273.

Schloss, C., & Alarid, L. (2007). Standards in the privatization of probation services. *Criminal Justice Review, 32*, 233–245.

Schnurer, E. (2015, March 11). When government competes against the private sector, everybody wins. *The Atlantic*. Retrieved from https://www.theatlantic.com/politics/archive/2015/03/when-government-competes-against-the-private-sector-everybody-wins/387460/

Shapiro, J. (2014, May 19). As court fees rise, the poor are paying the price. *All Things Considered*. Retrieved from http://www.npr.org/2014/05/19/312158516/increasing-court-fees-punish-the-poor

Southern Poverty Law Center (2016, December 13). Clanton residents settle lawsuit with private probation company. Retrieved from https://www.splcenter.org/news/2016/12/13/clanton-residents-settle-lawsuit-private-probation-company

Teague, M. (2016). Profiting from the poor: Offender-funded probation in the USA. *British Journal of Community Justice, 14*, 99–111.

Teague, M. (2011). Probation in America: Armed, private and unaffordable? *Probation Journal, 58*, 317–332.

Tonry, M. (1996). *Sentencing matters*. New York, NY: Oxford University Press.

Tonry, M., & Lynch, M. (1996). Intermediate sanctions. *Crime & Justice, 20*, 99–147.

U.S. Department of Justice Office of Inspector General (2017, April). *Office of the Inspector General U.S. Department of Justice Audit of the United States Marshals Service Contract No. DJJODT7C0002 with CoreCivic, Inc., to Operate the Leavenworth Detention Center Leavenworth, Kansas*. Washington, DC: U.S. Department of Justice.

von Hirsch, A. (1990). The ethics of community-based sanctions. *Crime & Delinquency, 36*, 162–173.

CHAPTER 12

Ethics and Forensic Science

Chapter Outline

CHAPTER LEARNING OBJECTIVES:

1. Explain what forensic science *is* and how it is organized.
2. Describe how forensic practitioners are hired and trained, and the value systems forensic practitioners tend to exhibit.
3. Identify the origins and purpose of the National Code of Professional Responsibility for Forensic Science and Forensic Medicine Service Providers.
4. Describe the ethical issues that are associated with forensic laboratory analytical procedures.
5. Explain the difference between science and law.
6. Identify the obligations of forensic practitioners to the larger field.
7. Describe whistleblowing in forensic science and provide examples of high-profile cases of whistleblowing.

INTRODUCTION

Consider the case of Han Tak Lee, 81, who spent 25 years in prison in Pennsylvania after he was convicted of murdering his daughter in an arson. In 2014, he was freed when his conviction was overturned after an appeals court ruled that the conviction was based on discredited theories of arson (see Balko, 2016). Or, take the case of Kirk Odom, who was released from prison in 2003 after serving 22 years for rape. In petitioning the court for Odom's release, the U.S. Attorney's Office for the District of Columbia indicated that DNA testing proved Odom was not the culprit and had been wrongfully convicted (see Cratty, 2012). Because of these cases and others highlighted in a series of stories on wrongful convictions that appeared in the *Washington Post* and the *New York Times* beginning in 2012, as well as pressures exerted by the Innocence Project in New York City, the U.S. Department of Justice in 2012 began what became a five-year review of thousands of criminal cases adjudicated in federal courts that involved FBI forensic experts to determine if defendants in them had been wrongly convicted as a result of those experts drawing conclusions unsupported by existing scientific techniques (Hsu, 2016).

Each day, in locations throughout this country, after police have responded to a call of a crime occurring and arrive on the scene, a process begins of searching that scene for evidence and collecting it. Some or all of the evidence recovered may then be submitted to one of more than 400 publicly operated crime laboratories in this country for various reasons, including to (1) identify and classify a substance, (2) determine a common or different origin of the evidence, (3) reconstruct the order of events and positions of those involved in the crime, and/or (4) compare an item of evidence (e.g., paint, glass, plastic, etc.) against a standard for purposes of identifying the item (Peterson, Sommers, Baskin, & Johnson, 2010). During calendar year 2014, the most recent year for which data are available, more than 4 million requests for evidence processing were submitted to these labs (Durose, Burch, Walsh, & Tiry, 2016). The evidence may then be used at trial as part of the state's efforts to convict defendants; that same evidence may also help undo those convictions.

This chapter examines ethical issues relating to forensic science—the application of science to legal issues arising in various forms of litigation (criminal, civil, and regulatory). In the chapter, I first provide you with an overview of what forensic science *is*, including the various disciplines that comprise it. Next, I discuss the hiring and training of forensic scientists, and examine the occupational culture of forensic science practitioners. Following this, I present an overview of standards and codes of ethics that exist for forensic laboratories and practitioners. I then examine specific examples of ethical issues and dilemmas that forensic scientists confront. I close the chapter by examining questions that have been raised about the legitimacy of certain forensic practices, and the ethical issues those questions have raised.

AN OVERVIEW OF FORENSIC SCIENCE AND ITS PRACTICE

Forensic science has been defined as "the application of scientific or technical practices to the recognition, collection, analysis, and interpretation of evidence in criminal, civil, or regulatory law proceedings" (President's Council of Advisors on Science and Technology, 2016, p. 1). It is most commonly used during two phases: (1) in police investigations to identify a likely perpetrator and (2) during the prosecution of specific individuals to help prove their guilt beyond reasonable doubt (Houck & Siegel, 2015). More recently, forensic science—especially DNA analysis—has also been used in postconviction challenges (Rittner, 2009).

The investigative and prosecutorial phases involve different standards for the use of forensic science (National Research Council, 2009). During investigation, relevant information can include that arising from well-established scientific knowledge as well as from exploratory approaches. During a prosecution, forensic evidence has to satisfy a more stringent legal standard. Many states and the federal courts, for example, require that forensic expert testimony be based on "reliable principles and methods . . . applied to the case" (President's Council of Advisors on Science and Technology, 2016, p. 21). Further, the Supreme Court ruled in the 1993 case of *Daubert v. Merrell Dow Pharmaceuticals* (509 U.S. 579) that judges are responsible for determining whether the reasoning or methodology underlying the forensic testimony is scientifically valid. It is during the prosecution phase that that important conflicts arise: judges decide the admissibility of scientific evidence based on *legal standards*, but the subject of the judge's inquiry is the *scientific validity* of the evidence/testimony, which is the province of the scientific community (Houck & Siegel, 2015).

The Disciplines of Forensic Science

The word "forensic" comes from the Latin *forensis*, meaning "to the forum or public discussion." A modern definition of forensic could be "relating to, used in, or suitable to a court of law" (Merriam-Webster, 2017). Thus, a forensic science is any science "used around the world to resolve civil disputes, to justly enforce criminal laws and government regulations, and to protect public health" (American Academy of Forensic Sciences,

TABLE 12.1 An Overview of Forensic Science

Why is it called *forensic* science?	From the Latin *forensis*, which means "to the forum" (the location where scholars and politicians would meet to discuss and debate issues including law); Because it uses the scientific method to solve problems
What are the differences between forensic science and "regular" science?	*Science*: Publish results in scientific journal for others to review—if results are incorrect, go back and try again *Forensic Science*: Present results in court to a judge/jury; Results not necessarily peer reviewed—they are reviewed by the "other side" in the case; If results are incorrect, innocent person can be wrongly convicted and sent to prison or executed
What does forensic science *do*?	Reconstructs past events; Reconstructs sequences of events to build a "story" about what happened; Seeks to link a suspect or defendant with a crime scene ("individualization")

Source: Crosby Independent School District (2017)

2017, p. 1). Forensic scientists become involved in legal proceedings when objective, scientific analysis is needed to answer one or more legal questions, find the truth, and seek justice (see Table 12.1). What's interesting is this: almost from its inception, forensic science has been associated with *government efforts* to identify perpetrators and prosecute defendants for crimes. The reason for this is that forensic operations—both historically and today—are typically housed in police departments or state-funded agencies (National Research Council, 2009). To be fair, such a characterization is technically incorrect, however: forensic science is *supposed* to be objective, unbiased, and can be used by *both* sides in *any* legal matter (see Houck & Siegel, 2015; Saperstein, 2009).

The American Academy of Forensic Sciences (AAFS), the largest professional association of scientists and practitioners involved in forensics in the world, identifies 10 separate disciplines as constituting the forensic sciences, including forensic anthropology, criminalistics, digital and multimedia forensics, engineering sciences, jurisprudence, odontology, pathology/biology, psychiatry/behavioral science, questioned documents, and toxicology (American Academy of Forensic Sciences, 2017). Some forensic scientists, however, have found it useful to group these areas into larger categories based on the shared characteristics of the disciplines involved. For example, John Barbara (2008) created a classification scheme for forensic science disciplines that encompasses four broad areas (see Table 12.2). Comparative disciplines (e.g., latent fingerprints, questioned documents, and firearms [including toolmarks]) can be grouped together since each involves the forensic scientist or technician comparing some piece of evidence with a known original. For example, when bullet casings are recovered at a crime scene, a test is conducted to decide if the recovered casings were fired from a recovered firearm or from a different gun. In latent fingerprint analysis, fingerprints recovered at the scene are compared to those stored in a database (e.g., the FBI's Automated Fingerprint Identification System, or AFIS) to identify a suspect. In questioned document analysis, the original document is compared to the suspect document. The analytical disciplines, a second area of Barbara's scheme, include forensic anthropology (facial reconstruction), controlled substances (drug chemistry), biology (DNA),

TABLE 12.2 Classifying the Forensic Science Disciplines

Category	Included Disciplines	Source of Commonality
Comparative Disciplines	Latent fingerprints; questioned documents; firearms; trace evidence;	Comparison of some piece of evidence with a known original
Analytical Disciplines	Drug chemistry; biology (DNA); toxicology; serology; etymology; anthropology; psychiatry/psychology	Use of various tools or equipment to analyze and reach conclusions about the nature of the evidence
Crime Scene Investigation (CSI)	Crime scene analysis	Identification of key features of the crime scene, including positions of persons involved, locations of evidence, etc. to reconstruct what occurred
Digital and Multimedia Forensics	Computer science and engineering; information systems; information technology; informatics	Identifying, recovering, analyzing, and presenting in court digital information stored on electronic devices

Source: Adapted from Barbara (2008)

psychiatry, trace evidence, and toxicology. In these instances, the forensic practitioner is using microscopes, other equipment, and/or statistics to analyze chemical, biological, or other properties of recovered evidence or people. Barbara assigns crime scene investigation (CSI) to its own category, and does the same for digital and multimedia forensics, although he notes this category overlaps with both the analytical disciplines and CSI.

Regardless of how its disciplines are identified or classified, at bottom forensic science can be conceptualized as the application of science to issues arising during litigation. It also consists of multiple disciplines ranging from those in the natural sciences (e.g., biology; chemistry; toxicology) and engineering (e.g., computer engineering), to the social sciences (forensic psychology), and medicine (e.g., odontology; pathology). As a result, it is perhaps better referred to as the forensic sciences. Further, these disciplines can be grouped together based on the characteristics of the analysis performed on the evidence: comparative, analytical, or investigative.

Armed with this basic knowledge, let's now consider the hiring and training of forensic practitioners and how such procedures relate to ethical issues concerning the practice of forensic science.

Forensic Scientist Hiring and Training

One of the major fallacies about forensic science promoted by television series like the *CSI* franchise is that forensic practitioners gather evidence at a crime scene, process (analyze) that evidence, and then arrest a likely perpetrator (Reavy, 2011; Tyler, 2006). In other words, the *same person* finds the evidence, collects and preserves it, analyzes it, and then arrests the presumed offender.

The reality of forensic science is much different. In the real world, there are multiple individuals whose job is to complete one part of an overall process that ultimately readies the evidence for presentation in court. For example, a crime scene investigator or criminalist (who is likely a police officer with multiple years' experience) secures the scene, and identifies, collects, and preserves evidence found there. She may also conduct **presumptive tests** at the scene—useful in determining the type of substance present, whether it's a toxin or a drug, whether it's a stain that contains body fluids, or even whether a dried red substance found in the kitchen is blood or ketchup (Carlyle, 2011). She then creates an inventory of evidence from the scene and stores it at a secure location at the police department before submitting it to a crime laboratory, where the evidence is then carefully checked in and stored, pending analysis. When the evidence is checked out and analyzed, the forensic technician doing so signs for it and then completes the appropriate analysis, which usually involves **confirmatory tests**, where instrumental analysis is performed to positively identify the contents of the submitted material (Saferstein, 2017). The technician's work—including a report—is then checked by a superior. The remaining evidence (if any) is then returned to the police, who again store it (or it may remain in the crime laboratory storage area). At the appropriate time, the evidence is again checked out and presented in court. At each check-in/check-out point, someone signs and dates a form indicating who removed/returned the evidence and what was done to it for the purpose of maintaining the chain of custody for the evidence. Removing and returning evidence is also limited to certain approved personnel, such as the lead investigator, prosecutor, or forensic technician.

In my experience, forensic science practitioners are either technicians or scientists. **Forensic technicians** typically secure, collect, and preserve evidence at a crime scene; reconstruct a crime scene and its features; and process evidence submitted to a crime laboratory. In the latter instance, the technician is performing actual analysis of recovered evidence using necessary tools or equipment such as a gas-chromatograph mass-spectrometer (GCMS), an analytical method that identifies different substances within a test sample. GCMS is typically used to identify illicit drugs, accelerants that may have been used in an arson, environmental pollutants, and explosives, among other substances. Forensic technicians typically possess at least an associate's degree. **Forensic scientists**, while also involved in processing evidence, spend more of their time engaging in basic and applied research, training new personnel on laboratory protocols and supervising them, and presenting scholarly work at conferences. They typically possess advanced degrees, including a doctorate or a professional degree (e.g., M.D.).

The hiring of both forensic technicians and scientists is usually done through civil service channels. Technicians typically need a minimum of a bachelor's degree (although in some labs, an associate's degree may suffice), in the natural sciences, in engineering, or forensic science. They complete background checks and drug tests, have their credit and driving records checked, and undergo polygraph and other examinations. Forensic scientists typically have earned at least a master's degree in forensic science, chemistry, or biology, or engineering; are familiar with lab protocols and have laboratory experience; and may possess specialized knowledge or technical expertise with one or more instruments. They also must have clean backgrounds and driving records, pass drug and polygraph tests, and possess good credit records.

Training of forensic technicians and scientists occurs through on-the-job training, in-service training, and continuing education (see Houck & Siegel, 2015). Before they will be allowed to perform their duties, practitioners receive on-the-job training conducted by more experienced colleagues or supervisors. New crime scene investigators typically assist experienced investigators for some probationary period, during which they learn proper procedures and methods for collecting, documenting, and preserving evidence. The length of this training varies by specialty (it's typically around six to nine months) and likely includes proficiency testing. Throughout their careers, forensic science practitioners will also have to keep pace with changes occurring in the field, particularly those relating to technological innovations and new tools/instruments that are developed. This is accomplished through annual in-service training occurring at the crime laboratory and via continuing education (discussed in the section "Obligations to Maintain Professional Competence" below).

The Occupational Culture of Forensic Practitioners

While existing research offers ample analysis of the occupational cultures of other criminal justice practitioners, I am unaware of any systematic empirical research on the occupational culture of forensic practitioners. That said, I don't think it would be inappropriate to assume that forensic practitioners likely possess value systems similar to those held by practitioners in policing, prosecutors' offices, or corrections. For example, because they work in the public sector in civil-service-type jobs, I think it safe to assume that forensic practitioners believe in not only the importance of public service, but also the "noble cause" of reducing crime by helping to identify and convict offenders. They thus self-select into the field, and after completing necessary hiring and training requirements, become involved in their assigned duties.

It also seems fair to assume that forensic practitioners evidence "correct" values, which are then enhanced through the hiring, initial training, and probationary process to the point where the practitioner is approved to work on actual cases according to job-related duties. And because many forensic practitioners work closely with police investigators and prosecutors' offices in putting together and executing cases against specific defendants, I think it also reasonable to assume that forensic practitioners likely share at least some of the same values previously described as possessed by police officers, correctional officers, and prosecutors. Finally, similar to what I described as occurring with other criminal justice practitioners, forensic scientists and technicians likely confront role conflict. On the one hand, they are usually employed by the state and routinely collaborate with police officers and prosecutors to "put bad guys in jail." They are also supposed to "seek the truth" and be bound by the objective results of their analyses, even if the results diminish the strength of the state's case against a defendant. Thus, like probation officers, they must balance these competing interests (see National Research Council, 2009).

Through a combination of anecdotal evidence and research that *has* identified some of the issues that have plagued forensic science in recent years and proposed solutions to them, a picture has emerged of the occupational-related values, attitudes, and norms of forensic practitioners. As a result, inferences might then be made concerning how the occupational culture of the forensic sciences affects practitioners as they confront various dilemmas arising from their work.

Jennifer Mnookin and her colleagues have outlined what might be considered the contours of an occupational culture in forensic practice (Mnookin, et al., 2010). First, let's consider the larger context in which forensic practice exists: adversarial justice and institutional ties between it and the state through publicly funded crime laboratories. As we saw with both prosecutors and defense counsel, adversarial justice is about *winning cases*, sometimes to the point of engaging in unethical or even illegal conduct to do so, all in the name of some "noble cause." Additionally, because the forensic sciences have long had institutional ties to the state (and its interests) through publicly funded crime laboratories, such ties have raised concerns over bias injecting itself into the work done by forensic practitioners (National Research Council, 2009). This context may thus create situations where forensic practitioners become willing or unwilling partners in the "noble cause" of "putting bad guys in jail," and thus caught up in the zeal that can sometimes color the "noble cause" of doing just that.

There is also the fact that the *practice* of forensic science—much as we saw with policing—is inherently conservative. What I mean here is not that forensic practitioners necessarily lean toward the right with their political ideology. Rather, what I mean is that forensic practitioners resist change. I reach this conclusion partly because the courts *allow* forensic practice to be driven by a **casework approach**, where, in their day-to-day work, practitioners use explicit, standard operating procedures (SOPs) and tacit knowledge developed through ongoing practice and training to complete their tasks (Doak & Assimakopoulos, 2007). This is illustrated when, during courtroom testimony, forensic practitioners justify their claims or conclusions based on their "training and experience" rather than on systematically collected data (Mnookin, et al., 2010). While "experience and training" may be legitimate as the basis for some types of knowledge, claiming "experience and training" as the basis for linking a handwriting sample or fingerprint to a specific defendant in a criminal case "is deeply problematic without robust feedback processes or mechanisms to identify mistakes" (Mnookin, et al., 2010, p. 745). If forensic practitioners have no independent way to verify whether a conclusion reached in a specific case is correct, they cannot learn from experience. They also cannot ever know when errors are made, nor can they adjust their practice to increase accuracy. In short, casework does not involve systematic research necessary to create a foundation upon which claims or conclusions can then legitimately rest (Mnookin, et al., 2010; National Research Council, 2009). The conservative nature of forensic practice is also illustrated when both practitioners and judges are "too willing to infer scientific validity from . . . longstanding use" of certain tools or instruments (Mnookin, et al., 2010, p. 747). Some forensic techniques have been in use for substantial periods of time, and the error rates associated with them are small relative to the frequency of use, which provides a degree of support for the accuracy of the technique. However, case information *alone* can never provide absolute assurance about truth, and longstanding use leads some in the field, including judges, to render as minimally important, systematic validation of longstanding use (Mnookin, et al., 2010). This helps foster a "we've always done it this way" attitude that is then resistant to change.

What this leaves us with is the reality that forensic science tends to be driven largely by practitioners, who likely share many of the same values and personal qualities of other criminal justice practitioners (e.g., police, prosecutors, and correctional officers). Their work occurs within a larger context of adversarial justice—a zero-sum game where there are winners and losers. Combined with this is the fact that institutional ties have long existed between the state and forensic laboratories that have earned implicit and explicit blessings from the courts, and that forensic practitioners overly rely on "experience, training, and longstanding use" as the basis for their claims and conclusions. This can lead to the practitioner finding herself facing conflicts over her role as objective scientist on the one hand and her commitment to the "noble cause" of reducing crime by "putting bad guys in jail" on the other. There are, however, ethical codes and standards to which forensic practitioners can look to for guidance. Let's explore these codes now.

FORENSIC SCIENCE STANDARDS AND CODES OF ETHICS

In 2009, the National Research Council (NRC) of the National Academy of Sciences released what many in forensic science considered an earth-shaking report on the status of the field in the United States (National Research Council, 2009). As part of a congressionally mandated review of forensic practices in this country, the 350-plus-page report identified serious and sometimes dramatic deficiencies existing in the nation's forensic science system and called for major reforms, including mandatory certification programs for practitioners; creation of a national oversight agency responsible for regulating forensic practice and laboratories; stronger standards and protocols for analyzing forensic evidence; new research programs; and more effective oversight of crime labs (Office of News and Public Information, 2009). Regarding ethics and the practice of forensic science, the NRC made the following recommendation (National Research Council, 2009, p. 215):

> The [oversight agency], in consultation with its advisory board, should establish a national code of ethics for all forensic science disciplines and encourage individual societies to incorporate this national code as part of their professional code of ethics. Additionally, mechanisms of enforcement for those forensic scientists who commit serious ethical breaches should be explored. Such a code could be enforced by a certification process for forensic scientists.

Note that it wasn't the case the NRC found there weren't codes of ethics for forensic practitioners. Many professional associations in forensic science have codes of ethics for their members, including the AAFS, the California Association of Criminalistics, and the Midwestern Association of Forensic Scientists, to name just three of them. The problem is that a national code of ethics for forensic practitioners, while it has been promulgated, has *not* been implemented, at least not as of this writing.

Let's move on and consider how forensic science responded to the NRC's call for a national code of ethics by discussing how the accrediting body for forensic laboratories and service providers adopted a national code for these facilities that was then incorporated into the accrediting process. I then detail how that code became the basis for creating a national code of professional responsibility for forensic practitioners and describe the ongoing efforts to implement that code at the national level. Let's get started.

Ethical Standards for Crime Laboratories

According to its website, the American Society of Crime Laboratory Directors (ASCLD, usually pronounced "azz-clad") is a nonprofit professional society of crime laboratory directors and forensic science managers dedicated to providing excellence in forensic science through leadership and innovation (American Society of Crime Laboratory Directors, 2017a). ASCLD's stated purpose includes fostering professional interests; developing laboratory management principles and techniques; acquiring, preserving, and disseminating forensic-based information; maintaining and improving communications among crime lab directors; and promoting, encouraging, and maintaining the highest standards of practice in the field (American Society of Crime Laboratory Directors, 2017b). During the late 1980s, the group developed a standards subcommittee whose charge was to evaluate the needs of the criminal justice system as they related to forensic services. The subcommittee eventually incorporated as a separate and distinct nonprofit entity with the acronym ASCLD/LAB (usually pronounced "azz-clad-lab") and was responsible for accrediting crime laboratories around the nation. Finally, in 2016, ASCLD/LAB merged into the ANSI-ASQ National Accreditation Board (ANAB) following the signing of an affiliation agreement. ANSI-ASQ now handles all forensic laboratory accreditation in the United States (Boler, 2016).

In 2008, ASCLD released specific guidelines for crime labs that were designed to "safeguard the integrity and value of our profession" and represented ASCLD's positions on what "each laboratory operation should strive to meet" (American Society of Crime Laboratory Directors, 2008). The position statement dealt with six areas, including ethics and objectivity. Concerning the latter, ASCLD's position was:

> ASCLD believes the practice of forensic science must be built on a foundation of ethics and objectivity. [L[aboratory managers and employees of forensic laboratories must avoid any activity, interest, influence, or association that interferes or appears to interfere with independent ability to exercise judgment. [P]rofessionals provide the basis for the examination of evidence and reporting of analytical results by blending . . . scientific and . . . statutory rules into guidelines for professional behavior. Laboratories must strive to ensure that forensic Science examinations are conducted [following] sound scientific principles and within the framework of the statutory requirements to which forensic professionals are responsible.
>
> —(American Society of Crime Laboratory Directors, 2008, p. 1)

In 2016, ANSI-ASQ released version 2.0 of a set of principles that are now part of accrediting standards for forensic laboratories in this country (ANSI-ASQ National Accreditation Board, 2016). The *Guiding Principles*, as they are referred to, have been adopted

> . . . with the hope that forensic management will use them in training sessions, performance evaluations, disciplinary decisions, and as guides in other management decisions [and] . . . that all personnel are equally aware of [them] and incorporate [them] into their daily work.
>
> —(ANSI-ASQ National Accreditation Board, 2016, p. 1)

The *Guiding Principles* for lab administrators and managers (1) describe ethical and professional responsibilities of forensic practitioners; (2) describe key areas and provide specific rules for them; (3) promote integrity; and (4) help increase public confidence in the quality of forensic services (ANSI-ASQ National Accreditation Board, 2016). Box 12.1 presents a condensed version of the *Guiding Principles* divided into three areas: professionalism, competency, and communication. As you will see, the ***Guiding Principles for Laboratory Directors*** was not only important for creating a set of ethical standards for crime laboratory managers, administrators, and staff. It also became the basis for a national-level code of ethics for *all* forensic practitioners.

BOX 12.1 ANSI-ASQ Guiding Principles for Laboratory Directors

Professionalism

Ethical and professionally responsible forensic personnel . . .

1. Are independent, impartial, detached, and objective, approaching all examinations with due diligence and an open mind.
2. Conduct full and fair examinations. Conclusions are based on the evidence and reference material relevant to the evidence, not on extraneous information, political pressure, or other outside influences.
3. Are aware of their limitations and only render conclusions that are within their area of expertise and about matters which they have given formal consideration.
4. Honestly communicate with all parties (the investigator, prosecutor, defense, and other expert witnesses) about all information relating to their analyses, when communications are permitted by law and agency practice.
5. Report to the appropriate legal or administrative authorities unethical, illegal, or scientifically questionable conduct of other forensic employees or managers. Forensic management will take appropriate action if there is potential for, or there has been, a miscarriage of justice due to circumstances that have become known, incompetent practice, or malpractice.
6. Report conflicts between their ethical/professional responsibilities and applicable agency policy, law, regulation, or other legal authority, and attempt to resolve them.
7. Do not accept or participate in any case on a contingency fee basis or in which they have any other personal or financial conflict of interest or an appearance of such a conflict.

Competency and Proficiency

Ethical and professionally responsible forensic personnel . . .

8. Are committed to career-long learning in the forensic disciplines which they practice and stay abreast of new equipment and techniques while guarding against the misuse of methods that have not been validated. Conclusions and opinions are based on generally accepted tests and procedures.
9. Are properly trained and determined to be competent through testing . . .
10. Honestly, fairly, and objectively administer and complete regularly scheduled relevant proficiency tests; comprehensive technical reviews of examiners' work; verifications of conclusions.
11. Give utmost care to the treatment of . . . items of potential evidentiary value to avoid tampering, adulteration, loss, or unnecessary consumption.
12. Use appropriate controls and standards when conducting . . . analyses.

Clear Communications

Ethical and professionally responsible forensic personnel . . .

13. Accurately represent their education, training, experience, and . . . expertise.
14. Present accurate and complete data in written reports and testimony.
15. Make and retain full, contemporaneous, clear, and accurate records of all examinations, tests conducted, conclusions drawn, in sufficient detail to allow meaningful review and assessment. Reports are prepared in which facts, opinions and interpretations are clearly distinguishable, and . . . clearly describe limitations on the methods, interpretations and opinions presented.
16. Do not alter reports or other records or withhold information from reports for strategic or tactical litigation advantage.
17. Support sound scientific techniques and practices and do not use their positions to pressure an examiner or technician to arrive at conclusions or results that are not supported by data.
18. Testify to results obtained and conclusions reached only when they have confidence that the opinions are based on good scientific principles and methods. Opinions are to be stated so as to be clear in their meaning. Wording should not be such that inferences may be drawn which are not valid, or that slant the opinion . . .
19. Attempt to qualify their responses while testifying when asked a question with the requirement that a simple "yes" or "no" answer be given, if answering "yes" or "no" would be misleading to the judge or the jury.

Source: Adapted from ANSI-ASQ National Accreditation Board (2016, pp. 1–4)

Practitioner Code of Ethics

Recall that in 2009, the NRC called for the establishment of a national code of ethics for all forensic practitioners that would include mechanisms of enforcement and sanctions for violators. The NRC also suggested that such a code could be incorporated into codes of ethics that professional associations in the field had developed for their members, and that the associations would then be responsible for devising enforcement mechanisms and sanctions for violations.

In 2010, the National Science and Technology Council's Subcommittee on Forensic Science developed a ***National Code of Professional Responsibility for Forensic Science and Forensic Medicine Providers*** (National Commission on Forensic Science, 2016a). In developing the code, the Subcommittee reviewed codes of ethics developed by forensic science organizations for use with members and identified four categories addressed by every code it reviewed: (1) working within professional competence, (2) providing clear and objective testimony, (3) avoiding conflicts of interest, and (4) avoiding bias and influence, real or perceived. The Subcommittee decided that the most broadly applicable existing code of ethics that could serve as the national code for practitioners was the *Guiding Principles of Professional Responsibility for Crime Laboratories and Forensic Scientists* discussed above. This decision was made because the principles outlined in the document were appropriate to work conducted in (specifically) federal forensic laboratories, and so the Subcommittee proposed that the *Guiding Principles* document be adopted as the national code of ethics for practitioners (National Commission on Forensic Science, 2016a). The Subcommittee also concluded that a core, essential element was lacking from the proposed national code—namely, an acknowledgment that violations of the code would occur—and that there had to be a mechanism for addressing the issue of violations, since oversight and enforcement are critical to compliance (National Commission on Forensic Science, 2016a).

To solve this problem, the Subcommittee recommended that all professional associations in the forensic sciences incorporate the national code into their membership codes of ethics and develop mechanisms for defining and acting against unethical behavior. The process would be designed to address all "adverse events" occurring—both intended and unintended—and would then involve the professional association with managing the reporting of, and corrective action(s) taken to remedy, these events (Bowers, 2015). In effect, while the code would be national in scope, enforcement of it would occur through mechanisms developed by professional associations and laboratory-accrediting entities, similar to what has been done with enforcing ethics in law and medicine.

Box 12.2 presents a condensed version of the *National Code of Professional Responsibility for Forensic Science and Forensic Medicine Providers* that existed as of this writing in early 2018. The code "defines a framework for promoting integrity and respect for the scientific process" among forensic practitioners and agencies (National Commission on Forensic Science, 2016a, p. 4). Practitioners and agencies must meet requirements 1–15, while requirement 16 refers to the responsibility of forensic science and forensic medicine management or administration rather than individual practitioners (National Commission on Forensic Science, 2016a, p. 4).

In March of 2016, the National Commission on Forensic Science recommended that the Attorney General (AG) of the United States pursue the following action(s) concerning

BOX 12.2 The National Code of Professional Responsibility for Forensic Science and Forensic Medicine Service Providers

1. Relevant education, training, experience, and area(s) of expertise should be accurately represented.
2. Be honest and truthful in all professional affairs; do not represent others' work as one's own.
3. Foster and pursue professional competency through . . . training, proficiency testing, certification, and presentation and publication of research findings.
4. Commit to continuous learning in relevant . . . disciplines and stay abreast of new findings, equipment, and techniques.
5. Utilize scientifically validated methods and innovative technologies, while guarding against use of unproven methods in casework and misapplication of generally-accepted standards.
6. Handle evidentiary materials to prevent tampering, adulteration, loss, or nonessential consumption . . .
7. Avoid participation in any case in which there is a conflict of interest.
8. Conduct independent, impartial, and objective examinations that are fair, unbiased, and fit-for-purpose.
9. Make and retain contemporaneous, clear, complete, and accurate records of all work in sufficient detail to allow meaningful review and assessment by independent professionals proficient in the discipline.
10. Ensure interpretations, opinions, and conclusions are supported by sufficient data while minimizing influences and biases for or against any party.
11. Render interpretations, opinions, or conclusions only within the practitioner's proficiency or expertise.
12. Reports and testimony should use clear and straightforward terminology, clearly distinguish data from interpretations, opinions, and conclusions, and disclose known limitations necessary to understand findings.
13. Reports and other records shall not be altered and information shall not be withheld for strategic or tactical advantage.
14. Document and . . . inform management . . . of nonconformities and breaches of law or professional standards.
15. Once a report is issued and the adjudicative process has commenced, communicate fully when requested with the parties through their investigators, attorneys, and experts, except when instructed that a legal privilege, protective order, or law prevents disclosure.
16. Appropriately inform affected recipients . . . of all nonconformities or breaches of law or professional standards that adversely affect a previously issued report or testimony and make reasonable efforts to inform all relevant stakeholders, including affected professional and legal parties, victim(s) and defendant(s).

Source: National Commission on Forensic Science (2016a, pp. 3–4)

implementation of the national code. First, the AG would urge all Department of Justice forensic service providers to adopt the code, and their management/administrators to create policies and procedures to enforce it. Second, the AG would urge *all* forensic science and medicine service providers, certification and accreditation bodies, and professional associations in the United States to adopt the code, and *their* governing boards, management, or administrators to create policies and procedures to enforce the code's standards. The policies and procedures would articulate a system that would protect individuals from retaliation when reporting suspicious, unscrupulous, unethical, or criminal actions. Additionally, the code would be reviewed annually and "signed off" on by all forensic service providers and associations. Finally, there would have to be an effective process to report and correct nonconformities or breaches of law or professional standards that adversely affected a previously issued report or testimony (National Commission on Forensic Science, 2016b).

In September of 2016, then Attorney General Loretta Lynch accepted the first recommendation from above. In a memorandum to the Department of Justice, Attorney General Lynch wrote:

> The Department is adopting a new code of professional responsibility for Department [of Justice] forensic laboratories. This code, which builds on the Department's Scientific Research and Integrity Policy and the Guiding Principles of Professional Responsibility of the American Society of Crime Laboratory Directors/Laboratory Accreditation Board, will apply to Departmental forensic examiners.
>
> —(Lynch, 2016)

The Attorney General, however, rejected the second recommendation. Subsequently, transition occurred from the Obama administration to the Trump administration, and current Attorney General Jeff Sessions announced on April 10, 2017, that (1) he would *not* renew the National Commission on Forensic Science (effectively ending it) and (2) he was suspending an ongoing Justice Department review of past forensic analyses in certain areas (e.g., hair and ballistics) used in criminal cases that was begun in 2012, pending review by the incoming administration and a strategy devised by an internal task force with input via public comments (Hsu, 2017).

In summary, ethical standards in the practice of forensic science have been a "hot button" issue for some time. For nearly a decade, practitioners, government agencies, scholars, judges, and attorneys labored to create a national code of ethics for forensic practitioners. These efforts resulted first in a national code of ethics for forensic laboratories that was incorporated into accreditation processes and policies for forensic labs. That code then served as the basis for creating a national code of ethics for all forensic practitioners. However, there were two issues that needed addressing: the code did not include a mechanism for reporting violations or procedures for responding to such reports, and there was no national body that would oversee these efforts. A positive development occurred when then Attorney General Loretta Lynch in 2016 mandated that all U.S. Department of Justice forensic service providers adopt the code and create and implement their own policies and procedures for enforcing it. However, efforts to implement the code nationally through incorporation into ethics codes for professional associations have stalled and the future is uncertain as to whether the national code will ever be implemented.

I've now provided you with a general overview of the forensic sciences, including the disciplines involved, the characteristics of practitioners, along with their hiring and training, and a sense of their occupational culture. I've also shared with you the emergence of a national code of ethics for the field. To conclude the chapter, let's now examine some examples of the types of ethical issues and dilemmas confronting forensic practitioners.

ETHICAL ISSUES IN THE PRACTICE OF FORENSIC SCIENCE

Forensic practitioners wear two hats. They are *scientists* relying upon standardized tools and methods to analyze evidence and reach conclusions about it. They are also embedded within the larger context of adversarial justice and are generally tied to agencies (crime labs) and individuals (police officers and prosecutors) representing the state, which is interested in obtaining a conviction in criminal cases. As a result, "forensic scientists face ethical challenges in virtually every facet of their career[s] and constant vigilance is necessary to avoid being tripped up at so many points along the way" (Siegel, 2012, p. 59).

This section of the chapter explores these ethical challenges and the steps practitioners can take to address them. The specific examples I've chosen include ethical issues concerning (1) analytical procedures commonly used in crime labs; (2) courtroom testimony and serving as an expert witness in trials; (3) practitioner obligations to the field; and (4) whistleblowing to uncover crime lab irregularities.

Laboratory Analytical Procedures

Those of you who recall laboratory exercises you completed in basic science courses like Introduction to Chemistry or Introduction to Biology may also recall there were protocols for conducting laboratory work (Bisen, 2014). **Lab protocols** (see Box 12.3) are typically lists of instructions for performing a particular analysis or experiment, and include not only instructions related to handling samples, but also instructions related to safety, proper analytical equipment to use, and how to avoid errors (Stanley, 2017). Forensic labs are no different. They also have developed protocols—often referred to as standard operating procedures (SOPs)—for analyzing evidence that include not only the above-named considerations, but also validation of the device or tool being used prior to using it and specific schemes for analyzing diverse types of evidence (Houck & Siegel, 2015; Saferstein, 2017). In some labs, forensic scientists or technicians must follow lab protocols in *all* cases, while in others, the scientist or technician may *choose* from available, validated tests, but has the freedom to perform whatever test(s) they feel are necessary in whatever order they choose (Siegel, 2012).

Finally, many forensic labs—especially those that are accredited—have in place protocols for reviewing the results of casework, ranging from a supervisor reading every lab report and examining data and documentation, to having other scientists in the lab verify results of selected cases, to having duplicate analyses of cases by two different scientists (see Federal Bureau of Investigation, 2006; Siegel, 2012). Ethical violations occur in forensic labs when practitioners fail to follow established protocols for analyzing evidence. Commonly occurring examples of these violations include insufficient analysis, "dry-labbing" (also known as "dry-benching"), "indiscriminate analysis," and "analyzing to fit the written law" (Augenstein, 2016; Gianelli, 2012; Houck & Siegel, 2015; Peters, 2013; Siegel, 2012). Below, I explore these issues in greater depth.

Insufficient Analysis

When the scientist or technician fails to perform sufficient testing of a sample of evidence to support conclusions reached about evidence in a case, she has engaged in *insufficient analysis* (Houck & Siegel, 2015). **Insufficient analysis** occurs if the analyst performs preliminary examination(s) of the evidence, but then fails to perform a final, confirmatory analysis that verifies the nature of the evidence and ultimately provides the data necessary to support the analyst's conclusion. It can also occur when the analyst skips preliminary testing and only conducts confirmatory tests, which is problematic because preliminary

BOX 12.3 Sample Lab Protocol

FTA DNA Purification Protocol

1. Sample application: Apply specimen to disk on FTA card and allow to dry completely.

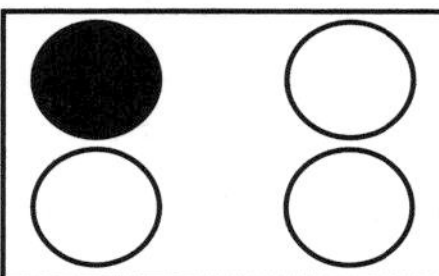

2. Disk removal: Punch out sample disk containing specimen from the FTA card.

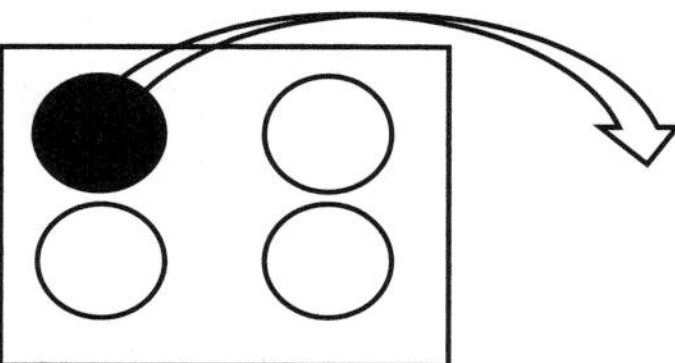

3. FTA purification reagent washes: Place specimen disk in PCR tube and wash three times with FTA Purification Reagent. Discard unused reagent after each wash.

4. TE^{-1} rinses: Wash twice with TE^{-1} buffer (10 mM Tris, 0.1 mM ETDA, pH 8.0) and discard used buffer after each wash.

5. Drying step: Dry disk in PCR tube.

6. Direct to PCR: Add PCR master mix directly to the disk and amplify.

Source: Adapted from Daniels (2015)

testing might have yielded data the confirmatory test missed. Siegel (2012) suggests that this violation occurs either because of poor ethical choice or from a lack of training.

Dry-Labbing (or Dry-Benching)

Another ethical violation that involves laboratory analytical procedures occurs when a technician *fabricates results* for a sample of evidence; that is, she fails to conduct the proper tests, known as **dry-labbing** (Allocca, 2015; Siegel, 2012). In some instances, dry-labbing occurs when results would be obvious—for example, the evidence is a small plastic storage bag containing a greenish-brownish leafy substance. In this case, the look and smell of the evidence is, itself, a good indication of the presence of marijuana. However, failing to conduct formal testing of the substance would miss the presence of other drugs either coating it or mixed with it (Siegel, 2012). Especially problematic is that dry-labbing almost always results in evidence favorable to the prosecution. In one gross example of dry-labbing, the Texas Court of Appeals in 2013 ordered a review of 5,000 drug cases in which a particular analyst was suspected of dry-labbing the evidence (Allocca, 2015). In rare cases involving a gross mix-up of cases, dry-labbing can be accidental. Sadly, the vast majority of occurrences involve *deliberate failure* by the technician or scientist to conduct a proper analysis (Siegel, 2012).

Indiscriminate Analysis

A third example of unethical behavior involving laboratory procedures is known as **indiscriminate analysis** (Houck & Siegel, 2015; Siegel, 2012). This problem arises when the analyst doesn't have a plan for conducting sufficient analysis, and instead uses every possible test for which the laboratory has resources, which results in overtesting of the evidence and a waste of time and resources (Houck & Siegel, 2015). Indiscriminate analysis is often done to impress the court, find already suspected results, or increase fees charged clients, and often ends up leaving the judge, members of the jury, and the attorneys in the case confused (Siegel, 2012).

Analyzing to Fit the Law

The final example of unethical behavior involving laboratory protocols occurs when technicians or scientists analyze evidence to meet the conditions of the law (Houck & Siegel, 2015; Siegel, 2012). **Analyzing to fit the law** occurs when a potential outcome of the analysis is preselected, via choice or manipulation, to conform the results to one or more conditions of the law that relates to the evidence, such as the weight of the sample or the level of blood alcohol content in a DUI case. By manipulating the sample, the analyst can cause the evidence to fit a specific category that carries a higher penalty for the defendant. For example, if a defendant is charged with possession of narcotics with the intent to distribute, the penalty depends on the quantity (weight) of the drugs present. If the quantity is close to the amount that triggers the higher penalty, the drug chemist may shade the weight to get over the trigger point and permit charging the more serious offense (or shade the results in the other direction, if that's what's desired) (Siegel, 2012). The unethical behavior is the act of "shading" results—either way—to obtain a desired outcome.

You have now seen some examples of unethical behavior that involve laboratory protocols and analyses. These all involve either improper manipulation of evidence to achieve a desired result or failure to conduct sufficient and/or proper analyses of evidence, leading to improper conclusions made about the evidence. These forms of unethical behavior can result in the court being confused (at best) and/or the defendant being improperly convicted (at worst). But the laboratory isn't the only place where unethical behavior by forensic practitioners occurs. It can also occur inside the courtroom itself. Let's now consider that issue.

Courtroom Testimony

Beyond conducting analyses of evidentiary samples and reaching conclusions about them, forensic practitioners also engage in an equally important activity, testifying in court, which separates forensic science from all other sciences (Bangerter, 2017; O'Brien,

Daeid & Black, 2015). From the outset, however, it's important to note that not all cases handled by forensic practitioners result in a trial. Recall from earlier chapters that more than 95% of all felony cases result in a plea bargain and thus avoid a trial. Further, not all felonies include forensic evidence, and even among them, not all the evidence has necessarily been analyzed. Thus, it is actually rare that the forensic practitioner working in a lab is called to testify in court.

Assuming we have a case that *does* go to trial, the forensic scientist or technician will receive a court order to produce the evidence in the case, known as a **subpoena *duces tecum***, that includes the name of the defendant in the case, jurisdiction in which the matter is being heard, date and time the analyst is expected to appear in court, and contact information for the attorney who requested the subpoena (Houck & Siegel, 2015). In practice, what this means is that not only must the technician appear at the location, on the day and time indicated in the subpoena, but all evidence in the case with which the analyst has worked must also be produced (e.g., laboratory reports the analyst generated and supporting documentation for them).

The Difference Between Science and Law

When the forensic analyst is called to court to testify, she enters a much different world than the world of science she normally inhabits. As shown in Table 12.3, there are major differences between science and law when it comes to such issues as the truth, communication, process, and goals (Bower, 2018). For example, in science, truth is served for its own sake. That is, the scientist seeks the truth as an end in itself, rather than for some other reward such as fame, wealth, or awards. In law, however, truth is served only as it relates to the client. During the adversarial process, each side presents the truth most favorable to its interests and tries to denigrate the truth favorable to the other side. Out of this clash comes THE TRUTH, or at least the *courtroom truth* emerges as determined by the judge or jury in the case after listening to both sides, considering the evidence, deliberating, and rendering a verdict (which, paradoxically, can be *false*, as occurs in wrongful convictions; see Dean, 2006).

Further, in science, communication is *open*. That is, through their reports, papers, and scholarly articles, scientists share their work with others and both expect and receive feedback that can sometimes be highly critical. But that's the point—through open communication and exchange, errors can be identified and new and better methods invented to investigate the world. In law, communication is different—it is *privileged*. What this means is that only some of the communication occurring among relevant parties in a case, especially communication between attorney and client, can be made public. Additionally, in science the process of creating knowledge is documented, objective, and

TABLE 12.3 Differences Between Science and Law

Issue	Science	Law
Truth	Serves the interest itself	Serves the interest(s) of client(s)
Communication	Open	Privileged
Process	Documented, objective, and systematic	Adversarial
Goal(s)	Socially valued goods/services; advance human knowledge; eliminate false beliefs	Serve the client(s); produce better arguments than opposition

Source: Bowen (2018, pp. 87–88)

systematic. The scientific method requires a step-by-step process that involves observation, collection of data, analysis, and interpretation. In law, the process is *adversarial*, a clash between the two sides presided over by an impartial arbiter, the judge, and confined within certain boundaries established by the rules of litigation—what is commonly referred to as the procedural law.

Finally, the goals of science and law differ as well. In science, the goal is to develop valued knowledge that can then be translated into a better understanding about the workings of the world, into valued services or products, etc. In law, the goal is to serve the client and win the case by producing better arguments than the other side.

Closing the Gap

Because science and law often clash, how does the forensic practitioner close the gap between them? Observers and practitioners have suggested several ways of doing this. First, the practitioner should not overstate to the attorney(s) involved her credentials—education, training, area(s) or expertise, and experience (Siegel, 2012). When called to testify, the scientist must be *credible* in the mind of the jury or judge—she is justified in presenting the information she does about the legal issue under scrutiny. Misrepresenting one's credentials can occur by claiming educational attainment that was either not earned or earned from a different institution than what is stated; claiming to possess professional certification that was not earned; misstating one's employment history; or misstating the number of times the scientist or technician had previously testified in court and in which courts that testimony occurred. Such misrepresentation is done for assorted reasons, including to impress the court, jury, or attorneys; to deflect challenges to opinions; or to intimidate opposing counsel (Siegel, 2012).

Misrepresenting credentials is problematic because doing so destroys the credibility of the scientist or technician, even if they properly conducted analyses of the evidence in the case. The thinking here is that if the practitioner is willing to misrepresent from where she earned her bachelor's degree, wouldn't she also be willing to falsify the results of the analysis she conducted? Sadly, because of limited resources and a willingness on the part of the courts to accept forensic practitioners at their word, the chances of getting caught are low, so the risk- reward equation may favor the reward in many cases (Siegel, 2012). Obvious solutions here are to conduct thorough background checks on prospective experts and sanction those caught misrepresenting their qualifications (Siegel, 2012).

A second way of closing the gap between science and law is for the technician to share with the attorney(s) that she is aware of, and took steps to mitigate, any bias that could have occurred in her analysis of the evidence (Bower, 2018; Venville, 2010). As described by Siegel (2012), two of the most serious types of bias affecting analysis of forensic evidence and its presentation in court are contextual bias and confirmation bias. **Contextual bias** occurs when forensic scientists or technicians become vulnerable to erroneous conclusions due to extraneous influences affecting their judgment (Thompson, 1995). That is, the analyst's objectivity is hampered because she develops expectations about the outcome of an examination based on extraneous information she possesses about the evidence (specifically) and the case (more broadly). Contextual bias seems particularly acute in pattern analysis fields such as fingerprint analysis, questioned documents, and ballistics (Venville, 2010), but can be addressed by limiting the analyst's access to case-specific information to minimize its contaminating effects. For example, does the scientist really need to know the defendant has prior convictions for distributing heroin to determine if the present sample being analyzed is heroin? **Sequential unmasking** can be used to mitigate contextual bias by controlling the order in which potentially biasing information is presented to the analyst, with irrelevant information (e.g., defendant has confessed; defendant has a criminal history) filtered out before the analyst receives the relevant details in the case (Reece, 2012).

Confirmation bias occurs when a second analyst is given the results of a colleague's work and is asked to replicate the analysis conducted by the first examiner (Kerstholt, et al., 2010). The bias arises here because the second scientist knows the results and conclusions reached by the first analyst, which may then affect her conclusions. Used as a quality control mechanism in many crime labs, such checks can create problems of their own, primarily by putting pressures on the second (or third) analyst. For example, Siegel (2012) asks what is supposed to happen if the second analyst disagrees with the results? What if the two are friends? What if the first examiner is the supervisor of the second? Confirmation bias can, however, be mitigated through **blind verification**, where the second (or third) technician is given all the evidence supplied the first, but #2 and #3 do *not* receive results achieved or conclusions reached by the first examiner (Ulery, Hicklin, Buscaglia, & Roberts, 2011).

A third way of closing the gap between science and law is for the forensic analyst to make sure the attorneys(s) involved are clear on what various terms used by the scientist in her testimony really *mean*. As explained by Siegel (2012), forensic science has been plagued by practitioners using imprecise terms when testifying, especially when associating crime scene evidence with a known source (the defendant). He includes the following terms as creating problems for forensics experts during testimony: "individualization," "consistent with," "similar to," "could not be distinguished from," "cannot be excluded," and the most commonly used term, "match" (Siegel, 2012, p. 65). Siegel argues the problem is that not only do forensic scientists disagree on the specific meanings of these terms, but the judge, attorneys, and members of the jury may impart a different meaning to a term used by the expert, especially if she fails to make clear what she means. Thus, Siegel (2012) argues, the analyst should be sure to explain—or ensure the attorney gets her to explain by asking appropriate questions—what is meant by the term being used. Such explanation provides context for the conclusion about which the expert is testifying and also gives the jury adequate information that allows appropriate weight to be assigned to the evidence.

In their testimony, forensic experts describe a two-step process used to analyze evidence. The first is to compare a questioned piece of evidence (e.g., a latent fingerprint, DNA left at the crime scene, a spent bullet casing) to an exemplar from a known source and ascertain whether they are so alike as to say that they "match." The second step is assessing the meaning of the match—what is the probability that the questioned and the known originated from the same source? For example, in the case of DNA, the known source would be DNA obtained from the defendant. The questioned item of evidence is DNA found at the crime scene. It then becomes the forensic expert's job to determine that the DNA obtained from the defendant and the DNA found at the scene matched. Then, the expert has to determine the *probability* that both came from the same source—the defendant in the case. As Michael Saks and Jonathan Koehler (2008) explained, in the best of all worlds, the forensic expert's work and the jury's or judge's task would be greatly simplified if both could assume that evidence matching a potential source resulted in unique and absolute identification of the source. The problem is that, based on current knowledge, *such an assumption is not possible*. They wrote (p. 205) that "[t]he concept 'individualization' exists only in a metaphysical or rhetorical sense. It has no scientific validity, and . . . is sustained largely by the faulty logic [equating] infrequency with uniqueness." As Siegel (2012, p. 66) has argued, "it is thus incumbent . . . [to] clearly define potentially unclear, ambiguous, and/or misleading terms of association including their limitations . . ."

In summary, forensic practitioners must close the gap between science and law by ensuring in their testimony that "limitations, errors, uncertainties, and weaknesses" in the analysis of a piece of evidence are summarized for a lay audience and made available for independent evaluation by other forensic experts (Siegel, 2012, p. 68). The question of ethics arises when experts use terms of art like "match" but fail to explain what the term means; when used in the forensics context, these terms differ from commonly understood meanings of them. However, if a forensic scientist wants to be biased in their scientific testimony, they can do so quite easily. They can offer deceptive or confusing testimony; present imprecise lab reports; fail to take a proper, scientifically indicated stance about the evidence; lie outright; over- or undersell the evidence; or equate the possible with the certain (Houck & Siegel, 2015). It thus becomes the job of the scientist or technician to work with the attorney(s) in the case to ensure that these problems do not occur (see Box 12.4).

Privatization of Forensic Services

As has occurred in the field of corrections, over the past 10–15 years increased privatization has been occurring in the delivery of forensic-based services in this country and elsewhere, especially in the United Kingdom (Lawless, 2010; McAndrew, 2012; Siegel, 2012). While still dwarfed by the number of publicly operated forensic laboratories, private, nonprofit, and for-profit forensic laboratories are becoming more common, and offer their services to parties involved in both civil and criminal litigation (McAndrew, 2012). Some labs are stand-alone facilities run by for-profit companies; others are organized as nonprofit facilities located either on or near the campuses of colleges and universities around the nation. Regardless of whether they are for- or nonprofit entities, these labs offer a wide variety of forensic-based services to clients on a fee-for-service or a larger-scale broad-based consulting arrangement, and a few of them are even accredited (Siegel, 2012).

BOX 12.4 Problems Faced by Forensic Experts When Testifying in Court

- Attorneys who want testimony supporting their client's position when results do not warrant such support;
- Evaluations that prove disadvantageous to the side that has retained the expert;
- Being approached for a combination of advice, evaluation, and expert testimony;
- Attorneys who waste the expert's (and the court's) time;
- Inconvenience or pressures on the expert created by the parties in the case (e.g., attorneys, agencies involved, clients or family, court schedules, travel, or accommodations);
- Distortion or impugning of the expert's reputation;
- Having an expert's testimony countered by one less qualified but given similar (or greater) weight by the court or the jury.

Source: Bowen (2018, p. 97)

Siegel (2012) has identified several ethical issues that surround forensic practitioners working for privately operated laboratories. One significant issue involves contextual bias, since the laboratory will know who has hired it. Additionally, because these labs are typically small operations with limited numbers of personnel, confirmation bias may be problematic as well. Siegel (2012) also suggested that the fees charged by private labs constitute an ethical issue. For example, in many forms of civil litigation, attorneys take cases on the basis of contingency-fee arrangements with the plaintiffs in them. What this means is rather than charging the client on a per-hour basis, the attorney agrees to receiving a portion of the damages awarded the plaintiff (33% to 50%, depending on the kind of case) as payment for their services. If the client loses and gets nothing, the attorney is not paid. Contingency-fee arrangements are often the only way a plaintiff can bring a civil action—the per-hour costs of legal assistance are simply too great otherwise. Siegel (2012) pointed out that in cases where a forensics expert is needed, the attorney and her client might be tempted to work out a contingency-fee arrangement for the expert's time and costs. Such arrangements with private experts are fraught with problems, not the least of which is exposing the expert to charges of bias in favor of the plaintiff. Such experts are often pejoratively described as **hired guns** who are being compensated for reaching conclusions favorable to the side paying them. A contingency-fee arrangement ultimately places the scientist or technician in the position of having a stake in the case outcome rather than being a neutral analyst. Siegel (2012) argues that fee arrangements should be explicitly negotiated at the beginning and be paid on an hourly basis regardless of case outcome.

A third ethical issue with privatized forensic services involves practitioners who work in public labs but are permitted to accept private consulting opportunities as long as doing so does not interfere with their work for the primary employer (Siegel, 2012). Often these opportunities involve civil cases or may even involve criminal cases occurring outside the jurisdiction served by the analyst's primary employer. The ethical issue here, according to Siegel (2012), is one of a potential conflict of interest: service to the public versus self-gratification of the scientist. Siegel noted that certain questioned document examiners can often make more money as forensic consultants in private civil cases than they can earn serving in that role full-time at the public laboratory, a very tempting opportunity indeed. Further, when engaging in these private consults, the analyst is actually running a separate business where she can charge the "market rate" for her services to offset the expenses she accrues and earn a profit. Thus, the analyst begins having to juggle her full-time work with consulting work, and that causes distractions and, ultimately, errors.

Obligations to Maintain Professional Competence

Recall that the *National Code of Professional Responsibility* indicates that all forensic service providers, whether technicians or scientists and regardless of whether they work in a publicly funded or private-sector lab, are supposed to foster and pursue professional competency through "training, proficiency testing, certification, and presentation and publication of research findings and should commit to continuous learning in relevant . . . disciplines and stay abreast of new findings, equipment, and techniques" (National Commission on Forensic Science, 2016a, p. 3). What this means in practice is that forensic practitioners are supposed to develop and then *maintain* the skills and competence necessary for them to do their jobs (Houck & Siegel, 2015; Siegel, 2012). To maintain a skill set, one must first obtain the necessary training and then pursue efforts aimed at ensuring that one's level of competence does not decline over the course of one's career. Failing to do so, according to Siegel (2012), violates one's obligations to the field. In fact, Siegel (2012) identified ethical issues associated with maintaining the competence of forensics practitioners that include keeping abreast of the latest developments in the field and continuing education practices. In this section, I examine these issues.

Keeping up with a Changing Field

Without question, the past 25–30 years have witnessed a sea change in the forensic sciences (Warrington, 2007). Over that period technologies created new tools such as digital cameras and camcorders; portable alternative light sources for detecting hair, fiber, and DNA evidence at crime scenes; superglue for processing fingerprints; personal computers; computerized databases of fingerprints and DNA; and so on. Laws and regulations also changed as the courts wrestled with emerging legal issues created by innovations in forensic science and the field worked to get its crime labs accredited (Cooper, 2013; Justice Project, 2008). The past decade in particular, ever since the NRC released its damning report on the state of forensic science in this country in 2009, has seen major changes occur in the field as it addressed criticisms raised by the report and implemented at least some of the report's recommendations (Butler, 2015).

PROFICIENCY TESTING. In its report, the NRC (2009, p. 215) identified proficiency testing and certification as mechanisms for enhancing quality control of forensic services and recommended that both be *mandatory* of all forensic service providers:

> [I]ndividual certification of forensic science professionals should be mandatory, and all forensic science professionals should have access to a certification process . . . No person (public or private) should be allowed to practice in a forensic science discipline or testify as a forensic science professional without certification [the requirements for which] should include, at a minimum, written examinations, supervised practice, proficiency testing, continuing education, recertification, adherence to a code of ethics, and effective disciplinary procedures.

Proficiency testing in forensic science has existed for some 40 years, but in recent years has become increasingly important as a tool for quality control and as a measure of both crime laboratories' and individual analysts' competency. **Proficiency testing** involves determining if an analyst is capable of satisfactorily engaging in routine examination of the type(s) of evidence for which the analyst has been trained (Koehler, 2008). Proficiency testing is currently a requirement of most accreditation schemes for forensic laboratories, as well as of certification procedures for individual forensic practitioners (National Research Council, 2009).

According to the National Research Council (2009), several types of proficiency tests exist. The primary distinction among them is whether the examiner is aware she is being tested (what's known as an "open" or "declared" test) or unaware that the sample being presented for analysis is a test sample and not from a real case (what's known as a "blind" test). Proficiency tests can be generated externally (e.g., by another laboratory, in what's called an "interlaboratory" test) or internally (e.g., the examiner's completed prior casework is randomly selected for reanalysis by a supervisor or another examiner, which is called a "random case reanalysis"). Finally, according to Koehler (2011) and Siegel (2012), proficiency testing should be (1) double blind—neither the analyst nor the supervisor should know the sample is a test sample, and (2) should mimic typical casework; that is, the test should be representative of the kinds of case(s) the forensic scientist normally receives and is asked to analyze.

Proficiency testing is not without critics (see Siegel, 2012). For example, law professor Jonathan Koehler has identified several deficiencies with them (Koehler, 2016). First, he argued there is no uniform agreement about the underlying goal of a forensic proficiency test. For example, for some, the goal is to measure the accuracy rate of forensic practitioners working with different samples under varying conditions. For others, the goal of proficiency testing is to determine whether an examiner can adequately follow laboratory protocols for evidence analysis. Finally, for a third group, the goal is to assess whether a *laboratory's* protocols are, themselves, adequate. Thus, if no consensus exists over the basic goal of proficiency testing, how is mandating that forensic service providers be tested on their proficiency going to ensure that forensic analysts possess the proper skills?

A second problem Koehler has identified with existing proficiency testing is that there are actually two types of proficiency tests (identified as Type I and Type II) that have different purposes. Type I proficiency tests, according to Koehler, serve *internal purposes* for the field. These tests identify strengths and weaknesses in both protocols and personnel for the internal purpose of improving forensic science casework by answering such questions as "Are training programs sufficient?" "Are laboratory protocols clear?" and "Are laboratory personnel able to follow protocols and generate results that competent others can also obtain?" (Koehler, 2016, p. 27). Type II tests, on the other hand, serve purposes primarily *external* to forensic science, as they are intended to measure casework performance information that is then shared with one or more external audiences. Thus, the primary goal of Type II tests is not to generate information that can then be used to improve forensic science. Instead, the goal of Type II proficiency tests is to provide information about the accuracy of forensic conclusions and opinions *for the benefit of those who use this information* (e.g., trial judges, prosecutors, police investigators, and defense counsel). Thus, for Koehler, while requiring proficiency testing is good, even if we decide what is the underlying goal, we also have to consider what is the ultimate purpose for which the test results will be used.

COMPETENCY TESTING. Another mechanism for ensuring that forensic analysts possess requisite skills and keep up with changes in the field is through **competency testing**. Formally, a competency test involves evaluation of an analyst's ability to perform work in any functional area prior to the performance of independent casework (Glossary of Forensic Terms, n.d.). Such tests establish that an analyst has acquired, currently possesses, and can demonstrate specialized knowledge, skills, and abilities in the standard practices necessary to conduct examinations in a discipline and/or category of testing prior to performing independent casework (National Research Council, 2009). As described by the National Research Council (2009), competency testing is integral to forensic training processes. Such a test is typically administered as part of a comprehensive assessment of an analyst's technical skills and knowledge concerning a newly validated technology, technique, or method. These tests usually include both written and/or practical exercises as part of a thorough evaluation of education, training, and practical experience.

CERTIFICATION. Finally, in its 2009 report, the NRC recommended that forensic scientists be certified to practice in their area(s) of specialization, in much the way that various boards certify medical doctors to practice specialty medicine. **Certification** is a credentialing process by which a nationally recognized external entity confirms a forensic science practitioner as having attained the professional competency necessary to practice in one or more forensic disciplines (Consortium of Forensic Science Organizations, 2013, p. 1). Additionally, certification provides the general public and the judicial system a means of identifying practitioners who have successfully demonstrated compliance with established requirements and ensures that professionals maintain technical proficiency and ethical standards of practice (National Commission on Forensic Science, 2016a).

In its 2009 report, the NRC argued that certification of individuals complemented the accreditation of forensic laboratories as part of a total quality assurance program and noted that in other areas of science and technology, practitioners (e.g., nurses, engineers, and some laboratory technicians) must be certified before they can practice. The NRC argued that the same should be true for forensic scientists who practice and testify. While *accreditation* primarily addresses a crime laboratory's management system, technical methods, quality of work, and staff training and education, *certification* is a process specifically designed to ensure the competency of individual forensic service providers. The NRC report noted that the American Bar Association recommended that the certification standards required of forensic examiners include written examinations, proficiency testing, continuing education, recertification procedures, an ethical code, and effective disciplinary procedures (National Research Council, 2009).

Beyond improving quality, the NRC argued that certification programs enhance the credibility of certificate holders. It also argued that the professional forensic science community is supportive of certification by pointing out that ASCLD recommends laboratory managers support peer certification programs that promote professionalism and provide objective standards. A number of disciplines within the forensic sciences offer certification (e.g., criminalists, document examiners, and odontologists, to name a few), and each has specific educational, training, experience requirements, along with competency tests—written and practical—proficiency testing, continuing education/active participation requirements via means such as scholarly publication and/or presentation, and membership in professional organizations. The problem is today, most forensic practitioners do *not* complete the somewhat costly process of certification because the profession does *not* mandate it and crime laboratories, the police, and the courts do *not* require it to engage in casework analysis (Siegel, 2012).

Continuing Education

The second area of concern expressed by Siegel (2012) relating to an obligation of the forensic practitioner to maintain her skills and competence involves continuing education; that is, short courses, readings, lectures, workshops, and other activities that provide additional or specialized information to professionals (Houck & Siegel, 2015). There are a number of ways continuing education can be obtained.

Perhaps the simplest way to obtain continuing education is for the practitioner to read the literature in her field, such as published articles and commentary appearing in both trade and scholarly journals and recently published books, including textbooks and reference books (Houck & Siegel, 2015; Siegel, 2012). Another method for obtaining continuing education is to participate in activities that expose one to current trends in the discipline and enhance awareness about them. Attending workshops and conferences is one time-tested way of gaining continuing education. For example, the AAFS routinely offers workshops at its annual meetings. Additionally, one can sit in on panel discussions devoted to trends or specific issues affecting the field. Forensic practitioners can also receive continuing education via online webinars and courses. For example, the National Institute of Justice (NIJ) sponsors a variety of online courses and workshops for practitioners. Many of these are offered by colleges or universities like West Virginia University or research institutes like the Research Triangle Institute (RTI) and are offered at no cost. These types of activities are available in virtually all areas of forensic science.

If there's a problem here, it's this: it's one thing to attend a professional meeting and take part in it by participating in workshops or presenting a research paper or poster. It is quite another to register for the conference and then spend the next several days playing golf or sight-seeing (Siegel, 2012). One can also sign up for an online course or workshop and do the absolute minimum amount of work to get through it and achieve the minimum passing grade (assuming there is grading). When it comes to continuing education, one surely gets out of it what one puts into it. It is also true that there is generally less "policing" of continuing education practices than there is of other behaviors (Siegel, 2012).

To summarize, there is little doubt that forensic practitioners have a duty to the field, the community, and to justice more broadly to develop and then maintain the skills and competence necessary for them to complete the duties assigned them. Maintaining these skills and keeping them up-to-date involves keeping abreast of developments in the field and pursuing continuing education. Proficiency and competence testing, along with certification, are three diverse ways of ensuring that forensic scientists and technicians provide evidence they possess the skills they are supposed to possess. While not perfect, testing and certification are clearly where the field is headed as it moves to address ongoing criticisms raised about its organization and operation. Additionally, pursuing continuing education by keeping on top of the current literature in the field, participating in workshops and conferences, or registering for and completing online courses is another way to ensure that the practitioner is equipped with the necessary skills to reduce errors and enhance the pursuit of justice.

Whistleblowing

Beginning in the late 1980s and continuing through the 1990s, Dr. Frederic Whitehurst was a Supervisory Special Agent (SSA) with the FBI and a noted authority on explosives who worked at the Bureau's crime laboratory in Quantico, VA. Beginning in the early 1990s, Dr. Whitehurst began complaining to his supervisors at the lab about shoddy practices occurring there. When his complaints went nowhere, he went public with them and officially become a "whistleblower" by highlighting to the public flawed forensic analysis and testimony involving lab personnel, including forensic aspects of the investigation into the bombing of the Alfred P. Murrah Federal Building in Oklahoma City on April 19, 1995 (Cohen, 2015). Now, some 30 years later and after several FBI Office of Inspector General (OIG) investigations into his claims; a more than $1.5 million whistleblower retaliation settlement with the FBI; lawsuits and litigation involving Freedom of Information Act (FOIA) requests he made of the Bureau; and continuing investigations of past cases involving the lab, Dr. Whitehurst is Principal of the Forensic Justice Project at the National Whistleblower Center in Washington, DC. He is widely considered the most noteworthy forensic whistleblower in American history (Cohen, 2015).

In recent years, both illegal and unethical behavior occurring in forensic labs has been uncovered by forensic practitioners working in them who came forward to detail the questionable behavior of one or more of their colleagues—or, as Jamie Downs has described the situation, forensic scientists "correcting the wrongs" that "required recognition of and owning the problems" (Downs, 2012, p. 400). This section of the chapter examines forensic whistleblowing that uncovered what Brent Turvey dubbed "forensic fraud" involving labs in multiple locations around this country (Turvey, 2013).

As you saw in Ch. 3, whistleblowing involves bringing to light, either within an organization (internal whistleblowing) or to outside parties (external whistleblowing) unresolved illegal or unethical behavior occurring in an agency. This can include reporting the wrongdoing to superiors or an Inspector General in the case of a federal agency; refusing to participate in the wrongdoing; testifying in legal proceedings about wrongdoing occurring in the agency; or leaking evidence of wrongdoing to journalists. Research suggests that "going public" is a whistleblower's response to her understanding that behaviors occurring within the organization are *harmful*—they interfere with others' rights, detract from the common good, or are simply unfair. "Going public" also involves the courage to call attention to a wrong occurring and a willingness to "take the heat" for doing so, including being ostracized, marginalized, or worse (Nadler & Schulman, 2006).

Whistleblowing by forensic scientists involves a process of discovering wrongdoing by one or more colleagues, identifying the wrongdoing as serious enough to warrant attention, coming forward and reporting the wrongdoing, and then living with the consequences of doing so (Downs, 2012). In discovering wrongdoing, the forensics whistleblower often recognizes "danger signs" in day-to-day operations of the laboratory: failure to follow protocols for evidence analysis; shoddy reports (some of which are based on shoddy analyses); and lack of quality control standards are all examples of "danger signs" that things are not quite right with the lab. The whistleblower then has to decide whether what she has observed constitute systemic problems rather than isolated instances. Mistakes occur—but are they systemic? If they are systemic, what's the potential cause? Is it a matter of a "rotten apple" or two spoiling the barrel, or is the barrel itself spoiled?

Coming forward involves relaying the whistleblower's concerns to appropriate supervisors within the lab. Effectively, rather than "passively accepting the status quo," the whistleblower takes a stand and refuses to allow things to continue as they have (Downs, 2012). The complainant has now become a protester against the wrongs of "the system" and attempts to effect change. They come forward for many reasons; the decision to do so may be an immediate one, after a final straw that "broke the camel's back," or out of concerns over liability for not reporting the problem (Downs, 2012). Once the whistleblower comes forward and reports the problem to supervisors, she then assumes action will be taken to address those concerns. Sometimes this happens and sometimes not—the whistleblower may thus have to be persistent as she makes her concerns known up the chain of command. Finally, and usually as a last resort, if the agency fails to adequately respond to the complaints of the whistleblower, she may decide to "go public," and contact third parties—typically journalists—about the situation.

The following three examples of recent, high-profile cases of forensic fraud uncovered through whistleblowing reveal the nature and scope of fraud that has occurred at some of the largest crime labs in this country:

- **San Francisco Crime Lab**. In March of 2015, a DNA consultant to the City of San Francisco's Office of the Public Defender filed a complaint with the San Francisco Police Department (SFPD), the FBI, and ASCLD/LAB over a Crime Lab analyst's "filling in the gaps" of an incomplete genetic sample and submitting it for comparison with a database of California offenders' DNA profiles. The doctored sample matched DNA in the database from a man named Marco Hernandez, whom prosecutors charged. The analyst's work was introduced into evidence at Hernandez's trial; he was later convicted and sentenced to prison even after the flawed DNA evidence had been uncovered. In March of 2016, after a six-month investigation, a government oversight panel consisting of 19 volunteer jurors traced major problems with the lab back to 2010 and found that the SFPD's management of the lab had resulted in bungled forensic science, theft in the drug-analysis lab, and the embarrassment of having two criminalists fail a national proficiency test (Sernoffsky, 2016).
- **Broward County (FL) Sheriff's Crime Laboratory**. In October of 2015, Tiffany Roy, an independent contractor employed by the Broward County (FL) Sheriff's Crime Laboratory (BCSCL) to assist the lab with analyses of DNA evidence, notified ASCLD/LAB of irregularities in how full-time lab personnel were conducting DNA analysis (the lab was accredited). In her complaint, she claimed that BCSCL was routinely using inconclusive DNA results to charge people with crimes. She explained to local media that best practices for DNA analysis had been made more stringent in 2011 but that the lab hadn't updated their procedures in line with the changes. Her complaint led to a full investigation by ASCLD/LAB. In April of 2016, ASCLD/LAB issued a ruling unfavorable to BCSCL, but BCSCL has appealed the decision (Iannelli, 2016).
- **Austin Police Department Crime Lab**. In 2012, Cecily Hamilton and Debra Stephens, two lab analysts working at the Austin Police Department's crime lab, went public with their complaints that the lab routinely circumvented standards and protocols for evidence processing in cases involving drug chemistry, DNA, and DUI. They also claimed that quality assurance personnel at the lab were underqualified and that staff were threatened with retaliation if they reported problems in the lab to supervisors. This began a saga that continues as of this writing, and has included closing the DNA lab, firing nearly all lab employees, and going through several directors of the facility (Hoffberger, 2016; Malek & Padraza, 2017).

To summarize, whistleblowing by forensic practitioners is both a difficult and complex decision that involves not just moral courage, but persistence. As forensic scientists and technicians go about their work in federal, state, and local crime labs, they face numerous pressures, including those arising from case backlogs. Some of them then either choose or feel driven to engage in forensic fraud to reduce the pressures. Colleagues and supervisors may notice protocol violations occurring and voice their concerns, that is, whistleblow, usually internally, but they may also choose to "go public" with them.

When doing so, they may then face a backlash from not only lab superiors, but from police departments and prosecutors' offices as well, resulting in either praise or condemnation. Usually, however, regardless of the tenor of the backlash, forensic whistleblowers will bring about positive change to a lab.

SUMMARY

This chapter examined ethics in the context of the forensic sciences, the multiple disciplines involved in addressing legal issues that arise in litigation. I began the chapter with an overview of these disciplines and a way of classifying them. I then turned attention to forensic practitioners, including the two main positions they occupy, their hiring and training, and their occupational culture. Here, I noted both the similarities of forensic practitioners with police and corrections officers' hiring, training, and occupational culture, as well as their differences. Next, I examined the standards and codes of ethics that have been developed for both crime laboratories and practitioners. One interesting point I made here is that both crime labs and forensic scientists have a nationally based code of ethics to guide their activities, although the latter has not been formally implemented as of this writing. I concluded the chapter by discussing examples of ethical issues in forensic science, including those surrounding analytical procedures commonly used in crime labs, courtroom testimony and expert witnesses, practitioner obligations to the field, and whistleblowing to uncover crime lab irregularities. Throughout the chapter, I referred to the seminal report by the National Research Council (2009) that was highly critical of the field, but that also offered multiple recommendations for moving forensic science forward.

To conclude this chapter, Thought Exercise 12.1 examines criticisms raised about the science behind forensic science—in particular, whether certain forensic disciplines can credibly claim to be scientifically based—and addresses the ethical issues raised by these fields and the evidence presented in court by practitioners in these areas.

THOUGHT EXERCISE 12.1

QUESTIONING THE SCIENCE BEHIND FORENSIC SCIENCE

As you saw from this chapter, the forensic sciences consist of multiple disciplines and analyses, conducted by different specialists, in a variety of settings (Houck & Siegel, 2015). For example, scientists perform DNA analysis in laboratories; police or technicians conduct fingerprint analysis at police departments; forensic pathologists trained in medicine conduct human autopsies in laboratory settings; criminalists or crime scene investigators analyze blood spatter patterns in the field. All of these analyses are routinely—and heavily—relied upon by prosecutors to help negotiate guilty pleas or prove cases against defendants (National Research Council, 2009).

In its 2009 report, the National Research Council (NRC) was highly critical of what is known as feature-comparison forensics, in which a suspect or defendant is matched with crime scene fingerprints, shoeprints, hair, fibers or tire tracks. A follow-up report in 2016 by the President's Council of Advisors on Science and Technology (PCAST) was again critical of "feature-comparison" forensics when considering its **foundational validity**—whether a discipline is repeatable, reproducible, and accurate—and its **validity as applied**—whether a discipline is actually being reliably applied in practice.

continued

The PCAST report assessed feature-comparison forensics with respect to these types of validity and considered whether each method was subjective or objective in nature, favoring objective methods because they contain protections against confirmation and contextual bias, as well as other forms of human judgment–based errors. Below are summaries of the PCAST findings (all references are to the President's Council of Advisors on Science and Technology [2016], with source page numbers indicated in parentheses).

Bite mark analysis. This technique involves an examiner determining whether questioned marks left on a victim were in fact left by teeth, and if so, the likelihood the marks were left by the suspect or defendant. Bite mark analysis *assumes* individuals have greatly differing dental characteristics and that mark-bearing surfaces (e.g., human skin) capture and retain the marks clearly enough to support reliable identification. PCAST was doubtful about this technique, arguing it was far from meeting the standards of foundational validity and had low prospects of developing into a scientifically valid method (pp. 8–9).

Latent fingerprint analysis. Latent fingerprint analysis involves comparing a complete or partial fingerprint impression left on items at a crime scene by an unknown subject with one or more known prints collected under controlled conditions from known subjects. Examiners may also analyze multiple unknown prints to determine a common source. Identification is determined by comparing features of the unknown print with that of a known suspect or by searching computerized databases to pinpoint an individual (p. 9). PCAST found that latent fingerprint analysis was a foundationally valid, subjective methodology but noted that substantial false positive rates exist. PCAST also expressed concern over the validity of these analyses, noting documented troubles involving contextual and confirmation bias, and the need for more rigorous proficiency testing.

Firearms analysis. Firearms analysis involves determining if ammunition recovered from a crime scene can be associated with a specific suspect firearm based on the toolmarks produced by the suspect weapon. This involves a two-stage analysis: bullets or cartridges must be included within permanent and predetermined class characteristics of a particular manufacturing process; and if that analysis leads to inclusion, the individual characteristics of the unknown bullet or cartridge are compared with the actual markings created by being fired from the suspect gun. PCAST found that foundational validity of firearms analysis had not been established and concluded that the courts were the final authority on whether firearms analysis should be admissible. PCAST also expressed concerns about contextual bias influencing these analyses.

Footwear analysis. Footwear analysis involves comparing a known shoe to a complete or partial impression recovered from a crime scene and determining whether the known shoe likely left the impression in question. Footwear analysis is also done in two stages: determining whether an inclusion exists based on comparison of class characteristics such as design, physical size, and general wear; and if inclusion exists, refining the association by looking at specific "identifying characteristics" or "randomly acquired characteristics" (such as marks on the shoe caused by cuts, nicks, and gouges from individualized wear). PCAST accepted that footwear analysis examiners could reliably determine class characteristics, but also found the discipline lacked foundational validity (p. 115).

Hair analysis. Hair analysis involves an examiner comparing the microscopic features of an unknown hair with hairs of a known source to determine whether a particular person may be the source of that hair. PCAST rejected hair analysis as a valid and reliable methodology.

There have now been two large-scale reports from independent commissions about 10 years apart sending the same message: many of the disciplines comprising the forensic sciences have questionable science behind them. *Yet, these forms of evidence continue to be collected, analyses of them completed, testimony about their value offered in courts across the nation, and defendants convicted due to the weight juries accord this evidence.* Concurrently, judges, prosecutors, and defense attorneys—not to mention juries—remain largely ignorant about the true nature of forensic evidence, the science behind it, and what that science means for the credibility of what's being paraded before them. I would argue that this situation leads us to a much larger question, namely, Is it ethical for the courts to continue to allow into evidence results of forensic analyses that have repeatedly been found to have questionable legitimacy?

What do *you* think?

KEY TERMS

Forensic science 347
Presumptive tests 349
Confirmatory tests 350
Forensic technicians 350
Forensic scientists 350
Casework approach 352
Guiding Principles for Laboratory Directors 354
National Code of Professional Responsibility for Forensic Science and Forensic Medicine Providers 356
Lab protocols 359
Insufficient analysis 359
Dry-labbing 360
Indiscriminate analysis 361
Analyzing to fit the law 361
Subpoena *duces tecum* 362
Contextual bias 363
Sequential unmasking 364
Confirmation bias 364
Blind verification 364
Hired guns 366
Proficiency testing 367
Competency testing 368
Certification 369
Foundational validity 373
Validity as applied 373

DISCUSSION QUESTIONS

1. With the development of the National Code of Professional Responsibility for Forensic Science and Forensic Medicine, can it now be said that forensic science has a national "code of ethics?" Explain why or why not.
2. Can housing a public crime laboratory (or having it affiliated with) a law enforcement agency like a local police department or the FBI be *ethically* justified? Explain why or why not.
3. Given the large number of wrongfully convicted defendants—particularly those convicted and sentenced to death—who have had their convictions overturned via DNA evidence, can it be ethically justified to establish new procedures such that, as part of the appeal in certain kinds of cases, the convicted offender is *automatically* entitled to have a new DNA analysis completed? Explain.
4. Does the public have a misguided perception of the role of forensic science in criminal cases? Explain.
5. Given its importance in many types of criminal cases, should annual training in the basics of forensics—especially DNA and digital forensics—be required of judges? Explain.

RESOURCES

National Institute of Justice Office of Investigative and Forensic Sciences (OIFS). According to its website, the OIFS is the federal government's "lead agency for forensic science research and development," and for administering programs that "facilitate training, improve laboratory efficiency and reduce backlogs." OIFS seeks to improve both the quality and the practice of forensic science through innovative solutions in support of research and development, testing and evaluation, technology, information exchange, and training resources. You can access the OIFS website by visiting https://www.nij.gov/about/pages/oifs.aspx

National Commission on Forensic Science. https://www.justice.gov/archives/ncfs

American Academy of Forensic Sciences (AAFS). https://www.aafs.org/

Forensic Magazine provides news and technical information to forensic professionals and crime scene investigators. https://www.forensicmag.com/

REFERENCES

Allocca, S. (2015, May 28). "Dry-labbing" and data integrity. *Forensics Magazine*. Retrieved from https://www.forensicmag.com/article/2015/05/%E2%80%98dry-labbing%E2%80%99-and-data-integrity-dr-ashraf-mozayani

American Academy of Forensic Sciences (2017). Types of forensic scientists. Retrieved from https://www.aafs.org/students/choosing-a-career/types-of-forensic-scientists-disciplines-of-aafs/

American Society of Crime Laboratory Directors (2017a). About us. Retrieved from http://www.ascld.org/about-us

American Society of Crime Laboratory Directors (2017b). Our history. Retrieved from http://www.ascld.org/about-us/our-history/

American Society of Crime Laboratory Directors (2008). Position statements, 2008. Retrieved from http://www.ascld.org/resource-library/ascld-policy-library/

ANSI-ASQ National Accreditation Board (2016). *Guiding principles of professional responsibility for forensic service providers and forensic personnel*. Milwaukee, WI: ANAB.

Augenstein, S. (2016, March 3). Lab tech suspended after allegedly "dry-labbing" drug evidence. *Forensic Magazine*. Retrieved from https://www.forensicmag.com/article/2016/03/lab-tech-suspended-after-allegedly-dry-labbing-drug-evidence

Balko, R. (2016, March 17). A trio of junk forensic science cases. *Washington Post*. Retrieved from https://www.washingtonpost.com/news/the-watch/wp/2016/03/17/a-trio-of-junk-forensic-science-cases/?utm_term=.5c41a01bc41e

Bangerter, M. (2017). The importance of forensic evidence in court. Retrieved from http://www.bangerterlaw.com/the-importance-of-forensic-evidence-in-court/

Barbara, J. (2008, June 1). Ethical practices in forensics. *Forensic Magazine*. Retrieved from https://www.forensicmag.com/article/2008/06/ethical-practices-forensics

Bisen, P. (2014). *Laboratory protocols in applied life sciences*. Boca Raton, FL: CRC Press.

Boler, J. (2016, April 26). ANAB merges forensics operations with ASCLD/LAB. *The Auditor*. Retrieved from http://www.theauditoronline.com/anab-merge-forensics-operations-ascldlab/

Bowen, R. (2018). *Ethics and the practice of forensic science* (2nd ed.). Boca Raton, FL: CRC Press.

Bowers, M. (2015, April 24). A cure for junk forensic science? Retrieved from http://scitechconnect.elsevier.com/junk-forensic-science/

Butler, J. (2015). U.S. initiatives to strengthen forensic science & international standards in forensic DNA. *Forensic Science International: Genetics, 18*, 4–20.

Carlyle, F. (2011, March 16). Seeing red: Presumptive tests for blood. *The Gist*. Retrieved from https://the-gist.org/2011/03/seeing-red-%E2%80%93-presumptive-tests-for-blood/

Cohen, A. (2015, April 4). Bad FBI science. The Marshall Project. Retrieved from https://www.themarshallproject.org/2015/04/24/bad-fbi-science

Consortium of Forensic Science Organizations (2013). Certification of forensic science practitioners. Retrieved from http://www.thecfso.org/advocacy/CFSO_Certification_Paper_201312.pdf

Cooper, S. (2013). The collision of law and science: American court responses to developments in forensic science. *Pace Law Review, 33*, 234–301.

Cratty, C. (2012, July 12). FBI, Justice Department reviewing forensic evidence in thousands of cases. *CNN Today*. Retrieved from http://www.cnn.com/2012/07/11/

justice/fbi-forensic-evidence-review/index.html

Crosby Independent School District (2017). Forensic science—law and ethics. Retrieved from http://crosby.esc11.net/cms/lib6/TX02216626/Centricity/Domain/235/Forensics_Law_and_Ethics.pdf

Daniels, D. (2015). DNA methodologies sterilization. Retrieved from http://slideplayer.com/slide/7444961/

Dean, C. (2006, December 5). When questions of science come to a courtroom, the truth has many faces. *New York Times*. Retrieved from http://www.nytimes.com/2006/12/05/science/05law.html

Doak, S., & Assimakopoulos, D. (2007). How do forensic scientists learn to become competent in casework reporting in practice? A theoretical and empirical approach. *Forensic Science International*, *167*, 201–206.

Downs, J. (2012). Whistleblowing. In J. Downs & A. Swienton (Eds.), *Ethics in forensic science* (pp. 399–424). Waltham, MA: Elsevier.

Durose, M., Burch, A., Walsh, K., & Tiry, E. (2016). *Publicly funded forensic crime laboratories: Resources and services, 2014*. Washington, DC: Bureau of Justice Statistics.

Federal Bureau of Investigation (2006). Quality assurance guide for the forensic analysis of ignitable liquids. *Forensic Science Communications*, *8*, 1.

Gianelli, P. (2012). The North Carolina crime lab scandal. *Criminal Justice*, *27*, 43–46.

Glossary of Forensic Terms (n.d.). Competency test. Retrieved from http://www.expert glossary. com/definition/competency-test.

Hoffberger, C. (2016, September 23). Crime lab cover-up? *The Austin Chronicle*. https://www. austinchronicle.com/news/2016-09-23/crime-lab-cover-up/

Houck, M., & Siegel, J. (2015). *Fundamentals of forensic science* (3rd ed.). New York, NY: Elsevier.

Hsu, S. (2016, February 25). Justice Dept. to expand review of FBI forensic techniques beyond hair unit. *Washington Post*. Retrieved from https://www.washingtonpost.com/local/public-safety/justice-dept-to-expand-review-of-fbi-forensic-techniques-beyond-hair-unit/2016/02/25/5adf0b8c-dbd4-11e5-81ae-7491b9b9e7df_story.html?utm_term=.c1c8da2a2496

Hsu, S. (2017, April 10). Sessions orders Justice Dept. to end forensic science commission, suspend review policy. *Washington Post*. Retrieved from https://www.washingtonpost.com/local/public-safety/sessions-orders-justice-dept-to-end-forensic-science-commission-suspend-review-policy/2017/04/10/2dada0ca-1c96-11e7-9887-1a5314b56a08_story.html?utm_term=.93a14c13dcc6

Iannelli, J. (2016, June 29). BSO crime lab could be mishandling crucial DNA evidence, whistleblower says. *Broward-Palm Beach New Times*. Retrieved from http://www.browardpalmbeach.com/news/bso-crime-lab-could-be-mishandling-crucial-dna-evidence-whistleblower-says-7881208

Justice Project (2008). *Improving the practice and use of forensic science*. Washington, DC: The Justice Project.

Kerstholt, J., Eikelboom, A., Dickman, T., Steel, R., Hessen, R., & van Leuven, R. (2010). Does suggestive information cause a confirmation bias in bullet comparisons? *Forensic Science International*, *198*, 138–142.

Koehler, J. (2016). Forensics or fauxrensics? Ascertaining accuracy in the forensic sciences. Retrieved from https://ssrn.com/abstract=2773255

Koehler, J. (2011). Proficiency tests to estimate error rates in the forensic sciences. Northwestern University School of Law Faculty Working Papers, Paper 24. Retrieved from http://scholarlycommons.law.northwestern.edu/cgi/viewcontent.cgi?article=1023&context=facultyworkingpapers

Koehler, J. (2008). Fingerprint error rates and proficiency tests: What they are and why they Matter. *Hastings Law Journal*, *59*, 1077–1089.

Lawless, C. (2010). *A curious reconstruction? The shaping of marketized forensic science*. London: Centre for Analysis of Risk and Regulation. Retrieved from https://core.ac.uk/download/pdf/219558.pdf

Lynch, L. (2016, September 6). Recommendations of the National Commission on

Forensic Science. Retrieved from https://www.justice.gov/opa/file/891366/download

Malek, C., & Padraza, L. (2017, September 18). The implosion of Austin's crime lab: A timeline. *Austin Monitor*. Retrieved from https://www.austinmonitor.com/stories/2017/09/the-implosion-of-austins-crime-lab-a-timeline/

McAndrew, W. (2012). Is privatization inevitable for forensic science laboratories? *Forensic Science Policy & Management*, *3*, 42–52.

Merriam-Webster (2017). Forensics. Retrieved from https://www.merriam-webster.com/dictionary/forensics

Mnookin, J., Cole, S., Dror, I., Fisher, B., Houck, M., Inman, R . . . Stoney, D. (2010). The need for a research culture in the forensic sciences. *UCLA Law Review*, *58*, 725–780.

Nadler, J., & Schulman, M. (2006). *Whistle blowing in the public sector*. Santa Clara, CA: Markkula Center for Applied Ethics.

National Commission on Forensic Science (2016a). Recommendation to the Attorney General: A national code of professional responsibility for forensic science and forensic medicine service providers. Retrieved from https://www.justice.gov/ncfs/file/839711/download

National Commission on Forensic Science (2016b). Views of the commission on certification of forensic science practitioners. Retrieved from https://www.justice.gov/ncfs/page/file/905897/download

National Research Council (2009). *Strengthening forensic science in the United States: A path forward*. Washington, DC: National Academies Press.

O'Brien, É., Nic Daeid, N., & Black, S. (2015). Science in the court: Pitfalls, challenges and solutions. *Philosophical Transactions of the Royal Society B: Biological Sciences*, *370*(1674), 20150062. Retrieved from https://www.ncbi.nlm.nih.gov/pmc/articles/PMC4581010/

Office of News and Public Information (2009, February 18). Badly fragmented forensic science system needs overhaul; Evidence to support reliability of many techniques is lacking. *News from the National Academies*. Retrieved from http://www8.nationalacademies.org/onpinews/newsitem.aspx?RecordID=12589

Peters, J. (2013, January 17). Crime labs botch tests all the time. Who's supposed to make sure they don't screw up? *Slate*. Retrieved from http://www.slate.com/blogs/crime/2013/01/17/crime_lab_scandal_crime_labs_botch_tests_all_the_time_who_s_supposed_to.html

Peterson, J., Sommers, I., Baskin, D., & Johnson, D. (2010). *The role and impact of forensic evidence in the criminal justice process*. Retrieved from https://www.ncjrs.gov/pdffiles1/nij/grants/231977.pdf

President's Council of Advisors on Science and Technology (2016). *Forensic science in criminal courts: Ensuring scientific validity of feature-comparison methods*. Retrieved from https://obamawhitehouse.archives.gov/sites/default/files/microsites/ostp/PCAST/pcast_forensic_science_report_final.pdf

Reavy, P. (2011, November 30). Forensic scientists shake their heads at TV "CSI" counterparts. *Deseret News Utah*. Retrieved from https://www.deseretnews.com/article/705395141/Real-forensic-scientists-shake-their-heads-at-TV-CSI-counterparts.html

Reece, E. (2012). Techniques for mitigating cognitive biases in fingerprint identification. *UCLA Law Review*, *59*, 1252–1290.

Rittner, N. (2009, March 16). Postconviction DNA testing is at core of major NIJ initiatives. *National Institute of Justice Journal*. Retrieved from https://www.nij.gov/journals/262/pages/postconviction.aspx

Saferstein, R. (2017). *Introduction to criminalistics* (12th ed.). New York, NY: Prentice Hall.

Saks, M., & Koehler, J. (2008). The individualization fallacy in forensic science evidence. *Vanderbilt Law Review*, *61*, 199–219.

Sernoffsky, E. (2016, June 1). Civil grand jury: SF crime lab shouldn't be run by police. *SFGate*. Retrieved from http://www.sfgate.com/crime/article/Civil-grand-jury-SF-crime-lab-shouldn-t-be-run-7957888.php#photo-7743959

Siegel, J. (2012). General forensic ethical dilemmas. In J. Downs & A. Swienton (Eds.), *Ethics in forensic science* (pp. 59–80). New York, NY: Elsevier.

Stanley, N. (2017). Definition of lab protocol. *Classroom*. Retrieved from http://classroom.synonym.com/definition-lab-protocol-6664852.html

Thompson, W. (1995). Subjective interpretation, laboratory error and the value of forensic DNA evidence: Three case studies. *Genetica, 96*, 153–168.

Turvey, B. (2013). *Forensic fraud: Evaluating law enforcement and forensic science cultures in the context of examiner misconduct*. Waltham, MA: Elsevier.

Tyler, T. (2006). Viewing CSI and the threshold of guilt: Managing truth and justice in reality and in fiction. *Yale Law Journal, 115*, 1050–1085.

Ulery, B., Hicklin, R., Buscaglia, J., & Roberts, M. (2011, May 10). Accuracy and reliability of forensic latent fingerprint decisions. *Proceedings of the National Academy of Sciences, 108*, 7733–7738. Retrieved from https://www.ncbi.nlm.nih.gov/pmc/articles/PMC3093498/

Venville, N. (2010). *A review of contextual bias in forensic science and its potential legal implications*. Melbourne, Australia: Australia-New Zealand Policing Advisory Agency.

Warrington, D. (2007, January 6). Thirty years of change. *Forensic Magazine*. Retrieved from https://www.forensicmag.com/article/2007/01/thirty-years-change

CHAPTER 13

Ethics and Criminal Justice Research

Chapter Outline

CHAPTER LEARNING OBJECTIVES:

1. Describe the Tuskegee Experiment and the ethical issues it raised.
2. Explain the role of science in human inquiry.
3. Identify the steps in the research process.
4. Explain the purposes of social scientific research and provide an example of each.
5. Describe the key characteristics of the Nuremberg Code, Helsinki Declaration, and Belmont Report.
6. Describe the major reasons scientists should care about research ethics.
7. Identify and provide examples of issues in research ethics.

INTRODUCTION

Human subjects-involved research (HSIR) has a long history that includes instances of unethical, and perhaps even illegal, research projects (see Beecher, 1966; Carome, 2016; Wrigley, 2015). In this country, one of the grossest examples of unethical HSIR was the then U.S. Public Health Service's study to record the natural history of syphilis that included researchers at what was then Tuskegee Institute (now Tuskegee University) (see Jones, 1993). Known as the "Tuskegee Study of Untreated Syphilis in the Negro Male," the project began in 1932 and didn't formally end until 1972, when the then Department of Health, Education, and Welfare (HEW) terminated the study. The end came after the Associated Press reported in 1972 that although the 600 African American men involved as subjects had freely agreed to participate, not only had researchers *not* informed the subjects of the study's real purposes, they had (1) overtly misled the men about the project; (2) failed to give infected subjects adequate treatment for the disease, even after penicillin became the drug of choice for treatment in 1947; and (3) never gave subjects the choice of leaving the study (see Jones, 1993). In 1974, a $10 million out-of-court settlement was reached in a class-action lawsuit filed against the government and the Tuskegee researchers by subjects and their families. As part of the settlement, the federal government promised to give lifetime medical benefits and burial services to all living participants (expanded in 1975 to include widows and children) and created The Tuskegee Health Benefit Program to provide them (Jones, 1993). The last living member of the study died in 2004, and the last widow, in 2009. As of August 2017, 12 children of the original subjects were still alive and receiving health and medical benefits now overseen by the Centers for Disease Control and Prevention (Centers for Disease Control and Prevention, 2017).

This chapter examines ethical issues that arise from HSIR, especially in the context of social scientific research generally and criminal justice/criminological research in particular. I begin the discussion by examining how knowledge is generated, how science is one way of generating it, and the rules of scientific research. My focus then shifts to social scientific research, such as that done in criminal justice, that involves human subjects. Here, I describe both the foundations and purposes of HSIR in social scientific research. Next, I examine codes of ethics in, and guiding principles for, HSIR, and review three primary examples of such codes: the Nuremberg Code (1947), the Helsinki Declaration (1964), and the Belmont Report (1979). I then devote the rest of the chapter to exploring specific ethical issues in HSIR, including informed consent, confidentiality, managing harm, conflicts of interest, researcher safety, and researcher integrity/misconduct. I conclude the chapter by examining ethical issues associated with the use of self-reports in the study of crime and delinquency.

THE RESEARCH PROCESS: AN OVERVIEW

Ethical issues arising from HSIR relate to a larger enterprise that constitutes one way of knowing about reality. This way of knowing involves an approach to discovering what is "real" or "true" based on specific criteria that have to be met, known as *science*. In science, "research" (whether human subject-involved or not) is a process one undertakes to discover reality that follows specific steps. Ethical issues surrounding research tend to involve not only the general process, but the steps comprising it. So, let's first see what science is all about.

Human Inquiry and the Role of Science

You "know" certain things like boiling water is hot to the touch and people living in Spain speak Spanish. The question for the moment is not so much about how broad or deep is what you know. Rather, the question is, *How do you know what you know?* That is, how do you *know* that boiling water is hot to the touch and that people living in Spain speak Spanish?

The answer is pretty straightforward: much of what you know is the result of someone telling you and you believing them (Babbie, 2016; Steup, 2005). For example, a friend who's just returned from a trip to Spain tells you the people living there speak Spanish; your father tells you, as a small child, that the Earth orbits around the Sun; your neighbor, who is a physician, tells you that engaging in unprotected sex can result in you contracting a sexually transmitted disease. In each instance, there is agreement and belief, rather than personal experience and discovery (such as the first time boiling water dripped on your hand and burned it).

A large component of our early socialization into this culture involves us learning to accept what those around us "know" (and failing to do so results in trouble fitting in) (Babbie, 2016). Thus, one way to "know" things is through what Babbie (2016) termed **agreement reality**. But there's also another way to "know" things, and that's through personal experience and observation (e.g., you observe the burns left by the hot water and experience the pain they cause), or what Babbie (2016) described as **experiential reality**: you know something because you observed it firsthand.

The problem is that some of what you "know" may actually *not* be true—and you may even suspect as much (e.g., "everyone knows" that very large cities are "dangerous places"). This leads to a dilemma: how can you know what's true and what's not? As humans wrestled with this question, over time they developed a way of knowing about reality using a systematic approach, based on criteria that have to be met before the reality uncovered is accepted, even if it is not experienced. This way of knowing is called *science* (Babbie, 2016).

In science, assertions must have both logical and empirical support; that is, they must make logical sense and must not contradict actual observations (Babbie, 2016). To illustrate, consider why a scientist "knows" that greenhouse gases (e.g., carbon dioxide, nitrous oxide, chlorofluorocarbons, methane, water vapor) facilitate global warming (see NASA, 2017). She knows this because the assertion makes logical sense: greenhouse gas molecules absorb sunlight, re-emit it in all directions, and warm the Earth's surface and lower atmosphere. She also knows that instruments monitoring greenhouse gas emissions in the lower atmosphere show that carbon dioxide levels have nearly doubled over the last 150 years (NASA, 2017). Thus, the scientist accepts the reality of something she has not personally experienced or observed, regardless of what others have told her. She accepts this reality because certain *standards* have been met. Those standards are the rules of scientific inquiry.

The Rules of Scientific Inquiry

Because science is a specialized approach to discovering reality based in logic and empirical evidence, rules have been established to guide the endeavor. In general, most scientists agree that the **research process** (also known as the scientific method) consists of the steps presented in Box 13.1.

Can you see where ethical issues might arise in the research process? For example, the problem you intend to investigate will likely determine whether human subjects will be involved. If the answer is "yes, they will," you will then have to follow protocols to mitigate the risk of harm occurring to your subjects.

Social Scientific Research

Scientific inquiry is not confined to the physical or natural world; it also includes the social world. Social scientific research, including that conducted to understand crime and the criminal justice system, is grounded in certain assumptions and foundations (see Babbie, 2016). First, social life is organized and ordered, and this organization can

BOX 13.1 The Research Process

1. *Identify a problem*: Here, you identify a specific topic you seek to investigate in some depth. For example, are rates of criminal victimization in the United States higher in cities than in rural areas?
2. *Review relevant literature*: In this step, you review what others have written about the problem you seek to investigate, noting the limitations of these prior studies. Thus, you analyze and synthesize what others have had to say about your problem. Doing this will help you to identify a hypothesis or set of hypotheses that will guide your project.
3. *Formulate a hypothesis (or series of hypotheses) or formulate a statement of the problem*: A research hypothesis is an educated prediction about the presumed relationship between variables; a statement of the problem reiterates the problem being investigated and a justification for studying the problem. Both of these are guided by the literature review.
4. *Select a research design*: The problem that you have chosen to investigate, including any hypotheses that you seek to test, will determine the research design or method you will employ to gather and analyze relevant data used to test hypotheses or address the problem you've identified.
5. *Collect the data*: Using the design you identified in Step #4, gather your data.
6. *Analyze the data and interpret the results*: Using the appropriate method you identified in the research design, analyze the data, and decide what the results mean as they relate to the problem you're investigating.
7. *Report your findings*: As a result of your analyses and interpretations of them, report your conclusions, along with any shortcomings relevant to your study.

be identified and understood. Second, this ordering creates observable patterns on which data can be collected and analyzed. Finally, the uncovered patterns can be understood through *theories*—presumed relationships among sets of identifiable variables—that can be tested and either rejected or fail to be rejected. In social science, just as is the case for science more generally, theories constitute the logical component, while the patterns observed constitute the empirical component. Thus, social science is still built upon the three foundations of science more broadly: theory, data collection and analysis, and interpretation.

Social scientific research has several purposes, including to explore, describe, and explain social phenomena (Babbie, 2016; Bryman, 2016). Exploratory research identifies new phenomena in the social world and targets it for future study. For example, in recent years, social scientists have become interested in the so-called alt-right movement in conservative politics and have begun exploring the origins and ideologies associated with this movement (see Brugge, 2002). Descriptive research examines social organization and its individual and institutional patterns and replaces speculation and impressions with empirical observation. Finally, explanatory research provides reasons for the existence of social phenomena in the form of probabilistic causal relationships among relevant factors.

According to Babbie (2016), some explanations in social science are *idiographic*, focusing on a particular case to fully understand and document what occurred in a single instance (e.g., why a particular young man joined a gang or how gun violence affected a family living in a public housing community in Detroit). The problem with **idiographic explanation** is that it is limited to the case at hand—generalization beyond that case is not warranted. Other explanations in social science explain an entire class of patterns or cases. These are called **nomothetic explanations** and involve focusing on a small number of

factors to understand why a larger-scale pattern exists and/or how it originated. The social scientist then generalizes her results to the entirety of the class of events under scrutiny (e.g., the correlates of sexual victimization of college women occurring on campus).

Scientific explanations are based on either inductive or deductive logic (Babbie, 2016). Those based on **inductive reasoning** move from the particular to the general or from a set of specific observations to the discovery of a pattern that represents some degree of order among all the given events. Inductive reasoning tells us that a pattern exists, not necessarily why it exists. Other explanations are based on **deductive reasoning**, which moves from the general to the specific. In other words, the reasoning moves from a pattern that might be logically or theoretically expected, to observations that test whether an expected pattern actually occurs.

To summarize, "research" refers to a step-by-step process associated with one mode of human inquiry, called "science." As an approach to uncover what is "real" or "true," science is based on the criteria of logic and empirical evidence. The research process describes a procedure for knowing that consists of a number of steps: a problem is identified, hypotheses about it are generated, data are collected about the problem and analyzed, and results are interpreted. Social scientific research is one form of scientific inquiry whose targeted problems relate to the social world, including crime and criminal justice. Social science research assumes that the social world is organized, that the organization creates patterns, and that these patterns can be understood through theories, some of which are inductively developed while others are deductive in orientation. Social research can then be used to explore emerging phenomena, describe patterns in existing phenomena, or explain how or why observed patterns exist. The knowledge generated by research can be idiographic (the focus is on a single case to fully understand the causes of what occurred in that case) or nomothetic (the focus is on a small number of factors to explain why a larger pattern exists and/or how it originated).

Now that you have an idea of what the research process is and how it works, when research involves human subjects—for example, testing the effectiveness of a new drug in treating opioid addiction—codes and guiding principles have been developed to ensure that subjects are not mistreated. In fact, these codes and guiding principles helped spur the development of research ethics more broadly. The following section discusses these codes and principles.

CODES OF ETHICS AND GUIDING PRINCIPLES IN RESEARCH

All forms of scientific research involve ethical dilemmas and concerns. However, HSIR research conducted by scholars in criminology and criminal justice is especially subject to ethical problems and concerns (see Israel, 2015; Johnstone, 2005). A starting point when discussing research ethics has typically been the ethical principles formulated primarily to guide biomedical research, and this section explores those principles. However, it's very important for you to realize that although these guiding principles were developed primarily to address ethical issues arising from biomedically based HSIR, most of them—if not all—also apply to HSIR in the social sciences, including criminology and criminal justice.

The Nuremberg Code

Shortly after World War II ended in 1945, the Allies organized an International Military Tribunal in Nuremberg, Germany (the birthplace of the Nazi party). The tribunal included a series of trials against alleged war criminals who were members of the German army and/or Nazi sympathizers who held powerful positions in government, the military, law, academe, and the economy (see Taylor [1992] for a firsthand account). The first trial, known as the **Doctors' Trial**, involved 23 physicians tried for crimes against humanity resulting from activities in which they participated during the war that included (1) planning and enacting the so-called Euthanasia Program aimed at people with severe psychiatric, neurological, or physical disabilities, and (2) engaging in pseudoscientific medical experiments that utilized thousands of concentration camp prisoners without their consent (Spitz, 2005). After five months of proceedings, 16 of the doctors were found guilty; seven of them were sentenced to death and executed in June of 1948 (United States Holocaust Memorial Museum, n.d.).

Guiding Principles

As a result of the Doctors' Trial, tribunal judges became convinced that protections were needed for HSIR that went beyond medicine's Hippocratic Oath and its maxim of "do no harm" (the convicted *were* medical doctors after all!). The judges developed a set of 10 guiding principles that centered not on the physician, but on the subject(s) involved in the research. As explained by Evelyne Shuster (1997), these principles—known as the **Nuremberg Code** (see Box 13.2)—included a new, comprehensive, and absolute requirement of (1) subjects giving their informed consent to participate in the research and (2) subjects having the right to withdraw their participation in the research. For many bioethicists, the unique (and most important) contribution of the Nuremberg Code was to merge medical ethics with the protection of human subjects *into a single code* that not only required physician-researchers to protect the best interests of their subjects but also proclaimed that subjects could actively protect themselves (Schuster, 1997; United Nations, 2017).

The Helsinki Declaration

The World Medical Association (WMA) was organized in 1945 in response to the atrocities perpetrated by Nazi physicians during World War II (World Medical Association, 2013). As explained by Bernard Fischer (2006), between 1953 and 1963, the association examined ethical issues in biomedical research, and its work culminated in the **Helsinki Declaration** (see Box 13.2 for a synopsis), which was first published in 1964 and has since been revised several times (Israel, 2015). In its current form (ca. 2013), the Declaration is organized into 12 sections and 37 separate paragraphs, which include a Preamble and a Statement of General Principles, along with substantive areas ranging from Informed Consent to Unproven Interventions in Clinical Practice (World Medical Association, 2013).

Guiding Principles

Fischer (2006) has suggested that three foundational aspects are preeminent in the Declaration. The first foundation was an overview, wherein the Declaration (1) defined HSIR, (2) indicated why it was necessary, and (3) stressed physician obligations to prioritize subjects' health. The second foundational area involved basic principles for biomedical research and reaffirmed certain aspects of the Nuremberg Code. What's notable here, according to Fischer (2006), was that the Declaration significantly expanded the Nuremberg Code's **principle of voluntarism** by arguing that subjects should give their consent only *after being fully informed* of a study's design, goals, funding sources, potential conflicts of interest, researcher affiliation(s), risks and benefits, and their right to withdraw. Also noteworthy was the Declaration arguing that only members of populations likely to benefit from the research should be recruited, and that vulnerable populations should not be used when other populations were available and appropriate (Fischer, 2006, p. 70). The third foundational area of the Declaration devoted itself to research combined with clinical practice and care. Highlights here included the Declaration stating that research combined with practice can only occur if doing so has the potential to diagnose and treat, and that in these cases subjects must be made aware of the aspects of their care that are experimental (Fischer, 2006).

The Belmont Report

The third code/set of guiding principles for HSIR is known as the **Belmont Report** (see Box 13.2), which devotes itself to HSIR that is funded by federal agencies in this country (e.g., the National Institutes of Health [NIH] or the Department of Health and Human Services [HHS]) (Israel, 2015). Published in 1979, *The Belmont Report: Ethical Principles and Guidelines for the Protection of Human Subjects of Research* articulated three principles (referred to as "basic ethical principles") governing HSIR and identified three sets of guidelines (referred to as "applications") useful in resolving ethical problems arising from HSIR (Office for Human Research Protections, 2016). Below, I provide you an overview of these elements.

Guiding Principles

According to the Belmont Report, basic ethical principles are foundational justifications for the myriad ethical prescriptions and evaluations of human actions that exist. These principles include (1) respect for persons, (2) beneficence, and (3) justice (Office for Human Research Protections, 2016; Office of Research Services, 2017). *Respect for persons* means that human subjects should be treated as individuals who make decisions about or deliberate for themselves concerning personal goals, and then act upon them. Persons unable to make such decisions (e.g., children or the physically or mentally infirm) should be protected from coercion by others and from all activities that harm them, where harm is related to the risks and benefits of the research. *Beneficence* involves doing "good" to the individual, understood to mean maximizing possible benefits and minimizing possible harms to research participants. Extending "do no harm" into research is understood in the Belmont Report to mean that one should not injure a single person, regardless of the benefits that others may gain. The problem is sometimes one cannot know that something is harmful until it is tried, and in doing so individuals will be exposed to risk of harm. Therefore, investigators must develop a plan that maximizes benefits and minimizes risks to the best of current knowledge (Office for Human Research Protections, 2016).

Finally, *justice* refers to whom the benefits and harms accrue (Office for Human Research Protections, 2016). During the 19th and early 20th centuries, the burdens (harms) of experimentation were borne by poor patients in charity hospitals, while the rewards (benefits) of improved medical care were realized primarily by wealthy patients.

During World War II, Nazi researchers' use of concentration camp prisoners was another example of injustice surrounding biomedical research. In research, both the benefits and the risks should be distributed in a just manner. To ensure this, the selection of subjects involved in the research needs to be constantly monitored to identify whether some pools of participants are being systematically chosen simply because they are easily available, are vulnerable, or are easy to manipulate, rather than for reasons directly related to the research problem being studied.

The Belmont Report also presented applications in practice, including those relating to *informed consent, assessing risks and benefits*, and *selecting participants* (Office for Human Research Protections, 2016; Office of Research Services, 2017). These applications are designed to ensure that the guiding principles of respect for persons, beneficence, and justice are put into practice when HSIR is occurring.

Crucial to ensuring that human subjects are respected and aware of possible benefits and risks is informed consent. Typically, **informed consent** is a document presented to a prospective subject that contains a written summary of the research project, including the protocols being used and a description of possible risks and benefits of participating. Once briefed on the project, the prospective subject—should she agree to participate—signs the consent form indicating her agreement to participate. Her signing, however, must *not* involve coercion or undue influence.

The **informed consent process** involves the following actions. The prospect is first provided adequate information about the project. Second, the subject is given adequate opportunity to consider their options of participating by having their questions answered, along with the researcher ensuring that the prospect comprehends the information she has been provided. Third, the prospect's voluntary agreement to participate is obtained, and fourth, the participant is provided additional information as needed (Office for Human Research Protections, 2016; Office of Research Services, 2017). In situations where prospects possess limited ability to understand information provided, the investigator makes special provisions that might include having a third party, able to understand the information and the prospect's situation, act on the subject's behalf.

Assessing possible risks and benefits requires a careful array of relevant data, including—in some cases—alternative means of obtaining the benefits sought by the project. This assessment serves several functions. For the investigator, it is a means for checking whether the proposed research project is properly designed. For a committee reviewing the project (see discussion of committee review of HSIR in the next section, "Impact of the Belmont Report"), it is a means by which it determines whether the possible risks presented to the subjects can be justified. Finally, for prospective subjects, the assessment assists in their determination of whether to participate (Office for Human Research Protections, 2016).

According to the Office for Human Research Protections (2016, p. 1), the requirement that research be justified on the basis of a favorable risk/benefit assessment bears a close relation to the principle of beneficence—"doing good." As used in the Belmont Report, "risk" refers to both a probability that harm may occur (e.g., the risk is "small" or "large") and the severity (magnitude) of the envisioned harm. "Harm" refers to a variety of negative outcomes, including those that are psychological, physical, legal, economic, or social in nature. The term "benefit" refers to something of positive value related to subjects' health or welfare but is not expressed in probabilities. Risk/benefit assessments are concerned with the probabilities and magnitudes of possible harm and anticipated benefits.

Participant selection relates to the guiding principle of justice, similar to how the principle of respect for persons finds expression in the requirement of informed consent, and the principle of beneficence finds expression in risk/benefit assessments. Justice gives rise to moral requirements that there be fair procedures and outcomes used to select research subjects; justice requires that receiving benefits and being subjected to risks be distributed fairly (Office of Research Services, 2017).

Impact of the Belmont Report

The Belmont Report's greatest impact was its incorporation into federal regulations concerning the protection of human subjects involved in research funded by federal agencies. In June of 1991, federal policy—known as the "Common Rule"—was codified into regulatory law and is found in Title 45 of the *Code of Federal Regulations* Part 46 (abbreviated as "45 CFR 46"). The **Common Rule** converted principles outlined in the Belmont Report into actual federal regulations for any HSIR funded by HHS and provided regulatory procedures for all research involving human subjects that was conducted, supported, or otherwise subject to regulation by any federal department or agency taking appropriate action to make the policy applicable to such research (Israel, 2015). At that point, a total of 18 federal agencies agreed to follow the Common Rule.

The Common Rule prescribes a variety of institutional structures, review mechanisms, and policies for review and oversight of HSIR, including creating **Institutional Review Boards** (IRBs) that are responsible for approving HSIR. Typically consisting of a panel containing a minimum of five researchers (the panel may be larger), IRBs meet on a regular basis (e.g., monthly) to review research projects submitted to them. Federal regulations require that IRBs follow written procedures for (1) conducting initial and continuing review of research and reporting its findings and actions to the investigator and the institution; (2) determining which projects require review more often than annually and which projects need verification from sources other than the investigators that no material changes have occurred since previous IRB review; and (3) ensuring prompt reporting to the IRB of proposed changes in a research activity, and (4) ensuring that investigators will conduct the research activity in accordance with the terms of the packet submitted to the IRB.

Until the IRB gives its approval, any project involving HSIR cannot commence. Further, once approved, and depending on the type of project, annual updates to IRB may be required. Additionally, if substantive change occurs, the investigator should submit an amendment to the original IRB submission, which is then reviewed by the panel. If there are concerns and/or questions relating to the amendment, another meeting with the investigator may be called. If there are enough objections, the IRB may suspend its approval of the project, pending remedies to their concerns being completed by the investigators. When the project is completed, the investigator may also submit a "final report" to the IRB. All of the documents for each project are then archived in case of institutional audit by the federal government.

Research institutions (e.g., colleges and universities; private "think tanks" involved in HSIR) have to comply with the Common Rule to remain eligible for funding provided by government agencies. Although the regulations apply to activities sponsored by a range of federal agencies, they were written primarily with biomedical research in mind, in the belief that the greatest risk to human subjects was typically associated with that type of research (Israel, 2015). However, to accommodate social and behavioral research involving human subjects (which is often, but not always, of minimal risk to human subjects), IRBs were given the prerogative of formally exempting some research, of conducting an expedited review, and of waiving the requirement of signed consent under certain reasonable circumstances (Israel, 2015). HHS-based changes to federal regulations concerning the protection of human subjects are scheduled to take effect in January of 2019 (Federal Register, 2018). The changes are designed to address broader types of research that use federal funds, such as behavioral and social science research.

BOX 13.2 Highlights of Major Codes and Guiding Principles Relating to Research Ethics

The Nuremberg Code (1947):

1. All participation in research must be voluntary.
2. The results of the research must be useful and unobtainable by other means.
3. The study must be rationally based on knowledge of the disease or condition to be studied.
4. It must avoid unnecessary suffering.
5. The study cannot include death or disabling injury as a foreseeable consequence.
6. Its benefits must outweigh its risks.
7. The study must use proper facilities to protect participants.
8. The study must be conducted by qualified individuals.
9. Participants may withdraw from the study if they wish.
10. Investigators must be prepared to stop the study should participants die/become disabled.

Source: Fischer (2006, p. 69)

The Helsinki Declaration (1964):

1. Research with humans should be based on the results from laboratory and animal experimentation.
2. Research protocols should be reviewed by an independent committee prior to initiation.
3. Informed consent from research participants is necessary.
4. Research should be conducted by medically/scientifically qualified individuals.
5. Risks should not exceed benefits.

Source: Office of the Vice Chancellor for Research & Economic Development (2017, p. 1)

The Belmont Report (1979):

ETHICAL PRINCIPLES FOR RESEARCH APPLICATIONS

1. Respect for Persons
   a. Individuals should be treated as autonomous agents.
   b. Persons with diminished autonomy are entitled to protections.
2. Beneficence
   a. Human participants should not be harmed.
   b. Research should maximize possible benefits and minimize possible risks.
3. Justice
   a. The benefits and risks of research must be distributed fairly.

APPLICATIONS FOR RESEARCH INVOLVING HUMAN PARTICIPANTS

1. Informed Consent
   a. Volunteer research participants, to the degree that they are capable, must be given the opportunity to choose what shall and shall not happen to them.
   b. The consent process must include three elements: information, comprehension, and voluntary participation.
2. Assessment of Risks and Benefits
   a. The nature and scope of risks and benefits must be assessed in a systematic way.
3. Selection of Participants
   a. There must be fair procedures outcomes in selecting participants.

Source: Medical Advocates for Social Justice (n.d., p. 1)

The changes are also intended to harmonize human subjects' policies across federal agencies (Office for Human Research Protections, 2017).

To summarize, because of Nazi physician and sympathizer atrocities during the Holocaust, a new field of biomedical research ethics emerged in the late 1940s. Important documents that have appeared since the 1940s, including the Nuremberg Code, the Helsinki Declaration, and the Belmont Report, articulate the ethical boundaries of HSIR. Each of these documents offers guiding principles for informed consent, mandates clear articulation of the risks and benefits to subjects, and supports subjects' right to withdraw at any time. Investigators must also ensure that special populations, such as those unable to give informed consent, are monitored and protected.

Now that you have a sense of the ethical issues associated with HSIR, let's consider Case Study 13.1, which describes ethical issues arising from conducting biomedical research on prison inmates. Use the framework for analysis (Ch. 5) to analyze the case from the perspective of virtue ethics (Ch. 2).

CASE STUDY 13.1 The Prison Warden's Dilemma

Adam Zapel is the current warden at the West Jefferson Correctional Facility, a maximum-security prison located in rural Jefferson County, AL, that houses over 700 inmates. Zapel has been warden at West Jefferson for about five years, during which time he has gained the respect of inmates and staff alike because he runs the prison in a firm but fair manner and is always looking to help the inmates.

Today, Warden Zapel has a meeting with Dr. Noah Lott, a medical researcher at the local university who appears to be on the verge of a cure for high blood pressure. After nearly 15 years of research and development, Lott has finally reached the point where the drug he's been working on is ready for testing on humans. The drug does, however, have potentially serious side effects, including damage to the lungs, liver, and even death from heart failure. Dr. Lott is convinced, however, that these risks are very low, based on other testing he's completed (not on humans).

The reason for the meeting is that Lott is seeking Zapel's cooperation in soliciting inmates from the prison who would *voluntarily* participate in a clinical trial of the drug in exchange for parole from the institution. At the meeting, Lott explains to the warden both the risks of harm for the subjects as well as the potential benefits that could be obtained should the drug prove successful (e.g., hypertension could be reduced, if not eliminated). Lott provides Zapel with a formal report from the Institutional Review Board (IRB) of the university with which Lott is affiliated that approved the project. Lott also shows Zapel a letter from Governor Paige Turner, which says she will ensure that parole is granted to the 50 inmates selected by Zapel in exchange for their participation in the tests. The letter says the governor will leave the final decision up to Zapel (i.e., he can reject Lott's proposal), and that she does not anticipate any problems from the parole board (i.e., its members are "on board"). Lott also reveals to Warden Zapel that if the proposed testing is rejected, there will be no further experiments because Lott's funding from the National Institutes of Health (NIH) has run out, and no other agency has expressed a willingness to continue funding his research.

Warden Zapel sees the potential good that could come from the experiment and already has in mind the inmates to which he might offer the option of participating. However, the possible risks of the drug trouble him, especially the possibility of death. Although the inmates he has in mind are either on death row or have received sentences of life in prison, the appellate courts have not heard all of their appeals, so if a study participant was to die because of the treatments, it could be that an innocent man died unnecessarily. The fact that some of the inmates would get a placebo yet still earn parole by participating in the study also troubles Zapel. After much thought, Zapel rejects the proposal.

Was Warden Zapel's behavior ethical?

ETHICAL ISSUES IN SOCIAL SCIENCE RESEARCH

Criminal justice researchers have not been given carte blanche to conduct their studies because the subject matter covered—problems in crime and justice—has been deemed as being especially important. Instead, they are *allowed* to conduct their research through a combination of good intentions on their part and a willingness to abide by constraints imposed on them when working with human subjects. Note that no *legitimate* social scientist would ever *deliberately* set out to harm others through their research. Sometimes—to their own horror—they realize the harm that is occurring and end the project (Philip Zimbardo's Stanford Prison Experiment, that was discussed in Ch. 10, is a good example). The problem is that sometimes criminal justice researchers may not see that harm can, in fact, occur, and need to be reminded of the ethical constraints that exist to try and avoid (or at least minimize) that harm. You may have the "best study ever" in technical or scientific terms, but if you ignore the ethical issues associated with it, you do so at your own peril and that of the larger discipline.

In this section, I examine some of the ethical issues confronting social science researchers—including those in criminology and criminal justice—as they seek to uncover new knowledge about the social world. I begin the section by explaining why criminal justice researchers should care about research ethics. I then discuss specific ethical issues surrounding informed consent, subject confidentiality, managing harm, conflicts of interest, researcher safety, and integrity and misconduct. The point of this section is to get you thinking about the ethical issues that come with generating new knowledge. This information will also help you critically evaluate the ethical foundations of studies in criminal justice or criminology you may read that used human subjects. Note that my purpose here is to provide you with an *overview* of several issues that scholars agree are important. For those interested in more thorough discussions of research ethics, I provide sources to consult in the Resources section of the chapter.

Why Care About Research Ethics?

The first point I want to make is this: anyone—*including students*—involved in criminal justice research should care about the ethics of their work, and *you* should care about *them* caring. As explained by Mark Israel (2015), there are at least four reasons you should care about research ethics.

First, research is supposed to generate trust—from other researchers, from institutions and governments, and perhaps most importantly, from the public—and promote integrity (Israel, 2015). Unethical research violates that trust, upends integrity, and creates a host of problems, including withdrawal of community support, damage to research institutions' credibility, and long-term harm to the researcher's reputation and ability to procure funding. If criminal justice researchers can assure colleagues (and other constituencies) that the research they conducted met the highest ethical standards, confidence in not only their results but also in the entire research enterprise increases.

Second, criminal justice researchers should also care about ethics because in doing so, one accepts the kind of accountability and professionalism increasingly demanded of researchers more broadly (Israel, 2015). Corruption, scientific misconduct, and impropriety threaten not only careers, but can lead to sanctions against miscreants, up to and including fines and/or imprisonment. Unethical behavior also causes diversion of institutional resources into monitoring research programs as part of an overall risk-management strategy and away from other deserving sources, jeopardizes professional researchers' ability to "police themselves," and subjects them to losing the benefits that come with belonging to a profession.

Third, Israel (2015) claims that criminal justice researchers should also care about research ethics as a result of new and more challenging ethical issues arising with advances in technology.

Turning first to new challenges linked to advancing technologies, consider the ethical implications of a research project that involves exabytes of data—say, for example, a 10-year study of calls for service received by the Los Angeles Police Department department to identify and predict "hot spots" of crime. How many thousands of people—and addresses—are identified in such data? How does the researcher obtain informed consent from the subjects? How do you protect their confidentiality? Looking to research codes, regulations and training materials may offer little comfort, as they may lag behind larger-scale change. As Israel (2015, p. 5) correctly observes, both individually and collectively, "researchers have little choice but to identify and work through the ethical issues as best they can, reflecting upon and justifying their decisions in these new environments."

Finally, researchers should care about ethics because doing so helps minimize the risks of harm to human subjects. Ethical research protects individuals, communities, and environments, and offers the potential to increase the sum of good in the world (Israel, 2015). What this means in practice is that researchers should always seek to avoid (or at least minimize) long-term, systematic harm to those same individuals, communities, and environments, even if doing so is inconvenient, time-consuming, and costly, whether in economic or other terms.

Now that you have a sense for why criminal justice researchers should care about research ethics, let's consider some specific ethical issues in HSIR conducted by those interested in problems relating to crime and justice.

Informed Consent

I'm hard pressed to think of a more important aspect of criminological and criminal justice research than obtaining informed consent from the people who are the subjects of a study (see Faden & Beauchamp, 1986). Informed consent is important because it involves researchers treating prospective subjects as autonomous, self-determining actors.

"Informed consent" means that one possesses knowledge about a subject or situation (Merriam-Webster, 2017a). A prospective subject can be considered to be informed when she has knowledge about the purpose(s) of a study, its methods, demands and risks, inconveniences, and possible outcomes, including whether and how results might be disseminated and data reused. Informed consent also involves one giving one's assent or approval (Merriam-Webster, 2017b). Putting the two together, informed consent involves a subject possessing adequate enough knowledge to give their assent to become involved in the research study (Israel, 2015). Sounds easy enough, right? Actually, it's a bit more complicated. Let's see why this is the case.

Accurate Information

Prospective participants must be *accurately* informed of the purpose, methods, risks, benefits, and uses of the research (Campbell, n.d.). In order for a prospective subject to make an *informed* decision about whether to participate in a research study, she has to first possess information that is *accurate*. What this means is the researcher doesn't "hide" anything from the prospective subject, but rather provides adequate summaries (in everyday language) of the purpose of the research (e.g., to understand how delinquent and criminal gangs recruit young men and women into their ranks); the methods being used (e.g., an in-person interview using a script of preselected questions); the potential risks of harm (e.g., psychological or emotional discomfort above what the subject might experience in a typical day); benefits (e.g., taking a personal stand against gang-related problems in your neighborhood); and potential uses of the research (e.g., to disrupt gangs).

Understanding

Second, the subject must *understand* this information and how it relates to their personal situation (Campbell, n.d.). Faden and Beauchamp (1986) have argued that a prospective subject can only make an informed decision if they have *substantial understanding* of all information that, in their view, is material to their decision to grant consent. In turn, substantial understanding occurs only if the subject *adequately comprehends* information that is material to her decision to participate, including the nature of the action (in this case, participating in the study) and the foreseeable consequences and outcomes of consenting (Faden & Beauchamp, 1986). Thus, the researcher must take steps to ensure that the subject adequately understands all material information relevant to the subject when making her decision to participate.

Voluntariness

A prospective subject must also make a *voluntary* decision concerning participation (Campbell, n.d.). What could impede a voluntary decision by the prospect? Some observers suggest that the two primary impediments to voluntary consent are *coercion* and *inducement*. The Belmont Report, for example, identified both coercion and inducement as challenges to ethically conducted research. It stated that coercion occurs "when an overt threat of harm is intentionally presented to obtain consent," while inducement occurs "through an offer of excessive, unwanted, inappropriate or improper reward . . . to obtain compliance" (Office for Human Research Protections, 2016, p. 8).

Relevant here are **incentives** researchers offer prospective subjects to get them to participate (Largent, Grady, Miller, & Wertheimer, 2013). According to proponents, incentives—referred to as "payment"—are appropriate for recruiting research participants. Critics contend that incentives, particularly those involving *monetary* considerations, undermine the voluntariness of participants' informed consent (Applebaum, Lidz, & Klitzman, 2009). The federal Common Rule for protecting human subjects offers little guidance, as it says simply that researchers should "minimize coercion or undue influence of subjects when obtaining informed consent."

While these arguments rage, individual researchers have to decide whether their incentives are "coercive" or constitute "undue influence." Say that you are studying how prescription pain medication helped spur spikes in heroin use and overdoses in a particular community. You are obviously interested in attracting opioid users into your study, so you include an incentive of $50 for those who participate. Say, too, that at least some of the prospects are suffering withdrawal symptoms when they see your recruiting advertisement. Are they not going to be "unduly influenced" by the $50 incentive to participate in your study? Researchers may thus find it difficult to assess whether potential participants do, in fact, have freedom of action (Israel, 2015). One possible solution, offered by Faden and Beauchamp (1986), would be for researchers to restrict their incentives to those that, on the one hand, would likely be welcomed (e.g., gift cards, t-shirts), but on the other, could be easily resisted by prospective subjects, should they wish.

Objections Surrounding Informed Consent

Many social scientists, while agreeing that obtaining informed consent is important, have objected—sometimes loudly—to having imposed on them a standardized process for obtaining consent that is based in quantitative, clinically oriented, biomedical research (see Dingwall, 2012; Schrag, 2011; White, 2007). Recruiting and interviewing residents of a public housing community to understand how underground economies for weapons or drugs develop in such locations is hardly the same as finding subjects to participate in clinical trials of a new drug aimed at controlling ADHD in young adults. In the former instance, researchers may use more open-ended, inductively based methodologies that include observation and unstructured interviews with residents, which may make it difficult beforehand for researchers to identify the potential risks for harm posed to subjects who participate (Heimer & Petty, 2010). Yet IRB protocols (see Box 13.3) often require that researchers—in both instances—use a similar procedure for obtaining informed consent, including having subjects sign a document as proof they have given their consent (White, 2007). Perhaps the American Association of University Professors (2000, p. 1) provided a good depiction of the concerns of social science researchers concerning IRB protocols relating to informed consent:

> [C]oncern has been expressed that explaining the purposes or the benefits of the research may run the risk of skewing the research results, because the subject can change his or her behavior based on the new knowledge. If, for example, subjects are told that a principal purpose of the research is to observe unobtrusively their conduct under stressful conditions, their behavior is not likely to be spontaneous. What can a researcher tell a subject about either the purpose or the benefits of the research if deceiving the subject is necessary to carry out the research? If the researcher is studying illegal or stigmatized behavior, obtaining consent may be infeasible or pose a greater risk to the subject than the research itself.

Israel (2015, p. 88) has identified multiple objections raised by social scientists to institutional norms for obtaining informed consent of human subjects, including:

- Research ethics' governance structures, such as IRBs, have mechanically adopted informed consent procedures, creating an artificial, culturally inappropriate, and occasionally dangerous bureaucratic process;
- Requiring participants to sign their names to informed consent documents potentially removes the protections that anonymity would provide should subjects make incriminating statements. But for the signed consent form, no identifying details would have been recorded. Instead of protecting participants, such a requirement places them at greater risk;
- Informed consent forms may actually compromise informed consent if written information is unclear or constructed without sensitivity. Standardized wording

BOX 13.3 Sample Online Informed Consent Form

WEB-BASED SURVEY CONSENT FORM

Who is doing this research study?
The person in charge of this research study is Professor Bonnie Fisher of the University of Cincinnati (UC) School of Criminal Justice.

What is the purpose of this research study?
This is a study looking at the prevention of dating violence and sexual violence on college campuses. Some questions may make you upset or feel uncomfortable and you may choose not to answer them. If some questions do upset you, at the end of the survey we will provide information for you, including people who may be able to help you with these feelings and resources on campus and in your community.

Who will be in this research study?
About 5000 randomly selected undergraduate students will take part in this study.

Are there any benefits from being in this research study?
Although you may not personally benefit from taking part in this research, your responses may help us understand more about college students' response rates to surveys about dating and sexual violence on your campus.

Are there any risks to being in this research study?
There is no physical health risk to study participation.

What will you be asked to do in this research study, and how long will it take?
You have a choice to complete the web-based questionnaire. If you do participate, you are free to skip any questions or discontinue at any time. The survey takes about 20–30 minutes to complete.

How will your research information be kept confidential?
Your responses will be kept confidential to the extent allowed by law. This study is protected by a Certificate of Confidentiality, which means that the researchers can refuse to disclose identifying information in any civil, criminal, or other proceeding, whether at the federal, state, or local level. Your responses will be kept in a database at UC on Professor Fisher's secured, password-protected computer, in her locked office for the duration of the project. After that, it will be deidentified and securely stored on Professor Fisher's computer. The UC Institutional Review Board reviews all research projects that involve human participants to be sure the rights and welfare of participants are protected. If you have questions about your rights as a participant or complaints about the study, you may contact Professor Fisher at (513) 556-5828 or Preventsv@gmail.com, the Chairperson of the UC IRB at (513) 558-5259, the UC Research Compliance Hotline at (800) 889-1547, the IRB, 300 University Hall, ML 0567, 51 Goodman Drive, Cincinnati, OH 45221-0567, or email the IRB office at atirb@ucmail.uc.edu.

What will you get for being in this research study?
Payment for your time in the form of a $5.00 Amazon gift card will be sent to you via email after you participate in the survey.

What are your legal rights in this research study?
Nothing in this consent form waives any legal rights you may have. This consent form also does not release the investigator, the institution, or its agents from liability for negligence.

Do you HAVE to take part in this research study?
No. However, by taking part in the web-based survey, you are providing your consent for your responses to be used in this study.

PLEASE KEEP THIS INFORMATION SHEET FOR YOUR REFERENCE.

Thank you for participating!

Source: Bonnie Fisher (personal communication, October 29, 2017)

can affect the quality of the research data by reducing responsiveness by subjects because they believe they are being tricked or because the form encourages researchers to overestimate the risks of potential harm to subjects;

- When researchers exercise excessive caution in negotiating informed consent, this can be interpreted as meaning that researchers distrust participants' capacity to make their own decisions.

Efforts to resolve these conflicts are ongoing. The National Science Foundation (NSF), in discussing informed consent protocols, has noted that requiring written consent could jeopardize the ability to conduct certain types of social scientific research (e.g., ethnographies) and has exempted from IRB protocols relating to informed consent, some types of research that it funds (National Science Foundation, 2017). Further, the Office for Human Research Protections (2003a) identified certain categories of HSIR involving "minimal risk of harm" to subjects as eligible for expedited review. What this means is that the chair of the IRB (or other designated member) conducts the review, but may not disapprove the project—that has to be done via full review. Finally, some institutions, including my former university, have created bifurcated IRBs, where one section handles approvals of social and behaviorally based research involving human subjects and the other section deals with biomedically based research (see Reynolds, 2000).

In summary, informed consent is both an important but controversial aspect of conducting ethically based HSIR, whether we're talking about biomedical or social scientific studies. The guiding principles here are those of respect, beneficence, and justice, while the guiding perspective is that the subject is capable of autonomous and self-directing decisions and actions. Generally, the procedure for obtaining informed consent is designed to ensure that the subject is given accurate information about the scope and nature of the study and has substantial understanding about, and adequately comprehends, what their consent involves. Finally, the consent obtained from subjects cannot be coerced, nor can incentives provided cause undue influence of subjects' decision-making. At the same time, conflicts between social scientists and IRBs have arisen over standardized protocols for obtaining informed consent. These scientists argue that the protocols may actually create problems for subjects, given the nature of some kinds of social scientific research, or skew results, as subjects behave differently than they would had they not known the exact focus of the study.

Confidentiality

Social scientists, especially those involved in studying crime and justice, will recruit subjects to reveal sensitive information about their behavior, such as involvement in illegal drug use or gang-related violence. In these instances, subjects will allow researchers to collect this information in exchange for (1) keeping subjects' names and other identifying information confidential, and (2) the information is being used solely for research purposes. As you can thus imagine, there are ethical issues surrounding **subject confidentiality** and the information that is shared by subjects with researchers and by researchers with others, especially when that information may have legal implications for the subjects.

Justifications for Confidentiality

In biomedical research, subjects recruited to participate in clinical trials of a new medication share sensitive information about themselves with researchers to obtain potential benefits, such as treatment of a disease. In social scientific research, investigators recruit subjects into studies where they will be asked to share confidential information in exchange for . . . *very little direct benefit* (Israel, 2015). For example, if I am a member of a juvenile gang and agree to share with you, Mr. or Ms. Researcher, information about how I was recruited into the group and descriptions of sexual assaults perpetrated during initiation rituals, what direct benefit is there for me in sharing this information? Additionally, what if other members find out that I have spoken about my experiences with someone doing gang research? However, if you are willing to guarantee that my personally identifiable information will be kept confidential and/or that what I said can't be linked to me (or at least that doing so would be very difficult), I might be willing to talk with you. In a sense, the benefit I accrue from talking to you is you keeping me unidentified or unidentifiable. The question then becomes possible justifications for keeping subjects' identities confidential.

There are at least three ethically principled justifications for confidentiality: consequentialist, rights-based, and fidelity-based (Israel, 2015). Consequentialist justifications argue that the potential positive consequences of maintaining subject confidentiality outweigh the potential negative consequences of not doing so. If subjects know that their identities and information are *not* being protected, they may be less willing to be forthright with what they reveal, which could jeopardize the validity of the project's results. Trust between researcher and subject is important; reneging on a promise of confidentiality not only jeopardizes that trust, it also jeopardizes the ability of future researchers to conduct similar studies. Rights-based justifications for confidentiality argue that every person has the right to limit access to his or her person—a right to privacy—that includes access to information about him or her. When I share sensitive information with you, Mr. or Ms. Researcher, I am explicitly granting you access to that information. However, if you then share that information with others without my consent, you have violated my right to that privacy, which is ethically problematic. Finally, fidelity-based justifications are deontological in orientation. That is, they argue that researchers have certain fidelity obligations to subjects, including honoring any promises made to them, such as keeping their identities confidential (or even anonymous). If subjects expect researchers will respect subjects' dignity and autonomy, researchers have an obligation to fulfill those expectations. As Israel (2015, p. 103) describes the situation, when a researcher offers a promise of secrecy to subjects, the researcher is both offering to give and perform something: they are giving their allegiance, and the performance is their keeping silent.

Protecting Confidentiality

To protect subjects' confidentiality, social scientists have used precautions that are methodological or legal in nature (Israel, 2015). Methodological precautions include administrative actions, such as not recording names and other identifying information at all; removing names and identifying details from confidential data at the earliest possible stage; or ensuring the security of data storage using locked file cabinets and password-protected datasets stored on computers. **Statistical confidentiality**, another methodological precaution researchers use to disguise/conceal personally identifying information stored in datasets, is accomplished by ensuring that the amount of information available about any particular individual never exceeds a sliding threshold that is adjusted upward as the sensitivity of the information increases (Duncan, Elliott, & Salazar-Gonzalez, 2011).

Legal precautions that social scientists use to preserve confidentiality include taking advantage of statutory protections and redacting data (Israel, 2015). One example of a statutory protection available to researchers is known as a **certificate of confidentiality** offered by government agencies such as the HHS. A researcher granted such a certificate can legally withhold from all parties not connected with the research the names or other identifying characteristics of individuals involved in the study. What this means in practice is that the researcher cannot be legally compelled to reveal such information in any federal, state, or local civil, criminal, administrative, legislative, or other proceedings (Office for Human Research Protections, 2003b). **Redacting data** occurs when the researcher agrees to hand over information to third parties, but in doing so, literally blacks out the sensitive information; various software programs are available to do this. Redacting can even be done with audio data, again using different software packages.

Because HSIR in criminology and criminal justice involves subjects revealing potentially sensitive information to researchers, protecting their identities is important. Justifications for confidentiality include principles based in consequentialist, rights-based, and deontological systems of ethics. Social scientists have used different methods to protect the confidentiality of their human subject data, including using administrative steps such as removing identifying information from datasets, using statistical confidentiality, or taking advantage of legal protections such as certificates of confidentiality. Researchers can also redact subject information shared with third parties.

Managing Harm

HSIR that is conducted ethically follows a guiding principle of "avoiding harm and doing good" in research studies. In general terms, "harm" has been taken to mean damage done to subjects, including physical, psychological, emotional, economic, or legal damage. Further, harm to subjects can also be direct or indirect. For example, direct harm to subjects involved in a clinical trial of a new medication would involve the medicine worsening symptoms or causing serious side effects. Indirect harm can occur too, such as a researcher failing to intervene after listening to members of a focus group discussing HIV/AIDS convince themselves that HIV can be contracted through casual contact (Kitzinger and Barbour, 1999). But what exactly is meant by "harm?"

Conceptualizing Harm

In the context of HSIR, **harm** can be considered as both an *event* and as a *state* (Belshaw, 2012). For example, you overconsume alcohol, damage your liver, and give yourself a headache; you drive too fast, hit a bridge, and end up in a coma; or you participate in a research study examining sexual assault and experience severe psychological and emotional distress. As Michael Belshaw (2012) explains it, in each of these cases, there is an *event*—drinking, driving, reliving the victimization—leading to a *state*—having liver damage and a headache, being in a coma, suffering an emotional breakdown. Further, the harmed state is significant; that is, you are different than you were before the event as shown by a decline in some aspect of your well-being (physical, psychological, emotional, etc.).

Harm is also conceptualized in HSIR in terms of its *probability* and *magnitude* (National Health and Medical Research Council, 2015). The probability of harm refers to the chance (i.e., the *risk*) the harm associated with the study will, in fact, occur. This is a judgment call on the part of the researcher, but there is a standard she can use: everyday risks associated with living (Emanuel, Abdoler, & Stunkel, n.d.). Anytime someone does something in daily life—drive a car, walk down the street, eat, or exercise—there is risk. Most times, in most cases, when we do something, the risk is small. When the possible harm associated with HSIR is no riskier than the possible harm of living everyday life, it is described as having "minimal risk." These types of research do not have to benefit *subjects* to be ethical, but they must at least have *social* value to make it worth using resources and taking the time of the subjects (Emanuel, et al., n.d.). In our case of subjects experiencing emotional distress as a result of sharing with a researcher details of sexual assault victimizations they experienced, compared to the everyday risk of experiencing such emotions, is the risk higher, lower, or about the same?

The magnitude of harm describes the seriousness of the change in well-being of the subject as a result of participating in the study. Again, this is a judgement call on the part of the researcher. She has to assess the nature of the harm and measure it on a scale from minimal to significant. When evaluating the ethics of HSIR, the risks to subjects must be balanced against the benefits to the subjects and/or the important new knowledge society will gain (Emanuel, et al., n.d.). This comparison is known as the **risk-benefit ratio**, where the riskier the study, the more benefit it must offer to be considered ethical. Researchers are also expected to adopt risk-minimization strategies (e.g., monitoring participants, maintaining a safety net of professionals who can provide support in emergencies, excluding vulnerable individuals or groups from participation, etc.) (Israel, 2015).

Empirical research conducted on the extent social science research causes a risk of harm to subjects and the magnitude of that harm is intended to help investigators make evidence-based, informed decisions about research protocols (Israel, 2015). For example, do subjects experience more or less distress when being interviewed one-on-one with the researcher or when completing a detailed survey? Determining which protocol reduces the risk of harm would thus become relevant to ethically justifying its use. Additionally, research indicates that **debriefing** can reduce stress and other harms caused to subjects involved in social scientific research (Dsowen, 2012). Formally, debriefing occurs after a participant has completed her participation in the research study and allows her to voice concerns or vent frustrations (Howitt & Cramer, 2011). Debriefing targets potential ethical problems relating to harm within a study, such as when deception is used, and detecting and dealing with the harm, distress, and confusion experienced by subjects (American Psychological Association, 2011). While some have questioned the effectiveness of debriefing if delayed, and that it may not take immediate effect, there is evidence that when done properly, debriefing removes stress and other harms caused in some kinds of social scientific research (Berscheid, Abrahams, & Aronson, 1967; Smith & Richardson, 1983).

To summarize, research ethics is extremely cognizant of the risks of harm caused to subjects. In research ethics, harm is conceptualized as both an event and a state; as something subjects can experience both directly and indirectly; and involves magnitude and probability. Harm is evaluated using a risk-benefit ratio that balances the possible risk of harm with the possible benefits, either to subjects or society more broadly. Finally, research conducted on how subjects involved in social science research experience the stress and distress of participating shows that debriefing subjects may help to reduce some forms of harm experienced by subjects.

Conflicts of Interest

You've no doubt heard about conflicts of interest leading to "bad" science in the case of biomedical research. The classic illustration of this is when researchers conduct industry-funded clinical trials of new drugs. Long-term, systematic, metareviews of the results of such trials reveal that when "big pharma" funds clinical trials, they are more likely to produce favorable results than in instances where the trials were funded by other sources (Gardner, 2015). "OK," you may say, "I can see where conflicts of interest could be problematic in *biomedical* research. But in *social scientific* research? I'm not following."

To illustrate, let me share a personal anecdote with you that may help. When I was first starting my academic career as a new assistant professor, I was asked to serve as a consultant in a legal appeal of Alabama's Habitual Felony Offender Act (HFOA). Briefly, the HFOA was passed by the Alabama legislature in 1980 and designed to deter and incapacitate recidivist offenders convicted of new crimes by enhancing their sentences, up to and including life without parole (LWOP), based on the number of prior felony convictions offenders had. The key to the legislation was that the HFOA was *mandatory*; that is, judges had no discretion in applying enhanced sentences to those with prior felonies who were convicted of a new felony.

What I was asked to do was conduct a statewide study of the extent to which judges actually followed the mandates of the HFOA. My study would be funded by lawyers handling the appeal of an offender who'd received a prison term of 40 years for, in effect, being a habitual bad-check writer. Around the same time, I had written several op-ed pieces for local and national media that were critical of so-called habitual offender statutes in general, and the HFOA in particular, and that's why I was contacted. So, in effect, I was offered a consulting opportunity that involved significant monetary remuneration by lawyers involved in an appeal of a statute about which I had been *publicly critical*. No conflict there, right? Well, there was, but here's how I handled it after speaking to senior colleagues and others outside the academy (e.g., my father) whose judgments I trusted.

First, I declined to accept payment of any kind for my services, so that removed any monetary incentive for "skewing" the results toward the people appealing the law. Second, I convinced the magistrate for the federal district court handling the case to hire me and another professor (selected by the state) from another university to work together to design the study. In effect, we would *both* be working *for the court* and would agree on the research design to be used for the study. Finally, while we would each write a separate report for the court, each of us would be allowed to read the other's report. Thus, with the help of others—especially my university—I took steps to *manage* the *perceived* conflict of interest I had in the case (in case you're wondering, the appeal was ultimately rejected; see *Jones v. White*, 992 F.2d 1548 [1993]).

Conflicts of interest occur when personal, financial, political, and academic concerns coexist and there is a potential for one interest to be illegitimately favored over others that have equal or greater legitimacy in a way that might make reasonable people feel misled or deceived (see Case Study 13.2). The key with conflicts of interest is the situation itself, rather than whether there has actually been misconduct (although that's quite possible). In other words, even if a study was done using a generally approved methodology, its results might be called into question *because* of the *perceived* conflicts that *may* exist involving, for example, the person doing the study and the entity funding the study. What *is* problematic is that researchers caught in a conflict of interest may end up appearing negligent, incompetent, deceptive, or all three. In my case, my university and I took steps to ensure that these claims could not be made about my involvement in the study relating to the HFOA appeal.

CASE STUDY 13.2 Conflicts of Interest in Criminological Research

In the late 1990s became known a case involving potential conflicts of interest that may have led to "bad" science concerning research conducted on recidivism of juvenile offenders.

The case involved ties between a then professor at a university in Florida and CoreCivic (formerly known as Corrections Corporation of America [CCA], one of the largest providers of private prison services in the world). The professor was a well-known supporter of privatization—some 175 favorable media quotes by him on private prisons were tallied in a 1997 *Wall Street Journal* article. Additionally, the professor was affiliated with a research center at the university that had received over $400,000 in funding from CoreCivic and another private prison service provider. He was also a board member of a realty subsidiary of CoreCivic, was being paid a summer salary of more than $25,000, an annual stipend of $12,000 plus $1,000 for each meeting of the trustees he attended, and $500 for every meeting of the Board's Compensation Committee he attended. Finally, the professor had the option of purchasing up to 5,000 shares of CoreCivic stock each year through April of 2007 at the initial offering price.

What raised the conflict of interest was that fact that the professor appeared as third author of a study published in a well-respected criminology journal in 1999. The article presented results of a one-year follow-up of offenders released from three Florida juvenile institutions, two of which were operated by Wackenhut Corrections Corporation and CoreCivic. The study compared matched samples of juveniles (a very powerful design) released from the two private institutions with those from a state-run facility. The authors reported that fewer youth from the private facilities had been rearrested and that they had been involved in less serious offenses after release. The authors granted that (1) the time period covered by the study may have been too short for adequate evaluation and (2) results may not have been generalizable to a population of more experienced offenders.

Flags were raised over the fact that (1) the article first appeared as an executive summary available on the Internet that did not include the professor as a coauthor, and (2) the report could be purchased for $10. While the report was professional in every way, several scholars raised questions about some of the language used in the report, including claims by the authors that they had "unequivocal" proof of the advantages of private prisons for lowering recidivism, and language that credited the authors with "well-deserved success." In the journal article version of the report, the professor failed to list his affiliations with CoreCivic or the university research center that was funded by it, while a second author failed to note *their* affiliation with the research center.

In 1999, the professor admitted to being involved in a conflict of interest and offered to stop his university research, pay a $2,000 fine, and resign as director of the research center. He maintained he had never disregarded his public duties to obtain private benefit, nor had he acted with corrupt intent or tried to hide his connections with the private corrections industry, having made disclosures to both the state and his own university. The fine was rejected as too low by Florida's ethics commission and the professor later offered to pay a $20,000 fine.

Sources: Geis, Mobley, & Schicor (1999, pp. 373–375); Israel (2015, p. 171); Tippett & Brooks (1997)

Although the chances that social scientists have financial stakes in the area they are studying are much less than in biomedical research (Israel, 2000; 2015), several issues relating to conflicts of interest in social scientific research are relevant and include considerations such as:

- What sort of financial arrangements should academics have with corporations, domestic or foreign government agencies?
- Should there be a limit on how much money an academic might receive from a private company or government agency?
- Should academics let companies or government agencies pay for their trips?
- Should academics disclose corporate or government affiliations when giving advice to the public or publishing research?

- Should academics with consultancies be able to act as reviewers for grant-awarding bodies if the research being funded may provide other academics with the expertise to act as a commercial competitor, or if the research might be critical of the reviewer's client?
- How should researchers distinguish between intellectual property that belongs to a client and that which belongs to the university?
- How is an academic society (e.g., the American Society of Criminology or the Academy of Criminal Justice Sciences) to deal with "huckstering" by members?

Contributing Factors

One reason cases like the one described in Case Study 13.2 are occurring and that such cases involve "significant" conflicts of interest is that many of the institutions within which social scientists work have increasingly developed an "enterprise culture" that stresses obtaining extramural funding (Israel, 2000; 2015). To give you an idea of what this means, David Matthews (2015) found that the proportion of total research income from grants and contracts awarded to higher education institutions in the United Kingdom that came from industry had increased by about $402.5 million between 1994–1995 and 2013–2014. In this country, Matthews (2015) reported that the proportion of university research funded by private industry had *tripled* between 1970 and 2000. For some in higher education, "corporate engagement in research is critical if universities are to continue their cutting-edge work" (McCluskey, 2017, p. 1). Yet, in reality, corporate backers have significant sway, including selecting specific kinds of studies and mandating that specific materials and techniques be used in exchange for their funding. As McCluskey (2017, p. 1) has argued, "[C]ompanies excel at creating the conditions most likely to give them the results they want."

To illustrate this new climate of "entrepreneurship" involving research at major universities, during my last decade as a full-time academic, especially after I became involved in cybersecurity and computer forensics and co-founded a research center that focused on those two areas, my university was especially interested in how discoveries made by colleagues and I could be "commercialized" or "monetized" into (1) royalties paid to the university by companies on patents we generated (and the university owned) and (2) start-up companies we created that would then be purchased by larger entities for a profit garnered by the university. For years, the concern by faculty working at research universities was "publishing or perishing." Beginning in the 1990s, the concern increasingly became an environment where researchers were expected to generate funding to help the university as state and federal sources continued to slash their support of higher education.

Other factors at work related to identifying conflicts of interest involve stronger efforts to identify and address them (Israel, 2015). One consideration is that the public's collective opinion of what constitutes a "conflict of interest" is expanding (Stark, 2000). What this means in practical terms is that the public may be less willing to excuse behavior that, rightly or wrongly, it considers a conflict of interest and about which it demands greater accountability. It may also mean that the public assumes (sometimes improperly) that a conflict of interest *automatically* means the science produced is somehow biased, which is simply not true.

Today there is greater involvement in institutional regulation of research and the conflicts of interest it may generate (Israel, 2015). At research universities, for example, IRB reviews are more likely now, than was the case a decade ago, to look for, identify, and seek clarification about conflicts of interest involving researchers. Research universities are also adopting "tougher" policies concerning disclosures of *potential* conflicts of interest involving researchers. To illustrate, in 2012, my former institution implemented new policies concerning conflicts of interest that stipulated that as part of the IRB review process, investigators would have to disclose any financial interests of $5,000 or more they, their spouses, or their dependents had acquired from any one entity in the previous 12 months for participating in any of the following activities:

- Professional studies, services, participation on boards of directors, or participation in manuscript review, grant/contract review, or academic program review for nonprofit/ philanthropic entities, professional societies, or professional associations, that are not affiliates of or affiliated with industry or other for-profit entities; and
- Seminars, presentations, performances, or board service for civic groups.

Additionally, as part of an annual ethics review process, investigators have to annually update all financial interests over $5,000 that developed during the previous 12 months (University of Alabama at Birmingham, 2017). Finally, academic journals that publish studies involving human subjects increasingly require a statement by the author(s) of any financial interests that could be perceived as biasing the results of the study (Ruff, 2015).

In sum, conflicts of interest pose significant threats to the ethical conduct of research in general, and HSIR in particular. Conflicts of interest occur when a researcher's personal, financial, political, and academic interests coexist, and one interest is illegitimately favored over the others, resulting in actual or perceived bias in the conduct of research. While conflicts of interest involving financial stakes for researchers in criminology and criminal justice are less likely to occur than in biomedical research, they nonetheless exist, need to be identified, and managed. The problem is that at many research universities, corporate-sponsored research has become an important source of revenue. Concurrently, the public is demanding greater accountability, and universities and other research-based institutions are implementing new governance policies geared toward identifying and addressing conflicts of interest. Academic journals have also adopted policies that require authors to identify conflicts of interest they may have involving the study being published.

Researcher Safety

Elijah Anderson is one of the preeminent urban ethnographers (one who studies people in their own environments using methods such as participant observation and face-to-face interviews) in this country. His work has included accounts of life in the inner cities of Chicago and Philadelphia that made great contributions to understanding the crime and violence often plaguing such places (his best-known work is probably *Code of the Streets: Decency, Violence and the Moral Life of the Inner City*, which, as of this writing, has been cited over 4,800 times by scholars around the globe). Anderson undertook that research with the understanding that he could be targeted and become a victim of the very crime and street violence he was studying. He thus assumed some risk in conducting the studies he did. Indeed, harm—be it physical or otherwise—can be linked to where the social scientist is doing her work, to the participants she is studying, to the sensitivity of the topic being studied, etc. (Israel, 2015). What does research ethics have to say about researcher safety/security in the context of conducting research involving human subjects, such as the work of Prof. Anderson and others like him?

Issues in Researcher Safety

I agree with Israel's (2015) observation that until *very* recently, researcher safety has been either ignored, denied, or taken for granted. The attitude has been that researchers are expected to "look after themselves" and address whatever the field throws at them with little to no support or training, and that, according to Sampson and Thomas (2003, p. 165), "issues of researcher health and safety are frequently under-emphasized and under-reported in both written and verbal accounts of fieldwork" (see also Johnson & Clarke [2003]).

This state of affairs seems odd for several reasons (Israel, 2015). One reason is that much of research ethics is concerned with protecting participants in the research process, including third parties who may suffer harm and receive little benefit. To exclude *researchers* from relevant constituencies potentially affected by the study is a major oversight, especially given the fact that the researchers themselves are *always involved*. A second oddity is that the safety of members of research teams working with researchers poorly equipped to care for themselves are even less discussed. Are *they* not worthy of consideration in terms of being exposed to risk for harm? Finally, in some countries like the United States and United Kingdom, it seems reasonable that occupational health and safety regulations be applied to the research enterprise to ensure that its members are at least aware of risks inherent in their work, and therefore be required to undergo training to mitigate them. Such is not the case, however, in either country.

Recent scholarship in this area has attempted to bring to the fore the kinds of safety risks faced by social science researchers involved in HSIR, especially those working outside laboratories (i.e., "in the field"). For example, Lee (1995) has argued that risks to researcher safety can be classified as being ambient or situational. **Ambient risks** are those embedded in the larger setting, say, the inner city of Detroit or a conflict zone in the Middle East. The risks exist because the location is itself risky, and that fact translates to an enhanced potential for harm not only to human subjects but to researchers. **Situational risks**, on the other hand, are attributable to the very presence of the researcher. For example, if I'm observing and speaking to teenaged boys playing basketball on a court in a public housing community in the inner city of Philadelphia, and I'm a 30-ish, white, male, my very presence triggers risk to my safety as people in the area don't know who I am or what I'm doing.

While true that a small number of social scientific researchers have been killed while conducting field research, a much larger number of them have been surveilled, harassed, and even assaulted by citizens or government officials. Researchers may experience physical and emotional stress when facing uncertain environments and compiling information that is both sensitive and challenging. Israel (2015) observed that social scientists may also experience changes in how they view themselves as a result of their work.

Projects can leave them exhausted or desensitized to others' suffering or leave them feeling guilty for extracting information without comparable reciprocity. Investigators may also experience their own trauma as they hear accounts by subjects about events they have themselves experienced.

Addressing the Risks of Harm

Researchers *can* take steps to address safety risks. For example, some researchers have heightened their own self-awareness, and created balance and connections with others to protect themselves against isolation. Others have created procedures whereby they speak with, and are counseled by, colleagues to alleviate emotional stress. Funding agencies, employing institutions, IRBs, and research managers can also play a role by adopting guidelines for researchers' safety (Dickson-Swift, James, Kippen, & Liamputtong, 2007). IRBs in particular can play a role by requiring researchers to stipulate in their IRB packets the self-care procedures being taken to help safeguard researchers' safety.

In summary, researcher safety is a neglected, but important, ethical issue in HSIR. Researchers, like research subjects, can experience many forms of harm. The risks for harm researchers experience can be tied to a specific location, as well as to their mere presence. Regardless of the nature of the risk encountered, until very recently, ethical research involving human subjects neglected to include considerations of researcher safety. While this is starting to change, concerns about researcher safety need to be better integrated into IRB reviews of HSIR.

Integrity and Misconduct

Dr. Marc Hauser was a prominent psychology professor at Harvard University whose research focused on understanding the processes and consequences of cognitive evolution in humans and primates. He had published some 200 articles in refereed scientific journals, had authored six books, and had received large research grants from federal agencies. In the summer of 2007, while he was out of the country, Harvard officials entered Dr. Hauser's lab and removed a computer that held documents and video recordings pertaining to his projects. They did so on the basis of a complaint filed by a member of his lab that alleged the psychologist had fabricated data and results in multiple experiments (see Gross, 2011). After a nearly five-year-long investigation, Dr. Hauser resigned from Harvard in 2011, and in 2012, the federal Office of Research Integrity (ORI) identified six instances where he had fabricated or falsified research findings in projects that had been funded by the federal government (Bartlett, 2011; 2012).

Sadly, researchers have been known to lie, fabricate data and results, copy the words of others and pass them off as their own, etc., whether human subjects were involved in the research or not. They failed to evidence honesty, truthfulness, or accuracy in what they did and how they did it. What this means is they lacked *integrity* in their actions and words, a situation that is clearly an issue in research ethics and to which I now turn my attention.

Let me begin by defining what I mean by **research misconduct**. To do so, I turn to the ORI, which has defined the term as follows:

> Research misconduct means fabrication, falsification, or plagiarism in proposing, performing, or reviewing research, or in reporting research results, [where] *fabrication* is making up data or results and recording or reporting them; *falsification* is manipulating

> research materials, equipment, or processes, or changing or omitting data or results such that the research is not accurately represented in the research record; and *plagiarism* is the appropriation of another person's ideas, processes, results, or words without giving appropriate credit. Research misconduct does not include honest error or differences of opinion.
>
> —(Office of Research Integrity, 2017, p. 1)

This definition is comprehensive in scope, as it is "organized around [intentional] misappropriation, interference, and misrepresentation and [addresses] collaborative/authorship disputes and sabotage in scientific laboratories" (Redman, 2017, p. 555). For misconduct to occur, according to the Code of Federal Regulations (42 CFR 93), there must be a finding by a committee that (1) a significant departure from accepted practices of the relevant research community occurred, (2) the misconduct was committed intentionally or knowingly, or recklessly, and (3) the allegations must be proved by a preponderance of evidence (i.e., proof by information that, compared with that opposing it, leads to the conclusion that the fact at issue is more probably true than not). The institution (e.g., college or university) bringing forward the complaint or the HHS has the burden of proof for making a finding of research misconduct.

Those being investigated for alleged scientific misconduct may be suspended from receiving federal funding, pending the outcome of the investigation (known as **suspension**); those found to have committed scientific misconduct may face a specified period of time (three years maximum) of exclusion from receiving federal funding, known as **debarment** (see United States Department of Transportation, 2017). There is a six-year limitation on bringing forward allegations of research misconduct. I will note here that not all scientists agree that even the most serious forms of scientific misconduct are detectable. For example, Bob Montgomerie and Tim Birkhead (2005, p. 19) argued that:

> [E]ven determining who is the perpetrator of clear cases of misconduct can be a tricky business. In general, scientists are poorly equipped to detect clever cases of misconduct, being more often awed by productivity, creativity, and apparent discovery than skeptical about interesting results. The legal, forensic, and psychological analyses needed to detect and be certain of serious cases of misconduct is such a daunting task that few scientists are willing to get involved. Moreover, wrongdoers are brilliant, charismatic individuals who have many supporters even in the face of what looks like clear evidence of malfeasance.

Frequency of Scientific Misconduct

One question you may have is, How frequently does scientific misconduct occur? As you can imagine, the answer absolutely depends on how the term "scientific misconduct" is defined and what behavior is included (e.g., if plagiarism is included, the percentage of scientists involved in misconduct increases significantly). That being said, the answer may be as few as 1 in 100,000 scientists (Steneck, 2006) or as many as 1 in 10,000 (Marshall, 2000). Danielle Fanelli, in an analysis of all published studies on scientific misconduct (N=18) that used surveys to identify self-reported misconduct by respondents and reported misconduct observed of scientists by respondents, found that (1) about 2% of scientists admit to having fabricated, falsified, or modified data or results at least once during their careers and as many as 34% admitted to other questionable research practices; and (2) about 14% had observed falsification, fabrication, or modification of data by others and 72% had observed other questionable research practices . She also found that misconduct was reported more frequently by medical/pharmacological researchers than by scientists in other fields (Fanelli, 2009).

Reasons Scientific Misconduct Occurs

You may also wonder why scientific misconduct occurs. For example, why would Dr. Hauser (from the above example), who had so much to lose, jeopardize his entire career by engaging in the type of misconduct in which he was found to have engaged? In reviewing the relatively scant literature on this topic, two themes seem to recur. The first is incredulity over why the question is even being asked. Those in this camp point out that *all* human activity is associated with misconduct, and that it may even be easier for scientists to do so because the entire scientific research enterprise operates on trust. Scientists can also be the victims of their own rhetoric: they have fooled themselves that science is a wholly objective enterprise unsullied by the usual human subjectivity and imperfections.

The second (and far more popular) explanation offered is based on a "cost/benefit" model. Here, the scientist's perceived costs might include personal anguish, official censure, difficulty in publishing research or obtaining grants, and loss of grants, research students, prestige, or employment. Perceived benefits might include new/better employment, prestige, increased salary, additional grants, and awards. Montgomerie and Birkhead (2005) note that in such a model, the "optimal" level of misconduct will depend on the scientist's perception of the costs; they further note that such a model is based on the perpetrator's *perceptions* of costs and benefits, rather than on the actual costs and benefits.

Preventing Scientific Misconduct

Given the seriousness of scientific misconduct for the integrity of the entire research enterprise and trust in its findings, what can be done to prevent this behavior? In a recent review of scientific misconduct and its implications, neuropsychologist Charles Gross (2016) discussed the following preventive measures: (1) whistleblowing, (2) training, (3) changing measures of success, and (4) adopting reproducible research tools. Let's consider each of these separately.

Whistleblowing by colleagues is the most common means of detecting scientific misconduct (Shamoo & Resnik, 2003). However, even when the whistleblowing is justified as a result of investigating the claims made, and despite the presence of protections for whistleblowers, the consequences for them of coming forward are often quite disastrous in terms of their income, research, personal relations at work, and future in science (Gross, 2016). Nonetheless, since whistleblowing remains a major weapon against scientific misconduct, encouraging the behavior—rather than punishing it—simply makes sense. This could be done, for example, by guaranteeing financial support and other resources—including a mentor—through receipt of the degree if the whistleblower was a graduate student in good standing. Postdoctoral fellows and technicians who whistleblow might be guaranteed a paid position for a stipulated period until they are able to find new support. Finally, institutional commitment to preventing career destruction of whistleblowers would send a strong message of support for such efforts.

Training in the **responsible conduct of research** (RCR), is another tool that can be used to prevent scientific misconduct, and one that is increasingly being adopted by colleges and universities, as well as by other institutions involved in the research enterprise (Gross, 2016). Training in RCR covers important topics including conflicts of interest, policies and practices relating to human and animal subjects and laboratories, mentor/mentee relationships, collaborative research, peer review, data acquisition and laboratory tools, research misconduct, responsible authorship and publication, and the scientist as a responsible member of society (Gross, 2016; National Science Foundation, n.d.). This training would occur at every level, from undergraduate students involved in research to senior research faculty members, and be mandated to occur a minimum of every four years. Gross (2016) argues that for participants, such training increases sensitivity, empathy, understanding, and awareness on a number of serious issues relating to the conduct of ethical research.

A third measure that could help prevent scientific misconduct involves growing efforts among scientists and research institutions to change measures of success. Specifically, what Gross (2016) is referring to here is changing success as measured by the *quantity* of a scientist's publications to a metric that focuses more on the *quality* of those publications. He notes that elite universities have begun moving in this direction by considering fewer papers in tenure and promotion decisions, while nominations to the National Academy of Sciences have been changed to require that a maximum of ten papers be submitted in the application process.

Gross (2016) suggests a final action that can be taken to help prevent scientific misconduct—individual researchers adopting **reproducible research tools** (RRT) in their work. RRT involves data and the computer programs used to analyze them being stored in an organized fashion (on a secured server), such that by clicking a link attached to a figure or a table appearing in a published scholarly article, readers can access the data and analysis that formed the basis for the figure or table (see Mesirov, 2010). RRT can be used in any scientifically based research project, and would be valuable for multiple purposes, including providing (1) a permanent, accessible history of the researcher's own data for further analysis, communication, and publication; (2) a common core of information for research collaborators; (3) the opportunity for laboratory colleagues to discuss and critique a project before the presentation and publication stages; and (4) a set of tools to scientific journals that enable all authors to submit all their data, experimental parameters, and programs used to analyze data as part of the review process by journal referees (Gross, 2016).

Scientific misconduct is a blight on the ethical conduct of HSIR specifically, and the scientific research enterprise more broadly. While the frequency of its occurrence is open to some debate, even if it occurs rarely it still causes damage to the offender, her colleagues, and to science more generally. Most scholars who have explored why the behavior occurs argue that it's the result of scientists weighing the perceived benefits of doing so against the perceived costs. Preventing such behavior involves efforts of whistleblowers willing to come forward, as well as efforts geared toward training in the responsible conduct of research, changing success measures from those involving the quantity of scholarly output to the quality of the output, and adopting tools that facilitate reproducibility of research.

SUMMARY

This chapter examined ethical issues arising from research conducted using human subjects. It began by exploring how we "know" reality and detailed one way we can know reality, science, and its assumptions and processes. I then shifted my attention to social scientific research and its workings, including its guiding assumptions and purposes. I explored in some detail post–World War II developments in research ethics in the form of three codes or sets of defining principles in HSIR: the Nuremberg Code, the Helsinki Declaration, and the Belmont Report. Each presented a set of guiding principles and practices that focus on the protection of human subjects and stress that subjects must provide their informed consent and always have the option of withdrawing their participation in a study. While these codes are geared primarily toward biomedical research, their principles and guiding practices apply to social science–based HSIR as well. The Belmont Report is especially important in this country, as its principles were incorporated into federal regulations (the Common Rule) and created a process for reviewing HSIR that features institutional review boards (IRBs).

I then turned my attention to examples of ethical issues in HSIR, including those relating to informed consent (ensuring that subjects are fully informed and comprehend the information provided); subject confidentiality (including justifications for it and steps taken to protect it); managing harm (including how harm is conceptualized and may be mitigated); conflicts of interest (what they involve and how they can be managed); researcher safety (an understudied but important aspect of harm) and managing it in HSIR; and scientific misconduct (including what it involves, its frequency, causal factors, and efforts to prevent it).

To end the chapter, let's consider Thought Exercise 13.1, which addresses an ethical issue in HSIR in the social sciences: the use of self-reports to study deviant behavior in general, and crime and delinquency in particular.

THOUGHT EXERCISE 13.1

ETHICAL ISSUES IN THE USE OF SELF-REPORTS TO STUDY CRIME

Among the methods available to researchers interested in the study of crime and delinquency are surveys that ask subjects to respond to questions about the extent and nature of their involvement in illegal behavior during a given period (e.g., "the past six months"). Known as self-reports, according to Delbert Elliott (2017), they: (1) were developed as a direct measure of criminal or delinquent behavior—as opposed to official reports of crime that measure police reactions to crime; (2) were first used in the 1940s but did not become entrenched in the field until the 1960s; (3) are generally believed to better capture the conceptual domain of crime and/or delinquency; (4) are based on offenders' own reports of their involvement in illegal behavior, whether known to law enforcement or not; and (5) avoid selective reporting and processing biases inherent in official record measures of responses to crime. They have now become a very commonly used method in criminological research, including longitudinal studies of juvenile and adult offending.

Ethical Issues in the Use of Self-Reports

David and Donald Bersoff (2000) are among the few researchers who have explored ethical issues in the use of self-reports, although the context they were considering was the use of self-reports in psychological research, particularly studies involving children. However, much of what they identify is also relevant to the use of self-reports in the fields of criminology and criminal justice. They note (p. 9) that issues relating to (1) informed consent, (2) privacy, and (3) confidentiality are all raised by self-reports. It is those issues that I'll be discussing here.

INFORMED CONSENT. Recall from the above discussion that consent given by subjects involved in research has to be informed and not the result of coercion or undue influence. Bersoff and Bersoff (2000) worry about the fact that survey research is exempted from IRB review *unless* the information obtained (1) can be linked to an identified respondent or (2) could reasonably place the subjects at risk of criminal or civil liability or be damaging to the subjects' financial standing, employability, or reputation. Bersoff and Bersoff argue that there are two problems with this policy. First, because self-reports often use open-ended questions, there is simply no way a researcher can anticipate the kinds of responses subjects might provide. The second problem is that federal guidelines are less stringent than are the ethical requirements of professional associations like the American Psychological Association (APA), which mandate that researchers inform prospective subjects of the nature of the research and factors that could influence their participation, such as limitations on confidentiality. The solution here, as they see it, is to require that all survey research have some sort of informed consent. At minimum, potential respondents should be informed about the topic and purpose of the research, the nature of the questions to be asked, the time required for participation, their right to skip individual questions or to withdraw from the study at any time without penalty, and whom to contact with questions or concerns about the study. Added to this would also be notification to the subjects of limits on the confidentiality of the data collected so that they understand that it is possible that third parties (e.g., a court) could subpoena the data.

PRIVACY RIGHTS. Bersoff and Bersoff (2000) correctly state that research participants have the right not to disclose information they may feel is too personal or sensitive (i.e., skip questions without prejudice), and this right is usually handled in standardized informed consent forms. But as a protection of subjects' privacy rights, permission to skip discomforting questions is not equivalent to being told the exact nature of the questions to be asked at the time of consent. For example, while many people would decline to participate in a study using a survey that included questions of an explicit, sexual nature, researchers can also manipulate them into answering these very questions by first asking them relatively innocuous sexually-related questions. Psychological research has clearly shown that once subjects have made commitments to a certain type of behavior (like answering a survey or even answering questions of a sexual nature on a survey), their wish to appear consistent and cooperative may impel them to continue even if doing so is ill-considered (this is called the foot-in-the-door phenomenon). Further, research also shows that if sensitive questions are ordered in a subtle gradient from tame to highly intrusive, once people have begun answering a set of such questions, they find it difficult to suddenly stop at a given question. After all, they just answered a slightly less provocative question (this is the slippery-slope phenomenon). While not arguing that such manipulation is common, Bersoff and Bersoff correctly point to the potential for its use when consent forms are absent or when complete disclosure of the nature of the questions to be asked is not provided to prospective subjects.

CONFIDENTIALITY. Finally, confidentiality is also an issue in self-report studies because subjects have a right not to have the information they voluntarily provide made public or used against them. Again, Bersoff and Bersoff (2000) note that this issue is typically addressed in the standard informed consent form, where a stipulation will be given that the information collected in the study will be kept strictly confidential *except as may be required by law*. Disclaimers such as these, because of their vagueness, place undue burdens on prospective subjects to (1) be familiar with laws regarding disclosures of information collected during research and (2) fully appreciate their (potential) lack of confidentiality rights given the nature of the research. The solution here is full disclosure: researchers explicitly spell out for subjects the conditions under which confidentiality may need to be broken (i.e., the limits on confidentiality).

Self-reports used to study crime and delinquency raise several ethical issues relating to informed consent and the protection of subjects from risk of harm—particularly harm that could arise should third parties like the courts obtain information collected by researchers that can be linked to specific individuals. Greater attention to these issues must be paid not only by IRBs but by individual researchers as well.

KEY TERMS

Agreement reality 383
Experiential reality 383
Research process 383
Idiographic explanations 384
Nomothetic explanations 384
Inductive reasoning 385
Deductive reasoning 385
Doctors' Trial 386
Nuremberg Code 386
Helsinki Declaration 386
Principle of voluntarism 387
Belmont Report 387
Informed consent 388
Common Rule 389
Institutional Review Boards 389
Incentives 394
Subject confidentiality 397
Statistical confidentiality 398
Certificate of confidentiality 398
Redacting data 399
Harm 399
Risk-benefit ratio 400
Debriefing 400
Conflicts of interest 401
Ambient risks 405
Situational risks 405
Research misconduct 406
Suspension 407
Debarment 407
Responsible conduct of research 409
Reproducible research tools 409

DISCUSSION QUESTIONS

1. Should the same guiding principles described for protecting human subjects involved in research be extended to protecting *animals* involved in research? Explain why or why not.
2. Compare the ethical principles articulated by the Nuremberg Code, Helsinki Declaration, and Belmont Report. Can you articulate common themes found across them?
3. Should undergraduate students conducting research, regardless of whether human subjects are involved, be required to take training in research ethics? Explain.
4. To understand how the IRB process works, attend an IRB review at your school and write a summary of what you observed. How does it compare with the process described in this chapter?
5. Because scientific evidence created through research may be used in criminal (or other) trials, should judges (in particular), prosecutors, and defense attorneys receive training in research ethics? Explain.

RESOURCES

To explore further the **codes and guiding principles** relating to the research process discussed in this chapter, see the following sources:

- *Nuremberg Code*: https://history.nih.gov/research/downloads/nuremberg.pdf
- *Helsinki Declaration*: https://www.wma.net/wp-content/uploads/2016/11/DoH-Oct2013-JAMA.pdf
- *Belmont Report*: https://phrp.nihtraining.com/codes/02_codes.php

For those looking for **comprehensive treatments of research ethics**, I suggest the following:

- Francis L. Macrina (Ed.) (2014). *Scientific Integrity* (4th ed.). Washington, DC: ASM Press. Available from Amazon books. Now in its fourth edition, the book is a widely regarded collection of readings on nearly all aspects of research ethics.

- Harriet A. Washington (2006). *Medical Apartheid: The Dark History of Medical Experimentation on Black Americans from Colonial Times to the Present*. New York: Harlem Moon. Available from Amazon books. This book was a National Book Critics Circle Award winner for nonfiction. Multiple starred reviews by such outlets as Publishers Weekly and Booklist.
- Maria K. E. Lahman (2017). *Ethics in Social Science Research: Becoming Culturally Responsive*. Thousand Oaks, CA: Sage Publications. Available from Amazon books. The work is a comprehensive guide to ethical concerns in research in a variety of social science disciplines.
- Ruth Faden and Tom Beauchamp (1986). *A History and Theory of Informed Consent*. New York: Oxford University Press. Available from Google Books. As of this writing, the book had been cited some 4,000 times by scholars—it is considered a "classic" treatise on research ethics.

REFERENCES

American Association of University Professors (2000). *Institutional review boards and social science research*. Retrieved from https://www.aaup.org/report/institutional-review-boards-and-social-science-research

American Psychological Association (2011). *Publication manual of the American Psychological Association* (6th ed.). Washington, DC: American Psychological Association.

Applebaum, P., Lidz, C., & Klitzman, R. (2009). Voluntariness of consent to research: A conceptual model. *Hastings Center Reports, 39*, 30–39.

Babbie, E. (2016). *The practice of social research* (14th ed.). Boston, MA: Cengage Learning.

Bartlett, T. (2011, July 19). Marc Hauser resigns from Harvard. *The Chronicle of Higher Education*. Retrieved from http://www.chronicle.com/article/Marc-Hauser-Resigns-From/128296

Bartlett, T. (2012, September 5). Former Harvard psychologist fabricated and falsified, report says. *The Chronicle of Higher Education*. Retrieved from http://www.chronicle.com/ blogs/percolator/report-says-former-harvard-psychologist-fabricated-falsified/30748

Beecher, H. (1966). Ethics and clinical research. *New England Journal of Medicine, 274*, 367– 372. Retrieved from http://wayback.archive-it.org/4657/20150930181806/ www.hhs.gov/ohrp/archive/documents/BeecherArticle.pdf

Belshaw, C. (2012). Harm, change, and time. *Journal of Medicine and Philosophy, 37*, 425–444.

Berscheid, E., Abrahams, D., & Aronson, V. (1967). Effectiveness of debriefing following deception experiments. *Journal of Personality and Social Psychology, 6*, 371–380.

Bersoff, D., & Bersoff, D. (2000). Ethical issues in the collection of self-report data. In A. Stone, J. Turkkan, C. Bachrach, J. Jobe, H. Kurtzman, & V. Cain (Eds.). *The science of self-report: Implications for research and practice* (pp. 68–82). Mahwah, NJ: Lawrence Erlbaum Associates.

Brugge, D. (2002). Pulling up the ladder: The anti-immigrant backlash. Retrieved from http://www.politicalresearch.org/2002/01/03/pulling-up-the-ladder-the-anti-immigrant-backlash/#sthash.1GCk6pE4.dpbs

Bryman, A. (2016). *Social research methods* (5th ed.). New York, NY: Oxford University Press.

Campbell, B. (n.d.). Informed consent in developing countries: Myth or reality? Retrieved from http://www.dartmouth.edu/~ethics/docs/Campbell_informedconsent.pdf

Carome, M. (2016, May 3). Outrage of the month: A steady stream of unethical human experiments. *The Huffington Post*. Retrieved fromhttps://www.huffingtonpost.com/michael-carome-md/outrage-of-the-month-a-st_b_9822610.html

Centers for Disease Control and Prevention (2017). U.S. Public Health Service Study of

Syphilis at Tuskegee. Retrieved from https://www.cdc.gov/tuskegee/after.htm

Dickson-Swift, V., James, E., Kippen, S., & Liamputtong, P. (2007) Doing sensitive research: What challenges do qualitative researchers face? *Qualitative Research, 7*, 327–353.

Dingwall, R. (2012). How did we ever get into this mess? The rise of ethical regulation in the social sciences. In K. Love (Ed.), *Ethics in social research* (pp. 3–26). Summerville, MA: Emerald.

Dsowen (2012, February 19). The importance of debriefing [Blog post]. https://dsowen.wordpress.com/2012/02/19/the-importance-of-debriefing/

Duncan, G., Elliott, M., & Salazar-Gonzalez, J. (2011). *Statistical confidentiality: Principles and practice*. New York, NY: Springer.

Elliott, D. (2017). Self-report crime surveys. Retrieved from http://www.oxfordbibliographies.com/view/document/obo-9780195396607/obo-9780195396607-0221.xml#obo-9780195396607-0221-bibItem-0003

Emanuel, E., Abdoler, E., & Stunkel, L. (n.d.). *Research ethics: How to treat people who participate in research*. Bethesda, MD: National Institutes of Health.

Faden, R., & Beauchamp, T. (1986). *A history and theory of informed consent*. New York, NY: Oxford University Press.

Fanelli, D. (2009, May 29). How many scientists fabricate and falsify research? A systematic review and meta-analysis of survey data. *PlosOne*. Retrieved from http://journals.plos.org/plosone/article?id=10.1371/journal.pone.0005738#pone.0005738-Marshall1

Federal Register (2018, April 18). Federal policy for the protection of Human subjects: proposed six-month delay of the general compliance date while allowing the use of three burden-reducing provisions during the delay period. Retrieved from https://www.federalregister.gov/documents/2018/04/20/2018-08231/federal-policy-for-the-protection-of-human-subjects-proposed-six-month-delay-of-the-general

Fischer, B. (2006). A summary of important documents in the field of research ethics. *Schizophrenia Bulletin, 32*, 69–80.

Gardner, B. (2015, June 4). Are financial conflicts of interest in medical research overblown? *New Republic*. Retrieved from https://newrepublic.com/article/121964/theres-more-one-kind-conflict-interest-medical-research

Geis, G., Mobley, A., & Schicor, D. (1999). Private prisons, criminological research, and conflict of interest: A case study. *Crime & Delinquency, 45*, 372–388.

Gross, C. (2011, December). On Marc Hauser: A case of scientific misconduct at Harvard. *The Nation*. Retrieved from https://www.thenation.com/article/disgrace-marc-hauser/

Gross, C. (2016). Scientific misconduct. *Annual Review of Psychology, 67*, 693–711.

Heimer, C., & Petty, J. (2010). Bureaucratic ethics: IRBs and the legal regulation of human subjects research. *Annual Review of Law and Social Science, 6*, 601–626.

Howitt, D., & Cramer, D. (2011). *Introduction to research methods in Psychology* (3rd ed.). Harlow, UK: Pearson Education Limited.

Israel, M. (2000). The commercialisation of university-based criminological research inAustralia. *Australian & New Zealand Journal of Criminology, 33*, 1–20.

Israel, M. (2015). *Research ethics and integrity for social scientists: Beyond regulatory compliance* (2nd ed.). Thousand Oaks, CA: Sage Publications.

Johnson, B., & Clarke, J. (2003). Collecting sensitive data: The impact on researchers. *Qualitative Health Research, 13*, 421–434.

Johnstone, G. (2005). Research ethics in criminology. *Research Ethics, 1*, 60–66.

Jones, J. (1993). *Bad blood: The Tuskegee syphilis experiment* (Rev. ed.). New York, NY: The Free Press.

Kitzinger, J., & Barbour, R (1999). The challenge and promise of focus groups. In R. Barbour and J. Kitzinger (Eds.), *Developing focus group research: Politics, theory and practice* (pp. 1–20). Thousand Oaks, CA: Sage Publications.

Largent, E., Grady, C., Miller, F., & Wertheimer, A. (2013). Misconceptions about coercion and undue influence: Reflections on the views of IRB members. *Bioethics, 27*, 500–507.

Lee, R. (1995). *Dangerous fieldwork*. Thousand Oaks, CA: Sage Publications.

Marshall, E. (2000). Scientific misconduct—How prevalent is fraud? That's a million-dollar question. *Science, 290*, 1662–1663.

Matthews, D. (2015, October 29). Is industry funding undermining trust in science? *Times*

Higher Education. Retrieved from https://www.timeshighereducation.com/features/is-industry-funding-undermining-trust-in-science

McCluskey, E. (2017, April 3). Public universities get an education in private industry. *The Atlantic*. Retrieved from https://www.theatlantic.com/education/archive/2017/04/public-universities-get-an-education-in-private-industry/521379/

Medical Advocates for Social Justice (n.d.). The Belmont Report. Retrieved from http://www. medadvocates.org/disciplines/ethics/belmont_report.html

Mesirov, J. (2010, November 26). Accessible reproducible research. *Science, 327,* 5964.

Merriam-Webster (2017a). Informed. Retrieved from https://www.merriam-webster.com/ dictionary/informed

Merriam-Webster (2017b). Consent. Retrieved from https://www.merriam-webster.com/dictionary/consent

Montgomerie, B., & Birkhead, T. (2005). A beginner's guide to scientific misconduct. *ISBE Newsletter, 17,* 16–25. Retrieved from http://browning.cm.utexas.edu/courses/ RCR/Montgomerie_Birkhead_misconduct.pdf

NASA (2017, November 1). Global climate change. Retrieved from https://climate.nasa.gov/causes/

National Health and Medical Research Council (2015, May). *National statement on ethicalconduct in human research*. Retrieved from https://www.nhmrc.gov.au/book/national-statement-ethical-conduct-human-research

National Science Foundation (n.d.). Responsible conduct of research. Retrieved from https://www.nsf.gov/bfa/dias/policy/rcr.jsp

National Science Foundation (2017). Informed consent in social and behavioral science. Retrieved from https://www.nsf.gov/bfa/dias/policy/hsfaqs.jsp#informed

Office for Human Research Protections (2003a). Expedited review procedures guidance. Retrieved from https://www.hhs.gov/ohrp/regulations-and-policy/guidance/guidance-on-expedited-review-procedures/index.html

Office for Human Research Protections (2003b). Certificates of confidentiality: Privacy protection for research subjects. Retrieved from https://www.hhs.gov/ohrp/regulations-and-policy/guidance/certificates-of-confidentiality/index.html

Office for Human Research Protections (2016). The Belmont Report. Retrieved from https://www.hhs.gov/ohrp/regulations-and-policy/belmont-report/index.html

Office for Human Research Protections (2017, January 19). Federal policy for the protection of human subjects. *Federal Register, 82,* 7149–7274.

Office of Research Services (2017). Basic principles of the Belmont Report. Retrieved fromhttp://www.rss.hku.hk/integrity/ethics-compliance/hrec

Office of the Vice Chancellor for Research & Economic Development (2017). History of research ethics. Retrieved from http://ors.umkc.edu/research-compliance-(iacuc-ibc-irb-rsc)/institutional-review-board-(irb)/history-of-research-ethics

Redman, B. (2017). Legacy of the Commission on Research Integrity. *Science and Engineering Ethics, 23,* 555–563.

Reynolds, D. (2000). Protecting the human subjects of social science research. *Bioethics Forum, 16,* 31–37.

Ruff, K. (2015). Scientific journals and conflict of interest disclosure: What progress has been made? *Environmental Health, 14,* 45–52.

Sampson, H., & Thomas, M. (2003). Risk and responsibility. *Qualitative Research, 3,* 165–189.

Schrag, Z. (2011). The case against ethics review in the social sciences. *Research Ethics, 7,* 120–131.

Shamoo, A., & Resnik, D. (2003). *Responsible conduct of research*. New York, NY: Oxford University Press.

Shuster, E. (1997, November 13). Fifty years later: The significance of the Nuremberg Code. *New England Journal of Medicine, 337,* 1436–1440.

Smith, S., & Richardson, D. (1983). Amelioration of deception and harm in psychological research: The important role of debriefing. *Journal of Personality and Social Psychology, 44,* 1075–1082.

Spitz, V. (2005). *Doctors from Hell: The horrific account of Nazi experiments on humans*. Boulder, CO: Sentient Publications.

Stark, A. (2000). *Conflict of interest in American public life*. Cambridge, MA: Harvard University Press.

Steneck, N. (2006). Fostering integrity in research: Definitions, current knowledge, and future directions. *Science and Engineering Ethics, 12*, 53–74.

Steup, M. (2005). Epistemology. In E. Zalta (Ed.), *The Stanford encyclopedia of philosophy* (Fall Edition). Retrieved from https://plato.stanford.edu/entries/epistemology/

Taylor, T. (1992). *The anatomy of the Nuremberg Trials: A personal memoir.* New York, NY: Knopf.

Tippett, K., & Brooks, R. (1997, April 30). Prison guru is criticized over job. *The Wall Street Journal*, pp. 1, 12.

United Nations (2017). *International covenant on civil and political rights.* Retrieved from http://www.ohchr.org/EN/ProfessionalInterest/Pages/CCPR.aspx

United States Department of Transportation (2017). Suspension and debarment: Frequently asked questions. Retrieved from https://www.fhwa.dot.gov/construction/cqit/ susdebqa.cfm#q01

United States Holocaust Memorial Museum (n.d.). The Doctors' Trial: The medical case of the subsequent Nuremberg proceedings. Retrieved from https://www.ushmm.org/information/exhibitions/online-exhibitions/special-focus/doctors-trial

University of Alabama at Birmingham (2017). UAB enterprise conflict of interest and conflict of commitment policy. Retrieved from http://www.uab.edu/policies/content/Pages/UAB-AD-POL-0000695.aspx

White, R. (2007). Institutional Review Board mission creep. *Independent Review, 11*, 547–564.

World Medical Association (2013, October 19). WMA Declaration of Helsinki. Retrieved from https://www.wma.net/policies-post/wma-declaration-of-helsinki-ethical-principles-for-medical-research-involving-human-subjects/

Wrigley, A. (2015, June 8). Human experiments—The good, the bad, and the ugly. *The Conversation*. Retrieved from https://theconversation.com/human-experiments-the-good-the-bad-and-the-ugly-39876

CHAPTER 14

The Future and Criminal Justice Ethics

Chapter Outline

CHAPTER LEARNING OBJECTIVES:

1. Describe the organizational context of criminal justice ethics.
2. Differentiate organizational policy from organizational procedure and provide examples of each.
3. Explain modeling ethics and its importance for enhancing ethical behavior by criminal justice practitioners.
4. Identify proactive strategies for ethics training in criminal justice agencies and explain why they are important.

5. Describe what hiring toward the community entails and how doing so can enhance ethical behavior by justice practitioners.
6. Explain how performance evaluations can be used as part of a comprehensive strategy for improving the ethics of criminal justice practitioners.

INTRODUCTION

This book has taken you on a long journey down the road of criminal justice ethics, but that journey is now ending. As you traveled down the road, you exited at various points, where you encountered:

- The field of ethics, including what ethics *is* and how ethics is distinguished from morality;
- Systems of ethics, including their guiding principles and how those principles can be applied to ethical issues arising from the practice of criminal justice;
- Moral dilemmas, including what they are and how they can be resolved;
- Moral reasoning, its processes, and guiding principles;
- A framework for analysis designed to help you use information at your disposal to reason through and reach a conclusion about the ethics of behavior by focusing on ideals, obligations, and consequences;
- Ethical issues involving police officers, including the tactics they use;
- Ethical issues associated with the punishment of criminal offenders;
- The courtroom workgroup and ethical issues associated with its members—prosecutors, defense attorneys, and judges;
- Institutional corrections, and the ethical issues associated with correctional officers and treatment staff working in prisons and jails;
- Community-based corrections, and the ethical issues involving its practitioners—probation and parole officers;
- The forensic sciences, and ethical issues associated with science in the courtroom; and
- Research ethics, and the ethical issues associated with using human subjects.

The road you took included signs and guides to help direct you. The signs included research and commentary from various disciplines, including philosophy, psychology, sociology, criminal justice, economics, and history. The guides were scholars in these disciplines who have identified, wrestled with, and tried to provide answers to the many ethical questions that arise from the practice of criminal justice. Some of the signs have been larger than others, and some probably did a better job of guiding you than did others. Regardless, I hope you learned that no one discipline has all the answers. Rather, many different orientations and perspectives inform the study of criminal justice ethics.

This last chapter is the final exit you'll take from the road you have been traveling and will conclude your journey into criminal justice ethics. At this exit, I ask you to look to the future of criminal justice ethics by exploring a prescription I believe can help heal the "disease" of immoral and unethical behavior that has infected the criminal justice system and its processes. I then close the chapter with a final Thought Exercise that examines the ethical implications of presuming people coming into the criminal justice system are guilty of the crime(s) with which they have been charged.

A PRESCRIPTION FOR THE FUTURE

Recall the many ethical issues surrounding criminal justice practitioners. With the police, the issues included how police officers are recruited, hired, trained, and retained; "noble cause" misconduct; and the tactics they use, especially deception. For the courts, the issues included prosecutorial misconduct; "zealousness" in defending criminal defendants; and assorted issues with the judiciary, including caseloads, delegating responsibilities, ambition, and doing justice. Turning to corrections, there are two sets of issues. In institutional corrections, the issues included reciprocity in supervision and corruption involving correctional officers. For treatment staff, the issues included respect for the dignity of prisoners, responsible care, and the integrity of relationships. Turning to community-based corrections (CBC), the issues included acceptable penal content; caseloads and workloads of probation/parole officers; arming probation and parole officers; offender-funded CBC; and for-profit privatized CBC. In forensic science, the issues included laboratory analytical procedures, courtroom testimony, privatization of forensic services, whistleblowing, maintaining competence, and "junk" science in the courtroom. Finally, in criminal justice research, the ethical issues revolved around the protection of human subjects. The list is long, indeed!

What do all of these issues have in common? *They all involve behavior and the breakdown of constraints on it.* How can these issues be addressed? One way would be to consider them singularly and develop appropriate responses to each. That is, you would assume that each is a separate issue that involves different dynamics and thus would involve different solutions. There is, I believe, a second, better option that I propose below. This "prescription for the future" is borrowed from Michael Caldero and John Crank's (2011) discussion about how to address noble cause misconduct by the police, with some tweaking. As I considered their recommendations, it dawned on me that much of what they recommend could actually be extended to include not just the police, but also the other areas of criminal justice—courts, corrections, forensic science, and research. As you'll see, the goal of this prescription is to help criminal justice practitioners behave more ethically, which can only occur if they receive a greater amount of training in ethics, if the training they receive is ongoing, and if the training they receive is not filed in the "waste of my time" folder. To see how this can happen, let's examine the specific parts of my prescription and how they might work in practice.

The Organizational Context of Criminal Justice Ethics

Across the preceding chapters, I have tried to highlight for you that criminal justice practitioners and researchers are embedded in an organizational context. Recall that the criminal justice *system* is typically conceptualized as a set of agencies—police, courts, and corrections—interacting with one another to process cases that come to their attention. Police departments, prosecutors' offices, public defenders' offices, the courts, prisons, probation and parole departments, and research institutions are all **organizations**, collectives of individuals organized into groups with identifiable boundaries and internal structures, engaging in activities designed to achieve a set of goals (Stojkovic, Kalinch, & Klofas, 2015). Thus, part of my prescription for the future is for you to keep in mind that criminal justice ethics occurs within *organizational settings*. What this ultimately means is that the structure, purpose, activities, and culture of criminal justice *organizations* will shape the ethics of criminal justice *practitioners*.

In any organization, one of its defining features is its structure. The great 19th-century German sociologist Max Weber argued that **organizational structure** can be conceptualized as a set of offices (e.g., ranks in a police department) organized into a hierarchy, with a clear division of labor, that is then guided or governed by formal rules (Weber, 1947). The hierarchy to which Weber refers is the organization's "chain of command," whose members have increasingly comprehensive authority to make decisions as they move from the bottom of the hierarchy to the top. For example, in the case of a police department, the chain of command stretches from shift sergeants, through lieutenants, precinct commanders, deputy chiefs, and, finally, the chief of police, who has the ultimate decision-making authority. Importantly, members of this hierarchy constitute the management team of the organization and are very important because they establish the ethical tone of the organization (discussed further in the section "Evaluate Agency Practices" later in this chapter).

The **division of labor** that Weber argued was part of an organization's structure refers to the fact that organizations possess a mix of interrelated labor processes that are both separated from one another, yet are coordinated by managerial authority (Scott, 1986). To illustrate, again consider the Federal Bureau of Prisons, the agency responsible for administering all of the federal correctional institutions in this country. Recall that in prisons, COs are responsible for security, resolving conflicts, insuring inmates attend required activities, etc. In turn, they have supervisors, who also have supervisors, usually a deputy warden. The warden is responsible for the entire functioning of the prison. In turn, she has a supervisor, and so on, up the Director level. Each of these technical pieces are coordinated into a coherent whole that revolves around a set of goals. An organization's division of labor is typically illustrated by its organizational chart (see Figure 14.1).

Finally, the formal rules of which Weber spoke are the written guidelines for how the agency and its members are supposed to behave as they go about their duties. These are typically found in the organization's "policies and procedures" manual. For an organization, a policy is a course of action or a guideline that's supposed to be followed by members of the organization, while a procedure outlines the steps that should be taken to implement a policy (State of New South Wales, 2009). A policies and procedure manual may include the following:

- Personnel practices (staff recruitment, training, holiday leave arrangements, promotions, performance appraisals, supervision);
- Complaints and disputes procedures;
- Occupational health and safety procedures;
- Conflict resolution processes;
- Communication policy;
- Delegations (who can make decisions about what, such as the approval process for spending money);
- Critical incidents procedures;
- Confidentiality policy;

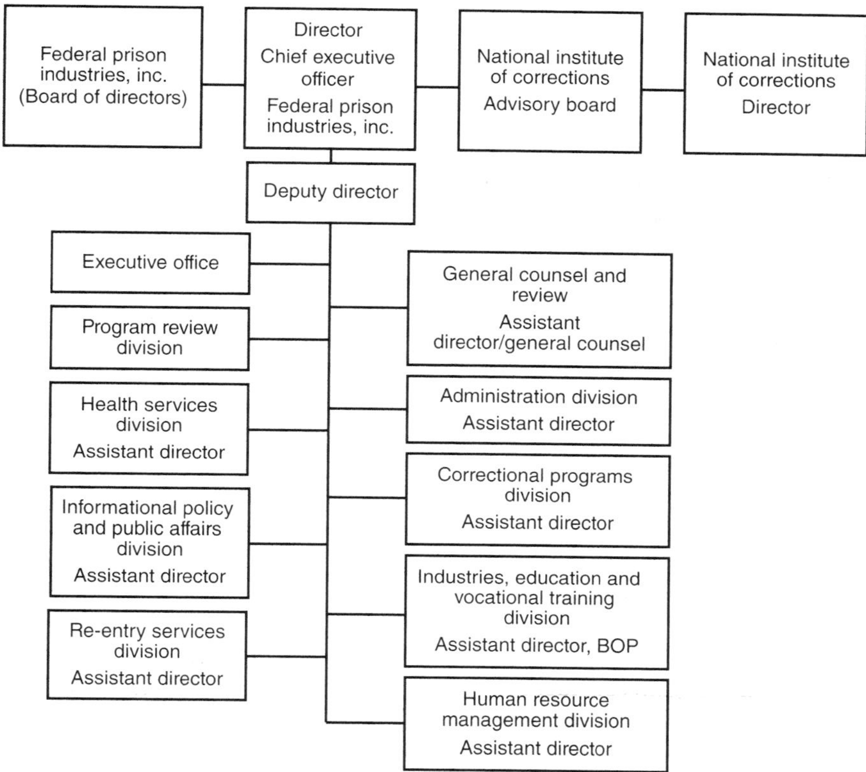

FIGURE 14.1 Federal Bureau of Prisons Organizational Chart (ca. 2013)
Source: Federal Bureau of Prisons (2014)

- Duty of care policy;
- Policy for coordinating /networking with external agencies.

Organizational purpose refers to the goals to be achieved by an agency that provide direction but also serve as constraints or limits on the behavior of members (Stojkovic, et al., 2015). The problem with criminal justice organizations is that they usually have many competing and conflicting purposes, what the great organizational theorist Herbert Simon described as the **complex goals** of an organization (Simon, 1964). For example, a circuit court has multiple purposes, including (but not limited to) timely processing of cases on the docket, ensuring defendants' rights are protected and that attorneys follow procedural rules, and protecting citizens' open access to court proceedings. For organizations like a public defender's office to be successful, the organization must try and achieve all of its goals. However, in the pursuit of its complex goals, what organizations learn is that it's unlikely to achieve 100% of its goals. Instead, what happens is that the organization will seek some (arbitrary) level of attainment of several goals simultaneously, instead of trying to maximize attaining each goal. Thus, while stated goals provide direction, they constrain an organization's ability to achieve all of them simultaneously.

The activities found in organizations are the formal and informal processes that are established and put into place to achieve organizational goals. For example, a prosecutor's office may have a goal of priority processing of sexual assault cases in its jurisdiction. To achieve this goal, the office may establish a special "team" of prosecutors, investigators, and forensic experts who work only on these cases and establish for themselves their own procedures to clear the cases quickly (and successfully) via plea bargains. Formally, the team is still following office rules and procedures to achieve the larger goals, but informally, they have established their own mechanisms for achieving the goal established for the team.

Finally, all criminal justice organizations have a culture, a set of assumptions and beliefs that create language, symbols, and folklore among members, and ultimately direct their behavior, especially in response to work-related problems they encounter (Stojkovic, et al., 2015). Members learn this culture through **occupational socialization**, the process by which members acquire the attitudes and behaviors of the agency, and this includes both formal training (such as that occurring at an academy) and informal interactions with peers, both on and off the job. The formal process is supposed to result in the member learning the organization's predominant belief system and rules: the "rights and wrongs," as well as the duty, responsibility, and personal character that's required by the organization of its members (Stojkovic, et al., 2015). It begins with recruiting and selection and continues through orientation and training. As you can imagine, the content of the agency's core belief system and rules has significant implications for the ethics of members' behavior. If command-level officers in a police department enculturate in line personnel a belief system depicting officers in the agency as "warriors," new officers quickly learn that excessive force and similar misbehavior will be tolerated. This, in turn, undercuts any socialization processes seeking to impose civil behavior and a public service mission on officers.

Supervisors and executives in criminal justice agencies thus continuously influence the socialization processes of personnel, both initially and over the long term (Stojkovic, et al., 2015). While criminal justice organizations are managed through an overall process, management functions are not limited to a specific office within an organization—those functions are spread throughout and across levels of the organization, ranging from line supervisors to executives. Coordination of these management activities thus becomes crucial when it comes to how much—or how little—ethics will be stressed. Managers lead organizations through a combination of vision, motivation, and inspiration (Stojkovic, et al., 2015). They are role models for how individuals are supposed to act as members of the organization. As a result, they have a duty to not only operate ethically themselves, but also to indoctrinate members with organizational ethics by prescribing and enforcing ethical behavior.

Criminal justice practitioners often face role conflict and ambiguity, conflicting expectations, and murky and sometimes contradictory goals. It becomes the "job" of managers, ranging from line supervisors to executives, to coordinate a vision of the agency that stresses ethics and provides necessary training and resources to ensure that both incoming and more experienced members of the agency learn and understand that ethics *matters* (see Case Study 14.1). Practically speaking, agency managers can ensure this occurs by modeling ethics in their everyday behavior. Let's see how this would work.

Modeling Ethics

The first challenge facing those like me who want to enhance ethics training for criminal justice practitioners is to *not* have the training "fall into that great reservoir of unapplied training knowledge that is shelved away into the cabinet called 'forget everything you learned in training—this is how we [actually] do it!'" (Caldero & Crank, 2011, p. 298). Instead, the training has to be meaningful and relevant. To ensure that both happen, lessons can be taken from juvenile justice and corrections, crime prevention programs, and elsewhere that show programs and training based on exhortation and manipulation of emotions, such as D.A.R.E. and "scared straight"-type programs, not only don't work

CASE STUDY 14.1 The Organizational Context of Ethics: The LAPD Rampart Scandal

The Rampart Division of the Los Angeles Police Department (LAPD) is located west of downtown Los Angeles, the most populous area of the city, and has a primarily Latino population. Between the 1970s and 1990s, it was one of the busiest divisions of the LAPD based on calls for service and arrests. In the late 1970s and 1980s, the area experienced a dramatic increase in violent crime, particularly gang-involved drug and weapon offenses. To address the problem, then LAPD chief Daryl Gates created special antigang units of elite officers called CRASH (Community Resources Against Street Hoodlums) units. Chief Gates intended for members of the units to get to know and mix with gang members for purposes of gathering intelligence on them that would then be used to prevent violent crime and arrest and prosecute those suspected of engaging in drug-related crimes or violence, especially firearm violence.

In the late 1990s, the Rampart Division experienced what is widely considered the worst instance of corruption in the history of the LAPD (Boyer, 2001). Now known simply as the Rampart Scandal, multiple investigations found that officers in the CRASH unit in the Rampart Division had framed innocent individuals by planting evidence and committing perjury to gain convictions, and had subjected suspects to excessive force, resulting in serious injuries. Officers were also involved in multiple crimes, including a bank robbery and the theft of $1 million in cocaine from an evidence room. Two officers were involved in a shootout that left one of them dead and the other disgraced. In 1998, one of the CRASH officers, Rafael Perez, agreed to cooperate with investigators looking into problems with the Rampart CRASH unit. In doing so, he implicated some 70 officers in serious wrongdoing (Kaplan, 2009).

Since the nearly two decades that have passed—and after one internal and three independent investigations of the Rampart Scandal issued reports, multiple criminal trials had been completed and civil lawsuits had been both tried and settled, and a consent decree had been arranged between the LAPD and the U.S. Department of Justice—the full extent of the corruption in the Rampart Division (or the larger department) is still not known (Blue Ribbon Rampart Review Panel, 2006). However, based on the several reports that have been released, it seems clear that the Rampart Scandal *not* happening would have been miraculous. For example, the LAPD's own Board of Inquiry found that shortcuts and other problems with recruitment and hiring processes associated with the department in the 1990s resulted in multiple officers involved with the scandal joining the department despite their questionable backgrounds—including gang-involvement while teenagers—that should have disqualified them (Los Angeles Police Department, 2000).

Further, according to University of Southern California law professor Eric Chemerinsky (2000), investigations into the scandal minimized its scope and nature, by largely ignoring general problems with CRASH units as a whole. He also argued that official investigations (a) failed to recognize the central problem as the culture of the LAPD, with its emphasis on a "code of silence" for officers about colleagues' misconduct that gave rise to and tolerated what occurred in the Rampart Division and elsewhere; (b) failed to consider the need for structural reforms in the LAPD, including reforms of the union, strengthening of the independence and powers of the department's Inspector General's Office, and creation of a permanent oversight mechanism for the department; (c) unduly minimized problems in the department's disciplinary system that affect every step from receipt of a citizen's complaint through adjudication of the complaint via a board of rights hearing; (d) failed to acknowledge serious problems with how the department handled excessive force cases, especially officer-involved shootings; and (e) failed to recognize broader problems in the criminal justice system in Los Angeles County, including the fact that prosecutors, defense attorneys, and judges bore shared responsibility for the convictions of innocence people (some 100 of these cases occurred and were later overturned). In short, both the structure and the culture of the LAPD became, for all intents, completely broken, resulting in miscarriages of justice, deaths and serious injuries, including to officers, and potentially irreparable harm to the relationship between the LAPD and residents in the Rampart Division (Gordon, 2011).

but lead to backfire effects like desensitizing subjects to using drugs or what life in prison is like (see Finckenauer & Gavin, 1999). On the positive side, what has been learned from these areas is that people take far more seriously the *actions* of others than they do their *words*. What this indicates is that meaningful and relevant training has to come from **modeling ethics**; that is, administrators, managers, and supervisors have to *model appropriate behavior* (Sterman, 1989).

If you think about this for a moment, it makes sense. To *be* honest, one must not lie. To *be* fair, one must not show favoritism. As Caldero and Crank (2011) explained, behavioral cues from higher-level organizational actors send strong messages to underlings and recruits about how to behave themselves. These cues then become models of behavior that are followed during interactions with colleagues, offenders, the public, etc. Caldero and Crank (2011) suggested that if executives, administrators, managers, and supervisors are serious about changing the ethics of their charges, they will have to take a long, hard look at their own behavior and assess the cues they are sending to others in their agency and modify their behavior accordingly. For example, recall from Ch. 6 that it is the chief of police who creates and enforces the "rules of the road" in his or her agency, including recruiting and training standards, supervisor accountability, internal control mechanisms, and the overall ethical climate of the agency (Ivković, 2005). The key is how the chief leads by example (Murgado, 2011), The same is true of executives in other agencies, including prosecutors' offices, probation departments, prisons, etc. Leading by example matters greatly.

Caldero and Crank (2011, p. 311) provided insight into this thinking by recounting an anecdote from a police commander with whom they were working on ethics training. The commander recounted to them his "90-10 rule," which held that 90% of the time, police officers act and think on a very high level, but 10% of the time, the flawed part of them rears its ugly head and gets them, the agency, and the entire occupation in trouble. It is to that 10% that attention must be paid.

If leading by example matters, executives, administrators, managers, and supervisors need to reflect on their own 10%, the part of themselves they don't tend to look at too closely, and assess what is happening with it. It may be that they are giving cues they don't recognize, and that they are uncomfortable with (Caldero & Crank, 2011, p. 313). I would suggest *all* criminal justice practitioners take a look at themselves and assess their 10%. Further, they must keep in mind that although they may not want to be role models, the nature of their work is such that that is exactly what they are, at least to many citizens. As a result, the cues they give to others matter greatly, as they show the world what they believe is right and wrong. If the goal is to change behavior, the work has to begin with those responsible for modeling appropriate behavior for others to follow. Unethical or illegal behavior can't be "fixed" by hiring new personnel (the typical "get rid of the few bad apples" solution). The fixing has to begin with the executives and experienced personnel who are already with the agency (Caldero & Crank, 2011).

Proactive Strategies

Most agencies in the criminal justice system—police departments, prosecutors' offices, prisons, etc.—have some internal mechanism for addressing complaints received about (alleged) improper behavior by those working at the agency. For example, as far as I know, all police agencies and sheriff's departments in this country have an internal affairs (IA) entity (department, division, unit, or squad—depending on the size of the agency).

The primary focus of IA is on controlling the behavior of officers employed by the department. When a complaint is received, IA begins a process that includes several steps, culminating in a finding about the allegation(s) (Roberg, Crank, & Kuykendall, 2000).

First, the unit reviews the complaint to establish whether the allegation(s) contained in it constitute(s) a violation of any law or department policy. If a determination is made that the allegation(s) *do* constitute a violation, IA then conducts interviews with the complainant and witnesses, and collects evidence relating to the event(s). IA also compiles background information on the complainant that may include a criminal background check. The purpose here is to assess the credibility of the complainant. The unit then interviews members of the department who may been involved in the incident(s) and records their descriptions of what occurred. Finally, IA will reach a decision on the allegation(s) that can take one of four forms: (1) sustained, (2) unsubstantiated, (3) unfounded, or (4) exonerated. A finding of "sustained" means that the allegation(s) found in the complaint were justified. A finding of "unsubstantiated" indicates that there was no sustaining evidence found regarding the allegation(s), so the truth or falsity of the allegation(s) cannot be determined. Complaints deemed "unfounded" mean that the investigation determined the alleged events contained in the complaint did not occur as stated by the complainant. Finally, an "exoneration" indicates that while what was alleged in the complaint was substantiated, the individual's behavior was either legal or within department policy (Roberg, Crank, & Kuykendall, 2000).

This IA entity can be either reactive or proactive (Caldero & Crank, 2011). A reactive unit is one that waits for a complaint to be filed before carrying out an investigation and is the traditional way IA units are organized, at least in police departments (Walker, 2006). Proactive units, on the other hand, try and prevent problems by instituting audits, stings, and other actions to identify and address misconduct before the misconduct becomes public (Noble & Alpert, 2009). It's important to note that IA is not involved in the day-to-day activities of the agency. That is, members do not respond to calls for service, nor do they investigate crime unless the offense(s) may have been committed by other police officers. Very important is the fact that IA tends to be disliked by line personnel, largely because their perceived role is solely to investigate and punish other police officers (Roberg, Crank, & Kuykendall, 2000). In effect, IA "polices the police."

Caldero and Crank (2011) suggested that IA units could be reoriented toward being **ethically proactive**. This would mean that as part of its operational mandate, members of the unit would routinely meet with representatives from other units/divisions/offices in the agency to discuss ethical issues. Their activities would also include identifying line personnel with special talents and recognizing them. The unit would also provide in-service ethics training that would include examples of ethically questionable activities, and discussion of them during training. Members of the unit would be reoriented away from investigating and charging other officers and toward coaching and mentoring colleagues. They would thus become the locus of professional development training within the agency. This reorientation would convey to employees that the agency cared about them as valued employees, and that through its activities, IA would help them improve their chances at promotion and make a positive and valued contribution to the agency and its mission.

The unit would thus help change the culture of the organization by being used for something other than punishing line personnel. By having the unit involved in training that would include complex, "real world" ethical problems faced by agency employees, it would be ethically proactive by describing for colleagues how to avoid ethical quandaries and providing training in doing so.

Hiring Toward the Community

One of the central issues in recruiting, hiring, training, and retaining criminal justice practitioners is finding individuals possessing cultural skills, especially in language or local linguistic skills, similar to the population(s) being served (Caldero & Crank, 2011). Many criminal justice agencies are actively searching for individuals with linguistic skills, as evidenced by employment opportunities for criminal justice practitioners who are bilingual in English and Spanish. To illustrate, during the week of October 9, 2017, Indeed.com listed 234 employment opportunities in four states for an entry-level "bilingual police officer," 180 opportunities for a "bilingual probation officer" at locations in five states, 52 opportunities at jails and prisons in 10 states for a "bilingual corrections officer," and 640 opportunities for a "bilingual attorney" with firms or state agencies in 10 different states. To attract recruits with these skills, one solution would be to give hiring preferences to them. To create incentives for employees already in the agency, one solution would be paying tuition costs of those seeking language training and/or offering bonuses for those who possess—and maintain—the skills (Caldero & Crank, 2011).

Beyond working to hire and retain practitioners possessing language skills, there is also a need to develop greater balance in the personal values and ideology of recruits and newer members of the agency. As you'll recall from Chs. 6, 9, and 10, recruits seeking careers in criminal justice agencies often possess values that revolve around the control of crime and the "noble cause" of getting criminals off the streets. During early training and initial occupational socialization of new members, these values are intensified. **Hiring toward the community** entails revamping the hiring and training process—from recruitment through graduation of an academy—to moderate the powerful influence of crime control ideology on behavior by encouraging a balanced perspective on the part of recruits and enhancing that perspective during training (Caldero & Crank, 2011).

One way to help encourage balance in the personal ideologies and values of recruits is by emphasizing the importance of **just means** during pre-employment screening, actual hiring processes, and training (Caldero & Crank, 2011). Recall that being a criminal justice practitioner, be it a police officer, prosecutor, probation officer, or correctional officer, sometimes involves resolving a means/ends dilemma and choosing improper (even illegal) means to obtain an appropriate end (e.g., arresting a suspect [in the case of police] or obtaining a conviction [in the case of prosecutors]). Just means can be incorporated into pre-employment and skills-based testing by including ethical decision-making as a component. For example, recruits could be presented with nonresolvable ethical dilemmas to test whether they recognize the complexities of these situations. Similarly, during oral interviews, nonresolvable ethical dilemmas could also be presented to applicants and discussed with them for purposes of identifying their ability to recognize ethical complexities. During training, instructors' use of "war stories" would be both discouraged and monitored (Caldero & Crank, 2011). Because trainers might be unaware of the effect of these stories on their charges, agencies could hold "training days" for instructors that would include a session on the power of war stories to imprint on new officers the traditions of the department. The result would be to ensure that instructors use stories that affirm substantive due process of law. Instructors would be monitored to ensure that "Black Swans" were not undercutting the process.

Finally, educational requirements also play a role in hiring toward the community (Caldero & Crank, 2011). America, especially its larger cities, is becoming an increasingly diverse country. This has created a working environment for practitioners that requires intelligence, quick thinking, and a breadth of human experience on their part. The increase in the diversity of the American citizenry means that practitioners are needed who have the capacity to think through problems in an increasingly multiracial, multi-ethnic, multireligious society. Caldero & Crank (2011) argue that a four-year college education is a minimal requirement for meeting the complex ethical demands that will be placed on police in the coming century, but I believe this can be extended to most other areas of criminal justice as well.

As Caldero & Crank (2011) argued, college-educated practitioners will be able to grasp the social complexities of the working environment they will encounter in the twenty-first century (see Thought Exercise 14.1). In policing, for example, research has consistently shown that a college education "generally has a positive effect on officer attitudes, performance, and behavior" (Novak, Cordner, Smith, & Roberg, 2017, p. 456). The key will be to establish a college education as a **bona fide occupational qualification** (BFOQ) for employment in a criminal justice agency like a police department, probation department, or correctional institution. I'll note here that the courts have upheld higher education requirements in policing as a BFOQ, for example, arguing that police decision-making requires an additional dimension of judgement; the courts have also applied this logic to other occupations such as airline pilots and those working in health-related professions, like nursing or occupational therapy (see Novak, et al., 2017, pp. 456–457).

THOUGHT EXERCISE 14.1

THE ADVANTAGES OF A COLLEGE DEGREE FOR DECISION-MAKING SKILLS

1. A college education develops a broader base of information for decision-making.
2. Course requirements and achievements indicate responsibility in the individual and a greater appreciation for constitutional rights, values, and the democratic form of government.
3. College education engenders in one the ability to be flexible in handling difficult or ambiguous situations with greater creativity and innovation.
4. Higher education develops a greater empathy for diverse populations and their unique perspectives.
5. The college-educated practitioner is assumed to be less rigid in decision-making and more readily accepts and adapts to organizational change.
6. The college experience will help practitioners better communicate with and respond to the concerns of citizen constituencies in a competent, humane, and civil manner.
7. College-educated practitioners exhibit more "professional" demeanor and performance.
8. The college experience tends to make the practitioner less authoritarian and less cynical with respect to the millieu of criminal justice.

Source: Adapted from Caldero & Crank (2011)

Because a four-year degree will increasingly become the minimum intellectual capital needed to participate in public life, criminal justice agencies should begin phasing in policies that limit hiring to applicants possessing a bachelor's degree, and at the level of supervisor and above, promote only those possessing a four-year degree. Thus, hiring toward the community involves working toward diversifying agency personnel not only in terms of race, gender, ethnicity, sexual orientation, etc., but also in terms of linguistic skills and values. Further, college-educated line personnel possess the necessary intellectual capital to be able to adapt more quickly to change, be more efficient and effective problem solvers, and be less authoritarian and cynical than their less educated counterparts. These efforts should also facilitate ethical conduct on the part of practitioners, as they will understand both the need for ethics and appreciate ethics training as part of a larger program to better connect their agency with the community being served.

Evaluate Agency Practices

One of the biggest problems in criminal justice is the lack of evaluation of how agencies are performing. Practitioners working in these agencies often do not know whether what they are doing "works," regardless of how "works" is defined (Caldero & Crank, 2011). In the context of policing, for example (but I'm convinced their comments can be more broadly construed), Jerome Skolnick and James Fyfe (1993) have argued that the inability of agencies to evaluate their effectiveness impedes innovation within and across them. Most police and other practitioners don't know whether what they are doing even works. When traditional ways of doing things *are* directly evaluated, results show these ways are often inefficient and ineffective.

One common practice in criminal justice agencies is to conduct annual performance evaluations of agency personnel (Reisig & Correia, 1997). Performance evaluations are instruments that assess the nature of the work process, specific accomplishments of employees, and public attitudes about agency performance more broadly (Caldero & Crank, 2011). Reasonable use of these evaluations is supposed to lead to improvement in one's job-related performance and direction, including directing employees on how they can adapt to change and innovation. The problem is they can also be used to punish practitioners who aren't performing in a way their supervisor(s) would prefer, to preserve the power advantage of boss over subordinate, and maintain the status quo in an agency (see Culbert, 2008).

Performance evaluations of individuals working in criminal justice agencies is complicated in two ways (Caldero & Crank, 2011). On the one hand, supervisors can unintentionally turn performance evaluations into an adversarial and hostile process. In part, this is because personnel systems that oversee criminal justice agencies tend to be oriented toward punishment more than reward. Line personnel failing to perform to some formal level of expectations may then encounter reprimands or find that their chances of being promoted are diminished. Consequently, poorly constructed or misused performance evaluations can have an alienating effect and encourage the development of secretive elements of line-level culture.

Second, performance evaluations often confront an **importance/usefulness dilemma** that can be described as follows: the more important is the performance evaluation for a candidate's career, the greater the likelihood evaluators are not going to provide useful distinctions among candidates (Caldero & Crank, 2011). Supervisors who use performance evaluations for reasons such as promotion or raises in base salaries (both of which are obviously important) and have to then work with both those who received the benefits (promotion; a raise) and those who did not tend to give similar scores to the candidates competing for the benefits. Even if the evaluator has a preference, he may not want to hurt the feelings or make enemies of those who didn't get the raise or promotion or their supporters.

The solution is to change the focus of performance evaluations from a tool used to assess how well someone is doing their job compared to others in the same unit, squad, division, etc., to using them as instruments to generate feedback for employees (Caldero & Crank, 2011). In this new environment, performance evaluations would be designed to provide useful and practical information to those being evaluated, regardless of the level they occupy within the agency (e.g., line, supervisory, executive) and not in comparison to others. Unlike the current practice of turning over performance evaluation information to superiors and personnel boards and placing a copy of the evaluation in the employee's permanent record, performance evaluations would now be used to *share constructive feedback* with employees. Additionally, because the feedback is constructive, little would be gained by incorporating these evaluations into an agency's promotion system. By removing them from the promotion process (or other benefit, like a raise in base salary), controversy over their results would be removed. Further, in this new system, performance evaluations can be conducted not only of individuals but also of teams, units, departments, etc. Finally, by changing their purpose, performance evaluations would be integrated into the culture of the agency as a positive tool, rather than as a way for supervisors to "stack the deck" against those they dislike for purposes of getting rid of them. No longer would these evaluations be feared and loathed. Rather, they would become part of a process that focused on helping employees grow and develop.

Under this new model, performance evaluation would also play an important role in organizational innovation by providing employees with job-related expectations that are consistent with the change(s) being sought (Caldero & Crank, 2011). Performance evaluations can then be used to assess how well employees are adapting to change by providing them with necessary feedback, along with identifying their concerns and questions. Thus, performance evaluations become tied to organizational purpose by allowing employees to see if and how innovations are viable and enabling problem solvers to reflect on successes and failures.

Finally, performance evaluation would be implemented on an agency-wide basis (Caldero & Crank, 2011). When senior-level administrators are evaluated, the process can show others that it is not punitive. The same is true as one moves down the hierarchy from top to bottom. If those at the bottom of the hierarchy see that positive results are occurring from of using performance evaluations in a positive manner, they will be less likely to resist their use and assume that the output is used solely to punish or as an impediment to promotion.

Changing the use of performance evaluations from a tool used to punish and diminish to one used to provide positive feedback designed to help employees grow would not only enhance organizational efficiency, it would also help change agency culture to one where evaluation is a positive aspect of working for the agency. By providing job-related expectations for employees, performance evaluations can be structured to focus on change, growth, and development rather than to discipline and punish.

SUMMARY

This chapter presented to you a prescription for addressing the many ethical issues confronting the criminal justice system, its processes, and its practitioners. Based on a set of recommendations developed by Caldero and Crank (2011) for addressing "noble cause" corruption in police agencies, my prescription further tweaks these recommendations by showing how they can be extended across criminal justice agencies and into the research arena as well. The goal of the prescription is to enhance ethical behavior by practitioners and researchers by altering the current "business as usual" orientation that, on the one hand gives lip service to ethics, but, on the other, fails to devote necessary resources to improve the ethical climate of criminal justice. Importantly, the prescription takes note of the fact that criminal justice ethics occurs in organizational contexts and is thus shaped and influenced by the structure, goals, activities, and culture of criminal justice organizations.

The prescription focuses on several areas, beginning with senior-level personnel modeling ethical behavior for the purpose of showing agency employees how to act ethically. Next, the prescription calls for agencies to reorient internal affairs (or similar units) toward becoming ethically proactive. What this means is that these units would become the locus of ethics mentoring, coaching, and training as part of the unit's operational mandate. Members of the unit would be reoriented away from investigating allegations of unethical/illegal behavior and toward promoting professional development in ethics for the agency. The third component of the prescription encourages agencies to hire toward the community being served, which includes working to balance the level of noble cause commitment of new recruits by altering hiring and training processes. Also included here would be preferential hiring of applicants possessing linguistic skills and four-year degrees. Finally, the prescription calls for agencies to alter their use of performance evaluations to become tools of positive feedback, providing useful and practical information to employees regardless of the level they occupy within the agency. These evaluations can also be integrated into agency efforts to facilitate change.

To conclude the chapter, I discuss the ethics of presumed guilt in the criminal justice system. When we presume guilt on the part of those coming into the system, we sully long-standing ideals upon which not only the criminal justice system was built, but also the entire country. Let's consider that issue in Thought Exercise 14.2.

THOUGHT EXERCISE 14.2

THE ETHICS OF PRESUMED GUILT

The young, bearded man dressed in jeans and a t-shirt had some idea why two Atlanta police officers with guns drawn were threatening to shoot him as he stepped from his beaten-up Honda parked in front of his new apartment building one evening in 2014. He repeatedly told the officers, "It's OK, it's all right—I live here," made no threatening moves, tried to remain calm, and did not raise his voice in protest. He did not resist as the officers grabbed and threw him on top of the trunk of his car or when one officer searched him and the other searched the car. He remained silent as officers kept him in a prone position at the rear of his car for 15 minutes while neighbors gathered to view the "dangerous criminal" that lived among them. When the officers determined that no crime had occurred and nothing incriminating turned up in a computerized background check, they told him to consider himself "lucky." While this was said as a taunt, they were right—he was lucky (see Stevenson, 2017).

The man who experienced this behavior is Bryan Stevenson, a Harvard-trained lawyer who founded and is Executive Director of the Equal Justice Initiative (EJI), a nonprofit public interest law firm in Montgomery (AL), whose award-winning work has been recognized by, among others, the Alabama Bar Association, the American Bar Association, the American Civil Liberties Union, the NAACP, and the American Psychiatric Association. Stevenson has been awarded 26 honorary degrees, authored an award-winning book, and given a TED talk. He is also African American.

Commenting on his experiences that evening in Atlanta, Stevenson (2017, p. 1) noted:

> What threatened to kill me on the streets of Atlanta wasn't just a misguided police officer with a gun, it was the force of America's history of racial injustice and the *presumption of guilt* it created. In America, no child should be born with a presumption of guilt, burdened with expectations of failure and dangerousness because of the color of her skin or a parent's poverty. Black people in this nation should be afforded the same protection, safety, and opportunity to thrive as anyone else. But that won't happen until we look squarely at our history and commit to engaging the past that continues to haunt us (emphasis added).

Stevenson's point about the presumption of guilt is important—it goes to the heart of many of the ethical issues confronting the criminal justice system. The presumption of guilt is even more problematic when it is combined with race.

Consider, for a moment, how, on seeing a photograph of the criminal suspect staring out at you from your TV screen during the local news, you *presume* he (or, in rare cases, she) is guilty. How often, on hearing about incidents like the one Stevenson experienced, have you *presumed* the police involved were guilty of excessive use of force or other misbehavior? I'm reminded of a quip I once heard from the late Supreme Court associate justice Antonin Scalia about an injustice he'd heard about. He suggested that the person involved "was probably guilty of *something*" and was, therefore, receiving his "just deserts." Have you ever felt that same way?

Criminal justice practitioners who presume guilt on the part of defendants coming into the criminal justice system create a variety of problems, not only for themselves, but for the system as a whole. For example, presumed guilt encourages police officers to circumvent both law and ethics and engage in noble cause misconduct in an effort to get the "bad guys" off the street (Kleinig, 2002). Presumed guilt leads to a lack of resources (e.g., investigators, forensic experts) for indigent defendants and their attorneys and reduces the effectiveness of legal representation in courtroom proceedings (Benner, 2009). Presumption of guilt helps sustain a plea-bargaining system that pressures defendants to plead guilty, sometimes to crimes they did not commit, and penalizes them for exercising their 5th Amendment right to a trial by jury (Bar-Gill & Ayal, 2009). Presumed guilt encourages crime control policies that result in the mass incarceration of citizens, especially young African American males (Alexander, 2012). Not only does the presumed guilt of defendants warp the ideals upon which our system of criminal justice was founded, it changes the obligations of most of those involved in the criminal justice system from ensuring that only the legally guilty are convicted to ensuring that *someone* is convicted and punished, preferably via imprisonment (Friedman, 1999). It also generates cynicism on the part of citizens toward the criminal justice system (Olsen & Huth, 1998). We all must resist the siren song of "presumed guilty" if we are to ever have a chance at achieving justice for all.

KEY TERMS

Organizations 419
Organizational structure 420
Division of labor 420
Complex goals 421
Occupational socialization 422
Modeling ethics 424
Ethically proactive 425
Hiring toward the community 426
Just means 426
Bona fide occupational qualification 427
Importance/usefulness dilemma 428

DISCUSSION QUESTIONS

1. Pick any one of the various characteristics of criminal justice organizations described above and identify its implications for the ethics of criminal justice practitioners.
2. Explore with some of your classmates the origins of "presumed guilty." Where did this attitude come from? Is it as great a threat to the criminal justice system as I make it out to be? Why or why not?

RESOURCES

Bryan Stevenson's most recent book is *Just Mercy: A Story of Justice and Redemption* (New York: Spiegel & Grau), which was #1 on the *New York Times* bestseller list (and won a bunch of awards). The book is a thrilling account of Stevenson's first case after founding the Equal Justice Initiative.

John Crank's ***Imagining Justice*** (New York: Routledge) is a call for all justice professionals to commit themselves to achieving justice and outlines how this can occur.

I can't end a book on criminal justice ethics and not recommend Harper Lee's ***To Kill a Mockingbird***. If you haven't read it, you've missed what many critics consider one of the best books of the *entire* 20th century.

REFERENCES

Alexander, M. (2012). *The new Jim Crow: Mass incarceration in an age of color blindness*. New York, NY: The New Press.

Bar-Gill, O., & Ayal, O (2009). Plea bargains only for the guilty. *Journal of Law & Economics, 49*, 353–364.

Benner, L. (2009). Presumption of guilt: Systemic factors that contribute to ineffective assistance of counsel in California. *California Western Law Review*, 45, 263–374.

Blue Ribbon Rampart Review Panel (2006). *Rampart reconsidered: The search for real reform seven years later*. Los Angeles, CA: City of Los Angeles.

Boyer, P. (2001, May 21). Bad cops. *The New Yorker*. Retrieved from https://www.newyorker.com/magazine/2001/05/21/bad-cops

Caldero, M., & Crank, J. (2011). *Police ethics: The corruption of noble cause* (Rev. 3rd ed.). New York, NY: Routledge.

Chemerinsky, E. (2000). The rampart scandal and the criminal justice system in Los Angeles county. *Guild Practitioner, 57*, 121–133

Culbert, S. (2008, October 20). Get rid of the performance review! *Wall Street Journal*. Retrieved from https://www.wsj.com/articles/SB122426318874844933

Federal Bureau of Prisons (2014). BOP org chart. Retrieved from https://www.justice.gov/jmd/functions-manual-federal-bureau-prisons-org-chart

Finckenauer, J., & Gavin, P. (1999). *Scared straight: The panacea phenomenon revisited*. Prospect Heights, IL: Waveland Press.

Friedman, D. (1999). Why not hang them all? The virtues of inefficient punishment. *Journal of Political Economy*, 107, S259–S269.

Gordon, M. (2011). *The thin blue line*. Los Angeles, CA: Matthew Gordon.

Ivković, S. (2005). *Fallen blue knights: Controlling police corruption*. New York, NY: Oxford University Press.

Kaplan, P. (2009). Looking through the gaps: A critical approach to the LAPD's Rampart Scandal. *Social Justice, 36*, 61–81.

Kleinig, J. (2002). Rethinking noble cause corruption. *International Journal of Police Science & Management*, 4, 287–314.

Los Angeles Police Department (2000). *Report of the Board of Inquiry into the Rampart area corruption incident*. Retrieved from http://assets.lapdonline.org/assets/pdf/boi_pub.pdf

Murgado, A. (2011, November 18). Leading by example. *Police*. Retrieved from http://www.policemag.com/channel/patrol/articles/2011/11/leading-by-example.aspx

Noble, J., & Alpert, G. (2009). *Managing accountability systems for police conduct*. Long Grove, IL: Waveland Press.

Novak, K., Cordner, G., Smith, R., & Roberg, R. (2017). *Police & society* (7th ed.). New York, NY: Oxford University Press.

Reisig, M., & Correia, M. (1997). Public evaluations of police performance: An analysis across three levels of policing. *Policing: An International Journal of Police Strategies & Management, 20*, 311–325.

Roberg, R., Crank, J., & Kuykendall, J. (2000). *Police in society* (2nd ed.). Prospect Heights, IL: Waveland Press.

Scott, A. (1986). Industrial organization and location: Division of labor, the firm, and spatial process. *Economic Geography, 62*, 215–231.

Simon, H. (1964). On the concept of organizational goals. *Administrative Science Quarterly, 9*, 1–22.

Skolnick, J., & Fyfe, J. (1993). *Above the law: Police and the excessive use of force*. New York, NY: The Free Press.

State of New South Wales (2009). Organizational policies and procedures. Retrieved from https://sielearning.tafensw.edu.au/MCS/CHCAOD402A/chcaod402a_csw/knowledge/policies/policies.htm#

Sterman, J. (1989). Modeling managerial behavior: Misperceptions of feedback in a dynamic decision making experiment. *Management Science*, 36, 321–339.

Stevenson, B. (2017, July 18). A presumption of guilt. *The New York Review of Books*. Retrieved from http://www.nybooks.com/articles/2017/07/13/presumption-of-guilt/

Stojkovic, S., Kalinich, D., & Klofas, J. (2015). *Criminal justice organizations: Administration and management* (6th ed.). Stamford, CT: Cengage Learning.

Walker, S. (2006). Police accountability: Current issues and research needs. Paper presented at the National Institute of Justice Policing Research Workshop, November 28–29, Washington, DC. Retrieved from https://www.ncjrs.gov/pdffiles1/nij/grants/218583.pdf

Weber, M. (1947). *The theory of social and economic organization*. New York, NY: Free Press.

INDEX